Trusted Criminals

White Collar Crime in Contemporary Society

THIRD EDITION

DAVID O. FRIEDRICHS
University of Scranton

THOMSON

WADSWORTH

Australia • Brazil • Canada • Mexico • Singapore • Spain
United Kingdom • United States

Trusted Criminals: White Collar Crime
in Contemporary Society,
Third Edition
David O. Friedrichs

Senior Acquisitions Editor, Criminal Justice:
   Carolyn Henderson Meier
Assistant Editor: Jana Davis
Editorial Assistant: Rebecca Johnson
Marketing Manager: Terra Schultz
Marketing Assistant: Jaren Boland
Marketing Communications Manager: Linda Yip
Project Manager, Editorial Production: Jennie Redwitz
Creative Director: Rob Hugel
Art Director: Vernon Boes

Print Buyer: Becky Cross
Permissions Editor: Bob Kauser
Production Service: Sara Dovre Wudali at Buuji, Inc.
Copy Editor: Kristina Rose McComas
Cover Designer: Bill Stanton
Cover Image: Left: Photodisc Red/Getty Images;
   right: Stone/Getty Images
Compositor: Integra Software Services
Text and Cover Printer: Malloy Incorporated

Library of Congress Control Number: 2006901123

ISBN 0-495-00604-1

Thomson Higher Education
10 Davis Drive
Belmont, CA 94002-3098
USA

For more information about our products, contact us at:
Thomson Learning Academic Resource Center
1-800-423-0563

For permission to use material from this text or product, submit a request online at **http://www.thomsonrights.com**. Any additional questions about permissions can be submitted by e-mail to **thomsonrights@thomson.com**.

For Jeanne

About the Author

David O. Friedrichs is Professor of Sociology/Criminal Justice at the University of Scranton. He was educated at New York University and taught for nine years at City University of New York (Staten Island). In addition to *Trusted Criminals*, he is the author of *Law in Our Lives: An Introduction* (Roxbury, 2001; 2006) and editor of *State Crime, Volumes I and II* (Ashgate/Dartmouth, 1998). He has published some 100 journal articles, book chapters, encyclopedia entries, and essays on such topics as the legitimation of legal order, radical/critical criminology, violence, narrative jurisprudence, postmodernism, crimes of states, and white collar crime. His articles have been published in many refereed journals in criminology, criminal justice, and sociology, as well as in numerous books. He is also the author of over 300 published book reviews. He served as editor of the *Legal Studies Forum* between 1985 and 1989. He has been active with numerous professional associations and has chaired or served on the committees of a number of these associations. He currently serves on the editorial boards of eight journals. He has been a visiting professor or guest lecturer at a number of colleges and universities, including Ohio University (as Rufus Putnam Visiting Professor), the University of South Africa, Hebrew University (Israel), and Flinders University (Australia). He has served as President of the White Collar Crime Research Consortium (2002–2004) and received the Lifetime Achievement Award of the Division on Critical Criminology of the American Society of Criminology in 2005.

Brief Contents

Contents

Foreword

One of the most well-established facts in criminology is the "age-crime curve," which holds that younger people commit more crimes than older people and that as criminally active young people begin to age, their level of criminality begins to wane. The age-crime curve explains a great deal about what we ordinarily think of as the subject matter of criminology: young and sometimes violent males. The age-crime curve explains why it does not surprise us to see our prisons filled with young adults, because we have come to expect that crime is a matter of youth.

And for the most part, this is not a false idea. But when it comes to "white collar" crime, a different notion emerges. For this kind of crime requires access to sources of significant money, especially through business, and it denotes the existence of a foundation of trust that is used to make the crime possible. Neither of these requirements—access and trust—seem to go with youth very well. It may take a few years in the business community to obtain access to the kinds of accounts that make really successful white collar crime lucrative, and it takes some years of work to generate the kind of trust that makes white collar crime possible. The people who defrauded so much in the case of Enron were middle-aged and older, citizens of repute. The people from WorldCom who bankrupted that company were the same. They had been active in business for long enough to gain reputations of some significance, and they had the kind of leverage that meant they could move large amounts of cash and credit on the strength of their signature.

White collar crime, then, is different from the kinds of crime that we usually study, for the ordinary rules do not seem to apply so well. Most white collar offenders are not kids; they are adults with years of experience in the world that they violate. Most white collar offenders are not poor but are instead either middle class or even affluent. Most white collar criminals are not socially disadvantaged but rather have the enormous social boon that allows them to prey on those who most trust them.

White collar crime is different in another respect. It is not studied with as much fervor as "street crime." This is curious because every scholar who writes about white collar crime will say that the total financial cost of this kind of crime far exceeds that of street crime; the likelihood of being a victim of white collar crime is far greater than the likelihood of ever being a victim of a serious street crime; and the damage done to people who suffer at the hands of white collar criminals can be every bit as devastating to one's quality of life as street crime. For these reasons alone, attaining a better understanding of the problem of white collar crime is an essential task of any student of crime and justice.

As editor of the *Wadsworth Contemporary Issues in Crime and Justice Series*, I am delighted to announce the publication of the third edition of *Trusted Criminals: White Collar Crime in Contemporary Society* by David O. Friedrichs. The *Contemporary Issues* series is devoted to furthering our understanding of important issues in crime and justice by providing an in-depth treatment of topics that are neglected or insufficiently discussed in today's textbooks. White collar crime is one of those topics, and this book is a classic examination of the problem.

This book will change the way you think about crime. It will show you how a better understanding of white collar crime will put the problem of street crime in a different perspective, and it will paint a picture of the criminal justice system that will leave you forever an advocate for better crime prevention of white collar offenses.

Professor Friedrichs is an internationally known scholar who has devoted his career to furthering our understanding of nontraditional crime and its consequences. His work has exposed the importance of costs of white collar crime, the impact of white collar victimizations, and the need for more effective public policy about white collar offenses. In this book, he brings together the most recent literature on white collar criminality—including recent studies of the exploding importance of technological crime—to inform the reader on the broad topic of white collar criminality with a confidence and comprehensiveness that no other text achieves. The work goes beyond an introduction and becomes an incisive examination of the phenomenon. Those who feel they have a good grounding in the area will find much in this book that is new and challenging; those who are neophytes to the topic will be stunned at how much there is to learn.

This third edition incorporates what we have learned from recent events in U.S. history, dominated by headlines about religious extremism, terrorism, and the war in Iraq. Friedrichs shows us that everyday headlines form the foundations for corporate and white collar criminality. He also shows us, through contemporary examples, the costs of this kind of crime, in matters ranging from the economics of everyday life to national security and international relations.

I commend this book to you. In the study of crime and justice, there is an enormous gap between the everyday material covered by popular news and other media and the dire and overwhelmingly harmful consequences of the "invisible" white collar criminality known to criminologists. This book will open your eyes and leave you forever informed about a kind of crime that matters far more than is commonly thought.

Todd R. Clear
Series Editor

Preface

More than 15 years have now passed since I began working on this book, and during that period of time the significance of white collar crime has become ever more clear. I have been gratified by the uniformly positive published reviews of this book and by the fact that it has been adopted for use in undergraduate- and graduate-level courses in the United States, Canada, Israel, Finland, Russia, and elsewhere. It has been translated into Japanese. And it continues to be widely cited by scholars writing about white collar crime. Many new developments pertaining to white collar crime and its control have occurred since the second edition of this book went to press in the summer of 2003, so a third edition seemed desirable at this time.

The original edition of this book was inspired by several considerations. Although white collar crime is immensely consequential, it has been relatively neglected by criminologists and is characterized by much conceptual confusion. When I began working on this text, only two books had been published that could be described as white collar crime texts, and neither of them systematically addressed the range of issues arising in connection with white collar crime and its control. Quite a number of white collar crime textbooks and readers have been published; however, a number of published reviews have identified this book as exceptionally comprehensive in its coverage, and I believe it remains the single most comprehensive survey of what is known about white collar crime and its control. This book is intended primarily as a text for advanced undergraduate- and graduate-level courses on white collar crime and closely related matters. However, it should be useful to scholars and other parties interested in white collar crime because it endeavors to clarify various conceptual and theoretical issues and to survey critically a large and unwieldy literature. It also aims to provide a relatively balanced presentation of the many controversies involved in white collar crime.

RATIONALES FOR STUDYING WHITE COLLAR CRIME

White collar crime—and more generally, the illegal, unethical, or deviant activity of respectable institutions and individuals—has been relatively neglected in the study of crime and deviance. Traditionally, criminology has focused on "street crime," not "suite crime." The sociology of deviance has emphasized the activities of "nuts, sluts, and perverts," not of corporate executives, physicians, and retail store owners, and this relative neglect has been generally reflected in the media. But one of the guiding premises of this book is that the range of activities that can fall under the heading of white collar crime is more pervasive and more costly to society than are conventional crime and deviance.

The study of white collar crime should obviously be of interest to students planning criminal justice careers and to people already employed in the criminal justice system. In recent years, white collar crime has received more attention from the criminal justice system, and there is reason to believe that this attention will increase in the years to come. As the investigation and prosecution of white collar crime increases, career opportunities for individuals well informed about this type of activity should expand. The prevention of some forms of white collar crime is also a major concern in the private sector, creating career opportunities in this realm as well. One of the many paradoxical characteristics of white collar crime that will be explored is that even though much white collar crime is committed within the context of legitimate governmental and business activities, careers combating such crime can be pursued in either the public or private sector.

The study of white collar crime is likely to be of interest to students of the social and behavioral sciences because white collar criminality, as it is defined here, often involves human behavior in its most devious and diabolical forms. This type of activity raises fundamental questions about human nature and responsibility. It forces us to confront the harsh realization that the distinctions between crime and order are not as great as we like to imagine and that those who benefit most from a stable social system often do the most to threaten its well-being. Few areas of human activity reveal more starkly the complex relationship between the creative and the destructive aspects of human nature than does white collar crime. We cannot fully understand our political, economic, and social institutions without attending to white collar crime, and our understanding of human psychology is deepened through the study of white collar criminals.

The law in the white collar realm that confronts pre-law and law students is especially dynamic and complex. The problem of corporate liability poses special difficulties, and the subtle and sometimes arbitrary lines of demarcation between criminal law and civil law are crucial aspects of the study of white collar crime.

A strong argument can be made that a deeper understanding of white collar crime should prove useful and relevant to students in any major. As citizens, employees, employers, and professionals, most of us are likely to be affected more by white collar crime than by any other type of criminal activity. And if we or the people with whom we have the most regular contact become involved in illegalities, such activities are likely to be some form of white collar crime.

Finally, if the problem of white collar crime is to be effectively addressed, many ordinary citizens must be aware of the nature of the problem and willing to engage with the forces involved in it. Certainly one objective of this book is to promote this consciousness and engagement.

NEW TO THIS EDITION

Much of the original organization of the book is retained, but I have also made a number of significant changes. First and foremost, updates drawing on published material through 2005 have been incorporated throughout the book. Altogether, over 600 new sources are cited in this edition. The period 2001–2006 has featured many big news stories, beginning with 9/11 and the response to it; Operation Iraqi Freedom; a series of natural catastrophes such as tsunamis, earthquakes, and fierce hurricanes; and the like. But white collar crime and its control have periodically resurfaced on the front pages or on television as the lead story at various points during this period.

The "corporate scandals" that surfaced, beginning with the collapse of Enron late in 2001, have been followed by high-profile trials for some of these cases, including those of CEOs and other top executives at Enron, WorldCom, Adelphia, Tyco, HealthSouth, and other firms. Important developments in these trials are addressed at different points in this edition but especially in Chapter 11.

Furthermore, during the recent period various forms of alleged massive fraud surfaced in the insurance industry, the hedge fund industry, the commodities industry, and other major segments of the world of higher finance. Accounting fraud was discovered at Fannie Mae, the mortgage giant. These emerging forms of fraud are addressed in Chapter 6.

Lifestyle celebrity Martha Stewart emerged from prison after serving time on obstruction of justice charges, and some former top executives were facing prison sentences as long as 25 years. The controversies that arose in connection with these sentences are addressed in Chapters 11 and 12.

The business community was responding to new initiatives against white collar crime in both cooperative ways and with resistance or protest. These responses are discussed in Chapters 9 and 12.

Cases of individuals and partnerships across the occupational spectrum engaged in financially fraudulent activity continued to surface, including a highly regarded school district superintendent who pleaded guilty to stealing some $2 million from his district. Chapter 4 on occupational crime attends to these developments.

In the political realm as well, ongoing allegations of state-based wrongdoing and corrupt dealings with military contractors and other private entities also surfaced. A majority leader of the House of Representatives was indicted on criminal charges relating to campaign fundraising activities. These activities of states and political figures are discussed in Chapter 5.

The demand for more effective responses to corporate crime and white collar crime generally intensified in at least some quarters, which is especially considered in Chapter 12. A significant level of concern with white collar crime and its control seems likely to expand in the years ahead.

Another important thrust of the new edition is the enhanced attention paid to some especially dynamic forms of white collar crime, including environmental crime and white collar crime in cyber space. For example, new studies that have explored evolving patterns of corporate compliance with environmental protection initiatives and some recent environmental initiatives adopted nationally and internationally are addressed. Also, identity theft has increased dramatically over the past two years, with cyber space implicated in a significant percentage of cases. The growing cost of illegitimate spam to American business has also increased exponentially. These developments are all addressed in this new edition.

Finally, the new edition features numerous new boxes, including:

- "Deep Throat" and the Watergate Case
- Designing a White Collar Crime Survey: Some Challenges
- "It's Legal But It Ain't Right"
- Halliburton, Vice President Cheney, and Iraq War Contracts
- Adelphia, HealthSouth, WorldCom, and Accounting Fraud
- Plagiarism and *Trusted Criminals*
- Stealing from the School District
- Extravagant Executive Compensation: Just Reward or Grand Theft?
- Military Contractors in Iraq: Corporate Warriors and the Halliburton Corporation
- Corruption in the Oil-for-Food Program
- Investment Banks: Wealth Producers or Large-Scale Fraudsters?
- Insider Trading and the Martha Stewart Case
- Fraudulent Conduct in the Mutual Funds and Hedge Funds Industries
- Advance Fee Frauds
- Diffusion Theory and Intermediate Fraud
- Low Self-Control and White Collar Crime
- Law Professor Stuart Green and the Moral Theory of White Collar Crime
- Protecting the Environment: Alternatives to Relying upon the EPA
- To Testify or Not to Testify?
- Can a Corporation Be Ethically Transformed? The Case of Tyco
- A "Chief Criminologist" for the SEC?
- Citizen Works Proposals for Cracking Down on Corporate Crime
- The Stakeholder Model for Corporations: Costco and Whole Foods

ORGANIZATION

This text provides a systematic survey of white collar crime and its control. It addresses many topics that tend to be either slighted or excluded in other texts on white collar crime. Chapters 1 and 2 address the historical development of the concept of white collar crime; crucial elements of white collar crime—trust, respectability, and risk; the role of the media and other agents in shaping our image of white collar crime; those who expose white collar crime, from whistleblowers to investigative reporters to criminologists; the challenges involved and the specific methods used in studying white collar crime; perceptions of white collar crime relative to other types of crime; the measurement of the costs and extent of white collar crime; and the victims of white collar crime.

Chapters 3 through 7 are devoted to systematic surveys of what we know about high-consensus forms of white collar crime, such as corporate crime and occupational crime, and about often-neglected cognate, hybrid, and marginal forms of white collar crime, including governmental crime, state-corporate crime, crimes of globalization, finance crime, technocrime, enterprise crime, contrepreneurial crime, and avocational crime. Two typically neglected and sensitive topics—universities and colleges as corporate criminals, and academics as white collar offenders—are covered in two of these chapters.

Chapter 8 offers a comprehensive survey and evaluation of the whole range of theoretical explanations for white collar crime, from demonological to postmodernist and from individualist to structuralist. Chapters 9, 10, and 11 provide a full treatment of the law and other forms of social control of white collar crime; the justice system response to such crime by many different entities, ranging from local police to federal regulatory agencies; and the adjudication of white collar crime, including the roles of grand juries, trial juries, prosecutors, defense attorneys, and judges, as well as a discussion of sentencing guidelines. Finally, Chapter 12 offers an exhaustive survey of the many possible responses to white collar crime, from the imposition of fines to the structural transformation of the social order.

SPECIAL FEATURES OF THIS TEXT

This text includes numerous boxes illustrating a wide range of white collar crime–related matters. It also includes summaries, lists of key terms with the page numbers on which the term is defined, and discussion questions at the end of each chapter. In sum, this book explores the conceptual, metaphysical, and methodological issues involved in the study of white collar crime. It delves into the character, causes, and consequences of this type of crime and explores the relationship of white collar crime and elite deviance to other types of illegal and deviant activity. This text examines the response of the law and the justice system to white collar crime and considers the prospects for deterring, preventing, and obliterating white collar crime.

A NOTE TO INSTRUCTORS

That considerable lack of consensus exists on matters pertaining to white collar crime is reflected by disagreement over usage of the text's central term: Should it be "white collar crime" or "white-collar crime"? The more common (and, from a strictly grammatical point of view, more correct) usage is "white-collar crime," but I have omitted the hyphen because it suggests too literal a reading of the term, which is better thought of as a metaphor. Interestingly enough, the seminal work in the field, E. H. Sutherland's *White Collar Crime*, did not use this hyphen (although even Sutherland was not completely clear on this matter and used a hyphen in his original 1940 article on white collar crime).

White collar crime is a problem in all contemporary societies. This text uses examples from the United States for most illustrative purposes. Obviously, the specific character of and response to the white collar crime problem varies from nation to nation, but many parallel patterns exist in all countries. References to other countries and societies are made and at least some of the foreign literature on the subject is drawn upon and cited, but as a practical matter, it was simply not possible to make a systematic, cross-cultural comparison. To date, white collar crime and the justice system response to it are far more fully documented for the American experience than for other countries, although the literature for such countries as Great Britain, Australia, and Canada is now considerable.

White collar crime courses are relatively new additions to the curriculum in most criminology and criminal justice programs, and they are offered under various titles and with a variety of approaches. Some instructors are especially concerned with identifying the broad varieties of white collar crime and the different theoretical explanations for them. Other instructors are far more concerned with white collar crime as a problem of social control and with the justice system response to it. This text was developed to accommodate the considerable diversity of perspectives on making sense of white collar crime. The order of the chapters is reasonably consistent with a conventional criminological approach to crime and criminal justice, but this arrangement inevitably has a certain arbitrariness. Each chapter was written to stand alone, and thus instructors can arrange the chapters to suit different approaches. For example, Chapter 9 on law and social control, Chapter 10 on policing and regulating white collar crime, and Chapter 11 on adjudicating white collar crime cases can be assigned up-front and followed by the substantive chapters on different types of white collar crime. A variety of rearrangements are clearly possible.

A test bank is available to all instructors who adopt this text. Also, a website now contains links to sites relevant to the focus of this book (these links were in Appendix B in the second edition and have been updated for the website).

All authors welcome responses to their work, and I am no exception. I have attempted to produce a book that is clear, accurate, informative, and thorough, but I recognize that some readers may have comments or suggestions. Any comments— positive or negative—and suggestions can be sent to me at the following address: David O. Friedrichs, Department of Sociology/Criminal Justice, University of Scranton,

PA 18510–4605. E-mail: friedrichsd1@scranton.edu. Comments and suggestions will be especially helpful for future editions of this book. Substantial comments and suggestions will be properly acknowledged in any new edition.

ACKNOWLEDGMENTS

The making of this book can be traced back several decades to my interest in crimes of the powerful and privileged in the 1970s. From the early 1980s on, I offered a white collar crime course, and beginning in 1990, I began systematic work on writing this text. Since I sent the original manuscript to the publisher in 1995, I have continued to follow developments relating to white collar crime and its control, updating my files. The second edition of this book was written principally in 2001–2002. The present edition was written principally during the course of 2005 but drew upon ongoing research from earlier years.

Many different individuals contributed in diverse ways to the making of this book over the course of many years. Perhaps my most basic debt is due to the numerous scholars and journalists whose work is cited throughout this text. I have learned a great deal from their prodigious labors and can only hope I have done justice to their efforts in my discussions of and references to their work.

Among those who have provided me with inspiration, encouragement, advice, materials, or useful feedback in connection with this project are the following: Anne Alvesalo, Menachem Amir, Richard Ball, Harold Barnett, Peter Benekos, Michael Benson, Thomas J. Bernard, Michael Blankenship, John Braithwaite, Ronald Burns, Kitty Calavita, Ronald Clarke, Frank Cullen, Rob Elias, Rob Faulkner, Marcus Felson, Jurg Gerber, Peter Grabosky, Stuart Green, Maria (Maki) Haberfeld, Frank Hagan, Stuart Henry, Stuart Hills, Drew Humphries, David Kauzlarich, Ron Kramer, William Laufer, Alfred McClung Lee, Michael Levi, Craig Little, Jarret Lovell, Michael Lynch, Gary Marx, Rick Matthews, Jeffrey McIllwain, John McNeill, Marilyn McShane, Robert Meier, Jim Messerschmidt, Dragan Milovanovic, Russell Mokhiber, Steve Muzzatti, David Nelken, Larry Nichols, Nikos Passas, Nicole Leeper Piquero, Gary Potter, Gary Reed, Nancy Reichman, Linda Robyn, Debra Ross, Jeffrey Ian Ross, Kip Schlegel, David Shichor, Neal Shover, Rashi Shukla, David Simon, Sally Simpson, Andreas Tomaszewski, Henry Vandenburgh, Diane Vaughan, David Weisburd, Mike Welch, Frank Williams, John Wozniak, and Peter Yeager. I appreciated the initiative of Carole Garrison of Eastern Kentucky University, Dawn Rothe of Western Michigan University, and Danielle McGurrin of Stonehill College in bringing me to their campuses for lectures on white collar crime, which inspired me to refine some of my ideas on the subject. Staff members of the National White Collar Crime Center were supportive during my two-year term (2002–2004) as president of the White Collar Crime Research Consortium, and I made various helpful contacts in this connection. Larry Nichols of West Virginia University has generously permitted me to include his listing of white collar crime films as an appendix. I am grateful to Paul Klenowski for taking on the revision of the Test Bank for this book. I apologize to others whose names I may have inadvertently omitted here. I am especially grateful to

Richard Quinney (Emeritus, Northern Illinois University) and Gilbert Geis (Emeritus, University of California–Irvine) for seminal inspiration in terms of my interest in white collar crime and for their encouragement and assistance. As always, I am also indebted to Martin D. Schwartz (Ohio University) for much ongoing encouragement, advice, and inspiration. I enjoyed working with Marty on a chapter on white collar crime and low self-control for a forthcoming book, during which time he discovered—perhaps to his surprise—that he knows something about white collar crime.

At the University of Scranton, the Faculty Research Committee, the Faculty Development Committee, and the University Travel Committee provided crucial support in several forms: annual faculty research grants, which enabled me to visit research libraries, acquire essential research materials, and defray numerous production costs; a sabbatical leave; summer grants at critical stages in the project; and travel grants that allowed me to attend and participate in professional meetings, where much current work is discussed and useful exchanges with professional colleagues occur. The Office of Research Services, including Dean Duncan Perry, Eileen Callahan, Eloise Libassi, and Maria Landis, has been helpful on a number of matters. The dean of my college, Joseph Dreisbach, has been supportive of this project in various ways. Within my own department, several colleagues have been helpful over the years, and I am especially grateful to my present chair, Harry Dammer, also a Thomson Wads-worth author, for various forms of encouragement and support. Bill Parente of Political Science, an even more compulsive clipper of newspapers than myself, has provided me with some items I missed and has been enjoyable company while we have both been serving time on the Fourth Floor of O'Hara Hall. I am also indebted to various reference librarians at the university's Weinberg Memorial Library, especially Betsey Moylan, Bonnie Strohl, Katie Duke, and Kevin Norris, for their assistance. A number of individuals associated with the university's Computer Service and PC Maintenance Center, including Gus Fernandez, Karl Johns, and Glen Pace, have been helpful in terms of computer hardware and software problems over the years. My former department secretaries, Judith Lestansky and Jean Hoppel, and my current department secretary, Gemma Davis, have provided efficient assistance on many aspects of this project. Gemma has been helpful in many ways. I have also benefited from feedback from many students I have had in my white collar crime course over the years, and for earlier editions of this book especially: Josianne Aboutanous, Ingrid Farally, Stuart Frasier, Erica Osuchowski, Marius Stan, and James Vadella. Matthew Gordon, a former student, sent me useful materials. Students in my Spring 2005 White Collar Crime class each completed assignments that were useful in revising this book, with the contributions of the following students especially helpful: Keith Brady, Jenelle Janowicz, Rob Lyons, Jason Mastony, and Sonya Standefer. Jenelle Janwicz assisted me with some tasks while this book was in production.

This edition of *Trusted Criminals* was completed during the period while I was Visiting Professor of Law at Flinders University in Adelaide, Australia, during a sabbatical in Spring 2006. I appreciate the role of Dean Gary Davis, Professor Mark Israel and Dr. Chris Symes, and Mrs. Sandra Brooks, in providing me with such a wonderful working environment and an altogether stimulating professional experience.

I visited many libraries over the course of research for this book. I am grateful to librarians at the NYU Law Library for making that collection accessible to me, and especially to the remarkable Phyllis Schultze of the Criminal Justice/NCCD Library at Rutgers University–Newark for numerous forms of assistance on this project. Phyllis is to my mind the premier criminal justice information specialist in the country, and I appreciate her assistance and friendship over a period of many years.

Several editors have been involved with this project. Cindy Stormer initiated the original edition of this book at Brooks/Cole, and Peggy Adams, Brian Gore, Shelly Murphy, and Sabra Horne worked on it after criminal justice titles were shifted to Wadsworth. I have enjoyed working with my current editor, Carolyn Henderson Meier.

I am grateful to the various editors and other personnel at Wadsworth for their encouragement and suggestions. I am especially indebted to Jennie Redwitz, the editorial production project manager, for her professionalism and efficiency in seeing this project through the production process, as well as to Sara Dovre Wudali at Buuji, for her unstinting work. Copy editor Kristina McComas has scrupulously reviewed every word of this text and has enhanced its clarity and accuracy in countless ways.

A number of external reviewers for Brooks/Cole and subsequently for Wadsworth provided me with some helpful advice, and I was much heartened by their very favorable and encouraging assessment of my work on this project. Reviewers for the first edition were William Clements (Norwich University), Lee Colwell (University of Arkansas, Little Rock), Jurg Gerber (Sam Houston State University), Richard Janikowski (University of Memphis), Sally Simpson (University of Maryland), and Kip Schlegel (Indiana University–Bloomington). Reviewers for the second edition were J. Price Foster (University of Louisville), John King (Baldwin-Wallace College), Patrick Mueller (Stephen F. Austin State University), Debra Ross (Buffalo State College), Kathleen Sweet (St. Cloud State University), and Henry Vandenburgh (State University of New York, Oswego). Those commenting on the third edition included Loretta Capeheart (Northeastern Illinois University), Christine Corken (Loras College), Michael Gilbert (University of Texas, San Antonio), Collin Lau (Chaminade University of Honolulu), Teelyn Mauney (University of Nebraska, Lincoln), Gerald Smith (University of Northern Iowa), and Henry Vandenburgh (now of Bridgewater State College). Quite a number of the specific suggestions from these reviewers were adopted in the course of writing and revising this book through its three editions.

Finally, various members of my large extended family have been supportive over the years. My father and mother, both now deceased, were always extraordinarily supportive and encouraging and an important source of inspiration for my professional work. My daughter Jessica directly inspired my interest in "crimes of globalization," following her junior year experience in Thailand, and my collaboration with her on an article on this topic, published in *Social Justice* in 2002, was especially gratifying. My son Bryan has in various ways been helpful to me, including as a willing listener and responder to some of my ideas. My wife Jeanne has brought joy into my life over a period of several decades now and has constantly reminded me in so many ways that there is more to life than working on a book. Jeanne has once again endured a book revision project. None of the three editions of this book would have been written without her loving support. For that reason, and because she makes our life together so wonderful, this book is once again dedicated to Jeanne, with much love.

1

The Discovery
of White Collar Crime

Martha Stewart, the celebrated founder of a multibillion dollar lifestyle empire, emerged from five months in a minimum-security prison in March 2005 (Hays 2005a, 2005b). She was required to wear a plastic monitoring device and was largely restricted to one of her homes (a Westchester mansion) for a five-month probationary period. Stewart, convicted of obstruction of justice charges related to alleged insider trading, hardly fit the traditional image of a criminal. Her offense was linked with a form of white collar crime. While many commentators felt that she deserved to be in prison, others claimed that her imprisonment was both unnecessary and unwarranted. Public perceptions of white collar crime tend to be more conflicted and confused than are perceptions of conventional forms of crime.

Consider the following list of situations:

- The world's largest retailer is accused of using illegal immigrant workers and cheating them on wages.

- An asbestos removal company is indicted on charges arising out of its practice of putting many people at risk by faking the asbestos removal.

- An energy corporation described as the nation's seventh-largest company collapses into bankruptcy amid allegations of massive fraud and insider self-dealing.

- A pharmacist is convicted of diluting cancer drugs to enhance his profits.

- A major defense contractor, formerly headed by the Vice President of the United States, is investigated for overcharging the government on Iraq contracts and cheating retirees on pensions.

- A bookkeeper embezzles from her employer to pay her bills.

- Several major pharmaceutical companies are accused of misrepresenting test results for their drug products, putting people who use these prescription drugs at risk.

- Doctors operating clinics in California are accused of filing some $1 billion in false claims.

- The world's largest software company is charged with illegal, anticompetitive practices.

- A priest is charged with stealing over a half million dollars in church funds.

- Insurance companies are accused of defrauding American soldiers heading for Iraq by selling them overpriced policies.

The situations listed here might seem to have little in common. They involve the very powerful and the relatively powerless, large-scale organizations and isolated individuals, enormous sums of money and relatively modest sums, the loss of numerous lives, and incremental, less apparent threats to long-term health. However, all these situations have several things in common. First, they do not include the forms of crime that typically come to mind when people think of crime: murder, rape, aggravated assault, burglary, car theft, or larceny. Second, the offenders or offending organizations enjoy a relatively high level of trust and respectability, at least when compared with organized crime and street criminals. Third, these situations have not been a traditional focus of the law and the justice system, which have responded to them in various ways. Fourth, they have all been considered forms of white collar crime, according to at least someone's conception of that complex term.

The term *white collar crime* is by now quite familiar to many people; it is also a source of considerable confusion. White collar crime can arise in unexpected circumstances. The many deaths associated with an earthquake in the state of Gujarat, India, would appear to be a natural catastrophe, wholly unrelated to white collar crime. But an Indian government report indicated that much of the loss of life could be attributed to shoddy building construction, a consequence of greedy developers paying off corrupt government inspectors to evade proper building codes (Bearak 2001). Furthermore, the term *white collar crime* is sometimes applied quite broadly. A well-known economist and columnist, Paul Krugman (2001a), characterized the tax-cut bill of President George W. Bush as a "fiscal scam" and "white collar crime, pure and simple."

EDWIN H. SUTHERLAND AND THE DISCOVERY OF WHITE COLLAR CRIME

Although Criminologist Edwin H. Sutherland is generally given credit for introducing the term *white collar crime* into the literature in 1939, recognition of this type of crime extends well back in history. Records from ancient times include identification of and sanctions against frauds carried out in the context of various types of commercial transactions.

In the 19th century, Karl Marx and Friedrich Engels (1848) insisted that the powerful and the privileged commit "crimes," loosely defined as consequences of the character of the capitalist economic system and the special status of the privileged within it. The American muckrakers of the early 20th century inveighed against the exploitative crimes of the "robber barons" and their confederates.

Sutherland (see Box 1.1) was apparently most directly inspired by E. A. Ross's (1907) *Sin and Society: An Analysis of Latter Day Iniquity* (Geis and Goff 1987). Writing shortly after the turn of the century, Ross, a prominent sociologist of his time, promoted the notion of "the *criminaloid*": the businessman who committed exploitative, if not necessarily illegal, acts out of an uninhibited desire to maximize profit, all the while hiding behind a facade of respectability and piety. Ross regarded these criminaloids as guilty of moral insensibility and held them directly responsible for unnecessary deaths of consumers and workers. At the outset of his book, Ross observed:

> The man who picks pockets with a railway rebate, murders with an adulterant instead of a bludgeon, burglarizes with a "rake-off" instead of a jimmy, cheats with a company prospectus instead of a deck of cards, or scuttles his town instead of his ship, does not feel on his brow the brand of a malefactor. (p. 7)

For Ross, the actions of criminaloids were threatening to a just and decent capitalist society, which Ross supported. Although his book enjoyed popular acclaim, it did not persuade the sociologists of the day to attend more fully to either criminaloids or white collar crime.

E. H. Sutherland's landmark American Sociological Society presidential address in Philadelphia in December 1939 was entitled "The White Collar Criminal." In this initial characterization of white collar crime, published the following year in the *American Sociological Review*, Sutherland alluded to "crime in the upper or white-collar class, composed of respectable or at least respected business and professional men" (1940: 1). A principal attribute of this type of crime is that it consists of "violation of

BOX 1.1   E. H. Sutherland: The "Father" of White Collar Crime Studies

E. H. Sutherland (1883–1950) is quite commonly regarded as "the most important contributor to American criminology to have appeared to date" (Gibbons 1979: 65). In addition to his seminal contributions to the study of white collar crime, he produced an influential textbook, formulated a major criminological theory (differential association), and published important works on professional crime and laws concerning sexual psychopaths. When Sutherland began publishing in the 1920s, American sociology was especially concerned with promoting its status as a legitimate social science, and it consciously distanced itself from the passionate moral exhortations of earlier sociologists (Geis and Meier 1977). Despite Sutherland's claim that his work on white collar crime was theoretical and scientific in purpose, his personal sense of outrage at corporate criminality was clearly a strong motivating factor for his work. Sutherland did not quarrel with the virtues of an openly competitive entrepreneurial form of capitalism as originally envisioned by Adam Smith. Rather, he was deeply angered by those behaviors and actions of "Big Business" that corrupted and threatened the laudable aspects of the American economic system (Sutherland 1949, 1983). Sutherland's value system combined a quintessentially American synthesis of entrepreneurial and progressive beliefs with his professional commitment to detached social scientific inquiry.

Sutherland's interest in white collar crime has been traced back to the 1920s, when he produced the first edition of his celebrated textbook *Criminology* (1924). His interest appears to have been motivated, in part, by his realization that the conventional criminological theories of his time focused almost exclusively on explaining lower-class criminality and provided little if any guidance for understanding the criminality of middle- and upper-class people (Cohen, Lindesmith, and Schuessler 1956). He came to believe that his theory of differential association, which attributed criminality to a learning process, was precisely the type of general theory that could usefully explain both lower-class and upper-class crime. Then, in 1929, with the crash of the stock market, the country entered a long period of economic distress. With so many Americans barely surviving, the crimes of the rich may well have appeared to be especially insidious. Throughout the 1930s, Sutherland collected data on crime by respectable individuals, especially embezzlers, and refined an emerging conception of white collar crime with his graduate students at Indiana University (Geis and Goff 1987). His election as president of the American Sociological Society offered him a unique opportunity to introduce and publicize the concept of white collar crime.

delegated or implied trust" (Sutherland 1940: 3). Examples of white collar criminality in business included various forms of misrepresentation, manipulation, embezzlement, and bribery. Sutherland suggested that white collar crime was a long-established American tradition, and he provided some evidence of its prevalence, its staggering financial costs, and the special vulnerability of its victims. Sutherland argued for the recognition of white collar crime as "real," even if convictions by criminal courts were not necessarily involved. He pointed out that the white collar classes have both special influence on the formulation of criminal laws and various means of minimizing the chances of criminal conviction.

During the 1940s, Sutherland undertook a major study that culminated in the publication of

White Collar Crime (1949), his last major contribution before his death in 1950. In this book, Sutherland focused on the 70 largest U.S. manufacturing, mining, and mercantile corporations with respect to the legal decisions (by criminal, civil, or administrative tribunals) against them concerning allegations of wrongdoing. Each of these corporations had one or more decisions against it, with an average of 14 decisions against each corporation during the course of its existence. However, no more than 16 percent of the decisions against the corporations emanated from the criminal courts. These decisions, in descending order of frequency, included restraint-of-trade violations, infringement of patent and other rights, unfair labor practices, fraudulent advertising, and illegal rebates. These findings led

Sutherland to conclude that 97 percent of the corporations, each with two or more adverse decisions, were criminal recidivists.

The main body of Sutherland's *White Collar Crime* consists of a systematic exploration of the specific forms of white collar crime committed by major corporations. Sutherland was especially venomous in his characterization of corporate fraud, profiteering, and tax evasion during World War II; he characterized white collar crime as a form of organized crime. Sutherland argued that the crimes committed by corporations were rational, deliberate, persistent, and much more extensive than prosecution of them indicated. Victims were often quite impotent to respond effectively to corporate crimes, which were difficult to prove, and corporations were well positioned to "fix" cases against them. Businessmen caught violating the law generally did not suffer a loss of peer status; in fact, businessmen as a group were commonly contemptuous of law, he noted. In their view, if they were technically in violation of certain laws, it was not because they were criminals but because the laws were bad.

The slow pace of development of white collar crime research in the wake of Sutherland's crucial contributions is somewhat mystifying. On the one hand, criminologists have generally acknowledged that Sutherland's *White Collar Crime* was one of the most important contributions to the field of criminology. On the other hand, for a long time this work was seldom cited and rarely emulated (Geis and Goff 1982). In addition to the ongoing conceptual confusion regarding the term *white collar crime*, for which Sutherland must assume some responsibility, this work can be faulted on other grounds. Even his admirers concede that Sutherland overemphasized an individualistic framework (and social-psychological factors) and largely ignored social structural factors (e.g., capitalism, profit rates, and business cycles). He failed to make clear-cut distinctions among white collar crimes, and he did not adequately appreciate the influence of corporations over the legislative and regulatory processes (Geis and Goff 1987; Meier 2001). Still, it is difficult to imagine the study of white collar crime without Sutherland's contribution.

DEFINING WHITE COLLAR CRIME

More than six decades have passed since Sutherland formally introduced the concept of white collar crime, but confusion about the meaning and most appropriate application of this concept continues (e.g., Green 2005; Helmkamp, Ball, and Townsend 1996; Nelken 2002). Why is this so?

First, a wide variety of terms has been used to characterize activities that could either be classified under the broad rubric of white collar crime or are closely linked with it. *Elite deviance* is one example. Other terms include *economic crime, commercial crime, business crime, marketplace crime, consumer crime, respectable crime, "crime at the top," "suite" crime, official crime and deviance, political crime, governmental crime, state (or state-organized) crime, corporate crime, occupational crime and deviance, workplace crime, employee crime, avocational crime, technocrime, computer crime, folk crime,* and *invisible crime.*

In some cases, different terms refer to the same activity; in other cases, they refer to specific types of crime. Obviously the invocation of so many different terms, interrelated in such a bewildering variety of ways, contributes to the general confusion about white collar crime. Each term is likely to have some unique connotations, and each tends to emphasize a particular dimension of white collar crime.

The terms *crime* and *deviance* have both been used to describe many of the activities discussed in this book. The choice has been made to emphasize the term *crime* because this term is more closely associated with doing harm to others than is *deviance* (Henry and Lanier 2001). Second, quite a bit of white collar crime unfortunately does not deviate from typical patterns of behavior (e.g., deception in the marketplace). Third, many white collar offenders avoid the stigma that is so central to the notion of deviance; they do not have a deviant self-identity or lifestyle. Box 1.2 compares conflicting views that have complicated achieving consensus on defining white collar crime.

Criminologists who study white collar crime have generally been in agreement that it (1) occurs in an legitimate occupational context; (2) is motivated by the objective of economic gain or

---

B O X 1.2   The Meaning of White Collar Crime: Some Issues under Debate

- White collar crime should only refer to violations of criminal law.

- White collar crime should only refer to acts committed by higher-status individuals and institutions.

- White collar crime should refer only to acts involving financial and economic activities.

- White collar crime should refer only to the acts of individuals.

- White collar crime should refer to forms of violations of the harm addressed by civil and administrative law as well as criminal law.

- White collar crime should refer to acts committed in the context of any legitimate occupation.

- White collar crime should refer to acts involving physical as well as financial harm.

- White collar crime should refer to the acts of organizations as well as individuals.

---

occupational success; and (3) is not characterized by direct, intentional violence.

On the other hand, these criminologists have also been divided on many issues, in terms of how they define white collar crime and which attributes of offenders they emphasize (Friedrichs 1992; Helmkamp, Ball, and Townsend 1996). In particular, they have been divided between those focused on exposing wrongdoing in high places and those who study occupational or fraudulent offenders (e.g., Simon 2006; Weisburd, Waring, and Chayet 2001). Lawyers and law professors inevitably stress the legalistic approaches to defining white collar crime (Green 2005).

In June 1996, the National White Collar Crime Center invited 15 white collar crime scholars (including the author of this book) to meet for three days in Morgantown, West Virginia, to engage in an intense discussion of the "definitional dilemma" pertaining to white collar crime. One day during lunch, one member of the group circulated a napkin with a proposed definition, inviting other participants to make amendments and revisions. The resulting definition reads as follows:

> White collar crimes are illegal or unethical acts that violate fiduciary responsibility of public trust committed by an individual or organization, usually during the course of legitimate occupational activity, by persons of high or respectable social status for personal or organizational gain. (Helmkamp, Ball, and Townsend 1996: 351)

It remains to be seen whether this somewhat convoluted definition gains wide acceptance. This text adopts a generally inclusive approach that recognizes that the term *white collar crime* can be used in many different ways.

A Multistage Approach to Defining White Collar Crime

A coherent and meaningful understanding of white collar crime must be approached in stages. The first, most general, definitional stage is *polemical*, the second stage is *typological*, and the third is *operational*. The traditional, "popular" conception of white collar crime—the illegal and harmful actions of elites and respectable members of society carried out for economic gain in the context of legitimate organizational or occupational activity—has an important polemical and pedagogical purpose. This conception challenges a popular tendency to associate criminality with inner-city residents, minorities, young men, and conventional illegal activities such as homicide, robbery, and burglary. The more complex and qualified the concept, the less effective it is likely to be in challenging conventional crime consciousness. It is not clear whether any of the many previously mentioned terms, all with somewhat more restricted connotations, can hope to achieve the easy recognition accorded white collar crime, which has been quite widely invoked for many decades.

In the second stage of conceptual development, the purpose of a criminological typology is to organize patterns of crime and criminal behavior into coherent or homogenous categories, to facilitate both explaining and responding to crime (Gibbons 2002). Because the patterns of actual lawbreakers are so varied, some commentators express a concern that typologies may distort reality rather than clarify it (e.g., Clarke 1990: 3). This concern is valid, but what are the realistic alternatives to typologies of some sort? Generalizing about "crime" or "lawbreakers" surely distorts reality even more.

The concept of "occupational crime" was first clearly identified by Quinney (1964) and was specifically defined by Clinard and Quinney (1967) as "violation of the legal codes in the course of activity in a legitimate occupation" (p. 131). They considered this formulation more useful than Sutherland's conception of white collar crime, which is restricted to high-status offenders. Following Newman (1958), among others, they recognized that crimes can be committed by farmers illegally watering down milk, by repair workers undertaking and charging for unnecessary repairs, and by a host of other non–white-collar workers who commit crimes within the context of their occupations. Following Bloch and Geis (1970), they differentiated among occupational crimes committed by individuals as individuals (e.g., doctors against patients), by employees against employers (e.g., embezzlers), and by merchants against customers (e.g., consumer fraud). Typically, occupational crime has been applied to acts in which financial gain or status is sought (or prevention of its loss is involved).

Clinard and Quinney (1973), in the second edition of their influential book *Criminal Behavior Systems*, designated corporate crime as but one form of occupational crime. This distinction has been the single, most influential typological scheme of white collar crime. It has been widely adopted within the field and by the more sophisticated media. Corporate crime was defined as "offenses committed by corporate officials for their corporation and the offenses of the corporation itself" (p. 188)—the type of crime Sutherland was concerned with in *White Collar Crime*. It is widely accepted today that the characteristics and consequences of corporate crime make it fundamentally different from the range of activities subsumed under the heading of occupational crime.

A somewhat parallel but hardly synonymous conceptual differentiation that was refined during the 1970s distinguishes between *organizational* and *individualistic* white collar crime (see, e.g., Schrager and Short 1977). The complex mixture of motives and objectives in organizational white collar crime is not easily conveyed by such a dichotomy (Reichman 1986). Various more fully differentiated typologies of white collar crime developed over the years have incorporated offender–victim relationships, offender attributes, offense context, offense form and objectives, nature of harm perpetrated, or some combination of these variables (Coleman 2002; Hagan 2002). We see, then, that different approaches can be applied to the challenge of formulating a typology of white collar crime. Despite the inevitably arbitrary and limited attributes of any classification scheme, typologies provide a necessary point of departure for any meaningful discussion of white collar crime. The synthetic typology offered in this text is adapted from some of the existing typologies but also encompasses the wide range of activities labeled as white collar crime. The principal criteria for differentiating between the types of white collar crime, broadly defined, are as follows:

- Context in which illegal activity occurs, including the setting (e.g., corporation, government agency, professional service) and the level within the setting (e.g., individual, workgroup, organization)
- Status or position of offender (e.g., wealthy or middle class, chief executive officer or employee)
- Primary victims (e.g., general public or individual clients)

- Principal form of harm (e.g., economic loss or physical injury)
- Legal classification (e.g., antitrust, fraud)

The typology that follows includes activities that some students of white collar crime would exclude, but at a minimum these activities have a close generic relationship with white collar crime:

1. *Corporate crime*: Illegal and harmful acts committed by officers and employees of corporations to promote corporate (and personal) interests. Forms include corporate violence, corporate theft, corporate financial manipulation, and corporate political corruption or meddling.

2. *Occupational crime*: Illegal or harmful financially driven activity committed within the context of a legitimate, respectable occupation. Forms include retail crime, service crime, crimes of professionals, and employee crime.

3. *Governmental crime*: A cognate form of white collar crime; a range of activities wherein government itself, government agencies, government office, or the aspiration to serve in a government office generates illegal or demonstrably harmful acts. Forms include state crime and political white collar crime.

4. *State-corporate crime, crimes of globalization, and finance crime*: Major hybrid forms of white collar crime that involve in some combination a synthesis of governmental, corporate, international financial institution, or occupational crime. *Finance crime* specifically refers to criminal activity in the realm of high-level finance, from banking to the securities markets.

5. *Enterprise crime, contrepreneurial crime, technocrime, and avocational crime*: "Residual" forms of white collar crime, or a variety of miscellaneous illegal activities that include more marginal forms of white collar crime. *Enterprise crime* refers to cooperative enterprises involving syndicated (organized) crime and legitimate businesses; *contrepreneurial crime* refers to swindles, scams, and frauds that assume the guise of legitimate businesses; *technocrime* involves the intersection of computers and other forms of high technology with white collar crime; *avocational crimes* are illegal but nonconventional criminal acts committed by white collar workers outside a specifically organizational or occupational context, including income tax evasion, insurance fraud, loan/credit fraud, customs evasion, and the purchase of stolen goods.

The third stage for defining white collar crime can be called *operational*. On this level, the objective of the definition is to provide a point of departure for focused empirical research or comparative critical analysis. In the positivist tradition, Wheeler and his associates (1988) provide one approach to an "operational" definition of white collar crime. For purposes of systematically comparing white collar criminals and "common" criminals, they define white collar crime as violations of eight federal crime categories: securities fraud, antitrust violations, bribery, tax offenses, bank embezzlement, postal and wire fraud, false claims and statements, and credit and lending institution fraud. Although they recognize that such an operational definition does not encompass a representative sampling of the total body of white collar crime, they consider it to reflect federally prosecuted white collar crime. If such an operational definition allows these researchers to make quantitative comparisons, then obviously any resulting generalizations must be qualified relative to the definition. Many empirical studies of white collar crime adopt much narrower definitions of specific types of white collar crime for purposes of quantitative analysis.

Such definitions, however, are not simply the purview of mainstream white collar criminologists dedicated to a scientific approach to the study of white collar crime. Critical criminologists have also formulated definitions of white collar crime that are intended to facilitate comparative analysis. Michalowski and Kramer (1987), for example, have defined *corporate transgressions* as violations of international standards of conduct (developed by the United Nations) by transnational corporations that result in identifiable social injury. It could be argued that such a definition raises some formidable interpretive questions, but its intent is to facilitate systematic, comparative analysis. Again, critical white collar criminologists have developed comparable but much more narrowly focused definitions for elite and corporate activities they consider criminal.

The concept of white collar crime is, in the final analysis, somewhat like a Chinese puzzle: Whichever way one turns with it, new difficulties and conundrums are encountered. Perhaps it is most easily defined in negative terms: It refers to illegal or harmful activity that is neither street crime nor conventional crime. More generally, white collar crime is a generic term for the whole range of illegal, prohibited, and demonstrably harmful activities involving a violation of a private or public trust, committed by institutions and individuals occupying a legitimate, respectable status and directed toward financial advantage or the maintenance and extension of power and privilege. We should give up the illusion that white collar crime can—or even should—have a single meaning or definition. Ideally, whenever a definition of white collar crime or cognate activities is advanced, it should be done so in conjunction with a clear indication of its purpose.

Trust and White Collar Crime

The notion of trust is a central one in contemporary social existence (Frankel and Gordon 2001; Gambetta 1988; Hardin 2002). The term *trust* has been defined in different ways; here it refers to confidence in a relationship that the other party will act honorably and fulfill legitimate expectations (Oliver 1997). Trust, in one formulation, is a secularized version of faith (Seligman 1997). It is involved in relationships with and between both individuals and organizations.

In the traditional world of our ancestors, life was largely confined to a small circle of people, primarily one's family, with whom one had longstanding, mutually interdependent relations. One of the central features of the modern world is that people typically spend much more time interacting with or are dependent on many individuals and organizations with whom they have narrower and more instrumental relationships (Misztal 1996). This applies to corporations that employ us, banks where we deposit money, stockbrokers with whom

we invest, retail businesses from which we purchase goods, physicians from whom we seek treatment, and so forth. Trust has become much more problematic in the modern world.

The diffusion of impersonal trust into a broad range of relationships and transactions creates countless opportunities for corruption, misrepresentation, and fraud. The broad extension of trust thus appears to be both unavoidable and necessary in a modern society, although a great deal of variability exists in the degree of trust involved in relationships and transactions. Donald Cressey (1980), the distinguished early student of white collar crime, argued that we must confront a fundamental paradox: If we attempt to curtail sharply the extension of trust in business relationships in the interest of reducing opportunities for white collar crime, we will also severely jeopardize legitimate business relationships and other interpersonal transactions.

Trust and its violation are certainly key elements of white collar crime. Sutherland (1940: 3; 1949: 152–58) characterized white collar crime as involving a "violation of delegated or implied trust." Susan Shapiro (1990: 350) has argued forcefully that *the* central attribute of white collar crime is the violation of trust, which then takes the form of misrepresentation, stealing, misappropriation, self-dealing, corruption, and role conflict. It is especially difficult to prosecute successfully the violations of trust that occur behind the closed doors of "suites," and the parties involved can often manipulate the organizational structure to conceal their misconduct (Shapiro 1990: 355). For lack of a term that better captures the common links among the broad range of white collar crimes, this book adopts the notion of *trusted criminals*, even though focusing on the nature of their offenses may be more important than making sense of the offenders themselves.

The adoption of the term *trusted criminals* and the recognition of the central role of trust in white collar crime should not be interpreted as an unqualified endorsement of the thesis that violations of trust differentiate white collar crime from other forms of crime. Trust and its violation are elements of other crimes, from confidence games to domestic violence. Conversely, the level of trust in white collar relationships and transactions is hardly absolute, although it is typically higher than in many other realms. Nevertheless, from a critical or progressive perspective, the essence of white collar crime resides in the harm done, not simply in the violation of trust.

The violation of trust has some significant consequences beyond the immediate losses suffered by victims of crimes. One of the most pernicious consequences of violations of trust—especially when committed by people in high places in government and in the corporate world—is the potential for an increase in distrust. To the extent that people become distrustful and cynical, the likelihood of cooperative and productive relationships is diminished. The long-term consequences of violations of trust, and the difficulties involved in restoring trusting relations, are relatively understudied. Still, the harmful consequences of the erosion of trust are surely diffuse and many.

Respectability and White Collar Crime

The idea of respectability has traditionally been closely associated with white collar crime. As noted earlier, Sutherland's (1940) initial characterization of white collar crime identified it as "crime in the upper or white-collar class, composed of respectable or at least respected business and professional men" (p. 1). This identification of white collar crime with respectability has been criticized because "respectability" is not easily defined, can be faked, and is not linked with specific norms for acceptable behavior (Shapiro 1990). Admittedly, the term *respectable* can be used in different ways, which causes some confusion. Dictionary definitions of respectable include worthy of esteem, of good standing, proper or decent, of moderate excellence, and of considerable size.

For our purposes, however, three different meanings of respectable must be distinguished: first, a *normative* meaning, or an assessment of moral integrity; second, a *status-related* meaning, that is to say a legitimate position or occupation; and third, a *symptomatic* meaning, or the outward appearance of acceptable or superior status. Obviously these different meanings are not synonymous; there are

dishonest (or morally unrespectable) stockbrokers and honest (but low-status) street people. The successful con artist projects an appearance of respectability but lacks either the required moral qualities or sufficient status. In the present context, the latter two meanings of respectable are invoked. No implication of moral integrity is intended; in fact, its absence among people who enjoy both the appearance and status of respectability is one of the core characteristics of white collar crime. When people object to the notion of *respectable criminals*, they are, of course, focusing on the moral meaning. From this point of view, people who commit crimes and perpetrate harms are never respectable. Even if those who are exposed as criminals may indeed lose their respectable status, it is important to recognize that often this status is precisely what enabled them to commit their crimes in the first place.

The more respectable people appear to be, the more likely they are to be trusted (Ball 1970). The more respectable people appear to be, the less likely they will be suspected of committing serious crimes. In a parallel vein, organizations such as corporations typically strive to be regarded as legitimate and respectable, with the view that such a perception will contribute significantly to their ability to compete effectively and maximize their profits. There may be many exceptions to these propositions, but they are valid generalizations.

Societies have ceremonies or rituals wherein respectable status is publicly acknowledged (e.g., graduation exercises). Other ceremonies—Garfinkel (1956) has called them *degradation ceremonies*—strip people of their respectable status. The criminal trial is perhaps the most obvious example; even though many who are brought to trial did not enjoy a truly respectable status to begin with, a criminal trial resulting in a conviction and a prison sentence formally transforms someone from a free citizen into an incarcerated felon. Commitment proceedings, formal expulsion processes, and other such rituals strip people of measures of respectability. Some evidence of the advantages of a respectable status for those who are processed by the criminal justice system will be offered in subsequent chapters.

Risk and White Collar Crime

The term *risk* has had a variety of meanings. Originally it was associated with a wager, or the probability of an event occurring; more recently it has come to mean great danger and alludes to negative outcomes exclusively (Douglas 1990; Feller 2005; Steele 2004). In the context of white collar crime, risk can refer to either meaning.

Risk applies to white collar crime in the original sense insofar as a calculated gamble is taken; the chances of being caught and punished are quite remote compared with the benefits that accrue from committing the crime. Although such calculations can play a role in most forms of crime, it is especially likely to be a central feature of much white collar crime. Evidence cited elsewhere in this book strongly suggests that in most cases the risk strongly favors the offender because the probability of detection, prosecution, and sanctioning is typically low.

Risk is also involved in an important class of white collar crimes in the second, more recent sense: as the assessment of chances of dangerous (even catastrophic) consequences of corporate and professional decision making. One distinctive element of much white collar crime is the absence of the *specific* intent to cause harm. Rather, the harm of much white collar crime is a function of making the pursuit of profit or economic efficiency paramount over all other objectives. More to the point, corporations and professionals have often been prepared to put their workers, customers, and the general public at higher risk of harm if their course of action is seen to enhance profit or result in lower risk of loss, or to achieve some other organizational objective. In 1972, the collapse of a mining company's dam in Buffalo Creek, West Virginia, led to the destruction of the community and the loss of many lives; in 1986, the explosion of the space shuttle *Challenger* destroyed the lives of seven astronauts, including an American schoolteacher, as millions of Americans watched on television. The extent to which such events were accidents or the avoidable outcome of decisions within complex organizations has been analyzed and debated (Erikson 1976; Vaughan 1996). At worst, criminally irresponsible decision making was involved.

The media play an important role in shaping perceptions of many modern hazards and tend to portray them as natural rather than human-made (Spencer and Triche 1994). The things we fear will harm us most often pose the least actual risk and vice versa (Glassner 2000). Most people, for example, tend to overestimate the likelihood of major nuclear power plant accidents and underestimate the hazards of lawn mowing (Clarke 1988: 23). Meier and Short (1985), in a seminal article on crime and risk, produced some evidence that citizens are increasingly conscious of the risk of becoming white collar crime victims.

The term *accident* is widely invoked for many fatal or harmful events, although this concept seems to have emerged only in the 17th century; in earlier times, fate, providence, witchcraft, God's will, and the like were blamed for misfortunes (Green J. 1997). Charles Perrow (1984) coined the term *normal accident* to refer to the accidents that complex modern technological systems inevitably produce. Perrow insisted, however, that we recognize that the choices underlying high-risk systems are knowingly made in deference to organizational goals. The costs of such choices should not be simply dismissed as accidents dictated by the technology itself or as human error. Rather, the nature of the risky choices built into these complex systems must be confronted. Today we are said to live increasingly in a *risk society*, with significant implications for our understanding of crime (O'Malley 1998; Rigakos 1999). Choices about risk occur within a social context that must be understood and analyzed (Alario and Freudenberg 2003; Tierney 1999). Ordinary citizens, workers, and consumers have too little input in these choices (Short 2001).

Serious efforts to impose legal controls on many important sources of societal risk date only from the mid-1960s and led to the establishment of federal regulatory agencies such as the Environmental Protection Agency and the Occupational, Safety and Health Administration (Priest 1990). Product liability, which focuses intensely on acceptable and unacceptable risk, has expanded greatly only in recent years and has now been identified as the largest subfield of civil law (Priest 1990: 210). The enormous growth of public and private law concerning risk assessment and the apportionment of blame for accidents has been vigorously criticized from many quarters as being economically inefficient and fundamentally unjust.

Risk assessment has been a big business for some time, although controversy persists over whether it is truly valid and objective (Huber 1990; Perrow 1984; Tierney 1999). The cost-benefit analysis that plays such a central role in much risk assessment undertaken on behalf of corporations is seen by some as fundamentally immoral (Teuber 1990). It attempts to impose a monetary value on human lives and accepts the loss of a certain number of lives as an economic necessity. The stress on assessing risk to individuals, as opposed to risk to populations, has also been criticized (Adler 2005). Some students of risk claim that workers make rational choices to engage in some risky occupations and that in a capitalist system the state should minimize its involvement in these choices (Viscusi 1983). But workers typically lack both the knowledge and power to make alternative choices or to modify dangerous working conditions (Draper 1984; Nelkin and Brown 1984). Employees who work in high-risk workplaces, when given the opportunity to express themselves, display considerable anxiety and anger over their circumstances (Nelkin and Brown 1984). Decision making about risks does not occur on a level playing field.

Corporations are more likely to take certain types of risks if they have reason to believe they can get away with it. For example, their concern for short-term financial gain means they are more likely to reduce risks involving worker safety than those involving workers' long-term health (Felstiner and Siegelman 1989). Workers and regulatory inspectors alike tend to respond more readily to hazards that pose immediate risks of direct injury than to the uncertainties of long-term or latent injuries (Hawkins 1990).

Corporations tend to accept higher levels of risk to employees than to the general public because accidents involving the public are more likely to get media attention (Hutter and Lloyd-Bostock 1990). But corporate concerns with keeping down costs can compromise public safety. Some commentators suggest the September 11, 2001 attacks might have been prevented if airlines had not been trying to save money on passenger screening procedures.

Decision making about risks is not, of course, restricted to corporations, although the scope of potential harm is especially broad in that realm. Many employees vested in corporate retirement funds have been forcefully reminded in recent years that top corporate executives often protect themselves from the risks of stock losses; the employees experience large losses (Uchitelle 2002). Physicians may impose unnecessary risks on patients either to maintain their control over a situation or for economic advantage. Other professionals such as stockbrokers may expose their clients to excessive financial risks to increase their own income from commissions. A basic issue in such cases is whether employees, patients, or clients were made fully aware of the risks involved before giving their consent for a riskier course of action. Criminal charges are quite uncommon in such cases due to the often formidable difficulty of demonstrating criminal intent.

Some level of risk may be an inevitable feature of modern existence. Certainly no reasonable person imagines that all risk of harm (physical or financial) can be eliminated from modern corporate and professional activities. An excessive aversion to risks carries costs of its own (Langewiesche 1998). But a substantial amount of evidence also demonstrates that corporations (and professionals) have too often imposed excessive risks on vulnerable parties, such that the costs outweigh any possible benefits. Clearly, making decisions involving risk can cross a line and become a form of criminal conduct: white collar crime. Box 1.3 explores the prevalence of white collar crime throughout the world.

COMPARING WHITE COLLAR AND CONVENTIONAL CRIME OFFENDERS

How do white collar and conventional crime offenders differ? Any attempt to answer this question must immediately acknowledge that both

BOX 1.3   Cross-Cultural and International Dimensions of White Collar Crime

White collar crime in at least most of its forms can be found in all countries, although some types of white collar crime (e.g., finance crime) may be more prevalent in developed countries and other types (e.g., corruption) may be more prevalent in less developed countries. The literature on white collar crime has been predominantly American, but in the English-language world a formidable literature also exists—in Great Britain, Canada, and Australia, in particular (e.g., Croall 2001; Grabosky 1989; Snider 1993). White collar crime has been especially associated with capitalist countries, but it has been shown to be well represented in communist countries, such as the former Soviet Union, communist Poland, and the People's Republic of China (e.g., Cebulak 1991; Rosner 1986; Zhang 2001). The form and character of white collar crime in countries with a capitalist economy is influenced by the culture and structure of opportunity in the particular country. For example, in Japan, white collar crime seems to be more group oriented than individualistic, as a reflection of cultural values and the organization of work (Kerbo and Inoue 1990; Walsh J. 2005). Some countries have engaged in much debate about white collar (or "economic") crime (e.g., Sweden); other countries have apparently declared the combating of white collar crime a high priority (e.g., Finland); and still other countries (e.g., Israel) have developed especially potent approaches to policing white collar crime (Alvesalo 1999; CJ International 1986; Lindgren 2002). As the world becomes increasingly globalized and borders between countries diminish in importance in many areas of business and trade, white collar crime must be understood in international terms (Martens 1991; Schlegel 2000). This text focuses principally on white collar crime and its control in the United States, as any systematic attempt to address white collar crime and its control around the world would require a book at least twice as long. Furthermore, a reasonably sophisticated understanding of white collar crime in other countries requires some familiarity with the history, culture, and legal systems of those countries. This text does refer to white collar crime and its control in other countries, when appropriate, and devotes some attention to globalized or international dimensions of white collar crime.

key terms cover a broad range of offenses and offenders. Nevertheless, some valid generalizations about differences are possible and useful to identify (Friedrichs 1999). In this context, then, white collar offenses include various forms of corporate and occupational crime as well as frauds such as contrepreneurial activity. Conventional crime includes such "index crimes" as murder, rape, robbery, burglary, aggravated assault, and auto theft.[1]

Age

Conventional crime offenders are disproportionately young, while white collar crime offenders are more likely to be middle-aged or older and to begin their offending at a later age (Benson and Kerley 2001; Holtfreter 2005). For example, about half of those arrested for index crimes are under age 25, and about a third are under age 21; for some conventional offenses (e.g., robbery), some 65 percent of those arrested are under age 25 (Federal Bureau of Investigation (FBI) 2005; Williamson 2000). If white collar crimes by definition include the actions of corporate executives, retailers, physicians, and entrepreneurs, among others, it should be obvious that they are typically middle-aged or older. Of course, many juveniles are employed (e.g., about half of those between ages 16 and 19), and a certain proportion of these juveniles commit work-related offenses such as shortchanging customers, giving away goods, and stealing from their employer (Wright and Cullen 2000). But such "occupational delinquency," although little studied to date, tends to incorporate relatively minor forms of white collar crime and constitutes a small proportion of the white collar crime problem.

---

1. Index crimes are those crimes used by the FBI to determine the incidence of crime in the United States.

Class

Conventional crime offenders are disproportionately lower class and poor, although in some interpretations it is society's response to the activities of the poor rather than their greater propensity for lawbreaking that determines the class profile of those arrested for conventional crimes (Chambliss 1973). Nevertheless, conventional offenses such as robbery and burglary are viewed as more concentrated in lower-class settings, and offenders are more likely to come from a lower-class background (Benson and Kerley 2001). As originally conceived of by Sutherland (1940), white collar crime is the crime of the upper or better-off classes. It is not the crime of the poor. Some students of white collar crime (e.g., Simon 2006) have focused principally on the crimes of the elite classes—rich corporate leaders and powerful political figures. Millionaires, even billionaires, have been accused of committing white collar crimes and in some cases have been convicted and imprisoned, as in the case of financier Michael Milken (Stewart 1991). The wealthiest man in Russia, Mikhail Khodorkovsky, was convicted on May 31, 2005, of fraud, embezzlement, and tax evasion, and was sentenced to nine years in prison (Chivers and Arvedlund 2005). Khodorkovsky, supposedly worth some $15 billion at one point, may well be the wealthiest man ever convicted of such crimes. In the United States, many of the accused executives in the early 21st-century corporate crime cases were worth tens of millions of dollars; some were worth hundreds of millions (Sorkin 2002c). They were wealthy by any standard.

The introduction of the concept of occupational crime has led to a way of thinking about white collar crime that substantially de-emphasizes the association with social elites and the upper class and stresses in its place the occupational context of the illegality. Occupational crime offenders are often middle class and in the broadest application of the term—illegality committed in the context of a legitimate occupation—may even be lower-class individuals employed in minimum wage jobs. However, the Yale University project on white collar crime, examining the class membership of those formally charged with white collar offenses, declared white collar crime to be principally "crimes of the middle class" (Weisburd, Wheeler, Waring, and Bode 1991). The more important thesis of the Weisburd et al. study is the claim that social status and class are much less of a factor in determining the seriousness of white collar crime than is control over organizational structures and resources. On this basis, managers are often more directly implicated in the most serious white collar crimes than are owners. In a study of over 1,000 occupational fraud cases, Kristy Holtfreter (2005a) reported that those involved in some forms of fraud—e.g., fraudulent statements—were significantly better off than those who committed other types of fraud (e.g., asset misappropriation). But the promotion of a view of white collar crime as essentially middle class also calls for an evaluation. First, on one level, this finding would be hardly surprising simply on the basis that there are far more middle-class individuals than upper-class individuals. The first question is this: What is their representation relative to a larger population? Second, is such a finding principally about those who commit what can meaningfully be called white collar crime or about how the criminal justice system chooses to define and process white collar offenders? A recent study of white collar offenders (Weisburd et al. 2001) acknowledges this issue but also recognizes that most of those actually charged with white collar offenses are not in fact members of the elite social classes. In part this finding is attributed to changes in the structure of work and occupations, extending to millions of middle- and lower-middle-class individuals with opportunities to engage in white collar crime. By any criteria, however, white collar crime offenders are significantly more likely to be middle and upper class than are conventional crime offenders.

Race

Racial minorities are disproportionately represented among those charged with several major forms of conventional crime. Over 25 percent of those arrested for index crimes in the United States are African Americans, although this group only constitutes about 12 percent of the American population (FBI 2005). Even more dramatically, African Americans have accounted for over half of those arrested for robbery (Williamson 2000: 43–44). American prisons are disproportionately populated by racial minorities, most of whom are in prison on conventional crime– or drug-related charges (Parenti 1999). African Americans and other disadvantaged minorities are highly unlikely to be charged with such white collar crimes as antitrust or corporate wrongdoing, although they are well represented among low-level white collar crime offenders guilty of embezzlement and fraud (Weisburd et al. 1991). According to Uniform Crime Report data, African Americans are as proportionately overrepresented for white collar crime arrests (over 30 percent in 2003) as for conventional offenses (FBI 2005). But the claim of Gottfredson and Hirschi (1990) that African Americans have a higher overall rate of involvement in white collar crime than do whites is highly misleading. Rather, they commit the types of low-level white collar crimes that are especially likely to be reported to the police, processed, and recorded in the FBI's Uniform Crime Report.

The kinds of fraud for which African American arrest rates are significantly higher than those of whites are often not occupation related, including welfare fraud (Steffensmeier 1989). Altogether, we have no truly reliable demographic data on the whole class of white collar offenders, but the data we do have strongly suggests that if African Americans are overrepresented for lower-level offenses, whites are overrepresented for middle- and high-level offenses (Harris 1991; Weisburd et al. 1991). When African Americans are accused of middle- or high-level offenses, either they or others on their behalf may invoke a claim of racist scapegoating (Nasar 1994). Such claims are not likely to be easily proven or disproved.

Gender

It is widely understood that males greatly outnumber females among conventional crime offenders (by at least six to one, in some estimates); all available evidence indicates that a parallel situation exists for white collar offenders. The exact dimensions of the proportional imbalance are not presently available, and some of the limited data reported are contradictory. But these data indicate that the female arrest rate for white collar crimes has been one quarter or one fifth of the male arrest rate (Manson 1986; Weisburd et al. 1991). In part, the kinds of crimes selected for comparison skew results in one direction or the other, especially as women are quite clearly better represented among those engaging in low-level frauds and underrepresented among those engaged in crimes of violence (Holtfreter 2005a). The male dominance of corporations and outside-the-home occupations, especially the more powerful positions, would seem to be clearly the single most important factor explaining the overall discrepancy or underrepresentation of female offenders (Braithwaite 1995: 225). Kathleen Daly (1989), in her survey of gender and white collar crime, has drawn the following conclusions: (1) The female share of corporate, or organizational, crime is low, with only 1 percent of the women's white collar crime cases (compared to 14 percent of the men's) falling into this category; (2) the female share of most forms of occupational crime is low, although for bank embezzlement it was 50 percent; (3) females were much less likely than males to work in crime groups and more likely to commit their white collar crimes alone; (4) the average gain from white collar crimes committed by females was much lower than that for males; and (5) females were much more likely to claim financial need of their families than males as a motivation for their involvement with white collar crime.

If the socialization of females and the job opportunity structure for women increasingly comes to resemble that for males, one would ordinarily expect that patterns of involvement in all forms of white collar crime will become more similar. We do not yet have studies that reliably establish whether women are less predisposed than men toward white collar criminality, although there are indications that this may be so.

Other Demographic Variables and Differences

White collar crime offenders tend to differ from conventional crime offenders on variables other than age, class, race, and gender. Obviously they are more likely to be employed, as employment is virtually by definition a precondition for the commission of white collar crimes (Weisburd et al. 2001). They are also more likely to be better educated, and a certain proportion are exceptionally well educated (Benson and Kerley 2001; Holtfreter 2005a). Insofar as they are older and more likely to be middle class and employed, they are more likely to be married and have more stable family situations. They are also more likely than conventional crime offenders to have community group and church affiliations (Benson and Kerley 2001). There are many exceptions to such generalizations, which are based upon limited samples of convicted white collar offenders, but as overall patterns they seem valid and are worth noting.

Criminal Careers

Conventional crime offenders are often viewed as engaging in multiple different forms of criminal conduct, of engagement in criminal activity over a period of years—sometimes indefinitely—and of being recidivists, or repeat offenders. The largest proportion of conventional crime offenders "age out" of such activity, however; as they get older, they are less likely to engage in such activities as robbery or auto theft.

By contrast, white collar crime offenders have commonly been regarded as committing only one form of white collar crime. The offense is typically viewed as a relatively isolated incident in a legitimate occupational career, with the crime not being repeated after the offender has been caught. In a study of those charged with white collar crime offenses in federal courts, Weisburd and colleagues (2001) challenge this traditional view of white collar crime offenders. They found that a significant percentage of white collar crime offenders had engaged in different forms of lawbreaking (both white collar and conventional), had multiple contacts with the criminal justice system, and were recidivists. It does seem to be true, unsurprisingly, that they are more likely to have begun their offending at a later age (Benson and Kerley 2001). However, white collar crime offenders processed by the criminal justice system are disproportionately engaged in low-level and fairly visible forms of fraud and are accordingly likely to have more in common with conventional crime offenders. We do not have sufficient reliable data to make truly valid comparisons between the career patterns of the whole spectrum of white collar crime offenders and conventional crime offenders.

THE SOCIAL MOVEMENT AGAINST WHITE COLLAR CRIME

Even though white collar crime continued to be relatively neglected for several decades after Sutherland's famous call for more attention to it, the situation began to change in the early 1970s. Sociologist Jack Katz (1980b) has argued that a social movement against white collar crime in the United States that emerged during this period was the most substantial attack on such crime since the early 20th-century Progressive Movement, which brought together rural populists, muckraking journalists, and organizations of civic-minded businessmen concerned about the excesses and outrages of big business. This "movement" was, in part, one response to disillusionment with and declining confidence in the political and business leadership, arising out of the Vietnam War protests, the Watergate crimes of the Nixon White House, and some high-profile cases of corporate misconduct (Friedrichs 1980a; Clinard and Yeager 1980). Emerging movements on behalf of minorities, consumers, and the environment highlighted social inequities and injustices and fed into increasing attention to white collar crime. Within the social sciences, conflict theory (and more specifically a neo-Marxist critique) directed more attention to the crimes of the state and the economic elites and to the disproportionate role of the rich and the powerful in the lawmaking process. Katz (1980b) argued that a variety of "moral entrepreneurs," including investigative reporters, legislators reacting to scandals, and federal prosecutors, both responded to and measurably raised public consciousness about white collar crime. Moral entrepreneurs are those who condemn a form of behavior and are in a position to mobilize people to demand legal action in response to it. The motivations on the part of politicians and prosecutors in particular were hardly fueled by moral outrage alone. To the extent that public concern with at least some forms of white collar crime increased, politicians and prosecutors could enjoy some career advantages by pursuing it (Cullen, Maakestad, and Cavender 1987). The need to reinforce confidence in the leadership and established institutions, and the need to reinforce the legitimation (or broad public support) of the system itself, also played an important role in the institutional response to white collar crime. On the other hand, one prominent student of corporate crime, Laureen Snider (2000), has declared the movement against corporate crime in the United States and Canada as largely defeated by the successful efforts of corporate interests to counter regulatory and justice system initiatives against their activities.

If there is a social movement against white collar crime today, it has not developed with any consistent momentum. In the more conservative 1980s in the United States, some curtailing of federal investigative resources and budgets of regulatory agencies occurred, and a dip in white collar crime convictions resulted (Caringella-MacDonald 1990; Poveda 1990). A number of large-scale white collar crime cases, from insider trading cases to the savings and loan frauds, received a good deal of attention. In the 1990s, federal prosecutors appointed by the Clinton administration expressed commitment to intensified efforts against white collar crime, and eventually they initiated some important cases, such as the antitrust case against Microsoft. But the Clinton administration on the whole adopted other priorities, and a series of allegations against Clinton and his close associates probably contributed to the derailment of any broader attack on white collar crime (Kramer and Michalowski 1995; Stewart 1996). A generally conservative Congress passed laws promoting an environment favorable to large-scale white collar crime (Labaton 2002b; Schwartz 2002). The George W. Bush

administration, early in the 21st century, was widely viewed as oriented toward the interests of business. It was criticized for seemingly retreating from aggressively pursuing environmental crime, and its decision not to pursue an effort to break up Microsoft strongly suggested that it would not aggressively pursue antitrust cases (Labaton and Lohr 2002). The series of corporate scandals early in the 21st century initially forced the Bush administration to proclaim its commitment to combating corporate crime (Walczak, Dunham, and Dwyer 2002).

The potential for a revived and more successful movement against corporate crime—and other forms of white collar crime—certainly exists. A grassroots social movement against white collar crime calls for a combination of activist activity in conjunction with a favorable political and economic environment (Almeida and Stearns 1998; Pellow 2001). However, the major war against terrorism, begun in September 2001, initially deflected public attention and justice system resources away from white collar crime. An economic downturn during this period also inhibited a social movement against white collar crime, with a concern about jobs and economic security taking precedence. By 2005, some of the momentum for reform of corporate governance, in the wake of the series of corporate scandals, seemed to be losing steam, with the Bush administration clearly not pushing the reforms (Eichenwald 2005b). Whether the considerable outrage initially emerging in response to the corporate scandals would eventually re-ignite a vigorous social movement against white collar crime remained to be seen (Rich 2002; Walczak, Dunham, and Dwyer 2002). The National White Collar Crime Center (see Box 1.4) is one response to concern with white collar crime.

IMAGES OF WHITE COLLAR CRIME: THE ROLE OF THE MEDIA

The media—television in particular—are a pervasive element of contemporary life. The media are a crucial source of our understanding of crime because few people experience a wide variety of

---

B O X 1.4 The National White Collar Crime Center

The National White Collar Crime Center (NW3C) was established in 1992 as the first federal entity exclusively focused on addressing white collar crime. It originated with the Leviticus Project Association, a multistate cooperative endeavor between law enforcement agencies, assisted with a federal grant, to share information and pool resources in the investigation and prosecution of white collar crimes. The NW3C provides research, training, and investigative support services to a range of entities pursuing white collar crime cases. Its member-

ship includes state and local law enforcement agencies, state regulatory agencies, federal agencies, national consumer advocacy organizations, and private businesses. The NW3C has sponsored a series of economic crime summits. Among other initiatives, it has established a White Collar Crime Research Consortium with the mission of promoting, through dedicated research, increased public awareness of the impact and burden of white collar crime on society. The author of this book served as president of the Consortium from 2002–2004.

---

crime firsthand (Surette 1998). Crime has been traditionally portrayed in the media mainly in conventional terms, with an emphasis on sensational, especially violent, crimes (Altheide 2002). This conventional, melodramatic, and sensationalistic bias serves the ideological function of deflecting attention from the structural and political sources of crime (Gitlin 1980; Humphries 1981; Potter and Kappeler 1998).

The news media have always devoted at least some space to the crimes of the rich and powerful, especially when scandalous circumstances are involved (Graber 1980; Papke 1987). Following the Watergate Affair, coverage of white collar crime increased (Gans 1979). But any increase in reporting on white collar crime was spotty (Evans and Lundman 1983). Reporting of corporate crime did not generally attribute criminal wrongdoing to the corporation. When 25 employees of a chicken processing plant died in a fire in North Carolina in 1991, the media attributed the tragedy to violations of safety regulations, but they did not characterize it as a crime despite the manslaughter conviction of the owner (Wright, Cullen, and Blankenship 1995). When 26 miners died in a Canadian mine explosion in 1992, the media focused on "harm," "charges," and "probes" but not on the criminal liability of the mining company itself (Goff 2001). When a deadly fire occurred in a dance hall in Gotesborg, Sweden, the newspapers largely neglected the role of organizers and promoters of

the dance (Burns and Orrick 2002). In the recent era, newspaper coverage of corporate crime cases remains quite limited, and it tends to shift attention away from the organization and onto the shoulders of specific individuals (Cavender and Mulcahy 1998). In another vein, a study of newspaper coverage of product liability cases against automobile manufacturers between 1983 and 1996 found that they mainly reported verdicts for plaintiffs receiving big awards, especially punitive damage awards; verdicts favoring the corporate defendants were rarely reported (Garber and Bowen 1999). But such coverage also conveys the false impression that product liability cases against corporations can be easily won.

The coverage of corporate crime on news telecasts has followed a pattern similar to that in the print media, with parallel inconsistencies (Potter and Kappeler 1998; Randall 1987). The great majority of the corporate crime stories were not aired at the beginning of the news telecast but were relegated to a later segment. Television coverage of these crimes concentrated mainly on the stories' early stages (initial revelation) and final stages (legal resolution). Coverage of white collar crime was not a consistent interest of the media during the 1980s (Randall, Lee-Sammons, and Hagner 1988); conventional crime and the "drug wars" were accorded more generous coverage. The looting of the savings and loan (S & L) thrifts, with losses of billions of dollars, was a major white collar crime story of the

1980s, but the media was slow to report on it and even then did not cover the story in great depth (Martz 1990b; Hume 1990). Of course, the corrupt and illegal doings of various Reagan administration members and their associates received some attention during the 1980s, as did the crimes of insider traders. In the 1990s, the sex scandals involving President Clinton (i.e., the Paula Jones and Monica Lewinsky cases) surely received more pervasive television coverage than did the Whitewater political corruption case or any of the corporate cases surfacing during this period (Friedrichs 2000a). From 2001 on, corporate scandals cases and other major white collar crime investigations were periodically big news stories but ultimately were overshadowed by the war in Iraq and other stories.

Overall, more dramatic crime stories receive greater coverage even if they are less objectively consequential (Burns and Orrick 2002). Furthermore, even when members of the public are exposed to media coverage of white collar crime, they continue to be far more concerned with conventional, interpersonal violent crimes (Altheide 2002; Graber 1980). The reporting of white collar crime seems to have a smaller impact on the audience than does the reporting of conventional violence.

The traditionally more limited media coverage of white collar crime may have several explanations, including the more indirect harm experienced by individual victims, public resistance to viewing corporations as criminal, and the fact that large and wealthy media organizations may not be inclined to link other large and wealthy organizations with criminality (Cavender and Mulcahy 1998; Evans and Lundman 1983). On a more practical level, media organizations may be intimidated by corporations that threaten directly or indirectly to withdraw advertising or institute defamation suits (Croteau and Hoynes 2001). Through marketing and advertising campaigns, corporations such as General Motors are able to influence public perceptions of their activities, somewhat countering any negative reports (Burns 1999). Altogether, the reporting of corporate crime is far less likely to produce the striking visual images (with oil spills a possible exception) on which the media (and television in particular) thrive. The

Microsoft antitrust case, for example, produced few vivid images for television coverage and was surely experienced as "boring" by many viewers. (Box 1.5 examines the "box office draw" of film and television portrayals of white collar crime.)

White collar crime trials are especially likely to be drawn out and dull and typically do not make especially lively copy (Grabosky and Wilson 1989). Because corporate crimes in particular are often highly complex, their coverage requires exceptionally knowledgeable journalists, but even skillful journalists do not always have the backing of their superiors to report on corporate fraud. Some further dimensions of such constraints on reporting this type of crime will be considered in more depth in a subsequent section on investigative reporting.

EXPOSING WHITE COLLAR CRIME

White collar crime, as a rule, is less visible than conventional crime. Although most conventional crime does not literally occur in that most public of places—the street—it does frequently come to the attention of the police because victims and witnesses report it and the police even observe some of it directly. White collar crime is generally far less visible—much of it, after all, takes place in suites, not streets—and many of its victims are not clearly aware that a crime has been perpetrated against them. "Witnesses" of white collar crime, who often do not realize that a crime has occurred, may be intimidated or confused about what to do in response to it. And our traditional frontline enforcement agencies (e.g., the urban police) have not been organized to monitor and respond to white collar crime. Accordingly, other "agents" play an especially important role in exposing white collar crime.

Informers and Whistleblowers

Informers (or *informants*) provide criminal justice system personnel with crucial information that can lead to the investigation, arrest, indictment, and conviction of law violators (Webster, in Reinertsen and Bronson

---

B O X 1.5   **The Media as Entertainment: White Collar Crime in Films and on TV**

Although countless films are about crime, such films have especially focused on personal violence offenders (especially murderers), conventional offenders and criminal gangs, organized crime (the Mafia), and political offenders, including terrorists. White collar crime has been the subject of a significant number of films, especially since 1970, but these films still constitute a small percentage of all films and, with isolated exceptions, are not among the most prominent films (Nichols 1999). In the major survey to date of films with white collar crime themes, Lawrence W. Nichols (1999) informs us that prior to 1960 such films tended to emphasize the moral conflicts and tragic possibilities involved with wealth and power; from the 1960s through the 1970s they were more likely to focus on political white collar crime; and only since 1979 has corporate illegality been a noteworthy focus of films. *Wall Street* (on insider trading) and *Erin Brockovich* (involving toxic wastes) are among the relatively few films in the recent era that addressed white collar crime issues and were quite successful commercially. (See the Appendix for a list of films with white collar crime themes.)

A common assumption is that television portrayals of crime concentrate disproportionately on conventional predatory offenders. When upper-class people are portrayed as criminals, the activity involved is more likely to be murder than corporate misdeeds (Box 1983). By the 1980s, though, businesspeople became

popular villains, arguably even television's favorite villains (Lichter, Lichter, and Rothman 1991). One study found that the ratio of "good" business executives to "bad" on TV was only 2 to 1, whereas for the police this ratio was 12 to 1, and for doctors 16 to 1 (Gitlin 1983: 268). Still another study found that businesspeople were five times more likely than those in other occupations to be represented as greedy (Lichter, Lichter, and Rothman 1991).

A traditional American ambivalence about businesspeople, who are both admired and reviled, is reflected in media portrayals. Businesspeople may be shown committing heinous deeds, but they are also portrayed as enjoying the "spoils" of their success: fancy cars and clothes, luxurious homes, glamorous parties, exciting recreational activities, and the like. Television conveys contradictory messages: It suggests that cheating and lying may "pay off" materially, but it also panders to the audience's appetite for seeing elites get their just deserts. Even if television viewers are entertained by villainous businesspeople and find them a satisfying vicarious target for their own hostility toward business generally, it is far from clear that this audience feels directly threatened by businesspeople–villains in the same way that it fears conventional predatory criminals. The specific influence of television's attention to the crimes of businesspeople on public perceptions of white collar crime, however, has yet to be fully investigated.

1990). Inevitably those who have the most specific and most incriminating information about illegal activity are themselves in varying degrees involved in it. The use of informers goes far back in history. Jonathan Wild (1682–1725) was a legendary English thief, fence, and informer who sent some 100 thieves to the gallows and ended up there himself (Marx 1988). At least since the time of Wild, informers have provided information in exchange for payment, a favorable arrangement concerning criminal charges against themselves, or both. Because white collar crime cases are relatively invisible, sophisticated, and complex, the use of informers is often indispensable.

Informers played a central role in exposing the Watergate crimes of the Nixon administration in

the 1970s, with lower-level officials assisting in making cases against high-level officials; in the series of Wall Street insider trading cases of the 1980s, with each cornered insider trader providing evidence against another wealthier and more powerful offender; in some of the corporate price-fixing cases of the 1990s, with corporate executives accused of wrongdoing providing incriminating information about their company; and in the corporate scandals cases in the 2000s, again with lower-level corporate executives offering incriminating evidence against former CEOs (Eichenwald 2000a, 2005c; Stewart 1991; Woodward and Bernstein 1977). Such informers are criminally implicated themselves and receive some form of

---

B O X 1.6   "Deep Throat" and the Watergate Case

In June 2005, arguably the most celebrated whistle-blower of the recent era was formally identified: "Deep Throat," the government insider who provided investigative journalists Bob Woodward and Carl Bernstein with crucial information and corroboration relating to the Nixon White House's involvement with and cover-up of the Watergate case, was identified as W. Mark Felt, the Number-Two man at the FBI during that period (Purdom 2005). The designation "Deep Throat" came from a celebrated pornographic film of that time. Considerable discussion ensued following the confirmation of Felt's role in this case (Seelye 2005): Was he a traitor or a hero? Was he motivated by his anger at not being appointed to succeed J. Edgar Hoover as Director of the FBI or by a patriotic sense of duty that high-level wrongdoing had to be exposed for the good of the country? If he knew of such wrong-doing, should he have addressed it within the justice system and resigned his position in protest, or was he right to play the covert whistleblower role he chose?

"consideration" from the criminal justice system in return for revealing what they know about illegal activity.

The use of informers in any criminal cases, including white collar crime, raises complex ethical questions (Marx 1988; Reinertsen and Bronson 1990). On the one hand, inappropriate lenience may be extended to informers who themselves have committed serious crimes, and informers may use their status as informers to commit additional crimes with some sense of immunity. On the other hand, viable criminal cases against major offenders often cannot be made without the assistance of informers, and the exposure of white collar crime is vitally dependent upon them. Some informants turn out to be manipulative con men (Connolly 1996). Mark Whitacre, the primary informant in a major price-fixing case involving the Archer Daniels Midland Company (maker of feed and grain additives), had not only defrauded his company but also reneged on agreements, admitted to having fabricated documents, and was hospitalized for mental illness (Eichenwald 2000a). Informants, then, are valuable but flawed exposers of white collar crime.

The *whistleblower* is a related crucial source of information needed for the detection, and ultimately the prosecution, of many white collar crimes, especially governmental and corporate varieties (Johnson 2002). Although whistleblowers have in common with informers an insider's perspective on the illegal activity, they are not crim-

inally implicated. *Time* magazine designated three whistleblowers as "Persons of the Year" for 2002 (Lacayo and Ripley 2002/2003). A whistleblower played a key role in the single most famous case of wrongdoing in the highest echelons of the federal government: the Watergate case (see Box 1.6).

White collar crime differs from many forms of conventional, organized, and professional crime insofar as the context within which it occurs has not typically been organized specifically to carry out an illegal or manifestly criminal operation. White collar criminals—whether in a government agency, a corporation, a retail business, or a professional service enterprise—may work with colleagues and associates who are not committed to the illegal activity or are directly opposed to it. Most of these associates, once they become aware of illegal activity, will not necessarily "blow the whistle," for many reasons (Miethe 1999). Probably foremost among these reasons is the self-preservation ethos: It is not generally in one's rational best interest to alert authorities on illegal activity occurring within one's organization, agency, corporation, or community. This is the lesson learned by the protagonist of Henrik Ibsen's late 19th-century play, *The Enemy of the People* (1882); he is persecuted by his fellow townsmen for exposing the dangerous pollution of their resort's "therapeutic baths" (MacNamara 1991). A fear of social ostracism, loyalty to one's organization and associates, belief in the company's rationales for unethical or illegal activity, denial that one knows enough or has the appropriate responsibility, and in some cases even fear for one's physical safety deter most people from becoming whistleblowers. On the other hand, senior corporate management sometimes reports wrongdoing by some of its own employees as part of a deal with prosecutors for corporate leniency or even amnesty (Laufer 2002). This has been referred to as "reverse whistleblowing." One study (Glazer and Glazer 1989) adopted the alternative term *ethical resisters* to distinguish those who blow the whistle for principled reasons from those who may do so for less than pure reasons—and in some cases for blatantly self-interested or instrumental reasons (e.g., to settle a personal score, to get rid of one or more personal competitors, or to attempt to deflect attention from the whistleblower's own wrongdoing or liability). In one case, a whistleblower in the computer industry then sold programs to and went to work for a competing company (Lohr 2003). Authentic whistleblowers are often courageous individuals motivated by moral outrage at illegal and often dangerous (or potentially dangerous) corporate policies and practices (Glazer and Glazer 1989, 1999; Johnson 2002). Rather than being ideological heretics and professional misfits, these whistleblowers tend to be conservative people who are dedicated to their work and genuinely committed to professional codes of ethics to which many others merely give lip service (Glazer and Glazer 1989).

Isolated individuals have long played the whistleblower role, but the Glazers (1989) argued that ethical resisters are a historically new group that emerged during the 1960s and 1970s in response to increasing concern over abuses of power and environmental threats. Some widely shown films of the past several decades had whistleblowers as heroes: *Serpico* (1973), *Silkwood* (1983), and *The Insider* (1999)—about police corruption, nuclear power plant safety, and deceitful tobacco company practices, respectively. Although these films largely adopted the image of the whistleblower as a loner, certain organizational and work-related conditions have been found to promote whistleblowing, including good access to information, relative autonomy from direct supervision, and norms

supporting professional expertise on technological matters (Miethe and Rothschild 1994; Perrucci, Anderson, Schendel, and Trachtman 1980). Women have been especially conspicuous among the whistleblowers in the corporate scandals of the 2000s (Abramson 2002; Hill 2002; Lacayo and Ripley 2002/2003).

Whistle-blowing has been characterized as a thoroughly social activity involving a network of relationships (Ling 1991). The term *whistleblower* has been most typically applied to those who inform outside agencies or entities of illegal or unethical actions of their company. Sometimes the term is applied as well to those who raise alarms internally. For example, Enron executive Sherron Watkins was celebrated as a whistleblower for sending a memo to the company's CEO challenging corporate accounting practices as highly questionable, but this memo only surfaced more publicly in the course of later investigations (Duffy 2002). In some cases, an organization or agency may expose wrongdoing by another entity. For example, the software company Netscape played a key role in the major antitrust case brought against Microsoft in 1998 by disclosing evidence to authorities suggesting that Microsoft attempted to intimidate the smaller company from developing its own Internet browser (Brinkley and Lohr 2001). Typically, however, whistle-blowing is most likely to occur in the absence of organizational channels for responding to concerns about illegal or unethical activity and with the perception of broadening collegial support for challenging such activity.

Although at least some whistleblowers have acted heroically, the response to them has hardly been uniformly positive (MacNamara 1991; Nichols 1991). Reactions to whistleblowers who seem to be motivated by greed and self-interest are likely to be negative in comparison with responses to those who seem to be altruistic and concerned with the well-being of others (Miethe and Rothschild 1994). Workers tend to support whistleblowers when direct threats to their health and well-being have been exposed, but when the dangers are less direct or imminent and the whistleblowing may jeopardize jobs or the local economy, workers are much less likely to be supportive (Glazer and Glazer 1989). The corporate scandals of the 2000s, especially the Enron case, inspired a wave of whistleblower reports to federal regulatory agencies and some recently established whistleblower hotlines (Banstetter 2002; Guernsey 2002).

As a rule, whistleblowers pay a substantial price for their courageous actions (Johnson 2002; Nussbaum 2002). According to one study, some 50 percent of a sample of whistleblowers suffered retaliation, and a significant percentage (between 10 and 20 percent) suffered traumatic personal consequences such as suicide, divorce, and the loss of a home, all of which were attributed to fallout from whistleblowing (MacNamara 1991). The literature contains many accounts of personal devastation experienced by whistleblowers, as well as retaliation from management in the form of blacklisting, dismissal, transfer, harassment, and threatened lawsuits (Associated Press 2002b; Eichenwald 1994b). In September 2005, the SEC was investigating charges that a high-tech corporation was retaliating against Wall Street stock analysts who challenged some of the company's claims (Morgenson 2005h). A vice president for marketing at Pfizer reported being increasingly isolated within the company after speaking out about drug-pricing practices (Berenson 2005a). A Pentagon whistleblower in the Halliburton case was threatened with demotion (Zagorin and Burger 2004). A former Wal-Mart executive claimed he was fired for exposing workplace violations such as mandatory 24-hour shifts and locked exits (Greenhouse S. 2005d). Tobacco industry whistleblower Jeffrey Wigand went from a $300,000 annual salary within the industry to an income of $30,000 a year as a teacher and anti-smoking activist (but reported feeling good about his life and work) (Ripley 2005). In some cases, whistleblowers have allegedly been shot at or even murdered (Maas 1973; Rashke 1981). Some whistleblowers who have been dismissed from their jobs have successfully sued for multimillion-dollar damages or reinstatement, and in rare cases they have even been formally vindicated by their company, complete with high-level apologies for their suffering (Eichenwald 1994b; Gerth 1988; Glazer and Glazer 1989). But more often they must move on to new jobs and careers and at least a small minority remain unemployed (and embittered) following the whistleblowing episode.

Traditionally, federal agencies and the courts have done rather little to intervene on behalf of whistleblowers (Johnson 2002; MacNamara 1991). Recently, some steps have been taken on both the federal and state levels to offer whistleblowers at least a measure of protection. The False Claims Amendment Act of 1986, which revitalized an 1860s law offering whistleblowers a monetary reward in the form of a percentage (15–30 percent) of funds recovered through a successful prosecution, has enabled a small number of whistleblowers to receive millions of dollars, a result that has proven controversial (Associated Press 2004; Seagull 1995). Two whistleblowers invoked the False Claims Amendment in alleging that the Custer Battles Security Company defrauded the allied military operation in Iraq out of millions of dollars (Eckholm 2005c).

The U.S. Supreme Court, in a 1998 decision, ruled against a corporate strategy to prevent whistleblowers from testifying against the corporation (*New York Times* 1998). Federal legislation in 1999 provided workers who complain about hazards with protection from job loss (Pear 1999b). Of course, the existence of such laws cannot be said to offer whistleblowers absolute guarantees of protection, insofar as a retaliatory dismissal or some other such action may be difficult or impossible to prove. The likelihood that whistleblowers will come forward is enhanced to the extent that public concern about corrupt and harmful conditions remains high, media attention is persistent, public interest groups are supportive, protective legislation is implemented, and the singular courage of whistleblowers is rewarded and celebrated.

Muckrakers and Investigative Reporters

Journalists historically have been a thorn in the side of the establishment because of their periodic exposures of wrongdoing by the powerful and privileged. The emergence in America of the so-called *muckrakers* in the early 20th century was an important development, for they firmly established the revelation of high-level wrongdoing as a legitimate journalistic enterprise (Serrin and Serrin 2002).

Lincoln Steffens's *The Shame of the Cities* (1904), a powerful exposé of municipal political corruption, has been credited with ushering in the muckraking era (Weir and Noyes 1983). Steffens refuted the then-commonplace notion that urban corruption could be blamed on the new waves of European immigrants, and he revealed the central role of established American businessmen in this form of corrupt activity (Palermo 1978). At about the same time, Ida Tarbell's landmark *The History of the Standard Oil Company* (1904) recounted the range of illegal and unethical actions that were integral to the formation of the richest and most powerful trust monopoly of its time (Brady 1984). Shortly after Tarbell's work came Upton Sinclair's *The Jungle* (1906), which exposed the shocking—literally sickening—practices in the meat-processing industry and was instrumental in promoting new laws. Even some of the films of this period engaged in muckraking. *Children Who Labor* (1912) exposed the exploitation of young children; other films, such as *The Reform Candidate* (1911), *The Grafters* (1913), and *The Land Swindlers* (1913) exposed corrupt politicians and businessmen (White and Averson 1979).

The period 1902–1912 has been referred to as the "golden age" of muckraking. During World War I and in the decades following it, the energy and visibility of muckraking seemed to go into decline, even though journalistic exposés of major forms of high-level crime and corruption were produced, especially in the 1930s. This decline has been attributed to the changing economics of journalism, some pressure from target corporations, growing public boredom with shrill social criticism, and a certain sense of disillusionment because adequate reforms had failed to result from the muckraking enterprise (Downie 1976; Geis 1993; Weir and Noyes 1983).

In the 1970s, muckraking experienced a formidable revival, although it became more commonly known as *investigative reporting*. The political activism and antiestablishment rhetoric so conspicuous on the university campuses in the late 1960s and early 1970s helped produce a generation of younger journalists who were either skeptical of or openly antagonistic toward establishment institutions. The unraveling Watergate Affair (1972–1974) and the enormous attention directed at two investigative reporters for *The Washington Post*, Bob Woodward and Carl Bernstein, played a role in inspiring a new wave of interest in investigative journalism.

The realities of investigative reporting are not as glamorous as popular public perception would have it. Investigative journalism is likely to be lonely, frustrating, tedious, expensive, time-consuming, sometimes hazardous, often controversial, and emotionally draining work; it can also be intensely satisfying and sometimes prestigious (Downie 1976; Shapiro 2003; Weir and Noyes 1983). But Americans have displayed some ambivalence toward muckrakers and investigative journalists. Many citizens see them as biased and unpatriotic and as contributors to excessive disillusionment and cynicism (Downie 1976). Investigative reporters for Tucson's *Arizona Daily Star* who exposed illegal practices in the popular University of Arizona football program were the target of much hostility and prompted significant retaliation by advertisers (Patterson and Russell 1986). Such news stories will inevitably offend some people in positions of power (Weir and Noyes 1983).

Investigative journalism remains a fairly limited enterprise today (Schultz 2003). Only a very small proportion of the nation's newspaper reporters could be accurately characterized as investigative reporters. The traditional focus of muckraking and investigative journalism has been political corruption; it has been much less active in examining private business (Downie 1976; Gans 1979; Shapiro 2003). It is not immune to the pervasive media bias that favors sensational stories about individual wrongdoing (which sell more papers and receive the most attention) over the unraveling of complex, involved forms of institutional wrongdoing that may be much more harmful (Levi 1987). If investigative reporting has become more common since the 1970s, it has also confronted an expanding range of constraints, including expanding government concern with secrecy, fear of libel suits, increasing concentration of the ownership of media outlets, and the growth of increasingly complex corporations, such as multi-nationals (Croteau and Hoynes 2001; Weir and Noyes 1983). Due to the considerable resources often needed to support investigative journalism, it has been undertaken mainly by major newspapers such as *The Washington Post* and *The New York Times*.

Much reporting is based upon press releases and is manipulated by powerful, wealthy sources. The business press as a whole played a limited role in exposing the financial wrongdoing in many major corporations during the recent era (Ledbetter 2003). These journalists were too often caught up in the "hype" of the bull market.

Newspapers in small cities and towns are limited mainly to exposing local political corruption, consumer fraud, and sometimes illegal or unethical practices of local public institutions and corporations. Campus newspapers occasionally address some forms of corporate wrongdoing, such as sweatshop labor (Einwohner and Spencer 2005). Some progressive or liberal publications of limited circulation have promoted investigative journalism: *Mother Jones*, *The Nation*, and *The Progressive* among them. Newsletters such as *Multinational Monitor* and *Corporate Crime Reporter* are dedicated to exposing the crimes of major corporations (Mokhiber and Weissman 1999). And of course the tradition of book-length exposés has continued. Books such as Rachel Carson's *The Silent Spring* (1962) about the destruction of the environment, Ralph Nader's *Unsafe at Any Speed* (1965) about unsafe automobiles, and Mary Adelaide Mendelson's *Tender Loving Greed* (1974) about scandalous nursing home practices have contributed significantly to inspiring investigations and new laws. Many discussions in this text draw on these books and others like them.

Historically, investigative reporting on television has been a limited undertaking. Periodically, and with considerable fanfare, the networks have produced documentaries such as *The Selling of the Pentagon*, which exposed questionable Pentagon public relations practices (Gans 1979). Some regular network "magazine" shows—*60 Minutes* is the best-known example—have also exposed various

white collar crime practices. Many newer shows, such as *20/20*, *PrimeTime Live*, and *Frontline*, have followed the lead of *60 Minutes*. Whenever *60 Minutes* has gone after federal agencies, including the Federal Trade Commission, Food and Drug Administration, Environmental Protection Agency, and IRS, it has typically encountered formidable resistance. The Defense Department even had a long-standing policy of noncooperation with *60 Minutes* (Madsen 1984). In some cases, *60 Minutes* has exposed major forms of corporate crime, including Kepone pollution of the James River by Allied Chemicals; the story resulted in a criminal indictment and a $13 million fine against the company. It has exposed harmful or illegal practices of major corporate sponsors, such as the Ford Company's defective Pintos (Madsen 1984). In recent seasons, *60 Minutes* and other such shows have run stories on con artists, whistleblowers, accused corporate fraudsters, bank fraud, dangerous toxins at the workplace, and tax shelters.

Most of the segments on these magazine shows are devoted to celebrity interviews and a range of rather prosaic foreign and domestic stories. *60 Minutes* was accused of having initially backed off running an exposé of pernicious practices of a major tobacco company because it was intimidated by the company's lawyers and had corporate ties with the tobacco industry (Alter 1995; Croteau and Hoynes 2001). Television networks have not made investigative reporting on a range of white collar crimes a staple. It remains a marginal offering, for several reasons. First, there is a significant degree of self-censorship: Networks are anxious about offending either a government whose regulatory agencies exercise considerable power over them, the traditionally conservative owners of their affiliate stations (who are unlikely to be enthusiastic about antiestablishment journalism), or the corporate advertisers upon whom they are so dependent (Hickey 1981). They are also concerned about possible lawsuits. ABC's *PrimeTime Live* was the target of a lawsuit after its reporter's used misrepresentations and hidden cameras to expose behind-the-scene unsavory and unsanitary food handling practices at a major supermarket chain (Food Line) (Bellafante 1997). Journalists and television executives are somewhat divided on the appropriateness of using deceptive practices to uncover dangerous activities of corporations and politicians (Starobin 1997). But the fear of litigation is surely a concern.

Beyond these basic inhibitions, many additional factors make investigative reporting of white collar crime typically unappealing to television network executives. Most white collar crimes do not provide vivid visual images. Investigating white collar crimes is time consuming, and many white collar crime stories cannot be covered in the brief TV segments typically available. The fairness doctrine requires equal time for editorial rebuttals, and TV executives fear lawsuits. Undercover reporting with the conspicuous paraphernalia normally used in TV production is difficult. Finally and most importantly, the popular appeal and ratings potential intrinsic to most such stories are low (Hickey 1981). As one TV executive has commented: "People get bored to tears with corruption stories unless they relate either to the White House or to some sex bomb in a Congressman's office" (Hickey 1981).

Some local television stations conduct a certain amount of investigative reporting, often focusing on municipal corruption and consumer fraud. A reporter for KHOU-TV in Houston, a local television news program, first reported on the defective Firestone tires, leading to a major recall (Rutenberg 2000). But local stations also face constraints similar to those of the networks and typically have more limited economic resources. In competitive local television markets, there is a strong temptation to go with sensationalistic exposés rather than in-depth investigations of complex white collar crimes.

Investigative reporting has also been represented in occasional television series that feature the news business. Because the scripts for these shows are often directly inspired by real cases and the audiences for these shows are sometimes large, they may be significant vehicles for raising consciousness about certain forms of white collar crime.

Some documentary filmmakers have over the years focused upon exposing wrongdoing in high places. In the recent era, Michael Moore has been the most famous of these filmmakers and perhaps the most controversial. His first documentary film, *Roger and Me* (1986) took a critical look at the policies and practices of General Motors; in 2004, Moore's film *Fahrenheit 9/11*, which criticized in harsh terms the presidency of George W. Bush, was widely viewed and both hailed and attacked (Moore 2005). A film entitled *Enron: The Smartest Guys in the Room*, based upon a best-selling book on the Enron Case, was released in 2005. The filmmaker Robert Greenwald has taken on media baron Rupert Murdoch and in 2005 was working on a new film: *Wal-Mart: The High Cost of Low Prices* (Halbfinger 2005). These documentary filmmakers uniformly claimed that they were attending to important stories either neglected or inadequately addressed by the mainstream news media.

No discussion of the role of journalism in exposing white collar crime would be complete without some discussion of the historical role of political cartoonists, especially in the realm of exposing political corruption. The authentic political cartoon seeks to do more than amuse. It attempts to produce a picture of reality that captures the essence of truth in a particular situation. It conveys a message and it seeks to create a mood (Press 1981). Insofar as cartoons are among the most widely read and easily understood parts of newspapers, they are clearly significant and potentially influential.

The earliest such cartoons were broadsides, flyers produced and posted for public consumption in the 16th century, and political cartoons have appeared in some form since then. In the latter half of the 19th century, Thomas Nast became the most celebrated American political cartoonist of his time. His brilliant cartoons of New York City's corrupt political boss, William Marcy ("Boss") Tweed of Tammany Hall, and his circle were widely credited with contributing to the fall of this political machine in the 1870s (Fischer 1996). In the late 19th century, Homer Davenport and Frederick Opper produced cartoons that attacked the large capitalist trusts of the time; their images of the trusts were widely reproduced (Press 1981).

Throughout the 20th century, political and editorial cartoonists have continued to produce memorable, powerful images of corruption in high places.

B O X 1.7   The Internet and White Collar Crime

Since the publication of the first edition of this book, the Internet has become a staple source of information for American households (Reuters 2002). A recent survey found that about 60 percent of those surveyed said they used the web regularly. Accordingly, it seems highly likely that a growing proportion of Americans are obtaining information on white collar crime and its control from the Internet. Online magazines such as *Slate* and news program websites such as CNN.com are increasingly common sources of information. A growing percentage of people now routinely use search engines such as Google to track down information on any topic of interest. Certainly a wealth of useful, up-to-date information is now available on the Internet. On the other hand, the provenance, or source, of this information is sometimes less clear—and less reliable—than that available through more established media. And the Internet itself is now the means through which a growing proportion of white collar crime is carried out and investigated. These aspects of the Internet are discussed elsewhere in this text.

From the late 1940s on, Herbert Block's (Herblock) cartoons were especially influential, exposing the dark deeds of Senator Joseph McCarthy and President Richard Nixon (Press 1981). From the 1970s on, editorial cartoonists had an endless series of targets, from Watergate to the "sleazy" doings of members of the Reagan administration to the political ties arising in the Enron case. Garry Trudeau's comic strip *Doonesbury* has been an especially widely circulated and discussed satirical critique of wrongdoing in high places.

Despite the much vaunted First Amendment rights enjoyed by American political cartoonists, it does not follow that such cartoonists operate entirely free of constraints. Publishers and their contacts in high places can exert direct or indirect pressures, and of course cartoonists often are forced to produce in the face of tight deadlines (Press 1981). There can be little question, however, that political cartoons can create powerful and enduring images of crime in high places. Box 1.7 considers coverage of white collar crime on a new information outlet, the World Wide Web.

The Consumer Movement, Public Interest Groups, and Labor Unions

An earlier section touched on the common claim that the general public has been relatively indifferent to white collar crime and discussed significant recent evidence indicating that the public perceives many forms of white collar crime as quite serious. Some exposure of white collar crime has resulted from the efforts of both individuals claiming to act on behalf of the public (or consumers) and public interest groups making parallel claims.

The exposure of frauds perpetrated on consumers is hardly a new enterprise. In 1880, for example, Anthony Comstock, a former special agent of the U.S. Post Office best known for his campaign to suppress vice, published *Frauds Exposed*. A book published in 1927, Stuart Chase and F. J. Schlink's *Your Money's Worth*, dealt with deceptive advertising and high-pressure sales and led to the publication of *Consumer's Bulletin* (Coleman 2002).

In 1911, the advertising industry had created vigilance committees "to rid itself of false claims, snake-oil salesmen, and fly-by-night operations" (Logan 1988: 29). One result is the establishment of Better Business Bureaus (BBBs), which today have 174 local branches. The BBBs, which claim to act on behalf of consumers, have distributed various publications exposing business frauds; mainly they have served as a complaint bureau for dissatisfied consumers. The online Better Business Bureau site claimed that in 2004 Better Business Bureaus in the United States and Canada provided service in some 60 million instances to both consumers and businesses. Because the BBBs are sponsored by businesses, however, they have often been seen as an instrument acting more on the behalf of business than of consumers, deflecting substantial consumer actions and focusing mainly on the most flagrant, small-scale business frauds. They have not played a significant role in exposing the wrong-doing of major corporations.

The environmental movement can trace its ancestry, to some extent at least, to the conservation movement that emerged in the late 19th and early 20th centuries. For much of the 20th century this movement was a limited enterprise, hardly a vigorous campaigner against corporate practices contributing to the destruction of the environment. In the final decades of the 20th century, however, grassroots environmental organizations began to play a significant role in raising consciousness about corporate environmental crime and in mobilizing responses to it (Burns and Lynch 2004; Cable and Benson 1993).

The emergence during the late 1960s and the 1970s of a public interest movement and of civil activism has been attributed to a number of factors. First, the relative prosperity of the period helped generate a perception that corporations could now afford to behave far more responsibly in producing safe products, improving working conditions, and limiting harm to the environment. On the other hand, an escalating rate of inflation promoted consumer anxiety and mistrust of business. The enormous increase in the number of young, well-educated people emerging from colleges during this period, after a sustained period of campus-based campaigns against a host of abuses of power and social injustices, created a large constituency receptive to critiques of big business (Vogel 1989).

Common Cause, a public interest group founded in 1970 and having a membership mainly composed of upper-middle-class whites, was concerned with combating undue power of special interests; it campaigned for federal election campaign reform and against the oil depletion allowance, among other issues (McFarland 1984). Other public interest organizations—supported by private contributions and dues, foundations, and tax benefits or government subsidies—promoted a range of environmental and consumer-related causes, not all

of them pertinent to white collar crime (Vogel 1989). Ralph Nader, in particular, and the public interest groups he established, played an especially significant role in the "movement" against such crime (see Box 1.8). Dr. Sidney Wolfe, a director at Public Citizen, has been a critic of the pharmaceutical industry and the FDA for more than 30 years (Harris 2005a). He has played a key role in the removal of numerous unsafe medicines from the marketplace.

Finally, workers have been among those who have suffered most from certain forms of white collar crime, especially in its corporate form. A long history of confrontation between management and labor exists, stretching back to the 19th century. Labor unions that emerged during the latter part of that century were principally concerned with gaining the right to strike and engage in collective bargaining as well as with fair wages, decent benefits, and job security. But labor unions have also played a role in exposing corporate practices that put workers in jeopardy (e.g., unsafe working conditions) and in managerial decisions that exploit workers financially or deprive them of jobs (Manheim 2000). In this sense, labor unions have played a role in exposing white collar crime.

The Role of Politicians and Political Institutions

Political institutions are both the locus of major forms of corruption and illegal activity and a principal instrument for the exposure and prosecution of such activity. Politicians and government office-holders are most typically the products of the same broad segment of society that produces white collar criminals. More narrowly, politicians often have a complex of close ties with corporations and businesspeople whose improper and illegal activities they are sometimes compelled to expose. Thus, the role of politicians and political institutions in exposing white collar crime must be understood in light of these complex ties among the constituencies involved. Illegal practices of marginal, quasi-respectable businesses and professionals that elicit much public indignation can be quite easily

---

BOX 1.8   Ralph Nader and the Consumer Movement

Ralph Nader is generally acknowledged to be the founder of the consumer rights movement. Nader was born in 1934 to a Lebanese American family that championed a strong political consciousness (*Current Biography Yearbook* 1986). As a teenager he read the muckrakers, and as a hitchhiking college student he became alarmed by the auto accidents he observed. At Princeton, he led a campaign against spraying campus trees with DDT. After acquiring a law degree from Harvard and serving in the army, he went into private practice for a brief time. Then, as a government staff lawyer in the mid-1960s, he undertook the research that led to the publication of his landmark study, *Unsafe at Any Speed* (1965). This book exposed long-standing automotive industry practices of knowingly producing and selling structurally defective automobiles, the result of placing profit-maximizing objectives over concern for consumer safety. The book led to congressional hearings and played an important role in the passage of the Traffic and Motor Vehicle Safety Act of 1966. The revelation that General Motors had engaged in a secret probe of Nader, in the hopes of discrediting him with compromising information about his private life or past political ties, only served to enhance Nader's status as an authentic hero to American consumers (Whiteside 1972).

In the years since he acquired his early fame, Nader has been a central figure in the revelation of a wide range of unethical and illegal corporate practices, and he has established various investigatory and advocacy organizations to promote consumer interests and safety. Nader's success has been somewhat mixed and his influence uneven during this period, as public interests and values have shifted, but he and his associates are credited with important roles in the establishment of the Environmental Protection Agency and the Occupational Safety and Health Administration, among other accomplishments. In 2000, Ralph Nader ran for President of the United States in a somewhat controversial Green Party campaign (and he ran again as an independent in 2004) (Colapinto 2001). In the early part of the 21st century, he continued to be actively engaged with a range of issues impacting on citizens and consumers.

---

condemned by politicians; however, the improper activities of major corporations, established professions, and government agencies themselves—to say nothing of fellow politicians—is more complicated. Some condemnation may indeed be idealistic, inspired by nothing more than the authentic outrage of the investigating politician; in other cases partisan motives, calculated and cynical political ploys, or pragmatic responses to powerful interest groups may be involved. Obviously, a mixture of motives may be involved in any particular case of political exposure, but these motives must always be carefully evaluated. Legion are the instances of rank hypocrisy of politicians' accusations of corrupt and illegal activities, in which the accusers themselves are revealed in time to have engaged in similar or worse practices.

Politicians have generally found it more attractive to attack street crime and call for "law and order" than to attack the crimes of powerful corporations, which may be among their biggest financial supporters. The legislative branch has played a role in exposing white collar crime primarily through congressional investigative committees. The first such committee was established in 1792 to investigate the defeat of General Arthur St. Clair at the hands of Ohio Native Americans (Schlesinger and Bruns 1975). Since then, such committees have investigated a range of issues at such times that a legislative response is deemed potentially appropriate. Committees investigated the corrupt dealings of congressmen in the Credit Mobilier affair in the 1870s and of cabinet officials in the Teapot Dome scandal of the 1920s. Other such committees looked into the monopolistic power of the trusts early in the 20th century and into the Wall Street financial manipulations that helped bring about the stock market crash in 1929.

In the latter part of the 20th century, the congressional committees that received the most public attention were those that exposed alleged wrongdoing in the White House, notably during the

Watergate hearings of the 1970s and the Iran–Contra arms hearings of the 1980s. Other congressional hearings during this period have explored specific white collar crimes such as oil company price fixing and investment banking check kiting, but these investigations have not inspired public interest that is even remotely equivalent to that directed at the political cases (Nichols 1990; U.S. Senate 1987). In the late 1990s, Congressional Committees held hearings on such matters as marketing practices in the software industry and safety standards of automobile and tire manufacturers. In 2002, seven different congressional committees held hearings on matters relating to the collapse of Enron and allegations of various forms of fraud (*New York Times* 2002b). Many of the Congress members involved, however, had either played a role in passing laws that facilitated the Enron-related misdeeds or had accepted substantial campaign contributions from the corporation and its executives (Labaton 2002b). Congressional committees can potentially raise public consciousness about particular forms of white collar crime and lead to useful new legislation; they have also been accused of being occasions for political grandstanding and of violating the rights of some witnesses. Investigative committees, whatever their abuses and objectives, are likely to continue playing a role in the exposure of white collar crime.

Criminal Justice Professionals and Academics (Including Criminologists)

The preceding sections have identified some significant agents in exposing white collar crime. Other parties also play important roles in the exposure of such crime. Some zealous prosecutors, for example, have put a high priority on bringing white collar crime to the attention of the public, although most prosecutors do not (Benson, Cullen, and Maakestad 1990b; Fishman 2005a). The role of prosecutors and other criminal justice personnel is explored more fully in Chapter 11.

Social scientists, and academic scholars generally, have also played a role in exposing white collar crime, a role that has sometimes been downplayed (Cullen et al. 1987). On the other hand, it has been suggested that the growing number of academics who have studied white collar crime have not been entirely successful in generating a public response, perhaps because they do not yet know enough and are not effectively communicating what they do know (Kramer 1989). Of course, a book such as this one draws heavily on the role of social scientists and academics generally in exposing white collar crime; this contribution is more systematically explored in Chapter 2.

Criminologists who have focused on white collar or corporate crime have been somewhat marginalized in academia (Mokhiber and Weissman 1999; Tombs and Whyte 2003). Some academics who have exposed alleged white collar crime have suffered repercussions. For example, a labor relations professor at Cornell University was sued for slander by the nation's largest nursing home company after characterizing the company as "one of the nation's most notorious labor law violators" (Greenhouse S. 1998a). Two business professors at Boise State University had their law journal article alleging abusive practices by the transnational corporation Boise Cascade retracted after the university publishing the journal was contacted by Boise Cascade (Monaghan 2001). Exposing white collar crime tends to involve risks not associated with exposing conventional street crime.

DISCOVERING WHITE COLLAR CRIME, IN SUM

This chapter has explored the "discovery" of white collar crime. Any serious study of white collar crime must be rooted in the recognition that there is still a great deal of confusion and dissension on how it should be defined. The "movement" against white collar crime, such as it is, has emerged more slowly and less vigorously than the long-standing social movement against conventional crime. We have seen that the media, which is such a pervasive element of contemporary life, have portrayed conventional crime and white collar crime quite differently, although growing attention has been accorded to at least some forms of white collar crime in more recent years. Finally, it is a premise of this chapter that the exposure of white collar crime tends to take a different form than the exposure of conventional crime, and it is worthwhile to systematically identify some of the agents who expose it.

KEY TERMS

criminaloid, 2	informers, 18	normal accident, 10	trusted criminals, 8
degradation ceremony, 9	investigative reporting, 23	respectable criminals, 9	whistleblowers, 20
elite deviance, 4	muckrakers, 23	risk society, 10	white collar crime, 2

DISCUSSION QUESTIONS

1. What are some of the principal elements of E. H. Sutherland's contribution to the study of white collar crime? What are some of the limitations of Sutherland's approach? What factors seem to have contributed to Sutherland's interest in white collar crime and to the relative disinterest of most other criminologists?

2. Identify some of the main issues involved in the challenge of defining white collar crime. What arguments can be made for and against favoring "white collar crime" over "elite deviance"? What are the benefits and drawbacks to a typological approach to white collar crime?

3. On what basis can white collar offenders be referred to as "trusted criminals," and what is the special significance of the concept of trust in relation to white collar crime? How do the notions of respectability and risk interrelate with the concept of white collar crime?

4. Which social developments may have contributed to a social movement against white collar crime, and which factors continue to act as constraints against any such movement? What role has the media played in shaping public perceptions of white collar crime, and what factors contribute to media distortions of such perceptions?

5. Identify the principal agents who expose white collar crime in contemporary society. What factors motivate people to expose such crime, and what factors inhibit them from doing so? What specific policy measures can be adopted to encourage exposure of white collar crime?

2

Studying White Collar Crime and Assessing Its Costs

The study of conventional forms of crime has vastly overshadowed and outpaced the study of white collar crime. Indeed, until the 1970s, criminologists devoted little attention to white collar crime (Geis and Goff 1982; Snider 2003). During the course of the 1970s, attention to white collar crime began to increase quite substantially. Initially, most of the white collar crime scholarship was a "criminology" of white collar crime concerned principally with its causes and patterns of behavior. Since 1980, a growing literature on the justice system's responses to and processing of white collar crime cases has developed; a vigorous literature on white collar crime law has also emerged. The literature on white collar crime expanded considerably during the final decade of the 20th century and into the 21st century (Coleman 2006; Croall 2001). Law professors and social scientists have made important contributions to this literature. Criminologists have been somewhat more active in the study of white collar crime than specialists in criminal justice (Robinson 2002b). White collar crime—and corporate crime specifically—remains underrepresented in criminology textbooks, journals, and the criminology curriculum (Lynch, McGurrin, and Fenwick 2004; Simpson 2003; Wright and Friedrichs 1991). Most criminologists continue to neglect white collar crime and are not well-informed about it.

UNDERLYING ASSUMPTIONS AND DIFFERENT PERSPECTIVES

In the course of learning about white collar crime, students are exposed to many assertions, claims, and characterizations. Upon what are these assertions, claims, and characterizations of white collar crime based? How can we best study and understand the many different dimensions of white collar crime?

We can begin by recognizing that all studies of white collar crime explicitly or implicitly adopt assumptions about such matters as the nature of reality, human nature, the basis of morality, and the character of society. Although these enduring philosophical issues cannot be adequately explored here, we can make a few brief observations specifically pertinent to the study of white collar crime.

First, to the extent that "reality" is a human production, we should recognize that the white collar classes have more influence over defining this reality than do less privileged members of society. Second, the social response to white collar crime has tended to adopt the view that humans are fundamentally rational but self-interested creatures, capable of making free choices for which they can be held accountable. Third, much moral hypocrisy permeates the realm of white collar crime. Elites in particular have often given lip service to moral absolutes but have rationalized their own unethical, illegal, and harmful activities. And fourth, the conventional view that law and social order are based on a democratic consensus is confounded by much evidence of the roles of power and conflict in shaping law and in maintaining social order. Some of these assumptions, which are worth bearing in mind at the outset of one's formal study of white collar crime, are explored more fully in other sections of this text.

It is necessary here to differentiate at least briefly between positivistic and humanistic approaches to the study of white collar crime. A *positivistic approach*, which draws on the tradition of the natural and physical sciences, generally assumes that white collar crime can be studied "scientifically." Positivistic students of white collar crime tend to adopt a conception of such crime as a violation of law, and they believe that we can best study white collar crime through systematic observation and measurement and through dispassionate, quantitative analysis. A *humanistic approach* generally rejects traditional scientific methods as inappropriate for the study of the human realm and looks instead to the tradition of the humanities. Humanistic students of white collar crime tend to focus on the social construction of the meaning of white collar crime, and they believe we can best study such crime through interpretive observation and qualitative methods.

SPECIFIC CHALLENGES IN THE STUDY OF WHITE COLLAR CRIME

The study of crime in a number of ways confronts researchers with difficulties not typical of many other areas of social and behavioral research. The contradictory complex of criminogenic (crime-producing) influences makes it more difficult to explain crime than, say, educational choices. The physical, financial, and emotional devastation crime causes make it more difficult to be dispassionate about it than, for example, about dating patterns.

The illegal or shameful character of criminal activities, and frequent extralegal responses of criminal justice agents to it, makes it more difficult to obtain valid and accurate data on crime than, for example, on household consumer practices. The study of white collar crime involves special difficulties within the broader category of criminological study.

The Complex Nature of White Collar Crime

We can begin by referring to the considerable lack of consensus on definitions and core concepts pertaining to white collar crime, as discussed in Chapter 1. This conceptual confusion is greater than in many other areas of criminological research and makes the formulation of testable hypotheses more difficult (Helmkamp, Ball, and Townsend 1996; Lynch, McGurrin, and Fenwick 2004). It also makes more questionable various types of comparison of studies conducted in different times and places.

Since the 1970s, the unit of analysis in white collar crime studies has increasingly shifted from the individual to the organization (Braithwaite 2001; Ermann and Lundman 2002; Gobert and Punch 2003). White collar crime is often complex, insofar as it may involve a large organization acting in concert with one or more organizations, numerous individuals occupying different positions in these organizations, and a series of complicated transactions—some of ambiguous legal status—carried out over a long period of time (Clinard and Yeager 1978; Simpson 2003). Given this complexity, researchers may need to understand aspects of many different fields, including economics, management, law, sociology, psychology, and organizational theory (Dinitz 1982; Geis 1984; Slapper and Tombs 1999). Students of white collar crime sometimes contend with such matters as bidding awards, auditing mechanisms, interlocking ownership arrangements, and codes of regulation (Clark and Hollinger 1977). By comparison, juvenile auto theft and most homicides are far more straightforward.

Problems of objectivity are arguably intensified in the realm of white collar crime if disputes over its very definition and the most appropriate legal responses to it are especially pronounced and if researchers are especially likely to be drawn to the field by moral outrage (Helmkamp, Townsend, and Ball 1996; Simpson 2003; Tombs and Whyte 2003). At least some students of white collar crime become advocates of specific white collar crime policies, whereas others feel that such advocacy is inappropriate for scholars.

Finally, conventional street offenders are typically more accessible (especially in detention) and perhaps more open about their illegal activities than are white collar offenders, the vast majority of whom are never processed by the system and in any case are more likely to feel shame about and deny criminality (Croall 2001; Geis 1984; Tombs and Whyte 2003). But Jack Katz (1997) suggests that elites may be quite accessible to study. Accordingly, it may be more difficult, but is not necessarily impossible, to compel powerful people and institutions to cooperate with a white collar crime research project.

Gaining Access for Research

To obtain the cooperation of an organization such as a corporation in a research project on some aspect of corporate crime, the research proposal must be presented in a nonthreatening way, must incorporate a framework and use terminology familiar to the organization, and must be seen as having some potential benefit or "payoff" for the organization (Yeager and Kram 1990: 133). In his study of corporate morality, Jackall (1988) was turned down by 36 corporations before 4 large corporations gave him access for his research. If the powerful consider the research findings distressing, they are more likely to be in a position to retaliate against the researcher (Williams 1989). Interviews of powerful people require special techniques that take into account accommodating time constraints, alleviating concerns about confidentiality, establishing empathy and credibility, and framing questions in forms most likely to elicit candid responses (Dexter 1970; Punch 1996; Williams 1989). It stands to reason that sophisticated people may be especially adept at providing misleading, self-serving responses to researchers' inquiries.

Obtaining Statistics

Because there is no real white collar crime equivalent to uniform crime report data, which exist for conventional crime, data with various limitations must be extracted from a wide range of sources, including governmental agency and annual financial reports, newspapers, and journals (Burns 2002; Clinard and Yeager 1978; Horn 2005). In official police crime statistical reports, corporate and occupational crimes are often lumped together, and white collar crime statistics in federal and state agency reports are divided among criminal, civil, and administrative agencies (Simpson, Harris, and Mattson 1993). Especially in the case of corporate crime, the data tend to be recorded only during an advanced stage of the proceedings, rather than immediately following the incident itself. Direct observation is the least effective method of monitoring control of corporate illegality because of the large number of actors involved and their dispersal over time and place (Shapiro 1984). Police departments report conventional crimes to the FBI but do not systematically tabulate or report white collar crimes (Horn 2005). With all these challenges in mind, Ronald Burns and Michael Lynch (2004) have identified a wide range of databases and data sources pertaining to environmental crime.

Obtaining Research Support

On a practical level, it has traditionally been easier to obtain research support for projects that explore conventional forms of juvenile delinquency and crime than for research on white collar crime, especially elite forms (Longmire 1982; Mokhiber and Weissman 1999; Snider 2003).The state and corporations that sponsor research may display some understandable discomfort with research that hits too close to home (Katz 1988; Punch 1996; Tombs and Whyte 2003). In the 1970s, the United States government funded some studies of corporate crime and other forms of white collar crime, but in the conservative era following the election of Ronald Reagan in 1980, much of this funding dried up (Snider 2003).

B O X   2.1   A Case Study: The Revco Medicaid Fraud Case

A clearer idea of the challenges confronting the white collar crime researcher can be acquired by looking at one specific example of such research. Diane Vaughan's *Controlling Unlawful Organizational Behavior* (1983) studied the Revco Medicaid fraud case in which a large drugstore chain in Ohio initiated a computer-generated double-billing scheme that cost the government $500,000 in Medicaid funds. Company officials, however, believed they were entitled to these funds because of perceived inequities they attributed to inefficient or unfair reimbursement practices.

Vaughan first developed a file on this case by "snowballing" bits and pieces of information, which led in turn to further leads. But Vaughan, trained as a sociologist, was confronted with an early obstacle posed by the need to master the many specialized languages involved in the case: the computer language of the Welfare Department's Division of Data Services, that department's "Medicaid language," and the financial language of the corporation (Vaughan 1983). Conversely, Vaughan's tendency to use sociological language had to be "translated" to become comprehensible to the personnel of these different organizations.

A second challenge involved the Revco Corporation's concerns about revealing secrets that would be useful to its competitors, as well as affecting employee morale and generating undesirable publicity. Thus, it resisted Vaughan's requests for access despite the fact that Revco was essentially claiming to be the victim in the case. Means of gaining cooperation from the various investigatory and prosecutorial agencies involved in the case also had to be negotiated; individual bureaucrats were reluctant to assume responsibility for providing access.

This led to a third basic challenge. The involvement of eight large, complex organizations in this single case required Vaughan to face difficult strategic and ethical choices: how to gain the trust and confidence of the various parties involved without revealing confidences, becoming intrusive, or becoming an advocate for any particular party. In analyzing the mass of often-conflicting information collected, researchers must be conscious of and resistant to different possible biases. Despite all these obstacles, Vaughan was able to produce an informative study of one corporation's encounter with and control of criminal conduct.

The difficulties involved in studying the Revco case failed to deter Vaughan (1996) from taking on the far more daunting task of studying the process involved in the decision to launch the space shuttle *Challenger* on an unusually cold day in 1986, resulting in the explosive destruction of the shuttle shortly after the launching and the death of all aboard it.

Whenever the government or corporations fund research on white collar crime, it seems relevant to ask whether such funders measure the researchers by some ideological standard and whether the researchers consciously or subconsciously adapt their research to accommodate the sponsor's perspective or interests. Box 2.1 offers a case study demonstrating some of the challenges inherent in white collar crime research.

RESEARCH METHODS FOR STUDYING WHITE COLLAR CRIME

We are all exposed through the media to reports of various types of white collar crime activities. These reports are largely a product of what we can call journalistic research. The quality and credibility of such reports vary greatly, as was discussed in Chapter 1. There is an intrinsic bias in much of the media toward the sensational; getting a good story often takes precedence over a balanced and thoroughly accurate representation of the facts. Even though journalists are trained to use sound methods for collecting and analyzing data, they must often contend with time and space constraints that preclude a full-fledged report of their findings.

Having said all this, we must also acknowledge the crucial role journalists play in facilitating our understanding of white collar crime. The journalistic role here is perhaps proportionally more important than in other types of crime. Major media enterprises have both the formidable resources and the access that are often required for effective investigations of the illegal activities of high-level governmental or corporate officials. Journalistic reports are drawn on and cited throughout this book. Mark Dowie's "Pinto Madness," originally published in *Mother Jones* in 1977, is but one outstanding (and award-winning) journalistic report that exposed a significant example of corporate misconduct and played a role in the response to this misconduct (Cullen et al. 1987). Journalists have played a major role in reporting on and analyzing recent corporate scandals and alleged wrongdoing (Cassidy 2002; Leckey 2004). Not only can such reports provide us with a vivid image of illegal activity but they can also generate hypotheses for further, more systematic study.

SCHOLARLY RESEARCH AND WHITE COLLAR CRIME

The formal study of white collar crime has used a variety of research methods. Many studies have used a combination of several different methods to explore some facet of white collar crime or to test a particular hypothesis. Accordingly, researchers might use a mixture of case study, interviews, direct observations, and analysis of secondary data (e.g., statistical information). These and other specific methods are discussed in the following sections.

Case Studies

The *case study* has been especially important in the field of white collar crime scholarship. The case study can be described quite simply as the in-depth study of a single case (or set of related cases), drawing upon a wide range of sources and resources, including court records, news reports, and interviews. A case study attempts to provide a relatively comprehensive exploration of the chosen case, going beyond the specific sequence of events involved in the case to identify the most convincing form of explanation for it as well. Within criminology, case studies were importantly featured by the "Chicago

School" (associated with descriptive, qualitative research) of the 1920s, and Edwin Sutherland himself produced a classical criminological case study, *The Professional Thief* (1937). The subject of this book was a professional thief, however, not a white collar offender.

The importance of case studies in the white collar crime field can be attributed, in part, to the relative paucity of data cutting across many cases. Perhaps, as well, the complexity of white collar crime renders an in-depth study of a single case especially appropriate. Journalists have played a disproportionately large role in the study of white collar crime, and journalism is especially drawn to the case approach because such a focus is more likely to produce colorful and dramatic copy. Case studies have also been a central feature of the business school curriculum, although here the emphasis is typically on successful businesses.

Gilbert Geis's (1967) "The Heavy Electrical Equipment Antitrust Cases of 1961" examined the prosecution of price fixing within a single industry; it has been widely cited in subsequent discussions of this form of crime (e.g., Faulkner, Cheney, Fisher and Baker 2003). In a research project directly inspired by Geis's work, Sally S. Simpson and Nicole Leeper Piquero (2001) undertook a case study of a more recent price-fixing conspiracy: that of Archer Daniels Midland (ADM) and competitors in the 1990s, involving the animal-feed protein additive, Lysine. Such an approach has been applied to other forms of corporate crime. For example, Cullen and colleagues' (1987) study of the Ford Pinto case has been an important contribution to the literature on corporate violence, and Ronald Kramer's (1992) study of the space shuttle *Challenger's* explosion has illustrated basic dimensions of state corporate crime. James Gobert and Maurice Punch (2003) explore a number of corporate crime cases as a means of demonstrating the complexities involved in prosecuting corporate crime.

The overriding advantage of the case study is that it can provide us with a concrete, rich understanding of the dynamics and realities of a particular white collar crime case. As Simpson and Piquero (2001) note, "The case study is a useful tool to assess what is known about a phenomenon, to develop empirical generalizations from observations that may be explored by others, to inform theory, and to identify new areas of research" (p. 186). Sometimes, however, the case study removes cases from their historical context (Croall 2001; Punch 1996). The principal limitation of the case study approach generally is that the particular case addressed may be quite atypical.

Experiments

The *experiment*, a method of study exemplifying a positivistic or scientific approach, has to date seldom been used in the study of white collar crime. Still, it is worth exploring whether this quintessentially positivistic method has any application to such study.

The classic experiment calls for an examination of the effects, if any, of an independent variable on a dependent variable. In its traditional form, a randomly selected experimental group and a virtually identical control group are tested before and after the experimental group alone has been exposed to the independent variable. This method has been used quite extensively in the behavioral sciences and has proven to be especially useful in the study of learning, memory, perception, and related matters. The *laboratory experiment* has been used rarely, if at all, in studying white collar crime; most of what we want to learn about white collar crime does not lend itself to such a highly controlled, specific setting. Nevertheless, the experiment has at least a limited potential usefulness in this field. In Stanley Milgram's (1963) famous experiment on authority and obedience, large numbers of subjects (ordinary people) complied with the experimenter's instruction that they should administer electrical shocks to other subjects when the latter apparently failed to accomplish a specific task. This experiment at least suggests that ordinary and even "good" people will often engage in "dirty work" if such specific actions are legitimated by some authority figure or occur in a particular context (Hughes 1964). The discussion of Milgram's experiment has centered on its relevance or

irrelevance for understanding participation in the Holocaust and parallel events (Miller 1986), but it is clear that one of the persistent themes in the study of white collar crime, especially its organizational or corporate form, is the involvement of "good" (or at least ordinary) people in "dirty" (or at least clearly illegal) activities.

The *field experiment* differs from the laboratory experiment insofar as it is carried out in a real-life setting rather than in a laboratory. Paul Tracy and James Alan Fox (1989) carried out a field experiment on fraudulent claims to insurance companies submitted by auto-body repair shops. Drivers were engaged to take damaged rental vehicles to 91 randomly selected auto-body shops in Massachusetts to obtain repair estimates. At each body shop, estimates of repair costs were obtained for two cars, one of which was said to be covered by insurance and the other of which was not. Although a number of variables were manipulated, including the driver's gender, "the key experimental variable was whether the damage was covered or not covered by insurance" (Tracy and Fox 1989: 596). The hypothesis—that repair cost estimates for vehicles covered by insurance would be inflated because drivers would have little incentive to go to the trouble of shopping around if the repair cost was not coming out of their pocket—was confirmed.

A third form of experiment, the *natural experiment*, allows the researcher to observe, but not manipulate, a real-world situation in order to identify the effect of some relevant independent variable. For example, a series of studies that compare annual injury rates in manufacturing plants subjected to regulatory inspections with those that were not constitutes a natural experiment to ascertain whether such inspections help reduce worker injuries (Gray and Sholz 1993). Of course, formidable methodological and measurement problems are involved in any such comparison.

Surveys

The *survey* is another major research method. This method is most readily associated with the study of opinions, attitudes, and beliefs but can also be used

---

B O X 2.2   Designing a White Collar Crime Survey: Some Challenges

A group of white collar crime specialists met in Pittsburgh in July 2004 to discuss some of the methodological challenges in designing and carrying out a new National Public Survey on White Collar Crime. Some of the issues that arose during the two-day workshop include the following: Are quantitative surveys of white collar crime victimization really valid, or would a qualitative approach be better? How does one discriminate between respondents who are true victims of white collar crime, as opposed to dissatisfied consumers or disgruntled employees? Are online surveys more likely to be productive than traditional mail or telephone surveys? When surveying a business, how does one best reach multiple people in the business? What is the best time frame to use for white collar crime victimization (e.g., "within your lifetime," "over the last 12 months'")? Is it better to use the word *theft* or *fraud* in exploring white collar crime victimization?

---

to explore experiences. The major challenge in survey research is obtaining a sample that is representative of the population about which one wants to generalize. A related challenge is obtaining a response rate high enough for the survey to be meaningful. Surveys may be carried out in person, over the telephone, or by mail. A third set of challenges centers on the problems of formulating questions that are not loaded, administering the survey in a way that minimizes problems of bias, and coding or interpreting the data in a valid way. Choices must be made about the benefits and drawbacks of using forced-choice and open-ended questions.

Surveys may investigate relative levels of fear of crime, attitudes toward punishment, perceptions of the fairness and effectiveness of the criminal justice system, personal patterns of involvement in illegal activity, experiences of crime victimization, and rationales for justice system responses to white collar crime. Surveys can contribute greatly to our understanding of white collar crime because we still have much to learn about patterns of involvement, rationalizations, and attitudes pertaining to white collar crime issues. In 2005, John Lane and April Wall (2006) of the National White Collar Crime Center supervised a survey of 1,605 American adults on experiences with and attitudes toward white collar crime. See Box 2.2 for a discussion of some of the specific challenges involved in constructing this type of survey.

Many other types of relevant surveys can be identified. For example, a 2004 survey of certified fraud examiners produced a profile on the position, gender, age, education, and criminal histories of perpetrators of occupational fraud (Wells 2004). Law enforcement officials have been surveyed on their role and activities in relation to Internet fraud (Burns, Whitworth, and Thompson 2004; Hinduja 2004). Federal judges have been surveyed to uncover the reasoning behind their sentencing practices for white collar offenders (Wheeler, Mann, and Sarat 1988). Surveys have also attempted to establish the stigmatizing and deterrent effect of criminal sanctions for white collar offenses. A variant on survey research uses questionnaires with scenarios or vignettes to uncover attributes of businesspeople more and less likely to engage in corporate violations (Piquero, Exum, and Simpson 2005). This approach has been labeled a *scenario methodology*.

Observational Research

Observational, or participant-observer, *research*, which involves direct observation of individuals, a group, or an organization over a period of time, has been quite useful in social science. To date it has been applied to white collar crime in a somewhat limited way because gaining access to either criminal enterprises or social control agencies is difficult. Blumberg (1989) analyzed the accounts of some 600 students who reported their experiences with deceptive practices in a range of retail businesses. Sometimes insiders—for example, former employees of Enron and Arthur Andersen, companies destroyed by fraudulent actions—provide what amount to observational studies of such organizational offenders (Brewer and Hansen 2004; Toffler 2003). Jackall's (1988) study of corporate morality and Vaughan's (1983) use of observation in the Revco Medicaid fraud case were mentioned earlier in this chapter.

Observational fieldwork has probably been most widely used in studies of regulatory agencies. Examples include studies of environmental regulatory agencies by Hawkins (1984) and by Yeager (1987) and of regulatory agencies focusing on working conditions by Braithwaite (1985b) and by Shover, Clelland, and Lynxwiler (1986). Although Susan Shapiro (1984) was able to observe the operation of the Securities and Exchange Commission from within, she also found that she had to overcome a rather high level of suspicion and distrust and that, in any case, much about SEC enforcement practices cannot be efficiently discovered by direct observation. To Shapiro it became quite evident that observational methods work much more successfully when applied to the social control of street crime than when applied to the social control of white collar crime.

Secondary Data Analysis and Event History Analysis

Much white collar crime research has involved the analysis of secondary data that were not directly generated or collected by the researcher. Such secondary data often take the form of statistical information collected by various official agencies. Clinard and Yeager's (1980) major study of corporate crime relied heavily on such data, and Wheeler and fellow researchers (1988) analyzed data on sentencing patterns for white collar offenders.

More recently, Michael L. Benson and Kent R. Kerley (2001), in their study of patterns of involvement with white collar crime, used data extracted from presentencing investigation reports. David Weisburd and Elin Waring (2001) also used such data in their study of the criminal careers of white collar offenders. Diana Bilimoria (2001), in a study of the relationship between compensation for corporate executives and corporate violations, analyzed available data on both of these variables. Henry Vandenburgh (1999), in his study of organizational deviance in the field of health care, used Texas Department of Health data to demonstrate that hospitals were bribing physicians to admit patients to their facilities. Michael Lynch, Paul Stretesky, and Ronald Burns (2004) analyzed Environmental Protection Agency (EPA) enforcement and census data to establish that violations of environmental laws occurring in poor, minority neighborhoods are less harshly punished than those occurring in affluent, white neighborhoods. Kristy Holtfreter (2005a) subjected a survey administered by the Association of Certified Fraud Examiners to analysis to examine differences between individuals involved in different types of fraud, as well as differences between organizational victims of such fraud. And in an approach they characterized as *event history analysis*, Sally Simpson and Christopher Koper (1992, 1997) used data from corporate files and government agencies to examine factors associated with corporate antitrust offending, as well as the types of sanctions that deterred such offenses.

The validity of any analysis of statistical data is limited by the quality and accuracy of the data. If presentencing investigation reports are used, for example, one must recognize that they only provide data on those formally processed by the justice system rather than the whole class of those who commit white collar offenses. Statistical data are open to a variety of interpretations. In evaluating any statistical analysis, researchers should ask themselves whether the appropriate statistical tests have been applied and applied correctly and whether all relevant variables have been incorporated into the analysis.

Archival Data Analysis and Historical Ethnography

The more complex a crime, the more likely it is to generate a large file of archival data, or written documents. Even if much white collar crime, and the justice system responses to it, is difficult to observe directly, often a mass of records is available.

Donald Scott (1989), in his study of the policing of corporate collusion, was able to reconstruct antitrust cases by systematically reviewing investigative files of the Antitrust Division of the Department of Justice (available through the Freedom of Information Act). Much of the evidence in such cases is documentary. As Barnett (1982) observed, corporate offenders have a bureaucratic need to maintain records, and this need may conflict with their desire to destroy incriminating evidence. Much the same can be said of various forms of governmental crime. The crimes of the Nazi regime were significantly reconstructed and continue to be investigated more than a half century later through examination of documentation produced by the Nazi bureaucracy. The White House tapes, which played a central role in the impeachment and resignation of President Richard Nixon, can be cited as classic proof of the fact that the desire to maintain a historical record can produce a fascinating record of elite crime in the making. In what she has described as *historical ethnography*, Diane Vaughan (1996) worked her way through the massive documentation relating to the *Challenger* launch decision—altogether, more than 120,000 pages of documents—to reconstruct the actual process leading to that fatal decision. Interviews with key figures involved were also used in this research. Matthew T. Lee and M. David Ermann (1999) used this same method—including the review of thousands of pages of recently declassified documents, trial transcripts, interviews, and a survey of the secondary literature—to produce a revisionist account of the decision-making process involved in the production and sale of the Ford Motor Company's notorious Pinto.

Among the principal limitations of archival data analysis are the selective nature of what is recorded in the first place and the incompleteness (through deliberate destruction or accidental circumstances) of the existing documentary record (Feder and Brick 2002). Still, because for many white collar crimes documentation is the single most credible and complete source of information, archival data analysis, especially if used in conjunction with a broader-ranging historical ethnographic approach, is an important method for studying white collar crime.

Content Analysis

Content analysis is a method that systematically analyzes the representation of something in the media "to find underlying forms and structures in social communication" (Sanders 1974: 12). Given the pervasive role of the media in our lives, it is important to analyze their treatment of white collar crime. In Chapter 1, several studies using content analysis were discussed. Lynch, Stretesky, and Hammond (2000) used content analysis to study newspaper reporting of environmental catastrophes. Ronald Burns and Lindsey Orrick (2002) conducted a content analysis of newspaper coverage of a case of corporate violence to determine how blame and culpability were assessed. This type of analysis, at least on an elementary level, is especially accessible to undergraduate students.

Comparative Studies of White Collar Crime

We live in an increasingly globalized world. Cross-cultural comparative studies become increasingly important in such a world. In a content analysis study with a specifically comparative focus, Lynch, Nalla, and Miller (1989) compared the reporting of the Bhopal disaster (the emission of poisonous gases from a Union Carbide plant in India in 1984, in which thousands were killed or injured) in Indian and American periodicals to determine whether the media in the two different countries were more likely to treat the incident as a "crime" or as an "accident." V. Lee Hamilton and Joseph Sanders (1996) used surveys to compare citizens' judgments of corporate wrongdoing in the United States, Russia, and Japan. And Henry N. Pontell, Stephen M. Rosoff, and Jason Lam (2001) reviewed various sources to compare insider trading in Japan and the United States. Such studies sensitize us to both parallels and differences in the response to white-collar crime in different countries.

B O X 2.3   Public Perception of White Collar Crime: How Serious Is It?

How serious a problem is white collar crime in the public view? The traditional view has been that white collar crime is perceived as less serious than conventional crime. This view was first advanced by pioneering students of white collar crime, including E. A. Ross (1907) and Edwin Sutherland (1949)—and it has endured in more recent times (Rosenmerkel 2001). Empirical research over the past several decades has challenged this view, however. As early as the 1950s, for example, some research found evidence of condemnation of white collar crime generally, identified disapproval of some specific white collar crimes (such as advertising misrepresentation and maintaining detrimental work conditions), and called for harsher sentences for at least some of these offenses (Aubert 1952; Newman 1953; Rettig and Passamanick 1959). Other illegal actions of businesspeople were defended, however.

Many studies examining perceptions of the *seriousness of crime* that have been conducted since the 1950s suggest relatively high levels of consensus in the ratings, especially among Americans (Grabosky, Braithwaite, and Wilson 1987; Warr 1989; Wolfgang, Figlio, Tracy, and Singer 1985). However, this consensus tends to be lower for white collar crime than for conventional violent crime and narcotics offenses

(Hauber, Toonvliet, and Willemse 1988; Miethe 1984). Perceptions of the seriousness of white collar crime vary by gender, race, socioeconomic status, occupation, and other factors (Grabosky et al. 1987; Hauber et al. 1988). Several studies from the late 1960s through the 1990s found that members of the general public regarded such white collar crimes as manufacturing unsafe products (e.g., pharmaceuticals or automobiles) and selling contaminated food as worse in some cases than armed robbery and arson, and majorities favored imprisonment for antitrust violators and embezzlers more often than for burglars or prostitutes (Cullen et al. 1985; Hauber et al. 1988; Holland 1995). White collar crimes involving fraud, illegal price fixing, or other purely financial losses tended to be regarded as less serious than those actually causing physical harm, although such a crime as obtaining money under false pretenses might be rated as more serious than housebreaking if a significant amount of money was involved (Levi 1987). Sean Rosenmerkel (2001) reported that for white collar offenses, seriousness is equated more with harmfulness than with wrongness. A survey of 1,605 U.S. citizens, conducted by the National White Collar Crime Center in 2005, found that many respondents regarded white collar crime as

---

Students' Role as Researchers

It is important to realize that, to date, far less basic data on white collar crime have been collected in comparison with the vast amount of data available on conventional crime and conventional offenders. Jurg Gerber and Eric Fritsch (1993) have suggested that students in white collar crime courses be assigned the project of collecting relevant data on white collar crime from such sources as *The Wall Street Journal, Standard & Poor's Register of Corporations, Directors and Executives, Who's Who in America, The Standard Directory of Advertisers,* and *The Statistical Abstract of the United States.* Students, then, have a role to play in advancing our understanding of white collar crime.

The preceding review makes no claim of exhaustively identifying the range of methods applied to the study of white collar crime. Rather,

it is an attempt to introduce the diversity of possible research strategies and some of the problems associated with them. These difficulties are further explored in the next two sections of this text. Box 2.3 considers research on how Americans perceive white collar crime.

MEASURING WHITE COLLAR CRIME: HOW PREVALENT IS IT?

There is no simple or especially accurate answer to the question of how much white collar crime occurs. Quantifying all forms of crime is difficult, and in the case of white collar crime, many difficulties are compounded. Consider the comparison in Box 2.4 of conventional crime and white collar crime rates.

no less serious than conventional crime (Lane and Wall 2006). Indeed, a majority regarded white collar crimes causing physical injury as more serious than armed robbery, and slightly more respondents regarded filing a false earnings report as more serious than robbery. Insurance overcharges and embezzlement were rated as more serious than burglary and car theft. Although survey results are not entirely consistent, at least some surveys suggest an increasing perception of white collar crimes as serious, especially if they involve physical harm to people (Goff and Nason-Clarke 1989; Lane and Wall 2006). Empirical studies have also produced evidence suggesting that perceptions of white collar crime are significantly influenced both by one's status and vantage point and by the victim's attributes.

Ultimately, perception of white collar crime is complex, and not only because the term *white collar crime* covers such a broad range of activities. Studies of perceptions of the seriousness of crime generally are plagued with methodological difficulties; they have typically used quite different measures of wrongdoing and classification of offenders and have used different types of seriousness scales or sampling techniques (Stylianou 2003). In some cases, these studies are also flawed by the adoption of narrow or conventional conceptions of white collar crime. Despite such limitations, the research on perceptions of crime is significant because it challenges the traditional assumption that the public generally does not regard white collar crime as especially serious. Even though the full meaning of the findings of these studies is still open to interpretation, the findings do not dispute the traditional claim that the crimes people fear most and that arouse their strongest visceral reactions tend to be violent personal crimes involving direct physical injury or death. It is not entirely clear that the perception of some white collar crime as very serious will translate into a willingness to impose harsh penalties on specific white collar offenders who appear highly respectable, express remorse, or have various plausible rationalizations for their actions (Grabosky et al. 1987). Nor is it clear under what circumstances perceptions of seriousness translate into willingness to actively support legislation that takes a tougher stance on white collar crime. In the final analysis, the measure of how seriously citizens regard white collar crime is provided not by what they think about it but by what they are willing to do about it.

Since the early 19th century, the analysis of crime statistics has served as an important basis for understanding and explaining crime. In the conventional view, the crime statistics collected by official agencies are regarded as quantitative measurements of crime and criminal justice system outcomes. A critical view today, however, contends that crime statistics are products of particular agencies and entities, each with ideological biases, strategic purposes, and finite resources (Beirne and Messerschmidt 2005; Selke and Pepinsky 1984).

In this view, understanding the process by which statistics are produced is more important than the resulting statistical data. In any case, statistics about criminal activity obviously should not be confused with statistics on criminal justice system responses to such activity (Reiss and Biderman 1980). Furthermore, there is considerable reason to believe that the statistics of official agencies direct much more attention to conventional crime than to white collar crime (Burns 2005; Wellford and Ingraham 1994). All general and comparative claims about the incidence and distribution of different types of crime must be approached with great caution and considerable skepticism.

Crimes are not uniformly defined, reported, or recorded, and the integrity and efficiency of criminal justice agencies varies. These problems are intensified in the case of white collar crime because legal definitions are especially likely to be variable or ambiguous and because victims of white collar crime are often unaware of their victimization. In the specific case of environmental crime, for example, much is not reported, and there is no centralized data on such crime (Shover and Routhe 2005). The different federal agencies do not adopt a uniform definition of white collar crime (Lybarger, Klenowski, and Kane 2001). Individuals who

B O X 2.4   Conventional Crime and White Collar Crime Rates

The overall trend for conventional crime between 1991 and 2005 was a decline or leveling off of such crime (FBI 2005). Despite the difficulties of measuring white collar crime, some statistics indicate recent rises in fraud and other forms of white collar crime (FBI 2005; Labaton 2002c; Lane and Wall 2006). Government and private lawsuits for securities fraud and other financial violations doubled between 1997 and 2001, as did the number of accounting and financial reporting cases opened by the Securities and Exchange Commission (SEC). A general rise in white collar crime cases is anticipated and reflects the explosion of new opportunities for fraud through the Internet, executive compensation schemes, and the aging and increasing educational level of the population.

become aware that they have been victims of a white collar crime often fail to report this victimization.

Several studies of victims of consumer fraud have documented that such victims are unlikely to report the crime to police; in one study, fewer than 1 in 10 victims of white collar crime reported this victimization to the police (Lane and Wall 2006; Rebovich and Layne 2000; Titus, Heinzelmann, and Boyle 1995). They often have a sense of futility about the police response, and they are often quite unaware of the existence of special fraud units set up to investigate these crimes. Many organizational victims of fraud (e.g., corporations) are especially reluctant to file reports because they fear negative publicity and a public loss of confidence in the organization (Levi 1992). Thus if victims of fraud and many other white collar offenses report an offense at all, they often report it to some entity other than the police. Accordingly, such data as exists on white collar crime victimization is dispersed among numerous different agencies, each with different forms of record keeping.

The FBI's Uniform Crime Report (UCR) has been the best-known source of national crime statistics in the United States. Ralph Nader has complained about the FBI's failure to collect and tabulate corporate crime data. So-called "index" crimes—conventional crimes such as homicide, forcible rape, aggravated assault, and burglary—are the principal focus of the Uniform Crime Report (Horn 2005; Lybarger et al. 2001). Although some forms of fraud and embezzlement are incorporated into the index crime categories, these crimes tend to be the less significant, smaller-scale white collar crimes or activities such as welfare fraud and passing bad checks that are not typically regarded as white collar crime at all.

In addition to the fact that many crimes of all types are never reported to the police, the UCR has many other limitations, including flawed operational definitions, lack of clarity, and nonstandardized data collection policies (Schneider and Wiersema 1990). Since the early 1970s, an annual *Sourcebook of Criminal Justice Statistics*, which collates data from the FBI and other federal sources, and National Institute of Justice reports have served as important sources for statistical information about crime. According to one study, arrests for three forms of white collar crime (forgery/counterfeiting, fraud, and embezzlement) rose in the United States from 287,025 in 1979 to a high of 415,151 in 1992 but dropped to 293,472 in 1999 (Lybarger et al. 2001). One analysis by the Bureau of Justice produced figures suggesting that prosecution and conviction rates for white collar offenders were comparable to or even higher than those for property crime offenders, that incarceration rates were slightly lower, and that the percentage incarcerated for more than a year was much lower (Manson 1986). However, since an unknown proportion of crimes defined as white collar cases in these statistics are in fact low-level frauds, such data simply do not tell us what percentage of the whole class of white collar offenders is arrested relative to the percentage of conventional property offenders arrested.

A large amount of statistical data on civil and administrative cases has also been collected, especially by the various regulatory agencies (Burns and

Lynch 2004). Many different state agencies today have been collecting data on various types of white collar crime. Those who favor restricting the definition of white collar crime to activities violating criminal law argue that inclusion of civil and administrative data leads to overcounting of white collar crime. On the other hand, sole reliance on data from criminal agencies vastly undercounts by any reasonable criteria the incidence and prevalence of white collar crime.

There are numerous problems with regulatory agency data. These agencies have considerable discretionary leeway in defining (and responding to) offenses. Of the offenses that in fact come to their attention—and many do not—various factors can affect how the offenses are classified and recorded. Because these agencies often focus their enforcement activities on corporations rather than on individuals, they are not likely to be reliable sources of data on individual offenders, and they are not organized to track either organizational or individual offenders over time (Reiss and Biderman 1980). Some of the statistics generated by regulatory agencies are cited at appropriate points in this book, but the limitations of such data should be kept in mind.

Victimization Surveys and Self-Report Studies

The limitations of official enforcement agency data for measuring white collar crime had become quite widely recognized by the 1960s. A broader measure of how much white collar crime is occurring would require that we examine the records of the whole range of regulatory agencies responding to some form of white collar crime. At a minimum, such records provide us with some understanding of enforcement patterns in response to such crime; they are somewhat less reliable on the actual incidence of such crime.

Many criminologists adopted the notion that crime data collected from sources less removed from the criminal event, rather than data processed by official agencies, was likely to be more accurate (Jackson 1990), and thus victimization surveys were

undertaken as one alternative to official data. The National Crime Survey (NCS), under the auspices of the Bureau of Justice Statistics, has annually surveyed a large sample of American individuals and households to determine whether they have been victims of crime over the preceding year. Not surprisingly, the NCS has revealed a much higher level of crime victimization than is indicated by the Uniform Crime Report, although some criminologists regard the UCR as more reliable for certain types of offenses (Jackson 1990). In the case of white collar crime, however, the usefulness of the survey is severely limited. A Natural Incident-Based Reporting System (NIBRS) established in 1991, may over time measure white collar crime more fully (Barnett 2003). But early in the 21st century, no national uniform white collar crime reporting system is in place.

One of the defining attributes of white collar crime is that victims are much more likely to be unaware of their victimization than are victims of conventional offenses. Someone who has been robbed is much more aware of his or her victimization than a person who overpays as a result of price fixing, for example. The greater ambiguity of the laws also makes it more difficult for victims to be clear about whether they have been victimized. Indeed, in the case of fraud it is possible for victimization to be overreported if survey respondents mistakenly interpret all instances of consumer-related dissatisfaction to be cases of criminal victimization. In privately conducted surveys, between one third and three quarters of the respondents reported having been deceived or defrauded by marketing schemes (Payne 2005b; Titus et al. 1995). In a *victimization survey* conducted by the National White Collar Crime Center of 1,169 American households, about one in three reported having been victims of some form of white collar crime in the previous year (Rebovich and Layne 2000). When this survey was replicated in 2005, almost half the households surveyed and one in three individuals reported being victimized by white collar crime in the previous year (Lane and Wall 2006). In the same survey, almost two out of three individuals reported being a victim of white

---

B O X 2.5   Measuring Specific Forms of White Collar Crime

There is no truly reliable way to measure the incidence of the many diverse forms of white collar crime, from antitrust infractions to violations of environmental law to Medicaid fraud to employee embezzlement. There is a need to collect and analyze data from a wide range of sources and to start developing sourcebooks for such data as a starting point to measuring various forms of white collar crime (Burns and Lynch 2004). Various estimates exist and will be referred to in this text where appropriate, but we must always try to identify the basis of these estimates.

Simpson and colleagues (1993) have suggested that we can more reliably measure corporate crime by developing a model that takes into account such factors as opportunities to commit offenses, interconnections among actors, and numbers of transactions. This is, admittedly, a complex challenge. Zimring (1987) has made an innovative proposal for measuring the incidence of insider trading, one form of white collar crime that is surely underreported. He has suggested sampling corporations that have made major announcements (e.g., about takeovers), using computers to construct baseline data on the volume of the corporations' stocks traded under normal circumstances, and then scanning for significant deviations from baseline trading figures in the period preceding such public announcements. Such an approach, he believes, could be applied to other forms of white collar crime, including the performance of unnecessary surgery. The resulting information might not identify individual offenders, but it could hypothetically provide us with reliable indicators about the distribution of white collar crime.

---

collar crime at some point in their lifetime. In these surveys, the largest number of victims reported the offense to the business involved in the crime (50 percent); other entities to whom the crime was reported included the phone company, a credit card company, a personal attorney, the Better Business Bureau, some other consumer protection agency, the district attorney, or the police. A National Fraud Survey administered by the Association of Certified Fraud Examiners in 2004 uncovered much information about patterns of fraud victimization (Wells 2004).

Self-report surveys, in which respondents are asked to report anonymously on their own law-breaking activities, have revealed much higher levels of illegal activity than are suggested by official data. However, for the most part these surveys have focused on the activities of juveniles (assault, theft, vandalism, illicit drug use, and the like) rather than on white collar offenses (Barlow and Kauzlarich 2002; Chambliss 1988b). Any such surveys directed at the population of white collar criminals would also encounter the problem that such offenders are especially likely to rationalize their conduct and may well deny even to themselves that they have violated laws.

Still, at least some self-report studies are pertinent to white collar crime. For example, surveys of self-reported noncompliance with income tax laws have been undertaken (Long and Swingen 1991). In a survey of middle managers who were retired and thus perhaps more candid about their activities, Clinard (1983) attempted to explore patterns of corporate lawbreaking, although he did not generate statistical data. Corporations may be required by regulatory agencies to file formal self-reports on selected offenses (Simpson et al. 1993). On the other hand, Zimring (1987) has suggested that researchers might produce some useful data by surveying white collar personnel and businesses not about their own offenses but rather about those of their competitors.

In principle, we could attempt to measure white collar crime through direct observation (Green S. P. 1997). Although such studies (e.g., of retailers and repair services) can provide estimates of the incidence or prevalence of white collar crime within certain spheres, most white collar crime simply cannot be observed directly. Box 2.5 suggests other strategies for measuring the incidence of some specific forms of white collar crime.

The Need for Reliable Data

Reliable statistical data on white collar crime can serve many useful purposes. They can broaden awareness of the true scope of the problem and provide a basis for obtaining more support for investigating and prosecuting white collar crime. Ideally, demonstrating that white collar offenders can be identified, successfully prosecuted, and punished can have some deterrent effect. To that end, various statistics are cited throughout this text.

Much still needs to be done to improve the quality of this statistical data. To date, the most exhaustive study of problems involved in the measurement of white collar crime is Reiss and Biderman's *Data Sources on White-Collar Law-Breaking* (1980). Among other recommendations, they called for greater standardization of definitions and recording practices, more reliable characterizations of the universe of offenders, and better coordination among the criminal, civil, and administrative agencies that collect statistics. Ronald Burns (2005) has undertaken preliminary steps in the development of a sourcebook on white collar crime. At the same time, from a critical perspective it is essential that we not rely exclusively on *official statistics* but instead exploit many alternative ways of measuring the true scope of white collar crime.

THE COSTS AND CONSEQUENCES OF WHITE COLLAR CRIME

The notion of the "cost of crime" is most readily associated with economic costs, which can only be roughly estimated. Many difficult questions are involved in measuring the economic costs of crime (Shenk and Klaus 1984), and for white collar crime it is substantially more difficult to measure than for conventional and many other forms of crime. First, the ongoing disputes about defining and identifying white collar crime, discussed in Chapter 1, complicate the process. Even though there is considerable agreement that billions of dollars were lost in the savings and loan crisis, for example, and government estimates suggested that criminal activity was involved in 70 to 80 percent of the insolvencies (Calavita and Pontell 1990), years of litigation have grappled with the question of what proportion of the losses can be attributed to criminal fraud and which proportion to poor judgment, bad luck, or even (as one prominent S & L director, Charles Keating, claims) to the ill-advised intervention of federal regulators (Carlson 1990a). The same problem applies to the corporate crime cases of the 2000s.

Second, as noted earlier, a much higher percentage of white collar crime is neither reported nor officially identified compared to conventional crime generally, and the costs of unreported crime are more difficult to measure. For example, major frauds against businesses may not be reported because they are embarrassing to the business (Levi 1987, 1992).

Third, there is no uniform way to measure costs even when a crime is identified and reported. If employees steal goods from a retail store, should the loss be calculated as the wholesale cost of the stolen goods, the retail value, or possibly different costs involved in their replacement? As Levi (1987) noted, it is especially difficult to assess the economic cost of bribe-related activity. For example, a relatively small bribe to a building inspector might ultimately lead to the immense costs associated with the collapse of a building. How does one measure the cost of corrupt activities of politicians and businesses that siphon off funds intended for reconstruction or relief of people harmed by repressive regimes, wars, and natural disasters, such as the December 2004 tsunami in Asia (Klein 2005)? The costs of such crimes are clearly immense.

Direct Costs

Some economic costs of white collar crime are clearly *direct costs*. Arson committed to defraud an insurance company may result in destruction of property of measurable value (again, however, we must differentiate among the original cost of the building, its current market value, and its replacement cost). Much conventional crime, and most white collar crime, involves the illegal transfer of assets from one party to another—fraud, by definition, increases the material well-being of one party at the expense of the other—and in these cases costs are typically defined in terms of the victims' losses.

Almost all crimes, and white collar crimes in particular, have winners or beneficiaries. For example, many stockholders benefit, however unwittingly, from corporate and securities-related crimes that enhance corporate profit and the value of stock. Corporations may benefit from the crimes of their employees, and employees may benefit from the crimes of their employers. Even legitimate businesses and professionals may profit from white collar crimes. Among the many profiteers are those who insure against such crime, sell security services, conduct investigations, repair or replace damage done by white collar crime (e.g., asbestos removal firms), treat victims of such crime, and provide legal representation. Those who write and teach about white collar crime might also be said to benefit from it.

A conservative argument contends that the direct costs of promulgating and enforcing laws prohibiting a wide range of improper, harmful, or intrinsically corrupt activities by corporations and politicians may outweigh the benefits (Machan and Johnson 1983). For example, if U.S. corporations are prohibited from bribing public officials in foreign countries to obtain lucrative contracts but corporations of other countries are not so constrained, U.S. corporations may well suffer from a competitive disadvantage. The results would include a reduction in foreign contracts, loss of American jobs, and possibly loss of foreign influence. Similarly, some conservatives claim that the costs of regulating environmental pollution, worker safety, and consumer products too often outweigh the benefits. Some corrupt acts—for example, telling a contractor the amount of the lowest competing bid so that he or she can underbid it—may actually save taxpayers money (Levi 1987). And the claim has been made that stringent restrictions on campaign fund-raising and private-sector careers following regulatory agency service deter some of the most qualified

people from running for election or re-election, or from accepting governmental appointments. On the liberal side, the costs of deregulation in the form of more corporate crime are greater by far than costs associated with regulation (Skeel 2005).

In the final analysis, the direct economic losses from all forms of white collar crime are immense and dwarf those of conventional crime. Some students of this issue have suggested that losses from some forms of white collar crime in the United States were in the range of $250 billion a year, compared to annual losses of some $4 billion a year from such conventional offenses as burglary and robbery. Recent estimates by the FBI and the Association of Certified Fraud Examiners put the annual cost of white collar crime in the range of $300 to $660 billion (Lane and Wall 2006:5). Another long-standing estimate of annual losses from frauds alone in the United States puts the figure at $40 billion (Copes, Kerley, Mason, and Van Wyk 2001; Press 1996; Rosoff, Pontell, and Tillman 2002). A figure of an estimated $48 billion in losses for identity theft has been produced (Lane and Wall 2006:5). Losses due to workplace theft have been estimated as high as $400 billion a year for the United States alone (Payne and Gainey 2004). Overall economic losses in the United States due to white collar crime have been estimated as high as $1 trillion annually (Schlegel 2000). Whether the economic losses due to white collar crime are more than 50 times greater than those due to conventional crime or only 10 times greater, most of those who have studied this issue would agree that they are certainly significantly greater.

It is difficult to estimate the economic cost of many major forms of white collar crime, such as tax evasion, environmental pollution, the sale of unsafe products, antitrust violations, and unfair labor practices. By any estimation, hundreds of billions of dollars are involved. Specific cases involving a single business, corporation, or failed thrift institution have sometimes involved losses of hundreds of millions, or billions, of dollars. Losses to ordinary workers and investors as a consequence of the collapse of Enron alone were estimated at up to

$50 billion (Greider 2002). Multiplied by the many other cases of corporate fraud during this period, estimated total losses well in excess of $100 billion are not far-fetched. The cost of treating diseases related to toxic exposure in the workplace adds up to tens of billions of dollars. Some specific estimates of dollar losses from white collar crime are provided in the context of discussions of particular forms of white collar crime in various chapters of this book.

Indirect Costs

Beyond the direct economic costs of crime are many significant *indirect costs*, although these costs are especially difficult to measure accurately. Among these indirect costs are higher taxes, increased cost of goods and services, and higher insurance rates (Shenk and Klaus 1984). Some econ-omists believe that the Enron collapse created industry-wide uncertainties that contributed significantly to slower job growth in subsequent years (Gross 2005). Furthermore, substantial sums must be spent in efforts to prevent or offer protection against crime. In the case of conventional crime, these expenses include the costs of locks, gates, burglar alarms, and the like. In the case of white collar crime, corporations and businesses with significant numbers of employees must typically spend money to screen out high-risk applicants from being employed in the first place, to purchase technology and hire internal personnel to maintain surveillance of employees, and to establish cumbersome procedures to minimize employee crime. On the other hand, because employees, customers, clients, and taxpayers are not especially well positioned to protect themselves against white collar crime victimization, these parties may expend some money to minimize their chances of being employed by or patronizing businesses and professionals who will subject them to illegal or fraudulent actions.

The costs of maintaining regulatory and justice systems to respond to white collar crime can also be included in the cost of this type of crime. The conventional criminal justice system expends proportionally less money on white collar crime than on conventional crime, despite the much greater cost of white collar crime. The average per-crime cost of responding to white collar crime is higher than the average per-crime cost of responding to conventional crime, both because of the greater complexity of white collar crimes and the greater defensive resources available to the perpetrators, especially if they are organizations. Of course, any attempt to gauge the costs of responding to white collar crime must take into account the many different civil, administrative, and private agencies other than criminal justice agencies that investigate and process this activity. Again, we must remind ourselves that many employees of these various agencies benefit from the existence of this type of crime.

In calculating the economic costs of white collar crimes, we could subtract from the total the amount of fines collected by the government, principally from organizations convicted in white collar crime cases (Levi 1987). In the insider trading cases of the 1980s, record fines were levied: $100 million against Ivan Boesky and $600 million against Michael Milken (Stewart 1991). In connection with the corporate scandals of the early 2000s, Wall Street firms agreed to pay billions of dollars in fines (Morgenson 2005a; Morgenson and McGeehan 2002). But these widely publicized figures and other large fines levied against corporate offenders may be somewhat misleading because tax write-offs can reduce substantially the final cost to the convicted party. In the savings and loan fraud cases, many of the guilty parties were ordered to repay hundreds of thousands, or even millions, of dollars. Because in many cases little, if any, of this money was actually collected (Pizzo and Muolo 1993), the gap between fines levied and restitution demanded (i.e., the net amount of money actually collected by the government) must always be taken into account. According to one commentator, underwriting profits for Wall Street investment banks are so much greater than their share of fines that fines are unlikely to deter the banks from wrongdoing (Bebchuk 2002).

Significant *residual economic costs* are also a consequence of white collar crime. In the case of conventional street crime, the loss of business for retail stores in high-crime areas is an example of a residual economic cost; an example in the case of white collar crime is a loss of investor confidence following revelations of insider trading or corporate financial manipulations, with consequent declines in stock values or increases in bond interest rates (Berenson 2002a; Levi 1987). Overall, a whole range of economic transactions are likely to become more costly to the extent that white collar crime precipitates diminishing trust.

Physical Costs

Even though the *physical cost* of crime—personal injury and loss of life—is most immediately associated with conventional predatory crime, the physical costs of white collar crime are substantial and, by one interpretation, exceed such costs for violent personal crime. The physical costs of white collar crime include death and injury from polluting the environment, from unsafe working conditions, and from marketing unsafe products. Even crimes ordinarily thought of as exclusively economic, such as fraud, may lead to substantial physical harm to people. For example, fraud involving governmental or nongovernmental aid agencies in third-world countries may lead to thousands of deaths from malnutrition. Those who argue for a more expansive definition of white collar crime would include the physical costs of illness and death from smoking. And if governmental crimes are included as well, the largest losses of life and physical injury result from acts of war and genocide.

·The physical costs of conventional violent crimes in the United States, as measured by the Uniform Crime Report, add up to more than 18,000 deaths and some 1 million serious injuries a year (Reiman 2004). It has been estimated that up to 200,000 Americans a year die from exposure to toxic pollution, and many animal species are devastated by pollution (Burns and Lynch 2004: 289; Shover and Routhe 2005). Figures from the U.S. Bureau of Labor Statistics and other sources suggest that more than 30,000 Americans die annually from work-related diseases and accidents, and nearly 3 million workers suffer other significant physical harm in the workplace (Reiman 2004). Because the entire population is vulnerable to conventional crime violence and because only less than half of the population in the labor force is vulnerable to work-related death or injury, the risks in the work context are much greater than from conventional violent crime. More than 12,000 deaths each year in the United States have been attributed to unnecessary medical operations alone, and close to 100,000 Americans are estimated to die annually from medical mistakes (Reiman 2004). Although it is obviously possible to question how many such deaths can be attributed to white collar crime specifically, it is also quite clear that the cost of white collar crime in lives and injuries is real and extensive.

Other Costs

Other types of "costs" and consequences of white collar crime are even more difficult to measure, even though they are also real and substantial. They include the cost of the psychological trauma of victimization, which is discussed in the section on victims of white collar crime.

The cost of crime to what has sometimes been called "the social fabric" is arguably the most difficult cost to measure. In the case of conventional crime, one such cost is the intensification of intergroup hostility and conflict. Various commentators have suggested that in the long run the most pernicious cost of white collar crime lies in the alienation it generates and in the distrust and erosion of confidence in major institutions it promotes (Meier and Short 1982). Some level of cynicism promotes elite crime, and elite crime then promotes even greater cynicism. Alienation, de-legitimation, and cynicism are significant costs of white collar crime.

VICTIMS OF WHITE COLLAR CRIME

The most common image of a crime victim is surely the victim of murder, rape, robbery, or burglary. There can be little question that people most fear being victimized by such crime. However, all of us are victims of various white collar crimes, often without being aware of it.

The concept of "victim" does not have a single, fixed meaning. Traditionally it has been most commonly applied to those harmed by deliberate acts of predation. More recently it has been more broadly invoked for large classes of people, including minorities and women, who are alleged to be exploited, abused, or persecuted in some way. In the broadest definitions of white collar crime or elite deviance, people who suffer from racism, imperialism, sexism, and the like are victims. An obvious drawback to such an inclusive meaning of victimization—that "we are all victims"—is that it strips the term of any coherent meaning (Karmen 2004). Even though the difficulties generated by broader applications of the concept of victim must be duly noted, official conceptions of "crime victim" reflect a middle-class bias emphasizing the victimization of innocent people by irrational and dangerous conventional offenders (McShane and Williams 1992). This narrowly restrictive conception of crime victims tends to reinforce the false notion that only this type of victimization is truly significant.

The victims of crime have been relatively neglected by the modern criminal justice system and by criminologists alike (Shichor, Schrest, and Doocy 2001). The criminal offender and the criminal justice agencies that respond to crime have been the principal focus of criminological theory and research. In more recent times, however, this has begun to change. In the 1970s, victimology emerged as a recognized specialization within criminology, although its roots can be traced to a number of earlier articles and books, from the 1940s on, that focused on crime victims. A victims' rights movement was a parallel development that also emerged during this same period.

Both victimology and the victims' rights movement have been almost exclusively directed toward victims of conventional predatory crimes (Karmen 2004). Both have been dominated by a conservative ideological outlook, and they have been more successful in promoting harsh penalties for conventional offenders than in truly helping

crime victims to recover from their experiences. They have largely ignored, or even deflected attention from, white collar crime victimization (Friedrichs 1983; McShane and Williams 1992). Victims of crimes of the state have been especially neglected (Kauzlarich, Matthews, and Miller 2001). Robert Elias (1986) has called for linking victimology with a conception of human rights and for attending to victims of consumer fraud, pollution, and other forms of suffering generated by social inequality and abuses of power. There is a need, then, for a more expansive conception of victims of crime.

All of us are victimized, in many capacities, by white collar crime. White collar crime victimization is especially diffuse, and victims' attributes are especially heterogeneous (Lane and Wall 2006; McShane and Williams 1992; Shichor et al. 2001). We are generally less likely to be conscious of this victimization than of conventional crime victimization. As workers or employees, we are victimized by hazardous and illegal conditions in the workplace or by managerial practices that illegally deprive us of our just compensation and other labor-related rights. As consumers, we are victimized by such corporate crimes as price fixing and the sale of unsafe products. As customers, clients, and patients, we are victimized by fraudulent and unethical practices of small businesses, entrepreneurs, and professionals. As citizens and residents of particular areas, we are victimized by corporate pollution. As taxpayers, we are victimized by defense contract frauds and by frauds involving thrift institutions with government-insured deposits. Among the many other classes of victims of white collar crime are business competitors, business partners, shareholders, investors, and pension holders. Of course, governmental entities and organizations, including corporations, are victims of certain forms of white collar crime as well (Shichor 1989). And a community can hypothetically be an indirect victim of white collar crime (Becker, Jipson, and Bruce 2000). But if all of us are victimized by white collar crime, some categories of people—such as the poor, people of color, and women—are disproportionately vulnerable to such victimization (Croall 2001; Lynch et al. 2002; Wonders and Danner 2002).

Many forms of white collar crime victimization, especially those involving the environment or the workplace, are defined as accidents or "disasters" and thus as beyond human control (Croall 2001; Walklate 1989). Victims themselves often accept this misleading notion, although much evidence suggests that many of these accidents and disasters are avoidable. Shichor (1989) differentiates among primary (personal) victims, secondary (organizational) victims, and tertiary victims (abstractions such as the community at large or public order). Vaughan (1980) has noted that direct victims of white collar crime are often surrogate victims for real but indirect victims who are not in a position to recognize their victimization. As an example, she cites a state welfare department that is defrauded by a private corporation; the welfare clients who lose services and the taxpayers whose tax bills are inflated are the ultimate but less visible victims. For some forms of white collar crime—for example, hazardous substances in the workplace or illegal pollution—it is especially difficult to establish three crucial parameters: (1) either intent to do harm or willful negligence that caused harm; (2) a direct causal link between health problems of workers or area residents and the hazardous conditions in the workplace or the illegal pollution; and (3) the time frame of harmful activity.

For at least some classes of white collar crime, each of a large number of victims suffers relatively minor losses. For example, a defense contract fraud or a price-fixing scheme may involve millions of dollars of losses, but each individual taxpayer or customer may lose only a few dollars or less. Of course, in these cases the cumulative losses are substantial and the physical harm over time can be considerable, and in some cases economic losses and physical harm are direct and great.

Even when victims of white collar crime are fully aware of their victimization, they are often more likely to be confused about how to report it and pessimistic about receiving meaningful assistance from the criminal justice system (Rebovich and Layne 2000). Those who report white collar crime are most likely to do so when they receive social support toward this end, believe the victimization was serious, and have

appropriate knowledge on reporting such victimization (Copes et al. 2001; Mason and Benson 1996). Victims of conventional crimes often have discouraging—sometimes even traumatic—experiences with this system, but the structure of mainstream criminal justice agencies makes them even less able to respond effectively to complex white collar crimes, and jurisdiction for white collar crimes is spread among many different types of government agencies.

When white collar crime cases are successfully prosecuted, the victims are not necessarily satisfied with the outcome. The great majority of victims of an investment fraud in one study expressed dissatisfaction with the handling of their case by the authorities (Shichor et al. 2001). In another study of white collar fraud cases, about half the victims thought the sentences were too lenient (Levi 1992). This study concluded that when victims pursue cases, they are principally motivated by a desire to promote general deterrence and adhere to their company's policy rather than by a desire to seek compensation or retribution. But to date there has been little serious study of white collar crime victims who pursue cases, and accordingly broad generalizations are not warranted.

The Role of the Victim

Victims of conventional crime have traditionally been thought of as passive and innocent elements of the crime. During the past three decades or so, research on victim proneness and provocation (or precipitation) has demonstrated that victims' attributes and actions can play a significant role in victimization, and for certain classes of offenses it can be difficult to draw sharp lines of demarcation between perpetrators and victims.

Although many crime victims may be wholly innocent, a significant number clearly precipitate the crime. Both extremes can distort the complex realities of the situation. The *victim blaming* tendency associated with at least one form of conventional crime, rape, has been strongly criticized by feminist commentators. Walsh and Schram (1980) argue that both white collar crime and rape cases provoke ambivalent responses; attention is shifted from exclusive focus on offenders to the circumstances in the cases. In both white collar crime and rape cases, victims may be stigmatized.

B O X 2.6 Organizations as Victims of White Collar Crime

A number of studies (see, for example, Hagan 1983; Kruttschnitt 1985; Levi 1991) have established that the victims of prosecuted white collar crime cases are more likely to be organizations than individuals and that organizational victims have more clout in court. Hagan (1983) attributes the greater success of organizational victims in achieving satisfactory outcomes for their cases more to their structural compatibility with criminal justice organizations than to their superior resources. Business organizations are especially well positioned to be able to quantify their losses and accordingly to be successful in obtaining restitution (Outlaw and Ruback 1999). As a result, Levi (1992) cautions, organizations' greater satisfaction with the outcome of their cases—relative to cases brought by individuals—may reflect differences in the types of cases pursued by organizations and individuals rather than a bias favoring corporations. But whatever accounts for this success, the victimization of

organizations has received a disproportionate amount of attention, and possibly a disproportionate measure of justice.

The size of the organization influences the type of victimization it experiences. Holtfreter (2005a) has found that smaller organizations are more vulnerable to asset misappropriation and larger organizations are more vulnerable to corruption. Organizations may experience various harmful consequences when they are victims of white collar crime. At a minimum, profits are likely to be diminished; losses may be incurred. In a certain percentage of cases, private corporations, businesses, and professional partnerships will be bankrupted and possibly dissolved as a consequence of being victimized. An organization that survives its victimization may be demoralized, and working conditions may undergo a considerable transformation. Individual victims of white collar crime, by contrast, may experience their losses directly and painfully.

Victims of rape may be blamed for sexually provocative behavior, whereas victims of white collar crime may be blamed for being greedy and self-interested. Such motivations clearly play a role in some classes of white collar crime victimization, as when people invest money in highly speculative ventures that turn out to be fraudulent. And victims of such white collar crimes as telemarketing or other forms of fraud are especially likely to blame themselves for their victimization (Levi 2001; Shichor et al. 2001). In other kinds of cases, such as employee injuries in hazardous workplaces, corporations have often offered the defense that the employee's own reckless and freely chosen actions caused the injury. Conversely, corporations and other types of organizations can play a role in inspiring their own victimization by their exploitative and unethical policies, as when corporations are defrauded by disgruntled employees.

Organizations accused of fraudulent activity may claim in response that they are exploited victims whose illegal actions were only undertaken defensively. In her study of a case in which the Revco Pharmaceutical Company was charged with defrauding the Ohio Department of Public Welfare with a

computer-generated double-billing scheme involving prescription charges for welfare beneficiaries, Vaughan (1980) shows us that from Revco's point of view, it was the victim of the welfare department's failure to make the timely reimbursements to which it was entitled. Small businesses engaged in illegal schemes may also view themselves or be seen more as victims of structural pressures imposed on them by large organizations (corporate suppliers and government regulatory agencies) than as victimizers (Sutton and Wild 1985). The complex character of many white collar crimes, especially those involving organizations, makes it possible to contest accusations of being the victimizer and claim victim status instead. Further, the very nature of white collar crime dictates that a somewhat disproportionate percentage of its victims are wealthy individuals or organizations, and such victims are somewhat less likely to generate sympathy than do many other classes of victims.

According to Levi (1991), the police are less sympathetic to corporate victims of fraud than to individual victims of fraud. Because most victims of white collar crime are not privileged members of society and are unfairly blamed for their victimization

(Walklate 1989), notions of victim precipitation and victim proneness are not readily applicable to the great majority of victims of white collar crime, especially corporate crime. Box 2.6 considers the outcomes for corporations and other organizations that are the target of white collar crime.

Specific Forms of Suffering of White Collar Crime Victims

The various costs of white collar crime were identified in a previous section. Here we consider the specific impact of these costs on victims, which range from financial losses to damage to physical and psychological health (Levi 2001). Although the economic costs of white collar crime have been pegged at billions of dollars, the losses to any individual victim of a specific white collar crime can range from the trivial (often spread among millions of victims) to financial devastation. Even within the framework of a particular white collar crime, the effect on individuals is not necessarily uniform. An investment fraud may wipe out one individual's life savings while another individual may lose a nominal amount of money. Contrary to one common perception, victims of fraud are not affluent as a group and may often suffer significant losses (Shichor et al. 2001). Victims of investment frauds reported that their planned retirements would have to be deferred, needed health services could no longer be afforded, and other projects for which they had long saved were no longer possible (Norris 1997; Whitaker 2005). Numerous Enron workers lost their jobs and savings, and felt angry and betrayed, following the collapse of the corporation in the wake of massive internal fraud (Bragg 2002). The same was surely true for other such corporate employees.

Although many programs now exist to facilitate restitution for victims of conventional crime, few such programs exist for victims of white collar crime (Eaton 1999a). If corporations are found guilty of some form of white collar crime, they may be required to make substantial restitution payments to victims. For example, Cendant, a large corporate franchiser operating Ramada Inn and Avis Car Rentals, among other businesses, agreed to pay its stockholders $2.8 billion for

their losses due to accounting fraud (Treaster 1999b). But victims of at least some corporate offenses, such as the Bhopal Union Carbide case in which thousands died or were disabled by the emission of poisonous gases, may have to wait for years to be compensated, and then the compensation is relatively modest (*New York Times* 1997). And in cases of individual fraud perpetrators, they have often spent or lost the money stolen and are unable to make restitution (Fried 1997a). Victims of such crimes are often dissatisfied with the amount of restitution granted them, which may amount to pennies on the dollar.

In a parallel vein, the physical impact of white collar crime takes many forms, including the development of painful, ultimately fatal conditions; physical maladies ranging from birth defects to sterility to cancer; and rather minor injuries and illnesses. There is no special reason to believe that the physical suffering associated with white collar crime, especially in its corporate form, is less intensely experienced than is conventional crime violence. In fact, the physical suffering is often more enduring in corporate crime cases (e.g., asbestosis).

The psychological trauma of victimization in conventional crimes such as rape, robbery, and burglary can be formidable, and sometimes it outweighs economic loss or physical injury. An enormous psychic cost is also involved in the anticipation of possible conventional crime victimization. The psychological suffering of white collar crime victims is likely to take a somewhat different course than that of conventional crime, although it is very real. First, the realization of victimization is likely to be more gradual, in some cases occurring years after the illegal event or process. Second, because direct physical confrontation is less likely, the white collar crime victim is somewhat less likely to have a sharply defined target for his or her anger. Third, a common psychological response to either the anticipation of or the experience of white collar crime victimization (of the more common economic type) is distrust or cynicism. In the case of victims of corporate or occupational violence—for example, individuals injured or made ill by unsafe products, dangerous working conditions, and environmental harm—

B O X 2.7 **Psychological Consequences of Fraud Victimization**

Psychological trauma is not limited to victims of physically injurious white collar crimes. It also occurs in conjunction with white collar crimes involving financial loss, although the degree of psychological trauma varies. In a study of victims of the failure of the Southern Industrial Banking Corporation (SIBC) due to gross mismanagement and fraud, Shover, Fox, and Mills (1994) found that the impact varied enormously, with victims fitting into three broad categories: the inconvenienced, the sobered, and the devastated. Those in the third category, the devastated, reported that the emotional and psychological damage was even worse than the financial loss, which often involved entire life savings. These victims made such comments as these: "Really, it destroyed our life. We're not happy people anymore. . . . I don't feel like a free human being anymore, . . . It's destroying us. . . . " (Shover, Fox, and Mills 1991: 13–14). Many of the

victims were disheartened by the feeble governmental response to their victimization, although this study found no evidence of significant, enduring de-legitimation of political institutions that could be traced to the victim's experience with SIBC. But clearly the effects of white collar crime victimization in this case parallel those of conventional crime. The largest number of victims (almost 40 percent) of another investment fraud reported anger and dismay over their victimization (Shichor et al. 2001). And still another study found that 29 percent of the 77 victims of a fraud suffered a major depressive episode within 20 months following their loss, compared to only 2 percent of a control sample (Ganzini, McFarland, and Bloom 1990). The victim of a bank failure caused by fraud wrote of losing her job, her home, and her husband (due to premature death) as a consequence of a white collar crime (Halbrooks 1990).

---

severe psychological trauma often accompanies the physical injury. (Box 2.7 explores in more depth specific psychological consequences of white collar crime victimization.)

Most of us probably have a stronger visceral fear of personal crime victimization and find the prospect of such sudden, direct, and extreme victimization more terrifying than corporate violence. Reiman (2004) suggests that a defender of the present legal order might explain this not only in terms of differences of directness but also by viewing corporate violence as a by-product of a legitimate pursuit in which victims have some choice in whether or not they are exposed to the violence. In response to this position, Reiman cites the many constraints on the choices of victims of white collar crime (e.g., workers frequently do not have realistic choices about where they work). Numerous accounts and experiences of victims of environmental pollution (e.g., the Love Canal case), unsafe working conditions (e.g., the Manville asbestos case), and unsafe products (e.g., the Ford Pinto case) fully convey the intense psychological suffering of these victims. If a victim attributes the harm to, for

example, a trusted employer, the sense of betrayal may well intensify the psychological damage incurred. As Box 2.7 demonstrates, many victims of white collar crime suffer from depression.

STUDYING WHITE COLLAR CRIME AND ASSESSING ITS COSTS, IN SUM

White collar crime and its control have been less thoroughly studied than conventional crime and its control. The study of white collar crime presents researchers with special challenges. Nevertheless, a wide range of research methods can be and have been applied to the study of white collar crime and its control.

In a parallel vein, it is more difficult to measure how much white collar crime occurs and how much it costs than is true of conventional crime. Various reasons for these difficulties have been identified in this chapter. At best, we have broad estimates. But by any reasonable measure, most if not all of those who have looked into this question would agree that the costs of white collar crime greatly exceed those of conventional crime.

White collar crime victimization is significant in terms of numbers and consequences. To date it has not been subjected to extensive and systematic study. We still have much to learn about the nature of the victim–offender relationship and the full range of consequences of white collar crime victimization.

There is a need, in particular, to understand more fully the reasons why this type of crime victimization does not inspire the same level of concern from either the public or the criminal justice system as conventional crime victimization. One of the key questions is whether public priorities concerning crime victimization are based on objective measures of harm or are fundamentally distorted by pervasive misrepresentations of such victimization.

KEY TERMS

archival data, 38

case study, 35

content analysis, 39

direct costs, 45

event history analysis, 38

experiment, 36

field, 36

laboratory, 36

natural, 36

humanistic approach, 32

indirect costs, 46

observational research, 37

official statistics, 45

physical costs, 47

positivistic approach, 32

residual economic costs, 47

secondary data analysis, 38

self-report surveys, 44

seriousness-of-crime surveys, 40

victim blaming, 50

victimization surveys, 43

DISCUSSION QUESTIONS

1. What are some of the specific challenges in studying white collar crime relative to the study of conventional crime? Can white collar crime be studied scientifically, or does it require a different type of approach? Why does the study of white collar crime ultimately call for a cross-disciplinary or interdisciplinary approach?

2. Identify some specific applications and limitations of three of the following methods for researching white collar crime: the journalistic approach, the experiment, the survey, observational research, the case study, secondary data analysis, archival data analysis, and content analysis. Then discuss how all three of the methods identified can be applied to the study of a single form of white collar crime.

3. Critically evaluate the traditional, common claim that the general public perceives white collar crime to be less serious than conventional

crime. What specific methodological questions can be raised about research on this question? Which specific factors have contributed to a growth in the perception that white collar crime is relatively serious?

4. What are the specific difficulties involved in measuring the amount and cost of white collar crime relative to such measurements applied to conventional crime? Which generalizations, if any, about the amount and cost of white collar crime do you regard as reliable? Discuss the concepts of *indirect costs* and *residual costs* of white collar crime.

5. Compare broad and narrow conceptions of the notion of victims of white collar crime. What are the specific reasons why victims of white collar crime have attracted less attention than victims of conventional predatory crime? Discuss the concepts of *victim blaming* and *organizational victims* in connection with white collar crime.

3

Corporate Crime

Since the mid-1970s, the term *corporate crime* has been widely invoked. It is seen as both a major form of white collar crime and a specific form of organizational crime (Friedrichs 2001b; Gobert and Punch 2003; Kramer 1984). An influential definition of corporate crime, by Marshall Clinard and Richard Quinney (1973), characterized it as "offenses committed by corporate officials for their corporation and the offenses of the corporation itself" (p. 188). Some of the implications of the concept of corporate crime—for example, whether corporations can be said to commit crimes and whether harmful acts involving corporations are crimes even if they are not prohibited by the criminal law—are considered elsewhere in this text. But because corporate crime was the focus of Sutherland's (1949) pioneering work on white collar crime, remains a principal concern of students of such crime, and is arguably the most consequential type of such crime, it seems appropriate to begin our review of the varieties of white collar crime with a discussion of corporate crime.

Before we explore corporate crime specifically, a brief review of the historical development of the corporation and its character today is in order.

THE HISTORICAL DEVELOPMENT OF THE CORPORATION AND CORPORATE CRIME

The legal idea of a corporation can be traced back to Roman times (Geis 1988). In the Anglo-American tradition, the earliest corporations, or "proto-corporations," were churches, towns, guilds, and universities, which over time came to be recognized as trusts with legal control over certain property (Coleman 1974; Stone 1975). The great trading corporations began to emerge in the 16th century, and in the 17th century the modern corporation, with specific corporate powers, can be recognized in the East India Company, founded in 1612 (Stone 1975).

The trading corporations of the 17th and 18th centuries played a central role in massively harmful acts; the devastation of Native Americans and the slave trading of Africans are two primary examples (Sale 1990; Williams 1966). Early corporations were also involved in specifically fraudulent and illegal activity. The so-called "South Sea Bubble" case in the early 18th century is a famous example. The South Sea Company was chartered in London in 1711 to engage in slave trade and commerce in South America. Investors lost large fortunes because the enterprise was fraudulent, driven by bribery, false financial statements, and stock manipulation (Balen 2003; Geis 1993; Robb 1990). The legislative response to the scandal (the South Sea Bubble Act of 1720) was an early form of recognition of the need for some legal controls on corporations, although such early laws were exceptionally clumsy and may have done more harm than good. The sale of corporate stocks was rendered more difficult.

The Industrial Revolution of the late 18th and 19th centuries eventually gave rise to immensely powerful and wealthy capitalist corporations, although during this period and into the 20th century relatively little regulation of these enterprises was effective (Clinard and Yeager 1980). The corporate empires of the *robber barons* (e.g., Rockefeller, Vanderbilt, Gould, Carnegie, and Frick) of the second half of the 19th century were involved in every manner of bribery, fraud, stock manipulation, predation against competitors, price gouging, exploitation of labor, and maintenance of unsafe working conditions, but these corporations were largely invulnerable to legal controls (Josephson 1934; Myers 1907).

In the late 19th century, the monopolistic practices of huge *trusts* (holding companies for a chain of corporations), such as Standard Oil, helped inspire the Sherman Antitrust Act. Through the early part of the 20th century, major corporations became increasingly national in character; since World War II in particular, mergers, the formation of conglomerates, corporate takeovers, and the growth of transnational or multinational corporations have been characteristic of corporate development (Bakan 2004; Clinard and Yeager 1980). If corporations no longer operate with the almost complete freedom of the 19th-century corporations of the robber barons, they are nevertheless powerful, and the notion of corporate crime is still very real.

THE CORPORATION IN MODERN SOCIETY

Corporations are a conspicuous feature of contemporary societies, especially in American society, and in many respects corporations are viewed in a posi-

tive way. They are widely regarded as the centerpiece of a free-market capitalist economy and as a powerful manifestation of entrepreneurial initiative and creativity. They are a major factor in the generally high standard of living Americans typically enjoy.

Millions of people are employed by corporations and regard them as their providers. Many young people aspire to become corporate employees. Corporations produce the seemingly endless range of products we purchase and consume, and they sponsor many forms of entertainment we enjoy, especially television. They are also principal sponsors of pioneering research in many fields and a crucial element in national defense. Corporations are important benefactors of a large number of charities, public events, institutions of higher learning, and scientific enterprises. And of course the major corporations in particular, with their large resources, are quite adept at reminding us of their positive contributions to our way of life. Thus, the very notion of corporate crime is jarring and disconcerting to many people, for it challenges a widely projected image of beneficence. In one recent major poll, two-thirds of Americans surveyed credited corporations for their economic prosperity (Court 2003: 11). However, three-fourths of these respondents expressed concern over excessive corporate power; a survey in 2004 found that some 75 percent of Americans had an image of corporations as "not good" or "terrible" (Rich 2004: 15).

The dark side of corporations has long been recognized. Karl Marx (1867) regarded the corporation (or *joint-stock company*) as one of the instruments of a capitalist system that exploits and dehumanizes workers and deprives them of a fair return on their labor. Marx and Friedrich Engels held capitalist corporations responsible for willful homicide and assault through the operation of industrialized enterprises that maximized the pursuit of profit and minimized the preservation of human life (Harris 1974).

With the great growth of the joint-stock corporation in the 19th century, Marx came to recognize that corporations were no longer fully controlled by those who "owned" them (i.e., the stockholders); in the Marxist view, the stockholder is a small-scale capitalist who has lost much control over his capital to those who actually manage the corporations (Mandel 1983). The corporate managers, who are often large stockholders as well, are in a position to advance their own interests and enrich themselves at the expense of workers and ordinary stockholders. But because in the Marxist view both managers and stockholders have a common interest in maximizing profit, they inevitably exploit workers and others as well. Many non-Marxists also recognize that the pursuit of profit is the principal rationale for the corporation, and they argue that it often takes precedence over all other considerations.

Major corporations have been accused of engaging in the "pathological" pursuit of profit, which for some of the largest corporations adds up to more than $100 billion a year, with sales exceeding the economies of many countries (Bakan 2004; Derber 2003). Corporate wealth is highly concentrated and is becoming even more so.

Corporate ownership and corporate-generated wealth have traditionally been concentrated in the hands of relatively few people, with about 1 percent of the population owning about half of the outstanding stock and trust equity in the United States, and two-thirds of the financial securities. The wealthiest 10 percent own some 90 percent of the stock (Wolff 2000). Although millions of Americans belong to pension plans that own large blocks of stock, the influence of these Americans over corporate affairs is essentially nonexistent. *Oligopolies* of a relatively few corporations dominating their market have replaced classical monopolies, which were outlawed in the United States by the Sherman Antitrust Act in 1890. In many industries (e.g., auto, tire, aircraft), a small number of corporations control up to two-thirds of the market. *Conglomerates*, a combination of centrally owned and controlled firms operating in different markets, have also become far more common, especially because of multibillion-dollar mergers in the 1980s and 1990s. Many of these conglomerates today are *transnational (multinational* or *global) corporations*, which produce goods outside of their home country. Although in a broad sense such corporations have existed for hundreds of years,

their number, importance, and influence increased greatly in the final decades of the 20th century, and this influence seems likely to increase in the 21st century.

Large corporations, by their very nature, are especially well positioned to take advantage of political corruption, the absence or paucity of regulatory controls, and the desperation for economic enterprise characteristic of many developing nations. Some of the *corporate transgressions* (harmful although not necessarily illegal actions) associated with transnationals operating in third-world countries include highly hazardous and dangerous working conditions at industrial facilities; exportation of unsafe products (often banned in developed countries); dumping of toxic wastes and other forms of environmental pollution; bribing and corrupting politicians; massive tax evasion by shifting profits to subsidiaries in countries with favorable corporate tax policies; and complicity in a range of human rights violations, including torture and assassinations, undertaken by repressive third-world governments and military or intelligence entities of developed governments (Michalowski and Kramer 1987; Simon 2006). (See Box 3.1.)

Even though desperately poor developing countries and their citizens may well derive some economic benefits from transnational economic activity in their countries, they are also clearly exploited and pay a high price, especially in terms of harm to health, for these benefits. These "corporate transgressions" have been condemned by United Nations codes (despite the efforts of transnational corporations to influence those codes) and are clearly injurious by any reasonable standard (Derber 2003; Michalowski and Kramer 1987). In view of the constant expansion of the global marketplace, the transgressions of transnational corporations are likely to become increasingly significant in the future.

Early in the 21st century, American corporations can be characterized as "the new sovereigns" (Mitchell L. E. 2002). Their worldwide pursuit of profit takes precedence over all other considerations. Their enormous resources give corporations great influence over politicians on all levels and play a major role in shaping public policy. A *power elite*

B O X 3.1   "It's Legal But It Ain't Right"

This chapter focuses on corporate crime, but many of the demonstrably harmful activities of corporations are in fact legal. In their book *It's Legal But It Ain't Right: Harmful Social Consequences of Legal Industries,* Nikos Passas and Neva Goodwin (2004) bring together a series of chapters on such corporate activities. The tobacco industry is an especially obvious candidate for a list of industries that cause immense harm not proscribed by law, but other legal industries that also cause great harm include those that produce or promote weapons, gambling, cheap food, and pesticides. Passas and Goodwin embrace the somewhat awkward term *negative externalities* to capture the huge costs that society must pay in some form for the inevitably harmful consequences of such legal products or services. In an increasingly globalized world, transnationals can engage in activities that are legal in developing countries—e.g., the use of child labor—and then profit greatly by selling their products in countries where such activities are outlawed. In one interpretation, the capitalist political economy is organized to produce a wide range of harms in the interest of generating wealth for the elite class (Tombs and Hillyard 2004). Corporations (like Enron) have been privatizing natural resources that should be public goods (Prashad 2002). Accordingly, many corporate activities are "crimes" in the broad sense of the term, without being illegal.

---

of the top people in the corporate world, government, and military have "interlocks," or a complex network of ties, that enable them to advance their interrelated interests and move quite easily between high-level private- and public-sector positions (Mills 1956; Useem 1983). The corporate elite in particular dominate the state through active pursuit of their own interests, coordinated corporate activities outside the government, and exploitation of economic conditions (Schwartz 1987). Despite the formidable political power of corporations, they have been relatively free of accountability and traditionally have been able to conceal much of their power-wielding activity (Bakan 2004; Bowman 1996). On all levels of government, powerful corporations play an important, if not always fully visible, role.

The large corporations so dominant in today's economic environment have transformed capitalism into something very different from the economic system envisioned by its principal philosopher, Adam Smith. In fact, in *The Wealth of Nations*, Smith (1776, 1937) condemned "the mean rapacity, the monopolizing spirit of merchants and manufacturers, who neither are nor ought be the rulers of mankind" (p. 460). Smith's conception of freely competing individual entrepreneurs has given way to a world dominated by huge, vastly powerful corporations, and the prevalence of authentic entrepreneurs has declined dramatically (Michalowski 1985).

Corporations are increasingly controlled by *paper entrepreneurs*, or investors who are principally concerned with short-term profit (Mitchell L. E. 2002; Reich 1983). These investors are far less likely to be strongly committed to product development or to the local communities in which corporate operations are based. Paper entrepreneurs have been the driving force behind the intensified wave of corporate takeovers since the 1980s, which has led to devastating personal consequences for millions of middle managers and ordinary workers who have lost jobs, benefits, or better salaries, and indirect consequences for taxpayers and consumers, who have absorbed lost revenue from vast debt-service payments or paid higher prices for products (Brooks 1987; Faludi 1990). Corporate takeovers and mergers often enrich top executives and investment bankers to the tune of tens (even hundreds) of millions of dollars, while thousands of company employees get pink slips (Morgenson 2005). Even though such corporate takeovers are not illegal—some parties have even defended them as beneficial—others argue that they are too often harmful and should be discouraged or prohibited (Henriques 1990b; Iseman 1986; Newport 1989).

In the bull market of the 1990s, corporate managers were under immense pressure to keep stock prices up, and they often did so by financial manipulations as opposed to product development. The bankruptcy in 2001 of the giant energy corporation, Enron, was one striking example of this trend (McLean 2001). In general, corporations in the United States today want to be left alone when business conditions are favorable and they are making money, but they want the government to bail them out when they get into trouble (Mintz and Cohen 1971, 1976). Enron lobbied aggressively for deregulation for many years, but when it faced bankruptcy—largely due to its corrupt financial manipulations—it sought a government bailout (Kadlec 2002a; Wayne 2002a). This has been called the "socialization of risk": Leave profit to the private sector and let the public sector absorb the risks.

A TYPOLOGY
OF CORPORATE CRIME

How can we best categorize the many different activities that can be encompassed by the term *corporate crime*? One approach is to adopt a typology emphasizing the primary victims: for example, the general public, consumers, employees, or a corporation's competitors. A second approach is to focus on the nature of the harmful activity: for example, corporate violence, corporate corruption, corporate stealing, or corporate deceptions. A third approach emphasizes the size or scope of the corporate entity: for example, crimes of transnational corporations; crimes of major domestic corporations; crimes of small, locally based corporations; or crimes of incorporated individual enterprises. A fourth approach has classified corporate crime according to the type of product or service involved: for example, crimes of the automotive industry, crimes of the pharmaceutical industry, crimes of the banking industry, or crimes of health care providers.

Other criteria can be taken into account in differentiating among corporate crimes. One criterion is the primary corporate agent of the criminal activity, such as the chief executive officer or principal executives, the middle managers, the corporate supervisors, or employees. One can ask which instrument or mechanism is used to initiate and commit the crime. Other criteria for classifying corporate transgressions emphasize the type of law invoked (criminal, civil, or administrative) or the specific legal class involved (e.g., antitrust, consumer protection, environmental).

The typology or classification we use is likely to be dictated by what we are seeking to explain or understand in a particular context. For purposes of this chapter, the major distinction is the type of activity; thus, we will examine corporate violence and corporate abuse of power, fraud, or economic exploitation. Within these two broad categories a further differentiation is made by type of victim. Accordingly, for corporate violence, we have corporate violence against the public, corporate violence against consumers, and corporate violence against workers. Within the category of corporate abuse of power, fraud, or economic exploitation, we have crimes against citizens, against consumers, against employees, against competitors, against franchisees and suppliers, and against owners or creditors. Other criteria, such as the type of product or service involved, are then incorporated into discussions of these types. The rationale for this scheme is not that these categories require separate and distinct theories—indeed, explanations tend to cut across the types—but rather that it enables us to organize and discuss the bewildering range of corporate crime activities with some coherence.

CORPORATE VIOLENCE

We have seen that violent crime is most readily associated with conventional predatory offenders, serial killers, mafiosi, and terrorists. Despite some reluctance to regard corporations as violent offenders, they are engaged in activities with violent consequences.

Corporate violence differs from conventional interpersonal violence in several ways. First, it is *indirect* in the sense that victims are not assaulted by another person. Corporate violence results from policies and actions, undertaken on behalf of the corporation, that result in the exposure of people to harmful conditions, products, or substances. Second, the effects of corporate violence are typically quite removed in time from the implementation of the corporate policy or action that caused the harm, and the causal relationship between the corporate action and the injury to health (or death) cannot always be clearly and definitively established. Third, typically in corporate violence a large number of individuals acting collectively, rather than a single or very few individuals, are responsible for the actions that result in physical injury or death. Fourth, corporate violence, virtually by definition, is motivated by the desire to maximize corporate profits (or survival) and minimize corporate overhead. The violence is a consequence rather than a specifically intended outcome of such motivations. Finally, corporate violence has traditionally inspired a far more limited legal and justice system response than has conventional interpersonal violence.

Corporate Violence against the Public: Unsafe Environmental Practices

Corporations' contributions to poisoning the environment may well be the most common form of corporate violence, although such crime has to date received rather little attention from criminologists (Burns and Lynch 2004; Lynch, Stretesky, and McGurrin 2002). There are, of course, many different sources of pollution, and corporations are hardly responsible for all of it (Blair 2001). Ordinary citizens as well as government operations on many levels can contribute to pollution. In New York State, two leading assembly members contended that the state government itself was the worst polluter, citing 450 violations of environmental laws at 267 state sites (Gold 1990). Still, corporations account for a disproportionately large share of the most dangerous pollution, and major corporations have been especially flagrant violators of environmental laws (Grant, Jones, and Bergesen 2002).

Through most of human history, the disposal of wastes of all kinds was little regulated or controlled. Obviously the lack of proper disposal of wastes contributed to highly unsanitary living conditions, the prolific spread of disease, and premature death. But it is not the case, as some might imagine, that concern over pollution is entirely modern. In 1290, for example, King Edward I of England prohibited the burning of coal while Parliament was sitting because it filled the London air with acrid smoke. In 1470, a German scholar, Ulrich Ellenbog, identified some adverse effects of exposure to carbon monoxide, lead, mercury, and other metals or substances (Bellini 1986). Similar and increasingly sophisticated observations of this type were made in subsequent centuries.

The modern problem of pollution, in contrast, is characterized in part by the dramatic increase in the production of toxic wastes, especially since World War II. In the United States, an exponential increase in the production of synthetic organic chemicals has occurred, with more than 300 billion pounds annually in the last quarter of the 20th century; the same is true for hazardous or toxic wastes, with 275 million metric tons produced (Regenstein 1986; Reiman 2004). Improper disposal of deadly wastes occurs an estimated 90 percent of the time.

The overall harmful consequences of such practices for the health of Americans seem evident to many observers. An estimated one-quarter of the U.S. population, or 56 million people, will develop cancer, and by some (admittedly controversial) estimates, 70 to 90 percent of all cancers may be environmentally related (Brownstein 1981; Regenstein 1986; Reiman 2004). Cancer is the only major cause of death that increased in prevalence in the 20th century. In addition to cancer, environmental pollution is associated with a range of other maladies and serious health problems, including heart and lung diseases, birth defects and genetic disorders, and sterility. Polluted air alone may jeopardize the health of some 35 million Americans and contributes to tens of thousands of premature deaths annually (Reiman 2004). Environmental pollution also has a devastating impact on wildlife habitats and endangered species (Shover and Routhe 2005). By any measure, then, corporate polluting of the environment is a serious crime.

Much evidence indicates that corporations either knew, or should have known, the inherent risks arising from their dumping of toxic wastes. Corporations have often opted for highly dangerous, low-cost methods of getting rid of such wastes. They have not been forthcoming with information on dangers concerning wastes and pollution; they have even engaged in deliberate deception. Corporations have typically denied responsibility for the harmful consequences attributed to their polluting practices and have resisted changing these practices until forced to do so (Barstow and Bergman 2003a, 2003b). And they have actively lobbied against environmental legislation. But some corporations have been convicted of or pleaded guilty to environmental crime charges: for example, McWane, Inc., a major manufacturer of cast-iron sewer and water pipes, in 2005 (Barstow 2005). Some specific forms of corporate polluting include release of toxic chemicals (including pesticides, herbicides, and oil) and air pollution.

Toxic Waste Some of the most notorious releases of toxic chemicals have occurred outside the United States. In one of these cases, a Japanese petrochemical corporation, Chisso, had for years been dumping a huge volume of poisons into the sea. In the 1950s, hundreds of residents of a small, nearby village, Minamata, developed severe brain and body dysfunctions, including birth defects, paralysis, blindness, and other horrendous consequences (Mokhiber 1988). In the Bhopal case in India, a massive poisonous chemical cloud was emitted from a Union Carbide plant in December 1984. Although estimates vary, it is generally believed that at least 5,000 people in the area died as a consequence; some 200,000 others were injured, 60,000 seriously and some 20,000 permanently (Pearce and Tombs 1989; Sarangi 2002). In both of these cases, subsequent investigation revealed that the corporations involved had been negligent or had cut corners on safety, had attempted to conceal or minimize their responsibility, and had avoided criminal prosecution

(cases were being resolved through civil lawsuits or settlements).

Within the United States, the Love Canal case is among the best-known cases of corporate pollution. In the 1940s, the Hooker Chemical Corporation bought the canal (near Niagara Falls), drained it, and began dumping into it a huge number of 55-gallon metal drums filled with highly toxic chemical wastes (Mokhiber 1988). Eventually the property was acquired by a local school board, and both a school and residential neighborhood were built in the area. Over a period of decades, school children and residents were exposed to noxious fumes and surfacing chemicals, allegedly resulting in a disproportionately high number of miscarriages, birth defects, liver ailments, and emotional disorders among this population (however, a direct causal link to the Love Canal chemicals was never conclusively established). The corporation's initial response was to attempt to suppress pertinent evidence and to limit its own legal liability, but eventually several hundred families were evacuated from the area, and Hooker Chemical was compelled to pay $20 million to former Love Canal residents. Box 3.2 recaps the infamous *Exxon Valdez* case.

The dumping of toxic wastes by cruise ships is another form of polluting the waters. In a recent year, the Royal Caribbean cruise line pleaded guilty to routinely dumping toxic waste and paid a fine of $18 million (Wald 1999b). Royal Caribbean initially tried to claim immunity from action by American courts because it flew a Liberian flag (Frantz 1999). Of course, the vast majority of its passengers are Americans, and the line had heralded on its ships the claim that it was committed to environmentally safe practices.

Corporations have long made deliberate decisions to produce and illegally (or improperly) dump toxic waste, despite the availability of much safer alternatives, because these practices are profitable for the corporations (Lynch, Stretesky, and McGurrin 2002). Furthermore, those who are victimized by these practices are disproportionately minorities and poor people who live in the closest proximity to the dump sites.

B O X 3.2 The *Exxon Valdez* and Prince William Sound

One of the worst cases of aquatic pollution occurred on March 24, 1989, when the oil tanker *Exxon Valdez* ran into a reef in Prince William Sound, Alaska, spilling 11 million gallons of oil into the sea, with devastating consequences for wildlife, the environment, and the region's economy (Davidson 1990; Labaton 1989a; Schneider 1991b). Complex questions of responsibility arose from this incident, but evidence emerged that the Exxon Corporation was aware that the ship's captain had a drinking problem and had reduced the size of the tanker's crew, leaving them fatigued. In 1991, Exxon agreed to plead guilty to a criminal charge and pay a $100 million fine, part of a civil and criminal settlement totaling more than $1 billion (Schneider 1991b). In September 1994, a federal grand jury in Anchorage ordered Exxon to pay $5 billion in punitive damages to Alaskans harmed by the *Valdez* oil spill; additional trials were anticipated (Schneider 1994). Remarkably, these outcomes had no significant negative effect on the corporation's earning prospects or stock price (Schneider 1991b; Schneider 1994). It was later divulged that Exxon had misled the jury in the case; it had secret agreements with seafood processor plaintiffs that they would return part of the punitive damages award (Salpurkas 1996). In November 2001, a federal appeals court overturned as excessive the $5.3 billion punitive damage award against Exxon (Nieves 2001). In 2003, another huge oil company, Texaco, went on trial in Ecuador for causing an ecological disaster by dumping billions of gallons of waste into open pits (Forero 2003).

Air Pollution It is well known today that automobile emissions constitute a significant proportion of the air pollution problem and that some cities—Los Angeles is a notable example—have generally unhealthful air conditions much of the year. What is less well known is that automobile companies deliberately promoted a situation in which nonpolluting public transportation systems were largely displaced by automobiles and buses in some areas (Mokhiber 1988). For at least a half century, the auto industry has actively resisted the imposition of clean air standards and the development of successful strategies for reducing smog (Doyle 2000).

In the 1930s, General Motors formed a subsidiary, United Cities Motor Transportation Co., to buy out the electric streetcar system in Los Angeles and replace it with buses. In 1949, General Motors and several other companies with a vested interest in gasoline-fueled transportation—for example, Standard Oil of California and Firestone—were convicted of violating antitrust law by criminally conspiring to eliminate electric transportation and monopolize the sale of buses.

The companies received only token fines of $5,000 apiece, and no one went to jail. When by 1970 the harmful environmental consequences of emissions from internal combustion engines were becoming more evident and the Clean Air Act was passed, another major auto manufacturer, Ford, spent a great deal of money lobbying against such initiatives and engaged in deceptive practices to avoid complying with emissions standards required by clean air legislation. In 1973, Ford pleaded no contest to 350 counts of criminal and civil charges pertaining to violations of the Clean Air Act and paid a combined $7 million fine (Doyle 2000; Mokhiber 1988).

Legal Challenges Continue Neither the environmental movement nor the implementation and enforcement of environmental protection laws has deterred major corporations from attempting to save money by illegal polluting. Major corporations have consistently been charged with polluting the environment, but it has often been difficult to pursue these cases as criminal cases.

Only a handful of businessmen have ever been sent to prison in pollution cases. In one such case, Russell Mahler, president of Hudson Oil Refining Company, was sentenced to one year in prison and fined $750,000 for violations of 22 counts of the Clean Streams Act (Chavez 1982). Mahler, a distinguished-looking Cornell graduate and to all

---

B O X 3.3 **Corporate Destruction of a Community**

One special form of "polluting" by corporations requires attention here, even though it differs from the conventional conception of such offenses.

When the Buffalo Creek dam burst in February 1972, the town of Saunders, West Virginia, was demolished (Erikson 1976; Stern 1976). The dam's rupture left 125 members of the community dead, and some 4,000 Buffalo Creek residents lost their homes. The dam had been used to contain mining wastes dumped over a period of many years by Buffalo Mining, which was owned by the large and powerful Pittston Mining Corporation. Even though for years citizens had expressed concern about the company's dumping practices, and despite a partial collapse of the dam that foreshadowed what was to come, Pittston

Mining attempted to absolve itself of basic legal responsibility by claiming that the rupture was "an act of God."

An inquiry after the disaster established that for many decades mining companies had been aware of the dangers of their dumping practices and that Pittston had specifically violated federal safety standards and ignored warnings about this dam's vulnerability. Despite this evidence, no grand jury indictment was directed at the corporation, and it eventually made a $13.5 million out-of-court civil settlement. The entire affair echoed a similar famous disaster in 1889—the Johnstown, Pennsylvania, flood, which caused the loss of more than 2,000 lives and was also attributed to the negligence of powerful corporate magnates.

---

external appearances a successful businessman, ran various companies in the oil reclamation business. But instead of legally and properly disposing of the toxic chemicals separated from oil wastes produced by various major corporations, Mahler's operation illegally dumped those wastes in city landfills, sewers, and other such locations. In one case, truck drivers for his company arranged to dump toxic wastes in a borehole behind a garage near Wilkes-Barre, Pennsylvania. The carcinogenic waste spilled into the Susquehanna River and contaminated the water supply of various northeastern Pennsylvania communities. When Mahler was confronted with the evidence of this illegal dumping, he initially attempted to arrange a cleanup in the hope—or expectation—that criminal prosecution could be avoided. In this particular case, the ploy was unsuccessful; Mahler actually went to prison. Box 3.3 examines a case in which corporate actions destroyed an entire town.

Corporate Violence against Consumers:
Unsafe Products

Although corporations hardly wish to inflict harm on consumers, they have in fact all too often done so when the drive to maximize profits or survive in the marketplace has taken precedence over a concern with consumer safety. An enormous range of consumer products—including many foods, drugs and medical devices, motor vehicles, household products, and cosmetics—have been identified as hazardous to various degrees (Brobeck and Averyt 1983). Tens of thousands of Americans are alleged to die annually from product-related accidents, and millions more suffer disabling injuries at a cost of more than $100 billion in property damage, lost wages, insurance, litigation, and medical expenses. In May 2005, the U.S. Consumer Product Safety Commission issued product recalls for 30 different products found to be potentially dangerous, including children's folding chairs, pacifiers, portable electric heaters, cribs, and utility vehicles. Even though certain products, such as lawn mowers, are intrinsically dangerous, much evidence suggests that corporations, in their almost single-minded pursuit of profit, have been negligent—sometimes criminally negligent—in their disregard for consumer safety.

Food Products In his influential novel *The Jungle* (1906), Upton Sinclair exposed the grossly unsanitary conditions in the Chicago meat markets. References in this novel to rats and even workers falling into the meat vats and becoming part of the final product inspired revulsion and helped bring into existence the Meat Inspection Act of 1906. Since that time, the public has come to assume that meat and other food products are inspected according to government standards to protect consumers, but much evidence indicates that throughout the 20th century, bribery of government meat inspectors and deception, through use of dyes and by other means, resulted in the foisting of much unhealthy meat on the American public (Kwitny 1979; Swanson and Schultz 1982). In the final decades of the 20th century, reports of unsanitary conditions in meatpacking plants, of marketing of unsafe meat, and of paid-off inspectors were still forthcoming, and millions of Americans were suffering from food poisoning as a result of such practices (Frank and Lynch 1992).

Of course, meat is hardly the only unsafe food product. Corporations entice millions of Americans, especially children, to consume misleadingly labeled foods with an unhealthy high sugar or fat content, and the widespread practice of processing foods with additives or irradiation may also increase the incidence of cancer among consumers (Curra 1994; Mindell 1987; Simon 2006). Because the consumption of food is an unavoidable activity, the questionable—and sometimes illegal—consequences of corporate practices in food production are especially far-reaching.

Pharmaceutical Products and Medical Devices
Even though "drug pushing" is most readily associated with sleazy inner-city dealers catering to the needs of vulnerable (often poor) people, pharmaceutical corporations can also be characterized as "pushers" insofar as they spend millions of dollars advertising the use of psychoactive drugs and encourage their sales representatives to use various inducements to persuade physicians to prescribe new drugs and other pharmaceutical products (Braithwaite 1984; Farrell 2004). At the core of this activity is a high, if arguably eroding, level of trust, for there are few commonplace products about which the typical consumer is less capable of making independent judgments.

The pharmaceutical industry has been accused of unsafe or unsanitary practices in the production and distribution of some of its products. It has aggressively promoted various painkillers, antidepressants and diet drugs, which are often overprescribed and have a variety of adverse consequences for users. Thalidomide, DES, and the Dalkon shield were especially notorious products.

In the case of thalidomide, some 8,000 babies whose mothers had taken this prescribed tranquilizer during their pregnancies were born grossly deformed in the early 1960s, mainly in Europe (Knightly, et al. 1979; Mokhiber 1988). Much evidence suggests that the principal pharmaceutical company involved, Chemie Grunenthal, had early indications of the drug's dangers (as well as its limited effectiveness), but the company continued to promote it as an over-the-counter drug until the enormous scope of harm being done had been widely publicized and it was forced to withdraw it from the market (Mokhiber 1988). A criminal indictment filed against Chemie Grunenthal in Germany in 1967 was dropped after the company agreed to pay a $31 million fine, and other pharmaceutical companies also eventually made civil settlements (Braithwaite 1984). In the late 1990s, thalidomide was once again being promoted as an effective drug for the treatment of some conditions, such as leprosy complications; whether a legally available thalidomide could be kept entirely from pregnant women remained to be seen (Cowley 1997).

DES, a drug discovered in the 1930s, was subsequently marketed by the pharmaceutical firm Eli Lilly as an effective agent in preventing miscarriages (Mokhiber 1988). Many thousands of daughters of women who took DES in the 1950s developed sometimes-fatal vaginal and cervical cancer and often experienced infertility or other serious reproductive problems; even some DES sons developed testicular abnormalities and fertility problems. Thousands of civil suits resulted, although no criminal indictment was ever produced in this matter. Considerable evidence exists concerning early corporate awareness of both the carcinogenic properties of DES and the danger it posed to fetuses

(Mokhiber 1988). The Food and Drug Administration (FDA) had relied on the pharmaceutical company's evaluations rather than on its own tests, and the FDA Drug Division Chief who approved the marketing of DES took a highly paid position with a drug company shortly thereafter (Mokhiber 1988). Ironically, it has never been established that DES is in fact effective in preventing miscarriage; it has been fully established, however, that the drug has caused (and continues to cause) enormous psychological anguish, profound reproductive abnormalities, cancer, and premature death.

The Dalkon shield was an intrauterine birth-control device sold in the 1960s by the A. H. Robins Company (Mintz 1985; Mokhiber 1988). Millions of these shields were distributed all over the world. Because the device was defective (bacteria were able to travel up the device's wick and into the womb), thousands of women were rendered sterile, gave birth to stillborn or deformed children, or suffered other reproductive system problems. Despite the fact that Robins had early indications of these problems, it neither voluntarily warned women nor withdrew the Dalkon shield from the market, because the product was highly profitable. After much stonewalling by the company, the FDA halted distribution of this product in 1974. Thousands of users sued, many lawsuits were settled with a long-term payout of approximately $1 billion, the corporation declared bankruptcy in 1985, and two top executives were found guilty of criminal contempt.

Many other dangerous drugs and pharmaceutical products have been inflicted on an unwitting public. Drugs such as Clioquinol, MER/29, Oraflex, and Selacryn, all developed since the 1930s for the treatment of such conditions as diarrhea, excessive cholesterol, arthritis, and mild blood pressure, were widely marketed, and in each case thousands of people suffered devastating side effects, from blindness and paralysis to death (Mokhiber 1988). Six executives of the C.R. Bard Co., the world's largest medical device manufacturer, were indicted in connection with the selling of untested heart catheters, responsible for at least one death and many emergency surgeries;

three of these executives were sentenced to prison (Hilts 1993a). Prison sentences in unsafe product cases are highly unusual, but in this case evidence was produced that the executives conspired to conceal the defects of their product and failed to report doctors' complaints about the product to the FDA.

In the 1990s, American Home Products (AHP) marketed a diet drug combination known as Fen-Phen, which was withdrawn from the market in 1997 after use of the drug was linked to the development of a fatal lung disease and heart problems (Mundy 2001). By 2005, the company—now Wyeth—estimated that it would cost some $21 billion to settle legal claims relating to Fen-Phen (Saul 2005a). Many users of this drug continued to be dissatisfied with the resolution of the cases against the company.

In the early years of the 21st century, allegations of unsafe pharmaceutical products targeted Earex (an anemia drug), Lotronex (for treatment of irritable bowels), and Clarinex (an allergy medication) (Grady 2002; Petersen 2002b; Pollack A. 2002). Pfizer's painkiller Celebrex was marketed despite tests suggesting possible links with heart attacks, and the safety of other popular painkillers was questioned (Harris 2005). The Merck Corporation was contending with lawsuits in 2005 over claims that its painkiller Vioxx played a role in heart attacks (Berenson 2005). The Guidant Corporation was accused of selling heart defibrillators despite knowledge of flaws (Meier 2005). The common element in all the pharmaceutical product cases was that the corporations put the pursuit of profits ahead of scrupulous concern for the health and safety of their products' users. Despite the fines, civil damages, and negative publicity experienced by the pharmaceutical companies, they have typically suffered no lasting damage and have continued to operate profitably.

Whenever pharmaceutical corporations run into marketing problems in developed Western nations or seek new markets, they turn to third-world countries, where safety standards are lax or nonexistent (Braithwaite 1984; Silverman, Ree, and Lydecker 1982). The Nestle Corporation's marketing of infant formula in less-developed countries is one of the better-publicized cases of these practices (Gerber and Short 1986). Claims alleged that millions of babies in these countries suffered or even died because their mothers were enticed into using infant formula without the knowledge, means, or conditions, including clean water, to use it safely. The protests and boycotts directed at Nestle were ultimately successful in compelling the company to abandon its aggressive marketing of infant formula in third-world countries.

Transportation Products and Services Americans have been described as having a longstanding love affair with the automobile, but there is a dark side to this relationship. Each year some 50,000 people are killed in automobile accidents that are typically blamed on driver recklessness or error, or on weather and road conditions. In recent decades, it has become more widely recognized that design defects in automotive products contribute to accidents and to fatalities. The automotive industry has put profits ahead of consumer safety for a long time.

In the 1920s, when the Dupont Corporation tried to interest General Motors in installing safer glass in its cars, the president of GM, Alfred P. Sloan, wrote back that he was not interested because such glass would not contribute to profit on the cars (Mintz and Cohen 1971). Another GM executive, John Z. DeLorean, speaking of his experience with the company several decades later, observed that "at General Motors the concern for the effect of our products on our many publics was never discussed except in terms of cost or sales potential" (Wright 1979: 6).

After the introduction of the Corvair in 1959 as a new sports car, it quite quickly became evident that this car had "oversteering" and engine-exhaust problems, and it was involved in a disproportionate number of accidents (Mokhiber 1988). GM was soon aware of the problems and chose not to address them. Inspired by this case, a young lawyer named Ralph Nader wrote *Unsafe at Any Speed* (1965), which succeeded in focusing public attention on the issue of auto safety.

In the years since Nader's book first appeared, many other cases of unsafe automobiles have surfaced, and automobile companies have been compelled to recall hundreds of thousands of defective cars (see Box 3.4).

Despite greater attention to safety features in more-recent years, unsafe vehicles still reach the market. Ford has been hardly the only company to have to contend with such charges. The auto industry generally has been accused of producing highly profitable SUVs that are both dangerous and environmentally harmful (Bradsher 2002). Early in the 21st century, millions of SUVs continue to be sold annually in the United States.

General Motors has portrayed itself in its advertising as greatly concerned with safety in automobiles, but its record is at odds with such claims (Burns 1999). In recent years, gas defects were identified in some GM pickup trucks, and the company acknowledged that antilock brakes on several million of its vehicles were defective (Bradsher 1999; Meier 1993). In the early 1990s, General Motors was found liable for gas-tank defects in some of its pickup trucks (Applebome 1993a; Meier 1992e; Meier 1993). As many as 150 fatalities were attributed to unsafe pickup trucks produced by GM (Thomas 1994). GM was compelled to recall many vehicles during this period. Although it is admittedly a complex challenge to disentangle motivations and actions in the automobile-defect cases, a recurrent pattern of unsafe automobiles strongly suggests that criminogenic tendencies are deeply ingrained in this industry.

Other segments of the transportation industry have been accused in defective-product cases. For example, the airline industry has been accused of flying planes with safety defects and of falsifying airplane maintenance records (Cushman 1990; Mokhiber 1988; Weiner 1990). A 1990 incident involving Eastern Airlines led to the first criminal indictment concerning airline maintenance. Greedy suppliers and inadequate government oversight were blamed for the use of defective or bogus aircraft parts on commercial airliners (Wald 1995). The cost-cutting maintenance procedures of a discount

---

B O X 3.4 The Ford Pinto Case

The Ford Pinto was at the center of the single most infamous defective automobile case ever (Cullen, Maakestad, and Cavender 1987; Dowie 1977; Mokhiber 1988).

Facing increasing competition from foreign imports in the late 1960s, Lee Iacocca, then president of the Ford Motor Company, called for the production of a car weighing less than 2,000 pounds and costing less than $2,000. In order to meet these requirements, the designers of the new car, the Pinto, placed the gas tank in the rear of the car.

In the early 1970s, after the car had been widely marketed, several Pintos were involved in rear-end collisions in which the gas tank exploded, burning some people to death. One such case, involving three Midwestern schoolgirls, led to the criminal prosecution of Ford. Investigation of the company in conjunction with this case revealed that Ford had made a calculated decision: It would be cheaper to pay civil damages arising out of these accidents than to recall the car and make it safe. Further, installation of a rubber bladder (cost: about $5) would have prevented the gas tank explosions.

Ultimately Ford had to pay millions of dollars of judgments in civil lawsuits and had to recall the Pinto at great expense, at a total cost estimated at some $100 million. Although Ford was acquitted in the criminal case—perhaps at least in part because the presiding judge ruled certain crucial pieces of evidence inadmissible—this case is commonly cited as evidence of the relative indifference of automobile manufacturers to the safety of drivers and their passengers. Safety features such as seatbelts and airbags are adopted only when the companies have been compelled to do so or it has become sufficiently profitable to do so.

The "standard account" of Ford's actions in this case, involving a calculated and cynical decision to foist an unsafe vehicle on the public and then to pay off claimants in accident burn cases rather than recall the Pinto, has been challenged by Matthew T. Lee and M. David Ermann (1999). They claim the Pinto case is better understood in terms of prevailing standards for auto safety at that time, rather than as an outcome of deliberate, conscious acts of indifference to the safety of Pinto drivers and passengers. But the persistence of such cases over many years is quite striking. In subsequent decades, Ford has been accused of producing other unsafe automotive products and knowingly using unsafe Firestone tires (Eisenberg 2000; Kunen 1994; Labaton and Bergman 2000; Meier 1992b). The Pinto case was simply the most widely exposed claim against the Ford Motor Company.

---

airline, ValuJet, contributed to a plane crash in 1996, killing 105 passengers and 5 crew members (Matthews and Kauzlarich 2000). Accordingly, airline practices can put unwitting airline passengers at risk.

Confronting a Far-Reaching Problem This review of corporate violence against consumers is highly selective. A legion of other unsafe, even deadly, products have been foisted on consumers by numerous corporations (see Box 3.5 on the controversy over tobacco products). These corporations have typically resisted acknowledging the unsafe character of their products and have largely avoided being held criminally liable for unsafe products.

Corporate Violence against Workers: Unsafe Working Conditions

Throughout human history, employers (and "masters") have often demonstrated a willful indifference to the health and safety of their employees (or servants and slaves). Friedrich Engels (1895) alleged that employers were guilty of murder because they knew perfectly well that the conditions to which workers were subjected would result in premature deaths. But for most of history, employers were not held liable for deaths, injuries, and illnesses suffered by workers as a consequence of workplace conditions; until very recently these deaths, injuries, and illnesses did not elicit a response from the criminal justice system. Workers, servants, and slaves who

---

B O X 3.5   The Production and Sale of Tobacco: Corporate Crime?

The use of tobacco has been described as the leading cause of preventable death in the United States, with some 400,000 premature deaths a year (Kluger 1996; Wolfson 2001). Worldwide, millions suffer ill health effects and premature death as a consequence of smoking or chewing tobacco. In addition to the direct harm to smokers, exposure of nonsmokers to "passive smoke" has been implicated as a cause of birth defects and other health problems (Brownlee and Roberts 1994; Cowley 1990). Smoking also exacts a staggering economic toll—billions of dollars toward medical costs, lost productivity, and the like (Wald 1988).

The harmful effects of tobacco on the health of those who use tobacco products has been well understood, at least since the 1960s. Yet the production and distribution of tobacco is not illegal and has been described as involving "victims without crime" (Brown 1982); accordingly, some would argue that tobacco corporations cannot be considered guilty of a form of corporate crime. Obviously many people consider smoking a free choice, and for millions it is a pleasurable activity. In this view, even if tobacco use has harmful consequences, the same could be said for many products that we do not proscribe by law, including alcohol and fatty foods.

Nevertheless, a number of allegations have been directed at the major tobacco companies. First, they have used their enormous economic and political clout to shield themselves from more legal restrictions on a demonstrably harmful product. Second, over a period of decades they concealed information and issued denials regarding the harmful health-related consequences of their product, despite clear evidence from their own laboratories and studies to the contrary (Hilts 1996; Rabe and Ermann 1995). Third, they deliberately

built addictives into cigarettes with the objective of broadening and deepening their customer base. Fourth, they have specifically targeted young people and other vulnerable constituencies with seductive advertising campaigns (Meier 1998a, 1998b). Fifth, tobacco use injures not only smokers but also large numbers of nonsmokers who are exposed to "secondary smoke." Sixth, economic benefits associated with the tobacco industry are overshadowed by the immense costs (e.g., higher health care costs) that tobacco inflicts on society.

From the early 1980s on, an antismoking (or tobacco control) movement grew with considerable momentum (White 1988). Individual lawsuits by smokers or former smokers, as well as class-action lawsuits involving the federal government and the states, were directed at the tobacco companies (Orey 1999). In June 2005, federal prosecutors wrapped up a major racketeering case against the leading tobacco companies, claiming that they had conspired against the public interest for decades (Janofsky 2005b). At the end of the 20th century, the tobacco companies agreed to pay 50 states some $200 billion to compensate them for increased health care costs emanating from tobacco use (Bragg 2000; Lacey 1999). In 2005, a federal appeals court ruled, however, that the government could not force the tobacco companies to turn over $280 billion in accumulated profits, and the Justice Department announced that it would seek only $10 billion, not the $130 billion originally suggested, from tobacco companies for antismoking programs (Janofsky 2005a; Janofsky and Johnston 2005). At some future time, the entire enterprise of producing and selling tobacco might well be regarded as one of the principal unpunished crimes of the modern era.

---

assaulted their employers have historically been punished in the harshest terms. Still, much evidence supports the contention that far more employees have been maimed and killed as a consequence of employers' actions than the reverse.

An investigative report in 2003 of McWane, Inc., one of the world's largest manufacturers of cast-iron sewer and water pipe, revealed that it was one of the most dangerous employers in America (Barstow and Bergman 2003a, 2003b). In the

previous seven years, 9 workers had been killed in McWane foundries, and at least 4,600 were injured, often seriously. According to various sources, work-related accidents and diseases have been the single greatest cause of disability and premature death in the United States today (Cullen, Maakestad, and Cavender 1987; Reiman 2004). Various studies by the government and private organizations have estimated annual deaths from work-related accidents and diseases at more than

30,000; some 3.6 million workers annually suffer from significant occupational accidents and diseases (Reiman 2004). The International Confederation of Free Trade Unions reports that in 2002 there were 2 million work-related fatalities and 160 million new work-related diseases worldwide (Brown 2002). According to recent estimates, 17 U.S. workers die each day due to work-related injuries; some 100 workers a year die as a consequence of intentional wrongdoing or gross indifference on the part of their employers or supervisors (Associated Press 2001a; Barstow 2003; Nordheimer 1996). While work-related deaths have declined in recent years, they have hardly disappeared.

No single reliable way to compile death and disease statistics exists. Job-related deaths may be either underreported or overreported, depending on the definition of "job-related." Some deaths may be due to worker negligence or freak accidents. But the number of work-related deaths remains significant, and many are preventable. Industries and businesses continue to resist the imposition of regulations that could make the workplace safer (Nordheimer 1996). In the interest of keeping labor costs low, much standardized manufacturing for American corporations is now carried out in factories located in developing countries. Workplace conditions in most of these factories are subject to little regulation, and conditions are often hazardous or deadly dangerous (Wonders and Danner 2002). For example, large numbers of women work in factories where they are exposed to hazardous chemicals without protective gear or adequate ventilation. American-based workers are more likely to be conscious of and concerned about hazardous working conditions than are workers in developing countries, but even American workers are often too fearful of being fired to file formal complaints (Nelkin and Brown 1984). Workers recognize that management is mainly concerned with external appearances and with the efficiency rather than the safety of the production process. Box 3.6 discusses the incidence of asbestosis among employees of one corporation. If the asbestos exposure of Manville workers is an especially well-known case, it is far from unique. The workers of many other industries, especially the mining, textile, and chemical industries, are routinely exposed to dangerous conditions.

In the coal mining industry, an estimated 100,000 deaths and 1.5 million injuries have occurred since 1930. Mining and quarry workers have the highest mortality rate due to "occupational trauma": 55 fatalities per 100,000 workers in the 1980s (Cullen, Maakestad, and Cavender 1987: 68). By the beginning of the 21st century, this death rate had declined to approximately 30 fatalities per 100,000, but mining remained the most dangerous occupation (Associated Press 2001a). The most dramatic of these deaths result from a mine collapse or fire. The deaths of 78 coal miners in 1968 in an explosion in a West Virginia mine helped to expose routine neglect of safety rules by mining corporations (Mokhiber 1988). Although this tragedy helped stimulate the passage of the Federal Coal Mine and Safety Act (1969), miners still die in fires and collapses and because of ventilation failures in which companies have flagrantly disregarded safety standards (Cullen, Maakestad, and Cavender 1987). For example, 26 miners were lost in the Westray mine explosion in Canada in 1992 (Goff 2001). Hundreds of thousands of miners have died or been permanently disabled by "black lung" resulting from exposure to dangerous mine dust (Mokhiber 1988).

In the textile industry, tens of thousands of workers have developed "brown lung" (byssinosis) from inhalation of dust; and in the chemical industry, millions of workers are routinely exposed to toxic and dangerous chemicals (Mokhiber 1988; Nelkin and Brown 1984). Typically there is evidence both of a long-standing awareness of dangers on the part of the corporations involved and of active resistance to regulatory and worker compensation laws. The relatively few criminal and civil penalties imposed on corporations in these industries for safety violations of federal standards have most typically been token fines; criminal prosecutions, even for intentional wrongdoing by employers, are rare (Barstow 2003). One exception is the Film Recovery Systems case (see Box 3.7).

B O X 3.6   Asbestos and the Manville Corporation

One of the most widely publicized cases of a corporate employer knowingly exposing employees to unsafe working conditions involved the Manville Corporation (originally Johns-Manville), a producer of asbestos products. The term *asbestos* refers to any of several silicate minerals that are extremely heat-resistant and unusually pliable, qualities that led to its widespread use for insulation and other purposes since ancient times. As early as the first century A.D., the Greek geographer Strabo and the Roman naturalist Pliny noted that slaves who worked with asbestos suffered from a lung disease; in the 20th century, the term *asbestosis* was applied to the crippling and ultimately fatal lung disease resulting from exposure to asbestos (Brodeur 1985). From at least the 1930s on, Manville had internal medical reports of asbestosis among its workers, but based on cost-benefit analysis it continued to produce and market this highly profitable product for several decades, concealing information about the health hazards even from its own workers (Brodeur 1985; Mokhiber 1988). The federal government and the insurance companies also knew of these dangers from this period or earlier (Grogan 2005). By the mid-1970s, thousands of asbestos workers were dying of asbestosis. Some 25,000 personal injury lawsuits had been filed against the company, and in 1982, Manville went into bankruptcy in anticipation of

potential liabilities of some $2 billion from such suits (Delaney 1992; Feder 1982; Mokhiber 1988).

Many asbestos workers and their families and friends were deeply embittered toward Manville, both for the original crime of knowingly exposing workers to dangerous asbestos dust and then for trying to evade responsibility. Other workers, concerned about their jobs and perhaps engaging in psychological denial, disparaged the dangers of exposure and denounced the lawsuits (Freedman 1982). No officers of asbestos-producing corporations were criminally indicted. In 2000, eight of the top asbestos-making corporations agreed to settle two large civil lawsuits for $160 million, but many federal and state cases remained unsettled (Labaton 2000a). In 2005, the president of the Asbestos Workers' Union estimated that approximately 7,000 Americans a year could be expected to die from asbestosis for decades to come, and he challenged efforts by the asbestos industry and its insurers to characterize themselves as victimized by the ongoing lawsuits (Grogan 2005). At least 1 million American workers were exposed to asbestos, but lawyers have been the primary beneficiaries of the lawsuits. The physical, emotional, and economic consequences of the asbestos tragedy are clearly going to persist for some time to come.

The Complexity of Determining Culpability
The issue of culpability can be complex in work-related accidents. It is hardly in the self-interest of corporations to seek to harm their workers deliberately. But workers are inevitably harmed—sometimes fatally—when corporate management limits or disregards safety precautions or imposes on workers production pressures that lead them to disregard such precautions, all in the interest of maximizing profit and minimizing costs. The absence of direct intent to do harm, the difficulty of pinpointing the specific cause of harm, the diffusion of responsibility for harm-producing corporate decisions, and the economic and political clout of corporations have combined to shield corporate employers from full-fledged liability for work-related injuries and deaths.

CORPORATE ABUSE OF POWER, FRAUD, AND ECONOMIC EXPLOITATION

Much corporate crime wreaks no violence but has vast political and economic consequences. In his landmark study of white collar crime, Sutherland (1949) focused almost entirely on *corporate fraud* that had economic rather than violent consequences. These offenses included restraints of trade; rebates; patent, trademark, and copyright violations; misrepresentations in advertising; unfair labor practices; financial manipulations; and war crimes. With respect to the last offense, Sutherland, writing during and immediately after World War II, examined

---

B O X 3.7 **The Film Recovery Systems Case**

Even though federal workplace safety laws have been in place since 1970, criminal prosecutions have been exceedingly rare, with only a handful of employers prosecuted for exposing workers to unacceptable risks (Glaberson 1990). The Film Recovery Systems case, originating in 1985, was the first case in which an employer was charged with murder in connection with a work-related death (Frank and Lynch 1992).

A Polish immigrant, Stefan Golab, died after being exposed to a cyanide solution used in the Film Recovery Systems factory in Illinois to recover silver from used photographic plates. The indictment of several company executives for murder (the company itself was charged with manslaughter) was based on

the fact that conditions in the factory were obviously unsafe and that these executives were aware of this fact. Three executives were convicted of murder and sentenced to 25 years in prison, and the company was fined $10,000. The convicted executives appealed the verdict and ultimately pleaded guilty to involuntary manslaughter charges, with brief prison or probation sentences (Associated Press 1995). By 1990, at least three state high courts had upheld the principle that employers can be criminally prosecuted for unsafe working conditions, and the convictions of two factory owners (and their corporation) in Brooklyn, New York, for exposing workers to unsafe conditions had been upheld (Glaberson 1990).

---

illegal profiteering and violations of other laws (such as embargoes and restraints on trade of war materials) committed by corporations during the war. He concluded that for large corporations, profits took precedence over patriotism.

Corporate abuse of power in the form of corruption of the political process has economic consequences for ordinary citizens. Corporations obtain favorable treatment on such matters as reducing their tax liability and increasing their freedom to raise prices or underpay workers. Corporations also use their immense economic clout to distort the political process in a system that claims to be democratic, and as a consequence, much policy ends up favoring the interests of corporations over those of ordinary citizens.

Direct bribery of governmental officials—legislators, in particular—has long been a common practice of corporations (Miller 1992; Noonan 1984). A great deal of corruption is less blatant; some takes the form of political campaign contributions (today, through corporate political action committees, or PACs) and aggressive lobbying (Bakan 2004; Khanna 2004; Lewis and the Center for Public Integrity 2000). When these various forms of influence compromise the state's control over harmful activities of corporations or when military interventions are undertaken on behalf of corporate interests,

physical and economic harm may result. The topic of corporate corruption of the governmental process is explored more fully in Chapters 5 and 6.

Crimes against Citizens and Taxpayers: Defrauding the Government and Corporate Tax Evasion

Federal, state, and local governments are major purchasers of corporate products and services, expending billions of dollars annually. Corporations with contracts to provide goods and services to the government have defrauded the government of billions of dollars; citizens and taxpayers ultimately foot the bill for these frauds. Defense and health-care–related expenditures are among the largest items on the federal budget.

Defense Contract Fraud   Defense contract frauds have been especially numerous and costly. The Department of Defense spends hundreds of millions of dollars a day and billions of dollars annually, with a disproportionate percentage of these expenditures going to a relatively small number of prime contractors. The whole system of awarding defense contracts has traditionally provided rich opportunities for fraud. A high percentage of new weapons-systems

---

B O X 3.8 Halliburton, Vice President Cheney, and Iraq War Contracts

The Halliburton Company is a giant energy corporation once headed by George W. Bush's vice president, Dick Cheney. In 2002, it agreed to pay the government $2 million in connection with inflated contract prices for maintenance and repair at a military base (Associated Press 2002a). Just prior to the initiation of Operation Iraqi Freedom in 2003, Halliburton was awarded a $7 billion, noncompetitive contract to rebuild Iraq's oil operation (Mayer 2004). Halliburton, described as the

biggest private contractor for American forces in Iraq, was subsequently accused of excess billing to the tune of millions of dollars on these contracts. In one case, a Halliburton subsidiary was found to have charged the U.S. government $2 million to transport fuel worth just $82,000 (Eckholm 2005a, 2005b) Altogether, audits conducted late in 2004 suggested that Halliburton had billed the U.S. government in excess of $100 million in connection with fuel contracts in Iraq.

---

contracts, for example, have been awarded without competitive bidding. Corporate contractors have charged unreasonable prices, collected tens of millions on cost overruns, falsified test data, double-billed the government and billed it for costs related to commercial contracts, and delivered defective products or systems (Simon 2006; U.S. Department of Justice 1989). A secret army of private military contractors, often run by retired military officers, obtains lucrative contracts with relatively little governmental oversight (Wayne 2005). The Halliburton Company is just one defense contractor that has been accused of defrauding the government in recent years (see Box 3.8). Literally billions of dollars have been wasted on "gold-plated" (i.e., unnecessarily sophisticated) weapons systems and other military hardware that failed (Isaacson 1983). In the early 1980s, the media widely publicized the Defense Department's gross overpayments for spare parts and tools. It paid $110 for a diode available elsewhere for 4 cents; $1,118 for a navigator's stool cap, which was subsequently priced at $10; $2,043 for a nut worth 13 cents; and $9,606 for an allen wrench available for 12 cents at hardware stores (Mohr 1983; Tolchin 1984). A nationwide investigation later that decade uncovered "rampant bribery" in military contracts (Magnuson 1988b).

Since then, many specific cases involving major defense contractors have come to light, including incidents in which Lockheed Martin, Rockwell International, Boeing, Unisys, and General Electric overcharged, double-billed, and defrauded the Defense Department of hundreds of millions of

dollars on contracts for transport planes, jet engines, and battlefield computer systems (Feder 1990; Fried 1991; Stevenson 1991b). Several aspects of the defense fraud cases are striking: The amount of money involved is large; the offenders are major corporations; these corporations do not seem to be deterred by publicized prosecutions; and the resolution of the cases typically involves a financial settlement rather than disqualification of the corporation from future government contracts. Defense contractors, not "national security," were the primary beneficiaries of the trillion-dollar defense-spending buildup of the Reagan era.

Defrauding the government—that is to say, the taxpayers—is hardly limited to defense contracts. In 2001, for example, a group of international construction firms was charged with rigging bids on U.S.-supported water projects in developing countries to reap 60 percent profits on the contracts (Eichenwald 2001a). In 2003, Exxon was ordered to pay almost $12 billion to the state of Alabama for depriving it of gas royalties, and the MCI phone company was banned from seeking federal contracts because of concerns about its integrity in financial dealings (Bayot 2003; Labaton and Feder 2003). Businesses that provide the government with goods and services in virtually all sectors of the economy have perpetuated fraud.

Health Care Provider Fraud Hospitals, including mental hospitals, rehabilitation centers, testing laboratories, and other medical facilities, are believed to defraud the government of billions of dollars annually through Medicaid and Medicare programs. In 1995, FBI Director Louis Freeh described health care fraud as the fastest-growing crime in the United States (Knight-Ridder 1995). In recent years, federal officials have estimated that medical fraud accounted for 10 percent of the annual $1 trillion U.S. health care bill, or approximately $100 billion a year; taxpayers footed a significant proportion of this bill (Sparrow 1998; Tillman 1998). Working under severe economic pressure during this era, hospitals have manipulated numerical codes for services rendered and demanded kickbacks from physicians for referrals; these illegal costs are ultimately included in the fraudulent, inflated bills submitted to federal health insurance programs (Sparrow 1996).

Criminal prosecutions for corporate health care provider fraud are complicated and relatively uncommon. In the late 1990s, Columbia/HCA Healthcare Corporation, the biggest hospital operator in the United States—with 350 hospitals treating 125,000 people a day and billing $20 billion annually—pleaded guilty to fraud for "up-coding," charging for improper services, and other forms of fraud, and was fined over $700 million in civil penalties (Gottlieb and Eichenwald 1997; Eichenwald 2000b). In 2000, several Medicare financial operators contracted by the government to handle Medicare billing were charged with fraud; eight operators paid $275 million to settle those claims (Pear 2000). In 2001, TAP Pharmaceutical Products was charged with manipulating the wholesale price of the drug Lupron so that doctors would receive more money from Medicare for prescribing it instead of a competing drug (Petersen 2001a). Later in the same year, two drug makers agreed to pay $875 million to settle fraud charges; this was the largest settlement to date for health care fraud (Petersen 2001c). In 2005, Staten Island University Hospital agreed to repay New York State over $75 million in connection with ongoing Medicaid fraud (Luo 2005). The hospital had made a similar concession some six years earlier.

Health care fraud is best understood in terms of the objective of reaping the largest possible profit and gain taking precedence over all other considerations. In his study of psychiatric hospitals in Texas, Henry Vandenburgh (1998, 1999) found that they adopted "business-first" methods, including the payment of substantial stipends to physicians for patient referrals and the adoption of aggressive marketing practices to increase patient loads. Quite inevitably, various forms of fraud arise as a consequence of such an orientation. Altogether, fraudulent activities across the whole spectrum of the health care industry have contributed significantly to the alarming rise in the national health bill.

Corporate Tax Evasion   Major corporations cost U.S. taxpayers huge amounts by evading their fair share of the tax burden. Sutherland (1949) identified a number of corporate tax evasion schemes, especially in conjunction with war profiteering, including padding cost figures (to reduce apparent profits), juggling financial data, and making fraudulent claims to the government on war-related expenditures.

The proportion of the federal tax burden borne by corporations declined during the latter part of the 20th century, while the proportion borne by individuals rose (Johnston 2003b). Major corporations with net incomes of hundreds of millions of dollars were paying virtually nothing in taxes, at least in part because of the success of corporate lobbyists in persuading legislators to adopt tax laws with devices such as depletion allowances, asset depreciation tables, and investment tax credits that favor corporations. The official tax rate means relatively little, however, because corporations also have highly paid, creative lawyers and accountants who enable them to maximize their liabilities and minimize their profits for the purposes of lowering their taxes. The corrupt energy giant Enron, while claiming massive profits, paid taxes in only one year between 1990 and 2000, while collecting hundreds of millions in tax refunds from the government (Johnston 2003b). This outcome was accomplished by setting up hundreds of subsidiaries in foreign countries, taking huge deductions for stock options, and manipulating financial records. Such cases abound. Almost two-thirds of major American corporations paid no taxes in the late 1990s (*New York Times* 2004a). Ordinary American taxpayers increasingly must make up the difference.

Despite legal reforms designed to address corporate tax shelters, they were still flourishing early in the 21st century, with few discovered (Johnston 2003). Large corporations were saving more than $14 billion through the use of tax shelters, many of them illegal. The IRS offered amnesty to corporations admitting use of such shelters. Corporations were also increasingly reincorporating offshore to minimize their taxes (Johnson and Holub 2003). Early in the 21st century, internal revenue resources are down, penalties are rare, and criminal prosecution even more rare. Tens of billions of dollars in tax revenue are being lost annually through the use of tax shelters and other accounting devices.

Throughout the recent era, American corporations have received various forms of corporate welfare, in addition to the many opportunities available to them for tax evasion (Bartlett and Steele 1998a, 1998b). In late 2001, following the September 11 attacks and the onset of a recession, a "stimulus bill" was introduced in Congress, calling for the repeal of the corporate minimum tax, retroactive to 1986 (Krugman 2001b; Morgenson 2001c). With the adoption of such a bill, some major corporations such as IBM and Ford stood to receive lump sum payments in the billions, and others, hundreds of millions. This type of legislation can be seen as more reflective of corporate political clout than as a demonstrably effective way to respond to an economic downturn. Although some critics of corporate taxes have complained that such taxes impose an unjust burden on investors and consumers and inhibit economic development, the fact is that many corporations have accumulated vast profits during a period when millions of ordinary taxpayers are struggling to pay their bills. Clearly, corporate tax evasion has contributed substantially to the national deficit. In 2003 and 2004, the U.S. Senate and House passed bills extending tax breaks worth hundreds of billions to corporations on profits earned abroad (Andrews 2003, 2004).

Supporters of these bills claimed American corporations would then invest more domestically, but critics argued there was no guarantee of such benefits for American workers.

Crimes against Consumers: Price Fixing, Price Gouging, False Advertising, and Misrepresentation of Products

Obtaining the highest-quality product at the lowest possible price was one of the principal rationales advanced by Adam Smith on behalf of a free-market economy. The idea was that freely competing entrepreneurs would need to enhance quality and reduce prices to stay in business, and consumers (whose welfare was Smith's primary concern) would benefit. Accordingly, when competing corporations join together and agree to fix prices at a certain level, this activity, known as *price fixing*, negates any such benefit to consumers.

Price Fixing Much of fixing prices does not involve a specific conspiracy but rather takes the form of *parallel pricing,* wherein industry "leaders" set inflated prices and supposed competitors adjust their own prices accordingly (Currie and Skolnick 1988). Parallel pricing, which is virtually beyond the reach of law, has been estimated to cost consumers more than $100 million annually.

Explicit price fixing was prohibited by the Sherman Act of 1890 as a form of "restraint of trade" (Clinard and Yeager 1980: 134). Sutherland (1949) identified at least six different methods for fixing prices and found evidence of numerous suits alleging this activity. In 1991, in recognition of the widespread violation of the price-fixing prohibition, Congress moved to reform the law to make the practice more difficult (Labaton 1991). For example, "vertical" price fixing, in which some manufacturers attempt to dictate retail price levels and lock out discounters, became vulnerable to lawsuits as a result of this reform.

Over the years, price-fixing conspiracies have been uncovered for virtually every imaginable product or service, including gasoline, vitamins, seeds, diamonds, soft drinks, food preservatives, infant formula, cardboard cartons, and airline tickets (Barboza 2004; Labaton 2001b, 2004b). One celebrated price-fixing conspiracy involved heavy-electrical-equipment manufacturers, including General Electric and Westinghouse, who conspired over a period of decades to fix prices on their products (Geis 1967; Herling 1962). Substantial fines (tax deductible, however, as business expenses) were imposed on the companies; several middle-level executives, who denied that their actions constituted a crime, went to jail briefly (for less than a month). Price-fixing cases that came to light in the recent era include an illegal scheme by major telephone companies to inflate prices on long-distance calls; the limiting of oil supplies and price fixing by oil companies in Western states; and the conviction of 43 dairy companies for fixing prices on milk contracts with schools and the military (Associated Press 1991; Henriques 1993; Sims 1990b). In 2004, the huge, politically well-connected Archer Daniels Midland Corporation negotiated to settle civil lawsuits for $400 million—it had already paid a criminal fine of $100 million fine—for fixing prices on feed additives (Eichenwald 2004; Simpson and Piquero 2001). Executives of this highly profitable company, earning several hundred million dollars in some years, had knowingly conspired with competitors for years; price fixing was a "standard operating procedure" within the company (Simpson and Piquero 2001: 181). In 1998, three former ADM executives were found guilty in the case (Eichenwald 1998a). ADM's price-fixing activity drove up the prices of processed foods, soft drinks, detergents, and other widely consumed products.

In 1999, seven of the world's largest drug companies agreed to pay $1.1 billion to settle a class-action lawsuit in connection with fixing prices on vitamins (Barboza 1999b; Labaton and Barboza 1999). Earlier, two of these companies, Hoffman LaRoche and BASF, had agreed to pay $700 million to settle criminal charges in the case, and in November 2001, these companies were fined $752 million by the European Commission (Meller 2001). In 2001, Nine West Group, a manufacturer

of women's shoes, agreed to pay $34 million for illegally fixing shoe prices since 1988. In 2002, Nintendo, the video game maker, was fined $147 million by the European Union for fixing prices on its products (Meller 2002). And in a case that received substantial publicity, top executives of the world's two leading art auction houses, Sotheby's and Christie's, were charged with collusion on commission fees charged to art sellers and on buyer's fees (McGinn 2000). The auction houses agreed to pay $512 million to settle the case against them (Vogel and Blumenthal 2001). The art buyers and sellers victimized in the auction houses case were principally affluent, but price-fixing activities cost consumers of more modest means tens of billions of dollars annually.

Price Gouging and Manipulation Charges of *price gouging*, or systematic overcharging, have also been directed at various industries and corporations when they take advantage of especially vulnerable classes of consumers or circumstances such as shortages. The pharmaceutical industry has long been accused of price gouging with huge markups (Braithwaite 1984; Pear 2004). This industry has a long history of promoting more-expensive brand name drugs over less-expensive, equivalent generic drugs (Hovenkamp 2004; Petersen and Walsh 2002; Simon 2006). It has lobbied against legislation that would make less-expensive imported drugs available to Americans (Stolberg and Harris 2003). Consumers are obviously more vulnerable to price gouging on prescription drugs than on, say, soda and snacks.

Price gouging clearly occurs in other industries as well, including the auto-rental, oil, meat, and infant-formula sectors (Barboza 1999a; Levine 1988; Pear 1992b). Enron engaged in fake trades to drive up energy prices in California (Oppel and Gerth 2002). In October 2002, a former Enron trader admitted to engaging in a conspiracy to manipulate the energy market in that state, driving up prices by millions (Eichenwald and Richtel 2002). Price gouging contributes to inflationary tendencies and costs consumers a great deal of money.

Corporations have defrauded consumers in other ways too. The Federal Communications Commission (FCC) shut down and fined a long-distance phone company, Fletcher, on charges of "slamming," or signing up customers by blatantly misleading tactics (Schiesel 1998b). Sears was charged with using improper practices in extracting payments for debts from customers (McCormick 1999). In a recent year, several credit card companies agreed to reimburse $300 million to customers who were overbilled or misled about interest rates (Leonhardt 2000). In 2004, Ford Motor Credit, a unit of the auto company, was sued in a class-action lawsuit claiming that its auto finance loans were discriminatory and misleading on interest (Peters and Hakim 2005). Astra-Zeneca, a pharmaceutical company, pleaded guilty to felony charges for having provided financial inducements to hundreds of doctors to prescribe its prostate-cancer drug (Petersen 2003a, 2003b). Pharmaceutical companies were increasingly becoming directly involved in patient care by devising treatment guidelines, but some commentators were concerned that these companies were mainly focused on promoting the use of their drug products.

False Advertising and Product Misrepresentation   In his chapter on *product misrepresentation* in advertising, Sutherland (1949) noted that prosecutions of *false-advertising* cases had proven difficult under the fraud laws due to the absence of major, highly motivated victims and problems of proving intent and damage. But with the passage of special laws such as the Pure Food and Drug Law (1906) and the establishment of the Federal Trade Commission (FTC), action against false advertising was somewhat facilitated. Even so, the law has defined "falsity" in advertising quite narrowly, and many forms of false advertising claims are not illegal (Preston 1994). Nevertheless, Sutherland (1949) found that many major corporations had been charged with false advertising for products, including such household names as Wheaties cereal, Morton's salt, Palmolive soap, Bayer's aspirin, Elizabeth Arden cosmetics, *Encyclopedia Britannica,* Goodyear tires, and Quaker State oil.

The history of corporations' blatantly false advertising claims and exaggerations or puffery is a long one (Fox 1984). In the more recent era, false claims have been made about Sears' dishwashers, Thompson Medical's Aspercreme, Sunoco 260 octane gas, Listerine mouthwash, Mobil's Hefty bags, and General Electric's incandescent light bulbs, among countless other products (Preston 1994). The FTC began to call for a more substantial response to this activity in the 1960s, but little change resulted. Today, many ads on the Internet are deceptive (Starek 1996). In 2002, the FTC was investigating the marketing practices of Verisign, Inc., a company that registers Internet addresses (Markoff 2002). The company allegedly used deceptive marketing to persuade rivals' customers to switch suppliers of domain names.

The basic response to false advertising has been to require a modification or discontinuation of a misleading advertising campaign, with criminal prosecutions rare (Cheng 2005; Fox 1984; Pear 2002). Altogether, U.S. consumers have been misled over the years into spending billions of dollars for products and services that fail to live up to advertisers' claims and in some instances actively harm consumers. In one especially notorious case, the Beech-Nut Nutrition Corporation, a major producer of baby foods, pleaded guilty to mislabeling as apple juice a cheap mixture of beet sugar, cane sugar, and corn syrup that contained little real apple juice, and marketing this product for babies (Traub 1988). The company was fined $2 million, and two corporate executives received jail terms. Kraft General Foods was charged with making misleading claims about the calcium content of its cheese products and was required by the FTC to modify its advertising (Preston 1994). In 2002, a pharmaceutical corporation, Pfizer, was accused of making misleading claims in advertisements for its cholesterol-lowering drug, Lipitor (Pear 2002). In 2004, the same corporation pleaded guilty to charges that it had marketed its epilepsy drug, Neurontin, for purposes not approved by the FDA (Farrell 2004). Pharmaceutical companies spend several billion dollars annually to advertise their products, and this spending has been growing at a faster rate than research-related spending. Many of the resulting ads are quite misleading. Even when clear economic or physical harm to consumers cannot be demonstrated, such cases are nevertheless a form of fraud.

Crimes against Employees: Economic Exploitation, Corporate Theft, Unfair Labor Practices, and Surveillance of Employees

It is widely recognized that employees steal from their employers (as discussed in Chapter 4), but it is less obvious to many people that employers can steal from their employees. In Karl Marx's (1867) view of a capitalist system, all employers (or owners of the means of production) were stealing from their employees because instead of the worker getting a full return on the value of his labor, the owner expropriated a part of this value in the name of profit. This theory of surplus value—the idea that the labor that goes into a product is what gives it value—has been widely disparaged by economists, but there can be little question historically that capitalist owners have exploited workers and in many instances underpaid them.

Economic Exploitation of Employees Various corporate efforts to drive down employee wages and benefits have been evident since the early 1970s, and real wages declined during the 1980s (Sheak 1990). The driving down of wages was accomplished by decreasing the number of high-wage union jobs and reducing wages of U.S. workers using such strategies as exporting capital, using more foreign components in domestic products, setting up offshore plants, extracting wage and benefits concessions from unions, hiring more part-time or lower-wage workers, and union busting. These activities can be regarded as "criminal" in the broader sense of the term. Some corporations, including Wal-Mart (America's largest corporation), have been charged with the specifically criminal act of hiring illegal immigrant workers as a cost-saving measure (Barboza 2001b; Greenhouse S. 2005). In

such circumstances, both domestic and immigrant workers tend to be exploited.

Corporate Stealing from Employees In some cases, thefts from employees clearly violate existing laws. Major corporations have been accused of cheating employees out of overtime pay, illegally denying workers their pensions, and even extorting money from employees falsely accused of theft (Associated Press 1988; Berg 1991; Hammer 1990). In 2002, Wal-Mart was accused of cheating employees out of hundreds of millions of dollars by requiring them to work after clocking out, with no additional pay. Wal-Mart managers then received bonuses for keeping labor costs down (Greenhouse S. 2002). Corporations and small businesses "steal time" from employees in various ways, including demanding their participation in corporate charitable events after hours (Snider 2001).

Many other cases of corporations stealing from their employees involve violations of minimum-wage laws, failure to make legally ordained social security payments on behalf of their employees, or improper use of employee pension funds. In 2004, the Halliburton Company was accused of using a legal loophole to reduce pension payouts to employees, urging them to take pensions early (Walsh 2004). Box 3.9 describes how employees lost their retirement savings in the Enron debacle. When corporations have been found guilty of having caused physical (and concomitant economic) harm to their employees, they have sometimes found ways to delay, minimize, or entirely avoid payments to the affected workers. Manville filed for Chapter 11 bankruptcy protection to protect itself from personal injury lawsuits alleging damage from exposure to asbestos (Delaney 1989, 1992).

Unfair Labor Practices Throughout much of the 19th century and well into the 20th century, corporate management has resisted, sometimes quite violently, the right of labor to organize, to strike, and to bargain collectively (Brecher 1974). Even though this right was recognized by the courts as early as 1842, a serious means of

B O X 3.9   The Enron Case and the Devastation of Employee Retirement Accounts

In December 2001, the Enron Corporation filed for bankruptcy. Enron was described as the seventh-largest American corporation in terms of earnings, with $60 billion in assets; this was described as the largest corporate bankruptcy filing in American history up to that time (Oppel and Sorkin 2001b).The subsequent bankruptcy of WorldCom was even larger (Romero and Atlas 2002). A large percentage of Enron employees lost their jobs—in the middle of a major economic downturn—and also lost $1.3 billion in retirement savings, since their retirement accounts were largely invested in Enron stock (Kadlec 2001b). Enron is not the only major corporation that has cajoled or coerced its employees into holding a high proportion of their retirement assets in their employer's stock (Krugman 2001c). In the case of Enron, the value of its stock declined over the course of a year from more than $90 to approximately 26 cents, or virtually nothing, per share; and Enron employees witnessed a decline of 90 percent or more in the value of their retirement portfolios (Kadlec 2001b). During a critical period of declining stock value in 2001, Enron employees were prohibited from withdrawing their retirement funds. Enron's politically well-connected chair, Kenneth Lay, and other top Enron executives earned hundreds of millions in salaries, bonuses, and stock options during a relatively brief time (Sloan 2001). Shortly before Enron's collapse, in connection with a prospective merger deal, Lay was formally entitled to a $60 million stock-option payout, which he only declined in the face of outraged protests by Enron employees witnessing the evaporation of their retirement funds (Sorkin and Atlas 2001). Mere days before the bankruptcy filing, Enron paid out some $55 million in "retention incentive" bonuses to 500 employees it described as crucial (Oppel and Eichenwald 2001).

The collapse of Enron was attributed, at least in part, to its taking on massive debt and to issuing highly misleading reports about its profits and overall finances (Sloan 2001). Much of the debt had been shifted into secret partnerships, which had the effect of grossly distorting the relationship between Enron's assets and profits, and its losses and debts. Members of its board of directors; its outside auditing firm, Arthur Andersen; and many stock analysts—all of whom might be said to have had some responsibility for failing to disclose or challenge Enron's grossly misleading financial statements—were all alleged to be compromised by profound conflicts of interest, including highly lucrative consulting and advising fees (Abelson 2001; Kadlec 2001b; Lashinsky 2001). Various federal agencies and Congressional committees investigated possible criminal activity in connection with this catastrophic corporate financial collapse. Similar circumstances arose in 2002 in connection with the collapse of WorldCom and other corrupt corporations.

implementation of the law did not come into being until the National Labor Relations Act of 1935 (Sutherland 1949). In addition to suffering physical harm at the hands of corporate private security forces and enforcers, workers collectively have also lost countless millions of dollars by being deprived of adequate and effective representation in negotiations with management. Corporations' discriminatory practices on the basis of race, ethnicity, gender, or age have caused equally massive losses to employees and potential employees. Of course in more recent years, a series of laws has rendered such discrimination less common and more vulnerable to legal action. But *unfair labor practices* have hardly been rendered extinct. In 2001, for example, the Smithfield Packing Company, the world's largest

pork processing plant, was found to have engaged in egregious and pervasive labor law violations; pro-labor workers were intimidated or fired (Sack 2001). In 2005, labor union officials in Colorado accused Wal-Mart of instituting a campaign of fear to defeat union organizing efforts among their employees in that state (Greenhouse S. 2005a).

Corporate Surveillance of Employees Yet another form of corporate crime against employees, the increasing use of intrusive technologies for *surveillance,* deserves mention here, although typically it would not be considered a form of corporate crime or violence. Einstadter (1992) has argued, however, that this activity is indeed a form of corporate theft, as it is an infringement on a traditional and important right to privacy. Furthermore, such corporate intrusiveness is said to contribute to a sense of alienation and estrangement in the workplace. The monitoring of employee e-mail, voice mail, and website visits has become increasingly common (Snider 2001). Of course, from the perspective of corporate management, this surveillance is necessary to combat another form of white collar crime, namely employee theft. At some point, however, the harms and injustices of such surveillance may exceed any legitimate purpose.

Crimes against Franchisees and Suppliers: Discount and Chargeback Frauds

Large corporations often have a considerable advantage in their dealings with countless small franchisees and suppliers. In 2005, the U.S. Supreme Court ruled against the Exxon Corporation in a case where gas stations did not receive promised fuel discounts from the corporation (Bloomberg News 2005). Exxon was expected to have to pay over $1 billion to the gas-station owners. Also in 2005, the Saks Fifth Avenue department store corporation was being investigated on claims that it had imposed improper "chargebacks" on its suppliers (Rozhon 2005). Chargebacks are deductions that large department store chains such as Saks take to reduce their payments to suppliers on the claim that the merchandise was defective or unwanted. Even when franchisees and suppliers suspect they are being taken advantage of or defrauded, they may be inhibited from challenging a large and powerful corporation, especially if their own financial well-being depends upon an ongoing business relationship with that corporation.

Crimes against Competitors: Monopolistic Practices and Theft of Trade Secrets

Competitors, especially smaller corporations, have historically been victims of unethical and illegal acts by large corporations. In the freewheeling capitalist economic environment of the 19th century, the robber barons used virtually every imaginable means to destroy their competitors, and they were often successful (Josephson 1934; Myers 1907). The Standard Oil Corporation, presided over by John D. Rockefeller, was perhaps the single most famous example of a corporation that ruthlessly undercut virtually all competitors; by the end of the 19th century, it had obtained a virtual *monopoly,* controlling 95 percent of the market. The Sherman Antitrust Act of 1890 (which is discussed in Chapter 9) was at least in part inspired by anger over the monopolistic practices of the large corporate trusts. Although full-scale private-sector monopolies like Standard Oil disappeared, monopolistic practices endured, in part because of weak enforcement of the Sherman Act and successive antitrust laws.

Sutherland (1949) identified two principal methods 19th-century corporations used to annihilate competitors: reducing their sales and increasing their costs. Competitors' sales could be reduced by undercutting them on price (predatory pricing) and by pressuring dealers, sales agents, unions, and other parties not to work with competitors. Competitors' costs could be raised by forcing up purchase prices on raw materials, making special deals with suppliers of such materials, pressuring lending institutions not to extend credit, and sponsoring direct sabotage of competitors. In the 19th century in particular, large corporations achieved an advantage over smaller competitors by obtaining rebates from railroad companies and other middlemen, who depended on the good graces of these larger corporations.

More recent studies of corporate crime (e.g., Clinard and Yeager 1980; Gordon 2002; Jamieson 1994) have found that anticompetitive practices are still quite common. One major antitrust case was directed at IBM, although the suit was eventually abandoned (DeLamarter 1976). More recently, competitors of Microsoft have complained of its anticompetitive practices (see Box 3.10), and the video game maker Nintendo has been the target of similar charges (Manes and Andrews 1994; Sheff 1994). Wal-Mart was found guilty of engaging in predatory pricing to undercut competing retailers (Jones 1993). In all such cases, the economic philosophy of the federal or state administration in

---

B O X   3.10   The Case against Microsoft

The antitrust case against Microsoft has surely been the largest such case of the recent era. Microsoft is the world's largest producer of software, and its cofounder and chairman, Bill Gates, was widely declared to be the world's richest man at the end of the 20th century, with a fortune estimated upwards of $50 billion. Insofar as Microsoft is widely viewed as having made important contributions to our economy and our whole way of life, the case against it has been somewhat controversial (Auletta 2001; Gordon 2002; Heilemann 2001).

Microsoft's MS-DOS and Windows operating systems provide basic command-and-control instructions for a majority of the world's personal computers. Because word processing, spreadsheets, games, and other software must be compatible with the Microsoft operating system, the company has a natural advantage over its competitors. The case against Microsoft was initiated by two such competitors, Sun Microsystems and Netscape. They complained to the U.S. Department of Justice that Microsoft was engaging in prohibited anticompetitive practices. More specifically, Microsoft was accused of signing contracts with manufacturers of computers and Internet-access suppliers that excluded their principal rivals from key channels of distribution for their products. Microsoft was alleged to have traded on inside information from companies it did business with, offering these companies special discounts and misleading its competitors.

And by bundling its browser with its industry-standard Windows operating system, Microsoft was accused of violating a 1995 consent agreement it had signed with the government.

When Gates testified in a deposition in this case, he claimed memory lapses that tended to stretch credibility, and his performance was widely viewed as awkward and unconvincing. But the broader claims made by Gates in his testimony before Congress in 1998 that software manufacturers (led by Microsoft) had created 2 million American jobs, contributed $100 billion to the economy, and generated an awesome technological transformation in American life were persuasive to some Americans. Microsoft attributed its great success to the production of innovative products and effective marketing, not unfair and anticompetitive practices (Lohr 1998). The Department of Justice's antitrust division began investigating Microsoft in 1993 and negotiated a consent decree with the company the following year (Markoff 1994). When major competitors complained several years later that Microsoft had violated the terms of the decree and had in fact engaged in egregious anticompetitive practices, the Justice Department initiated an antitrust suit against Microsoft, ultimately joined by 18 states. In a provisional opinion issued in November 1999, Federal Judge Thomas Penfield Jackson ruled in a finding of fact that Microsoft had stifled innovation through its immense monopoly power, had reduced competition against

---

power is an important factor in determining the form and intensity of the justice system response.

As Sutherland (1949) observed, corporate illegalities directed at competitors can take a number of different forms, including patent, trademark, and copyright infringements. In the current information age, the theft of ideas and technology has probably become more important than ever. In one case in the 1980s, representatives of the Hitachi Corporation, after an investigation by the FBI, ultimately pleaded guilty to the theft of corporate secrets from IBM (Stewart 1987). (Thus, IBM has been both an accused perpetrator of anticompetitive practices and a victim of corporate theft by a competitor.) In another case in the

1990s, a high-level executive of Volkswagen, Jose Lopez, who formerly headed General Motors' auto parts purchase division, was accused of stealing thousands of pages with trade secrets from his former employer (Andrews 1997; Meredith 1997). Lopez was subsequently indicted on criminal charges, and Volkswagen agreed to pay General Motors $100 million to settle claims in the case.

Still another form of anticompetitive practice involves interference with contractual agreements. In a well-publicized case in the 1980s, Texaco was accused of improperly undercutting a competitor, Pennzoil, in the acquisition of Getty Oil; specifically, Texaco was found to have fraudulently induced Getty Oil to break a contract with

itself, and had caused harm to consumers (Brinkley 1999). A subsequent mediation effort presided over by Federal Judge Richard Posner to attempt to arrive at a mutually acceptable resolution of the government's concerns was unsuccessful; and in April 2000, Judge Jackson ruled that Microsoft had violated the Sherman Antitrust Act by maintaining a monopoly for its PC operating system, by attempting to monopolize the web browser software market, and by attempting to quash innovation (Brinkley 2000a). In June 2000, Judge Jackson ordered the breakup of Microsoft. Naturally, Microsoft appealed this ruling. In July 2001, a federal appeals court upheld the finding that Microsoft was a monopoly and engaged in anticompetitive practices, but it also held that Judge Jackson had displayed a bias against Microsoft and had made inappropriate comments to the press, so it ordered the case reheard by another judge. In September 2001, the Bush administration Justice Department announced that it would no longer seek the breakup of Microsoft. Some commentators speculated that Microsoft's formidable lobbying and generous contributions to the Republican campaign had played a role in this decision (Cohen 2001). In October 2001, the U.S. Supreme Court rejected Microsoft's petition to have the case against it thrown out due to Judge Jackson's misconduct, while a federal judge newly appointed to the case ordered the government and Microsoft to engage in settlement talks (Labaton 2001c). In a November 2002 decision,

this federal judge approved an antitrust settlement largely favoring Microsoft and rejecting the calls of nine states for stiff measures against Microsoft (Harmon 2002c; Lohr 2002b). It did require Microsoft to share more technical information with rivals. Critics were concerned that the ruling would allow Microsoft to continue pursuing many anticompetitive practices. In 2005, Microsoft was ordered to pay $775 million to IBM in connection with its anticompetitive practices (Markoff 2005). This was ironic because in an earlier era, IBM itself had been accused of such practices.

The case against Microsoft echoed in some respects an antitrust case almost a century earlier against Standard Oil. In this earlier case as well, one company was accused of monopolizing its industry, which was quite central to the economy of its time. And in the earlier case, the founder of Standard Oil, John D. Rockefeller, was also widely described as the world's richest man. In 1911, the U.S. Supreme Court ruled against Standard Oil, and shortly thereafter it was broken up into 33 new oil companies. In 1982, another major American monopoly, American Telephone and Telegraph, was also broken up into smaller companies. Despite the abandonment of the breakup remedy by the Bush Administration, it remains to be seen whether in the long run Microsoft continues to dominate the software market as a single company or is successfully challenged.

Pennzoil, thereby stripping Pennzoil of rights to a billion barrels of oil reserves (Petzinger 1987). The civil court proceeding resulted in a judgment against Texaco of $11 billion (the largest such judgment in U.S. history), although Texaco ultimately settled with Pennzoil for $3 billion. In the 2001 case involving the collapse of the giant energy corporation, Enron, the company accused another major energy company, Dynergy, of self-serving manipulations in the context of merger talks, as Dynergy stood to profit from the collapse of Enron (Oppel and Sorkin 2001a). Enron initiated a civil lawsuit against Dynergy.

Finally, it is clear that in addition to defrauding consumers, false advertising and misrepresentation

of products can harm competitors to the extent that the offender gets away with such false claims. Altogether, then, crimes against competitors can take many forms, and at least some of the resulting losses are passed along to consumers.

Crimes against Owners and Creditors: Managerial Accounting Fraud, Self-Dealing, and Strategic Bankruptcy

In this section, we examine how the owners of corporations can themselves be victimized by corporate crime. Adolph Berle and Gardiner Means's *The Modern Corporation and Private Property* (1932) is commonly given credit for advancing the thesis that ownership in the modern corporation is separated from management or from direct control (although this point was hardly original, as Karl Marx made it in 1867 in *Das Kapital*). The owners, of course, are the stockholders, whereas management consists of the executives who run the corporation and typically also own some of its stock.

The interests of a corporation's managers may not coincide entirely with those of other stockholders. For example, when corporations register abroad in places like Bermuda, investors may lose the right to sue executives and directors who abuse their positions (Johnston 2002c). In an earlier period, the compensation of corporate executives was highly correlated with company size, so managers tended to focus on corporate growth (Powell 1986). Some commentators criticized managers as more concerned with protecting their jobs and executive perks than with increasing stock value. More recently, however, a great emphasis on stock price has led to (1) vast compensation packages in terms of pay, stock options, forgivable loans, insurance policies, and the like being awarded to CEOs and top executives; and (2) massive financial manipulations of corporate financial data to keep the stock price rising or prevent its falling (Lowenstein 2002; Rozhon and Treaster 2002). With executive compensation linked to stock price, these executives have been provided with strong incentives to manipulate financial data (Eichenwald 2002a; Leonhardt 2002c). The issue of excessive compensation for top corporate managers is better characterized as activity against the interests of the corporation rather than activity undertaken on behalf of the corporation. Accordingly, it is addressed more fully in the following chapter on occupational crime. Admittedly, the lines of demarcation between actions undertaken for and against the interests of the corporation can become blurred. Corporate managers may not have complete freedom of action, but they do have significant opportunities for *self-dealing*. In principle, corporate boards of directors exercise some oversight and control over managers, but directors are often allies of or beholden to the

CEO, and in any case they are not especially well positioned to police the managers (Atlas 2002; Henriques and Fabrikant 2002; Powell 1986). Enron's board included many individuals with lucrative consulting contracts with the corporation or with other conflicts of interest (Abelson 2001). The need for more independent corporate boards, truly committed to the interests of the corporation's stockholders and other stakeholders, is an obvious challenge. As they are presently constituted, boards cannot be depended on to ensure that corporations neither engage in illegal activity nor defraud their owners, the stockholders.

From the earliest stages of corporate history, insiders have often defrauded investors and would-be owners through false financial statements, stock price manipulations, and other such strategies. The 18th-century case of the "South Sea Bubble" is one example. In the modern era, the Equity Funding case was one of the most notorious and widely reported cases of corporate crime in which the owners (or stockholders) were the primary victims of managerial fraud. Equity Funding, an insurance company developed from modest origins in the 1960s, attracted large numbers of investors with greatly inflated claims of assets (Dirks and Gross 1974; Soble and Dallos 1974). Ultimately, more than 50,000 bogus insurance policies were created (with the aid of computers), and some $200 million in nonexistent assets were claimed as a means of inflating stock prices and attracting additional investors. This celebrated case foreshadowed the many forms of corporate financial misrepresentations in the years ahead.

In the bull market of the 1990s, corporate management felt increasing pressure to produce high levels of profit and growth and keep the company's stock prices high. Testimony for the increasing frequency of such corporate crimes was presented in a 1992 front-page story in *The New York Times*, "Falsifying Corporate Data Becomes Fraud of the 90s," and a decade later this problem was worse than ever (Henriques 1992; Schoenberger 2001). The executives involved may have been seeking self-preservation, or they may have been setting up an outright swindle. Misstatements of financial data by corporations became quite common, especially by

B O X   3.11   Adelphia, HealthSouth, WorldCom, and Accounting Fraud

If Enron Corporation received the most attention in the "corporate scandal" cases from 2001, several other cases of massive financial misrepresentation and accounting fraud also received much front-page coverage and resulted in several high-profile trials: Adelphia, HealthSouth, and WorldCom. Adelphia Communications is the sixth-largest cable company in America, based in Coudersport, Pennsylvania (Lowenstein 2004). The founder of the company, John Rigas, and two of his sons, Timothy and Michael, were tried in 2004 on charges that they masterminded a scheme to falsely represent company earnings and to conceal from investors the billions they borrowed from the company. Prosecutors claimed that the Rigases used their publicly held company much like a personal piggy bank (Meier 2004). When the company filed for bankruptcy protection in 2002, it declared over $18 billion in debt. John and Timothy Rigas were convicted of conspiracy and fraud in a federal trial, and in 2005 they were given stiff prison sentences (Farzad 2005b).

HealthSouth is one of the nation's largest providers of outpatient surgery, diagnostic, and rehabilitative health services. Richard Scrushy was a former respiratory therapist who built up this corporation over a period of years and became chief executive officer and chairman of the corporation's board (Abelson and Freudenheim 2005; Freudenheim and Lichtblau 2003). Scrushy was indicted, along with other executives, on charges of having overstated HealthSouth's assets by billions in an effort to meet expectations of Wall Street stock analysts and keep the price of the stock high. Scrushy was the first CEO indicted under the provisions of the Sarbanes-

Oxley Act of 2002—passed in the wake of the Enron revelations—which imposes a duty on CEOs to ensure that the corporate financial statements they are signing are not fraudulent. During his 2005 trial in Alabama—home state of HealthSouth—five former chief financial officers of the corporation testified that Scrushy oversaw the accounting fraud. In June 2005, Scrushy was acquitted of the fraud charges against him.

WorldCom, having absorbed MCI, was the second-largest telephone company when its top officers were charged with a massive $11 billion fraud involving gross misrepresentation of the corporation's finances over a period of years (Feder and Eichenwald 2004). Bernard J. Ebbers, the former CEO tried in 2005 on federal charges of fraud, conspiracy, and filing of false claims, was a former Mississippi gym teacher, milkman, and bouncer who built up the corporation from a tiny service provider; he was convicted on all charges and sentenced in July 2005 (Belson 2005). During his trial, Ebbers, who received hundreds of millions of dollars in compensation from WorldCom and was at one point a billionaire, claimed to understand neither the finances nor the technology of the company he ran (Belson and Schiesel 2005). The jury did not buy this. WorldCom's bankruptcy filing was the largest in American history, greater even than Enron's.

In each of these cases CEOs from humble origins built up multibillion dollar corporations, received massive compensation, and sold tens or hundreds of millions of dollars of their corporation's stock for great profit but also actively directed or participated in gross misrepresentations of corporate finances, with multibillion dollar losses to investors and huge costs to many other parties.

software and "dot.com" companies (Andersen 2000). The list of major corporations conceding fraudulent accounting or gross misrepresentation of corporate finances, sometimes to the tune of billions of dollars, has simply grown from year to year. The Enron case was arguably the highest profile such misrepresentation, with off-the-books partnerships playing a key role in concealing massive debt and allowing for wholly false portrayals of the corporation's true financial state (Eichenwald 2005) (see Box 3.11).

Many other such cases can be identified, however. In 2000, the Chairman of Micro Strategy was accused of fraud by the SEC for reporting profits but not losses (Norris 2000c). In 2001, the former chiefs of the huge Cendant corporation—which controls Avis Rental Cars, Days Inn, Century 21 Real Estate, and other entities—were accused of reporting $500 million in phony profits (Norris 2001b). Accounting irregularities at Cendant were ultimately estimated to cost stock- and bondholders some $14 billion (Morgenson 2004b). In 2001,

Albert Dunlap, who achieved some fame in the 1990s as "Chainsaw Al," a ruthlessly efficient CEO who streamlined bloated corporations to produce record profits, was accused by the SEC of having directed a huge accounting fraud as head of the Sunbeam Corporation by reporting false profits and through other manipulations of financial statements (Norris 2001c). In 2002, Xerox had to reclassify more than $2 billion to correct previous misstatements of finances, and in 2003, six executives from the company agreed to pay millions of dollars to settle accusations of accounting fraud (Deutsch 2002; Norris 2003a). In 2004, financial documents of Nortel Networks, a telecommunications giant, were subpoenaed due to suspected accounting irregularities (Belson 2004a). Also in 2004, Lucent Technologies was accused of fraudulently reporting some $1.2 billion in revenue (Belson 2004b). And during the same year, the former CEO of Computer Associates International and other company executives were indicted in connection with major accounting fraud, including alleged backdating of billions of dollars of contracts, and seven executives of Symbol Technologies were indicted for overreporting revenue in a case called "breathtaking in its scope" by the prosecutor (Berenson 2004e; Lohr 2004). In 2005, Time Warner Inc. agreed to pay $300 million to settle charges that its AOL unit had overstated revenue over a period of years (Fabrikant 2005). Also in 2005, the drug maker Bristol-Myers agreed to pay close to $300 million to settle allegations about its accounting practices (Saul 2005b). In 2005 as well, charges were brought against high-level executives of Qwest Communications International in connection with an alleged $3 billion accounting fraud, and the insurance giant A.I.G. was being investigated on allegations of having grossly inflated its claims about revenue over a period of years (Browning 2005a; Feder 2005).

The list of such companies seems quite endless. In 2004, 253 companies had to restate their annual financial reports, an increase of over 20 percent from the previous year and a record number for a five-year period (Glater 2005). The trials of John and Timothy Rigas of Adelphia, Bernard Ebbers of WorldCom, and Richard Scrushy of HealthSouth were arguably the three highest-profile trials of CEOs for financial statement misrepresentations or gross accounting fraud during these years (see Box 3.11). Typically in these cases, corporate management collected salaries and bonuses in the millions and sold lucrative stock options while stockholders ultimately lost large sums due to drastic declines in stock price.

Finally, corporations may commit crimes against their creditors by using various strategies to evade payment of debts and obligations. Whereas bankruptcy was regarded historically as a desperate, stigmatized last resort for businesses (and individuals), in recent years some major corporations have pursued what Delaney (1992) labeled *strategic bankruptcy* to avoid meeting certain burdensome financial obligations, including, in some cases, obligations to creditors. Texaco, for example, took advantage of bankruptcy laws to force a settlement with a major creditor, Pennzoil. In some instances, corporate managers use various strategies to manipulate the data representing the corporation's financial status (Delaney 1994). Creditors might also be considered victims of some of the many corporate takeovers in the 1980s, insofar as the parties who profited from these takeovers pulled so much capital out of these corporations that some went bankrupt (Eichenwald 1991). Of course, employees and shareholders are also victims of corporate bankruptcies.

ARE UNIVERSITIES AND COLLEGES CORPORATE CRIMINALS?

Because much study of corporate crime has emanated from universities, it seems only fair to ask whether universities and colleges themselves are guilty of corporate crime. According to *The Chronicle of Higher Education* (2002), academic institutions in many parts of the world are plagued by corruption, with admissions and diplomas awarded only through bribery. Many large American universities are organized in ways that are not too dissimilar from major corporations, although they are not focused on making a profit. Some emerging for-profit institutions of higher education have been accused of inflating enrollment numbers and other unethical activities (Brown 2004). In the wake of the corporate scandals, internal auditors are reported to have gained influence at traditional universities and colleges (Fain 2005). Because universities often have huge financial commitments and are engaged in vigorous competition with comparable institutions, they have been accused of some forms of corporate crime. Furthermore, American universities in recent years have been accused of compromising their integrity and independence by accepting corporate sponsorship of research, with corporations sometimes dictating the terms for the research and even attempting to control publication of findings (Croissant 2001; Washburn 2005). Stanford University was criticized in 2003 for establishing a $225 million Global Climate and Energy Project, principally sponsored by Exxon Mobil and other major corporations (Blumenstyk 2003). Critics expressed concern that this research entity would produce findings consistent with the interests of major energy corporations and support their public relations claims about environmental concerns. Enron financed a research center at Harvard, the Harvard Electricity Policy Group (HEPG), which then produced many reports promoting deregulation of California's energy markets (Washburn 2005: xvii). We now know that Enron traders exploited this deregulatory environment to defraud California energy consumers. Overall, corporate ties with large universities in particular have increased, and in such circumstances various conflicts of interest can arise.

Various prestigious research institutions have been accused of charging numerous improper items and activities (e.g., parties, trips, furniture) to federal research grants (DePalma 1992a; Pear 1992a). With increasing frequency, research results heavily subsidized by American taxpayers are being patented for private profit (Washburn 2005).

Some well-connected colleges have been accused of lobbying Congress directly for research money, with political clout taking precedence over peer review and scientific criteria in the awarding of grants (Weiner 1999). Health care centers and medical schools affiliated with the University of Pennsylvania and Yale were implicated in improper Medicare or Medicaid payments (Johnston 1995; Zielbauer 2001). Institutions of higher learning have also been accused of cheating taxpayers by making fraudulent claims in connection with federal student-aid programs (Deloughry 1991; DePalma 1991; Lueck 1993). The most blatant cases of such fraud are associated with proprietary trade schools and religious schools, but other types of educational institutions have sometimes been involved. Winerip (1994) has reported that altogether the federal government loses up to $4 billion annually from waste, fraud, and loan defaults in college and university student-aid programs.

Some critics of higher education (e.g., Anderson 1992; Sykes 1988; Washburn 2005) claim that universities and colleges are defrauding students by not providing the quality of education promised; instead, undergraduate students in many institutions are taught by overworked, underpaid, and poorly supervised graduate students or teaching assistants. Such institutions are said to make basic misrepresentations (on admissions processes, facilities, programs, and career placement) to prospective students, with a major focus on generating profit (Applebome 1992). Universities and colleges have also been investigated for alleged price fixing of tuition (Jaschik 1990; Leslie 1989). A controversial Justice Department investigation focused on the claim that MIT and seven other Ivy League colleges engaged in price fixing in connection with financial aid offers to admittees (Fendrich 1992). Only MIT chose to fight these charges—unsuccessfully—although this antitrust action was criticized as misguided on the premise that bright, financially needy students actually benefited from the agreements among the colleges (DePalma 1992b, 1992c; *New York Times* 1993). Universities and colleges have also been accused of engaging in price fixing of faculty salaries and exploiting part-time faculty and graduate teaching assistants (Kean 1994; Mundy 1992; Washburn 2005). And the University of Wisconsin–Madison was accused of using a fraudulent photograph in its admissions brochure to represent diversity (Clegg 2000).

College and university athletic programs, in particular Division I programs, have been accused of exploiting student athletes by using them for economic gain without attending to their educational needs (McMillen 1992; Monaghan 1991; Sperber 2000). Of course, college athletic programs, in which millions of dollars are often at stake, have periodically been accused of various violations of NCAA rules (e.g., recruiting enticements) and of being generally corrupt.

All colleges and universities, especially private ones, depend to a significant degree on donations from individual benefactors. Many prominent institutions of higher education have been accused of accepting large donations from notorious white collar criminals, including war criminals, international arms dealers, corporate offenders, insider traders, and tax evaders (Mundy 1993; Washburn 2005). A *Chronicle of Higher Education* article in 2003 estimated that American colleges and universities had "received gifts worth well over $100 million from companies and individuals who have been investigated and indicted, or convicted, of white-collar swindling" (Pulley 2003: A32). The individuals include A. Alfred Taubman (Christie's), Bernard Ebbers (WorldCom), Kenneth Lay (Enron), and Dennis Kozlowski (Tyco). Many leading American universities, including Stanford, Vanderbilt, Rockefeller, and Carnegie-Mellon, carry the names of 19th-century robber barons. Universities today sometimes find themselves in the embarrassing position of having prominent buildings on their campuses named for individuals who have been convicted of white collar crimes.

And even if universities are not readily associated with corporate violence, they have been charged with inadequately protecting students against violent crime and exposing them to hazardous conditions in university laboratories (Colino 1990; Kalette 1990). Following the deaths of experimental subjects, researchers at Johns Hopkins University and at the University of Pennsylvania were accused of violating human research protection rules (Kolata 2001; Washburn 2005).

Nothing in this discussion is intended to suggest that the corporate crimes of universities and colleges are likely to approximate the scope of other corporate crime reviewed in this chapter. Surely the singular mission of institutions of higher education provides them with less incentive and less opportunity for corporate crime. Still, the common tendency to overlook these institutions in discussions of corporate crime is not warranted.

CORPORATE CRIME, IN SUM

This chapter has surveyed what we know about corporate crime, which has been the primary form of white collar crime for E. H. Sutherland and many other scholars in the field. Corporations have played a central role in the history of modern societies and continue to do so today. The complex and contradictory character of corporations was addressed at the outset of this chapter.

Because the crimes of corporations encompass a wide range of activities and take quite different forms, a typology of corporate crime has been produced here. On the one hand, we have corporate crimes of violence; this section addressed the myth that corporate crime is nonviolent crime. On the other hand, we have corporate crime that takes the form of abuse of power, fraud, and economic exploitation. These crimes also victimize not only the public, consumers, and employees but also taxpayers, competitors, shareholders and creditors, among others. This chapter documents the extraordinary scope of the financial devastation caused by corporate crime. Discussion of the crimes of universities—corporations of a kind—concluded this chapter.

KEY TERMS

conglomerates, 57

corporate crime, 55

corporate fraud, 70

corporate surveillance, 78

corporate transgressions, 57

corporate violence, 59

false advertising, 76

joint-stock company, 56

monopoly, 79

paper entrepreneurs, 58

power elite, 57

price fixing, 74

price gouging, 75

product misrepresentation, 76

robber barons, 56

self-dealing, 82

strategic bankruptcy, 84

transnational corporation, 57

trusts, 56

unfair labor practices, 77

DISCUSSION QUESTIONS

1. Identify the historical origins of the corporation and the principal elements of the contradictory status of the corporation in contemporary society (i.e., as a positive and a negative force). What are the principal sources of corporate power, and what are the principal differences between the nature of contemporary and early capitalist corporations?

2. What are the main criteria for a typology of corporate crime? Which criteria do you regard as most significant, and which as least significant? What are the benefits and limitations of discussing and studying corporate crime without relying upon a typological approach?

3. Identify and discuss the most common pattern or stages involved in corporate violence. What are the worst specific consequences of corporate violence, and which claims about corporate violence seem least warranted? Which industries seem to have the worst records of corporate violence, and why?

4. How are corporate abuses of power, corporate fraud, and corporate economic exploitation interrelated? Which segments of society seem to bear the largest burden from these forms of corporate crime, and which segments seem least vulnerable? Which of these forms of corporate crime concern you most, and which concern you least, and why?

5. Is the characterization of universities and colleges as corporate criminals warranted? Why would you expect institutions of higher education to be more or less criminal than other types of corporate entities? Which forms of university or college corporate crime, if any, do you regard as most unjustly neglected by our system of law, and why?

4

Occupational Crime and Avocational Crime

Our society expects that adults, for the larger part of their lives, will have a legitimate occupation—that is, some legal way of earning a living. An official U.S. government publication recognizes more than 20,000 occupational titles, each reflecting some degree of prestige and power (Hodson and Sullivan 2002). Legitimate occupations also provide different sorts of opportunities to engage in fraud and include occupational subcultures that either promote or constrain illegal activity.

The concept of occupational crime was first clearly defined by Clinard and Quinney (1967) as a "violation of the legal codes in the course of activity in a legitimate occupation" (p. 131). Typically, the concept of occupational crime has been applied to acts in which financial gain or status is sought (or their loss prevented) in the context of performing one's job. Considerable confusion has arisen with the interchangeable invocation of the terms *occupational crime, occupational deviance*, and *workplace crime* (Friedrichs 2002b; Mars 2001a). The position adopted here is that it makes the most sense to restrict the term *occupational crime* to financially oriented offenses committed by individuals within the context of a legitimate occupation and specifically made possible by that occupation. The term *occupational deviance* can be applied to activities deviating from norms of employers, professional

associations, or coworkers within an occupational setting, such as malingering or sexual harassment. The term *workplace crime* can be best applied to conventional forms of crime, such as rape or robbery, that occur at the workplace. Even though the boundaries between white collar crime and other forms of illegality committed in an occupational context can indeed be blurred, this chapter focuses on the financially oriented illegalities committed primarily by middle- and upper-class individuals within the context of a legal occupation.

White collar crime scholarship has focused on corporate crime, but some commentators argue that small business crime has been relatively neglected and should receive more attention (Barlow 1993; Sutton and Wild 1985). Others have noted that those actually charged and convicted of white collar crimes are disproportionately ordinary members of the middle or lower middle class with relatively modest incomes, such as small business owners, shopkeepers, restaurateurs, market traders, used-car salespeople, and employees (Croall 2001; Weisburd et al. 2001). Some are no longer gainfully employed when charged with a white collar crime offense. The reasons for this apparent contradiction are explored in other chapters, and Chapter 8 considers ways in which large corporations may create a "criminogenic environment" that facilitates crimes by smaller businesses and enterprises. Large businesses are often in a position to take advantage of smaller businesses, sometimes in illegal ways. Wal-Mart, the nation's largest retailer, was found guilty in Arkansas of "predatory pricing," or selling certain items below cost to destroy smaller competitors; whether or not Americans on balance benefit from the existence of Wal-Mart is a matter of ongoing controversy (Jones 1993; Reich 2005). Major corporations can also be victimized by retail operations with which they do business. For example, a Long Island car dealer bilked General Motors out of some $422 million in connection with loans for vans that did not exist (Richardson 1996b). Small businesses, then, can be both white collar crime victims and victimizers.

Clearly, the vast amount of occupationally based illegality committed by small businesses (e.g., retail and service businesses), professionals, and employees of a broad range of enterprises is significant, and the incremental financial and physical harm caused by occupational crime is substantial. Most of us encounter such forms of white collar crime quite directly. Indeed, if readers of this book ever contend with temptations and pressures to engage in white collar crime, it is especially likely to be associated with the pursuit of a conventional, legitimate occupation. Accordingly, we will review some forms of occupational crime in this chapter, beginning with small business crime.

CRIMES BY SMALL BUSINESSES: RETAIL CRIME AND SERVICE FRAUD

Retail businesses are often thought of as victims of crime, whether by pilfering or embezzling employees, by shoplifters, or by robbers and burglars. But retail businesses of all sizes, from large department stores to "mom-and-pop" neighborhood stores, may themselves engage in a wide range of deceptive and illegal activities, including deceptive and fraudulent advertising, illegal pricing practices, sale of fraudulently represented merchandise, purchase

and resale of stolen goods, exploitation of employees through exposure to hazardous conditions or nonpayment of social security taxes, evasion of sales taxes, and payoffs to inspectors and other public officials. On just one of these offenses, criminal tax violations, some of the following activities are quite common in the restaurant industry: underreporting income; overstating deductions; keeping two sets of books; making false entries in records; claiming personal expenses as business expenses; claiming false deductions; failing to pay employment taxes; and hiding assets (Dino 2004). Even though relations between buyers and sellers have traditionally been guided by the *caveat emptor* (let the buyer beware) doctrine, it is not the case, as some people assume, that the law has always uniformly upheld this doctrine (Geis 2005a; Hamilton 1931; Scheppele 1988). Although consumer movements and other forces have recently been quite successful in challenging the caveat emptor doctrine, sellers continue to be in a position to take advantage of consumers in a variety of ways.

Retail Crime

The pervasiveness of deceptive business practices—often illegal, always unethical—has been documented by Paul Blumberg in *The Predatory Society* (1989). Over a 15-year period (1972–1987) Blumberg collected essays on the work experiences of more than 700 City University of New York (CUNY) students. Among the 638 respondents whose essays were analyzed, 71 percent reported that the business they worked for engaged in some form of deception. Although some of these deceptions were rather minor and commonplace (e.g., misleading advertisements), about 25 percent involved serious deceptions, such as misrepresenting an inferior product as a more expensive one. For example, some gas stations inflate the octane rating for lower-octane gas they sell, cheating U.S. drivers out of millions of dollars nationwide; nonkosher food is sometimes labeled as kosher and sold at higher prices.

Blumberg identified other deceptive practices in *retail crime*. Adulteration of products (e.g., tap water sold as spring water) is an ancient and still common

---

B O X 4.1   Occupational Crime as Violence: Drug Dilution and Fake Asbestos Removal

A Kansas City, Missouri, pharmacist, Robert Ray Courtney, pleaded guilty in February 2002 to diluting drugs prescribed for a large number of cancer patients (Jones 2002). By diluting the drug, the pharmacist greatly enhanced his profits. At the time he was originally charged, he was reported to be worth $10 million (Belluck 2001). The dilution of the drug may well have contributed to the premature death of some patients, and the pharmacist, who was stripped of his pharmacy license, was facing more than 100 wrongful death lawsuits in addition to a prison sentence of 17 1/2 to 30 years without parole. In a somewhat similar case, a Westchester, New York, pharmacist was charged with providing heart patients with cheaper, less effective forms of medication than those prescribed and customers contending with infertility with fewer pills than

had been prescribed (O'Connor 2005). While these cases may be unusual, they illustrate the more general theme that trusted professionals can cause real physical harm, even death, when they put profits over other considerations.

A father-and-son team that operated one of New York's largest asbestos removal firms was charged with having ordered their workers to fake asbestos removal and follow-up air tests, with practices of crudely ripping asbestos from walls, producing thick and dangerous asbestos dust (York 2004). The unsafe procedures saved on labor costs and accordingly greatly enhanced the firm's profits. Those exposed to asbestos fibers in the air are at risk for developing asbestosis and cancer, which can lead to premature and painful death.

---

practice. "Short-weighting" (e.g., providing less meat than the customer pays for) seems to be the norm. Other forms of retail deception include bait-and-switch tactics, in which consumers are lured by sale prices for items that are not available and then are sold higher-priced items; bar-code prices that do not reflect advertised sales prices; and the collection of "taxes" for nontaxable items.

Some deceptive practices are especially disturbing because they not only cost consumers money but also impinge directly on their physical well-being. Many of Blumberg's students found themselves in work situations in which a variety of techniques and practices had been developed to conceal food spoilage (e.g., soaking meat in salt and vinegar, and using "cosmetic surgery" to conceal mold). Unhygienic food-handling practices were widely reported, and restaurant owners often paid off health inspectors to avoid fines or closures.

If the responses of Blumberg's students can be taken as representative, they would strongly suggest that some level of deception is the norm for small business and entrepreneurial practices. A few more recent illustrative cases of such activities can be mentioned: Some restaurants in New York City were found to be inflating charges and falsifying tips

on credit card slips; some small businesses were found to be stealing employee health benefits; vendors who supply food to New York City schools were found to have fixed prices on these food orders; Blockbuster video rental stores were found to have assessed predatory late charges on customers; tax preparation businesses were accused of defrauding low-income customers of a federal tax credit by arranging deceptive, high-cost loans (Fabrikant 2001; Johnston 2002g; O'Brien 1998b; Sullivan 2000; Tillman and Indergaard 1999). Moving companies have been accused of demanding far more than original estimates once they reach the customer's destination and then refusing to release the customer's possessions until the company is paid (Tresniowski, Kapos, and Comander 2004). Box 4.1 recaps the case of a pharmacist who diluted cancer drugs to enhance his profits and the case of a father/son asbestos removal firm that potentially exposed thousands of people to disease and death.

Defrauding Vulnerable People

An especially disturbing form of consumer fraud victimizes the most vulnerable people. In a landmark study conducted in New York City in the early 1960s, David Caplowitz established that *The Poor Pay More* (1967). The poor were overcharged (especially on days that welfare checks arrived), were sold inferior or shoddy goods, and were victimized by deceptive credit practices, complicated consumer contracts, and lawsuits threatening wage garnishment. Despite new laws and consumer affairs initiatives, these fraudulent practices—always unethical, sometimes criminal—are hardly extinct. A Department of Consumer Affairs report in New York City, undertaken some 25 years later, found that shoppers in poor neighborhoods were paying almost 9 percent more for food than shoppers in middle-class neighborhoods; a poor family of four spent $350 a year more than an equivalent middle-class family for the same groceries (Landa 1991). Retail merchants are undeniably victims of many crimes in poor neighborhoods, including looting during riots, but the daily exploitation of poor consumers in such neighborhoods generally receives less attention. The most vulnerable workers arc also often exploited by shop owners, especially in lower-income neighborhoods. A 2005 survey of immigrant workers in Brooklyn, New York, who worked in discount stores, found that many were paid well below the legal minimum hourly wage (Greenhouse S. 2005). Immigrant workers may be afraid to file complaints and risk losing jobs or having their residency status challenged, and overwhelmed state regulatory agencies are often unable to properly investigate these cases. Victims of natural disasters also are especially vulnerable to fraud by contractors when they attempt to rebuild (Davilo, Marquant, and Mullings 2005). This concern intensified after major hurricanes in September 2005, in the Gulf states.

The recently bereaved and the seriously afflicted or dependent elderly are also among the most vulnerable of consumers. In her best-selling *The American Way of Death*, originally published in 1963, Jessica Mitford shocked the American public by exposing the unscrupulous practices of the funeral industry. Although many of these practices, which often involved subtly persuading bereaved survivors to contract for much more elaborate funeral and burial arrangements than they could afford,

were not necessarily illegal, they were highly unethical. Some 10 years later, Mary Adelaide Mendelson's *Tender Loving Greed* (1974) exposed scandalous practices in the nursing home industry. Mendelson's investigation uncovered many blatantly illegal practices whereby nursing home operators maximized their revenue (much of it coming from Medicaid and Medicare programs) while minimizing costs by inadequately feeding, clothing, and sheltering nursing home residents. Such problems are extensive today in the home health care business and in adult homes for the mentally ill (Levy 2003; Payne 2003). Billing for services never rendered, overcharging, embezzlement, bribery, and forgery are also found in businesses caring for these vulnerable people.

Service Business Fraud

Repair service businesses have an especially notorious reputation for cheating customers, and they are often well positioned to do so. In an oft-cited study conducted in 1941 under the sponsorship of *Reader's Digest*, a car in perfect mechanical condition (except for a detached coil wire) was taken to 347 different auto repair shops across the country; some 63 percent of the shops overcharged, inventing unnecessary work and lying about the mechanical condition of the car. A much later replication of this study found that most shops overcharged from $2 to $500 (Blumberg 1989). Such auto repair frauds are hardly restricted to small, independent service stations. The California Department of Consumer Affairs charged the chain of Sears Roebuck auto repair centers with systematically defrauding customers by performing unnecessary service and repairs (Fisher 1992a, 1992b). Consumer Affairs investigators made 38 visits to 27 Sears auto repair centers, and on 34 of these visits unnecessary services or repairs were recommended. Sears employees were under pressure from their supervisors to sell a certain amount of such services and repairs every day.

In fairness to the auto repair business, not all studies have confirmed high rates of dishonesty. Jesilow (1982b) found that only 10 percent of the more than 300 auto repair shops he visited recommended replacing a battery that simply needed recharging. A New York State Department of Motor Vehicles investigation of Goodyear and Sears repair shops found abuses in only a few of them (Fisher 1992a). However, in recent years American consumers were spending $90 billion a year on car repairs, with between 25 and 50 percent wasted on fraudulent or incompetent work (Belsky 1996).

Service fraud is hardly restricted to auto repairs. High rates of unnecessary repairs (up to 70 percent) have been found in investigations of television, type-writer, and watch-repair shops (Anonymous 1971; Blumberg 1989). An appliance store owner on Long Island was jailed on charges of having cheated customers out of up to a million dollars over a period of years by doing unnecessary or exorbitantly priced repairs (Healy 2003a). With computers, in particular, most users have no way to evaluate malfunctions, and a significant number of computer stores apparently take advantage of this situation (Maren 1996). Consumer affairs investigations and insider accounts alike suggest that in some of these businesses, making unnecessary repairs or overcharging is the norm, not the exception. And in some cases, repair fraud or mistakes can result in injury or death. A pool mechanic on Long Island, New York, was indicted on charges of criminally negligent homicide, alleging that his failure to install a $1.44 plastic exhaust pipe led to the death by carbon monoxide poisoning of the prominent tennis player Vitas Gerulaitis, who was staying in a friend's poolside guesthouse (Carvajal 1995). Surely fraudulent auto repairs have also played a role in fatal car accidents.

By any measure, then, U.S. consumers expend billions of dollars annually as a consequence of retail and service-related frauds. Of course, a great many small businesses are honest. The extent to which small businesses engage in fraudulent conduct is not simply a function of the integrity of a businesses' owner but also depends on the owner's self-perception (as a professional or businessperson), the nature of the community within which the business operates, the importance of a "good reputation," and the type of product or service. Richard Quinney (1963), for example, found that pharmacists who regarded themselves primarily as businesspeople were more likely to commit prescription violations than were pharmacists whose primary self-

identification was as professionals. Furthermore, it is obviously easier to cheat people on prescription drugs than on vegetables. A survey in New York City found vast differences among pharmacies on prescription prices; a heart medication sold for $5.37 in one pharmacy and for $39.95 in another (Steier 1993).

Many consumers are unaware that they have been victimized, and even when they suspect fraud, they are quite justifiably skeptical that reporting the abuse will lead to effective action. All consumers, regardless of how vigilant they are, will periodically be "robbed" by unscrupulous retailers and entrepreneurs.

CRIMES BY PROFESSIONALS: MEDICAL, LEGAL, ACADEMIC, AND RELIGIOUS CRIME

The professions generally enjoy great prestige in our society. Doctors, lawyers, and scientists, for example, are typically looked up to in their communities.

Use of the term *profession* in several different ways has created some confusion (Freidson 1986: 21). In the broader sense, *profession* is virtually a synonym for a full-time occupation, as in "professional waitress," "professional wrestler," and "professional criminal." In the narrower sense, which is adopted here, the term *profession* refers to occupations characterized by higher (graduate-level) education and training; specialized technical knowledge and skills; a high degree of autonomy; monopolistic, or near monopolistic control over services offered to clients and patients; substantial authority over clients and subordinates; legal responsibilities and professional codes of ethics; licensure and accreditation requirements; a fundamental claim to the attributes of a "calling," with altruistic and public service goals; a professional subculture with its own language and generalized value system; and professional associations that promote the interests of the profession and are charged with policing it (Freidson 1986; Hodson and Sullivan 2002). The classic "liberal professions" were medicine, law, and the ministry, and college professors and scientists are widely regarded as members of this professional elite.

Many other occupational groups, including accountants, engineers, pharmacists, nurses, social workers, and at least some categories of administrators and managers claim professional status. They also share some important attributes and enjoy at least some of the privileges of the traditional professions (Freidson 1986). The term *semi-profession* has been applied to some of these occupational groups, such as pharmacists and nurses (Sullivan and Hodson 2002). Indeed, the relatively high level of prestige, autonomy, trust, and income enjoyed by those accorded the status of professional has led an even wider range of occupations to pursue "professionalization" in the hopes of sharing in these advantages.

On another plane, many who claim professional status actually have little real autonomy but must instead respond to the demands of powerful clients upon whom they are financially dependent (Freidson 1986). Indeed, many physicians, lawyers, and scientists are increasingly constrained in their decision making by the fact that they work for large corporations or are funded by powerful governmental and private agencies (Derber, Schwartz, and Magrass 1990). The truly autonomous solo practitioner is relatively rare today.

Members of the medical, legal, academic, and clerical professions have enjoyed a privileged status. Their specialized knowledge puts professionals in a different position from that of entrepreneurs, retailers, and salespeople. As patients, clients, and students, people typically defer to the judgments of professionals much more readily than they do as consumers or customers because they perceive they have less reason to be confident in their own judgment. The "gray area" encompassed by the notion of "professional opinion" is especially broad and ambiguous; professionals can be guilty of providing either too little of their service or too much. The interests of their patients, clients, or students are all too often at odds with their self-interest (Smith R. G. 2002). *Conflicts of interest* frequently arise for professionals. The gap between the sometimes sanctimonious claims about "a calling" and disinterested service to public welfare renders the unethical, fraudulent, and illegal practices of some proportion of the liberal professions especially disturbing.

Medical Crime

The medical profession has generally enjoyed great prestige in the United States. Physicians enjoy an image of ultrarespectability and professional self-assurance (Rothman 1978: 71). Physicians are well compensated, are typically accorded a high level of trust, and exercise unusual power or "professional dominance" over patients (Freidson 1970).

Not everyone agrees that such trust is warranted. One professor of medicine who was harshly critical of his own profession suggested that doctors should be no more trusted than used-car salespeople (Mendelsohn 1979). On the one hand, physicians are expected to use their power to benefit their patients, and perhaps the larger community as well; on the other hand, physicians in a capitalist society are seen as profit-seeking entrepreneurs. This is part of the "structural contradiction" in the physician's role (Draper E. 2003a; Jesilow, Pontell, and Geis 1992). Even so, the popular images of "physician" and "criminal" would appear to be polar opposites. Even though E. H. Sutherland (1949: 12) noted a number of illegal acts committed by the medical profession, he stated that it was "probably less criminal than other professions." Still, much evidence suggests that many physicians engage in activities that are (or ought to be) defined as *medical crime* (Liederbach 2001).

The recognition that physicians should be held accountable for any grievous harm they cause to their patients extends back to ancient times, and specific diatribes against physician fraud date from the 1600s (Jesilow et al. 1985). Even though the medical profession has been given substantial powers to police itself, it has traditionally seemed far more concerned with promoting and protecting its own interests than with protecting the public from incompetent, unethical, and fraudulent physicians (Bonner 2005; Harmer 1975; Pontell, Jesilow, and Geis 1982). Historically, in fact, the American Medical Association has been quite indifferent to such medically harmful activities as cigarette smoking and dangerous environmental pollution. It opposed legislation that might produce less expensive prescription drugs and has been extraordinarily timid in encouraging the reporting, investigation, and prosecution of physician crime (Harmer 1975; Geis, Pontell, and Jesilow 1988). The long-standing position of the medical profession is that medical crime is a minor problem.

Among the specifically illegal and unethical activities engaged in by physicians, psychiatrists, and dentists are fee splitting, or taking and offering kickbacks; price fixing; conflicts of interest arising through ownership of clinics and pharmacies; cooptation by corporate employers; unnecessary operations, tests, and other medical services; conducting controversial and often harmful forms of experimental surgery without patients' consent; false and fraudulent billing, especially Medicaid and Medicare fraud and abuse; filling of illegal prescriptions; false testimony in court cases; the production of iatrogenic diseases (i.e., diseases inadvertently induced by medical intervention); fraudulent activity relating to medical license exams, diplomas, and scholarships; medical research fraud; tax evasion; and outright quackery. Let's consider some of the more significant forms of medical crime.

Medical Crime as Violent Crime   The performance of unnecessary surgery is arguably the single most disturbing form of medical crime, insofar as it can be considered violent occupational crime. Most operations (perhaps 80 percent) are elective procedures. Some studies have suggested that up to 15 or 20 percent of the several million operations performed annually in the United States may be unnecessary, and the percentage of unnecessary operations has increased in recent years (Jesilow et al. 1985; Leape 1989). By one account, some 16,000 patients die annually in the United States from unnecessary operations (Reiman 2004).

The most common forms of unnecessary surgery have involved removal of tonsils, hemorrhoids, appendixes, and uteruses; heart-related surgery (e.g., coronary bypasses, pacemaker implants); and caesarean section deliveries—all at an annual cost of billions of dollars and many lives (Angier 1997; Barron 1989; Grisanti 1989). In at least some cases, surgeons performing clearly unnecessary operations have caused paralysis, blindness, or other forms of permanent injury (Jesilow et al. 1985; Ortega 1997; Reiman 2004). A New York City eye doctor

admitted in 2003 that he had performed numerous unnecessary procedures on residents of homes for the mentally ill (Levy 2003a, 2003b). Although admittedly it is not always easy to identify "unnecessary surgery," various studies indicate that the amount of surgery is more a function of an oversupply of surgeons, the availability of reimbursement for particular classes of surgical patients, and the type of hospital than of the medical needs of a patient population (Lanza-Kaduce 1980; Nash 1987). For example, Americans are several times more likely to have certain kinds of surgery than are their British counterparts; Medicaid patients are twice as likely as the general population to have operations.

The traditional American fee-for-service reimbursement system and the absence of effective peer review procedures are among the criminogenic conditions promoting unnecessary surgery. In extreme cases, harmful (and nonconsensual) forms of psychosurgery (e.g., lobotomies), sterilizations of retarded women, and experimental surgery on women's sex organs have been performed out of an apparently sincere belief in the benefits of the surgery (Harmer 1975; Wachsman 1989). Surgeons may often be "true believers" in surgery, but the harm they can do is quite well established and not likely to be subject to formal legal action. Indeed, when a New York physician was sentenced to jail for "reckless endangerment" leading to a patient's death, this was described as a rare penalty for a physician (Nossiter 1995).

Medical Crime as Fraud   Medicaid and Medicare fraud by physicians has been characterized as an especially "pure" form of white collar crime because it occurs within the context of routine occupational activity, is not easily discovered, and can often be covered up and denied (Pontell et al. 1982).

The losses from Medicaid and Medicare fraud are enormous. Estimates of overall annual losses in the United States due to health care fraud or abuse have ranged as high as $100 billion, with a substantial proportion of these losses in Medicaid and Medicare programs but with no truly reliable way to measure the current level of fraud (Jesilow et al. 1992; Payne 2005c; Sparrow 1998). In one estimation, some 3 percent of the nation's physicians routinely commit outright fraud, with a much larger percentage engaging in improper, ambiguous billing (Rosenthal 1990). Whatever the actual amount, Medicaid and Medicare fraud clearly drains off medical resources, deprives patients of needed care, and in some cases leads to direct injury of patients through unnecessary and harmful operations (Pontell, Jesilow, Geis, and O'Brien 1985).

Overutilization, or billing for superfluous and unnecessary tests and other services, is perhaps the most common form of medical fraud, and it is especially difficult to prove and prosecute successfully (Jesilow et al. 1987). Some evidence suggests that many physicians do not regard Medicaid or other forms of insurance fraud as criminal behavior; rather, they see it as an understandable, even justifiable, response to the perceived low payment schedule of Medicaid and other insurance programs. Specific techniques used in this type of fraud, especially by "Medicaid mills" in poor neighborhoods, include "ping-ponging" (referring patients to several different practitioners when their symptoms do not warrant such referral), "family ganging" (extending several unnecessary services to all members of a patient's family), "steering" (directing patients to the clinic's pharmacy to fill unneeded prescriptions), and "upgrading" (billing for services more extensive than were actually performed) (Birenbaum 1977; Payne 2005c; Pontell et al. 1982). An investigation in Florida in 2001 disclosed that recruiters delivered thousands of poor children to dental clinics for "treatment" billed to Medicaid (Canedy 2001). A dentist in New York City was accused in 2005 of defrauding Medicaid of over $1 million, claiming to perform almost a thousand procedures a day (Levy and Luo 2005). In recent years, physicians have become especially creative in the use of "code games"—that is, "unbundling" interrelated medical procedures—to run up overcharges estimated to total billions of dollars (Knight-Ridder Newspapers 1990b). Therapists are also sometimes involved in such fraud (Evans and Porche 2005). Furthermore, billing fraud is not restricted to Medicare and Medicaid programs. In

2005, Blue Cross and Blue Shield plans exposed a scheme to bilk them out of more than $1 billion by sending patients from 47 states to California for unnecessary surgical and diagnostic procedures (Pear 2005a). The costs of such frauds are inevitably passed on to other parties who participate in these plans. Some doctors have also been accused of making numerous false diagnoses of asbestosis and silicosis, in connection with lawsuits against various corporations (Parloff 2005). It is somewhat ironic that corporations that have victimized workers and consumers by exposing them to asbestos and sand particles have themselves been victimized by such frauds, as have those who actually have these conditions and are accordingly deprived of their fair share of civil lawsuit settlements.

Some physicians have inherent conflicts of interest, insofar as they own the laboratories, diagnostic imaging centers, and physical therapy clinics to which they refer their patients; in such cases the cost of services is higher as a consequence (Pear and Eckholm 1991; Pear 1991). In a related vein, physicians have actively promoted medical devices produced by companies in which they have invested (or have stock options), and some physicians have been paid as much as $4,000 per patient by pharmaceutical companies for enlisting patients in pharmaceutical research, or they have accepted payments to prescribe certain drugs (Abelson and Glater 2003; Eichenwald and Kolata 1999a, 1999b; Harris 2004). Vermont, in 2002, became the first state to require pharmaceutical companies to disclose their gifts (such as free vacations in Florida), to physicians (Petersen 2002a). Still another conflict of interest arises for company doctors, who have often been found to put the company's interest above that of their worker patients (Draper E. 2003).

Altogether, then, substantial economic losses result from medical crime and fraud. For all kinds of reasons, enforcement efforts have been remarkably lax, and many practical or ideological problems have hindered successful investigation, prosecution, and punishment of Medicaid fraud (Jesilow et al. 1992). Success in dealing with medical fraud may require a fundamental transformation of the health care system.

In addition to the offenses discussed in this section, physicians have been accused of various other occupationally related crimes, ranging from narcotics addiction to sexual abuse of patients. Clearly a great many physicians are dedicated and honorable professionals. Still, physicians have abundant opportunities for various abuses because of the generally high level of trust patients extend to them, and they have also enjoyed substantial immunity from being called to account for these abuses.

Legal Crime

Legal crime may sound like an oxymoron; for our purposes, it refers to lawyers engaging in criminal conduct in the course of discharging their professional duties. Lawyers are officers of the court and as such are sworn to uphold the law; they also encounter some unique opportunities to break laws.

The legal profession has attempted to project an altruistic image, and many lawyers claim that the ethical standards of their profession are high. Their critics, in contrast, have long claimed that the nature of legal education and the conditions of legal practice promote an attenuation of conscience and much unscrupulous, unethical, and illegal activity (Jack and Jack 1992; Stern 1980; Zitrin and Langford 1999). Conflicts of interest are pervasive in legal practice (Shapiro 2002). The general public is sometimes skeptical of the motives and trustworthiness of lawyers, and public awareness of unethical conduct by lawyers appears to be increasing.

In some cases, lawyers have clearly crossed the line between representation of those charged with illegal acts and participation in illegal activity (Taylor 1985; Weiser 1997a). For example, a former prosecutor who defended a client in a drug case pleaded guilty to aiding in money laundering by his client's drug cartel (Stout 1995). In some cases, lawyers have become directly engaged in criminal activities, such as insurance fraud claims arising out of fake car accidents (*New York Times* 2001). While crooked lawyers dedicated to illegal enterprises certainly exist, they are quite rare. It is far more common for lawyers to become involved with, facilitate, or help cover up illegal enterprises while maintaining their primary commitment to the conventional and legitimate tasks of a lawyer.

Legal Crime as Fraud Lawyers may victimize their clients in a variety of ways. Lawyers have periodically been accused of stealing money— sometimes substantial amounts—from clients or colleagues. The *power of attorney* granted to lawyers, their control over escrow accounts, and their frequently intimate knowledge of and access to clients' finances provides them with a host of opportunities to commit this type of theft. The crimes can be quite sensational, in some cases involving the theft of millions of dollars from client's accounts (Behar 1992; Margolick 1992; Weiser 1997e).The lawyers involved in such cases include prominent members of the bar.

The intangibility of a lawyer's work provides special opportunities for overbilling clients (especially those with means), and at least some of this activity crosses the line into criminality. John Grisham's popular novel *The Firm* (1991) features overbilling, among other crimes committed by members of a rich and powerful Memphis law firm. In 1994, a close associate of President Clinton, Webster Hubbell, resigned as associate U.S. attorney general and subsequently admitted that he stole $394,000 from his law partners and various clients by filing false expense vouchers and overbilling; he pleaded guilty to two counts of mail fraud and tax evasion (Labaton 1994b).

A lawyer in Boston was disciplined for charging $50,000 to defend a 21-year-old in a drunk-driving case (Shao 1996). A lawyer-appointed guardian for an elderly woman in a nursing home billed her estate $1,275 for taking the woman out for an ice cream cone (Fritsch 2001). A lawyer who earned several million dollars suing failed savings and loan institutions was sentenced to 33 months in prison for defrauding the government with inflated bills in these cases (Weiser 1997a). Lawyers in the antitobacco litigation have been accused of extraordinary greed, with lawyers in Texas collecting over $3 billion (a former attorney general of the state went to jail for attempting to defraud the tobacco fund); one lawyer received $14 million for 70 hours of work, or about $200,000 an hour (Beam 2004). It

---

B O X 4.2   Lawyers and the Abuse of Political Power

In recent American history there has been no more dramatic illustration of "legal crime"—of lawyers involved in illegal activities—than the Watergate affair. The break-in at the offices of the Democratic Party in the Watergate complex and a range of other illegal acts carried out by the Committee to Re-Elect the President, who was Richard Nixon, and by high-level White House officials, involved lawyers on all levels and at each stage of the enterprise.

President Nixon, who resigned in the face of virtually certain impeachment for alleged obstruction of justice following the arrest of the Watergate burglars, was himself a lawyer. But so were many of his high-level associates, quite a number of whom went to prison in Watergate cases. His vice president, Spiro Agnew—also a lawyer—had to resign and pleaded no contest to tax evasion charges (Cohen and Witcover 1974; Woodward and Bernstein 1977).

Edwin Meese III, a close political associate of President Ronald Reagan and attorney general during his second term of office, was accused of improprieties in connection with both the investigation of the Iran-Contra arms case and the Wedtech fraudulent defense contract case (Martz 1987; Magnuson 1988a). Under formidable public pressure, Meese resigned as attorney general.

President William Jefferson Clinton and his wife, Hillary Rodham Clinton, were both lawyers. They were investigated along with several lawyer associations in connection with a land deal known as Whitewater from their earlier life in Arkansas, and President Clinton was subsequently impeached but not removed from office for lying under oath in connection with his involvement with White House intern Monica Lewinsky (Church 1994; Friedrichs 2000a). After leaving office in January 2001, President Clinton was investigated for awarding pardons to individuals with ties to donors to his campaign or library (Johnston and Lacey 2001).

---

has generally proven difficult to establish criminal intent in such overbilling or excess billing cases.

Legal Crime as Collusion   Lawyers may also engage in activities that specifically aid and abet the crimes of their clients. The ethics code of the American Bar Association both requires lawyers to keep in strict confidence any knowledge of a client's past crimes and prohibits lawyers from advising or assisting a client in the commission of any illegal or fraudulent act (Taylor 1983). The line between maintaining lawyer/client confidentiality and becoming party to illegal activity can be extremely thin. In a case that emerged in the early 1980s, a prominent New York City law firm—Singer, Hutner, Levine, & Seeman—was accused of complicity in a scheme by a client, O.P.M. Leasing Services, Inc., to defraud banks and other lenders of $210 million (Taylor 1983). It was ultimately revealed that even after it learned of its client's fraudulent lease closings, the law firm had continued to represent O.P.M. Leasing in fraudulent dealings, resulting in further losses of $15 million.

A number of major insider trading cases of the 1980s involved criminal charges against lawyers who passed on privileged information about pending corporate takeovers (Frantz 1987; Stewart 1991). Additionally, several leading law firms implicated in some of the massive savings and loan frauds during the same decade paid fines of more than $40 million each to settle the government's accusations that they had acted improperly in representing fraudulent thrifts (Cushman 1993; Hughes 1993; Nader and Smith 1996). It is difficult to imagine that billions of dollars could have been stolen from the S & Ls without the connivance or negligence of lawyers and other professionals. Lawyers were also quite directly involved in structuring off-the-books partnerships and other transactions for Enron and other corporations that contributed to investor losses of billions of dollars (Cottle 2002; *New York Times* 2002g). A high-level lawyer for the Tyco corporation was the target of allegations that he failed to inform the corporation's board of the CEO's wrongdoing (Rozen 2002). Although lawyers who do legal work for corporations are supposed to represent the interest of the corporation itself, they often do the bidding of the corrupt corporate executives who hire them. Box 4.2 shows this concept at work in the political arena.

It is important to examine the criminal activities of highly placed lawyers because such activities are likely to have especially damaging consequences. Lawyers operating in the political arena have substantial power and influence, which sometimes are applied corruptly (Green 1975; Nader and Smith 1996). The highly paid, typically bright lawyers who help corporations hide their immensely harmful activities and successfully defend them when they are criminally charged may be responsible for great harm.

Empirical studies of violations of ethical standards by lawyers have indicated that disbarred lawyers are most likely to be "marginal" solo practitioners (Arnold and Kay 1995; Parker 1982; Reasons and Chappell 1987). According to one study, the offense for which such lawyers are most likely to be punished is misappropriation of client funds and related activities (Reasons and Chappell 1987). Such activity is not restricted to marginal members of the profession, although they may be more vulnerable to exposure and punishment. Lawyers on all levels are especially well positioned—and perhaps especially tempted—to commit a range of illegalities, including bribery, perjury, conspiracy, and theft.

Academic Crime: Professors, Scientists, and Students

The "ivory tower" of academe is often considered to be removed from the real world and is rarely thought of as a significant locus of crime. Professors and research scientists tend to be regarded as benign and harmless creatures. Thus, two cases in the 1980s were widely reported precisely because they were so unusual. A prominent Tufts University biochemist, Dr. William Douglas, was convicted of murdering a prostitute he had paid with grant funds, and in another case, the head of New York University's Anthropology Department, Dr. John Buettner-Janusch, was convicted of using university laboratories to manufacture and sell illegal drugs (Carpenter 1989; McFadden 1987). Somewhat less sensationally, a survey of academic criminologists found that a significant percentage of them had engaged in various forms of illegal and deviant behavior, some of which were

occupationally related (Zaitzow and Robinson 2001). In any case, an academic text on crimes by members of other professions would seem to have a special obligation to consider the crimes of academics.

The fact that professors engage in less occupationally related crime than do doctors and lawyers is probably more a function of fewer opportunities for such activity than a matter of greater personal integrity among professors. Crime and deviance by academics has not been studied much to date, and definitional or conceptual disputes persist on the specific parameters of such crime and deviance (Thompson 2002). The principal types of *academic crimes* of professors and research scientists include plagiarism; misuse of or embezzlement of university discretionary funds or research grants; forgery or fraudulent claims about credentials; unresolved conflicts of interest in connection with grants, peer reviews, or evaluations of students; pilfering and unauthorized photocopying; gross negligence in the fulfillment of teaching responsibilities (e.g., failure to teach the course for which students enrolled); exposing students or research subjects to unsafe or harmful conditions or procedures; and fabrication of scholarship or the use of fraudulent data in research studies (Bayer 2001; Heeren and Shichor 1993). Some of this activity is "exogenous," or pertinent to occupational opportunities, and some is "endogenous," or a violation of professional norms (Douglas 1992; Heeren and Shichor 1993). The distinction is clarified by Douglas (1992): "A great scientist who happens to steal money, while continuing to be meticulously honest in his scientific work, is a thief, not a scientific fraud" (p. 77). Of course, the converse of this example is also possible.

Plagiarism, the use or misappropriation of the ideas or words of others without giving them credit, may well be the "purest" form of academic white collar crime, insofar as ideas and knowledge are the principal currency of the academic world. Allegations of plagiarism surface periodically, although formal charges are relatively rare (Buranen and Roy 1999; Green R. G. 2002; Mallon 1989; Mooney 1992). A prominent contributor to the white collar crime literature was accused of plagiarism in 1999,

---

B O X   4.3   Plagiarism and *Trusted Criminals*

While undertaking research for this edition of *Trusted Criminals*, the author of this book consulted an encyclopedia of white collar crime. When he read one of the entries, it seemed to him that whoever had written it was quite familiar with the relevant literature, until he realized that the entry had clearly been plagiarized from the second edition of this book. In fact, all 40 paragraphs of the entry had been copied, with only a scattering of minor modifications. The publisher of the encyclopedia was contacted, and the "author" of the entry eventually admitted to the plagiarism and returned to the publisher the fee paid to him. It seemed especially brazen to commit a form of academic white collar crime in connection with producing an entry for an encyclopedia of white collar crime.

---

although the allegation was vigorously contested (Leatherman 1999). In 2002, two prominent historians—Stephen Ambrose and Doris Kearns Goodwin—were accused of having plagiarized passages in their best-selling books, and in 2004, two prominent Harvard Law professors—Charles J. Ogletree, Jr., and Laurence Tribe—were accused of having plagiarized material from other legal scholars (Kirkpatrick 2002a, 2002b; Rimer 2004). (See Box 4.3.)

In collaborative research, disputes sometimes arise over the "ownership" of ideas or formulas generated by the research. A researcher at the University of South Florida was jailed for "stealing" his own notebooks that were produced in connection with research on extracting ammonia from clay (Jaroff 1997). He had refused a judge's order to turn them over when a corporation complained that he was stealing trade secrets protected by their contract with his university. On the other hand, academics are sometimes accused of improper or illegal conduct reflecting fundamental conflicts of interest. A Florida criminologist was alleged to be guilty of conflicts of interest in evaluating private prisons in which he held stock (Geis, Mobley, and Shichor 1999). Two Harvard University scholars were targets of a civil suit filed by federal prosecutors who claimed that they abused government-financed positions as advisors for Russia's economic reforms to enrich themselves and their spouses (Goldberg 2000).

Outright embezzlement, a more conventional form of white collar crime, is hardly unknown in the academic environment. In some cases, misuse of college funds or research grant money is alleged.

The newspaper *The Chronicle of Higher Education* periodically reports on cases of professors or college administrators charged with misappropriation of college funds and similar offenses, although other university officials, including college presidents, seem to be involved more often than professors (Leatherman 1995; Mogul 1997; Perez-Pena 1995). Such administrators and employees often have better opportunities than professors to embezzle or obtain improper payments. In 2005, however, a George Washington University engineering professor was accused of having embezzled almost $600,000 in federal grant money, in part to finance his extravagant lifestyle (e.g., living in a $2 million mansion) (Fogg 2005). Also in 2005, a Yale economist—ironically, an expert on corporate governance—resigned in the face of accusations that he had embezzled $150,000 by double billing the university for travel and other expenses (Salzman 2005). Some academic researchers have taken advantage of the special access they have to rare and valuable artifacts and manuscripts to steal these items and sell them for profit (Honan 1995). An Ohio State University professor was accused of stealing and selling manuscript pages and prints from ancient books, offering them for sale to a rare book dealer. Of course occupationally related theft is not restricted to those in higher education but may occur in other divisions of the educational system (see Box 4.4).

Academic Crime as Fraud   Fraud by research scientists (who may or may not also be professors) has come to light relatively recently (Davis 1989;

B O X 4.4   Stealing from the School District

In June 2005, Frank A. Tassone, a former superintendent of an affluent (Roslyn) Long Island, New York,
school district, was charged with having conspired with
a roommate to inflate bills—to the tune of hundreds
of thousands of dollars—sent to the school district for
various alleged services and products (Lambert 2005b).
Altogether, over $11 million had been stolen from the
school district over a period of years by various
schemes, with some $2 million of this loss attributed to
the superintendent (Lambert 2005a). In September
2005, he pleaded guilty to the charges (Vitello 2005).
Pamela Gluckin, a former school district business man-

ager, was alleged to have stolen some $4 million. Items
billed to the school district by the superintendent and
the business manager included over a million dollars in
cash advances as well as mortgage payments, airline
tickets, hotel bills, jewelry, pet supplies, and custom
tailoring. To the outrage of district taxpayers and parents, when the school board had originally discovered
some of the embezzlement of the business manager, it
had allowed her to quietly repay the money and leave,
without pursuing criminal charges. The embezzlement
victimized students in the school district as well as its
taxpayers.

LaFollette 1992). Science, which has as its principal
raison d'être the search for truth, is typically thought
of as self-policing, and fraud has traditionally been
considered quite negligible.

Indeed, the scientific establishment has tended
to deny that scientific fraud is a significant problem
(Brainard 2000; Dong 1991). It has proven difficult
to develop reliable data on the extent of scientific
fraud, which principally takes the form of fabricat-
ing, manipulating, and suppressing data (Davis
1989; LaFollette 1992; Zuckerman 1977). But
researchers may also be co-opted by corporate
sponsors, who play an increasingly conspicuous role
in university-based research. The tobacco industry
and the energy industry have paid researchers to
downplay the dangers of smoking and global
warming respectively (Washburn 2005). A review
of over 1,000 clinical trial studies, published in
2003, concluded that when research is industry-
sponsored, it is significantly more likely to reach
conclusions favorable to the industry than when the
research funding comes from some other source
(Washburn 2005: 84). The conscious or subcon-
scious skewing of research results to accommodate
corporate sponsors is a serious concern.

Claims that outright scientific fraud is rare,
whether or not they are accurate, have not typically
been based upon scientific research (Gunsalus
1997). The first detailed national study in 1993 on
research fraud and other forms of misconduct in

science suggested that such activities are not especially rare; some 6 to 9 percent of faculty and
students in various disciplines report direct knowledge of plagiarism or falsified data (Hilts 1993b). In
a survey of 3,000 scientists reported in 2005, one
third of the respondents admitted to overlooking
flawed data and not reporting data at odds with
their claims (Monastersky 2005). New technologies
of information transmission have facilitated scientific plagiarism and fraud, and in an era in which
more and more scientists are scrambling for fewer
research dollars, the pressures that contribute to
data manipulation have intensified (Bell 1992;
LaFollette 1992). Among the most celebrated cases
of scientific fraud are those of Cyril Burt (falsified
data on twins were used to demonstrate the inher-
itability of intelligence), William Summerlin (inked
patches were drawn on laboratory mice to falsely
convey the impression of successful skin grafts
between genetically different animals), John Darsee
(data on drugs administered to dogs were falsified to
indicate a reduction in the risk of heart attacks),
Stephen Breuning (psychopharmacological data
pertinent to controlling the behavior of mentally
retarded children were falsified), and Thereza
Imanishi-Kari and David Baltimore (data on gene
transplants and the immune system were allegedly
faked in a paper in which a Nobel laureate was
listed as coauthor) (Davis 1989; Sarasohn 1993;
Sykes 1988; Zuckerman 1977). In a case disclosed

in 2002, a Bell Laboratory physicist was accused of faking data in published research on what appeared to be important insights on electrical resistance changes and temperature (Chang 2002). Another recent case involved a physicist at the prestigious Lawrence Berkeley National Laboratory, alleged to have produced fraudulent data relating to the creation of the heaviest elements, 116 and 118 (Johnson 2002; Monastersky 2002). In both of the latter cases, the falsifications surfaced when other laboratory scientists were unable to reproduce the results. There was some chagrin at the failure of the coauthors and journal reviewers to detect the falsifications (Kolata 2002).

Some of these cases have been hotly contested. In the case of Cyril Burt, for example, Joynson (1994) and others have argued that the case against him was either flimsy or false. In the case involving Nobel laureate David Baltimore, a federal appeals court in 1996 dismissed charges of scientific misconduct against him and his colleagues, and a major study of the case characterized it as one of terrible injustice (Kevles 1998; Kolata 1996b). Only one of the scientists mentioned in the preceding paragraph, Stephen Breuning, was sentenced to a jail term, apparently the first such sentence for falsifying data (Davis 1989). Because his research involved a federal grant, federal fraud charges were filed. Vulnerable retarded children were actually treated on the basis of Breuning's falsified findings, an especially disturbing aspect of that case. Similarly disturbing is a 1994 case in which a Canadian researcher was accused of falsifying data in a study of breast cancer; the results had influenced treatment strategies for women with cancer (Altman 1994). When a Johns Hopkins laboratory worker died after taking part in an asthma research study, the university began investigating possible violations of its policies on research involving human subjects by one of its researchers carrying out cancer research in India, with possible harmful effects for experimental subjects (Associated Press 2001b). Such cases justify the classification of scientific fraud as a potentially violent form of white collar crime. In addition, the influence of corporate sponsors over scientific research may hinder the open circulation of research findings about harmful products and conditions.

Student White Collar Crime What of student white collar crime? First, it is important to realize that even though many traditional students may also hold part-time (or even full-time) jobs, such jobs are typically held to make school financially possible; thus, a student's primary occupation or principal pursuit is being a student. Students, of course, commit various illegal acts that have nothing to do with white collar crime, including vandalism, drunkenness, illicit drug use and transactions, car theft, petty larceny, assault, and rape. Many of these acts occur on campus, and students have numerous opportunities to engage in acts such as date rape. But much of the more conventional illegality and deviance of students, especially if it occurs on college campuses, has been treated as the "sowing of wild oats" or hushed up by college officials concerned about negative publicity (White 1993). This may be especially true if the students are from higher social classes, are attending an elite school, or are star athletes. Stuart Hills (1982) has speculated that college students' experiences of lawbreaking, which often involve peer-supported rationalizations and lenient reactions from college officials, may facilitate adult white collar crime.

Student white collar crime, then, is best defined as illegal or harmful conduct committed specifically in the context of their student role, for gain or advantage. The clearest example of such crime is cheating. Academic cheating is clearly commonplace in primary and secondary schools (Gross 2003). A study of elite prep schools, which produce a disproportionate percentage of the nation's business elite, specifically identifies such activities as buying homework and obtaining a copy of an upcoming examination as forms of white collar crime (Cookson and Persell 1985). Depending on the perceived seriousness of the activity, punishment ranges from restriction of privileges to expulsion. Colleges are also concerned that many applicants engage in "resume fraud" by making false claims about their achievements and activities (Marklein 2003). Inflated resumes may deprive other accomplished but honest students of admission to competitive colleges.

Various studies have indicated that cheating is epidemic among students on all levels in America and abroad (Desruiseaux 1999; Vowell and Chen 2004). A 2002 survey of 10,000 American high school students found that 43 percent agreed with the statement "A person has to lie or cheat sometimes in order to succeed" (Marklein 2003: D1). In a survey of more than 12,000 American high school students, conducted in October 2002, 74 percent reported having cheated within the previous year, (Gross 2003). In a survey of high-achieving high school students, 80 percent admitted to having cheated at least once, and about half did not believe that cheating was necessarily wrong; 95 percent of the students who admitted cheating had never been caught, and some 90 percent of college students reported that they believed that those who cheated never paid the price for it (Kleiner and Lord 1999). Although the frequency of academic cheating is variable relative to many different factors, some studies suggest that it has increased dramatically over the past half century, with current reports showing from 50 percent to as high as 98 percent of respondents admitting to some incident of cheating (Gross 2003; Kleiner and Lord 1999; McCabe 1992; McCabe, Trevino, and Butterfield 1999). One study of college students found that one third could be described as "hard-core" cheaters (Collison 1990). A brisk market in the sale of college term papers has developed (Goldin 1995). A physics professor at the prestigious University of Virginia used a computer program to establish that 60 term papers submitted to him were nearly identical and clearly reflected cheating (Schemo 2001). But professors often feel constrained from taking action against cheaters, with the possibility of being targets of lawsuits if they are found to have made false accusations (Schneider 1999). New technology, especially the Internet and the immense resources available through it, has greatly increased the opportunity for cheating; in part, the increasing practice of doing research on a home-based computer instead of in the school library may enhance plagiarism (Laird 2001). At the same time, new software provides a more efficient means of identifying plagiarized work.

Students seem to have conflicting feelings about academic cheating; some students brag about it, and others discreetly conceal it from disapproving peers (Labeff, Clark, Haines, and Dickhoff 1990; Moffatt 1989). Academic cheating takes different forms, including cheating on exams, homework, and term papers. But students who engage in one such form of cheating do not necessarily engage in all forms of cheating (Michaels and Miethe 1989). Gender appears to make some difference in the factors that influence students to cheat (Tibbetts 1997). Female students were found to be significantly less inclined toward cheating than male students.

Much academic cheating appears to be a response to situational pressures (e.g., not enough time to write one's paper) and fortuitous circumstances (e.g., finding oneself in a position to see the answers on another student's exam). Cheating in relation to college may involve entrance or scholarship exams. In June 2005, an assistant superintendent in charge of exams in a Long Island (New York) school district was accused of assisting his son in cheating on a Regent's examination (Lambert 2005c). Cheating in the form of making fraudulent claims on college applications, including those directed at the most prestigious colleges, is also not uncommon (Hernadez 1995). College admissions officers have become increasingly concerned—especially at highly competitive colleges—with "essay fraud" (Healy 2000).

Some academic cheating may be virtually inevitable because "grades often matter . . . more to the students than the substance taught in courses, at least in some of the courses" (Moffatt 1989: 297). For college students, passing grades are essential, and good grades are obviously advantageous in many respects. The opportunities for cheating are often readily available, and the likelihood of getting caught or suffering any significant penalty is slim. Some studies have found that academic cheating in college is correlated with parental pressure to raise grades, poor study habits, opportunity to cheat without detection, and the condoning of cheating by significant others (Michaels and Miethe 1989; Vowell and Chen 2004). Such cheating can continue in graduate or professional school education. For example, a ring taking advantage of time differences between California and New York was found to be selling answers for graduate school admissions exams to graduate school applicants (Richardson 1996c; Weiser 1997b).

Obviously, academic cheating does discernible injury by distorting and downgrading the achievement of honest students and possibly by depriving them of grants, awards, and positions they might otherwise receive. The experience of academic cheating may also contribute to the making of adult white collar criminals. Endorsing Hills's thesis, Michaels and Miethe (1989) observed that "cheating to receive institutional rewards also may generalize to other organizational settings after graduation, with cheaters subsequently relying on similar adaptations in carrying out their responsibilities in business, industry, and government" (p. 880). A Rutgers University study found that students majoring in economics were more likely to cheat than students in other majors (Collison 1990).

Cheating is not the only form of student white collar crime. College students not infrequently cooperate with their parents in ethically questionable, even overtly fraudulent, activity to obtain financial aid, and defaults on government-backed student loans have exceeded 20 percent (Ostling 1992). Student aid programs often include loopholes that some students take advantage of; in one especially extreme case, a foreign student obtained more than $400,000 in student loans (Burd 1999). Because college students are especially likely to be proficient in the use of computers, they are likely to be well represented in software piracy (Lewis P. H. 1994). U.S. agents have raided several prestigious campuses to crack down on such activity (Shenon 2001). Abuses, if not outright embezzlements, of student government funds by student government officers are not unknown (Gonzalez J. 1991). Two Harvard University students were accused of embezzling $100,000 from Harvard's famous Hasty Pudding Theatricals Club to finance vacations and purchase fancy goods (Belluck 2002a). Student white collar crime is a significant problem in its own right and arguably an important breeding ground for adult white collar criminality.

Religious Crime

For some, the notion of *religious crime* may be the most disturbing of all forms of crimes by professionals. In the eyes of the faithful, religious leaders are primary sources of moral guidance and inspiration. They typically take sacred vows to uphold religious doctrine that uniformly denounces theft, violence, and exploitation. The sacred, as Durkheim (1912) emphasized long ago, occupies a special realm in human affairs, quite removed from profane, conventional objects, activities, and rituals. By invoking the name of God or Jesus, religious leaders may generate a bottomless well of trust among gullible believers. Accordingly, those who commit crimes from behind the shield of a religiously ordained status violate a special, sacred form of trust. Religious crime has a long history, and no single faith has a corner on the market (Barnhill 2005).

Some members of the ministry of various faiths may take on the attributes of professionals, whereas others may lack those attributes. Some of the most financially successful ministers are also the least educated, and their ministries are more a function of personal charisma than of specialized knowledge or skills. Some of these ministers appear to have more in common with entrepreneurs than with professionals in the conventional sense, and even less in common with traditional spiritual leaders.

Some religious leaders—or those claiming such a status—have defrauded believers and used offerings or donations for corrupt purposes. Televangelists have been especially vulnerable to the accusation that they exploit their audience to personally enrich themselves. In a widely publicized case in the 1980s, televangelist Jim Bakker and the PTL ministry raised over $100 million a year from viewers; it later surfaced that Bakker and his wife Tammy were drawing large six-figure salaries and indulging themselves in every imaginable extravagance with viewer donations (Shepard 1989; Tidwell 1993). In October 1989, Bakker was convicted of fraud and conspiracy charges and received a long prison sentence. In 1998, Henry J. Lyons, the president of the National Baptist Convention, USA, was charged with theft and in 1999 received a 5½-year prison sentence (Bragg 1999a; Niebuhr 1998). He was found guilty of swindling millions of dollars from companies doing business with his church and with stealing money donated to rebuild Baptist churches set afire by racists in the South. In 2006, a former Roman Catholic priest pleaded guilty to stealing close to $150,000 from his parish (Associated Press 2006). The Roman Catholic Church hierarchy's cover-up of cases of priests molesting young children has received much attention in recent years but generally falls outside the realm of white collar crime. One incentive for the cover-up, however, was the hope of sparing the Church massive payments to victims.

Some allegedly religious enterprises—for example, Scientology—have been accused of being organized principally to defraud large numbers of people out of millions of dollars by a combination of seductive appeals, illusory treatment programs, and intimidation (Behar 1991). With all due respect for the predominantly good work that clergy of all faiths have done, especially reprehensible frauds have been committed by invoking religious claims.

EMPLOYEE CRIME

Employees stealing from their employers is one of the more common images of white collar crime. From the perspective of employers, unsurprisingly, such crimes are the heart of the white collar crime problem.

Even though most of us think of "employees" as lower-level workers, strictly speaking an employee is anyone who is being paid by another individual, a group of owners, or a business; thus, this definition also applies to high-level executives and managers. Indeed, higher-level employees are best positioned to steal from a company on the largest scale, and by some estimates, executives and managers are responsible for the largest proportion of losses businesses suffer at the hands of their employees (Coleman 2006). When managers steal, losses average $250,000 (Winter 2000). This is far higher than average losses from lower-level employees. A Wal-Mart executive in charge of addressing employee theft had stated that employees who stole

should be shot; he was subsequently accused of misappropriating some $500,000 in corporate funds and property for his own benefit (Farzad 2005a).

Executives and managers are often in a position to award themselves huge bonuses and a wide range of exceedingly expensive "perks," such as country club memberships, a private jet, and condominiums (Altheide, Adler, Adler, and Altheide 1978). In cases such as expense-account padding, the perks are clearly illegal; in other cases they are distributed as part of the company's compensation system. Is the extravagant compensation awarded CEOs and other top executives just reward for their work or theft on a grand scale? (See Box 4.5). Even though outright thefts are commonly associated with low-level employees such as bank tellers, the amount of money high-level executives of publicly owned companies embezzle tends to dwarf the embezzlements of ordinary employees. For example, Robert Vesco is alleged to have "misappropriated" some $224 million of other people's (mainly, stockholders') money from Investors Overseas Services (Dorman 1975). At least part of the massive losses in the savings and loan cases can be attributed to embezzlement on a grand scale by highly placed banking executives (Pizzo, Fricker, and Muolo 1991). The chief financial officer of Day-Lee Foods, Yasuyoshi Kato, embezzled $100 million over several years to finance a lavish lifestyle; he received a 63-month prison sentence (Murr 1997). In 1998, the head of BankBoston's International Client Business in New York disappeared with $66 million; a Citibank executive in the same year was arrested for embezzling $10 million to finance high living on the Upper East Side and in the Hamptons (Davis, Keil, and Keil 1998; Kleinfeld 1998).

John Clark and Richard Hollinger (1983: 1) define employee theft as "the unauthorized taking, control or transfer of money and/or property of the formal work organization perpetrated by an employee during the course of occupational activity which is related to his or her employment." On the most mundane level, this includes cashiers who do not ring up friends' purchases and ticket-takers who do not tear up tickets and then collude with someone in the box office to resell them. At its most extreme, employee theft may involve systematic embezzlement of millions of dollars over an extended period by someone occupying a key position. If executives and managers are best positioned to steal millions, sometimes lower-level employees succeed in doing so as well. In 2004, for example, a former Goldman Sachs (investment banking house) secretary was found guilty of having embezzled at least $7 million from her employers (Sorkin 2004b). She forged transfer authorizations from her boss's accounts.

Even though other forms of white collar crime may be more harmful and costly than employee theft, it is clearly pervasive and by some accounts has been increasing (Winter 2000). A great deal of employee crime is not readily discovered, and even when discovered it may not be reported to any official agency. Because no agency collects and publishes statistics on the range of activities encompassed by the term *employee crime*, only rough estimates based on diverse sources and statistical extrapolations are available for study.

Estimated annual losses due to employee crime in the United States have been as high as $400 billion, although such estimates vary widely, with most in the $5 billion to $10 billion range. Thus, employee crime accounts for about 1 percent of the gross national product and inflates the price of consumer items by 10 to 15 percent (Clark and Hollinger 1983; Irwin 2003; Miller and Gaines 1997). According to one study, an embezzling worker in a small business steals an average of $127,500 (Irwin 2003). However, a hospital locks foreman stole up to $6 million from his employer by setting up phony companies to bill them for security supplies (Lambert 2004). By all accounts, employee theft is responsible for the largest percentage—perhaps as high as 75 percent—of *inventory shrinkage*, goods and supplies that are delivered and paid for but cannot be accounted for by sales or stockroom surveys (McCaghy and Cernkovich 1987). Catering company employees managed to steal some 400,000 miniature liquor bottles, or about $1.5 million worth, from an American Airline facility at a New York City airport (Kilgallon 2003). Employees steal far more

from most businesses, on the average, than shoplifters, burglars, or robbers.

Employee theft can lead to lost employee benefits, defaulted loans, and intensified mistrust within the business (Sieh 1993). According to a survey reported in 2003, one quarter of 500 small businesses have caught their employees stealing (Irwin 2003). In another survey, almost half the workers polled admitted to illegal or unethical behavior on the job over the preceding year, and at least some of this behavior involved employee theft (Jones 1997). A significant percent of juveniles who are gainfully employed report engaging in such crime, either in the form of giving away goods and services (26 percent) or helping a coworker steal an employer's property (9 percent) (Wright and Cullen 2000). Some self-report surveys have indicated that between 75 percent and 92 percent of all workers supplement their legitimate incomes in technically illegal ways, a good proportion of which involves some form of theft from their employers (Mars 1982). Furthermore, a vast amount of fraud exists in the workers' compensation system, which is funded by employer premiums; cheating is involved in an estimated 20 percent or more of the claims (Kerr 1991b).

Forms of Employee Theft

In the broadest possible sense, all employees steal from their employers. They use office supplies and machinery for personal purposes, make personal phone calls on a business phone, use a company car for personal reasons, and use company time for personal business or for unauthorized recreation (Snider 2001). In addition to a formal paycheck, then, many employees view such activities as *wages-in-kind* (Ditton 1977). Some such wages-in-kind, such as tips, are regarded as perfectly legitimate; others, like letting relatives help themselves to store goods without charging them, cross the line into theft. Employees perceive their acquisitive actions as either theft or something else according to the amount of money or material taken, the method used, and the degree of complicity with other employees (Clarke 1990). Admittedly, much ambiguity is involved here, and on the pettiest

---

B O X 4.5 Extravagant Executive Compensation: Just Reward or Grand Theft?

The extraordinary compensation awarded CEOs of major corporations has been one of the big stories of the recent era. In 2004, CEOs of 179 major corporations were paid an average of close to $10 million a year, a 12 percent increase from the previous year; average labor compensation rose less than 5 percent during that year (Moriarty 2005; Samuelson 2005). Over a 10-year period CEO pay tripled, and over a 20-year period increased almost twentyfold, while a rising number of Americans—6 million—were without health insurance (Kristof 2005). During this same period, the pay of Army privates—individuals asked to put their lives on the line on behalf of their country—averaged less than $30,000 a year (Stein 2005). At 100 major corporations, bonuses rose 46 percent in 2004, to a median of over $1 million (Kristof 2005). Some executives received hundreds of millions of dollars in compensation. There is much evidence that these pay packages cannot be attributed to executive performance in any meaningful sense but rather reflect the control of CEOs over corporate boards and compensation committees (Bebchuk and Fried 2004; Moriarty 2005). Exorbitant compensation has often been awarded even when the company has been losing money and the stock value has declined dramatically (Deutsch 2005; Morgenson 2004; Oppel and Eichenwald 2001). For example, during a year when net income at Eli Lilly declined almost 30 percent and shareholder returns declined greatly, the CEO received a 41 percent boost in pay, to more than $12 million a year (Deutsch 2005: 12). During a year when the stock price of John Hancock declined over 30 percent and earnings dropped some 15 percent, the CEO of the company received over $21 million in pay, up from $8 million the year before (Treaster 2003). In the many cases where CEOs collected millions in bonuses and stocks to reward them when their company reported high profits, they failed without exception to return this money when it later came out that the financial statements had been false (for example, the CEO of El Paso received almost $10 million in compensation in 2001 when his company

reported profits of $93 million; it later came out that the company had actually lost close to $450 million that year!) (Glater 2005c; Norris 2003b). By analogy, if a bank accidentally deposited millions of dollars in your personal account, should you be allowed to keep the money when the mistake is discovered? Banks uniformly say no.

A CEO of Orbitz had an unusual clause built into his contract that would award him large cash bonuses even when shareholder losses on the companies stock were increasing (McGeehan 2003). And many CEOs have negotiated immensely extravagant "golden parachutes" and retirement packages for themselves, even in circumstances where they have lost their jobs due to poor performance. Philip Purcell received $113 million after losing his job as head of Morgan Stanley, and Carly Fiorina received $21 million after losing her job as head of Hewlett-Packard (Gasparino 2005c). Famously, Michael Ovitz received some $140 million after being forced to resign after slightly more than a year as president of the Walt Disney Company; this payment became the focus of a major shareholder's lawsuit (O'Brien 2005). John F. Welch, the celebrated former CEO of General Electric and a contemporary business leadership icon, was awarded the use of a fancy Manhattan apartment, wine, food, laundry services, toiletries, newspapers, basketball and tennis tournament tickets, and satellite television services, all as part of a retirement package (O'Brien 2005). Welch was worth some $700 million at this time. These perks often seem quite absurd in light of the wealth of the recipients. Oracle gave Lawrence Ellison, its chairman, $8,360 for "personal fitness expenses" at a time when he was estimated to be worth some $50 billion (Berenson 2004a). Charles K. Gifford, on retiring as CEO of Bank of America, was to receive over $38 million in stocks, $16 million in cash, over $8 million in "incentive payments," over $3 million a year for life (with over $2 million a year for life to his wife, if he predeceased her), 120 hours of free flight time on company jets, an office and secretary, and rights to buy

---

level, neither employees nor employers are likely to characterize such activities as "stealing."

Employee theft occurs on a number of different levels. *Pilfering* refers to petty theft, *larceny* to unauthorized taking of something of value. *Chiseling* refers to

cheating or swindling, *fraud* is theft through misrepresentation, and *embezzlement* refers to "the destruction or fraudulent appropriation of another's money or merchandise which has been entrusted to one's care" (Altheide et al. 1978: 91). As a matter of law, these

60 Red Sox tickets a year (O'Brien 2005). Many other such examples could be given.

Corporate mergers have been a major theme of the recent era in big business, but who benefits from these mergers? There is much evidence that the top corporate executives—and the investment bankers—are the primary beneficiaries. The merger of the Gillette Company with Procter & Gamble resulted in pink slips for thousands of Gillette employees, but the CEO of Gillette, James Kilts, cleared close to $170 million (Morgenson 2005e). The present and former top officers of Toys "R" Us also stood to clear some $170 million—with over $60 million to the CEO—in a buyout deal. The CEO of MBNA could anticipate a pay-out exceeding $150 million when his company was bought by Bank of America (Creswell and Dash 2005). Many other such examples could be cited. Meanwhile, merger activity resulted in the loss of almost 80,000 jobs in the first quarter of 2005 alone.

In the series of trials involving top executives of corporations that had reported hundreds of millions of dollars—or billions of dollars—of false financial information, a quite uniform defense claim of the former CEOs has been: "I don't understand corporate accounting, I didn't know about the accounting fraud, and I had nothing to do with it" (Eichenwald 2005c; Norris 2005a). This has been true of cases involving former CEOs of Adelphia, Cendant, and WorldCom, among other companies. One can only wonder whether these executives claimed such ignorance and lack of awareness of what was going on in companies they supposedly ran when they requested hundreds of millions of dollars in compensation from their corporate boards.

In June 2005, L. Dennis Kozlowski, former CEO of Tyco International, and Mark H. Swartz, former chief financial officer of the corporation, were convicted on charges of fraud, conspiracy, and grand larceny for stealing $150 million directly from the corporation and obtaining in excess of $400 million more by artificially inflating the value of corporation's finances, while sell-

ing their stock (Sorkin 2005b). Tyco International, a multibillion dollar conglomerate that acquired hundreds of companies, was one of the hottest stocks of the 1990s, but its stock declined 80 percent, or approximately $100 billion, in the first six months of 2002 (Eisenberg 2002a; Rashbaum and Berenson 2002). Kozlowski, a police detective's son from Newark, New Jersey, became a major symbol of rampant greed among top corporate executives. He had arranged for the corporation to pay for extravagant apartments and mansions, $12 million for decorating one of these apartments (including a notorious $15,000 umbrella stand and a $6,000 shower curtain), and $10 million for the art for the apartment, as well as a multimillion dollar birthday party for his wife, jewelry, and many other such items (Sorkin 2005a; Stewart 2003). Kozlowski had earlier been indicted for having evaded more than $1 million in New York sales taxes in connection with $13 million of art purchased for his Fifth Avenue apartment in New York (Berenson and Vogel 2002). Altogether, Kozlowski was facing serious prison time.

Nor was the case of Kozlowski and Tyco entirely unique. In Canada, media baron Conrad Black, former CEO of Hollinger International, was charged along with an associate of looting his company of some $400 million over a period of seven years—or some 95 percent of the corporation's profits during that time (McNish and Stewart 2005). Black spent the company's money on multimillion dollar homes, private jets, rare artifacts, servants, and parties.

Walking into a bank with a gun and demanding money from a teller is one way to steal money; walking into a corporate boardroom and demanding that a board compensation committee made up of cronies, consultants, and even relatives approve compensation of millions—sometimes tens of millions or hundreds of millions—is another way to steal money. The principal differences are that the second way of stealing money pays much better and is far less likely to result in criminal prosecution and imprisonment.

---

crimes incorporate different elements. Although employers may well focus on the criminal aspects of these acts, employees who engage in them may see them differently, describing them as "salvaging," "fringing," "borrowing," "fiddling," and "leveling" (Horning 1983: 699).

Employers' Responses to Employee Theft

Some employee theft is tolerated, sometimes even encouraged, by employers to compensate for low wages and poor working conditions (Ditton 1977; Zeitlin 1971). Indeed, some evidence suggests that

---

B O X 4.6   Union Leaders Who Steal from Their Union Members

Labor unions were originally established to enable workers to gain fairer wages, appropriate benefits, and better working conditions. Certainly unions have succeeded in achieving significant concessions from employers on behalf of their membership. Sadly, however, many corrupt union leaders have been more concerned with enriching themselves than with the well-being of their membership. Several recent examples occurred in New York City. In 1997, the president of a health care workers' union ran up more than $100,000 in questionable hotel and restaurant charges. The following year, the former president of the carpenters' union was convicted of stealing $50,000 from a fund for unemployed carpenters. In

1999, officials of a construction workers' union were alleged to have wasted or stolen more than $50 million from a benefits fund. And in 2000, the head of a union of low-paid school cafeteria and crossing guards, who typically earn less than $20,000 a year, was sentenced to three to nine years in prison for stealing more than $2 million from the union to finance a fancy lifestyle, including junkets abroad with relatives (Greenhouse 1999; Rohde 2000). It seems especially shameful that union officials who should be representing union workers in their dealings with exploitive employers are instead stealing from their own employers, the union members.

---

such theft contributes to worker satisfaction and productivity, especially in marginal jobs (Mars 1982). But workers who engage in minor employee theft as a "fringe benefit" are somewhat compromised by their participation, and as a result they are less well positioned to organize and make militant demands for better wages. In this sense, employers may actually profit or save money from a certain amount of employee theft.

Many employers are unlikely to involve the police when they discover significant employee thefts because to do so risks disrupting relationships and productive patterns at work, exposing improper or even illegal practices of the employer, and possibly garnering bad publicity if arrests and criminal trials ensue (Clarke 1990; Holtfreter 2005d). Other employers, on the other hand, may take strong measures to prevent employee theft, investigate it vigorously, and punish it harshly—especially when cheap labor is plentiful or when employee theft is of a form and level that reduces profits or renders managers vulnerable to claims of incompetence (Mars 1982). Managers and employers may use various forms of surveillance to minimize employee theft and uncover it when it occurs. Box 4.6 examines thefts of labor union funds.

Alternative Forms of Employee Crime

The growing problem of theft of ideas, designs, and formulas—that is, of trade secrets—is another form of employee crime (Bequai 1978). In the long run, the theft of a unique design or formula, if it reaches a competitor, can cost an employer far more than the direct theft of money or material property. Such theft, which may be motivated by hostility to the employer or by financial payoffs from competing companies, can be expected to become an increasingly costly problem in the current "information revolution." Not all employee crime against the employer takes the form of theft. For example, employees may commit acts of *sabotage*, the deliberate destruction of the employers' product, facilities, machinery, or records (Holtfreter 2005d; Mars 2001b). According to Hodson and Sullivan (2002), "The word *sabotage* originated in the 1400s, in the Netherlands, where workers would throw their sabots (wooden shoes) into the wooden gears of the textile looms to break the cogs" (p. 105). Workers may commit sabotage to conceal their own errors, to gain time off or more pay, or to express their contempt and anger with their work and employer. The most extreme forms of sabotage are likely to occur in settings in which workers are especially alienated or believe they have been unfairly exploited and mistreated.

Dishonest resumes may also be said to victimize employers. A deceased director of recruiting for Lucent Industries lied on his resume about degrees earned and a past criminal record (Romero and Richtel 2001). Al Dunlop, a high-profile CEO of a major corporation, concealed earlier job dismissals from his resume (Norris 2001d). Many other such cases could be cited, including a new head coach for the Notre Dame football team who claimed a degree he had not earned and a nonexistent career as a college football player (Fountain and Wong 2001). Although specific harm caused to an employer by such misrepresentations cannot always be easily identified, at a minimum they tend to cause embarrassment and inconvenience.

Some Factors in Employee Theft

Not all employees are equally likely to steal from their employers or commit sabotage. Differences in personal integrity are clearly an important factor. Different forms of employee theft or deviance spring from different motives; workers who steal may do so only for themselves or to "altruistically" facilitate the thefts of relatives and friends (Hollinger, Slora, and Terris 1992). In some rare cases, employees who believe their employer is engaging in dangerous or unethical practices may steal or commit sabotage to expose or hinder the employer's operation. Still, only a small minority of employee theft is motivated by altruistic or idealistic objectives.

The most extensive study of employee theft, sponsored by the National Institute of Justice, found that employees who commit theft are more likely to be young (ages 16–25), male, and unmarried (Clark and Hollinger 1983). According to one study (Boye 1991), workers who expect to leave a job soon are more likely to steal. Personal attributes, however, appear to be considerably less important than both a range of situational and structural factors characterizing the workplace and employee responses to and perceptions of these factors.

A well-known study by Horning (1970) of 88 blue-collar employees of a large Midwest electronics assembly plant found that they strongly discriminated among company property, personal property,

and "property of uncertain ownership." *Company property* refers mainly to basic, bulky components and tools (e.g., power transformers and electric drills), which are quite closely monitored. *Property of uncertain ownership* refers mainly to small, inexpensive, and expendable components and tools such as nails, bolts, scrap metals, pliers, and drill bits. *Personal property* refers to monogrammed clothing, wallets, jewelry, personally modified tools, and the like. (Some personal property, such as lost money or misplaced, unmarked clothes, falls into the category of property of uncertain ownership.) Not surprisingly, workers were most likely to take property of uncertain ownership, and in this study, more than 90 percent admitted to having pilfered such property. Most of the workers (about 80 percent) felt it was wrong to steal company property, although a significant minority were not necessarily so inhibited. Finally, these blue-collar workers quite uniformly condemned the theft of personal property, and virtually all of them (99 percent) claimed that such theft rarely if ever occurred.

Unanticipated personal circumstances and the availability of a wide range of rationalizations can also play an important role in employee theft. In *Other People's Money* (1953), a pioneering study of embezzlement, Donald Cressey interviewed 133 embezzlers and defrauders and determined that the existence of secret financial problems (e.g., gambling losses, a mistress) increased the likelihood that individuals in a position of trust would embezzle. Even though they knew perfectly well that embezzlement was illegal, they also strongly rationalized their actions as "borrowing" with the intention of eventually paying the money back. They also tended to find some grounds of "justifying" their actions (e.g., "I'm entitled to the money"), or they denied being able to help it (e.g., "I got into a situation in which I had no other alternative").

A subsequent study by Dorothy Zietz (1981) found that female embezzlers were more likely to be motivated by family-related financial emergencies and problems than were male embezzlers. Zietz's study recognized, in fact, that employees who embezzle can be motivated by a range of circumstances and objectives. Some embezzlers deliberately

---

B O X 4.7   Donkeys, Wolfpacks, Vultures, and Hawks: A Typology of Employee Theft

Gerald Mars (1982), a British social anthropologist, developed a typology, based on the closeness of supervision and the presence or absence of a strong work group, to characterize the variety of workplace thieves. "Donkeys," such as cashiers, are closely supervised and have weak group ties; they are most likely to "steal" time and to engage in creative accounting. "Wolfpack" members (e.g., longshoremen) are closely supervised and have strong group ties; they engage in elaborate, systematic pilferage. "Vultures" (e.g., cab drivers) are weakly supervised and have strong group ties; they often organize stable, ongoing systems of pilferage. "Hawks" (e.g., professionals) are both weakly supervised and typically weakly integrated into work groups; they are especially likely to engage in abuses related to time and expense accounts.

---

seek out positions that will provide them with opportunities to embezzle, with the goal of enhancing their lifestyle, making up for childhood deprivations, or attempting to satisfy the demands of a spouse or lover. Others may be motivated by altruism (the desire to help others), fantasies, weak character, simple greed, or some combination of these factors. Studies of embezzlers have highlighted the complex interrelationship among opportunistic, situational, and personal factors that can generate some forms of employee crime.

Conditions in the Workplace and Employee Crime

Perhaps the most important factors influencing the form and level of employee theft involve workplace conditions such as the size of the organization. Smigel (1970), in an oft-cited study, found that his respondents were more prepared to steal from large organizations than from small ones. First, stealing from a large organization could be more easily rationalized on the grounds that such organizations are especially exploitative and are far less likely in any case to suffer measurable harm from conventional levels of theft. Second, the larger the organization, the smaller the risk of being caught.

Other studies (see, for example, Clark and Hollinger 1983) have found that employees' dissatisfaction with the company or with supervisors was associated with higher rates of employee theft. American workers in particular deeply resent affronts to their dignity and self-respect in the workplace, and

significant anecdotal evidence suggests that much employee theft and sabotage is inspired by this resentment (Altheide et al. 1978). Clearly, the more alienated the employees are, the less likely they are to be inhibited from committing theft and sabotage against employers. In Box 4.7, a British social scientist offers a vivid typology of employee crime.

The conditions conducive to employee theft vary widely among occupations. Bank clerks, for example, generally have greater difficulty "skimming the product" they handle than do low-level employees in many other fields (Mars 1982). In some fields, relatively low-level employees may prefer to pass up promotions if the increased pay and constraints of the higher position will not compensate for reduced opportunities to steal (Mars 1982). Other students of employee deviance and theft (see, e.g., Altheide et al. 1978; Snizek 1974) have supported Mars's finding that work-group norms are an especially important factor in determining the scope and form of employee theft.

According to the most ambitious study in this area, opportunity to steal is a major determinant of employee theft, and those who have the greatest access to things worth stealing are most likely to do so (Clark and Hollinger 1983). The single most important predictor of employee theft, according to this study, is the perceived likelihood of getting caught. The vast majority of workers who steal (95–99 percent, depending on the type of business) are not caught, although again most of this theft is occasional and relatively petty. Deterrence of employee theft appears to be less a function of a vigorous security presence than of a clearly articulated policy on employee theft, good inventory control, pre-employment screening, and action taken against identified thieves. An overriding conclusion of Clark and Hollinger's study is that employee theft and deviance must be understood principally in terms of factors inherent in the workplace rather than external factors. Employees' perceptions of the quality of the workplace milieu are a significant factor in whether or not theft occurs, and informal workplace norms tend to govern the type and amount of such theft.

AVOCATIONAL CRIME AND WHITE COLLAR CRIME

One class of illegal activities that is not white collar crime in the strict sense, even though it has a generic relationship to it, can be labeled *avocational crime* (Geis 1974). The most common dictionary definition of an avocation is a hobby or occasional occupation. In this context, avocational crime refers to occasional economic crimes committed by respectable members of society outside of an occupational context.

The concept of avocational crime has some similarities with the concepts of occasional property crime, folk crime, and mundane crime. Clinard and Quinney (1973) defined *occasional property crime* as amateur, small-scale property theft or destruction. Ross (1961) and Wilson (2001) have used the term *folk crime* to apply to everyday deviance, such as traffic violations and poaching, that does not reduce the status of the violator and is generally considered relatively harmless. Gibbons's (1983) somewhat related concept of *mundane crime* was applied to commonplace, innocuous, often dull or routine opportunistic forms of lawbreaking with relatively low visibility.

The preferred use here of the term *avocational crime* over the related terms emphasizes that the illegal activity occurs outside of an occupational context. Even though avocational criminals do not necessarily enjoy a respectable status, it is significant that so many of them are considered respectable and hold legitimate occupations. Indeed, a respectable status often provides special opportunities for engaging in this type of illegality. The people involved, their motivations, and the consequences of avocational crime are often similar or identical to occupational white collar crime.

Avocational crimes includes evading personal taxes; defrauding insurance companies; providing false statements in connection with personal loans and obtaining credit; defaulting on payments of debts; evading customs; stealing services (e.g., telephone calls, tolls, tickets for travel or entertainment events); stealing copyrighted material (e.g., audiotapes, videotapes, software, printed matter); and purchasing stolen ("hot") goods. We could include shoplifting and defrauding of retailers and wholesalers (e.g., rebate and coupon abuse) in this list, but the people who engage in these offenses are less likely to commit white collar offenses. Altogether, the entire range of illegal activities committed by "respectable" members of society for financial advantage or to avoid financial disadvantage, in their roles as citizens, taxpayers, consumers, insured parties, and travelers, can be considered avocational crime.

Income Tax Evasion

Some scholars of white collar crime (see, e.g., Green 1997; Coleman 2006) have classified *income tax evasion* as a form of occupational or individual white collar crime. But strictly speaking, the obligation to pay income taxes applies to income from whatever sources and is not limited to that from a legitimate occupation. Indeed, income earned outside the occupational context—from investments or rental properties, for example—is most likely to be involved in income tax evasion (Braithwaite 2005; Johnston 2003a).

Federal tax laws require taxpayers to file a timely return, report tax liabilities accurately, and make a timely payment of taxes due; employers are additionally required to withhold the appropriate amount of taxes from their employees' paychecks (Gordon 1996; Long 1981). Failure to comply with tax law may take different forms, including failure to file, nonreporting of income, underreporting of income, and false or misrepresented claims of deductions. Noncompliance with tax laws is a major problem in many countries (Braithwaite 2005; Hasseldine and Li 1999). In the United States, tax revenue lost from noncompliance has been estimated to be approaching $300 billion annually (McGinn 2002). This is serious money.

Tax evasion, which is defined by the Internal Revenue Service (IRS) as an act involving deceit, subterfuge, and concealment, is, of course, illegal. On the other hand, tax avoidance, the arrangement of a taxpayer's affairs to minimize tax liability, is legal (Burnham 1989; Thurman and Vose 2001). The complexity of tax law makes it difficult to distinguish clearly between tax evasion and tax avoidance or between fraudulent and "aggressive" tax planning (Braithwaite 2005; Long 1981).

Income tax (individual and corporate) provides two thirds of federal tax revenue, with an additional one fourth coming from employment taxes. The corporate share of the income tax burden has fallen steadily, especially since World War II (Braithwaite 2005; Johnston 2003b). From the beginning, there have been interpretive ambiguities about classifying different forms of income and eligibility for various deductions. Corporations and well-off individuals, with access to high-priced lawyers and accountants, have obviously been best positioned to take advantage of these interpretive ambiguities (Johnston 2003b; Stern 1972). Many millionaires or even billionaires have paid only trivial taxes on stupendous incomes by taking advantage of provisions in the tax code that allowed large-scale deductions. The IRS has been more vigorous in the pursuit of tax protesters—those advocating tax evasion—than of tax straddlers—those using illegal tax shelters. In recent years, wealthy and middle-income individuals have used tax shelters, offshore charge cards, trusts, and partnerships to minimize their tax bill, often in ways that are illegal (Braithwaite 2005; Dentzer 1984; Johnston 2003b). Such devices are sometimes successfully challenged by the IRS; in 2005, the IRS was pursuing a case against Presidio, a firm that sold tax shelters to some of the wealthiest Americans and allowed them to shield billions of dollars of income (Browning 2005b). The tax laws themselves privilege some classes of taxpayers over others and generate some noncompliance among taxpayers who resent perceived inequities.

Early in the 21st century, an outgoing IRS Commissioner declared that the tax agency was losing its war on tax cheats (Johnston 2003b). The IRS devoted more resources to investigating tax cheating by poor wage earners than by wealthy people who derive income from partnerships and trusts, although much evidence suggested that tax cheating was epidemic among affluent citizens (see Box 4.8). Early in the 21st century, some $800 billion in American money was on deposit in one tax haven, the Cayman Islands; 2 million Americans were using offshore accounts to evade taxes (Johnston 2003c; McGinn 2002). More specifically, offshore credit and charge cards billed to a Caribbean bank facilitates tax evasion, by some estimates totaling $20 billion annually (Johnston 2003c). The chances of working poor people being audited in 2001 was 1 in 47; for people earning more than $100,000, it was 1 in 145; for corporations, it was 1 in 233; and for participants in partnerships, it was 1 in 400 (Johnston 2003e)! The focus on poor tax payers arose out of a Republican concern with misuse of the earned income tax credit. Virtually unprecedented Congressional criticism of IRS audit practices, responding to taxpayer complaints, led the IRS to back off some of its more aggressive auditing tactics, and staff and funding cuts further reduced the probability of taxpayers being audited (Johnston 1998a; McGinn 2002). These developments provided taxpayers with rationales to cheat and lower perceived risk in doing so.

One study of tax compliance suggested that a complex of factors, including opportunity, convenience, and interpretations of the law, is often involved in tax evasion and that a series of decisions rather than a single one leads to noncompliance (Smith and Kinsey 1987). The tax laws themselves are often complex, onerous, arbitrary, confusing, and illogical, and accordingly promote a certain level of evasion (Duke 1983). According to a study reported in 2005, the more prevalent an individual perceives tax evasion to be, the more inclined that individual will be to commit tax evasion (Welch

---

B O X 4.8   A Record Case of Individual Tax Evasion

In February 2005, Walter Anderson, a prominent owner of telecommunications companies, was arrested and charged with evading taxes on at least $450 million in income (Johnston 2005a). By some accounts, his unreported income was several times this figure. Over one five-year period, he was accused of having failed to pay over $200 million in taxes. In 1998—a year during which he reportedly earned some $125 million—Anderson reported a total income of less than $70,000 and paid less than $500 in taxes. Over a period of many years, he apparently filed no tax returns at all.

Walter Anderson was accused of being the biggest tax cheat in American history (Johnston 2005a). He was an early employee of MCI and then founded his own long-distance company as well as several space travel companies. He traveled in private jets and made various multimillion dollar deals. Anderson, who never married, cultivated a low public profile and created at least seven aliases. Using some of these aliases, he set up offshore corporations as one means of concealing his ownership of various telecommunications companies.

---

et al. 2005). Given the relatively low risk of audits and the rather mild sanctions, the real issue may be why so many people comply with tax laws (Smith and Kinsey 1987). Authentic corporate compliance with the tax laws appears to be more limited than individual compliance.

One principal response of the IRS to tax evasion has been to target especially prominent Americans for criminal prosecution; the expectation is that the inevitable publicity will have a deterrent effect on ordinary taxpayers. Many eminently respectable citizens—including a former dean of the Harvard Law School; a president of the National City Bank of New York; a police chief of Providence, Rhode Island; and a vice president of the United States (Spiro Agnew)—have been prosecuted on tax evasion charges (Carson 1973; Cohen and Witcover 1974). Baseball star Pete Rose, country singer Willie Nelson, and billionaire hotel owner Leona Helmsley were among those pursued in recent high-profile cases (Desnoyers 2005; Glaberson 1989b; Smith 1990). Albert J. Pirro, a prominent Republican businessman, real estate lawyer, and husband of Westchester, New York, Chief Prosecutor Jeanine Pirro, was sentenced to 29 months in prison (Chen 2000). He improperly deducted $1.2 million of personal expenses as business expenses. This case received substantial press coverage. And tax evasion cases are not uncommonly interrelated with other forms of white collar crime. For example, a high-level Enron executive pleaded

guilty to tax evasion; he failed to report improper kickbacks related to Enron partnership deals (Eichenwald 2002i). Sometimes the tax evasion cases are the easiest to make against major white collar offenders.

Despite the IRS's best efforts, a conviction for tax evasion seems to have less of a stigmatizing effect than conviction for most comparable economic crimes. The perceived inequities, complexities, and contradictions of the tax laws clearly provide opportunities for evasion and a range of rationales for doing so. The relationship between compliance and noncompliance with income tax laws and other laws specifically applicable in the corporate or occupational setting is worthy of much more substantial investigation.

Other Forms of Avocational Crime

Insurance fraud is widely recognized to be a growing problem in the United States and other Western nations. The literature on insurance fraud estimates that as much as 20 percent of all insurance claims are fraudulent; for some types of claims (e.g., auto theft), it may be considerably higher (Ericson and Doyle 2004; Kerr 1992a, 1993). In a recent year, it was estimated that insurance fraud cost American consumers some $120 billion a year (Ericson and Doyle 2004: 101). Arrests for making such claims are rather uncommon and mostly involve ordinary citizens, including schoolteachers, grandmothers, and other unlikely parties (Sloane 1991a). Various professionals—including doctors, lawyers, insurance adjusters, and police officers—may be involved in facilitating false injury, damage, and theft claims (Healey 2003b; Kerr 1993). Even though a certain proportion of insurance fraud is carried out by organized crime or professional criminals, and of course some fraudulent claims are made within a legitimate business context (e.g., a failing business is "torched" by the owner, who then collects insurance), much insurance fraud generally is avocational crime committed by respectable middle- or upper-class members of society.

Many false claims involve relatively minor inflations of actual damages or losses, and many people do not consider such activity to be a significant offense (Romano 1992). However, some false claims are substantial and incorporate fraudulent medical histories, arson for profit, and major exaggerations of injuries (Walsh 2005). A related form of insurance fraud is "rate evading": registering vehicles in neighboring states with lower insurance rates (Kennedy 2003).

Avocational crime is treated here as a form of crime with a marginal relationship to white collar crime. It occurs outside of an occupational context, although of course a great deal of parallel activity such as tax evasion, insurance fraud, and theft of services occurs specifically within such a context. Many who engage in avocational crime have legitimate occupations and a respectable social status, and in this regard avocational offenders are identical to white collar offenders. Some avocational crime is facilitated by occupational status, although it is not wholly dependent on it. Avocational crime also has in common with much corporate and occupational white collar crime the primary objective of maximizing financial advantage or minimizing a financial disadvantage.

Much avocational crime is, on the whole, even less stigmatizing than virtually all forms of white collar crime, at least in part because the primary victims are most typically the government or large corporations and because the losses appear to be more "abstract" than for other forms of theft or fraud. It has also been given low priority, for the most part, by the criminal justice system, and it receives relatively modest media attention. The specific nature of the relationship between avocational crime and white collar crime, and how involvement with one influences involvement with the other, merit further study.

OCCUPATIONAL AND AVOCATIONAL CRIME, IN SUM

Occupational crime, surveyed in this chapter, is generally recognized as the other major form of white collar crime, in relation to corporate crime. Such crime encompasses the whole spectrum of fraudulent practices committed by those engaged in retail and service-related businesses, with some classes of people—for example, the recently bereaved—especially vulnerable. In this chapter, we have also seen that professionals and semiprofessionals engage in various forms of white collar crime. Although this review focused on several high-profile professions, any profession could be subject to the same sort of analysis. The crimes of professionals are significant because the unusually high level of trust professionals generally enjoy places them in a position to cause substantial harm to clients and patients. The high prestige of many professionals tends to shield them from criminal accusations and convictions in all but the most blatant and egregious cases.

Much significant crime is committed by employees against their employers. Clearly, a complex of factors can interact in different ways to encourage or deter employee crime. A high level of opportunity to steal may be offset by a high degree of loyalty and job satisfaction. Conversely, a significant amount of employee theft may occur when levels of hostility to the employer are high, even if opportunities to steal are somewhat limited and risky. Altogether, if we are to understand employee crime, we must attend to a complex of structural factors, plus personal interaction between employer and employee. But it is the highest-level employees who are best positioned to steal the largest amounts of money from employers.

Finally, some attention in this chapter was given to avocational crime, which occurs outside of an occupational context but parallels occupational crime in terms of those who engage in it and their motivations. Altogether, this chapter demonstrated that significant crimes are committed within the context of the whole range of legitimate occupations.

KEY TERMS

academic crime, 98

avocational crime, 111

caveat emptor, 89

conflicts of interest, 93

embezzlement, 107

employee crime, 104

fraud, 107

income tax evasion, 111

insurance fraud, 113

inventory shrinkage, 107

legal crime, 96

medical crime, 93

occupational crime, 88

occupational deviance, 88

plagiarism, 98

power of attorney, 96

profession, 92

property of uncertain ownership, 109

religious crime, 103

retail crime, 89

sabotage, 108

wages-in-kind, 107

DISCUSSION QUESTIONS

1. What are the benefits and drawbacks of adopting Green's definition of occupational crime as "any act punishable by law through opportunity created in the course of an occupation that is legal"? How does occupational crime differ from corporate crime? What are the major forms of occupational crime?

2. Discuss the principal evidence on the scope of retail crime and factors that tend to promote or inhibit it. Compare the crimes of small businesses that sell products with those that provide services. Which type of small businesses are best positioned to engage in unethical and illegal activity, and why?

3. Identify the principal defining elements of the professions. Which attributes of the professions promote illegal conduct and which attributes should inhibit it? What do medical crime, legal crime, academic crime, and religious crime, as defined in this text, have in common, and how do they differ? Which profession's crimes disturb you most, and why? Is student white collar crime a relatively trivial problem or a substantial problem?

4. Discuss the principal problems involved in defining employee crime and measuring its scope accurately. Which forms of employee crime are most harmful, and which are least harmful? Identify the main factors that seem to promote a high level of employee crime and the main factors that influence employer response to it.

5. What is the relationship of avocational crime to white collar crime, and how do they differ? Can you identify any hypothetical ways in which avocational crime and occupational crime might interact directly? Which factors inhibit a more vigorous response to avocational crime?

5

Governmental Crime
State Crime and Political White Collar Crime

The problem of governmental crime will surely be one of the major challenges of the 21st century. "Governmental crime" is a disquieting notion. Government is, after all, the entity that produces, implements, and administers a society's laws. People like to think the government is there to protect them from crime and to deter, incapacitate, punish, and rehabilitate criminals. The worst crimes, in terms of physical harm to human beings, abuse of civil liberties, and economic loss, have been committed by individuals and entities acting in the name of the government, or the state. We are easily so overwhelmed by the contemplation of crimes of the state that we retreat into a state of denial (Cohen S. 2001). By some estimates, more than 350 million people worldwide—a staggering number—died in the 20th century because of deliberate actions of the state (Falconer 2003; Heidenreich 2001). Although war accounts for many of these deaths, a large proportion of them are attributed to genocides, massacres, and mass executions (Jones 2004; Markusen 1992; Shaw 2003). In addition, a great deal of nonviolent crime with major consequences is committed by governmental officials, either for political or economic gain.

What we here consider governmental crime in the broad sense is not always crime in the narrower legal sense of the term. We must distinguish among those governmental or political actions prohibited by the state's laws, those defined as criminal by international law, and those regarded as criminal on some other criteria of harmfulness not necessarily recognized by either the state's laws or international law. If we concede to the state the exclusive prerogative of defining crime, many harmful activities perpetrated in the name of states, or by governmental officials, will not be defined as crime (Kauzlarich and Friedrichs 2003; Kauzlarich, Kramer, and Smith 1992; Ross 2003). On the other hand, applying the term *crime* too broadly to any and all forms of governmental activity at odds with some group's value system also has costs (Green and Ward 2004). The absence of agreement on defining governmental crime must be acknowledged.

In this chapter, the term *governmental crime* is used as a broad term for the whole range of crimes committed in a governmental context. The term *state crime* denotes harmful activities carried out by the state or on behalf of some state agency, whereas *political white collar crime* refers to illegal activities carried out by officials and politicians for direct personal benefit.

The term *political crime*, which has been labeled a "broad and ill-defined category" (Allen, Friday, Roebuck, and Sagarin 1981: 201), has most typically been associated with crimes such as treason, sedition, disobedience of mandated service (e.g., draft dodging), and illegal protests (Turk 1982). Crimes committed by or on behalf of the government have been classified most typically as a type of political crime (Clinard and Quinney 1973; Hagan 1997; Ross 2003). But an important distinction must be made between those who commit crimes against the state from without and those who do so from within. This chapter is concerned with crime carried out by those within the government—and not with political crime carried out by individuals or political groups that lack governmental status.

Governmental crime goes beyond Sutherland's original conception of white collar crime, but it is often so intimately interrelated with it that no survey of white collar crime can neglect it. Governmental crime is closely related to white collar crime carried out by corporations, professionals, businesspeople, and others because the parties involved enjoy a respectable status, occupy a position of trust, most typically have moderate or higher incomes, and do not regard themselves as criminals. Clearly, a symbiotic relationship, a mutual interdependence, exists between much governmental and traditional white collar crime, a thesis explored more fully in Chapter 6.

Even though political white collar crime is often motivated by the desire for financial gain, the extension or maintenance of power plays a much larger and more central role in state crime. When violence occurs as an element of state crime, it is likely to be much more direct than the violence of corporate crime. Although violation of trust is a key element in white collar crime generally, in the case of state or political white collar crime a public trust is violated, whereas corporate and occupational crime involve a violation of an essentially private trust. Accordingly, some commentators regard governmental crime as worse than corporate and occupational crime.

Admittedly, we cannot always easily discriminate between those who commit crimes on behalf of the state and those who use their state or governmental position to commit offenses for their own personal benefit, but it still seems useful to differentiate between, for example, genocidal actions and accepting bribes. Michalowski (1985) produced a typology that differentiates between crimes committed by those in political power and those outside government, between crimes that benefit individuals and organizations (including government), and between crimes committed for economic and political gain.

Prosecution of state crime and political white collar crime may involve some unique difficulties, especially when the accused are part of the lawmaking and enforcement apparatus. Indeed, any claim that governmental crimes have been committed is especially vulnerable to the charge of ideological bias, and at least some governmental actions will be defended as desirable policy by some and castigated as a criminal form of repression by others. When they are exposed, state crime and political white collar crime may become the focus of considerable public interest and outrage because of the conspicuous public profile of governmental and political officials (Geis and Meier 1977; Simon 2006). No corporate or occupational crime has ever generated the level of public attention directed at the Nuremberg Trials and Watergate hearings. If public anger and concern over Enron's collapse was high, this could be attributed in part to the company's formidable political clout and close ties with high-level political officials, including the president (Duffy and Dickerson 2002). On the other hand, much avoidance and indifference has also characterized public responses to some of the worst crimes of states (Cohen S. 2001; Smith R. W. 2004). By any measure, American public interest in international tribunals on genocide in Kosovo and Rwanda, and ongoing genocide in Darfur (Sudan), was limited.

Traditionally, the study of governmental crime has been relatively neglected by criminologists, perhaps even more neglected than the study of corporate and occupational crime (Green and Ward

2004; Kauzlarich and Kramer 1998; Ross 2003). Why is this so? It is difficult to gain access to and study the politically powerful; the forms of harm and lawbreaking perpetrated in the name of the state or by government officials are often complex; and many members of society are resistant to regarding states and government officials as criminals. The somewhat limited examination of governmental crime in this text is more a reflection of the fact that such crime is less central to what is ordinarily defined as white collar crime than a judgment of its relative importance. On the contrary, the worst of all crimes have been governmental crimes.

GOVERNMENTAL CRIME: SOME BASIC TERMS

Some terminology of governmental crime requires definition because these terms are used in quite different ways. Even though *abuse of power* is perhaps the broadest charge associated with governmental crime, it has no fixed meaning. The most obvious, least problematic instances of abuse of power occur when the state or its agents violate laws to accomplish some improper or prohibited objective. In its broader meaning, abuse of power occurs when the state assumes and exercises power it ought not to have. When FBI agents engage in surveillance or break-ins specifically prohibited by law, abuse of power in the first sense is involved. The institution of an Emergency Act that enabled South Africa's apartheid government to arrest and detain dissidents involved abuse of power in the second sense. The full range of governmental abuses of power entails many forms of harm, including violations of universally defined basic human rights (Cohen 1993; Ishay 2004; Ross 2000). Even though in its broadest sense abuse of power includes acts of economic corruption, limiting the use of the term to acts involving the extension or maintenance of power can avoid some confusion.

A second basic concept associated with governmental crime is *corruption*. In the English language of Shakespeare's time, the expression "to corrupt" had both sexual and political meanings, and today's dictionaries offer many different definitions (Heffernan and Kleinig 2004; Heidenheimer 1977). Political corruption most typically involves the misuse of political office for material advantage, although it also encompasses acts undertaken for political advantage. It has been applied narrowly (as the violation of specific laws, typically for some form of payment) and more loosely as deviation from ideal or expected patterns of behavior (Kratcoski 2001; Lowenstein 2004).

Even though the term *corruption* has negative connotations, some regard a degree of political corruption as inevitable and functional (Heffernan and Kleinig 2004; Lieberman 1972). Political corruption in some form can be found in all but the most primitive societies, and we have records of such corruption from the earliest times, such as the Code of Hammurabi from Babylon, ca.1700 B.C., and the book of Exodus in the Old Testament (Alatas 1990). Standards for defining corruption vary over time and across cultures, and actions that might be considered corrupt by one standard may be regarded as acceptable by another (Heffernan and Kleinig 2004; Quah 2003). Corruption is frequently practiced by the same people who condemn it rhetorically.

Bribery is probably the activity most closely associated with political corruption. In his magisterial book, *Bribes*, John T. Noonan, Jr. (1984) states that "the core of the concept of a bribe is an inducement improperly influencing the performance of a public function meant to be gratuitously exercised" (p. xi). Even though bribery is specifically a legal concept, its various meanings include those defined by moralists, those defined by written law, those defined by law in practice, and those defined by commonly accepted practices (Noonan 1984). Although the specific definition of bribery varies among societies, the concept reaches far back in history and cuts across virtually all existing societies.

Finally, the concept of *political scandal* is important to our understanding of state crime and political white collar crime. In a liberal democratic society, major governmental crime is likely to be exposed in the context of a political scandal, and in one view, political scandal is possible only in such a society

(Heilbrun 2005; Markovits and Silverstein 1988). Such scandals are most likely to occur when a basic division of power exists in society, when a major external threat to the society is lacking, and when politicians violate widely supported norms about proper conduct in political office (Barker 1994; Neckel 1989). In a democratic society, the political opposition and the media play the major roles in creating and sustaining political scandals, although the effects of ongoing scandals on the political system are often modest or limited (Szasz 1986a). Because political scandals tend to focus attention on the people involved, they do not necessarily undercut the legitimacy of a political state; they may even enhance it if the perceived wrongdoers are swiftly and justly punished (Logue 1988). However, the most recent research indicates that exposure of corruption diminishes belief in the political system and reduces interpersonal trust (Seligson 2002).

Political scandals are more likely to lead to criminal prosecutions than to fundamental, enduring reforms. In David Simon's (2006) interpretation, recent American political scandals were the result of secret, illegal (or unethical) acts of government agencies, with demonstrably harmful effects; were subjects of official government hearings or investigations; left unanswered questions; and were interrelated with each other and with other forms of crime and deviance. The Enron case was both a corporate and political scandal: Conservative politicians heavily lobbied by Enron and other major business lobbyists—and beneficiaries of their huge campaign funding donations—blocked efforts to pass laws that might have prevented some of the egregious practices that led to the collapse of the corporation and billions of dollars of losses (Berke 2002b; Borosage 2002).

GOVERNMENTAL CRIMINALITY ON AN EPIC SCALE

In the view of one ideological tradition, *anarchism*, the state is inherently aggressive and fundamentally unnecessary (Krimerman and Perry 1966; Shatz 1971; Wolff 1976). At its most extreme, anarchism holds that the state is a criminal enterprise. This anarchist perspective has not been widely adopted.

If unjustly depriving people of their property, their way of life, and their very lives is regarded as criminal, then imperialistic conquests and state-sanctioned wars are governmental crimes of extraordinary scope. Indeed, in one interpretation the United States was founded upon a crime, insofar as Columbus's "discovery" in 1492 led to the conquest of paradise (Sale 1990). As early as 1542, we find a Catholic priest, Fr. Bartolome de las Casas, protesting the abuses committed against indigenous people in the new world (MacKay 1996). The literature documenting many of the state-sponsored crimes committed by those who came after Columbus is formidable, especially concerning the destruction of Native American peoples and the slavery trade involving African Americans (see, e.g., Brown 1971; Davidson 1961; Mohawk 2000). These historical crimes were once celebrated as triumphs of Western civilization.

The waging of war has been even more destructive than imperialistic endeavors. Over time, the state became the largest and most efficient user of violence, a dubious distinction it originally shared with bandits and pirates (Heyman 1999; Jones 2004; Tilly 1985). Pacifists regard war in any form as criminal; others have distinguished between just and unjust wars (Walzer 1977). A leading contributor to the contemporary "just war" dialogue, Michael Walzer (2004) now argues that we must also attend to *jus post bellum*, or justice after war. Since the middle of the 19th century, various countries have joined together to ratify agreements prohibiting or outlawing particular acts during times of war (Falk, Kolko, and Lifton 1971; Neier 1998). In addition to uncalled-for aggression and crimes against peace, over time the following have been identified as *war crimes*: the use of poisonous gases, biological and chemical weapons, nuclear weapons (see Box 5.1), and mines; indiscriminate attacks against civilians, carpet bombing, and "collateral damage" to civilian targets; gratuitous attacks on dams, dikes, waterworks, and nuclear stations; wanton destruction of property and pillage

B O X   5.1   The Threat of Nuclear War as Crime—and Other Weapons of Mass Destruction

Waging a nuclear war may well be the penultimate state crime. An all-out nuclear war has the potential to create a "nuclear winter" that would destroy the planet's environment, leading to the obliteration of humanity, the "death of death" (Schell 1982, 2003b). The whole issue involving possession and possible use of nuclear arms has generated an enormous literature exploring a range of complex questions about the objectives of developing and producing nuclear weapons, their impact on international relations, and the best strategy for minimizing the possibility of a nuclear war.

It is quite remarkable that the vast criminal potential in the use of nuclear weapons has been neglected by criminologists and criminal justicians (Harding 1983; Friedrichs 1985; Kauzlarich and Kramer 1998). Although international law does not prohibit possession of nuclear weapons, the threatened and actual use of such weapons is prohibited by international law and by the Charter of the United Nations (Burroughs 1997; Kauzlarich and Kramer 1998). The traditional nuclear weapons policy of the United States can certainly be interpreted as a violation of such codes, charters, and historical agreements on the conduct of armed conflict (Lichterman and Cabasso 2002). The Soviet Union began to develop its own nuclear weapons shortly after the United States did, and by the beginning of the 21st century various other countries—including India, Pakistan, Israel, and North Korea—had nuclear weapons; Saddam Hussein's Iraq had attempted to develop

them (Butler 2001; Easterbrook 2001; Schell 2001). No weapons of mass destruction were found by occupying American forces in Iraq; in 2005, North Korea's claims that it was developing nuclear weapons were of special concern (Becker 2005). Following the September 11th attack on the United States, concern also intensified that international terrorists would be able to obtain and use nuclear weapons (Allison 2004; Dodd and Hager 2001; Erlanger 2001).

The potential use of other *weapons of mass destruction* (WMD) by states and terrorist organizations was also a growing concern. The United States and the Soviet Union had taken the lead early in the 20th century in the development of biological and chemical weapons (Miller, Engelberg, and Broad 2001). Although the United States abandoned these programs in 1969, the Soviet Union continued to develop such weapons in secret, as did Iraq and other countries. By the early 21st century, fear of their use by terrorists had intensified.

At a minimum, students of white collar crime should consider how involvement with the nuclear arms race relates to and is distinctive from governmental crime generally. How are the motivations of those who might initiate a nuclear war or the use of other weapons of mass destruction similar to and different from the motivations of white collar criminals of all types? Does it make any sense to raise the issue of nuclear warfare in the context of a survey of white collar crime?

(theft); enslavement, forced labor, enforced prostitution, and systematic rape; hostage taking, genocidal actions, use of death squads to murder civilians, reprisal killings, and collective punishment; use of child soldiers; and mistreatment of prisoners of war, including torture (Gutman and Rieff 1999). Inevitably, however, only captured members of the losing side have been brought to account for war crimes (Neier 1998).

The Vietnam War

U.S. involvement in the Vietnam War has been widely condemned as criminal by many people all over the world, including a significant number of Americans during the course of the war (Willson

2004; Young 1991). Billions of pounds of bombs were dropped on Vietnam, and millions of Vietnamese were killed, wounded, orphaned, or uprooted by the war. Hundreds of thousands of U.S. soldiers were wounded and traumatized, and tens of thousands lost their lives. In addition to staggering human costs, the Vietnam War had major enduring psychological, social, political, and economic costs (Starr 1998). Any benefits from waging war in Vietnam have been difficult to identify.

In one view, the U.S. engagement in the Vietnam War was illegal under U.S. law because Congress never specifically declared war, as required by the Constitution (although it did pass resolutions and appropriate funding for the war). Among the specific accusations of illegality by U.S.

forces are the use of napalm during air strikes, chemical warfare, torture of prisoners, burning of villages, illegal detention of civilians, bombing of hospitals and dikes, moral corruption, and sabotage of the Vietnamese economy. Some observers consider the destruction of millions of arable acres and hardwood forests to be an ecological crime of immense proportions.

The 1968 massacre of 504 Vietnamese men, women, and children in the village of My Lai (more correctly, Son My) by Lt. William Calley and his troops is the single most infamous episode of American criminality in Vietnam; it was hardly unique, however (Anderson 1998; Willson 2004; Young 1991). The subsequent trial and conviction of Lt. Calley, who served 35 months of house arrest on a military base, were widely criticized as deflecting attention from the far more substantial crimes of those higher in the chain of command, including the president and his associates. Richard Nixon, president during the latter period of the war, and Henry Kissinger, his secretary of state, have both been accused of duplicitous acts and complicity in perpetuating the war, mass murders, and other crimes occurring in the context of the war (Berman 2001; Hitchens 2001; Jacobs 2004). But no president, cabinet officer, or other high-level civilian or military official involved in the pursuit of the Vietnam War has ever been required to provide a formal defense for his policy decisions, and of course none has ever stood trial for war crimes.

U.S. Military Activity in the "New World Order"

More recent U.S. military ventures, including the invasions of Grenada and Panama, the mining of the Managua (Nicaragua) harbor, the Gulf War against Iraq, participation in the NATO action undertaken in the former Yugoslavia on behalf of Kosovo in 1999 on humanitarian grounds, actions in Afghanistan in 2002 as part of a war against international terrorism, and "Operation Iraqi Freedom" in 2003, were all criticized in some quarters as criminal actions (Halberstam 2001; Massing 2002; Schell 2003a). (See Box 5.2.)

Despite some history of antiwar mobilization—most conspicuously during the Vietnam War—the more enduring theme in American culture has resisted the imputation of criminality to American acts of war. U.S. political leaders have traditionally rejected, and are likely to continue to reject, the prospect of judgments of an international court concerning their military actions (Ignatieff 2005; Keller 2002; Russell 2005). In July 2002, the permanent International Criminal Court was formally in business, ratified by more than 70 nations, but not the United States, with jurisdiction to adjudicate allegations (against individuals, not nations) of war crimes, genocide, and crimes against humanity (Crossette 2002; Simons 2002). The Bush administration and some in Congress refused to support this endeavor, with the claim that American soldiers on peacekeeping missions could conceivably be indicted. Critics noted the many safeguards against politicized prosecutions and expressed the view that the Bush administration actually feared that American policymakers could be held accountable by this court.

FORMS OF STATE CRIMINALITY

State criminality, as a specific subtype of governmental crime, takes many forms and occurs on many different levels. When some form of state criminality becomes a dominant force in the operation of the state, we may be justified in labeling the state a *criminal state*.

In one view, a criminal state is any state successfully labeled as such by one or more other states that are either victorious over it or have the political power to impose such a label (Jenkins 1988). In modern history, Nazi Germany may be the single most prominent case of a state widely labeled as criminal because its criminality was virtually its defining feature (Luban 1987). But many other states have been candidates for this designation, from the Soviet Union to Saddam Hussein's Iraq. Many have characterized the United States as a criminal state due to its actions in the Vietnam

---

B O X 5.2   Post-9/11 Initiatives: Protecting Us against Terrorism or Perpetrating State Crimes?

The attack on America on September 11, 2001, result-ing in the collapse of the World Trade Center towers, substantial damage to the Pentagon, and the loss of several thousand lives, was a terrorist crime wholly at odds with what we mean when we refer to white collar crime. It was surely not about financial gain, and it also differed from white collar crime by perpetrating intentional harm through violence. But strong evi-dence indicated that the terrorists were affiliated with Osama bin Laden's Al Qaeda organization, which in turn was supported or at least harbored by the Taliban government of Afghanistan. Accordingly, the U.S. government declared Taliban Afghanistan a criminal state and launched a military attack in the fall and winter of 2001–2002. Subsequently, in his 2002 State of the Union address President George W. Bush identified several other states—Iraq, Iran, and North Korea—as part of an "axis of evil," or implicitly criminal states. The supreme religious leader of Iran in turn character-ized the United States as "the world's greatest evil" (Fathi 2002). Needless to say, the Taliban leadership and their allies also characterized the United States as a criminal state. A major poll conducted in many Islamic nations in 2002 found that only 9 percent of

people regarded the U.S. action in Afghanistan as morally justifiable; it seems reasonable to infer that many among the vast majority who did not regarded the United States in some sense as a criminal state (Stone 2002). Israel is clearly viewed as a criminal state by many Palestinians and their supporters, and the United States, as a major supporter of Israel, is seen as deeply complicit in the perceived crimes of Israel.

"Operation Iraqi Freedom," initiated in Spring 2003, was also at least partly rationalized by the Bush administration on the basis of claimed complicity of Saddam Hussein's regime with the 9/11 terrorists, but the legality and morality of the preemptive attack of Iraq has been a subject of ongoing controversy (Aronowitz and Gautney 2003; Dudziak 2003; Schlesinger 2004). Subsequently, the alleged long-term detention and alleged torture of many accused Taliban fighters at Guantanamo Bay in Cuba was severely criticized in many quarters as a form of state crime on the part of the United States; the Guantanamo Bay detentions were defended by the Bush administration as legitimate and necessary for addressing the ongoing terrorist threat (Judt 2005). In Iraq, many specific actions of the occupying U.S. forces—most famously,

---

and Gulf wars and the war against the Taliban in Afghanistan (see Box 5.2).

Accusations of state criminality are subjective and likely to incorporate an ideological dimension. The distinctions made here among some idealized types—the criminal state, the repressive state, the corrupt state, and the negligent state—are useful only in capturing the essential dimensions of a state's criminality. Predation, repression, corrup-tion, and negligence often coexist in varying degrees within any given state. We first consider the concept of the criminal state.

The Criminal State

The controversial notion of a criminal state is most commonly applied to the ultimate criminal enter-prise wherein the state is used as an instrument to commit crimes against humanity, such as genocide.

Even though the term *genocide* was coined as recently as World War II, such atrocities have taken place in some form throughout history in all parts of the world (Jonassohn and Bjornson 1998; Jones 2004). Some have applied the term *genocide* so broadly that it encompasses such policies as family planning and language regulation in schools, but most commonly it refers to a deliberate state policy of mass killing directed at some identifiable group of people (Chalk and Jonassohn 1990). The term *ethnic cleansing* has also been invoked in the recent era to describe large-scale killing of such groups (Mann 2005). Among the most prominent cases of genocide and ethnic cleansing in the 20th cen-tury are the hundreds of thousands of Armenians massacred in Turkey in 1915 (historically denied by the Turkish); millions of members of various groups liquidated in the Soviet Union during the Stalin regime (1922–1953) and in the People's

the sexual debasement and torture of detainees at Abu Ghraib prison—were also harshly condemned by many as clear violations of the Geneva Codes and as further acts of state crime (Greenberg and Dratel 2005). The Bush administration continued to defend the occupation itself while characterizing Abu Ghraib and other such events as aberrant acts of individual soldiers.

On the domestic front, the passage of the USA Patriot Act and a general expansion of investigative powers of criminal justice agencies, as well as increasing use of detention or deportation of many individuals alleged to have some kind of terrorist ties, were also both widely supported and widely criticized (Brown 2003). Were these initiatives necessary and effective policies for an ongoing war on terrorism, or were they forms of overreach by an increasingly autocratic administration, with basic infringements of American civil liberties and privacy rights? Conflicts on such matters were likely to be an ongoing characteristic of a post-9/11 America.

More generally, the United States has been characterized as a "*rogue*," "thug," "terrorist," or criminal state by some American critics, not only by foreigners. For example, William Blum (2000) noted that the United States has developed and sometimes used weapons of mass destruction, including nuclear, biological, and chemical weapons, and has engaged in sweeping bombing campaigns in many countries; has supported many repressive dictators (even perpetrators of genocide, such as Pol Pot) and many terrorists (including bin Laden when he was fighting the Soviet Union), as long as they have been viewed as advancing causes consistent with American interests; has been complicit in attempts to overthrow numerous popularly supported governments and populist movements around the world; has been the locus of training (i.e., the School of the Americas, at Ft. Benning, Georgia) for perpetrators of gross human rights violations in Latin America; and has been a party to assassinations, torture, kidnapping, looting, and the perversion of elections in many different countries. Noam Chomsky (2001) has characterized the United States as a "leading terrorist state" for its military actions in Nicaragua, Sudan, and elsewhere. Stephen Richards and Michael Avery (2000) have characterized the United States as a "thug" state based on what they characterize as increasing and unwarranted use of intelligence and police power.

Republic of China under Mao Tse-tung (1949–1976); up to 200,000 Hutus in the impoverished African country of Burundi killed by the politically dominant Tutsis in 1972 and after; up to 2 million Cambodian urbanites, members of the intelligentsia, and others murdered during the regime of Pol Pot and the Khmer Rouge (1975–1978); at least 500,000 Rwandans (primarily Tutsis) killed by government forces in 1994; and tens of thousands of ethnic minorities killed in Croatia, Bosnia, and Kosovo throughout the 1990s, primarily by Serbs.

The *Holocaust* perpetuated by the Nazis during World War II is perhaps the single most dramatic, fully documented, and extreme case of genocide ever, arguably unique in its scope and ambition, an appropriate candidate for the designation "the crime of the 20th century" (Friedrichs 2000b). It has been credibly estimated that between 5 million and 6 million Jews died at the hands of the Nazis, and many others (e.g., the mentally retarded, homosexuals, and gypsies) were also systematically exterminated (Hilberg 1980; Levin 1973). In addition to these crimes against humanity, the surviving Nazi leadership put on trial in Nuremberg after the war faced charges of war crimes and crimes against peace (Glaser and Possony 1979). The Nazi regime launched unprovoked attacks on other countries; committed numerous assassinations, acts of plundering, and other such criminal acts; and utterly subverted human rights. Do these acts constitute white collar crime? Box 5.3 considers that question.

The *Nuremberg Trials* generated some controversy over the question of whether the Nazi leaders could be tried by the Allies when no fully recognized international criminal law existed and whether some of the Nazis' alleged war crimes were substantially different from those committed by the Allies (Douglas 2001; Langenbacher 2004;

BOX 5.3   Adolf Hitler: The Greatest White Collar Criminal of the 20th Century?

What is the relationship between the criminal state (and genocide more generally) and white collar crime? John Braithwaite (1992), arguably the most accomplished white collar crime scholar today, has written that Adolf Hitler was "the greatest white-collar criminal of our century" (p. 100). In justifying this designation he wrote, "I trust that is it obvious that Hitler's genocide was a crime and fits Sutherland's definition of white-collar crime" (p. 107). But Sutherland's work on white collar crime dealt with it almost exclusively as a corporate and entrepreneurial activity for economic gain. Despite the fact that Sutherland's famous 1939 speech was made while Hitler was near the height of his power and that his 1949 book was published shortly after the full scope of Hitler's crimes had been revealed to the world, Sutherland made no references to Hitler in his work on white collar crime. His book's chapter on "war crimes" deals exclusively with the violation of wartime regulations and other (e.g., tax-related) laws by business people.

Some might argue that classifying Hitler and other tyrants as "white collar criminals" trivializes the enormity of their crimes by giving them membership in a group largely composed of price-fixing executives and embezzling employees. In this sense, it is preferable to consider genocide and related monstrous crimes not as white collar crime but rather as a cognate type of crime with a generic relationship to it—as a form of governmental crime that is the ultimate expression of the abuse of power, position, and trust (see Friedrichs 1996 for an elaboration on these themes).

Sklar 1964; Taylor 1970). Although some parties felt that the Nazi leadership should simply be shot without trial, the arguments in favor of a trial prevailed. Most of the Nazis were convicted and sentenced to death; several were sentenced to prison terms ranging from 10 years to life. In the years since the Nuremberg Trials, the argument that they made an important symbolic statement by administering justice to the guilty in an orderly way seems to have gained wide acceptance (Luban 1987).

Since the post–World War II trials, it has proven difficult to bring perpetrators of genocides and ethnic cleansing to justice, and much of the world has been quite indifferent to these events. However, in 1999 a Spanish court attempted to extradite former Chilean head of state Augusto Pinochet to stand trial on charges involving the alleged beating, burning, caging, binding, starving, and sodomizing of victims of state persecution during his time in office (Hoge 1999). General Pinochet had taken power as part of a military coup against a democratically elected president, Salvador Allende, a socialist, and Pinochet's government ruthlessly attempted to purge socialist elements from Chile's government (Webber 1999). Arrested in England, Pinochet was ultimately ruled

to be unfit at age 84 to stand trial and was sent back to Chile (Hoge 2000). He was subsequently found fit for trial in Chile and was acquitted in one such case (*New York Times* 2005d). In 2005, he was still facing other charges in Chile.

Special tribunals were formed to try those accused of genocidal activity in Rwanda and in Bosnia and the Balkans (Booth 2003). In June 2001, Slobodan Milosevic, the former Yugoslav leader, was turned over to the United Nations for trial in The Hague, becoming the first former head of state to be brought before an international war crimes court to answer for actions committed during his regime (Hagan 2003; Simons 2001). In 2006, Milosevic died in jail, after denying his guilt and declaring the U.N. charges against him to be lies, attacking NATO's bombing of his capital as the real war crime, and claiming that his own actions involved a war against terrorism within his country. This trial established an important precedent for holding heads of state responsible for war crimes and other state crimes committed by their government. Saddam Hussein, in 2005, was awaiting trial for such crimes in Iraq.

Although the crimes of Pol Pot of Cambodia were especially monstrous, he was never tried prior to his death in 1998; it took the United Nations 18 years to recognize the crimes that took place in the "killing fields" of Cambodia, and more than 25 years after they ended, no Khmer Rouge leader had yet been brought to justice (Fawthrop and Jarvis 2004; Short 2005). The alleged killing of between 300,000–400,000 people in the Darfur region of Sudan and the displacement of some 2 million people in 2003–2005 elicited little attention from the United States or other countries (Kristof 2005; Power 2004; Simons 2005). In 2005, the United Nations Security Council asked the new International Criminal Court to begin investigating these crimes.

The United States has refused to subject itself to the judgment of international courts and ignored a World Court finding that it had engaged in illegal acts of war involving the mining of Nicaraguan territorial waters in the 1980s (Ignatieff 2005; Kahn 1987). Furthermore, the United States was one of the few countries unwilling to endorse the establishment of a permanent *International Criminal Court* as a means in the 21st century of bringing perpetrators of state crime to justice (Mullins, Kauzlarich, and Rothe 2004; Russell 2005). The long-term consequences of this stance remained to be seen.

The Repressive State

A second form of state criminality takes the form of a *repressive state*. This state does not go so far as waging a formal campaign of genocide, but it systematically deprives its citizens of fundamental human rights.

The idea of *human rights* is rooted in ancient tradition; the Bible is but one early source (Ishay 2004). Our current understanding of human rights is principally a product of the writing of Enlightenment philosophers such as Thomas Hobbes, John Locke, Charles-Louis Montesquieu, and Jean-Jacques Rousseau, who argued in various ways that humans were naturally entitled to what the Declaration of Independence so eloquently called "Life, Liberty and the Pursuit of Happiness." These ideas became increasingly influential

in the Western world in the 18th century. In one sense the American and French revolutions were precipitated by a perception that a people—the American colonists and French "Third Estate," respectively—were being "criminally" deprived of fundamental human rights, by the British monarchy in the one case and the French *ancien régime* in the other.

Although efforts to promote human rights as an international concern have been made since the early 19th century, until World War I the matter of human rights was essentially a domestic concern. Many of the world's governments have made little effort to acknowledge fully and guarantee the range of rights considered an entitlement in most Western democracies today. The widespread condemnation of slavery and the promotion of certain rights of minorities, aliens, and prisoners of war in the 19th and 20th centuries were notable exceptions to this general proposition (Driscoll 1989; Ishay 2004).

The United Nations was formed after World War II, partly in response to the gross and conspicuous abuse of the most fundamental human rights by the totalitarian governments of the time. Though the United Nations Universal Declaration of Human Rights of 1948 identified a long list of fundamental human rights—from the right to life, liberty, and the security of person to the right to work and to leisure—the United Nations has not been able to impose these standards on any government. The rhetoric of human rights is a major source of current notions of international crime (Cohen 1993; Ross 2000), but states around the world almost universally deny that they are guilty of any such crimes.

South Africa, dominated for 300 years by the white minority and culminating in the establishment of the *apartheid* system of formal racial discrimination, was a premier example of a repressive state (Hayner 2002; Sparks 1990). In the latter half of the 20th century—before the establishment of a democratic system and the election of Nelson Mandela as president in 1994—South Africa was regarded by much of the world as a pariah and was the target of widespread sanctions. Although apartheid South Africa has been called a "criminal state," it differed from Nazi Germany in that repression rather than extermination was its central objective.

Repression and the deprivation of rights can occur in any political system, including a Western democracy, but in the 20th century they were most closely associated with dictatorships. The principal motivating factor in the imposition of a repressive system of government is the extension or retention of power, often for its own sake. Repression of rights has certainly facilitated blatant economic exploitation, but this combination has contributed to the downfall of a number of "traditional" dictatorships, including that of the Shah of Iran, Anastasio Somoza of Nicaragua, Ferdinand Marcos of the Philippines, and François Duvalier of Haiti. To many Westerners, the Communist dictatorships of the Soviet Union and the Eastern bloc nations exemplified the repressive state, and surely the repressive elements of these systems ultimately contributed to their political downfall.

In the second half of the 20th century, numerous "modern" dictatorships emerged in developing or third-world countries, and many of them endured for decades. These modern dictators have often come to power in coups or revolutions conducted against traditional right-wing monarchies or dictatorships in the name of promoting broader social justice, a goal they accomplish at least to some degree, along with promoting some sense of national pride and purpose (Rubin 1987). But modern dictators "most often continue or intensify injustice, fear, torture, discrimination, lack of liberty, pervasive material and spiritual corruption, poisonous propaganda, violent hatred, xenophobia, economic decay and aggression" (Rubin 1987; 263). A list of the world's 10 worst dictators in 2005 included: Omar al-Bashir of Sudan; Kim Jong II of North Korea; Than Shwe of Burma (Myanmar); Hu Jintao of China; Crown Prince Abdullah of Saudi Arabia (since deceased); Muammar al Qaddafi of Libya; Pervez Musharraf of Pakistan; Sparamurat Niyazov of Turkmenistan; Robert Mugabe of Zimbabwe; and Teodoro Obiang Nguema of Equatorial Guinea (Wallechinsky 2005).

The fundamental hypocrisy of allegations of repression in revolutionary third-world dictatorships by the United States and other Western democracies that had previously tolerated or actively supported corrupt, repressive right-wing dictatorships in these countries is a recurring theme. After some of the repressive dictatorships supported by the United States were overthrown in the 1970s and 1980s, considerable controversy ensued over whether the governments that replaced them (e.g., the Sandinistas in Nicaragua and the Islamic fundamentalists in Iran) increased or diminished the level of state repression or criminality.

The Corrupt State

A *corrupt state* refers to a government used as an instrument to enrich its leadership. The case of the Philippines under Ferdinand Marcos provides one well-documented example of a corrupt state. For two decades, the leadership engaged in the systematic enrichment of the president, his family, and his cronies with billions of dollars at the expense of the country's general welfare (Carbonell-Catilo 1986; Kang 2002). During the 30-year reign of the Somoza family in Nicaragua, family members and allied families were alleged to have accumulated a fortune of some $1 billion, including ownership of much of the country's best land and control of two dozen important industries (Herman 1982; Rubin 1987). Although Marcos and Somoza had to flee their countries when their regimes collapsed, neither was ever brought to justice.

Corruption is virtually an institutionalized part of the political system in some countries. Among the countries identified as being especially corrupt in recent years are Cameroon, Nigeria, Indonesia (see Box 5.4), Azerbaijan, Uzbekistan, Ukraine, Honduras, Tanzania, Yugoslavia, Paraguay, and Kenya (O'Brien 1999c; Markovskaya, Pridemore, and Nakajima 2003). China, an emerging economic superpower by 2005, was plagued by massive corruption on the part of the political and economic elite (Barboza 2005; Qinglian 2004). If systematic corruption is carried out by the leadership of the country, we can claim a corrupt state exists.

One can identify many other examples of corrupt states. The former president of South Korea

---

B O X 5.4   Suharto and the Looting of Indonesia

In Indonesia, Suharto governed as president for 32 years, and during this time he and his family are believed to have acquired $73 billion, with some $15 billion of this fortune still in their control after Suharto was forced from office in 1998 (Colmey and Liebhold 1999).

Suharto's immediate family controlled major banks, real estate, shipping, oil and gas exploration, petrochemicals, auto production, hotels, and transportation systems, among other enterprises (Meyer 1998). In one estimate, 80 percent of major contracts went to Suharto's children and friends. Although he accomplished some economic and political gains for his country, Suharto ultimately failed to differentiate between the interests of his family and those of the state (Erlanger 1998). Suharto was formally charged with corruption in August 2000 (Mydans 2000). In 2004, Suharto was at the top of a list of embezzling leaders of the world's countries (Agence France-Presse 2004).

---

was arrested late in 1995 and charged with accepting hundreds of millions of dollars in bribes while he was in office (Kang 2002; Kristof 1995). The family of Pakistani Prime Minister Benazir Bhutto was accused in 1998 of acquiring a fortune in excess of $100 million, in part by soliciting huge bribes from foreign corporations (Burns 1998). Leaders in war-ravaged Bosnia were alleged in 1999 to have stolen up to $1 billion in relief aid and embassy funds (Hedges 1999).

Many African nations are widely regarded as pervasively corrupt, and some of the leadership spectacularly so (LaFraniere 2005; Williams 1987). After Mobutu Sese Seko became president of Zaire, he allegedly accumulated assets of $3 billion and built 11 palaces for himself (Lamb 1987). While Mobutu was stealing billions from his country, most of the people of Zaire were living in desperate poverty, reduced to eating a single meal a day, and the country was disintegrating physically and politically (Wrong 2001). Mobutu's government was overthrown by rebel forces in 1997, and he died in exile shortly after. General Sani Abacha of Nigeria also stole billions of dollars from a country afflicted with widespread poverty and other severe social problems (Masland and Bartholet 2000). Abacha died of a heart attack in 1998 at age 53, while participating in an orgy with several prostitutes. Charles Taylor, president of Liberia for six years, was alleged to have stolen or diverted some $100 million of his country's wealth (Weiner 2003a). His country was then ranked the poorest in the world.

In 2005, efforts were being made in some African countries to address the problem of corruption more effectively (LaFraniere 2005). Pervasive corruption was inhibiting outside aid by developed countries and was also stalling economic development, generating cynicism and bitterness among citizens, and contributing to circumstances of desperate poverty for many of these citizens.

Polls in Latin America in 2005 indicated that Latin Americans regarded corruption as their most serious problem (Rohter and Forero 2005). This was an enormous source of frustration and disillusionment in this region, with one poll suggesting that a majority of Latin Americans would prefer economically efficient dictatorships over corrupt and inefficient democracies. By some estimates, some 15 percent of annual growth in Latin American countries was deflected by corruption, and foreign investors were being scared off by this problem. People in Brazil were especially disheartened that corruption seemed to escalate rather than decline following the coming to power of Lula da Silva, a former union leader who ran on a platform to restore integrity to the government. But corruption was a pervasive problem in many other Latin American countries, including Peru, Ecuador, Argentina, Paraguay, Bolivia, Costa Rica, Guatemala, and Mexico.

In the case of developing African countries, various factors contribute to corruption, including the absence of a civil service "work ethic," extreme economic inequality, a lack of disciplined leadership, extensive bureaucratic powers, cultural norms favoring tribal loyalties over integrity, and the absence of countervailing forces such as opposition parties or a free press (Hope 1987). If political corruption is to be diminished (if not eradicated) in these countries, a fundamental transformation of the entire administrative structure and related cultural norms must take place.

State Negligence

If state corruption describes a situation in which the political leadership proactively loots the country's wealth, *state negligence* describes a situation in which "crimes of omission" are committed. The state fails to prevent loss of human life, suffering, and deprivation that are in its power to prevent (Barak 1991). The concept could even be extended to apply to circumstances in which the state's finite resources are wasted on a vast scale through gross bureaucratic inefficiencies, negligence, and incompetence.

Of course, it can be difficult to distinguish among malfeasance (doing something you are prohibited from doing), nonfeasance (failing to do something you are required to do), and misfeasance (performing a permissible act in an improper manner) (Gardiner 1986). Surely many people would object to extending the concept of criminality to include negligence and wastefulness, which are never subject to criminal prosecution if no demonstrable fraud is involved. But it may be worthwhile to examine such criminality and to ask ourselves both how it differs from "proactive" forms of criminality and whether it should and could be formally defined as criminal. Attention to wasteful and negligent governmental practices promotes appreciation of the enormous costs to taxpayers of poor governmental stewardship, incompetence, and inherently distorted priorities and policies.

The most serious form of negligent state criminality involves the unnecessary and premature loss of life that occurs when the government and its agents fail to act affirmatively in certain situations. In the international realm, this claim arises most starkly in relation to genocide. David Wyman (1984) claimed that during World War II, U.S. leaders knew about the Nazi death camps and were criminally negligent in failing to act more aggressively against the Nazis' systematic genocide. In *A Problem from Hell*, Samantha Power (2002) has documented many other occasions when the United States has had both the knowledge and the means to intervene in cases of genocide abroad and has failed to do so. These claims raise complicated and contentious questions.

On the domestic front, the infant mortality rate in the United States generally declined during the 20th century, but it rose, especially among poor African American families, in the early 1980s in conjunction with the Reagan administration's reductions in maternal and infant health care programs (Boone 1989). Although many factors contribute to the relatively high infant mortality rate among poor African American families in America, government negligence appears to be one contributing factor. More recently, claims were made that states were lax in testing for lead poisoning in poor children (Pear 1999c). Poor children are especially likely to be exposed to lead (for example, from chipped paint in rundown tenements), and such exposure can lead to serious neurological and health-related problems.

In a similar vein, the political leadership in the United States has been accused of responding too slowly and ineffectively to the AIDS epidemic as it evolved in the 1980s; thousands of deaths might have been prevented with a more potent response (Shilts 1987). The derelict actions of the U.S. government, and state and local governments as well, have been attributed to the fact that AIDS first surfaced in America in the gay community and has continued to afflict disproportionately several underprivileged and stigmatized social groups, including drug addicts and prostitutes. Even though it is acknowledged that many other parties bear responsibility for this tragic epidemic, some AIDS activists have called political leaders "murderers" because they could have implemented more effective preventive policies in response to this new "holocaust" and failed to do so (Kramer L. 1989). Rates of AIDS infection in China, Ethiopia, India, Nigeria, and Russia were rising so rapidly early in the 21st century that by 2010 an estimated

50 million to 75 million people could be affected in these countries, posing a large security risk to their regions as well as to the United States (Altman 2002).

Gregg Barak and Robert Bohm (1989) have argued that the "crime of homelessness"—the state's failure to enact laws and formulate policies that provide all people of limited means with affordable housing—should concern us more than the crimes of the homeless. Stuart Henry (1978) classified the existence of an underground economy as a state crime of omission, charging that the state's failure to control the distribution of wealth at the source forces many people into an underground economy, a predicament that makes them especially vulnerable to illicit drug use and involvement in conventional criminal activity. In addition, the sheer wastefulness of many government programs, amounting by some estimates to hundreds of billions of dollars over only three years, can be regarded as crimes of negligence (Diamond 1986; Hershey 1984).

Examples of government wastefulness include pork barrel projects, overly generous federal pensions, lax loan collection procedures, inefficient subsidies, and the maintenance of unnecessary military bases. Furthermore, early in the 21st century, government auditors alleged that many federal agencies could not account for billions of dollars of federal funding under their control (Brinkley 2002). Some $33 billion in erroneous payments for Medicare and other programs were sent out by these agencies.

The concept of state negligence (or wastefulness) could be extended to include inadequate or inefficient governmental responses to poverty in general, to crime, to environmental degradation, and the like. Governmental negligence is principally a consequence both of ideological commitments to favoring particular programs and constituencies over others (e.g., defense spending over antipoverty programs or businesspeople over homeless people), and of decisions of political expediency (i.e., choosing those policy initiatives most likely to produce political dividends). Accordingly, the concept of state negligence may be seen by some as too remote

and tangential to be linked with white collar crime in any meaningful way. But if harmful, even fatal, consequences and unnecessary economic losses occur because of the negligent or wasteful practices of government officials, such results are certainly criminal in the humanistic sense and should be included in the roster of the principal forms of governmental crime.

STATE-ORGANIZED CRIME

In a presidential address to the American Society of Criminology, William J. Chambliss (1989) defined the concept of *state-organized crime* as "acts defined by law as criminal and committed by state officials in pursuit of their job as representatives of the state" (p. 184). Chambliss specifically excluded criminal acts that benefit individual officeholders. Even though state-organized crime is carried out on behalf of a government entity, the lines between individual and organizational benefit cannot always be so easily drawn.

Piracy is one of the earliest forms of state-organized crime. There is evidence that corrupt governors cooperated with pirates in Ancient Greece and Rome, and during the Middle Ages the Vikings operated as pirates on behalf of Scandinavian governments (Mueller and Adler 1985; Peterson M. J. 1989). During the 16th and 17th centuries, the British, French, and Dutch governments arranged for pirates such as Sir Francis Drake to attack Spanish and Portuguese ships returning from the New World laden with vast mineral riches; the state got a share of the loot in return for protection and sponsorship (Chambliss 1989; Jachel 1981; Peterson M. J. 1989). During the colonial period in America, corrupt governments in New York City and Charleston, South Carolina, cultivated and protected pirates (including the notorious Edward Teach, or "Blackbeard") and profited accordingly (Browning and Gerassi 1980; Mueller and Adler 1985). Of course, state policy was not uniformly supportive of piracy, and during certain periods governments were actively hostile toward it (Jachcel 1981). But the overall history of relations between governments and pirates suggests that plundering is overlooked or actively encouraged by the state when it benefits from such activity.

Chambliss (1989) identified various other forms of state-organized crime, including state complicity in smuggling, assassinations, criminal conspiracies, spying on citizens, diverting funds illegally, selling arms to blacklisted countries, and supporting terrorists.

Terrorism, including assassination, torture, and kidnapping, although commonly thought of as crimes of individuals and groups outside of government, has often been carried out by agents of the state on behalf of the state (Stohl and Lopez 1984). Indeed, the term *terrorism* was first applied to the post–French Revolution government, which ruled by intimidation (Stern 1999). In the modern era, states have been accused of carrying out terrorism directly when they engage in massive bombing of civilian populations. For example, the British bombing of Dresden and the American bombing of Hiroshima and Nagasaki during World War II have been described in these terms. At the same time, Nazi Germany and Imperialist Japan also engaged in massive terrorizing of civilian populations (Stern 1999). Stalin's brutal actions against citizens of his own state, the activities of the Guatemalan government over a period of decades, and Saddam Hussein's chemical warfare against Kurds in northern Iraq are all offered as examples of direct forms of state terrorism. In the early 1980s, an estimated 90,000 Latin Americans "disappeared" at the hands of state forces (Herman 1982). Even though *wholesale* acts of terrorism the state wages against citizens of other countries, its own citizens, and independence or revolutionary movements may be much more consequential, such acts receive less scholarly attention than do conventional forms of *retail terrorism* (Green and Ward 2004; Herman 1982; Barak 1990). We must also consider the relationship between wholesale and retail terrorism (Pillar 2001). On the one hand, conventional terrorists may justify their activities by reference to the alleged terrorism of the United States; on the other

hand, if the United States is to combat conventional terrorism effectively, it must seek cooperation from states that have either engaged in state terrorism or have supported some forms of conventional terrorism.

Many countries have directly or indirectly sponsored state terrorism and independent terrorist groups. The United States has sold billions of dollars worth of arms and ammunition to *client states* all over the world; those countries have used these munitions for state terrorist activities and for training hundreds of thousands of military and police personnel (Blum 2000; Cottam and Marenin 1989; Herman 1982). In El Salvador in the early 1980s, for example, more than 10,000 people were murdered in a single year by government forces supported by the United States, and as many as 70,000 may have been kidnapped and tortured to death between 1981 and 1988 (Agee 1988; Herman 1982). It seems unlikely that the countless murders committed by "death squads" in El Salvador and other U.S. client states can be attributed to "out of control" security forces. Without in any way minimizing the crimes of "conventional" terrorists, such as Timothy McVeigh in Oklahoma City and the 9/11 suicide plane hijackers, it is clear that much of the worst terrorism—in terms of human suffering— has been carried out on behalf of the state (Chomsky 2001; Green and Ward 2004; Herman 1982).

The White House and State-Organized Crime

Some of the most significant state-organized crime in the United States emanated directly from the White House. Investigation of the *Watergate* affair in the 1970s revealed that the Nixon White House was involved in a range of improper and illegal "political policing" endeavors (Wise 1976). At the specific insistence of President Nixon, secret wiretaps were used against journalists and government officials suspected of being "disloyal" to the White House agenda in Vietnam and elsewhere. This improper wiretapping scheme, which the president and his associates later attempted to justify on national security grounds but had never properly authorized, provided a basis for one of the articles of impeachment drawn up against President Nixon. The exposure of the so-called "White House Plumbers" also contributed to Nixon's downfall. Over several years, a group of special operatives, including former New York City police officers, CIA agents, and anti-Castro fighters, engaged in various highly questionable or blatantly illegal "investigations"; the most notorious was the break-in at the office of the psychiatrist (Dr. Lew Fielding) of Daniel Ellsberg, a former defense analyst who made the Pentagon Papers public (Wise 1976). The White House Plumbers were controlled by high-level Nixon aides operating from within the White House.

In the 1980s, the single most celebrated case of state-organized crime was the *Iran-Contra Affair*, or "Irangate" (Draper 1991; Pfost 1991; Simon 2006). At the heart of this case was the authorization, emanating from the White House, of the sale of weapons to Iran in exchange for funds to arm and support the Contras, who were fighting to overthrow the Sandinista government in Nicaragua. The principal illegality involved was violation of the Boland Amendment, which had expressly prohibited such covert aid to the Contras. The Iran-Contra enterprise, in fact, violated both Article 1, Section 9 of the U.S. Constitution, which requires that all funds raised by the U.S. government go through the Treasury and be approved by a congressional act, and the 19th-century Neutrality Act, which prohibits military expenditures against governments with which the United States is not at war.

The Reagan administration's involvement in the Iran-Contra scheme was broadly rationalized by invoking the promise of democracy in Nicaragua and a concern with human life. But the United States had supported the Somoza dictatorship, hardly a bastion of democracy, for decades, had boycotted the 1984 Nicaraguan elections (given a stamp of approval by international observers), had sought aid for the Contras from decidedly nondemocratic countries, and had attempted to circumvent constitutional constraints in the United States to provide aid to the Contras.

The Iran-Contra case involved a conspiracy to violate the Boland Act, to defraud the government of money and power, and to commit perjury before Congress and obstruction of justice. A major congressional investigation and an independent prosecutor's investigation focused on the case.

Allegations of improper use of White House power hardly ended with the Reagan administration. The administration of his successor George H. W. Bush was alleged to have participated in arranging arms shipments and other payments to the regime of Saddam Hussein in Iraq, which was covered up after the administration initiated the Persian Gulf War against Iraq (Hagan 1997). The administrations of Presidents Bill Clinton and George W. Bush have also been targets of claims of complicity in crimes on a large scale in connection with military interventions in Sudan, Kosovo, Afghanistan, and Iraq; support for sanctions against Cuba, Iraq, Haiti, and Serbia; failure to intervene in genocidal campaigns in Rwanda; and other forms of state activity (Chomsky 2001; Garfield 2002; Power 2002). In 2005, with increasing evidence surfacing that the American people were quite deliberately deceived with false claims of weapons of mass destruction in Iraq and of Iraqi 9/11 connections, George W. Bush was being compared with other presidents who lied to the American people—e.g., Richard Nixon on Watergate and Vietnam (Herbert 2005). Ralph Nader had already called for Bush's impeachment over the war in Iraq (Lueck 2004). But to date none of the claims identified here have been formally pursued by either domestic or international tribunals.

State-Organized Crime and Federal Investigative Agencies

Some of the most significant state-organized crime is carried out under the auspices of governmental agencies with investigative powers, including the Central Intelligence Agency (CIA), the Federal Bureau of Investigation (FBI), and the Internal Revenue Service (IRS). The FBI in particular plays an important role in the investigation and prosecution of some of the most significant white collar crime. In recent years, though, charges have surfaced that these agencies have engaged in forms of governmental crime.

The Central Intelligence Agency The CIA was established after World War II to prevent another Pearl Harbor, a surprise attack on U.S. territory, and in response to the emerging "Cold War" (Jeffreys-Jones 1989; Whitaker 2000). An intelligence agency by definition engages in covert operations that, at least sometimes, are of doubtful legality in the context within which they occur.

In 1975, a congressional investigation uncovered clear evidence that the CIA had periodically violated its own charter (Johnson 1985; Prados 1986; Wise 1976). The violations included illegal opening of U.S. mail over several years; prohibited surveillance of various domestic dissident organizations; assassination plots against foreign leaders; unlawful stockpiling of deadly poisons and conducting dangerous, mind-altering experiments with unwitting subjects; complicity in the Watergate affair; and assisting in the bribing and blackmailing of foreign leaders. Over a period of decades, the CIA intervened improperly in the affairs of many countries, funneling support to corrupt, totalitarian political leaders (including Panama's notorious Manuel Noriega) it viewed as supportive of U.S. policies while aiding in the downfall of other political leaders regarded as threatening to U.S. corporate interests (Jeffreys-Jones 1989; Kempe 1990; Prados 1986). CIA involvement in overthrowing the democratically elected, leftist government of Salvador Allende in Chile in 1973 is one of the best-documented cases of the latter type of intervention. This type of CIA operation has helped generate anti-American sentiments in many parts of the world.

The CIA has been accused of having a right-wing bias and of placing its own interests ahead of other considerations, including compliance with the law. Many Americans have supported CIA operations and objectives and have viewed CIA personnel in heroic terms while vilifying their Soviet counterparts in the KGB (Andrew and Gordievsky 1990; Ranelagh 1986). The fall of the Soviet Union has arguably reduced the importance of this form of support for the CIA. With the 9/11 attack on America, two different forms of criticism were directed at the CIA. On one hand, it was faulted for having failed, perhaps due to insufficient attention to human intelligence gathering, to anticipate and expose the attack plot; on the other hand, it was known to have supported the Taliban mullahs who shielded the Al Qaeda terrorist network during the Afghanistan war to expel the Soviets (National Commission 2004; Rashid 2000; Schoenfield 2001). In an environment of intensified fear of terrorism, however, many Americans were likely to be more concerned with effective intelligence gathering by the CIA, by whatever means, than with possible illegal or unethical acts by CIA agents.

The Federal Bureau of Investigation Throughout most of the legendary reign of J. Edgar Hoover (1924–1972) the FBI generally enjoyed a reputation for integrity and high professional standards. After Hoover's death in 1972, revelations of improper and illegal FBI activities became much more frequent. It emerged that the FBI had been engaging in warrantless wiretapping and unauthorized domestic spying for decades (Theoharis 2004). Much FBI activity focused on suppressing political views at odds with those of the conservative Hoover.

While still a young U.S. attorney, Hoover had been appointed FBI director at a time when the small government agency was plagued by corruption charges. The FBI (originally, the Bureau of Investigation) had participated in controversial dragnet raids on draft dodgers and radicals during World War I, and its highest officials had been charged with hindering the investigations of war contractor fraud and the corrupt Teapot Dome dealings (Poveda 1990). Although the FBI and Hoover were not immune to criticism during the years up to 1972 (and especially during the tumultuous 1960s), Hoover was by any measure enormously skillful in promoting a favorable public image of the agency and in maintaining relationships with powerful politicians.

Following Hoover's death, the FBI became much more vulnerable to criticism, in part as a consequence of a Nixon administration initiative to reform government intelligence agencies (Poveda 1990). In the mid-1970s in particular,

FBI involvement in various abuses or outright illegalities came to light. From the mid-1950s on, the FBI had engaged in extralegal and illegal disruption and destabilization of dissident political groups through *COINTELPRO*, the umbrella name for various counterintelligence programs (Richards and Avery 2000). Close to 300 surreptitious entries and burglaries were conducted between 1942 and 1968 against at least 14 domestic organizations. Over many decades, Hoover maintained secret files on public officials, a practice that amounted to an implicit, if not explicit, blackmailing scheme. Through several different administrations, the White House was allowed to use the FBI to gather political intelligence for partisan purposes. Some internal financial corruption occurred; FBI agents accepted kickbacks from an electronics firm, and agency personnel performed personal services for Hoover. Finally, informants were used as agent provocateurs to instigate illegal actions by dissident groups (Poveda 1990; Simon 2006).

Even though the exposure of scandalous FBI practices in the 1970s ultimately reduced the FBI's autonomy and almost certainly imposed some constraints on illegalities and corruption, it is not clear that such patterns have been eradicated. Between 1981 and 1985, the FBI engaged in extensive investigation of more than 100 individuals and groups opposed to the Reagan administration's Central America policies (Jacoby 1988). In the 1990s and early in the new century, the FBI was criticized for making certain files available to the Clinton White House and for complicity with organized crime (Butterfield 2002a; Stewart 1996). On the other hand, the FBI has sometimes mounted undercover operations and used deceitful tactics to produce evidence against powerful and sophisticated white collar and governmental criminals (Marx 1988). Evaluation of some of the FBI's "dirty tricks" may be shaped by biases regarding the targets of the operations.

Following 9/11, the FBI was criticized for its sluggish response to suspicious activities (and persons) and for failing to uncover the terrorist plot (National Commission 2004; Theoharis 2004). Subsequently, the FBI adopted some practices in the "war on terror" that were criticized as infringing on American civil liberties and privacy rights: for example, "Project Carnivore," an Internet surveillance program that is highly intrusive (Ventura, Miller, and DeFlem 2005). Was the FBI negligent in failing to anticipate 9/11, or was it perpetrating a form of state crime in its response to that event? In one view, the allocation of FBI resources was far from optimal.

Thus far, our examination of state-organized crime has concentrated on the federal and state levels. But "state-organized" crime also occurs at the local level in the form of police crime.

Police Crime

Among governmental crimes committed by relatively low-level officials, *police crimes* tend to be especially consequential. It may be useful to distinguish between police crime as a form of state-organized crime involving the abuse of power and police crime as occupational crime, primarily corruption (Barker and Carter 1986; Ross 2003), but it is not always possible to differentiate between organizational and personal motivations or objectives.

The history of police crime is long and varied, involving violations of constitutional rights, excessive use of force, and related illegal acts to fulfill state or departmental objectives (Walker 1980, 1983). This abuse of police power has been disproportionately directed toward minorities, the poor, political dissidents, and members of the counterculture (Green and Ward 2004; Platt and Cooper 1974; Skolnick 1969). Many of the major urban race riots in the 1960s and since were precipitated by abuse of African Americans by white police officers; the 1991 Rodney King case, in which the brutal beating of a man pulled over for speeding was videotaped, is only one of the more recent and widely publicized of a long line of such incidents (Levy 1968; National Advisory Commission on Civil Disorders 1968; Roberg and Kuykendall 1993).

The most serious form of police brutality is the sometimes-fatal misuse of deadly force (Fyfe 1988; Sherman and Langworthy 1979). In one high profile case, several New York City police officers fatally shot an immigrant, Amandou Diallou, 41 times as he was reaching for his wallet while standing in a building doorway (Robinson 2002a). Historically, police brutality has rarely been prosecuted and only in recent decades has this situation improved with the establishment of civilian review boards, citizen mobilization, and a more attentive press. An ongoing debate focuses on whether the improper use of force is ever justified to control crime. This has been called the *"Dirty Harry" problem*, reference to a Clint Eastwood film character called "Dirty Harry" Callahan, a police inspector who uses blatantly illegal actions to force information out of a sadistic kidnapper (Klockars 1980). Such tactics are regularly featured on television police dramas, such as *NYPD Blue*.

Police brutality is not the only form of police abuse of power. The Mollen Commission reported in 1994 that New York City police officers frequently committed perjury, made searches without warrants and false arrests, and tampered with evidence (Sexton 1994). Perjury in court testimony was especially common and was known among the police as *testilying*. The officers crossed the line into illegality either to achieve the department's crime-fighting objectives more efficiently or to advance their own careers.

Police crime has received a fair amount of attention, but other low-level criminal justice personnel succumb to the temptations to commit occupationally related crimes (Henderson and Simon 1994; Parenti 1999). Abuse of authority and various forms of corruption occur within all components of the criminal justice system, including the courts and correctional institutions.

POLITICAL WHITE COLLAR CRIME

Earlier in this chapter, we defined political white collar crime as governmental or political party officials engaging in illegal and improper activity for personal gain (e.g., economic enrichment or political advantage) rather than to advance some state goal. Political white collar crime is also committed on behalf of political parties, rather than simply for personal gain.

Political System Corruption

Free elections and competing political parties are defining elements of Western democracies, and most observers would agree that such systems avoid some of the extreme abuses of power associated with one-party systems. But the electoral process and interparty competition in such societies promote their own forms of corruption. In the progressive view, democracy is something of an illusion in a system in which a small *power elite* controls decision making and the general population is largely indoctrinated with the "official line" by a compliant press (Chomsky 2002; Mills 1956; Tombs and Whyte 2003). Nevertheless, at least some differences in policy preferences exist between the two major parties in the United States, and competition is a real element in the electoral process.

Once politicians gain the power of office, they more often than not attempt to hold onto it (see Box 5.5). Incumbency has advantages: enhanced name recognition, the capacity to implement programs for and grant favors to special interests and constituents, a well-documented record of accomplishments, and voters' tendency to prefer stability over change. It has never been illegal for politicians to propose, endorse, or push through policies and programs that, despite questionable value, still benefit special interests and constituents, as long as no direct *quid pro quo* ("this for that") exists.

Corruption in the Electoral Financing Process

We tend to view political corruption in individualistic terms because it is easier and more reassuring to focus on individual wrongdoers. Etzioni (1988a) related this tendency to the misleading personality cult prevalent in the media, Americans' pride in their system of government, and the failure to recognize that the beneficiaries of corruption have managed to legalize most of it. The financing of elections,

---

B O X 5.5   The Watergate Affair

The single most famous contemporary case of political crime motivated by the desire to stay in power is the Watergate affair, which ultimately led to the resignation of President Richard Nixon. Watergate had two primary aspects: a break-in and burglary in June 1972 and the broad range of abuses of power by the Nixon administration, including illegal surveillance, dirty tricks, cover-ups, and enemies' lists (Emery 1994; Silverstein 1988). For one commentator (Hitt 2004: 1) Watergate established the "template" for later public and private sector scandals: "the fallen giant, the whistle-blower, the dogged journalist, the arrogant lieutenants, the little people left twisting in the wind."

The original incident was a break-in at the Democratic National Party Headquarters in the Watergate complex in Washington, DC, carried out by individuals affiliated with the Committee to Reelect the President (CREEP) and the White House itself. Initially the Nixon White House tried to dismiss the whole matter as a "third-rate burglary" in which they had no part, but over the course of the next two years, a massive cover-up conspiracy, with Nixon directly involved, ensued. Investigative reporters (especially Bob Woodward and Carl Bernstein of *The Washington Post*), a special prosecutor, and congressional investigative committees uncovered this conspiracy, including the direct involvement of numerous highly placed Nixon administration and reelection campaign officials. Impeachment proceedings were initiated against Nixon, who in August 1974 resigned the presidency rather than face virtually certain removal from office. Although Nixon was controversially pardoned and excused from criminal liability by his successor, Gerald Ford, many of his close associates went to prison.

One explanation of Watergate is that Nixon and his associates were uniquely corrupt and unprincipled and that the origins of Watergate can be traced to Nixon's paranoia and flawed personality. An alternative view is that the Watergate crimes were products of a political system that imposes high expectations on presidents but frustrates them with checks and balances; in such a system, maintaining, exercising, and extending power takes precedent over integrity and compliance with the law. In this view, most recent U.S. American presidents have authorized similar evasions or violations of law (Silverstein 1988). As is often the case, both views reflect a measure of truth.

One of the remarkable aspects of Watergate is that direct personal enrichment played almost no role. The Watergate crimes focused on maintaining power and punishing political enemies. From the outset, every effort was made to cover up illegal acts and shield higher-level conspirators from criminal liability. The individuals ultimately accused in the Watergate case professed to be motivated by concern for the welfare of the country or by political loyalty; in at least some cases, career ambitions or the inability to say no to a superior may have played a role.

Still, financial gain was not entirely absent from the affair. The wealthy corporations and individuals (principally the "new money" rich) who violated campaign-contribution laws by funneling large sums of money to CREEP surely anticipated long-term financial benefits from having a conservative administration indebted to them (Sale 1977). Thus, Watergate can also be seen as the concerted effort of businessmen and politicians to profit from the maintenance and extension of Nixon's political power.

---

especially legislative elections, and the related practice of legislative lobbying are two integral parts of the political system that promote corruption.

Until the final few decades of the 20th century, campaigns were generally fairly inexpensive, involving the costs of traveling to give speeches and manufacturing campaign buttons and posters (Jackson 1988). More recently, especially with the advent of television, the cost of campaigning has increased exponentially. The major–party presidential candidates now spend a combined several

hundred million dollars during the course of the campaign (Lewis 2004: 2). Since the federal election financing reforms of the early 1970s, which imposed strict limitations on the amount of money individuals could donate to campaigns, *political action committees (PACs)* became a vastly more important element in the financing of elections (Berke 2002a; Etzioni 1988a; Makinson 1990). Although any interest group can put together a PAC, wealthy corporations in particular have used this device to funnel tens of millions of dollars to political candidates, especially incumbents and chairs of powerful legislative committees. This form of *legalized bribery* not only gives incumbents an enormous financial advantage over challengers but it has been demonstrated to influence legislators' voting records as well (Etzioni 1988a; Lowenstein 2004; Makinson 1990). Defense contractors and energy company executives, to name but two examples, have used the political campaign financing system to successfully promote their interests, at a cost to taxpayers in the billions of dollars. Furthermore, until quite recently, members of Congress could transfer PAC money left over from their campaigns into their personal accounts or use it however they chose.

Large corporations and wealthy individuals were able to continue making huge donations to political parties despite the post-Watergate political financing reforms because they were unrestricted in the amount of *soft-money* donations. This money is supposed to be used only to promote issues, not specific candidates, but it has proven quite easy to find ways to promote specific candidates through "issues-focused" advertising. In the 2000 election, $500 million in unlimited donations was raised by both parties (Clymer 2002). And those who donated extravagant sums of money to the major political parties expected in many cases to enjoy special access and influence as a consequence (Lewis 2004). In December 2003, the U.S. Supreme Court narrowly upheld the law (McCain-Feingold) passed the previous year by the U.S. Congress imposing limits on "soft-money" political campaign donations (Greenhouse 2003). It remained to be seen whether this initiative to combat political corruption would succeed. Well-heeled corporations and individuals certainly continued to find ways to get large sums of money to favored parties and candidates.

Election financing abuse can be considered a white collar crime issue even when laws are not specifically violated. Clearly, the line between a "bribe" (an illegal payoff for an explicit vote) and a "contribution" (a legal donation with an implicit understanding) is exceptionally thin, and to date no member of Congress has ever been indicted simply for accepting PAC money.

Political White Collar Crime in the Executive Branch

No U.S. president has been convicted of using this high office for personal enrichment, but many are alleged to have engaged in unethical or specifically illegal conduct for economic gain before, during, and after their term of office. Even George Washington is alleged to have engaged in suspect land deals early in his career (Miller 1992; Wines 1997). Various 19th-century presidents were linked with bribery scandals, and recent presidents, including Eisenhower, Johnson, Nixon, Ford, Reagan, and Clinton, have allegedly accepted generous gifts or exorbitant honorariums from foreign leaders or admirers, evaded taxes, accumulated private fortunes by selling political influence, or appropriated secret funds for personal use (Garment 1992; Miller 1992; Wines 1997). Although President Clinton was accused of various offenses, including perjury, which gave rise to his impeachment, these charges for the most part did not allege personal enrichment (Cowan 2001; Friedrichs 2000a; Turley 2000). On leaving office, President Clinton accepted immunity from prosecution on criminal charges after conceding that he had given false testimony (Lewis N. A. 2001).

President George W. Bush has been accused of having profited throughout the course of his career as a businessman from family connections and sweetheart contracts, with ordinary investors or taxpayers at a disadvantage. As governor and president he has consistently rewarded his wealthy individual and corporate supporters (Lewis C. and Center for Public Integrity 2000; Lizza 2002). Under one interpretation, President Bush and his associates committed the ultimate theft, of the presidency itself, in the tactics used in connection with the disputed Florida vote in the 2000 presidential election (Kaplan 2001). As the Enron scandal emerged, the numerous close ties between President Bush and Enron were revealed (Rich 2002; Yardley 2002). Following the arrest of Bush's former chief of federal procurement policy in September 2005, and in the wake of various revelations of "cronyism" and corrupt dealings within Administration networks, one commentator was comparing these networks unfavorably with those that surfaced during the administration of Warren Harding (Rich 2005a). Federal auditors during this period stated that the Bush administration was guilty of purchasing favorable new coverage of some of its policies (Pear 2005b). Such dissemination of "covert propaganda" specifically violated federal law.

Vice presidents have sometimes been targets of accusations of wrongdoing. Schuyler Colfax, vice president in Ulysses Grant's first administration (1869–1873), was accused of accepting bribes and was politically ruined, even though he was never formally charged (Kohn 1989; Noonan 1984). One hundred years later, Spiro Agnew, Richard Nixon's first vice president, was formally accused of having accepted payoffs from Maryland contractors, whom he had favored as governor of that state (Cohen and Witcover 1974). As part of a complex negotiated deal, Agnew was forced to resign and to plead no contest to one charge of tax evasion. In the present era, Vice President Dick Cheney was accused of giving major energy company executives, including those of Enron, special access to the committee he chaired on energy policy (Van Natta and Banerjee 2002). Cheney had formerly been CEO of the energy giant Halliburton, a target of various alleged forms of wrongdoing.

Many other high-level members of various presidential administrations have been charged with specific criminal acts. Samuel Swartout, a New York Port customs collector during Andrew Jackson's two administrations, was charged with having embezzled more than $1 million (Miller 1992). The Buchanan administration, which immediately preceded Lincoln's presidency, was compromised by much graft, kickbacks, and overpayments (Hagan 1992). The Grant administrations after the Civil War were notoriously corrupt; specific charges of fraud or accepting bribes were directed at Grant's ambassador to Great Britain; his secretaries of war, the navy, and the interior; and his presidential secretary (Browning and Gerassi 1980; Miller 1992). In the famous *Teapot Dome* scandal during the Harding administration

(1921–1923), the secretary of the interior accepted bribes for turning over leases of government oil fields to private oil companies to exploit for their own profit; Harding's attorney general, Veterans Bureau director, and alien property custodian were also charged with corruption and fraud (Kohn 1989; Miller 1992). In many subsequent administrations, high-level aides or officials were charged with some form of personal corruption (Miller 1992); for example, Truman's military aide Harry Vaughn was alleged to have accepted a freezer, and Eisenhower's chief of staff Sherman Adams, a vicuña coat.

The Nixon administration is notorious with respect to governmental criminality and wrongdoing, and perhaps more close Nixon associates went to prison than did the cronies of any other president. Still, it is rather striking that the numerous serious charges against Nixon's associates, including perjury, burglary, bribery, illegal surveillance, altering evidence, and the like, were almost wholly devoid of elements of personal enrichment.

In contrast, the Reagan administration's pervasive "sleaze factor" was characterized by a "cashing in" mentality, and it may have been the most corrupt of all presidential administrations (Hagan 1992). This cashing-in mentality is best exemplified by the case of Michael Deaver, Reagan's deputy chief of staff. Deaver left the White House in 1985 and immediately engaged in influence peddling for exorbitant fees, collecting millions of dollars from foreign governments and corporate clients in return for "access"; in one case, he allegedly received $250,000 for making a single phone call (Martz 1986). Deaver was ultimately charged with violating laws prohibiting lobbying by recently retired federal officials and was convicted of lying about his activities (Beckwith 1987).

More than 200 members of the Reagan administration—including his first and second attorney generals, his first national security advisor, his schedule maker, his CIA director, his deputy secretary of commerce, his federal aviation administrator, his secretary of the navy, his deputy defense secretary, his secretary of the interior, his director of the U.S. Information Agency, and his head of the Veterans Administration—were investigated for ethical or criminal misconduct; personal enrichment was involved in many of these cases (Brinkley 1988; Ross J. I. 1992). In 1996, Reagan's former interior secretary, James Watt, facing 25 felony charges of illegal influence peddling, pleaded guilty to one misdemeanor charge (Johnston 1996). But such cases of alleged personal corruption, which typically received substantial media coverage, are less significant than the more subtle and sophisticated forms of institutionalized corruption carried out from within many executive branch departments.

In the case of one cabinet-level department, Housing and Urban Development (HUD), an estimated $4 billion to $8 billion was defrauded or wasted during the 1980s, and the department was riddled with corruption and mismanagement (Waldman 1989). The essence of the HUD scandal was that a large number of lucrative grants were dispensed to or on behalf of Republican Party benefactors, well-connected political figures, and members of Congress. The extraordinary hypocrisy of the HUD scandal is obvious: Members of an administration that campaigned against big government and government waste engaged in large-scale waste of taxpayers' money. Programs intended to assist poor Americans were milked by wealthy developers, private interests, highly paid consultants, and influential politicians for their own benefit, and homelessness in America increased dramatically during a period when HUD money was being ripped off and wasted (Waldman 1989). In this case, a form of state-organized crime was driven by the symbiotic relationship between incumbent politicians concerned with staying in office and special interests determined to profit from their ties to and support for those incumbents.

In the mid-1990s, corruption was alleged to be widespread in farm-aid programs and in connection with immigration matters (Engelberg 1994; Frantz 1994). Webster Hubbell, who had served as the third-highest official in the Clinton Justice department, served 18 months in prison after pleading guilty to tax evasion. He subsequently faced further charges arising out of payments made to him by Clinton supporters, allegedly to dissuade him from

testifying against the president (Gerth and Labaton 1997; Labaton 1998). Five cabinet secretaries in the Clinton Administration—the secretaries of Labor, Interior, Housing, Agriculture, and Commerce—were investigated by independent counsels or the Justice Department for various allegations of corrupt dealings and influence peddling (Johnston 1998). And several high level members of the George W. Bush administration, including Secretary of the Army Thomas E. White and top advisor Karl Rove, held substantial Enron stock, had significant ties to the company, and were suspected by some of improper actions in relation to this bankrupt corporation (Van Natta and Wayne 2002). The complex intersection of big money and major governmental power on this level generates endless opportunities for corruption.

Corruption in State Government   Corruption at the state level dates from the early history of the American colonies. Benjamin Fletcher, one of the first governors (1692–1698) of New York, was driven from office by charges of pervasive corruption, including giving protection to pirates for payoffs, making huge land grants to friends and associates, and intimidating voters at the polls with armed thugs (Browning and Gerassi 1980). Such a pattern of corruption was present in many colonies and persisted into statehood after the American Revolution.

In the course of the 20th century, 15 American sitting governors or former governors were indicted or convicted of such charges as conspiracy, fraud, perjury, bribery, racketeering, and income tax evasion (Applebome 1993b; Kohn 1989; politicalgraveyard.com 2002). These charges typically involved accepting stocks or taking bribes from contractors and others doing business with the state in return for political favors. In 1993, Governor Guy Hunt of Alabama was convicted of felony charges in connection with converting a $200,000 inauguration fund for personal use and was immediately ousted from office (Applebome 1993b). In 1996, Governor Jim Guy Tucker of Arkansas was convicted of felony mail fraud; in 1997, Governor Fife Symington of Arizona was convicted of fraud in connection with the filing of misleading financial statements; in 2000, Governor Edwin Edwards of Louisiana was convicted of fraud and racketeering (politicalgraveyard.com 2002; Purdom 1998). In 2004, former Governor John G. Rowland of Connecticut pleaded guilty to a federal corruption charge, admitting he had accepted $107,000 in gratuities and had failed to pay taxes on them; in 2005, he was sentenced to a year and a day in federal prison (McFadden 2004; Yardley and Stowe 2005). In the fall of 2005, former Governor George Ryan of Illinois was tried on various charges, including racketeering conspiracy, in connection with claims of granting lucrative state contracts to friends and receiving gifts, cash, and luxury vacations from them (Wilgoren 2005). One or more other governors during this period was suspected of or being investigated for some form of corruption.

Corruption on the state level is hardly restricted to governors. Countless other state and county officials have been charged with various forms of corruption, and some have been sent to prison. For example in 2005, Robert Janiszewski, former county executive of Hudson County in New Jersey, was sentenced to 41 months in prison for accepting bribes (Smothers 2005). Many other such cases could be cited in this context. The level of prosecution of such officials has certainly increased recently, although it is not clear whether the overall level of corruption itself has in fact increased.

During the colonial period in the 18th century, local governments were often guilty of embezzling, taking bribes, and reserving for themselves the right to rent out city property and sell liquor for profit (Browning and Gerassi 1980). In the 19th century and into the 20th century, city governments were often largely run by political bosses or party machines that virtually institutionalized corruption (Steffens 1904; Steinberg 1972). Some commentators have even suggested that at least some of this corruption was an inevitable and functionally positive response to the weaknesses and inadequacies of official city governments (Wilson 1961). Even so, it is clearly true that such corruption costs taxpayers a great deal of money and has generated distrustful and cynical attitudes toward local government.

Perhaps the single most famous example of political machine corruption is New York City's *Tammany Hall*, established in 1789 and a major force in the city's political life for the next 150 years. One early Tammany Hall leader, George Washington Plunkitt, bluntly called the systematic corruption he and his associates practiced "*honest graft.*" He has been quoted as observing, "I seen my opportunities and I took 'em" (Miller 1992: 239). Although many of the city's bosses got away with accumulating large private fortunes through corrupt dealings, Tammany Hall reached its apex in the 1870s under the leadership of William Marcy ("Boss") Tweed (Ackerman 2005). Primarily by exercising control of the department of public works, Tweed and his associates, known as the *Tweed Ring*, defrauded the City of New York of up to $200 million through vastly inflated purchases and repairs, false vouchers, fictitious bills, and other such devices. They became so greedy and obvious in their theft of the city's assets that public outrage finally led to criminal prosecutions (Browning and Gerassi 1980; Kohn 1989; Miller 1992). Tweed was eventually convicted on 204 criminal counts and died in prison in 1878.

One view holds that urban political corruption has generally declined during the 20th century because of such factors as civil service reforms (which reduce patronage), the welfare state's displacement of the urban machines, the decreasing power of white ethnic groups as new minorities emerged, and the increasing importance of television advertising, which diminishes the role of the party organization (Tager 1988). But if such factors decreased somewhat the scope of municipal corruption, they hardly eliminated it, and new forces provided new opportunities and incentives for corruption. New York City seems to experience a cycle of corruption scandals every five to seven years (Anechiarico 1990).

One cycle of municipal corruption occurred in the late 1980s during the administration of Mayor Ed Koch (Newfield and Barrett 1988). Such corruption has been an ongoing problem. In February 2002, 18 New York City tax assessors were indicted in a bribe scheme stretching back several decades, which involved taking in millions of dollars of bribes to lower property tax assessments on large office buildings and residential apartment houses (Bagli and Rashbaum 2002). It was estimated that these activities cost the city well over $150 million in lost tax revenue, with the burden passed on to other tax payers and those dependent upon city-funded programs. In 2002, Vincent (Buddy) Cianci, the popular, long-term mayor of Providence, Rhode Island, was sentenced to more than five years in prison for federal racketeering charges arising out of corrupt practices in the mayor's office (Belluck 2002b). In 2003, Joseph P. Ganim, Mayor of Bridgeport, Connecticut, was tried on federal corruption charges, with allegations that he was a shakedown artist extracting cash and gifts from city contractors (von Zielbauer 2003). In 2005, Michael Zucchat, the acting mayor of San Diego, was found guilty of corruption charges (Pollack 2005). Other mayors have faced such charges as well.

The persistence of corruption tends to support the primacy of structural or institutional causes over individualistic, "bad apples" explanations. In view of the repeated historical failure of reform movements and criminal prosecutions to eradicate municipal corruption, it is likely to endure on some level in the foreseeable future.

Political White Collar Crime in the Legislative Branch

Members of the legislative branch of the government have always had a broad range of opportunities for corrupt dealings. James Madison, one of the founding fathers and the fourth U.S. president, believed that the Congress was less corruptible than the executive branch in part because of its large number of members and diluted power (Noonan 1984). But from the beginning, state legislators have often found irresistible the temptation to benefit personally from their legislative actions.

In 1795, several Georgia legislators acquired shares in a company seeking legislative action that would transfer to it millions of acres of Indian land. Although the legislators involved were punished at the polls at the next election, they could not be criminally prosecuted because at that time Georgia had no law against bribery (Noonan 1984). Until after the Civil War, neither effective federal laws nor adequate means of investigating the whole range of corrupt legislative practices existed, and even such venerated statesmen as Henry Clay and Daniel Webster accepted large loans or retainers from special interests.

The *Credit Mobilier* affair, which surfaced in 1872, was perhaps the first major public scandal concerning congressional corruption (Noonan 1984). Credit Mobilier was a holding company organized in 1864 to coordinate the westward expansion of the Union Pacific railroad. Shares in the company were made available to many congressmen at nominal cost (or were given as a gift) by the company's founders, including Congressman Oakes Ames, and Congress enacted a bond capitalization of the scheme that greatly enriched the shareholders. Although considerable public indignation and a congressional investigation resulted once the scheme was revealed, no congressmen were criminally prosecuted, and only two, including Ames, were even censured.

In the 130 years since the Credit Mobilier affair, major congressional corruption scandals have erupted periodically, and some forms of corruption have become virtually institutionalized. Some of the specific ways in which lawmakers become lawbreakers include use of official status to evade arrest (for drunken driving and other such offenses); "junketing" (taking trips to exotic locations at the taxpayers' expense, often on the superficial pretext of making a legislative study); double billing, in which both a private corporation and the government are billed for the same item; using the franking (free mailing) privilege for political or personal purposes; using official congressional staff for purely political or personal purposes; and a broad range of conflict-of-interest offenses (Green 1984; Lewis E. 1998). There are many documented instances of legislators promoting legislation that benefits special interests who have paid them off, either directly through low-cost loans or through retainers to law partners. In some cases, their own investments are directly affected.

An especially dramatic scandal, the *Abscam* case, was revealed in 1980. In the late 1970s, the FBI had set up a bogus company (Abdul Enterprises) and spread the word that wealthy Arab sheiks were prepared to engage in various shady deals (Noonan 1984). Seven members of Congress ultimately indicted for accepting bribes in some form (e.g., $50,000 cash) from the "Arab sheiks" were expelled from Congress or forced to resign and were convicted of various charges; several of them, including Senator Harrison Williams of New Jersey, were sentenced to prison terms. The FBI videotapes of the legislators accepting bribes marked the first time such evidence was available in the long history of congressional bribe taking. However, the claim that the FBI had engaged in entrapment introduced controversy into the case.

The passage of legislation benefiting special interests who donate generous sums to the campaigns of members of Congress is surely the most enduring and costly form of legislative crime (Lewis and The Center for Public Integrity 1998; Palast 2003). Some commentators suggest that campaign finance reforms did indeed lead to a significant decline of corruption in Congress, which was replaced by excessive partisanship (Tolchin and Tolchin 2001). But the Abscam affair was hardly the last case of direct forms of congressional corruption. In 1996, Dan Rostenkowski, the powerful chair of the House Ways and Means Committee, pleaded guilty to mail fraud arising out of the House Post Office Scandal of the late 1980s, with a 17-month prison sentence as part of the deal (Rosenbaum 1996). In 1997, Speaker of the House Newt Gingrich was cited for serious ethics violations, involving tax-exempt financing of some of his activities, and agreed to pay a $300,000 fine (Clymer 1997). Gingrich was pressured to give up his office in 1998 in the face of allegations of adultery, and he left Congress (Tolchin and Tolchin 2001). Ironically, he had spearheaded an investigation of ethics charges against an earlier Speaker of the House, Democrat Jim Wright. In April 2002, Ohio Congressman James A. Traficant Jr. was found guilty of racketeering and corruption as a consequence of soliciting bribes from businesspeople and kickbacks from members of his own staff (Clines 2002). To some members of Congress, the lure of corruption is

apparently more potent than any deterrent effect of the threat of disgrace, conviction, and imprisonment.

In September 2005, House Majority Leader Tom DeLay was indicted for conspiracy to violate state election laws and was forced to step aside from his leadership post; he was also still being investigated in connection with violation of Congressional rules on accepting free travel from lobbyists and with the hiring of his wife by a lobbying entity (Shenon and Hulse 2005; Tumulty 2005). Jack Abramoff, a prominent lobbyist with whom DeLay had close ties, was the target of a Justice Department criminal investigation for defrauding Native Americans of tens of millions of dollars in fees, among other things.

Political White Collar Crime in the Judicial Branch

Of the three branches of government, the judicial branch has probably been the least tainted by claims of corruption, but it has not been free of such claims. Concerns over judicial misconduct date back to the earliest civilizations, and judges are known to have accepted bribes in Ancient Rome and during medieval times (Noonan 1984). One of the most famous cases involved Sir Francis Bacon, who served as Lord Chancellor during the reign of King James I of England and was charged in 1621 with accepting bribes in return for favorable decisions. Bacon was fined but later pardoned. Judges in the United States have been charged with many crimes, including bribery, extortion, obstructing justice, income tax evasion, embezzlement, fraud, and abuse of authority (Ashman 1973). Many judges so charged have been forced to resign; others have been impeached, censured, disbarred, and convicted of crimes. A few went to prison.

Criminal prosecutions of federal judges have been rare (Jackson 1974). One federal judge in the 1980s was convicted of income tax evasion, sentenced to prison, and impeached, and another was impeached for soliciting a $150,000 bribe (Johnston 1989). State court judges and local judges have far more often been charged with milking estates for personal enrichment, making corrupt arrangements with bail bondsmen, and accepting outright bribes (Jackson 1974). For example in August 2002, a Brooklyn, New York judge, Victor Barron, pleaded guilty to accepting a bribe of $18,000 from a lawyer in return for a favorable judgment in a civil case involving a $1.6 million fee for the lawyer (Glaberson 2002). In April 2003, another State Supreme Court justice in Brooklyn, Gerald Garson, was charged with accepting bribes in divorce and custody cases (Newman 2003). Prosecutors complained of a "culture of corruption" in the matrimonial section of the court. In August 2005, a New York state judge was arraigned on charges of money laundering with mob figures (Rashbaum 2005). The judge had self-published a book on his judicial career.

Judges are obviously in a position to abuse their considerable power. If it is in fact true that outright criminal behavior is rare among judges, it may be that the daily contact with lawbreakers in their courts raises their awareness of the harmful consequences of lawbreaking. Because judges are relatively well compensated and enjoy considerable prestige, they have relatively less to gain and much more to lose by engaging in criminal conduct. Furthermore, it is tempting to believe that the procedures for selecting judges succeed more often than not in advancing individuals of above-average integrity. But there is also some reason to believe that prosecutors and other criminal justice personnel are reluctant to go after judges and that judges are reluctant to turn on each other (Jackson 1974). Clearly, cases of judicial crime and corruption are especially disturbing, given a judge's role of passing judgment on others convicted of criminal behavior. Box 5.6 addresses corruption in another sector of the law enforcement system—police departments.

GOVERNMENTAL CRIME, IN SUM

Governmental crime has been defined here as a cognate form of white collar crime. It obviously has many attributes similar to those of corporate crime and occupational crime, and it is driven by similar motivations. There are numerous interrelationships between governmental criminals and corporate white collar criminals because people move back and forth between the public and private sectors. The differences between governmental and private-sector white collar crime are principally differences of emphasis; the enhancement or extension of power is somewhat more important in the former case, whereas the maximization of profit (or the prevention of loss) is relatively more important in the latter case. The ultimate scope of harm may be greater in governmental crime cases.

The first half of this chapter addressed crimes committed on behalf of the state. The clearly interrelated concepts of state criminality, state repression, state corruption, and state negligence need not be considered synonymous. If economic corruption was hardly unknown in Nazi Germany, it is because that state focused instead on extending its geopolitical boundaries and exterminating its perceived internal enemies. On the other hand, although the Indonesian government under Suharto was involved in genocidal actions against the people of East Timor, the Suharto family was principally focused on enriching itself through massive corruption and plundering of state assets. In the case of the recent history of the People's Republic of China, state repression with broad deprivation of basic human rights and freedom is widely viewed as the principal problem, although certainly negligence, corruption, and even genocidal actions have also been alleged. Problems of state negligence are especially evident in the case of wealthy nations. Many allegations of genocide, repression, and corruption have been directed at the United States by both external and internal critics. Iraq under Saddam Hussein was accused of genocidal policies toward the Kurds and aggressive warfare against Kuwait; it was widely believed to be developing weapons of mass destruction, including nuclear weapons, and was certainly guilty of practicing various forms of repression and denying people their basic human rights (Pollack K. M. 2002). Further, Saddam Hussein and his associates spent hundreds of millions of dollars on their own lavish palaces and lifestyles and stole

---

B O X 5.6   Police Corruption as a Form of "Political" White Collar Crime

Although ordinary police officers are no longer appointed to their jobs by a purely political process, they are among the lower-level personnel in the political or governmental system. For well over a century, commissions formed to investigate charges of police corruption have found evidence of significant levels of such wrongdoing. In this context, corruption refers to illegal and improper behavior on the part of the police to personally enrich themselves. The Lexow Commission in the 1890s uncovered much police corruption in New York City, as did the Knapp Commission in the 1970s, the Mollen Commission in the 1990s, and other investigations in between (Roberg and Kuykendall 1993). Police corruption is a problem in many countries, and in some countries it is highly organized and entrenched (Green and Ward 2004; Kratcoski 2001). Such corruption may involve corruption of authority (e.g., accepting discounts), kickbacks, opportunistic theft (e.g., of arrestees), shakedowns (e.g., of traffic offenders), protection of illegal activities, fixes (e.g., of traffic tickets), direct criminal activities (e.g., burglary), and internal payoffs (e.g., sale of work assignments) (Barker 1996). It is useful to distinguish between police personnel who actively seek bribes and kickbacks, engage in "shakedowns," and even steal for personal gain ("meat eaters"), and those who accept minor gratuities, meals, and the like from businesses and individual entrepreneurs on their beat ("grass eaters") (Knapp Commission 1973). The more serious corruption has been most frequently associated with vice, or "victimless crimes." Police officers can rationalize that their corrupt activity in this realm does no harm because the laws are largely futile and they are only victimizing criminals.

Twelve police officers affiliated with the Harlem precinct were arrested in New York City in April 1994 on charges of forcing drug dealers to pay them protection money and beating up dealers who did not cooperate (Krauss 1994). These arrests followed earlier arrests of officers for drug dealing.

Such corrupt activity occurred in many precincts. Police in virtually every large city engage in this type of corrupt activity. Some police abuse of power and corruption is simply wrongdoing by a few "crooked cops" on the police force. Police work is likely to attract at least some individuals who enjoy bullying others or those join the force with the intention of exploiting special opportunities to enrich themselves. However, police crime may well be more fully explained by systemic factors that promote it and tend to shield it from exposure (Sherman 1978; Roberg, Crank, and Kuykendall 2000). Police officers enter police work somewhat idealistically and subsequently undergo a process of socialization to the harsh realities of their jobs; the result is often cynicism. Officers are also likely to internalize powerful norms, especially loyalty to their fellow officers, that tend to discourage cooperation with investigations of corruption. Police work is also especially fraught with unusual opportunities and temptations to abuse power or corruptly benefit financially.

Police crime has received a fair amount of attention, but other low-level criminal justice personnel are hardly immune to the temptations to commit occupationally related crimes (Henderson and Simon 1994). Abuse of authority and various forms of corruption occur within all components of the criminal justice system, including the courts and correctional institutions.

---

billions of dollars from the Iraqi treasury, while most Iraqis suffered terrible deprivations (Byron 1991; Liu, Nordland, and Thomas 2003). Saddam Hussein's Iraq was guilty of state criminality, repression, corruption, and negligence, arguably in equal measure.

State-organized crimes were discussed principally in terms of government entities that commit crimes in the form of abuses of power, from White House officials to CIA agents to ordinary police.

In the second half of this chapter, various forms of political white collar crime were surveyed.

Corrupt acts of political parties or of political officials in the executive, legislative, or judicial branches to advance their own power or economic interests were addressed here.

The existence of governmental crime generates some challenging questions: Does governmental crime produce structural conditions that promote white collar crime? Does it generate a moral ambience that facilitates the rationalization of white collar crime? If the government is committing crime, who polices the government?

KEY TERMS

Abscam, 140

abuse of power, 118

anarchism, 119

apartheid, 125

bribery, 118

client states, 130

COINTELPRO, 133

corruption, 118

corrupt state, 126

Credit Mobilier, 140

criminal state, 121

"Dirty Harry" problem, 134

genocide, 122

governmental crime, 116

Holocaust, 123

honest graft, 139

human rights, 125

International Criminal Court, 125

Iran-Contra Affair, 131

legalized bribery, 136

Nuremberg Trials, 123

PAC (political action committee), 135

police crime, 133

political crime, 117

political scandal, 118

political white collar crime, 116

power elite, 134

repressive state, 125

rogue states, 123

soft money, 136

state crime, 116

state-organized crime, 129

state negligence, 128

Tammany Hall, 139

Teapot Dome, 137

testilying, 134

Tweed Ring, 139

war crimes, 119

Watergate, 130

weapons of mass destruction, 120

wholesale/retail terrorism, 130

DISCUSSION QUESTIONS

1. Distinguish between the concepts of governmental crime, state crime, and political white collar crime. Identify as well the special significance of the following concepts: abuse of power, corruption, bribery, and political scandal. In what respects are the first set of concepts controversial, and how do they relate to the traditional concept of white collar crime? Why has governmental crime been relatively neglected by criminologists?

2. What can be said in favor of, and against, the proposition of characterizing imperialistic conquest, warfare, and the threat of nuclear war as forms of governmental crime? Differentiate between a criminal state, a repressive state, a corrupt state, and a negligent state, with examples of each. Why is it useful or not useful to break down some major forms of governmental crime in this way?

3. Identify the specific meaning of Chambliss's concept of state-organized crime, and discuss some of its specific historical manifestations. How does "wholesale" terrorism differ from "retail" terrorism? Which case of contemporary American state-organized crime did you find most disturbing, and why?

4. How does political white collar crime differ from state crime or state-organized crime, as defined in this text? How are the various crimes of the police best classified? How does a structural account of political white collar crime differ from the "bad apples" account, and which account do you find most persuasive?

5. What are some noteworthy examples of executive branch, legislative branch, and judicial branch political white collar crime? Can you identify factors unique to each branch that contribute to corrupt activity, or do the same factors seem to apply uniformly to all three branches? Why has it proven so difficult to obliterate political white collar crime?

6

State-Corporate Crime, Crimes of Globalization, and Finance Crime

Some major forms of white collar crime are not easily classified as corporate, occupational, or governmental crime. They are hybrids that combine attributes of two or more of the established forms of white collar crime. In this chapter, we consider three especially significant hybrid types: state-corporate crime, crimes of globalization, and finance crime.

STATE-CORPORATE CRIME

Much illegal governmental activity has connections with private enterprise. Many linkages exist among the "power elites," and many "interlocks" occur between public and private entities. Kramer and Michalowski (1990) called for recognition of *state-corporate crime* that "occurs at the interstices of corporations and governments" (p. 3). They define this type of crime as follows:

> State-corporate crimes are illegal or socially injurious actions that occur when one or more institutions of political governance pursue a goal in direct cooperation with one or more institutions of economic production and distribution. (p. 3)

The premise for the concept of state-corporate crime is that modern states and corporations are profoundly interdependent. A theory of state-corporate crime focuses on how state and corporate managers engage in cooperative endeavors that "result in death, injury, ill health, financial loss, and . . . cultural destruction, all the while being insulated from the full weight of criminalization for these actions" (Kramer, Michalowski, and Kauzlarich 2002: 266). Since the concept was introduced in 1990, it has been applied to a range of specific cases (Michalowski and Kramer 2006; Friedrichs 2002a), including the Holocaust (see Box 6.1). In 2005, the California-based energy corporation Unocal agreed to settle a lawsuit against it that charged the company with complicity in the torture, murder, and rape of Burmese villagers by government soldiers in that country to enable the company to build a gas pipeline (Eviatar 2005; Shamir 2004). Corporations in cooperation with governments continue to play a role in state-based violence.

B O X 6.1 State-Corporate Crime, Nazi Germany, and the Holocaust

The torture and murder of millions of people, principally European Jews, by Nazi Germany is by any criteria among the most monstrous crimes in history. Although Hitler and his Nazi henchmen rightly receive most of the blame, many major corporations also played a role (Matthews 2006). Most of these corporations were German, but some were American, including ITT, General Motors, Ford Motor Company, and IBM. Within Germany, the I. G. Farben Company, a huge chemical combine, built a slave labor camp adjacent to the notorious Auschwitz concentration camp and controlled a company that produced the poisonous Zyklon B gas used in the death camps (Borkin 1978). Only a handful of I. G. Farben executives were convicted of crimes against humanity after World War II (and they received relatively light sentences), and the corporation once again became an enormously powerful and profitable entity. Even though I. G. Farben's wartime actions occurred under extraordinary political circumstances and may well have involved complex and conflicting motivations (Hayes 1987), its use of slave labor and the production of poisonous gas were nonetheless criminal enterprises involving cooperation between a state and a corporation.

Other German corporations played an important role in both the rise of Hitler and the Nazis to power and the exploitation of conditions in Nazi Germany for profit. German corporations helped fund Hitler and the Nazi Party in the apparent belief that the Nazis could restore order in Germany, and they had the false confidence that once Hitler came to power they would be able to influence and manipulate him to their advantage (Turner 1969). Although big business could not control Hitler, many large corporations and businesses cooperated in the "Aryanization" program of the Nazi state, which included dismissing Jewish executives and employees and taking over Jewish business assets, to the economic advantage of these corporations (Hayes 1998; Stallbaumer 1999). And large German corporations such as Daimler-Benz and Krupp played a crucially important role in arming the Nazis for the aggressive wars they launched against neighboring countries (Gregor 1998; Manchester 1968). Many companies also employed slave labor in business operations often set up adjacent to Nazi concentration camps.

In recent years, the complicity of American or American-based corporations has increasingly come to light (Matthews 2006). The international conglomerate ITT had divisions in Germany that produced essential communications and armaments networks and equipment for Nazi Germany; after World War II, ITT sued the United States government for war damages to some of its German operations (Sampson 1973). IBM facilitated the massive Nazi German effort to identify and deport Jews and other perceived enemies of the state to concentration camps with its Hollerith machines; Thomas Watson Sr., the founder of IBM, accepted a medal from Adolf Hitler (Black 2001). Subsidiaries of Ford and General Motors built trucks for the Nazi war machine and used forced or slave labor in Germany to enhance profits (Billstein, Fings, Kugler, and Levis 2001).

The space shuttle *Challenger* disaster is a high-profile example of alleged state–corporate crime (Kramer and Michalowski 1990; Kramer 1992; Shukla and Bartgis, forthcoming). *Challenger* exploded just minutes after it was launched on January 28, 1986, killing all seven astronauts aboard, including schoolteacher Christa McAuliffe. This fatal explosion was officially designated a tragic accident attributed to the failure of O-ring seals. But Kramer and Michalowski (1990) claimed that a complex of governmental and corporate pressures led to an avoidable tragedy. Some parallel concerns were raised following the *Columbia* space shuttle disintegration on February 1, 2003 (Glanz and Wong 2003).

On the one hand, NASA was under continual pressure during a period of diminished political and economic support for the space program to produce a successful launch of the reusable space shuttle as soon as possible. NASA's response to these external pressures was to approve various compromises in the design of the craft; it was also apparently eager to have the *Challenger* in orbit while President Reagan delivered his State of the Union address, which would have allowed him to note that an ordinary American schoolteacher was in orbit even as he spoke.

For its part, the Morton Thiokol Corporation, the primary contractor on the project, was eager to meet NASA's tight deadlines (and retain its profitable contracts) and pushed ahead with production of the space shuttle despite tests indicating problems with the O-ring seals. Additional pressures to launch were generated by previous postponements due to bad weather and the great public interest generated by the inclusion of a schoolteacher on the flight, and thus the January 28 launch date became a high priority.

A presidential commission investigating the tragedy later uncovered clear evidence that Morton Thiokol engineers had expressed strong reservations about launching in the cold weather anticipated for that day, and a simple experiment performed by a commission member, the eminent physicist Richard Feynman, clearly demonstrated that the O-ring seals lost resilience when subjected to cold temperatures. But the dissenting engineers were overruled by corporate and agency superiors who refused to heed the warnings of danger. Although the presidential commission had harsh words for the decision makers involved in this tragedy, none was ever criminally indicted.

The *Challenger* launch decision was a complex case, and Diane Vaughan (1996), in an exhaustive study of the case, concluded that it occurred not because those involved made knowingly wrong decisions but rather because an ingrained culture of decision making led them to accept the risks involved in the launch. Disasters of this sort are surely complex, and we should exercise caution in explaining them. But in this case, it seems fair to say that a congruence of state and corporate objectives promoted organizational values and practices that inevitably had tragic consequences.

Other examples of state-corporate crime include the Iran-Contra Affair, which involved governmental personnel and private arms dealers, and defense contract frauds resulting from a cooperative enterprise between military or political officials and private defense contractors (Kramer and Michalowski 1990; Michalowski and Kramer 2006) (see Box 6.2). Environmental crimes committed in conjunction with U.S. nuclear weapons production are a form of state-corporate crime because they are a collective product of interaction between a government agency (the U.S. Department of Energy) and private corporations (Kauzlarich and Kramer 1993, 1998). Aulette and Michalowski (1993) described a 1991 explosion and fire at the Imperial Food Products chicken processing plant in Hamlet, North Carolina, which killed 25 plant workers and injured 56, as a state-corporate crime, due to the complicity of a range of state agencies and the food-processing corporation. Matthews and Kauzlarich (2000) classified the crash of ValuJet Flight 592 in the Florida Everglades in 1996, which killed 105 passengers and 5 crew members, as state-corporate (or "state-facilitated") crime because the Federal Aviation Administration (FAA) failed to adequately enforce safety regulations and a private airline cut costs by contracting maintenance to a company (Sabretech) that placed an improperly inspected oxygen canister on the flight. The canister caught fire and exploded. Robyn (2002) has described the exploitation of natural resources on a Native American reservation as a form of state-corporate crime involving a state agency and a private corporation, Exxon. Military contractors with close ties to state officials have also been accused of a form of state-corporate crime (see Box 6.2).

Strictly speaking, state-corporate crime reflects the fulfillment of mutually agreed-on objectives of a public agency and a private entity achieved through cooperative illegal activity. Kramer and Michalowski (1990) noted that state-corporate crime also occurs on the international level, as in the involvement of ITT with harmful governmental or military activities in Chile (Sampson 1973), and on the local level (e.g., state involvement with private operators of hazardous waste disposal operations). States and private corporations have been accused of complicity in the devastating consequences of some natural disasters such as earthquakes when their corrupt practices lead to shoddy construction and the unnecessary loss of lives and property in such circumstances (Green 2005). The awarding of hundreds of millions of dollars worth of contracts on a nonbidding basis following a major hurricane might also be suspected of involving a form of state-corporate crime (Lipton and Nixon

---

B O X   6.2   Military Contractors in Iraq: Corporate Warriors and the Halliburton Corporation

Military functions have been increasingly "outsourced" to private companies, who use their close government connections to obtain lucrative contracts, then often overcharge the government for their services, and are party to abusive practices due to a lack of oversight (Singer 2003, 2004). The privatized military functions include logistics, troop training, convoy escorts, and interrogations.

In 2003, a group of businessmen with close ties to President Bush—including his former campaign manager—set up a firm (New Bridge Strategies) to advise companies on how to obtain lucrative re-construction contracts in Iraq following "Operation Iraqi Freedom" (Jehl 2003). Custer Battles, a security firm that won a $100 million contract to provide security services, was subsequently accused of billing the occupation authority for nonexistent services, or grossly inflating bills for services provided (Eckholm 2003). Very large, noncompetitive contracts of some $10 billion for work in Iraq were awarded to Kellogg, Brown & Root, a subsidiary of Halliburton (Eckholm 2005b; Mayer 2004). Halliburton was especially

well-connected politically and was formerly headed by Vice President Dick Cheney. In 2005, Halliburton was accused of "war profiteering," with Pentagon audits raising questions about a staggering $1 billion of bills from the company (Eckholm 2005b). For example, the Army was billed for 20,000 daily meals in a dining room where only 10,000 were being served. In one especially notorious case, the U.S. government was charged $27 million to transport fuel worth just $82,000 (Eckholm 2005a). Altogether, the Halliburton case exemplified the opportunities for massive fraud that exist for politically well-connected defense contractors.

Did a form of state-corporate crime influence American policy in relation to 9/11? In *House of Bush, House of Fraud*, Craig Unger (2004) has argued that long-standing business ties between the Bush family (an "American dynasty") and the royal house of Saud in Saudi Arabia prevented President George W. Bush from confronting the House of Saud about the Islamic militants in their country and the threat of a Saudi Arabian–based Al Qaeda.

2005). Above all, the concept of state-corporate crime compels us to recognize that some major forms of organizational crime cannot be easily classified as either corporate or governmental and that these interorganizational forms of crime may be especially potent and pernicious.

CRIMES OF GLOBALIZATION

Sutherland's classic *White Collar Crime* (1949) examined its title subject within a national frame-work. Although some of the corporations he wrote about certainly had international subsidiaries and transnational activities, Sutherland made little refer-ence to illegal corporate or business activity of an international scope. If we accept the premise that we live in an increasingly globalized world, how-ever, we must also focus on the global character of some white collar crime. A United Nations Report

in 2005 makes the point that people in developing countries are especially vulnerable to globalized forms of white collar crime, in part due to weak regulation and limited government resources for addressing such crime (Secretariat 2005). The dis-cussion of multinational corporations in Chapter 3 addressed some dimensions of globalized white collar crime, and we broaden that focus here. The *antiglobalization movement* contends that large-scale crimes are being carried out in the name of global-ization. The United States was a strong supporter of the North American Free Trade Agreement in 1993, and has generally promoted global free trade but has also been accused of causing harm to farm-ers, merchants, and consumers in many countries when it protects its own interests against free trade (Weiner 2003b). Its lavish subsidies of its own farmers cause immense harm to farmers in poor, developing countries and have been declared illegal by the World Trade Organization; steel tariffs imposed by President George W. Bush in 2002,

---

BOX 6.3   Corruption in the Oil-for-Food Program

Following the first Gulf War against Iraq in the early 1990s, economic sanctions were imposed on that country by the United Nations (Halliday 2004; LeBillon 2005). Critics of the sanctions have argued that hundreds of thousands of Iraqis—disproportionately children—died from malnutrition and lack of medicine as a consequence of these sanctions; accordingly, the sanctions have been characterized as "genocidal" by some of these critics. These critics claimed that economic sanctions were most harmful to vulnerable constituencies that the international community is committed to assisting (e.g., women, children, the sick, and the elderly) while failing to bring down the targeted regime or the powerful elites. This was certainly the case with Iraq. In response to this type of critique, however, a program was set up by the United Nations to enable Saddam Hussein to trade Iraqi oil for food. But by 2005, ongoing allegations were claiming that various oil companies had made secret deals to profit from this program, kickbacks to and skimming by Saddam Hussein and his associates was pervasive, and some well-connected individuals (including a son of UN Secretary General Kofi Annan) also made deals to profit improperly from the Oil-for-Food program (Hoge 2005a, 2005b; Preston and Miller 2005). Apparently, relatively little in the way of food or medicine got to the beleaguered Iraqi people. Insofar as the United Nations is an international institution with some global responsibilities, its failure to ensure that ordinary Iraqi citizens were the primary beneficiaries of the Oil-for-Food program was one form of a crime of globalization.

---

to protect the American steel industry, were subsequently also declared illegal by that organization (Becker 2003; *New York Times* 2004b). The claim of free trade in the world today is highly misleading, as trade is actually "rigged" in many ways to favor the interests of powerful and wealthy nations and transnational corporations.

Global or international institutions sometimes adopt policies that fail to address human suffering in the world or that aggravate existing suffering (see Box 6.3). More specifically, international financial institutions such as the International Monetary Fund and the World Bank are alleged to be complicit in major crimes against large numbers of people in developing countries (Darrow 2003; Friedrichs and Friedrichs 2002). The alleged crimes have important elements of white collar crimes although they do not correspond with the classic parameters of such crime. On the one hand, *crimes of globalization* are consequences of policy decisions of high-level officials of major financial institutions and government agencies who are attempting to realize positive outcomes (or avoid losses); although it is not typically their specific intent to cause harm, their policy decisions can have devastating financial and human consequences for large numbers of

especially vulnerable people. On the other hand, crimes of globalization do not necessarily involve either the direct pursuit of profit or directly fraudulent activity, as would be true of much white collar crime.

The policies and practices of *international financial institutions* (IFIs) can only be understood in the context of the notion of *globalization*. The invocation of the term *globalization* has become ubiquitous, and the literature on globalization has expanded exponentially, although the meaning of the term is far from settled (Hay and Marsh 2000; Schaeffer 2003; Weinstein 2005). The term has been in wide use since the 1960s (Busch 2000). In one sense, globalization is hardly a new phenomenon if one means by it the emergence of international trade and a transnational economic order. But globalization has become a buzzword of the transition into the new century due to the widely perceived intensification of certain economic, political, and cultural developments (Chase-Dunn, Kawano, and Brewer 2000; Schaeffer 2003). The phenomenal growth in the importance and influence of transnational corporations, nongovernmental organizations (NGOs), intergovernmental organizations (IGOs), international financial institutions, and special interest

---

B O X 6.4 **Sweatshops in Developing Countries: Criminal Enterprises or Economic Opportunities?**

Much criticism has been directed at so-called *sweatshops*, factories in developing countries where employees, often women and sometimes children, work under miserable conditions for pitiful wages (e.g., 60 cents an hour) to produce clothing and other products sold to Westerners in trendy stores at high prices (Esbenshade 2004; Rose 2004). Some products carry the names of celebrities, like Michael Jordan and Kathy Lee Gifford, who have been paid millions for their endorsements. Nike, the Gap, and other immensely profitable corporations are supplied by these sweatshops. Critics contend that these corporations, and others who profit from sweatshops, are complicit in a form of global crime akin to profiting from slavery.

Sweatshop conditions can lead to untimely deaths. In May 1993, the worst industrial fire in the history of capitalism occurred at a toy factory outside Bangkok, killing at least 188 and injuring 469 (Greider 1997). The loss of life exceeded that of the famous Triangle Shirtwaist Company fire of 1911 in Manhattan, where some 146 young immigrant women died when trapped in the factory. Americans worry about the safety of their children's toys but are often indifferent to the fate of children producing these toys in foreign sweatshops (Greider 1997).

On balance, some commentators suggest, sweatshops do more good than harm, providing desperately poor people with a better income (Kristof and Wu Dunn 2000). The monitoring of sweatshops to encourage safe and fair practices, rather than boycotts or attempts to shut them down, is seen as more humane and effective.

---

groups is a conspicuous dimension of contemporary globalization (Mazlish 1999; Shapiro and Brilmayer 1999; Valaskakis 1999). Ordinary people lose control over their economic destiny (Greider 1997). World markets increasingly overshadow national markets, barriers to trade are reduced, and instant tele- and cyber-transactions are becoming the norm (Chase-Dunn et al. 2000; Jackson 2000; Scheuerman 1999). In the broadest possible terms, globalization refers to the dramatic compression of time and space across the globe.

There are many "winners" in the move toward an increasingly globalized economy, but those winners are disproportionately wealthy multinational corporations while the losers are disproportionately poor and disadvantaged, including indigenous peoples in developing countries (Frank 2000). (See Box 6.4.)

Globalization contributes to an overall increase in economic inequality, fostering poverty and unemployment for many (George 2000; Kahn 2000; Shapiro and Brilmayer 1999). It has been characterized as a new form of the ancient practice of colonization (Dunne 1999). Falk (2004) argues that the logic of globalization is dictated by the well-being of capital rather than of people.

Globalization clearly has many different dimensions. Those most pertinent within the realm of white collar crime include the following: (1) the growing global dominance and reach of neoliberalism and a free market, capitalist system that disproportionately benefits wealthy and powerful organizations and individuals; (2) the increasing vulnerability of indigenous people with a traditional way of life to the forces of globalized capitalism; (3) the growing influence and impact of international financial institutions (such as the World Bank) and the related, relative decline of power of local or state-based institutions; and (4) the nondemocratic operation of international financial institutions, taking the form of globalization from above instead of globalization from below.

The Role of the World Bank in a Global Economy

The international financial institutions that play such a central role in contemporary globalization have become prime targets for criticism for their policies and practices. These international financial institutions include the World Trade Organization, with a primary mission to foster trade; the International

Monetary Fund, which seeks to maximize financial stability; and the World Bank, primarily focused on promoting development (Darrow 2003; Stiglitz 2002). These institutions have many ties with each other, and the lines of demarcation between their activities can become quite blurred. Collectively, much evidence suggests that they have acted principally in response to the interests of developed countries and their privileged institutions rather than in the interests of the poor (Sjoberg, Gill, and Williams 2001; Smith and Moran 2000; Stiglitz 2002). The focus here is principally on the activities of the World Bank.

The *World Bank*, formally the International Bank for Reconstruction and Development (IBRD), was established at the Bretton Woods Conference in 1944 to help stabilize and rebuild economies ravaged by World War II. Eventually it shifted its focus to an emphasis on aiding developing nations (Darrow 2003; Johnson 2000). The Bank makes low-interest loans to governments of its member nations and to private development projects backed by those governments with the stated aim to benefit the citizens of those countries. The World Bank (2000) claims to contribute to the reduction of poverty and to improved living standards in developing countries. Today the Bank is a large, international operation with more than 10,000 employees, 180 member states, and annual loans of $30 billion (Finnegan 2000).

The World Bank was established, along with the International Monetary Fund, at the behest of dominant Western nations with little input from developing countries (Kapstein 1998/1999; Rajagopal 2003). It is disproportionately influenced by or manipulated by elite economic institutions and has been characterized as an agent of global capital (Greider 2000). In developing countries, it deals primarily with the political and economic elites of those countries with little direct attention to the perspectives and needs of indigenous peoples, a practice for which it has been criticized by U.S. senators (Caufield 1996; Rajagopal 2003; Rich 1994). It has loaned money to ruthless military dictatorships engaged in murder and torture and denied loans to democratic governments overthrown by the military (Rich 1994). It favors strong dictatorships over struggling democracies because it believes that the former are more able to introduce and see through the unpopular reforms its loans require (Caufield 1996). World Bank borrowers typically are political elites of developing countries and their cronies, although repaying the debt becomes the responsibility of these countries' citizens, most of whom do not benefit from the loans. In this reading, then, the privileged benefit disproportionately from dealings with the World Bank relative to the poor.

The World Bank and Crimes of Globalization

The World Bank has been characterized as paternalistic, secretive, and counterproductive in terms of its claimed goals of improving people's lives. It has been charged with complicity in policies with genocidal consequences, with exacerbating ethnic conflict, with increasing the gap between rich and poor, with fostering immense ecological and environmental damage, and with the callous displacement of vast numbers of indigenous people in developing countries from their original homes and communities (Dugger 2004; Rich 1994). Critics claim that many less developed countries that received World Bank loans are worse off today in terms of poverty and that the severe austerity measures imposed on borrowing countries, deemed necessary to maximize the chances of Bank loans being repaid, impact most heavily on the poorest and most vulnerable citizens (Johnson 2000; Rajagopal 2003). The building of dams has been the single most favored World Bank project, but even its own experts concede that millions of people have been displaced as a result of these dams (Caufield 1996; Rajagopal 2003). In many of these projects, resettlement plans have either been nonexistent—in violation of the Bank's own guidelines—or have been inadequately implemented. In one notorious case in the 1970s, antidam protesters in Guatemala were massacred by the military; this atrocity is not mentioned in the World Bank's report on the project (Caufield 1996).

B O X 6.5 **The Dam at Pak Moon: A Case of Global Crime by Jessica Friedrichs**

The World Bank helped finance the building of a dam on the Moon (or Mun) River in eastern Thailand in the early 1990s (Friedrichs and Friedrichs 2002; Vallabhaneni 2000). The process of planning, constructing, and operating this dam was undertaken without obtaining input from the fishermen and villagers who lived along the river. The construction of the dam had a detrimental effect on the environment, flooding the adjacent forests; this effect violated the World Bank's own policies on cultural property destruction. Many edible plants upon which locals were dependent for their sustenance and for income were lost. Villagers who used the river waters for drinking, bathing, and laundry developed skin rashes. Most importantly, a severe decline in the fish population occurred. As a consequence, the way of life of indigenous fishermen dependent upon abundant fish for food and income was annihilated. Resettlement of the fishermen and compensation for their losses was wholly inadequate. Traditional communities began to disintegrate. Many of those affected by these developments organized protest villages and engaged in other actions calling for the Thai government and the World Bank to take responsibility for the devastation they caused by building the dam, which cost far more than expected and has generated far less electricity than was anticipated.

At a World Bank meeting in Berlin in 1988, protesters called for the establishment of a Permanent People's Tribunal to try the World Bank (and the International Monetary Fund) for "crimes against humanity" (Rich 1994: 9). An American anthropologist has characterized the forced resettlement of people in dam-related projects as the worst crime against them, short of killing them (Caufield 1996). An American biologist characterized the World Bank's report on the environmental impact of a dam project in a developing country as "fraudulent" and "criminal" (Rich 1994). These allegations certainly apply in the case of the Pak Moon dam (see Box 6.5).

The World Bank's complicity in these allegations is best understood in terms of the Bank's criminogenic structure and organization. The historical charge of its charter has called upon it to focus on economic developments and considerations, not other kinds of consequences of its policies and practices (Rich 1994). Accordingly, throughout its history it has avoided addressing or taking a strong stand on human rights (Caufield 1996; Darrow 2003). Furthermore, it has focused on an ill-defined mission of promoting "long-term sustainable growth" as a rationale for imposing much short-term suffering and economic losses (Rich 1994). This orientation has led the World Bank to adopt and apply somewhat one-dimensional economic models to its project-related analyses, with insufficient attention to many other considerations and potentially useful insights from other disciplines. And once the projects are initiated, they tend to develop a momentum that often marginalizes or negates any real adjustments in response to reports indicating negative environmental or social effects (Vallabhaneni 2000). The underlying incentive structure at the Bank encourages "success" with large, costly projects. Bank employees are pressured to make environmental and social conditions fit. The World Bank has in common with other international financial institutions a structure that rewards its personnel for technical proficiency rather than for concerning themselves with the perspectives and needs of the ordinary people of developing countries (Bradlow 1996; Dugger 2004).

In terms of their own career interests, World Bank officials are rewarded for making loans and moving large amounts of money, rather than relative to any human consequences of these loans, and they have not been held accountable for the tragic human consequences of their projects (Rich 1994).

Though the World Bank has not been a signatory of international human rights treaties, it is subject to the imperatives of international law; at a minimum it is obliged to ensure that it does not exacerbate conditions impinging on human rights

(Skogly 2002). The president of the World Bank from 1995–2005, James Wolfensohn, expressed some interest in addressing concerns of antiglobalization protesters and shifting more attention away from controversial infrastructure projects and more toward public health and education projects but with only mixed success (Becker 2004; Mallaby 2004). In 2005, Paul Wolfowitz, a Bush administration official and a primary architect of "Operation Iraqi Freedom," was appointed the new president of the World Bank (Becker 2005; Krugman 2005). In light of his background and political views, there was a concern that he would be more committed to promoting American as opposed to global priorities. The World Bank does not set out to do harm, but its mode of operation is intrinsically criminogenic and it functions undemocratically. Its key deliberations are carried out secretly, and it is insufficiently accountable to any independent entity. The World Bank is at a minimum criminally negligent when it: (1) fails to adequately explore or take into the account the impact of its loans for major projects on indigenous peoples; (2) adopts and implements policies specifically at odds with the protocols of the UN Universal Declaration of Human Rights and subsequent covenants; or (3) operates in a manner at least hypothetically at odds with both international law and state law. Raising consciousness about the criminal aspects of activities of international financial institutions is both an academic pursuit and activism on the part of the world's poorest peoples. Ideally, external pressures on international financial institutions such as the World Bank lead either to substantive internal reforms or the demise of such institutions.

FINANCE CRIME

"Behind every great fortune is a crime."
—BALZAC (BOONE 1992: 199)

We use the term *finance crime* to refer to large-scale illegality that occurs in the world of finance and financial institutions. Finance crime may be committed on behalf of major financial institutions, such as banks, or for the benefit of individuals occupying financially privileged statuses, such as investment bankers. Even though students of white collar crime have typically classified some activities discussed here as forms of corporate crime or occupational crime, it may make more sense to consider finance crime separately for three reasons. First, vast financial stakes are involved; single individuals or financial organizations may illegally acquire tens of millions, hundreds of millions, or billions of dollars. Second, finance crime may have parallels with corporate crime and is closely entwined with corporations and finance networks but has some different dimensions as well. Finally, finance crime quite directly threatens the integrity of the economic system itself.

Banking/Thrifts Crime: The Savings and Loan Mess

The physical structure and ambience of banks is intended to convey ultimate respectability and trust, for literally hundreds of billions of dollars are entrusted to the banking system. The critical importance of banks to the economy and the catastrophic financial consequences of bank failures led to the creation of a large regulatory structure intended to oversee and police banking operations. All too often, however, bank regulators have been closely allied with bank directors in promoting banking interests instead of protecting bank customers (Greenwald 1980; Thornton, Coy, and Timmons 2002).

Substantial evidence shows that banks from their earliest days have engaged in fraudulent activities (Robb 1990). Much evidence supports the contention that banks, thrifts, and other institutions that perform financial services have unethically and illegally deprived customers of far more money than bank robbers and embezzlers have stolen from them. By some estimations, banks have deprived customers of billions of dollars of interest through deceptive policies and practices pertaining to checking accounts and mortgage escrow accounts

(Berenson 2003b; Greenwald 1980; Mrkvicka 1989). Banks have a role in the long history of misleading people in solicitations for credit card customers about special fees and the real, long-term interest rates they will pay (McGeehan 2004). Bank credit card customers pay millions of dollars of fees they had not anticipated, due to fine print they overlooked in their contracts, allowing the issuer to double and triple interest rates with little warning. In recent years, as the adult credit card market has become largely saturated, credit card companies have aggressively wooed college students, even high school seniors (Geraghty 1996). Needless to say, many of these inexperienced and immature consumers with limited income get themselves deep into debt. If credit card companies and banks marketing these cards are not breaking laws, they may be seen as engaging in ethically questionable practices.

Some alleged practices involving credit cards do violate laws. In 1998, the federal government filed antitrust charges against Visa and MasterCard for restricting banks from offering competitors' cards (Gilpin 1998). In 2002, a class action suit initiated by retailers alleged that Visa and MasterCard had joined forces to monopolize the market for debit cards and designed debit cards (with higher transaction fees) to look almost exactly like credit cards, which confuses merchants (Bayot 2002). This lawsuit was settled in May 2003, with Visa and MasterCard agreeing to pay several billion dollars to retailers and to accept possible future restrictions on the use of their signature debit cards (Bayot 2003b). In addition to credit cards, many banks also sell mutual funds through affiliated brokerages, but some customers have complained that they have not been clearly informed that the investments are not insured or backed by the bank and that sales and management fees may be charged (Ringer 1994). Some banks, including Bank of America, were investigated for complicity in illegal mutual fund trading (Atlas 2003).

Banks and other lenders have often taken advantage of generally unsophisticated borrowers with modest incomes who need to pay their bills or want to buy a house (Azmy 2005; Kirchhoff 2004; Moss 2004). Lenders have discovered that "subprime loans"—or loans to financially marginal people—can be very profitable. Unsolicited loan checks sent to people through the mail often get financially desperate people in trouble; in other cases, the checks are stolen from mailboxes and cashed in by another party, causing major headaches for the addressee (Hershey 1999). Mortgage borrowers often discover they were misled on escalating interest rates and fees, and they end up with monthly payments they cannot afford. In some cases, these borrowers have attempted to consolidate their debts with new, high-interest mortgages (Moss 2004). Some of these people end up losing their homes. The Coalition for Responsible Lending estimated that *predatory lending* costs borrowers $9 billion annually in excessive fees and interest rates (Thompson 2001). A home equity lender, First Alliance Mortgage Corporation, agreed to pay $60 million to 18,000 people it had allegedly deceived with extremely high fees and interest rates (Henriques 2002). Although many of the most unscrupulous loans are made by independent finance companies, they are often backed by banks or the banks buy up their loans and profit from them.

Banks have allegedly made billions of dollars improperly by requiring mortgage lenders to maintain excessive balances in their escrow accounts. The Fleet Mortgage Group, the country's largest private home mortgage company, agreed to refund approximately $150 million to 700,000 homeowners required to make excessive escrow payments (Sack 1993). In 2003, it was alleged that many banks were encouraging customers with low balances to overdraw their checking accounts because these banks earn billions of dollars in overdraft fees (Berenson 2003b). The Bankers Trust Company pleaded guilty to federal criminal charges that unclaimed customer checks and credits in the millions of dollars were diverted into the bank's own accounts, making these accounts appear more profitable (Weiser 1999).

In 2003 and 2004, Freddie Mac and Fannie Mae—as the two government-sponsored mortgage giants are known—were investigated for various forms of accounting fraud (Berenson 2003c; Morgenson 2004c; O'Brien and Lee 2004). These two enterprises carry well over a trillion dollars worth of home mortgages and accordingly play a central role in American home ownership. Their top executives are exceedingly well compensated—with over $20 million a year in the case of Fannie Mae. Serious problems with Freddie Mac and Fannie Mae could have a profound effect on the real estate market and potentially could create huge numbers of mortgage foreclosures.

Banks have also been implicated in a wide range of illegal acts intended to enhance their (or their officers') profitability, including bribery, fraud, money laundering, and violations of the bank secrecy act (Morgenson 2004c; Pollack 2003; Villa 1988). *Money laundering* has been described as the criminal practice of taking ill-gotten gains and moving them through a sequence of bank accounts, so they look like legitimate profits from legal businesses (Bonner and O'Brien 1999). Russian organized crime is believed to have channeled billions of dollars through the Bank of New York in a money-laundering operation. Although the bank itself denied any complicity, one or more officials at the bank must have facilitated these transactions. And a bank in the Cayman Islands was identified as engaged in large-scale money laundering to conceal from the Internal Revenue Service deposits made by wealthy Americans (Smothers 1999b). A New York bank, U.S. Trust, was fined $10 million in 2001 for violating secrecy laws and failing to keep appropriate records for its trading units (Brick 2001). At least one bank, the Ali Taqwa Bank, is suspected of being a financial network supporting the terrorist organization of Osama bin Laden, Al Qaeda (Eichenwald 2001b). Banks wittingly and unwittingly facilitate many forms of crime.

Some banks operate primarily as investment entities, and banks are often intimately involved in the investment activities of major corporate customers. When banks are directly involved in investment and trading activities, they may encourage their brokers and traders to aggressively pursue and maximize profits. This promotion of and rewarding of high profit margins can backfire

spectacularly. In 1995, the venerable British investment bank Barings collapsed—after 230 years in business—because Nicholas Leeson, a rogue trader in the Singapore office, lost approximately $1 billion in unauthorized, exceedingly risky trading in international securities (Chua-Eoan 1995a; Fay 1999). Leeson went to prison for several years, but the bank itself surely bore some responsibility for inadequately supervising a relatively inexperienced trader who had been well rewarded for trading that appeared to be highly profitable. Many innocent parties lost jobs and investment funds in this debacle. Also in 1995, trader Toshihide Iguchi in the Japanese investment bank Daiwa Bank, Ltd., managed to lose more than $1 billion in unauthorized bond trading (Truell 1995b). In February 1996, the bank pleaded guilty to covering up these losses, instead of reporting them to federal regulatory agencies, as American law required (Associated Press 1996). The bank paid a fine of $340 million. In 2002, John Rusnak, a trader for a Baltimore bank, a unit of Allied Irish Banks of Dublin, was shown to have losses of about $700 million in trading (Fuerbringer 2002). He had agreements to use the names of two major American banks, Bank of America and Citibank, in carrying out his trades. Again, the bank seemingly rewarded trading that appeared to be highly profitable while failing to adequately supervise it. But investment banks also foster or are complicit in quite direct forms of fraudulent activity (see Box 6.6).

Banks have been the instruments of massive frauds perpetrated by their owners, executives, and boards. One observation by California's Savings and Loan Commissioner Bill Crawford is especially apt: "The best way to rob a bank is to own one" (Black 2005a; Calavita and Pontell 1990: 321). In recent years, the most blatant and extensive instances of such "bank robbery" occurred in the savings and loan *thrifts*.

The S & L Frauds The losses incurred by the savings and loan (S & L) thrifts throughout the 1980s may constitute the "biggest bank robbery" ever (Black 2005a, 2005b; Calavita, Pontell, and

---

B O X 6.6 Investment Banks: Wealth Producers or Large-Scale Fraudsters?

Investment banks—based in the Wall Street district of Manhattan and elsewhere—are prestigious and powerful financial institutions, with high-level executives who are richly compensated. They like to put themselves forth as central players in the creation of wealth in capitalist societies who put the interests of their clients first. In *The Greed Merchants*, former investment banker Philip Augar (2005) challenges this characterization of these banks and seeks to demonstrate that the investment banks are ridden with conflicts of interest and all too often put their own interests and profits first and foremost. Specifically, the investment banking industry wages for 1980–2000 added up to more than $500 billion—a staggering amount—with shareholders and customers subsidizing a vast proportion of this pay-out (Augar 2005: 62). By simultaneously advising both buyers and sellers in merger transactions, investment banking institutions are obviously in a conflict-of-interest situation. Indeed, they aggressively promote mergers—even when such mergers impose great costs or losses on investors, workers, and consumers—because they generate huge fees for the investment banks. They have allocated hot initial public offering (IPO) shares to top executives of corporations in return for these executives steering lucrative corporate business to the investment banking houses. Frank Quattrone, one of the most successful investment bankers of this era, was convicted in 2004 of obstruction-of-justice charges for emailing associates to "clean up those files" in the face of a criminal investigation on just this practice (Sorkin 2004c; Sorkin 2005c). Mr. Quattrone, who appealed his conviction, earned over $100 million in 2000 alone for his investment banking activities. In May 2005, financier Ronald O. Perelman was awarded $1.45 billion from the investment bank Morgan Stanley when a jury in Florida agreed with his claim that the bank had defrauded him in a 1998 deal (Thomas 2005b). Morgan Stanley was accused of not sharing with him negative information it had about Sunbeam when Perelman made a huge investment in that company.

Major investment banks were deeply implicated in the corporate scandals involving Enron, WorldCom, and other corporations that vastly misrepresented their finances (Augar 2005; Sale 2004). They were accused of either inadequately overseeing huge loans to such corporations or being directly complicit in fraudulent applications of such loans. In 2004, two major investment banking firms, Citicorp and J. P. Morgan Chase, each agreed to pay WorldCom investors over $2 billion, and in 2005, they each agreed to pay Enron investors similar amounts to settle lawsuits about their complicity in these major corporate fraud cases (Cresswell 2005a, 2005b). Among other things, they had helped structure the controversial and arguably illegal off-balance-sheets partnerships that played a central role in the collapse of Enron. The banks found themselves in the awkward position of being both representatives of Enron creditors and targets for creditor lawsuits. These banks were also accused of having misled investors: Jack Grubman, a star telecom analyst for the Salomon Smith Barney unit of Citigroup, was alleged to have upgraded his investment opinion of AT&T at a time when the bank was seeking major investment fees from this corporation; allegedly, the bank's chair did a personal favor for Grubman in return (*New York Times* 2002h). In April 2003, Grubman agreed to accept a lifelong ban from the securities industry and pay a multimillion dollar fine (Labaton 2003b). At the same time, J. P. Morgan Chase was also sued by international investors who lost large sums of money with a trading firm (Evergreen International Spot Trading) that used an account with the bank that was inadequately supervised (Gaylord 2002). Rather than being effective generators of wealth who earned their huge fees, investment banks have been portrayed by critics as greedy institutions all too often complicit in massive frauds.

Tillman 1997; Waldman 1990). The S & L failures can hardly be attributed to criminal conduct alone, but such conduct clearly played an important role. Government estimates suggested that criminal activity or outright fraud was involved in 50 to 80 percent of the failed S & Ls; fraud or criminal misconduct was the decisive factor in 30 to

40 percent of these failures (Calavita, Pontell, and Tillman 1997; Kerry 1990; Waldman 1990). Such misconduct was, perhaps unsurprisingly, almost certain to be involved in the biggest S & L losses.

Total thrift failure losses due to criminal fraud and waste have been estimated at $250 billion, and with interest payments over several decades, the cost of resolving the crisis may eventually exceed $1 trillion (Bartlett 1990; Martz 1990a; Silk 1990; Waldman 1990). By 1999, the bailout of the thrifts had already cost taxpayers some $165 billion (Labaton 1999a). The $165 million loss from just one failed S & L (Centennial) is several times greater than the total take of $46 million from 6,000 bank robberies reported by the FBI in 1985 (Hagan and Benekos 1991).

Thousands of people lost large sums of money directly; in some cases, retired people lost their life savings by purchasing from thrifts uninsured bonds that were ultimately declared worthless (Martz 1990a). Beyond such immediate victims and long-term costs to taxpayers, the S & L frauds added to the national budget deficit; deflected billions of dollars that might have been spent on education, health care, and environmental projects; and limited credit available to legitimate borrowers, who paid higher rates for loans (Martz 1990a).

For decades, the savings and loans were popular depositories for small savers and a major means for enabling millions of Americans to become homeowners. In the 1970s, however, the rapid inflationary rise in the cost of living made the low, fixed interest rates paid by the S & Ls increasingly unappealing to depositors and rendered the higher but still relatively modest interest earned on mortgages increasingly unprofitable. Various other changes in the banking system provided potential depositors with more attractive options than those offered by thrifts. As a consequence, the management of these institutions, facing large losses, exerted political pressure to deregulate the S & Ls and allow them to compete aggressively in a changing economic environment. Thrifts deregulation took place over a period of time, culminating in the 1982 Garn–St. Germain Act, which raised the federal deposit guarantee from $40,000 to $100,000 and allowed the S & Ls to offer much more competitive rates, attract huge "brokered" packages of deposits, and make a broad range of investments and loans, including unsecured commercial loans (Glasberg and Skidmore 1997b).

Because the new guarantee pertained to accounts and not to individuals, wealthy people could protect as much of their savings as they wished. Many S & Ls, eager to attract as much of this money as possible, offered unrealistically high interest rates. Because they were stuck with many low-paying, fixed-interest mortgages, they were bound to go broke unless their loans to highly speculative development enterprises paid off (Gordon 1991: 66). They did not.

New regulatory accounting practices encouraged risk, and by some measures the S & L industry became unregulated rather than simply deregulated (Hagan and Benekos 1991). These changes and a new rule allowing a single stockholder (instead of at least 400) to own a federally insured thrift created an extraordinary range of opportunities for dangerously speculative and blatantly fraudulent activity. As one commentator (Solomon 1989: 27) remarked about the Garn–St. Germain Act, "Before the ink was dry on the new act, the staid thrift industry was invaded by all manner of promoter, swindler, land speculator, junk bond player and money launderer." But many thrift executives and their professional associates, who may have previously operated in essentially legitimate ways, could not resist crossing the line into blatant criminality to take advantage of the new opportunities.

Calavita and colleagues (1997) classified the various forms of illegality in the S & L frauds as "unlawful risk taking," "looting," and "covering up." *Unlawful risk taking* refers to exceeding the practices legally available to the S & Ls, even in the deregulated 1980s. Huge loans were made to developers engaged in highly speculative projects; the borrowers did not necessarily put any of their own money into these projects, and they did not even pay the origination fees (Pilzer and Deitz 1989). If the projects succeeded, investors stood to make a great deal of money; if they failed, the developers simply defaulted on the loan, and the taxpayers were stuck with the bill. A great many defaults occurred. Making these high-risk loans was attractive to the S & Ls because they could report high short-term profits from such new business, and the bankers could give themselves large bonuses. One bank awarded $22 million in bonuses over four years; at another, $3 million in kickbacks was paid for arranging one large loan (Pilzer and Deitz 1989). Deregulation produced a criminogenic environment that was bound to escalate the level of illegal activity.

Calavita and fellow authors (1997) have characterized *collective embezzlement* as a relatively new and understudied form of crime by a corporation against itself. As deposits began to pour into the S & Ls in huge amounts, executives and directors began to siphon off an extravagant percentage of this money for themselves. Erwin Hansen, head of Centennial Savings and Loan in California, threw a $148,000 Christmas party, circled the globe on private airplanes, purchased antique furniture, renovated a house for $1 million, bought expensive artwork, and maintained a fleet of luxury cars—all at the expense of the thrift (Pizzo, Fricker, and Muolo 1991). Don Dixon, owner of Vernon Savings and Loan in Texas, bought a $1 million beach house in California, traveled on two jets costing $200,000 a year to operate, took his wife on a gastronomic tour of Europe at a cost of $22,000, and bought a 112-foot yacht for $2.6 million—all, apparently, at the expense of the thrift (Pilzer and Deitz 1989; Pizzo et al. 1991). These two cases were hardly unique (Gorman 1990; Hershey 1990a; Nash 1990a). Altogether, many executives used a complex of ingenious strategies to loot S & Ls for their own personal benefit, even as those institutions were losing large sums of money.

Finally, the S & Ls engaged in massive deceptions to conceal their fraudulent activities and insolvency from outside examiners. In addition to trading around bad assets, S & Ls kept separate books, engaged in phony transactions to maintain a fictitious impression of net worth, and set up loans so that they would appear to be current when in fact they were phony (Calavita et al. 1997). Highly paid accountants, lawyers, and appraisers aided in these deceptions (Waldman 1990: 48), and in many cases, political pressure and bribery were used to deflect accurate examinations of the thrifts' activities and prevent appropriate actions in response to fraud or irregularities. Box 6.7 presents one of the most infamous S & L cases.

The Wide Net of Responsibility for the S & L Failures   Beyond the S & L officers who directly engaged in fraudulent and illegal activity, other parties must be held responsible for facilitating the thrifts debacle: investment bankers who dumped junk bonds on S & Ls, co-opted accountants, a generally disinterested media, negligent regulators, "free-market" ideologues, and corrupt politicians (Black 2005b; Hume 1990; Pizzo 1990).

Fraud and the S & L Bailout   By the time President George H. W. Bush took office in 1989, it was widely recognized that a massive bailout of the S & Ls was necessary. A new agency, the Resolution Trust Corporation, was established to sell the assets of hundreds of failed thrifts (Gorman 1990). By 1990, there was growing concern that millions were being lost daily because of the slow start on the bailout effort. It became clear then that the government's efforts to unload billions of dollars of seized assets—from failed thrifts to vast real estate holdings acquired through default—made the opportunities for corrupt special deals almost unlimited (Labaton 1990b). The bailout was corrupted by political considerations, with socially and politically well-connected banks broadly assisted while an African American–owned bank with many charities and nonprofits as depositors was allowed to go bankrupt (Glasberg and Skidmore 1997a).

Many buyers of the failed thrifts' assets were property developers and speculators who had defaulted on loans on these properties and thus were obviously in a good position to know their real value. A federal judge awarded a Californian S & L more than $900 million in one case against the federal government. On the other hand, in late 2001, one of the nation's wealthiest families, the Pritzkers, agreed to pay the federal government $460 million for their failed management of Superior Bank (Barboza 2001a). This family was one of the parties to the ongoing lawsuits by S & L owners against the federal government.

The Criminal Justice Response to S & L Fraud   Investigating and successfully prosecuting S & L crimes proved difficult. The crimes were highly complex, and the line separating outright

---

BOX 6.7   The Charles Keating Case

Arguably the most widely publicized S & L fraud case involved Charles H. Keating Jr. and Lincoln Savings and Loan, alleged to be one of the most thoroughly corrupt S & Ls.

Although Lincoln Savings and Loan's recorded assets increased from less than $1 billion to more than $5 billion between 1982 and 1988, it reported losses in excess of $800 million in 1989 when its total losses exceeded $2 billion (Nash and Shenon 1989; Nash 1989c). In late 1989, the Resolution Trust Corporation filed a $1.1 billion civil racketeering suit against Keating and his associates, alleging fraud, insider dealing, illegal loans, and a pattern of racketeering (Morgenthau 1989); the Securities and Exchange Commission and FBI investigated criminal charges as well. Lincoln was accused, among other things, of "manufacturing profits" from sham land sales to businesses that were bought at inflated prices in return for big loans. Keating allegedly paid himself and family members $34 million from the Lincoln Savings and Loan in the three and a half years before its demise (Nash 1989a). Some 23,000 people bought more than $200 million in bonds in Lincoln's parent company from bank officials who falsely touted the bonds as either guaranteed by the government or absolutely safe. Older people sank their life savings in these bonds, and an order of nuns invested their retirement fund (Nash 1989b). They all lost their money when the thrift failed.

When federal regulators recommended that strong regulatory action be taken against Keating in 1987, five U.S. Senators—Alan Cranston, Donald Riegle, John Glenn, Dennis DeConcini, and John McCain—to whom Keating had donated $1.3 million in campaign contributions, met with regulatory bureaucrats who then effectively backed off (Nash 1989a). When asked whether he believed his campaign contributions would influence the senators to act on his behalf, Keating had replied candidly, "I certainly hope so" (Carlson 1989a: 27). One apparent consequence of the senators' intervention was a two-year delay in the closing of the Lincoln Savings and Loan, at an additional cost of $1.3 billion to taxpayers.

In 1990, Keating claimed he had done nothing wrong and blamed incompetent regulator interference as the source of the problems (Carlson 1990a). Others condemned Keating as "a financial pirate" and a "financio-path of obscene proportions" (Morgenthau 1989; Nash 1989b). In 1992, Keating was sentenced in a California proceeding to 10 years in prison for defrauding S & L customers, and in 1993, he was convicted of 73 criminal counts in a federal prosecution (Stevenson 1992a; Sims 1993). After serving almost five years in prison, Keating's federal and state convictions were overturned on appeal, on the grounds that in the federal case jurors had improperly learned about his conviction in the state case, and in the state case the trial judge (Lance Ito, who presided at the O. J. Simpson murder trial) had improperly instructed the jurors (Associated Press 1999; Zagorin 1997). In April 1999, Keating pleaded guilty to four federal fraud counts to resolve the case against him (Mrozek 1999).

---

fraud from bad business judgment or mismanagement is not always well defined. Much of the evidence was buried in millions of financial documents that required sophisticated special knowledge to decipher (Behar 1990; Johnston 1990).

Most of those convicted in S & L cases were minor players, and in many of the cases involving losses in the millions of dollars, only probation and relatively modest fines were imposed (Webb 1990). By the Justice Department's own guidelines, the appropriate jail time for these crimes was less than that imposed for conventional bank robbery, and the fines imposed were less than the total amount stolen (Pilzer and Deitz 1989; Pizzo et al. 1991).

Only a few harsh prison sentences were given to S & L fraudsters (Hayes 1990). According to William Black (2005a, 2005b) it is far from clear that the "control frauds" that characterized the S & L failures have been fully understood or that the lessons from this debacle have been well-learned. See Box 6.8 for a case of global bank–related crime.

Insider Trading

Insider trading became a major symbol of the excesses of the 1980s; in one commentator's view, it is "the representative white collar crime" of that decade (Coffee 1988a: 121). Early in the 21st century,

---

B O X 6.8   The BCCI Case

The S & L failures were not the only recent cases of major bank-related fraud. The Bank of Commerce and Credit International (BCCI) case that emerged in the early 1990s has been characterized as "the largest corporate criminal enterprise ever, the biggest Ponzi scheme, the most pervasive moneylaundering operation" (Beaty and Gwynne 1991). With losses estimated in the $15 billion range, the bank has been called "the world's most corrupt financial empire" (Truell and Gurwin 1992), "the world's sleaziest bank" (Potts, Kochan, and Whittington 1992), "the dirtiest bank of all" (Beaty and Gwynne 1991), and "the bank of crooks and criminals international" (Adams and Frantz 1992).

BCCI was founded in Luxembourg in 1972 by a charismatic Pakistani, Agha Hasan Abedi. It was the first multinational third-world bank. Operating secretively and with little regulatory oversight, it quickly established branches in more than 70 countries around the world, acquired assets of some $20 billion to 30 billion, became a major force in world financial centers, and was backed by the immensely wealthy ruler of Abu Dhai, Sheik al-Nahyan.

In 1991, the bank was shut down after investigations in several countries resulted in charges of corruption, bribery, money laundering, gun running, drug smuggling, terrorism, and massive outright theft. BCCI apparently catered to notorious dictators, including Saddam Hussein, and to international drug dealers, such as the Medellin drug cartel. A complex web of strategies—phony loans, unrecorded deposits, secret files, illicit share-buying schemes, and shell companies—were used to loot the bank of billions (Lohr 1991). Bribery was one key to BCCI's success in infiltrating or taking over banks in many countries and in escaping accountability for so long.

The BCCI pleaded guilty to federal and state charges of racketeering, fraud, larceny, and falsification of business documents and agreed to forfeit $550 million, the largest such forfeiture in a criminal case to date (Johnston 1990). The chief executive of BCCI, Swaleh Naqvi, pleaded guilty to sweeping federal fraud charges in July 1994, admitting responsibility for losses of $225 million in the United States alone (Labaton 1994a). Investors, depositors, and small businesses—disproportionately located in third-world countries—lost $12 billion due to the criminal and negligent activities of BCCI and its subsequent closure. Several U.S. banks associated with BCCI collapsed, exacting huge losses on taxpayers (Truell and Gurwin 1992).

---

concern over insider trading had revived (Labaton and Leonhardt 2002; Thomas 2004). Even if insider trading has not historically been a focus of students of corporate and occupational crime, it is an especially "pure" form of white collar crime. Violation of trust may be a principal attribute of white collar crime, but such a violation virtually defines insider trading. Vast amounts of money, sometimes hundreds of millions of dollars, have been involved in insider trading cases. The median gain in a typical case has been more modest, about $25,000 (Szockyj and Geis 2002). At least some of those engaged in insider trading are wealthy people; most tend to be more privileged than the typical white collar offender. Many other cases of insider trading involve individuals of more moderate means simply looking for a quick profit on an investment or to avoid losing money.

Insider trading in a broad sense may be as old as the marketplace; individuals with *privileged information* have always made investment and trading decisions on the basis of such information. And throughout most of history, nothing has prohibited taking advantage of privileged information. Even with the emergence of the modern corporation, the common law generally did not prohibit corporate insiders from trading on the basis of their privileged information (Pitt 1987). In the wake of the corporate scandals of the 2000s, some commentators have called for a more expansive conception of insider trading or insider deals. High-level corporate executives of Enron, WorldCom, and numerous other corporations profited hugely by unloading stocks at or near their peak value, while ordinary investors often held on (Norris 2002b). At least some of these executives attempted to protect themselves from technical violations of insider trading laws by establishing prearranged trading plans (Altman 2002). But they have clearly profited from insider information. More broadly still, they benefited from insider dealing to garner massive compensation packages from their corporate boards.

Prohibitions of insider trading originate principally with the advent of federal securities laws. Although no specific statutory definition of insider trading exists, SEC regulations and judicial opinions have generally defined it as trading on the basis of material nonpublic information (Pitt 1987). The current laws against insider trading have their roots in a 1909 U.S. Supreme Court decision, *Strong v. Repide*, 213 U.S. 419, which established a "disclose or abstain" rule (i.e., a company official must disclose his special knowledge when purchasing company stock or abstain from purchasing such stock), and in the antifraud provisions of the federal securities regulations of the 1930s (Lynch and Missal 1987: 22; Pitt 1987: 6). The Insider Trading Sanctions Act, passed in 1984, and the Insider Trading and Securities Fraud Enforcement Act, passed in 1988, were intended to strengthen initiatives against insider trading (Gunkel 2005). Both acts accord much discretion to the SEC in specifically defining insider trading.

At least some conservative economists adopt the view that insider trading is a legitimate element of a free-market economy and should be legalized, although polls support the view that Americans favor fair markets over marginally more efficient ones (Cheng 2005b; Gilson 1987). Others have suggested that the seriousness of insider trading as a form of crime has been overstated (Rider 2000). The overriding rationale for prohibiting insider trading is that it creates a fundamentally unfair market that defrauds those without access to the information or deters large numbers of potential investors from entering the marketplace because they believe it is "fixed" (Giuliani 1990: 13; Kuczynski and Sorkin 2002). But it is also obviously true that no market can provide all potential investors with truly equal access to material information, especially in a world of electronic trading connections and 24-hour markets (Labaton and Leonhardt 2002; Makin 1986). The

exchange of tips among the well-heeled and well-connected is common (Kuczynski and Sorkin 2002). The line between privileged and nonprivileged information can be quite blurred.

Nevertheless, insider trading laws attempt to neutralize the advantages that violate either a basic trust or specific requirements for confidentiality. In this context, the courts have had to grapple with the question of defining "insider" and clarifying who may and who may not trade on inside information. Szockyj and Geis (2002) have identified three broad categories of illegal insider traders: (1) corporate officers, directors, and owners who trade or tip on inside knowledge; (2) outsiders who trade on confidential information when they have a fiduciary duty to the source of their information; and (3) anyone who has confidential information relating to a trade or merger and trades on that information. In a 1996 case, a U.S. Court of Appeals ruled in favor of a lawyer who traded on information from a client of his firm on the basis that the lawyer did not owe a duty to the stockholders of the takeover target corporation whose stock he purchased (Norris 1996). But in *U.S. v. O'Hagan* (1997), the U.S. Supreme Court reversed this decision, upholding a "misappropriation" theory of insider trading, reasoning that the lawyer had misappropriated privileged information (Labaton and Leonhardt 2002; Vashita, Johnston, and Choudhury 2005). The specific scope of privileged information is not entirely settled, however.

The Pursuit of Insider Trading Cases   Through most of the 20th century, the practice of passing inside tips was probably quite common and was not prosecuted (Clarke 1990). The principal legal developments and prosecutions of insider trading cases occurred during the 1980s, when a number of spectacular and highly publicized cases directed much attention to this form of crime. From 1934 to 1979, the SEC initiated only 53 insider trading enforcement actions; in the seven years from 1980 to 1987, it brought 177 actions (Szockyj 1990).

During the 1980s, a number of factors increased the visibility and newsworthiness of insider trading. The financial markets became more

---

B O X 6.9   The Corporate Takeover Controversy

The insider trading cases of the 1980s can be properly understood only in the context of the wave of corporate takeovers occurring at the time. In 1974, the International Nickel Company successfully broke a long-standing taboo against hostile corporate takeovers when it acquired the Electric Storage Company. In 1975, an SEC ruling that commissions on stock transactions were negotiable instead of fixed led to a sharp downturn in Wall Street revenues (Reich 1989). Corporate takeovers, including hostile ones, came to be seen as an important new source of income on Wall Street. Leveraged buyouts, in which a company's management joins with investment bankers to buy out the company's shareholders and take the company private, became especially popular. Between 1978 and 1988, the percentage of Wall Street profit provided by mergers, acquisitions, and leveraged buyouts rose from 5 percent to approximately 50 percent (Reich 1989). During three years in the early 1980s, some 9,000 companies or divisions worth $480 billion changed hands (Cooper 1987). Because the value of a company's stock invariably rises—sometimes quite dramatically—when the company becomes a takeover target, it is not difficult to understand the enormous temptation to acquire and trade on inside information about a planned takeover.

A new breed of *risk arbitrageurs* played a central role in the takeovers of the 1970s and 1980s. Traditionally, *arbitrage* refers to the practice of trading on different markets to take advantage of the possibility of buying in one market a stock that can be sold at a profit in another market (Reichman 1989). A risk arbitrageur such as Ivan Boesky, who during the early 1980s was "King of the Arbitrageurs," would buy up stock in companies that were takeover targets in anticipation of higher stock values. Clearly, illegally acquired inside information on prospective takeovers provides the arbitrageur with a large advantage.

Whether the takeovers themselves were on balance beneficial or detrimental to the national economy and whether restrictions should be placed on corporate takeovers have been hotly debated (Johnson 1986; Brooks 1987; Adams and Brock 1989). Defenders of hostile takeovers involving corporate raiders argue that raiders identify companies with assets that are undervalued on the stock market due to bad management; that raiders make these companies more efficient and profitable by buying them out and getting rid of inefficient managers, practices, and divisions; and that accordingly, shareholders gain (Icahn 1986; Newport 1989; Samuelson 1987).

Critics of hostile takeovers have argued that nothing economically useful emerges from takeovers and that they actually damage the system by diverting attention from the hard work of developing and producing better products (Galbraith 1986; Reich 1989). In this view, relatively few people—mainly raiders, insiders, investment bankers, and brokers—benefit from the takeovers, and those few derive grossly excessive profits. The RJR Nabisco leveraged buyout, for example, produced some $1 billion in fees for investment bankers, and Michael Milken alone earned at least $550 million in one year based on activities substantially involving takeovers (Burrough and Helyar 1989; Stewart 2001). Corporate raiders have walked away with tens of millions of dollars, perhaps even hundreds of millions, in "greenmail," which is what a target company pays corporate raiders to sell their acquired stock.

Meanwhile, ordinary taxpayers must make up part or all of the tax revenues lost from enormous post-takeover or buyout corporate interest payment deductions. Consumers often end up paying significantly higher prices when companies are under intense new pressure to reduce a heavy debt load. Tens of thousands of employees lose their jobs or take major pay cuts; their communities suffer the consequences when divisions are shut down or sold to pay off such debt (Cooper 1987; Faludi 1990; Reich 1989).

---

vulnerable to insider trading by virtue of the dramatic growth in both the trading capacity of institutions and corporations and in tender offers or takeover situations (see Box 6.9) (Augar 2005; Szockyj 1990). New types of securities, the greater use of options, and a higher level of international trading also facilitated insider trading during this period. Altogether, a broader variety of professionals became directly involved in the securities markets, information networks expanded, and traditional securities market controls broke down (Reichman 1989; Zey 1993). At the same time, President

Reagan's new SEC chair, John Shad, and the SEC's enforcement division head, John Fedders, were seeking a way to distinguish their administration of the agency from the previous one, which had focused on international bribery and corporate fraud. They were also eager to enhance the credibility of the SEC and respond to critics who alleged that it did not take a sufficiently tough stand on insider trading. Moreover, insider trading was unpopular in the business world. In 2002, the SEC and federal prosecutors assumed a renewed interest in insider trading with a new wave of high-profile cases (Labaton and Leonhardt 2002).

Szockyj and Geis (2002) have reviewed the character and outcome of 425 insider trading cases pursued by the SEC and Department of Justice from 1980 to 1989. Most involved individuals, although in some cases brokerages were named. Most were addressed civilly; criminal cases were referred to the Department of Justice. Civil cases were typically settled by disgorgement (giving up) of the illegal profit, plus a fine equal to that profit (in 20 percent of the cases the fine was less than the profit). Defendants were often allowed to settle without admitting guilt and accordingly avoided the stigma of a criminal conviction. The relatively small number of cases that were pursued as criminal cases were not necessarily granted lenience; in more than half the cases, incarceration resulted. In most cases, opportunity to commit insider trading was an important factor; relatively little effort or skill was typically involved.

The Victims of Insider Trading Clearly, the primary victims of insider trading are institutional and individual investors who bought or sold stock at a loss, failed to realize a profit, or overpaid for stock because of insider trader manipulations. The losses may range from thousands of dollars for individual investors to millions of dollars for institutional investors. Because the pension funds of millions of Americans are heavily invested in the stock market, a large class of unwitting victims of insider trading exists. Once they learn that a company is targeted for a takeover bid, insiders can buy up large blocks of the company's stock,

driving the price up and costing the takeover entity a large amount of money it ordinarily would not have had to pay. Investors that lack insider information may be misled and may accordingly buy or sell at a disadvantage, though some investors inadvertently profit. The substantial direct losses of some investors are but a part of the cost of insider trading; the loss of confidence in the integrity of the market is another very real cost.

The Wall Street Insider Trading Cases of the 1980s The most spectacular and widely publicized insider trading cases began to unfold in 1985 with an anonymous letter to Merrill Lynch claiming that one of its traders in Caracas was trading on inside information (Stone 1986). This tip led to an SEC investigation of a small bank in the Bahamas, Bank Leu, through which the trades were executed. The investigation revealed that one of the bank's clients had engaged in a pattern of exceedingly profitable trades correlated with corporate takeovers. This client, further investigation revealed, was Dennis Levine, a 33-year-old investment banker with Drexel Burnham in New York. Levine came from a modest middle-class background in Queens, attended Baruch College of City University, and with a combination of raw ambition, aggressiveness, and charm had quickly worked his way through a series of executive positions with prestigious investment banking firms, including Smith Barney and Lehman. At age 32, he was appointed a managing director of Drexel Burnham with a high six-figure salary.

In 1979, Levine began to establish a small network of friends, business associates, lawyers, and investment bankers, all of them intimately involved in corporate takeover deals, to trade confidential information on pending takeovers that could be used for highly profitable stock trading. Levine assumed that his trades, executed through the Bahamian bank and transacted with a pseudonym ("Mr. Diamond"), would not be traced back to him as an insider (Frantz 1987). By 1985, Levine's personal account at Bank Leu had surpassed the $10 million mark; altogether Levine acquired more than $11 million from his illegal investments. But

Levine had rather recklessly continued his insider trading activities even after learning of SEC inquiries, arrogantly assuming that he was too shrewd to be caught.

After Levine was arrested and confronted with the evidence against him, he began to provide government investigators with information about his associates in insider trading deals. On June 5, 1986—just three weeks after his arrest—Levine pleaded guilty to one count of securities fraud, two counts of income tax evasion, and one count of perjury (Frantz 1987). He settled SEC charges against him by agreeing to pay $11.6 million and by accepting a permanent injunction against working in the securities business. He was allowed to keep his $1 million Park Avenue apartment, BMW, and $100,000 in bank accounts.

Those implicated by Levine included investment banker Martin Siegel and arbitrageur Ivan Boesky, a model for the Gordon Gekko character in the film *Wall Street* (Glaberson 1987; Stewart 1991). Boesky agreed to pay a $100 million fine, received a three-year prison sentence, and was barred from the securities business for life (Kilborn 1986). Both Siegel and Boesky received relatively light prison sentences for cooperating with authorities.

The Michael Milken Case   Some of the information provided by Ivan Boesky led to the most spectacular securities market prosecution of them all, that of Michael Milken and Drexel Burnham (Byron 1990; Greenwald 1990; Kornbluth 1992; Stewart 1991). Milken became a key figure in the hyperinflated financial market of the 1980s as the "Junk Bond King."

In the 1970s, Milken had come to recognize that vast amounts of money could be raised through issuing and selling high-yield, high-risk *junk bonds*. Such bonds can be issued by smaller, less established companies that do not qualify for blue-chip bonds. They pay higher interest because they are viewed as more prone to default, but during the 1980s, the actual rate of default was quite low. These junk bonds were widely used to finance the wave of corporate takeovers during the

1980s, and they were bought up by S & Ls and many mutual funds.

Operating out of Drexel Burnham's Beverly Hills office, Milken was extraordinarily successful in developing and selling such bonds and in advising companies seeking to expand or to take over other companies. He and his associates became immensely wealthy; in 1987, he was reputed to have personally earned $750 million. Then the Wall Street insider trading cases led to an investigation of the activities of Drexel Burnham and Milken. In 1988, Drexel Burnham pleaded guilty to violation of federal securities laws and agreed to pay a $650 million fine (Labaton 1988). This plea was entered in the face of a prospective federal racketeering (RICO) prosecution that could have resulted in the confiscation of the firm's total assets. In February 1990, Drexel Burnham collapsed anyway—after 152 years in business and a period in the 1980s when it was the most profitable investment banking house on Wall Street (Greenwald 1990).

Although the criminal investigation of Milken initially included charges of insider trading, it ultimately resulted in his pleading guilty to six felony charges of securities fraud and conspiracy in 1990, including manipulating securities prices, filing false information and false reporting with the SEC, engaging in overcharging of a mutual fund, and filing a false tax return (Eichenwald 1990b; Stewart 2001). In connection with Boesky, Milken was accused of having allowed Boesky to "park" stock with him to enable Boesky to avoid filing forms required of those holding more than 5 percent of a corporation's assets; Milken received $5 million in "consultation" fees from Boesky for this service. Milken long resisted any settlement of the charges against him, paying lawyers $1 million a month to fight the charges, and consequently he lost some of the leverage he might have had by settling earlier.

As part of his agreement, Milken paid a $600 million fine and was sentenced by Judge Kimba Woods to 10 years in prison. This seemingly harsh sentence was ultimately reduced in return for Milken's cooperation in related cases, and he served only 22 months in a minimum security prison. By some estimates, Milken earned as much as $275,000 an hour during his years as a financier; as a prison inmate, he was entitled to earn about 40 cents an hour for his labors. Despite the huge fine he paid, Milken retained a significant portion of his fortune, which at one point was estimated to exceed $1 billion (Stewart 2001). Not long after his release, Milken was teaching a finance course to admiring MBA students at UCLA (Clines 1993). In subsequent years, he spent a fortune to become a major influence in medical research, education, and economics, largely through his Milken Institute and through global conferences he sponsored (Pollack 1999). He discovered that he had prostate cancer while in prison, and this inspired an interest in sponsoring searches for a cure for this disease (Andrews 1996). Between 1993 and 1996, Milken earned $92 million for "facilitating" business deals, despite having earlier signed an agreement banning him for life from the securities industry (Stewart 2001). It was puzzling to some that Milken would risk reimprisonment by violating the terms of the agreement and that leading businessmen would pay him such extravagant fees. In 1998, Milken agreed to pay the SEC $47 million to settle the charges involved in the alleged violation of the agreement, although he neither admitted nor denied these charges (Truell 1998). Milken's efforts to obtain a pardon from President Clinton in his final days in office were unsuccessful (Stewart 2001). The SEC and the U.S. Attorney's office in New York objected to the pardon bid on the basis that Milken had attempted to obstruct justice and had given false and misleading testimony in connection with the case against him.

Some see Milken as a greedy villain who caused much harm in the securities markets, while others view him as a misunderstood financial genius who helped to build the economy and was made a scapegoat for the financial excesses of the 1980s (Kornbluth 1992; Fischel 1995; Stewart 1991). The SEC estimated that his illegal actions cost investors $1 billion or more (Stewart 2001). Although some corporations (e.g., MCI and Turner Broadcasting) benefited greatly from junk bonds and their dealings with Milken, many other companies collapsed into bankruptcy due to high debt, workers lost jobs, and free competition in the markets was seriously compromised.

Insider Trading since the 1980s Various insider trading cases surfaced during the 1990s, including one involving an investment banking house compliance officer and another involving a former investment banking firm CEO who provided insider information to his stripper girlfriend (Fuerbringer 1997; Trillin 2000; Weiser and McGeehan 1999).

In 2002, an especially high-profile case of alleged insider trading surfaced involving Dr. Sam Waksal of ImClone (a biotech company) and his good friend, Martha Stewart (Peyser 2002). (See Box 6.10.) Waksal was alleged to have tipped off a number of relatives and friends directly or indirectly that the FDA had failed to approve a major new ImClone drug for the market; when this news became public, the stock price plunged. In June 2003, Waksal was sentenced to seven years in prison in this case (Hays 2003). Also in 2002, reporting of an investigation of possible insider trading by President George W. Bush as an energy company executive in 1990 resurfaced (Bumiller 2002b). In 2004, a father and son settled insider trading charges, based on the father (a bakeries company executive) advising the son (a stockbroker) to sell stock in the company on the basis of the father's inside knowledge of the company's deteriorating financial condition (Thomas 2004). In 2005, in a somewhat unusual case, a well-known penny stock trader and an FBI agent were convicted of securities charges for trading on confidential information, when the trader used information supplied by the agent on criminal investigations to make illegal profits (Dash 2005a). Also in 2005, Lawrence Ellison, CEO of the Oracle company, agreed to pay $100 million to charity to settle insider trading allegations; and Bill Frist, majority leader in the Senate, was being investigated on possible insider trading charges arising out of his sale of stock in a corporation founded by his family (Glater 2005h; Kirkpatrick 2005). During this period, the SEC was pursuing about 50 insider trading cases a year.

B O X   6.10   Insider Trading and the Martha Stewart Case

Arguably the highest profile insider trading case of the recent era involved the lifestyle and homemaking magnate Martha Stewart, one of the most celebrated women in America (Glater 2004a; Toobin 2004). Although she was at one point estimated to be worth something in the neighborhood of $1 billion, she apparently could not resist the temptation to unload Imclone stock for a savings of some $50,000 when information originating with her friend Samuel Waksal came her way and indicated that an impending announcement would lead to a sharp decline in the value of the stock. Although some people expressed sympathy and support for Ms. Stewart, the lawyer–novelist Scott Turow (2004) reminds us that those who bought her Imclone stock lost money: "Martha Stewart ripped her buyers off as certainly as if she'd sold them silk sheets that she knew were actually synthetic." But contrary to a widespread public impression, Martha Stewart's criminal trial was for "obstruction of justice" charges in connection with her testimony to federal investigators looking into the insider trading case and not for the somewhat more difficult to prove insider trading charges. She was convicted in March 2004 and subsequently sentenced to five months in a minimum security prison, to be followed by five months of house arrest (Hays 2004; Hays and Eaton 2004). This case exemplified the axiom that it is often the attempt to cover up the original offense that will get you into more trouble than the original offense itself (Berenson 2004b). Although in 2005 Martha Stewart was reported to be moving forward with her life following her release from prison, by any measure the cost to her of trading on inside information was huge (Hays 2005b). It remained to be seen whether this highly publicized case would deter others from engaging in insider trading.

Finance Crime and Financial Markets

In addition to insider trading, many other unethical and illegal activities occur within financial markets: a massive check-kiting scheme against banks, masterminded by the prestigious brokerage firm, E. F. Hutton (Sterngold 1990); systemic cheating of customers by Chicago commodities traders (Padgett 1989); phony bidding in U.S. Treasury bonds by the celebrated Salomon Brothers investment bank (Eichenwald 1992); the selling of hundreds of millions of dollars of municipal bonds by a Merrill Lynch financial strategist with a fundamental conflict of interest (Wayne 1996); a *derivatives* investment scheme that bankrupted Orange County, California (Sterngold 1995; Wayne and Pollock 1998); a long-running fraud within a rigged foreign currency marketplace (Fuerbringer and Rashbaum 2003); the sale of illegal tax shelters by a major accounting firm, KPMG (Glater 2005g); and the revelation of significant fraud in the mutual fund and hedge fund industries (see Box 6.11). These cases were mostly resolved by fines, although the Merrill Lynch financial analyst received a 33-month prison sentence.

An immense amount of fraud occurs in connection with the sale of stocks, and some of this activity is addressed in the next chapter as a form of contrepreneurial fraud. In some cases, however, major financial institutions are involved, and a classification of finance crime may be warranted. In 1993 and 1994, a huge brokerage firm, Prudential Securities, Inc., agreed to pay $371 million in restitution and fines to settle a wide range of fraud charges for conduct over at least a decade (Eichenwald 1993a, 1993b, 1994a). Prudential was charged with lying to investors about risks, returns, and losses; inadequately supervising subsidiaries and employees; abusing client trust; and "churning," a persistent problem in the securities field involving the practice of unauthorized, excessive trading in clients' accounts to increase brokers' commissions. In 1994, federal prosecutors investigated possible systematic defrauding of large institutional investors in connection with the sale of limited real estate partnerships (Eichenwald 1994a). The 1981 Reagan Tax Reform bill created a boom in opportunities to sell tax shelters and limited partnerships to investors seeking to reduce their tax liability (Webber 1995). The Prudential case has been

---

B O X 6.11   Fraudulent Conduct in the Mutual Funds and Hedge Funds Industries

---

Beginning in Fall 2003, a series of revelations of wrongdoing in the mutual funds industry surfaced and received much attention (Labaton 2003a; Quinn 2003; Thottam 2003). That significant levels of fraudulent and unethical conduct occurred in this segment of high finance was especially disturbing because some 100 million Americans have some $7 trillion invested in mutual funds, which often constitute a significant portion of their financial assets. Altogether, investors pay funds an enormous amount—some $70 billion a year during the current era—in fees. But during this recent era, there were years when ordinary investors were losing hundreds of billions of dollars on their investments while fund managers were getting rich during the same period. Municipal funds were widely assumed to be heavily regulated for just this reason (Labaton 2003b). Investigations from 2003 on indicated that about half of the funds were breaking rules intended to protect investors.

Various types of manipulations within mutual fund trading were exposed, all benefiting fund managers and privileged investors while putting ordinary investors at a disadvantage or imposing losses on them (Labaton 2004a). In some cases, payouts or kickbacks were paid to brokers to steer customers into certain mutual funds. High fees were charged to investors without always being clearly identified to them. With so-called "soft dollar commissions," fund managers were passing along much of their normal overhead to investors. Top executives of funds were trading in and out of their own funds and skimming profits for themselves. This type of rapid, short-term trading is known as "market timing." Fund managers were also

providing privileged information to large or important customers, a form of insider trading. They allowed these customers in some cases to engage in after-hours—after the close of market—trading, to their considerable advantage. This activity is known as "late trading."

Many civil lawsuits on behalf of investors were initiated against mutual funds, with many of these lawsuits resolved through a settlement. In a few cases, individual mutual fund managers or traders were pursued. In 2004, Richard Strong, founder of Strong Capital Management, agreed to a lifetime ban from the financial industry and paid a $60 million fine after admitting his own trading worked against the interest of his investors (Atlas 2004). Strong, reported to be worth some $800 million, avoided criminal charges through this action. In another case, a Bank of America broker, Theodore Siphol, was criminally prosecuted for allowing a hedge fund company to trade mutual funds after the market closed (Glater 2005f). Siphol managed to beat some charges in a trial in 2005 but faced further criminal prosecution. Clearly much wrongdoing occurred within the mutual fund industry, with relatively little accountability for those responsible for it.

Hedge funds are entities that raise large pools of money from wealthy individuals and asset-rich institutions and seek high rates of return with sharp investment strategies (Anderson 2005a). But these funds are largely unregulated and accordingly are ripe for frauds. Two principals of one such fund, the Bayou Group, pleaded guilty to criminal charges of fraud in September 2005 (Anderson 2005b). Much of the money in their $450 million fund had disappeared by that time.

---

characterized as "the largest investment scandal in history"; hundreds of thousands of investors lost homes, retirement funds, and massive proportions of their savings (Eichenwald 1995b, 1996a). In the later 1990s, ongoing litigation focused on Prudential's efforts to avoid turning over some documents and the pursuit of punitive damages by investors who lost money. Prudential was accused of new cheating in relation to the settlement agreement it had signed earlier to avoid paying what it really owed (Hanley 1997; Treaster 1997a). Subsequently Prudential, the nation's fourth-largest securities

brokerage, worked on recovering from this debacle, but there was little evidence that wrongdoers within the company suffered specific consequences from their involvement.

Systematic defrauding of customers of stock traders has been an ongoing enterprise. In 2005, the U.S. attorney's office in Manhattan was investigating allegations that individual traders at the New York Stock Exchange were engaging in illegal trading—for example, trading ahead of their customers' orders or obtaining inferior prices for their customers' orders—to enhance their own profit at the expense of their customers (Anderson 2005a). The year before, five trading firms had paid $240 million in penalties in connection with such charges.

Stock Analysts and Conflicts of Interest Many investors have historically relied upon the advice and recommendation of stock analysts while making their investments. Such investors have presumably assumed that these stock analysts are savvy students of the financial markets who make investment recommendations based on objective analysis of financial data and a wide range of market conditions affecting particular stocks. They might assume that these analysts have a vested interest in providing accurate forecasts because their own reputations depend upon being right more often than they are wrong. More cynical investors have recognized that stock analysts may profit directly from pushing certain stocks. But in the wake of the collapse of Enron in 2001, the full scope of conflicts of interest inherent in the activities of many leading Wall Street stock analysts was broadly revealed (Augar 2005; Kadlec 2002b; McGeehan 2002c). Billions of dollars of losses were generated by stock analysts who hyped stocks with questionable or blatantly false claims (Berenson 2003a; Gasparino 2005a).

Many stock analysts maintained a "buy" recommendation on Enron and other "new economy" stocks long after these stocks began to fail. Why? In essence, Wall Street analysts were part of firms that derived the largest share of their income from underwriting and arranging IPOs of new companies. These firms' research departments are quite unlikely to be self-supporting but can contribute greatly to the profit margin by producing favorable reports on stocks of companies whose business the firms are seeking. Furthermore, companies are especially likely to give their underwriting business to firms with "star" analysts who they believe will successfully promote their stock. Ethically, stock brokerage and investment banking should remain separate operations, but much evidence exists that this separation is routinely breached.

Executives generally profit enormously if their companies' stock prices rise; accordingly, they will not be favorably disposed toward Wall Street firms with analysts who disparage their stock. Stock analysts, then, would often function as sales representatives promoting a company's stock instead of as disinterested and impartial analysts. In return, the analysts who helped bring business to their firms were rewarded with huge bonuses, sometimes earning tens of millions of dollar annually. In some cases, stock analysts even owned stock in companies whose stock they promoted, and accordingly they profited greatly from a run-up in the stock price.

In early 2002, New York Attorney General Eliot Spitzer launched a criminal investigation of Wall Street firms after evidence surfaced that stock analysts who were recommending that their clients buy a stock were at the same time disparaging the companies involved and their stock in e-mails among themselves (McGeehan 2002e). Congress was also exploring these conflicts of interest, including the claim that some of the Wall Street firms were compelled to invest in Enron partnerships and accordingly had a strong vested interest in endorsing Enron stock (Oppel 2002d). The CEO of Merrill Lynch issued a public apology following revelation of this practice (McGeehan 2002c). The Wall Street firms were contending with other allegations of illegal or unethical practices to improve the appearance of their funds' performance, including possible antitrust violations in setting fees for initial public offerings of stocks and buying additional shares of stocks in companies already well represented in their portfolios at the end of the year or the fiscal quarter (Gasparino 2005a; Hakim 2001). On April 28, 2003, the nation's 10 biggest investment firms agreed to pay $1.4 billion to settle charges of grossly misleading investors (Labaton 2003b). In 2005, further payments of billions of dollars were paid out to settle investor claims (Cresswell 2005a, 2005b). Many stock analysts were complicit in huge losses for investors.

Pension funds have also been victimized by stockbrokers acting as investment consultants and money managers, sometimes suffering millions of dollars of losses due to undisclosed fees and other fraudulent practices (Morgenson and Walsh 2005). The Chattanooga Pension Fund in Tennessee discovered a loss of $20 million in its fund in 2005 in just such a case. Some individual investors have sued stock brokerages such as Merrill Lynch on the claim that they lost much money due to fraudulent research and claims by the brokerage (Anderson 2005b). In such a case in 2005, a Florida couple was awarded $1 million for their losses, but it is quite difficult for individual investors to win these cases. And whole cohorts of corporate employees have suffered large losses to their pension funds when money managers have shifted their assets from safer to riskier investments (Walsh M. 2005). United Airlines' pension plan virtually collapsed in such circumstances, but the money managers walked away with fees of some $125 million over a period of five years.

Insurance Industry Fraud The multibillion dollar insurance industry is also at the heart of our financial system in the sense that people rely heavily on insurance as a buffer against catastrophic accidents, illnesses, and fatalities and as a source of retirement income. This industry has been the target of recurrent and persistent accusations of self-dealing, unsound investments, unsuitable or misleading policies, and high-pressure sales techniques (Dooling 2005; Quint 1995). The offshore insurance companies have been especially successful in avoiding regulatory oversight and have been involved in large-scale frauds (Tillman 2002). In January 2005, New York attorney general Eliot Spitzer reported that his office had uncovered evidence of massive wrongdoing on the part of insurance companies and their brokers, taking the form of systematic fraud and market manipulation (Treaster 2005b). For example, brokers who were supposed to provide unbiased recommendations on coverage to their customers often steered them to insurance companies that provided the brokers with incentive commissions. Marsh and McLennan, the largest insurance broker in the world, settled such bid-rigging charges for $850 million, and its CEO, Jeffrey W. Greenberg, was forced to resign (Treaster 2005b). During the same period, the global insurance giant AIG (American International Group) was under investigation for alleged massive fraud in the form

of "sham transactions" that hid losses and inflated the company's apparent net worth, and its CEO, Maurice Greenberg—father of Jeffrey—was also forced to resign (Kadlec 2005). The financial misrepresentations and manipulations of these insurance companies, while enriching their top executives, put the interests of their clientele in jeopardy. For example, a Virginia physician had to dissolve his practice when he was unable to pay a $750,000 malpractice judgment because his malpractice insurance company (Reciprocal of America) had collapsed after its vast financial representations were exposed as fraudulent (O'Brien and Treaster 2005). Company executives pleaded guilty to fraud charges, but both doctors and patients suffered devastating financial consequences.

As a consequence of the McCarran-Ferguson Act of 1945 and potent lobbying, the insurance industry has been relatively unregulated. Because the income of agents depends significantly on commissions from selling more insurance to clients or inducing them to switch policies, churning is also a problem in this industry. Prime America Financial is but one major insurance company accused of selling insurance by deceptive or phony policy illustrations; it was also accused of recruiting agents through a pyramid scheme that allows recruiting agents to share in commissions (Quint 1995). Metropolitan Life was required to pay hundreds of millions of dollars to settle suits that customers were cheated by deceptive sales practices (Meier 1999). A standard tactic involved persuading customers to exchange older policies for newer ones, with the false claim that the newer policies were cheaper and offered better coverage. In 2005, sales of annuities to older people were being investigated for potential fraud (Morgenson 2005d). Prospective and present retirees are invited to free "investment seminars," where they may be persuaded to liquidate their stocks and bonds for annuities. While annuities are suitable investments for some people, they can carry commissions of up to 12 percent, and holders pay stiff penalties if they do not keep them for at least 15 years. Accordingly, some who buy these annuities from aggressive salespeople believe they were tricked and defrauded.

BOX 6.12 The Martin Frankel Case

Insurance companies acquire large pools of assets, which make them especially tempting targets of fraudsters. In one of the more spectacular cases of such fraud in the late 1990s, more than $200 million in insurance premiums was siphoned off by Martin Frankel, who had created or taken control of several insurance companies (Kahn 1999a; Kahn and Finkelstein 1999). Frankel grew up in a middle-class family in Toledo, Ohio, and attended the University of Toledo, though he failed to graduate. In the 1980s, he got involved in money management. Following an SEC investigation in 1992, Frankel was banned for life from the securities industry, due to flagrant misrepresentations of his money management activities. Frankel ignored this ban and in the 1990s began acquiring small, troubled insurance companies in the South. The state agencies charged with regulating insurance companies are often not well equipped to supervise them effectively. Frankel began stripping the companies he acquired of assets under the pretext that he was successfully investing these funds. He also set up a phony charity (the Saint Francis of Assisi Foundation) through a contact at the Vatican but rather than making philanthropic donations, he attempted to use this foundation and the Vatican connection to take control of insurance companies (Stanley 1999). During this time, Frankel was living a lavish, if somewhat bizarre, life in a Greenwich, Connecticut mansion, often with young women he contacted through personal ads in sex magazines. As investigators began to close in on him, Frankel set a fire in his mansion to attempt to destroy documents and fled to Europe in a private plane, with millions of dollars in diamonds. He was arrested in Germany in September 1999 and returned to the United States to face various charges. With the fraud exposed, policyholders with the insurance companies involved experienced considerable anxiety over whether their policies would be honored (Treaster 1999a). In May 2002, Frankel pleaded guilty to 23 federal counts of racketeering and wire and securities fraud (Zielbauer 2002). In December 2004, Martin Frankel was sentenced in a federal court to a prison term of almost 17 years (Cowan 2004). His lawyer had tried to elicit sympathy for him by referring to the pitiful conditions of his present life, and Frankel himself pleaded for leniency on the grounds that he suffered from a mental illness, but the judge in the case was unmoved.

Insurance companies have been accused of jeopardizing the financial well-being of clients by reselling policies to weak (or insolvent) companies, cheating taxpayers by evading legally mandated responsibilities to elderly workers who are covered by Medicare, and using questionable means to avoid insuring vulnerable classes of clients, such as potential AIDS patients (Kerr 1992c; Knight-Ridder Newspapers 1990a; Scherzer 1987). In an era of managed care, insurance companies sometimes attempt to deny coverage to customers; a widow of a man who died after their insurance company denied treatment won a $119 million punitive award against the company (Johnston 1999a). State Farm was found to have breached its contract with its policyholders by requiring that body shops use lower-priced generic parts for auto crash repairs rather than the parts made by the auto manufacturer; the company was ordered to pay policyholders $456 million (Wald 1999c). The company claimed that using the higher-priced manufacturer parts would ultimately cost its clients more through higher premiums. In some cases, insurance companies may victimize each other. In one case, the chair of U.S. Aviation, an insurance company, was found guilty of trying to make other insurance companies pick up the costs of an airplane crash (Bryant and Meier 1996). Box 6.12 presents another example of wrongdoing in the insurance industry.

HYBRID WHITE COLLAR CRIME, IN SUM

This chapter surveys several major forms of white collar crime that are not properly classified as corporate crime, occupational crime, or governmental crime. The term *state-corporate crime* has only been introduced into the criminological literature quite recently, but it has been recognized as usefully capturing cooperative state and corporate forms of harm and lawbreaking. A number of historical and contemporary cases that illustrate this concept were discussed in this chapter. In the present global economy, there is reason to believe that this form of crime will become even more significant.

The concept of *crimes of globalization* is an even more recent addition to the criminological literature, and it remains to be seen whether it will be widely adopted. But the section of this chapter devoted to crimes of globalization advanced the argument that the policies and practices of international financial institutions such as the World Bank can have immensely harmful consequences that require criminological attention and that in an increasingly globalized world will be viewed as a significant form of white collar crime.

The term *finance crime* has been adopted here to encompass the massive forms of wrongdoing that occur in the world of high finance, from investment banks to insurance companies to the mutual funds industry. These financial institutions operate at the heart of our economy, and are accordingly positioned to bring about massive financial losses.

The forms of white collar crime addressed in this chapter have become increasingly significant in recent years and illustrate the increasingly hybrid character of much white collar crime. The networks connecting governments, corporations, and various elements of the financial markets will likely be major features of white collar crime throughout the 21st century.

KEY TERMS

antiglobalization movement, 148

arbitrage, 162

collective embezzlement, 158

crimes of globalization, 149

derivatives, 166

finance crime, 153

globalization, 149

insider trading, 159

international financial institutions, 149

junk bonds, 164

money laundering, 155

predatory lending, 154

privileged information, 160

risk arbitrageurs, 162

state-corporate crime, 145

sweatshops, 150

thrifts, 155

unlawful risk taking, 157

World Bank, 151

DISCUSSION QUESTIONS

1. What are the defining attributes of state-corporate crime, and what are some good examples of such crime? With regard to one specific example, what were the key elements that produced this state-corporate crime? Why would you anticipate an increase or decline in state-corporate crime in the future?

2. What arguments can be made for and against the concept of crimes of globalization? How

do crimes of globalization intersect with and differ from other major forms of white collar crime? Is the Pak Moon dam story about a crime of globalization or something else? Is the World Bank, in your view, in any sense a party to criminal activity?

3. Why is finance crime separated from corporate crime and occupational crime as a form of white collar crime? What are some specific

activities carried out by or through banks that are either illegal or unethical, or both? What forces or developments in the larger society have contributed to the development of bank or thrifts crime?

4. Which dimensions of insider trading are "time honored" and which are more recent? What is the nature of the basic controversy over insider trading and corporate takeovers? Which factors have limited the response to insider trading, and which specific factors led to a wave of prosecutions in recent decades?

5. What are some of the specific types of unethical and illegal activities, other than insider trading, that occur within the financial markets (securities and bonds) or financial services (e.g., the insurance business)? Why does finance crime represent an especially potent threat to society?

7

Enterprise Crime, Contrepreneurial Crime, and Technocrime

Once we move beyond relatively high-consensus forms of white collar crime, we begin to consider illegal activity on the margins of those crimes. The terms *enterprise crime*, *contrepreneurial crime*, and *technocrime* refer to hybrids of white collar crime and organized crime, professional crime, and corporate or occupational crime, respectively. These types of crime range along a continuum connecting white collar crime with other forms of criminal activity or are interrelated in some way with that activity.

ENTERPRISE CRIME: ORGANIZED CRIME AND WHITE COLLAR CRIME

The term *enterprise crime* is adopted here to provide a framework within which more familiar, related terms—organized crime and syndicated crime—can be discussed. Ultimately, the interrelated dealings of legitimate businesspeople, political officials, and syndicated racketeers take the form of an "enterprise."

The term *organized crime* is familiar, but there is considerable confusion about its meaning. In its broadest use, the term could refer to any organized illegal activity, including organized professional theft, business theft, terrorist groups, motorcycle gangs, and "racketeers" who extort money by intimidation and violence (Abadinsky 2005; Albanese, Das, and Verma 2003; Barlow and Kauzlarich 2002). It can easily be confused with the concept of organizational crime, an umbrella term for crimes of corporations and government agencies (Adler, Mueller, and Laufer 1998). It is most commonly associated with the *Mafia*, or *La Cosa Nostra*, an alleged national syndicate of criminals of Italian descent engaged in systematic illegal enterprises involving the sale and distribution of illicit drugs, gambling, prostitution, loan sharking, labor racketeering, and other such activities (Cressey 1969; Finckenauer and Albanese 2005). In this view, organized crime operates as a "criminal corporation." Whether or not a unified national syndicate exists has been vigorously debated in the organized crime literature for several decades. Many who study organized crime express skepticism (Barlow and Kauzlarich 2002), and some contend that it is more accurately characterized as relatively autonomous local syndicates or families engaged in systematic illegal enterprises, possibly with informal ties (Abadinsky 2005; Hagan 2002). Perhaps the easiest solution is to refer to the popular image of Mafia-type syndicates, whether local or national, as *syndicated crime* and use the term *organized crime* more broadly, especially to refer to certain alliances to be discussed shortly.

Several features are commonly associated with syndicated crime. It is a self-perpetuating organization with a hierarchy, a limited membership, specialized roles, and particular obligations, especially a vow of secrecy (*omerta*). It conspires to gain monopolistic control over certain illegal enterprises in a particular area and uses the threat of or actual force, violence, and intimidation as a primary instrument for achieving its aims. With a primary objective to acquire large-scale financial gain at relatively modest risk, the crime syndicate seeks to protect itself from prosecution by corrupting the political and legal system. Its success results from providing goods and services for which there is a demand but no legal supply.

The celebrated syndicated crime leader Meyer Lansky once boasted, "We're bigger than U.S. Steel." Indeed, the annual gross income of syndicated crime has been estimated in recent years to exceed $50 billion, or 1 percent of the GNP, and some estimates run as high as $250 billion (Berger, Free, and Searles 2001; Rowan 1986).

Other students of syndicated crime downplay the ethnic and family-related dimensions and adopt instead the concept of an illicit business enterprise that differs from legitimate businesses principally in terms of its degree of involvement with illegality and the perception of its illegitimacy (Albanese 1998; Block and Weaver 2004). This view of syndicated crime is especially relevant for exploring its relationship to white collar crime. Dwight Smith (1978) argued that businesses are conducted across a "spectrum" of behaviors shaped by market dynamics. Both corporate crime and syndicated crime can be seen as ways of conducting business illegally, and both reflect political processes that dictate that certain forms of entrepreneurship must be constrained and prohibited. In this view, ethnicity and conspiracy can play a role in both white collar and syndicated crime.

Legitimate businesses and syndicated crime engage in many of the same activities (e.g., lending money) but in ways that are somewhat arbitrarily defined as legal or illegal (e.g., the amount of interest charged). In *Organized Crime and American Power* (2001), Michael Woodiwiss has argued that the term *organized crime* can be appropriately applied to the activities of many legitimate businesses. When savings and loan institutions become a vehicle for engaging in "collective embezzlement," the line between white collar crime and syndicated crime is erased. Calavita and Pontell (1993) suggested that if we focus on the nature of the offenses rather than on the people involved, it becomes evident that much of the thrifts crime in the 1980s constituted a form of organized crime.

William Chambliss (1988b) advanced a related view of organized crime, defining it as a coalition of politicians, law enforcement officers, businesspeople, union leaders, and racketeers (see also Block and Weaver 2004). For Chambliss, the essential attribute of organized crime is a network of alliances operating a range of corrupt and illegal enterprises; people often become involved with the network through a somewhat serendipitous pattern of casual contacts in pursuit of moneymaking opportunities (Chambliss 1988b). Chambliss discovered such a network during an investigation in Seattle, and he believes similar networks exist in other U.S. cities.

This way of thinking about organized crime, widely adopted by progressive criminologists, views it as both a product of and an important ongoing element of a capitalist political economy (Quinney 1979; Simon 2006; Woodiwiss 2001). The contradictions of the capitalist economy—countervailing pressures to acquire and consume and make a profit, to legitimize the system, and to maintain order—generate circumstances in which racketeers, businesspeople, and government officials all benefit from cooperating in carrying out or tolerating criminal schemes (Chambliss 1988b).

Syndicated crime performs important functions for corporate enterprises and the capitalist political economy. On the one hand, it consumes many services and goods, invests in many legitimate businesses, and deposits a huge amount of laundered money in mainstream banks. On the other hand, it suppresses dissatisfied workers via labor racketeering, oppresses the restless unemployed with a parallel opportunity structure, and represses impoverished inner-city residents through the distribution of illegal drugs (Simon 2006). The "sweetheart contracts" that syndicated crime–directed unions negotiate with businesses, guaranteeing labor peace while cheating workers out of wages and other benefits, are an especially good example of the mutually beneficial crimes perpetrated by legitimate businesses and syndicated crime against relatively powerless workers (Hills 1980). Altogether, syndicated crime and capitalist institutions coexist profitably.

This way of characterizing the economic role of syndicated crime is obviously controversial and much at odds with a mainstream economic perspective. An alternative interpretation focuses on stifled competition, deflected capital, lost jobs, billions in economic costs, and destruction of the work ethic in inner-city neighborhoods (Inciardi 1980b; Rowan 1986). Perhaps the most accurate assessment of the economic impact of syndicated crime acknowledges that it cuts both ways. It benefits some elements of the capitalist political economy while harming others.

The Relation between Governmental Crime and Syndicated Crime

Important networks and interrelationships exist among politicians, government employees, and syndicated crime figures. The survival of syndicated crime may depend on the cooperation or connivance of some governmental officials (Block and Weaver 2004; Chambliss 1988b; Simon 2006). Corruption in many U.S. cities, from police officers taking payoffs to high-level city officials awarding lucrative contracts for bribes, involves a strong syndicated crime element. Many other investigations have uncovered evidence linking governors, state legislators, judges, and various other government

officials with syndicated crime. Some commentators place special emphasis on the increasingly global character of such networks (Block and Weaver 2004; Hagan 2002; Van Duyne 1993).

On the national level, ties between government agencies and syndicated crime go back at least as far as the early half of the 20th century. During World War II, Charles "Lucky" Luciano, one of the most powerful syndicated crime figures of his time, apparently assisted U.S. Naval Intelligence in preventing sabotage and unrest on the New York docks. During the 1960s, the CIA enlisted the cooperation of syndicated crime in its attempt to overthrow Fidel Castro (Rhodes 1984; Simon 2006). If conspiracy theorists are to be believed, these entities also arranged the assassination of President John F. Kennedy. CIA-syndicated crime cooperative ventures—for example, relating to drug trafficking—supposedly continued during the Vietnam War period and after.

In the realm of politics, syndicated crime has both played a role in corrupting the electoral process via bribes, delivery of votes, and fixes and provided campaign contributions and other services to candidates in return for cooperation or immunity in criminal enterprises (Barlow and Kauzlarich 2002; Hills 1980). On the other hand, in one interpretation the prosecution of racketeers—from Al Capone in the 1930s to today—occurs primarily when their activities directly threaten the interests of corporate and governmental elites (Pearce 1976; Woodiwiss 2001). In this view, government officials' response to syndicated crime is significantly influenced by their own political agenda.

In the critical or progressive view, then, organized crime must be understood both as a product of a capitalist economy and as the illegal activity of a network of interdependent businesspeople, government officials, and racketeers. It is quite often intimately intertwined with white collar crime.

Historical Roots of Organized Crime

Organized crime is hardly a new phenomenon. Piracy, which dates from the ancient Greeks and Romans, might be regarded as the first form of organized crime (Browning and Gerassi 1980; Chambliss 2004). Significant networks of organized criminals were operating in 16th- and 17th-century London (if not earlier) and in the Massachusetts Bay Colony by the end of the 17th century (McMullan 1982; Browning and Gerassi 1980). John Hancock, the celebrated first signer of the Declaration of Independence, apparently operated an organized crime cartel that engaged in large-scale smuggling in the pre-Revolutionary colonies (Lupsha 1986).

The syndicated form of organized crime is often considered to have its roots in various criminal organizations such as the Mafia, which emerged in southern Italy no later than the 16th century. These crime cabals—also known as *la Camorro, L'Unione Siciliana*, the Black Hand, the Honored Society, and La Cosa Nostra—began to surface in New Orleans, New York, and other U.S. cities by the end of the 19th century (Abadinsky 2000; Ianni and Reuss-Ianni 1972; Inciardi 1975). Through much of the 20th century, Italian-American syndicated crime was widely regarded as the dominant form of authentic organized crime in the United States, although clearly syndicated crime entities developed among other ethnic groups as well (Finckenauer and Albanese 2005). Prohibition, which occurred between 1919 and 1933, provided an ideal opportunity for the dramatic growth and expansion of syndicated crime because it created enormous demand for a product, alcoholic beverages, in the absence of a legal supply (Lupsha 1986; Schneider 2005b). In one commentator's view, Prohibition largely turned the alcoholic beverage industry over to criminals (Schelling 1973). It also led to much more systematic contact between the underworld and the upper-world and in this respect established a firmer and more enduring basis for the mixture of syndicated and white collar crime. Founders of some of the great 20th-century North American fortunes, including Samuel Bronfman of Seagrams, Moe Annenberg of the Nationwide News publishing dynasty, and Kennedy family patriarch Joseph P. Kennedy, are alleged to have greatly enhanced their fortunes during this period,

partly through involvement with bootlegging, bookmaking, and other syndicated crime activities (Fox 1989).

The repeal of Prohibition hardly diminished the potency of syndicated crime. In subsequent decades, a vast range of opportunities for making money illegally—gambling, drugs, loan sharking, and labor racketeering—evolved with new areas of opportunity, including arson for hire, credit card and real estate frauds, the pornography business, the theft and sale of securities, and cigarette bootlegging (Nelli 1986). The World War II black market also generated a new set of opportunities for syndicated crime. Despite persistent investigations of and campaigns against syndicated crime during much of this period, it has certainly survived into the early years of the 21st century.

The presence in syndicated crime of certain 19th-century ethnic groups (e.g., the Irish and Eastern European Jews) has become less visible as others, including Russians, African Americans, Jamaicans, Hispanics (especially Cubans and Colombians), and various groups of Asians, have become more conspicuous (Abadinsky 2000; Finckenauer and Albanese 2005). As Bell (1962) argued in a frequently cited article, syndicated crime was an important, if unorthodox, ladder of mobility for immigrant and minority groups for whom legitimate ladders of mobility were restricted. This view recognizes direct parallels between the large-scale legitimate gambling enterprise known as the stock market and the gambling ventures run by syndicated crime (Schelling 1973). The objectives of those involved in syndicated crime thus parallel those of individuals in legitimate occupations, and syndicated crime is simply seen as an unorthodox form of white collar crime.

Transnational organized crime—a hybrid of corporate, syndicated, and street forms of crime—appears to be growing (Edwards and Gill 2002). The specific attributes of organized crime in different parts of the world vary, as does the extent of involvement of organized crime with legitimate businesses and institutions.

BOX 7.1   Joe Valachi of La Cosa Nostra and Carl Kotchian of Lockheed

The parallels between syndicated crime and white collar organizational crime continue today. Jay Albanese (1982) compared two separate testimonies before Senate investigative committees: in the 1960s, testimony by Joseph Valachi, reputed member of La Cosa Nostra; and in the 1970s, testimony by Carl Kotchian, president of the Lockheed Corporation. Valachi was the first "insider" to confirm (truthfully or otherwise) the existence of a national syndicated crime network; Kotchian was the first high-level insider to testify openly about secret corporate payments or bribes to foreign governments to secure major contracts. Applying the framework of Smith's "spectrum-based theory of enterprise," Albanese has argued that the Valachi and Kotchian testimonies revealed parallel concerns between syndicated crime entities and corporations in conspiring to make bribes: Both seek to create a favorable climate (or protection) for their business and to maintain their dominance over competitors in the marketplace.

The Relation between Syndicated Crime and White Collar Crime

One thesis concerning the connections between syndicated crime and white collar crime suggests that the methods used to establish the great industrial empires and sprawling Western ranches of the 19th century were fundamentally no different from the methods used by 20th century mafiosi and syndicated crime members. As Gus Tyler (1981) observed:

> Original accumulations of capital were amassed in tripartite deals among pirates, governors, and brokers. Fur fortunes were piled up alongside the drunk and dead bodies of our noble savages, the Indians. Small settlers were driven from their lands or turned into tenants by big ranchers employing rustlers, guns, outlaws—and the law. In the great railroad and shipping wars, enterprising capitalists used extortion, blackmail, violence, bribery, and private armies with muskets and cannons to wreck a competitor and to become the sole boss of the trade. (p. 277)

In this view, the 19th-century robber barons and cattle barons were the forerunners of 20th-century organized crime. For much of the 20th century the descendants of the robber barons occupied the pinnacle of the social hierarchy, and prestigious universities and foundations have been named after such robber barons as Vanderbilt and Rockefeller; is it possible, one commentator asks, that one day similar tributes will be paid to syndicated crime figures (Abadinsky 1981)? Such recognition seems unlikely, but the analogy is provocative. Box 7.1 explores a similar parallel.

Ferdinand Lundberg (1968), a prominent student of the crimes of the rich, has argued that corporate criminals "make Mafias and Crime Syndicates look like pushcart operations" (p. 131). It has also been suggested that La Cosa Nostra, whether or not it is a national syndicate, performs functions similar to those of a Rotary Club or other such association for white collar businesspeople: It facilitates business contacts and promotes the interests of business generally (Haller 1990). David Simon (2002), in *Tony Soprano and the American Dream*, suggests that the values and activities of the fictional Tony Soprano and his syndicated crime confederates are consistent with a broader American theme that tacitly endorses unethical means to achieve the "American dream" of material success. That syndicated crime may elicit a harsher legal response than white collar crime and have a more negative image may be attributable to ethnic and class biases.

The general public perception of syndicated crime has in fact been somewhat ambivalent. An enduring fascination with the Mafia, "the mob," is evident from the public's response to such films as *The Godfather* and *Goodfellas* and the HBO series

The Sopranos (Simon 2002). As a rule, "mobsters" seem to inspire less visceral fear and hatred than do predatory street criminals. Despite such ambivalence, syndicated crime mobsters do not enjoy the same status of respectability that white collar offenders do, and they are more vulnerable to suspicion, investigation, and conviction on that score alone.

Although students of organized crime are divided on many issues, they uniformly agree that syndicated crime infiltration of and interrelationships with legitimate corporations and businesses has increased over the decades (Hills 1980; Nelli 1986; Ruggiero 2002). Legitimate businesses provide both a front and an important tax cover for illegal activities; they provide employment for associates and relatives who are on probation and parole; they can be transferred more easily to dependents and heirs; and they can provide a more secure source of income and profit (Anderson 1979). Altogether, increasing involvement with legitimate businesses can reduce the exposure of syndicated crime figures to prosecution and may also reflect an aspiration for greater respectability. Although such infiltration is often denounced by politicians and journalists, it is not entirely clear that society as a whole is better off when syndicated crime reinvests in illicit enterprises alone.

The involvement of syndicated crime with certain classes of legitimate and quasi-legitimate businesses, including vending machines, construction, nightclubs, casinos, and pornography, has long been recognized. An investigation of New York City's building trades and construction industry in the 1980s uncovered evidence of pervasive syndicated crime involvement, including extortion, bribery, theft, fraud, and bid-rigging (New York State Organized Crime Task Force 1988). The syndicate's infiltration and takeover of the meat industry, cheese-processing plants, garment factories, banks, stock brokerages, and unions have come to light (Kwitny 1979). The consequences of such infiltration include the dumping of unhealthy food products into ordinary supermarkets, inflated prices for consumers, and lower wages and benefits for workers.

A Senate committee chaired by Estes Kefauver in the 1950s identified some 50 types of business, from advertising and appliances to theaters and transportation, with a syndicated crime presence. A congressional investigation in 1970 identified 70 areas of economic activity with syndicated crime involvement (Nelli 1986). More than 20 years after the Pennsylvania Crime Commission (1991) first began investigating organized crime in that state, it concluded: "There is a prevailing influence of organized crime in certain legitimate industries and unions in Pennsylvania." In the late 1990s and early years of the 21st century, there was evidence of increasing movement of syndicated crime into such areas as health insurance, identity theft, credit card fraud, and prepaid telephone cards (Raab 1997; Secretariat 2005). In 2004, federal investigators claimed that organized crime figures had defrauded consumers out of over $200 by "cramming" bogus charges on their telephone bills (Rashbaum 2004). This movement of organized crime into "billing fraud" was something new. Box 7.2 explores arson for profit as another connection between syndicated and corporate crime elements.

Hazardous Waste Disposal

The business of disposing of toxic waste has been heavily infiltrated by syndicated crime because of its long-standing domination of the garbage-carting and disposal business (Block and Scarpitti 1985; Reuter 1993; Szasz 1986b). The illegal disposal of hazardous waste costs only a fraction (perhaps 5 percent) of the cost of safe and legal disposal; less than 20 percent of these wastes are disposed of properly (Szasz 1986b). Illegally disposed of hazardous waste, whether in the ground or in waterways, endangers the health of people exposed to it. Corporations that generate hazardous waste strongly lobbied against laws that would impose substantial liability on them for the effects of improper or illegal disposal. They also contracted with hazardous waste haulers they likely knew would not dispose of the waste legally and properly. Law enforcement efforts have been directed mainly at hazardous waste management businesses

---

BOX 7.2   Arson as a Form of Enterprise Crime

Arson for profit is an especially harmful crime, each year causing more than $2 billion in direct losses of commercial property and some $10 billion in indirect losses, such as jobs, business income, taxes, and municipal costs (Goetz 1997; Rhodes 1984). Arson also traumatizes nearby residents and results in the deaths of hundreds of citizens and firefighters annually (Brady 1983). In a study of the epidemic of commercial arson in Boston in the 1970s, Brady (1983) found evidence of mutual involvement of legitimate businesses and syndicated crime racketeers. When banks began to engage in discriminatory "redlining" of mortgages in inner-city neighborhoods, about half of the city's arsons occurred in the growing numbers of abandoned buildings in these neighborhoods (Brady 1983). Arson-for-profit crimes impact disproportionately on poor people and have not been a priority for law enforcement agencies (Goetz 1997).

Syndicated crime racketeers would secure mortgages for abandoned buildings by agreeing to buy them at inflated prices; they would then insure them and arrange for the buildings to be "torched." The bank would profit by collecting from the insurance company; the insurance company would pay the claims, raise its premiums, and discourage further investigation because it feared greater state regulation and the perception that it resisted paying claims. Because most insurance companies do not have enough arson investigators to pursue cases effectively and can face possible lawsuits when they deny claims (Rhodes 1984), government investigators would often be paid off. In this sense, then, arson for profit can be regarded as a form of organized crime activity that has a devastating effect on some urban communities. Because arson emanates out of a symbiosis of corporate profiteering, gangster racketeering, and government corruption or ineptitude (Brady 1983), it is more a hybrid form of white collar and syndicated crime than an activity of mafiosi and lone arsonists for hire.

---

that can be linked with syndicated crime, although other waste management corporations may engage in the same types of harmful and illegal practices (Carter 1999). The pervasive illegal disposal of hazardous waste lends especially strong support to the network model of organized crime because it comes about through interdependent ties, corruption, and ineptitude of corporations, politicians, regulatory bureaucrats, and traditional syndicated crime entrepreneurs (Block and Scarpitti 1985; Szasz 1986b). This activity, which may well cause more harm than such syndicated crime enterprises as gambling and prostitution, is an especially clear example of a hybrid type of white collar/organized crime.

The Relation between Syndicated Crime and Finance Crime

A long history of ties exist between syndicated crime and financial institutions. The theft and manipulation of stocks and bonds by syndicated crime have been major problems since the early 1970s (Abadinsky 2005; Sullivan and Berenson 2000). Crime-infiltrated brokerages may be especially aggressive in artificially pumping up and then dumping stocks (Schneider 2005b; Weiser 1998b). "Penny stock" fraud is also widespread. Obtaining and then selling these stocks and bonds requires a certain level of cooperation from brokerages, investors, and other legitimate parties. "Pumping and dumping" and securities-related fraud is also quite widespread apart from syndicated crime involvement, and the lines of demarcation between white collar crime and organized crime can be especially blurred (Griffin 2002). In *Born to Steal: When the Mafia Hit Wall Street*, Gary Weiss (2003) has argued that syndicated crime infiltration of Wall Street may have played a significant role in the spectacular run-up of the stock market in the 1990s, which if true was the ultimate "pump and dump" scheme.

The long-standing practice of laundering the huge sums of money generated by illegal enterprises obviously requires some complicity on the part of banks, which benefit from these large deposits (Block and Weaver 2004; O'Brien 1999b;

B O X 7.3   The Looting of the Thrifts and Syndicated Crime

The looting of savings and loans in the 1980s was arguably the most costly of all white collar crimes. In an especially widely read exposé of the S & L frauds, Pizzo and colleagues (1991) claimed to have found evidence that individuals associated with syndicated crime were directly or peripherally involved with a significant number of the defrauded thrifts. The S & L frauds can be characterized either as a form of organized crime or as an illustration of the blurred

lines between syndicated crime and white collar crime, carried out by a network that included businesspeople, confidence men, government officials, and (among others) individuals with syndicated crime ties (Brewton 1992; Calavita and Pontell 1993; Pizzo et al. 1991). Taking advantage of opportunities to get in on business-related frauds is quite consistent with the recent history of syndicated crime.

Thornburgh 1990). Up to $1 trillion is laundered each year by concealment of the sources of illegally generated cash as it is moved through legitimate accounts. However, in one commentator's view this activity is far less of a threat to global security than deregulation of global markets (Rawlinson 2002). Does the involvement of syndicated crime in at least some proportion of money laundering lead to disproportionate attention to such activity?

Box 7.3 considers syndicated crime's involvement in the savings and loans frauds of the 1980s. No one is likely to confuse WorldCom's CEO Bernard Ebbers, who was convicted of massive accounting fraud at his company, with the late John Gotti, the most notorious syndicated crime figure of this era. There is a difference in style, in the degree of involvement in illegal enterprises, in the typical character of these enterprises (e.g., illicit narcotics, gambling, and labor racketeering as opposed to complicity in the issuing of fraudulent financial statements), and in the level of direct intimidation or violence.

On the other hand, many connections exist between organized crime and white collar crime, and the boundary lines between them have blurred considerably. In a 1983 interview (Laub 1983: 153–54), criminologist Donald Cressey speculated that at some point early in the 21st century we would no longer be able to tell the difference between white collar crime and organized crime. To date, this prediction probably has not come true, but it may do so in the future.

CONTREPRENEURIAL CRIME: PROFESSIONAL CRIMINALS AND WHITE COLLAR CRIME

Like the term *organized crime*, the term *professional criminal* is familiar but vague. In its broadest use, the term is applied to anyone who engages in criminal activity regularly; in this sense it has been used interchangeably with *career criminal*. Some commentators object to using "professional," as in *professional killer*, for able or skilled criminals (Hagan 2002).

However, a narrower conception of the term *professional criminal* has been quite widely accepted in the criminological literature, including Sutherland's classic *The Professional Thief* (1937), a first-hand account of the criminal life by the pseudonymous criminal "Chic Conwell." Some of the attributes of professional criminals Sutherland identified include highly developed skills for committing crime; high status in the criminal world; socialization into professional crime values and knowledge through association with others; alliances with other professional criminals, commonly in the form of a mob; and shared values and professional pride with such associates. Professional criminals attempt to minimize the risk of arrest, prosecution, and imprisonment by carefully planning their crimes, avoiding violence, and putting in the "fix" with corruptible law enforcement and political officials. Among the activities of

---

BOX 7.4   Joseph "Yellow Kid" Weil and the Big Con

The elaborate big cons engineered by the legendary Joseph "Yellow Kid" Weil have become less common (Sifakis 2001). Weil was an elegant, sophisticated man with a formidable knowledge of banking, mining, financing, and other fields. He would move from city to city representing himself as a successful businessman or a representative of powerful interests. He would establish ties with wealthy individuals and financial institutions and proceed to defraud them of large sums of money by enticing them to invest in some phony scheme (Weil and Brannon 1957). Weil claimed that his victims were not only well heeled but sufficiently greedy to risk making a fast dollar by questionable means.

The old-fashioned big con could be characterized as a form of crime that victimizes people who are predisposed to commit white collar crime. Although Weil's particular style of professional crime may indeed have declined or disappeared, vast amounts of money are still stolen by con artists in the guise of entrepreneurs. Today's white collar contrepreneurs, however, victimize people with ordinary or modest incomes; of course, some contrepreneurs target institutions such as the thrifts as well. Furthermore, activities of high-level executives for corporations such as Enron, WorldCom, and Adelphia—and their associates in the world of high finance—could be viewed as engaging in a big con on a monumental scale.

---

professional criminals, according to Sutherland, are theft, picking pockets ("cannons"), shoplifting ("boosting"), switching jewels on inspection and stealing them ("penny-weighting"), hotel burglaries, check forgery ("laying paper"), shakedowns, and short and big "cons."

Of all these activities, the *big con* intersects most fully with white collar crime as a form of *contrepreneurial crime*. Francis (1988) coined the term *contrepreneurs*—combining "con artist" with entrepreneur—to refer to white collar con artists. The contrepreneur carries out a swindle while appearing to be engaged in a legitimate enterprise.

Historical Origins of Professional Crime

The origins of professional crime have been traced back to the disintegration of European feudalism during the late Middle Ages (1350–1550), when a certain proportion of the newly disenfranchised turned to robbery, poaching, banditry, and other outlaw practices (Inciardi 1975). Professional crime in subsequent centuries took on many guises in many places.

In the American tradition, frontier bandits such as Jesse James in the 19th century and bank robbers such as John Dillinger in the 20th century have been regarded as one class of professional criminals. Such criminals have long been romanticized

through penny novels, films, and television dramatizations. *The Sting*, a 1973 film featuring Paul Newman and Robert Redford, is a prominent example of an entertainment that portrays contrepreneurs in a sympathetic light. Box 7.4 introduces a real-life contrepreneur.

The question of whether professional crime is in decline is a controversial one (Hagan 2002; Walker 1981). In his exhaustive study of the historical sources on professional crime, Inciardi (1975) concluded that it entered a decline at least as recently as the 1940s, when increasingly sophisticated crime prevention and detection technology was introduced. Others (see, for example, Hagan 2002; King and Chambliss 1984; Staats 1977) have argued that professional crime has simply adapted to changing conditions and opportunities. The boundaries between professional crime and occupational crime have eroded. Check and credit card fraud have replaced such activities as safecracking as professional crime activities of choice.

The Relation between Professional Crime and White Collar Crime

Several significant parallels exist between professional criminals and white collar offenders. Both are prepared to take risks to make money, both are prepared to violate laws to maximize profit, and both seek to immunize themselves by bribing or financing the campaigns of politicians or becoming informants for law enforcement officials (King and Chambliss 1984). The classic professional criminal, like the white collar offender, relies on skill and planning, rather than direct force or intimidation, to achieve an illegal objective; and both need to convey an aura of respectability and inspire some level of trust to carry out their crimes successfully. In both cases, rationalization is important. Professional criminals argue that legitimate businesspeople are no more honest than they are, and corporate criminals often contend that their competitors are not complying with the law either.

In one sense, professional criminals may feel they can assume a stance of moral superiority over white collar criminals. According to Sutherland's (1937) "Chic Conwell,"

> [Con mob members] believe that if a person is going to steal, let him steal from the same point of view that the thief does: do not profess honesty and steal at the same time. Thieves are tolerant of almost everything except hypocrisy. This is why defaulting bankers, embezzlers, etc., are despised strongly by the thief. (p. 178)

A similar point was made by Chambliss's informant, the "box man" (safecracker) Harry King, who expressed contempt for the hypocrisy of conventional businesspeople (King and Chambliss 1984). On the other hand, Sutherland's Conwell claimed that other professional thieves harbor the hope of getting out of thievery and into a legitimate occupation, and Chambliss's "box man" tired of "rooting and rousting about" and ultimately committed suicide when a "straight" job as a probation counselor failed to come through.

What are the differences, if any, between the classic professional criminal and the contrepreneurial white collar criminal? First, there may be a difference in self-identity. Professional criminals are likely more accepting of their outlaw status, whereas white collar criminals may be more likely to regard themselves primarily as businesspeople. Second, the professional criminal is more likely to

make a deliberate decision to become involved in criminal activities, while the white collar criminal may drift into fraudulent enterprises. Third, the professional criminal typically attempts a pure theft of money from a vulnerable victim or mark, whereas the white collar criminal defrauds by giving something of little or no real value in return for money. Contrepreneurial white collar crime in some respects is a true hybrid of elements of classic professional crime and occupational white collar crime, although often there is no practical difference between what these criminals do.

Fraudulent Businesses: Swindles, Scams, and Rackets

A vast number of enterprises are swindles, scams, or rackets that annually cost consumers, investors, and other unwitting parties billions of dollars. Although "the operator," as one commentator (Gibney 1978) calls him or her, has been an enduring figure in U.S. history, current conditions continuously nurture and promote completely new realms for fraudulent activities. Are these activities properly classified as white collar crimes?

In some cases, the fraudulent activity is more appropriately described as organized crime or professional crime; in other cases, a designation of white collar crime is clearly justified. Certainly many of the offenders affect the appearance of "white-collar" entrepreneurs or businesspeople and are so perceived by others. Their activities are commonly designated as white collar crime by the FBI and other law enforcement agencies.

Businesses range along a continuum extending from the wholly legal and ethical on one end to the blatantly criminal and unscrupulous at the other end. Obviously a good many enterprises fall somewhere between the extremes (see Box 7.5 for one example). Still, a basic premise applies to all businesses: Their success depends significantly on conveying an image of legitimacy and respectability. And, of course, the entire spectrum of enterprises shares the objective of making money. It is sometimes difficult to discriminate

BOX 7.5   The Fence

In certain respects, fences illustrate the intersection between legitimate business and outright criminality. *Fences* buy stolen goods from burglars, thieves, and others who acquire them and sell them to consumers or businesses for resale. Fences may also play a key role in bankruptcy frauds, in which an apparently legitimate business orders merchandise from suppliers and then sells it through fences, avoiding payment to the suppliers by declaring bankruptcy (Bequai 1978).

Even though fences commit the offense of receiving stolen property, they typically operate legitimate businesses and are seen (and see themselves) primarily as legitimate businesspeople

(Steffensmeier 1986). Although fences are more likely to be classified as professional criminals than as white collar criminals, they do not fit entirely well into either category. Fences have available to them a large number of rationales: "If I didn't buy the stolen goods, someone else would," or "I only make money because conventional businesses and consumers knowingly buy stolen merchandise, if they can get it at a good discount." And legitimate businesses are important customers for them. In some respects, the fences' "hot goods" customers are the opposite of the defrauded consumer: They benefit at someone else's expense rather than being exploited.

---

between fundamentally legitimate and illegitimate businesses.

Fraud

Reports of fraud appear early in recorded history. Laws prohibiting fraud were known in the 4th century B.C. in ancient Greece (Drapkin 1989). An account from this time describes a ship owner attempting to defraud someone by seeking a cash advance for a ship laden with corn, when all along the intent was to scuttle the ship instead of delivering the corn (Clarke 1990). We have clear accounts of consumer fraud (e.g., adulterating food and wine) from the first century A.D. in ancient Rome (Green 1997: 224), and we have much evidence that such schemes have been practiced throughout the Western world since then. The book *The Founding Swindlers* alleges that some of America's founding fathers were engaged in various forms of fraudulent activity involving land (Royster 2000).

In the late 18th century, former magistrate Patrick Colquhoun inveighed against various "sharpers, cheats, and swindlers," including pawnbrokers, auctioneers, merchants who use false weights and measures, and other defrauders, in his *A Treatise on the Police of the Metropolis* (1795, 1969). In the late 19th century, Anthony Comstock, a special agent for the Post Office who is best known

for his "suppression of vice" campaign, published *Frauds Exposed* (1880, 1969) in which he documented numerous consumer frauds, including stock market swindles, phony mining companies, bogus lotteries and contests, and the peddling of worthless merchandise or cures. In the latter part of the 20th century, Robert S. Rosefsky's *Frauds, Swindles and Rackets* (1973) provided a "red alert" for contemporary consumers, identifying such frauds as "get-rich-quick" schemes, home improvement rackets, land swindles, and "E-Z" credit offerings. Rosefsky identified assorted other swindles and schemes, including phony charities, long-lost heir searches, magazine subscription rackets, referral schemes, dancing lesson rackets, phony contests, travel deceptions, phony auctions, reducing salon rackets, phony employment agencies, and tax preparation shysters. See Box 7.6 for consumer advice from a reformed contrepreneur.

Fraudulent businesses, many of which operate as mail-order businesses, prey upon human vanity, fantasy, loneliness, insecurity, and fear. During hard economic times, when people are desperate for money or savings, get-rich-quick schemes tend to flourish (Bohlen 1997; Kerr 1991a). The elderly, the unemployed, and people with poor credit histories are especially vulnerable to fraud from a variety of sources: contractors promising to make their homes safe, people promising to enrich them,

---

B O X 7.6   A Contrepreneur's Advice to Potential Victims

One of the most sensational and widely reported contrepreneurial cases in recent years involved Barry Minkow, who as a 16-year-old set up a carpet cleaning business, ZZZZ Best, in the garage of his parents' home (Domanick 1989). This business ultimately defrauded customers, investors, and financial institutions of millions of dollars, and in 1988, Minkow was convicted on 57 counts of stock, bank, and mail fraud. He served about eight years in a federal prison. Minkow now works as a radio show host and consultant on fraud prevention. His book *Buyer Beware: How to Avoid*

Cons, Swindles, Frauds, and Other Trickeries (1997) provides readers with advice on how to avoid being victimized by a wide range of rackets, including credit card fraud, financial planning, job searches, 900 numbers, telemarketing, and weight-loss scams. In his most recent book, *Cleaning Up—One Man's Redemptive Journey through the Seductive World of Corporate Crime* (2005), Minkow recounts the story of how he became involved in a massive scam and how he has worked to expose just such scams since his release from prison.

---

firms promising lucrative foreign employment, and companies offering easy loans or second mortgages (Brenner 1993; Lesce 2000; Wald 1992). The FBI has estimated that the elderly are conned out of $40 billion a year (Church 1997). New immigrants are especially vulnerable to fraud by contrepreneurs who charge them exorbitant fees with false claims that they can facilitate the naturalization process or obtain work permits for them (Hedges 2000; Kennedy 1997; Pristin 2000). Even wealthy potential immigrants have been defrauded by consulting firms exploiting a program providing residency visas for foreign investments in excess of $500,000 (Schmitt 1998). Contrepreneurs who exploit immigrants are rarely caught or successfully prosecuted, mainly because many illegal immigrants fear reporting their victimization to government authorities or cooperating with prosecution. Some fraudsters, such as fugitive tax protesters, focus on defrauding major businesses or the government as an expression of their hostility to "the system" (Brooke 1996; Meier 1995).

Entrepreneurs who sell basically legitimate products may also fraudulently play on people's fears to sell their products, such as costly cribs, expensive alarm systems, and other safety or security products. Products may be inflated in price and may not live up to their billing. Other products and services are inherently dubious. Consumers are enticed into making payments, which can range

from fairly modest to quite substantial, with the misrepresented prospect of obtaining lucrative modeling contracts for their child, selling their musical compositions, publishing their book and having it sold in bookstores, promoting their invention, winning a contest, making money from home-assembled products, or being identified as an heir of a deceased, unknown relative or of an unclaimed bank account of such a "relative" (usually someone with the same surname but not related). Most Americans have received notices informing them that they have won a prize or enticing them to enter a sweepstakes; these offers are typically misleading at best and could be outright frauds (Frantz 1998b; Purdy 2005c). In one case, an elderly man committed suicide after spending more than $100,000 on sweepstakes and other contests; in another case, an elderly women subscribed to 60 magazines in the hopes of winning sweepstakes. Elderly victims have flown across the country to claim sweepstakes prizes they believed they had won, on the basis of misleading letters (Crisp 1997; Frantz 1998b). Prominent celebrities such as Dick Clark and Ed McMahon have been involved in promoting mass-mailing sweepstakes (Quinn 1999). In the recent era so dominated by the Internet, millions of Americans (including the author) receive virtually daily e-mail communications from someone conveying the impression that they have won a foreign lottery or will receive

---

BOX 7.7 Advance Fee Frauds

The term *advance fee frauds* has now been applied to the ubiquitous efforts to entice e-mail recipients into providing financial accounts information and funds in return for a promised multimillion dollar lottery prize or a very large share of unclaimed funds (Chen 1998; Schneider 2005a; Smothers 1996). These schemes are believed to have originated in Nigeria in the mid-1980s but currently are also coming from other countries. Such schemes have been estimated to net between $100 million and $250 million a year from people foolish or desperate enough to provide advance fees or bank account numbers in response to these letters. In some cases, those who respond to such enticements have ultimately been lured into making a trip to Nigeria or some other African country, where more money may be extorted from them or they may even be held for ransom. In some cases, victims have supposedly been physically harmed or even killed. Many victims fail to report their victimization to authorities, perhaps because they are embarrassed, fearful of being charged with some form of wrongdoing, or naively harbor the hope of getting their money back.

---

millions of dollars for assisting in getting some funds out of a foreign country (see Box 7.7). Consumers who respond to the various enticements typically lose their money and fail to realize their objective, and many may suffer emotional distress as well. Fraudulent charities (see Box 7.8) are among the most twisted of these crimes.

Ponzi and Pyramid Schemes One of the most famous swindles in U.S. history took place in 1919, when Charles Ponzi, an Italian immigrant, began advertising that he could return large profits to investors because he had learned how to take advantage of the international currency and postage markets (Zuckhoff 2005). The claim was that international postal reply coupons purchased in a poor country such as Italy could be redeemed at a much higher rate in the United States. As word spread of rapid, dramatic profits returned to early Ponzi investors, millions of dollars began to pour in. Ponzi, however, was not investing the money; he was spending it on himself and paying off early investors with some part of the money pouring in from newer investors. Eventually, of course, the scheme was exposed, many people lost their money, and Ponzi went to prison. But the *Ponzi scheme* itself has proven to be remarkably durable.

In some cases, the perpetrator of a Ponzi scheme is taking advantage of an "affinity" with the victims, who may be fellow immigrants, church or club members, or relatives and friends (Finkelstein 2000; Fried 1997b; Sachs 2001). It has been estimated that con artists have stolen over $2 billion a year recently from church members after securing endorsements from clergy or even posing as pastors (Fields–Meyer 2005). High returns are promised; some early investors may receive payoffs, but most of the "invested" money is spent on a lavish lifestyle for the perpetrator.

A special variant of a Ponzi scheme, called a *pyramid scheme*, continues to be perpetrated on new generations of naive investors. A large number of fraudulent businesses over the years have enticed people to make investments, purchase dealerships, or buy expensive products on the premise that they will make back their money many times over by bringing in other customers or dealers (Navarro 1996). In one case, Glenn Turner established the Dare To Be Great Company, which was charged with defrauding thousands of consumers out of their money by inducing them to purchase multilevel distributorships for cosmetics and self-improvement courses; he used the grossly misleading lure that they could earn up to $200,000 a year (Bequai 1978). The cosmetics industry seems to be especially prone to such practices (Springen 1991). In another case, Charles Groeschel, who headed the Association of Individual Ministries, lured some 2,000 victims into a securities investment pyramid scheme with the claim that God endorsed it;

BOX 7.8   Charity as Fraud

Arguably the single most disturbing form of contrepreneurial fraud involves fake advocacy and charitable organizations. Telemarketing firms sometimes retain 85 percent or more of the funds they raise, without informing donors that such a high percentage of their contributions goes toward "administrative" costs (Greenhouse 2002). The American Relief Organization raised $665,844 in 2001, supposedly for needy Native Americans, but only $6,424—or less than 1 percent of the money raised—went to these supposed beneficiaries (Stamler 2003). A professional fundraising company raised over $428,000 for the International Narcotic Enforcement Officer Association, but the association only received some $57,000—or about 13 percent—of this total (Bartosiewicz 2004).

United Way of America is a huge charitable enterprise with many legitimate accomplishments, but in 2002 the Washington, DC, United Way Office was challenged on accounting practices that appeared to inflate contributions and conceal expenses (Johnston 2002e; Strom 2002). Some charities have for-profit units that can be used to line the pockets of insiders (Abelson 1998). Health charity programs have been accused of benefiting their executives and staffs and the medical establishment rather than disease victims or the general public (Bennett and DiLorenzo 1994). A popular "charitable" feast in New York City, the San Gennaro Feast, was alleged to be a largely for-profit enterprise for insiders (Barry 1996). In other cases, top officials of charitable entities may simply steal from the charitable funds (Fried 1996b; Richardson 1996a; Swarns 1997). A United Way president and two aides were convicted on federal charges of having stolen more than $600,000—subsequently spent on personal luxuries—from the fund (Arenson 1995). In 2003, a former vice president of a United Way in Michigan pleaded guilty to embezzling almost $2 million from the charity, largely to support an interest in quarter horses (Strom 2003).

Wealthy and sophisticated individuals and institutions are sometimes duped. Some leading financiers supported New Era Philanthropy, which claimed to be raising money—through investments—for religious and educational institutions, which in turn invested substantial sums of money with this same organization (Ditzen, Dobrin, and Eng 1995; Mercer 1995). Its investors lost large sums of money when the fraud was exposed, and the founder was sentenced to prison.

In the wake of national tragedies such as plane crashes, both legitimate and illegitimate charities surface, claiming to be collecting money for victims or their families (Swarns 1996). After the 9/11 attacks, hundreds of products were sold with the claim that the proceeds would benefit 9/11 victims' families; many of these sales campaigns were misleading and failed to disclose what proportion of the money would go to the charities (Barstow and Henriques 2002). In 2003, for example, a Queens, NY man pleaded guilty to defrauding businesses and individuals by falsely claiming that he was raising charitable funds for families of police officers killed in the 9/11 attacks (Weiser 2003). In 2005, there was concern about fraudulent charitable appeals in the wake of the devastating tsunami catastrophe in Asia and after Hurricane Katrina in the American gulf-coast states (Becker and Strom 2005; Zeller 2005b). Some spam e-mail from fraudsters during this period claimed to be raising such charitable funds.

Associate Ministers moved up to Ministers in this scheme (O'Brien 1998a). Despite recurrent exposés, multilevel distributorship scams continue to surface.

Investment Frauds Losses due to investments in fraudulent schemes and securities are especially widespread and substantial. By some estimates, Americans lose more than $2 billion annually investing in low-priced *penny stocks* (Barboza, Eaton, and Henriques 1999). These stocks are sold through a series of gross misrepresentations, with insiders pumping up the stock price and then dumping it at its peak, leaving other investors with huge losses. Investors lost millions when the Canadian Mining Company made fraudulent claims that it had discovered a huge deposit of gold in a remote part of Indonesia (Spaeth 1997). Steve Hoffenberg of Towers Financial was sentenced in 1997 to 20 years in prison for bilking investors out of hundreds of millions of dollars they thought were invested in bonds and notes backed by a collection agency

---

B O X 7.9   Pump and Dump: The Jonathan Lebed Case

Jonathan Lebed, a 15-year-old New Jersey schoolboy, realized several hundred thousand dollars in stock investment profits in 2000 by planting bogus hype in Internet investment chat rooms. In effect, he would purchase stock in a company, circulate information indicating that the stock would rise dramatically, and then sell the stock when he had succeeded in driving its price up (Kadlec 2000; M. Lewis 2001a, 2001b). This strategy, known as *pump and dump*, has been widely practiced to defraud investors. In this case, the novel feature was the age of the offender and the effectiveness of using an Internet chat room to carry out the scheme. Lebed was the first minor ever charged with fraud by the SEC, but the charges were dropped in return for giving up some $285,000 in

profits and interest that could be directly linked with the chat room hype. He retained substantial profits from other stock investments, where the SEC was unable to make a direct connection with fraudulent activity. Due to the youth of the accused, this case received much attention in the media. Lebed was apparently regarded as a hero by some of his peers, and his father, driving a Mercedes given to him by his son, declared himself proud of his son. This case demonstrates that someone with a computer and Internet access can manipulate the market by spreading false information. Of course, some observers also point out that investors who purchased stocks on the basis of unsubstantiated chat room messages deserved some blame for their losses.

(Eaton 1997c). Patrick Brennan was convicted in 1999 of defrauding more than 10,000 investors (many elderly) of $600 million, with claims to be financing leases on office equipment (Eaton 1999b; Weisman 1999). Another Brennan, Robert, was charged in 2000 and 2001 with money laundering and other frauds related to a long-standing scheme to sell penny stocks in dubious companies through First Jersey Securities (Hanley 2001b; Smothers 2001). "Cold-calling" salespeople pushed such stocks, pumped them up, and sold them at illegally inflated prices. Of course, the losses due to such schemes are dwarfed by the losses to investors as a consequence of massive accounting fraud at Enron, WorldCom, HealthSouth, and other such major corporations, as discussed in Chapters 3 and 6. Box 7.9 profiles a youthful practitioner of investment fraud.

The bull market of the late 1990s, facilitated by growing use of the Internet for investing, led to much investment fraud (O'Brien 1999a; Smith 2004; Spragins 1997). A more depressed securities market early in the 21st century would create pressures of its own for fraud.

Home Improvement and Ownership Frauds   A whole range of home improvement projects, from roofing to basement waterproofing, lend

themselves especially well to fraudulent schemes (Purdy 2005). Some contractors are outright con artists; many others are marginal contractors who mislead customers, do incomplete or shoddy work, and declare bankruptcy or engage in some other subterfuge to avoid settling claims. Energy-related home improvement has been especially prone to abuse. A standard approach in these frauds has included gaining entry into homes on false pretexts, such as posing as inspectors, and then frightening homeowners with claims that their furnace is dangerous or does not meet current pollution emissions standards.

Frauds relating to home ownership, mortgages, and apartment rentals are also common. Real estate brokers have preyed upon people desperate to get apartments by collecting commissions, deposits, and rents for unavailable apartments (Bagli 1997). Builders, appraisers, and mortgage brokers have conspired to sell poorly constructed homes at inflated prices with misrepresentation of tax obligations to prospective homeowners (Baker A. 2001). In some cases, nonprofit organizations have been accused of taking advantage of federal programs to foster home ownership, luring vulnerable people into committing themselves to dilapidated homes without the resources to keep them (Pristin 2001).

Thousands of lower income New Yorkers were lured into believing they could afford homes in the Poconos, in Monroe County, Pennsylvania, with many of these homes going into foreclosure (Moss and Jacobs 2004). In all these cases, victims may lose both money and homes.

Land Sale Frauds In the 1920s, many people who bought "land" in Florida eventually discovered that their land was underwater. Fifty years later, land sale fraud was especially prevalent in Arizona and New Mexico. Losses of billions of dollars are involved; some such swindles have netted $200 million (Bequai 1978; Lindsey 1979).

The basic scheme in these cases is to entice prospective retirees and other investors with attractive brochures of beautiful developments complete with landscaping, golf courses, and lakes. Through the use of high-pressure sales tactics, people are persuaded to pay exorbitant prices for arid desert plots that turn out to be virtually worthless when promised development plans never materialize. These schemes have been carried out by people linked with organized crime, by professional criminals, and by legitimate real estate brokers who cross the line into white collar crime.

Travel Scams and Time-Share Vacation Resorts In a practice that became widespread in the 1980s and continues today, millions of Americans received postcards informing them that they had won a glamorous vacation to Florida, Hawaii, or Las Vegas (Pauly 1987). People who responded to such inducements would often be persuaded to pay a fairly substantial "travel club" or "service" fee before receiving their "prize." The free vacation would turn out to have so many absurd restrictions that it would be useless to the recipient, who then could often be persuaded to pay additional fees to "upgrade" the arrangements. Recipients often ended up with no vacation or with one for which they paid a substantial amount of money. Similarly, millions of people receive inducements to buy into time-share vacation plans (Lyons 1982). Consumers who respond to blatantly misleading announcements about "prizes" that will be awarded if they visit the time-share resorts are subjected to high-pressure sales pitches. Many respondents commit themselves to expensive plans that do not deliver what they promise, and they rarely if ever receive the prizes they have been promised.

Employment Agency and Education-Related Scams Unemployed people and individuals hoping to get better jobs have paid fees (sometimes in the thousands of dollars) to "employment agencies" that guarantee them jobs, sometimes abroad (Booth 1993; Minkow 1997). After sending in their money, many clients never hear from the agency again, or they receive sloppily prepared résumés or outdated lists of jobs or corporate contacts. In most cases, applicants do not obtain jobs.

Some similar scams involve fraudulent claims relating to education. One variation of this scam involves an "educational consultant" who collects thousands of dollars (from young people in particular) in return for the false promise that the consultant will ensure their placement in a medical or dental school (Bequai 1978; Minkow 1997). A G.E. Career Center in New York City was exposed in 2002 for charging people $125 to obtain high school equivalency diplomas, which turned out to be bogus (Newman 2002). Some correspondence schools or vocationally oriented schools lure students, especially minorities and veterans, with promises of a valid educational or training curriculum that will lead to guaranteed jobs, when in fact the education or training is worthless and no jobs result. Financial assistance companies that claim they will enable high school students to obtain scholarships and grants are sometimes fraudulent enterprises (Hoover 2003). Between 1996 and 2003, close to 300,000 clients who had been defrauded out of almost $50 million were identified.

Telemarketing or "Boiler Room" Scams In recent years, scam artists using various telemarketing schemes were bilking U.S. citizens out of an estimated $40 billion annually ($50 billion with Canadians taken into account) (Bacon and Roston

2003; Shover and Coffey 2005). The National Consumers League estimated in 2002 that successful telemarketing frauds extract an average of $845 from each victim (Payne 2005b: 799). These operations may offer tempting investments (e.g., in rare coins, oil or gas leases, or diamonds), prizes, vitamins, and the like. Even though they may be placing a call from a shabby office, successful telemarketers convey to the recipient of their call an image of a booming, established business enterprise. Some relatively new telemarketing scams include enticements for "cash loans" in which callers are charged $49 for a generic information package on how to apply for bank loans; "one-shot" credit cards, in which callers pay a fee for a card that then turns out to be usable only once; bogus health product promotions, such as water purifiers; and penny-stock offerings based on misleading information about new small companies (*Consumer's Research* 1990; Eaton 1997d; Minkow 1997). The common elements of *telemarketing fraud* are a smooth, polished line to generate trust and interest; persuading the victims to provide a credit card number or to forward payment before they receive anything; the failure to give consumers what they expect; and the difficulty of prosecuting the offenders, who may move around frequently (Holcomb 1986; Meier 1992a; Payne 2005b). Although predatory telemarketers have some attributes in common with traditional professional criminals, they are more likely to come from middle-class and entrepreneurial backgrounds and more easily simulate an appearance of being engaged in a legitimate business (Shover, Coffey, and Hobbs 2003). In one case, a former U.S. Attorney and commodities regulator was convicted of engaging in telemarketing fraud (Smothers 2000). In another case, a telemarketing organization was charged with selling questionable and overpriced protection—against telemarketing fraud (Fried 2001)!

Schemes to Defraud the Wealthy Victims of investment scams are not always naïve, poorly educated elderly people or naturally gullible parties,

as some might imagine. Middle-class individuals seeking a high return on their investment can be susceptible, too. Some 6,000 people who invested $350 million in Colonial Realty in the 1980s, for example, lost much of their money when the operation turned out to be fraudulent (Judson 1992). In 1994, a California man was accused of bilking thousands of investors, who mistakenly thought they were investing in tax-sheltered low-income housing projects, out of as much as $130 million (Eaton 1994). The money was never invested, and the investors faced both the loss of their money and possible back taxes.

Some victims of investment frauds are quite affluent. New Yorker David Bloom, shortly after graduating from college, persuaded 100 well-off individuals to invest $10 million with his Sutton Investing Group (Blum 1988). Bloom used most of the money to buy millions of dollars worth of art, a house in the Hamptons, a $139,000 Aston Martin Volante convertible, and other luxury items while investors were misled with phony investment statements. Dana Giacchetto, financial advisor to Leonardo DiCaprio and other well-known Hollywood film stars, spent millions entrusted to him for investment to finance a lavish lifestyle, featuring dinner bills in the thousands of dollars, six-figure airplane and helicopter fares, and the like (Wong 2001; Wong and Eaton 2001). He received a five-year prison sentence. In 2005, a stockbroker and former agent for hip-hop stars was accused of defrauding them of several million dollars (Leeds 2005). During the same year, Alberto Vilar—a prominent philanthropist and patron of the arts—was jailed after wealthy investors claimed he stole millions of dollars from them; in the same year, Hakan Yalincak, a 21-year-old NYU senior was jailed when he tried to cash a forged $25 million check after raising millions from investors for apparently fraudulent purposes (Fishman 2005b; Wakin 2005). Also during 2005, two hedge fund managers, operating out of fancy offices in Palm Beach, Florida, were believed to have defrauded wealthy investors out of some $200 million (Cresswell 2005a).

Even highly sophisticated stock brokerage firms can be vulnerable to investment fraud. In the early

---

B O X 7.10 **When Fraud Leads to Violence**

Contrepreneurial crime and fraud generally are regarded as nonviolent crimes focused on financial gain. But violence can arise, sometimes perpetrated by victims or contrepreneurial competitors and sometimes by desperate contrepreneurs attempting to avoid exposure. Two stock promoters involved in the promotion of penny stocks were found murdered in New Jersey in October 1999 (Henriques 1999). Both of the deceased had been accused in the past of frauds relating to investments. Violence among people involved in stock frauds appears to be increasing. In 2000, a decorated Army captain, John Law, was charged with having flown home from a posting in Italy to murder a young couple he had defrauded in a land investment deal (Flynn 2000). Contrepreneurial crime is not by definition violent crime, but it can lead to violence.

1990s, a Nigerian grifter who had acquired an understanding of the logistics of high-level trading was able to trade some $1 billion in bonds and notes through major brokerages without putting up a nickel of his own money (Pooley 1993); the embarrassed brokerage houses lost hundreds of thousands of dollars. A stockbroker in 2005 who claimed to have various famous basketball players as clients was accused of stealing at least several million dollars from brokerage houses for which he worked, to support an extravagant lifestyle (Thomas 2005a). In 2005, a Greenwich (Connecticut) developer was accused of defrauding banks out of millions of dollars for loans but hiding evidence of earlier loans that had not been paid off (Cowan 2005b). In another case that is essentially check kiting on a grand scale, a Long Island car dealer borrowed $1.75 billion from General Motors to finance thousands of nonexistent cars, defrauding the company of several hundred million dollars (Fritsch 1992). That a corporation of this size can be so massively defrauded is surely a sobering realization. The success of contrepreneurs depends significantly on their ability to convey an aura of respectability and trust and to have credibility with financial institutions and investors. Time after time, apparently reputable individuals have used their positions to defraud investors or organizations of huge amounts of money. Occasionally, these frauds end violently. (See Box 7.10.)

TECHNOCRIME, INCLUDING COMPUTER CRIME

Computers and other forms of modern technology play an increasingly central role in many white collar crimes, and this role will surely expand in the future. It is difficult to overstate the rapidity with which new forms of technology have been introduced and disseminated in our society. By the early 1990s, information technology had become the single largest industry in the world; by the beginning of the 21st century, more than $100 billion in financial transactions were taking place online annually (Gegak 1997; Grabosky, Smith, and Dempsey 2001; Vohra 1994). In 1991, there were only a few Internet hosts or websites, but by 2005 there were at least 200 million (The Secretariat 2005: 5). Distribution and use of other forms of modern technology as well—VCRs, for example—have also experienced exponential growth. High technology is one of the defining elements of this era, sometimes labeled the "Age of Information." The influx into our lives of increasingly sophisticated forms of technology has been acclaimed by technocrats as a substantial benefit and lamented by techno-skeptics as harmful. Even as modern technology speeds up and facilitates many routine and complex tasks, it also tends to divide society in new ways—into those who have access to technology and those who do not. It provides greater occupational mobility for some and unemployment for others. In the realm of crime and criminal justice, it offers new and greater protection and security, even as it becomes a formidable instrument for committing new forms and levels of fraud, embezzlement, and other crimes. It provides the criminal justice system with powerful new tools and enables those who control such tools to engage in massive invasions of privacy and other abuses.

Technocrime Defined

The term *technocrime* is somewhat broader than the more familiar term *computer crime*, as it encompasses crime facilitated by any sophisticated form of technology (Bequai 1987; Jacobson and Greca Green 2002). Technocrime has been described as a subset of white collar crime or, alternatively, as a distinctly new form (Parker 1980; Wasik 1991). The terms *cybercrime*, *Internet crime*, *network crime*, *information crime*, and *electronic theft* have also been used to refer to crimes carried out with computers or in cyberspace (Smith, Grabosky, and Urbas 2004; Wall 2003; Williams M. 2005).

Of course, not all illegalities committed with technology are white collar crimes. For example, technocrime committed by spies engaged in espionage activities, and in some instances by terrorists, are not white collar crimes. Nor is use of computers for the dissemination of child pornography, or the use of the Internet by pedophiles to solicit victims, white collar crime (Hollinger 2001). Computer hacking is often a sophisticated form of vandalism committed by "electronic delinquents" or "technopaths" who break into computer systems simply for the challenge or to cause mischief (Bequai 1987; Nicholson 1990; Purdy 2005a). Such cybercrime has huge economic consequences. For example, worldwide losses due to viruses, including loss of productivity, are estimated at up to $12 billion annually (Speer 2000). The spam or junk e-mail that is now estimated to make up as much as 80 percent of all e-mail, is not necessarily illegal but must be addressed and deleted in some form at enormous cost (Flynn 2004; Hansell 2003). The problems associated with spam have become so

great that lawsuits, legislation, and legal prosecutions of spammers are beginning to occur.

The cost and sophistication of high technology ensure that such computer crime is especially well represented in the white collar world. Computers play a central role in insider trading by helping to hide illegal profits and market positions, by facilitating transfer of money to offshore bank accounts, by parking stocks, and by concealing stock ownership (Reichman 1993). Today at least 80 percent of financial transactions in the United States are conducted electronically (Gegak 1997; Sessions 1991). Cyber payment systems facilitate money laundering and other forms of financial crime (The Secretariat 2005). Computers clearly create a vast new arena for criminal activity.

Computer Crime

Computer crime has been most simply defined as an illegal act wherein computers and computer technology are used to commit the offense (Jacobson and Greca Green 2002: 274; Williams M. 2005). Computer hardware is protected by the same laws that protect other forms of physical property, but the electronic information inside a computer represents a new form of property less clearly protected by traditional laws (Michalowski and Pfuhl 1991). Accordingly, the introduction of computers has created new forms of electronic and magnetic "assets" and a new language as well (Grabosky et al. 2001; Parker 1980). A computer may be the tool of a crime (e.g., embezzlement) or the target of a crime (e.g., theft of services). Categories of computer crime include: internal computer crimes (e.g., sabotaging programs), telecommunications crimes (e.g., hacking and illegal bulletin boards), computer manipulation crimes (e.g., embezzlements and frauds), computers in support of criminal enterprises (e.g., facilitating illicit drug distribution), and hardware/software thefts (e.g., software piracy, thefts of computers and chips, and thefts of trade secrets) (Hollinger 2001; McEwen 1990a).

The theft of a computer itself is simply a conventional crime with a high-tech target. An increasing proportion of theft today, however, takes the form of stealing information, pirating software and electronic products, and copying "intellectual property" (e.g., music) without authorization. Some of this activity is outright theft in a conventional sense, but much bootlegging and unauthorized copying are now so widely diffused and accepted in many circles that they have a "contested" status as deviance or crime (Zernike 2003). Major corporations have adopted different positions on this issue. Media companies such as Disney want their intellectual property protected from unauthorized copying; technology and Internet companies want to promote technological innovation and facilitate copying (Harmon 2002a). At least some music companies have begun initiating legal actions against those who engage in illegal file-sharing (Harmon 2003). Some commentators fear that young Internet "pirates" who can easily bootleg music will get in the habit of bootlegging many other things and become more insensitive to theft and cheating generally (Bowie 2005; Schwartz 2001). If much bootlegging or unauthorized copying has nothing to do with white collar crime, certainly some such activity is carried out in a business or occupational environment, and practices acquired in one's personal life may well carry over into one's professional life.

An estimated one third of business software is pirated, with an estimated loss to software producers in 2002 of over $13 billion, assuming that users would have purchased the software if they had not been able to acquire it illegitimately (Wallace, Lusthaus, and Kim 2005: 276). Microsoft and other software companies regard themselves as seriously threatened by such activity and have launched an aggressive war against software piracy (McGuire 2001). Once again, we have an example of a corporation, Microsoft, that has been accused of committing a form of white collar crime (antitrust) but is also a victim of white collar crime.

Increasing reliance upon "digital money" from the mid-1990s on and the explosive growth of business transactions carried out on the Internet have generated broad new opportunities for criminal conduct (Grabosky 2001; Mann and Sutton 1998;

Williams M. 2005). In one especially direct form, we have Internet scams involving auctions, investments, health products, selling on your own, travel bargains, Internet access, credit card fraud, and home businesses (*U.S. News & World Report* 2000).

Although many of these scams are enduring forms of contrepreneurial crime, the relative anonymity of the Internet can facilitate these crimes. For example, eBay has become a $5 billion-a-year business, bringing together sellers and buyers in an auction format (Schwartz and Dobrzynski 2001). Shill bidding, or bidding on one's own auction to drive up bids, is prohibited but clearly occurs. Sellers may receive payment and then never ship the product, ship damaged products, or sell products not accurately described. On the other hand, businesses that pay billions of dollars to Google and other search engines to advertise and steer potential customers to their websites have become increasingly concerned about "click fraud" (Ives 2005). These advertisers must pay for each "click" on their ads but believe that in some cases, competitors or other parties are deliberately driving their advertising costs up by fraudulent clicking.

The Internet has also facilitated identity theft (see Box 7.11) and the theft of confidential information. The scope of such theft has increased dramatically in recent years as sophisticated criminals find various ways to defraud businesses using the Internet (Grabosky 2001; Stone 2001; Tedeschi 2001). On the other hand, a considerable amount of computer or cybercrime is carried out by or through businesses or by people within the context of a legitimate occupation, victimizing consumers and individuals.

It is difficult to estimate accurately losses due to computer crime, much of which is not reported—or even discovered—but by any estimate the losses are in the billions (Jacobson and Greca Green 2002). In a recent survey, average losses of $2 million were reported due to computer crime; companies that lost proprietary information or were victims of financial fraud reported average losses of between $4 million and $6.5 million per incident (Tedeschi 2003). The use of computers greatly increases the potential size and scope of

BOX 7.11   Identity Theft as White Collar Crime

Identity theft has been one of the fastest growing crimes in recent years, with an estimated 3.2 million Americans as victims each year, according to the Federal Trade Commission (Rivlin 2005). The current epidemic in identity theft has been attributed to the rapid growth of the Internet and digital finance, the vast expansion of consumer credit, and the limited response of the justice system and regulatory system (O'Brien 2004). Much of this theft involves stolen credit card numbers and unauthorized charges to credit cards, with a rapidly expanding international black market for the sale of stolen credit card (and bank account) information (Zeller 2005a). "Phishing" is one technique for extracting personal financial information for fraudulent purposes, when Internet users click on e-mails or pop-ups requesting such information that appear to come from recognizable corporations such as Microsoft (Hansell 2004). Worldwide losses due to identity theft and fraud have been estimated in the "double-digit billions," with American financial institutions alone sustaining close to $50 billion in annual losses (Levy and Stone 2005; O'Brien 2004; Richtel 2002). Although victims of identity theft can avoid the losses charged to their accounts by establishing that they are not responsible for the charges, they often endure significant emotional distress and years of inconvenience to repair their credit standing. The cost

of such "repair" is adding up some $5 billion a year for American consumers. And in some cases, consumers have been defrauded by responding to what appears to be a notice about a fraud (Hafner and Flynn 2003). An e-mail message directs recipients to a website to correct an alleged problem with fraud by entering credit card and Social Security information, which is then used to defraud them!

Does identity theft have anything to do with white collar crime? Such theft is a classic example of a hybrid form of crime. Access to privileged identity information is often gained by someone in an occupational setting and passed along to others. In November 2002, authorities in New York announced the breakup of an identity-theft ring that stole and traded on the credit histories of 30,000 people (O'Brien 2002; Weiser 2002b). A former "help desk" worker for a company providing software to banks and other companies to obtain credit histories played a key role in this identity theft case, possibly the largest to date. In June 2005, millions of Americans were put at risk for identity theft and fraud when CardSystems Solutions, a payment processor, admitted to a major security breach in its system (Dash 2005b). Accordingly, the negligent actions of legitimate financial institutions can play a significant role in identity theft and fraud.

thefts; the average computer crime loss is many times greater than the average amount netted in a bank robbery (Michalowski and Pfuhl 1991). However, bank robberies are almost always reported; many computer crimes, especially those involving more modest losses, are not. The biggest losses inevitably occur when computer crime is committed as a matter of corporate policy. One of the largest corporate frauds in U.S. history occurred in the 1970s, when officials of the Equity Funding Insurance Co. created billions of dollars of phony policies and assets with the assistance of computers (Bequai 1987).

The use of computers enables people working in certain occupations to use a "salami technique"— that is, to steal small amounts of assets from many sources. The total stolen is often quite substantial,

but detection is minimized because such a small amount (sometimes pennies) is stolen from so many individual accounts (Judson 1994; Schjolberg and Parker 1983). As is true of much white collar crime, computer crime offenders tend to deny they are criminals and may alternatively see themselves as "problem solvers." Such rationalization is more likely when the victim of computer crime is an organization and the spoils of the crime are somewhat intangible and accessed electronically (Parker 1980). A small proportion of computer crime committed by employees is motivated by a desire to avenge perceived mistreatment by the employer. In a similar situation, a provider of computer software was charged with attempting to destroy a client's program by introducing a virus into it in the aftermath of a billing dispute (Schemo 1993).

Other examples of computer crimes committed by employees include programming a bank computer to ignore an overdraft in the programmer's account; stealing merchandise by manipulating a computerized inventory bank; stealing computer time to run one's own business; using computers to extract business trade secrets and then selling them to competitors; and manipulating computer records to embezzle funds from employers or customers. For example, accountants for Cisco System broke into the company's computer and issued themselves $8 million worth of stock (Tedeschi 2003). The rapid increase in the use of computers on all levels of government suggests that computer crimes against the government by its own employees are likely to increase greatly (Bennett 1987; Grabosky et al. 2001). The enormous size of many government financial programs renders them especially vulnerable to computer crime.

Computers also play a role in tax fraud and evasion, either within a business context or on the part of individual taxpayers. Stew Leonard, owner of a large dairy store in Connecticut, pleaded guilty to defrauding the government of $17.5 million in taxes, with the store's computer playing a central role in hiding cash discrepancies (Levy 1993). Now that the IRS has come to encourage the expanded use of electronic filing of federal income tax forms, it must also confront a growing problem of fraudulently filed electronic returns, which can be more difficult to verify than returns with documentation on paper (Hershey 1994). Although computer programs have long been used to check returns more efficiently, it is clear that electronic filing enhances some opportunities for fraud.

It has proven quite difficult to respond effectively to computer crime (Lewis 2004). Only a small proportion of it is discovered, let alone reported. Because it is carried out electronically, evidence is often hidden deep within the bowels of a computer system, and in some cases it may be quickly erased. The recent growth of wireless data technology (Wi-Fi) has made it even more difficult to solve cybercrimes, as fraudsters can patch into other people's networks that have not been protected by encryption (Schiesel

2005). In many cases, victims of computer crime are reluctant to report their victimization. Banks and other businesses do not want the vulnerability of their computer systems publicized, and in any case, they may have little confidence in the ability of the criminal justice system to respond effectively to this type of crime. Finally, public consciousness of and concern with computer crime are relatively small because of its novelty and lack of directness.

The Law and Computer Crime

Computer crime has a relatively recent history. The first recorded computer crime case occurred in 1958, and the first federal prosecution occurred in 1966 (Bequai 1987). Despite increasing publicity about computer crimes, prosecutions for such crimes are relatively few in number, constituting a fraction of prosecutors' caseloads (Jacobson and Greca Green 2002; Michalowski and Pfuhl 1991). However, many offenses involving computers are prosecuted through ordinary common law statutes, and there is no centralized bank of computer crime statistics.

Laws specifically prohibiting computer crime are quite recent and not easily enforced. Traditional criminal laws are not always applicable to crimes committed by manipulation of electronic software. Most state and federal laws specifically applicable to computer crime came into being in the 1980s; by the early years of the 21st century, all 50 states had passed some form of computer crime laws (Conly 1990; Wallace et al. 2005). In 1986, Congress passed a Computer Fraud and Abuse Act, intended to make the use of computers for fraud and theft a felony in cases not covered by state laws (Ross 2005). These laws were enacted either because legislators recognized a rational need for them or because lawmakers were responding to a perceived threat to established property and authority relations posed by illicit access to a new and ambiguous form of information (Hollinger and Lanza-Kaduce 1988; Michalowski and Pfuhl 1991). In 1996, the passage of the National Information Infrastructure Protection Act eliminated some of the common defenses in computer crime cases; in 2000, the Internet False Identification Prevention Act focused on one significant form of computer crime. In the wake of the 9/11 attacks, the USA Patriot Act added some amendments to the 1996 law (Wallace et al. 2005). These acts provided government agencies with broader powers to investigate computer frauds and authorized harsher penalties for offenders. To date, the practical impact of computer crime laws has been limited at best, though their symbolic and ideological importance may be more substantial.

The Pursuit of Computer Crime Cases

Investigation and prosecution of computer crime require specially trained personnel and tend to be quite time consuming. In 2002, the FBI had 270 agents working on its computer crime task force and was planning to expand to 700 agents (Tedeschi 2002). It is clear that criminal justice agencies on all levels must devote more resources to technocrime. Private Internet police, including accountants, play a significant role in the prevention and detection of computer crime and may refer findings to federal authorities after catching offenders in a "sting" action (Tedeschi 2002). But it is often necessary to resolve computer crimes privately and informally, in part because special complications arise if cases are pursued through the criminal justice system (Smith et al. 2004). Defense lawyers, for example, often challenge the admissibility of computer-related evidence (Jacobson and Greca Green 2002; Schjolberg and Parker 1983). Additional legal reforms are needed to successfully address computer crime.

Other Types of Technocrime

Automatic teller machines (ATMs), telecommunications systems, facsimile machines, and other forms of technology also provide a range of opportunities for misappropriation or theft. A significant proportion of such technocrime is committed by people who cannot be classified as white collar criminals; for example, those who steal from ATMs are unlikely to fit the profile of white collar offenders unless they are bank employees taking advantage of inside knowledge and access.

Advances in all forms of copying technology have provided new opportunities for organized and professional crime, particularly in counterfeiting and distributing video and audiotapes. Of course, such copying, and unauthorized copying of computer software as well, is so widely engaged in by private parties that it hardly requires documentation (Harmon 2002a; McGuire 2001).

Millions of Americans also engage in airwave piracy through the use of satellite dishes, illegal chips, and the simple expedient of wiring onto a cable line (Lieberman 2002). Further, the theft of telephone service—through the use of "blue boxes" simulating telephone system beeps, altered cellular phone chips, and unauthorized use of corporate switchboards—costs telephone companies and other victimized parties millions of dollars (Grabosky and Smith 1998; Ramirez 1992). Much of this activity is regarded as relatively harmless "folk crime." At least some proportion of technocrime either occurs in an occupational context or is committed on behalf of corporations. Rapid, sophisticated photocopying machines facilitate the theft of trade secrets by corporations and by employees seeking financial benefit from the use of such information (Bennett 1987). Telecommunications companies are directly or indirectly complicit in "slamming," or the unauthorized switching of a long-distance carrier, which collectively can cost telephone customers a huge sum of money (Dodge 2001b). Predatory telemarketing—discussed earlier in this chapter—is greatly facilitated by digital technology and automatic dialer technology (Bacon and Roston 2003). Businesses of all sizes can be victimized by technocrimes, but they commit some of it as well.

The distinguished University of Pennsylvania criminologist Marvin Wolfgang was quoted in 1987 as predicting that "by the turn of the century, the main concern of criminal justice will be information crime" (Bennett 1987: 109). In the face of terrorism threats and other serious forms of crime, this may appear to be an overstatement, but the growing significance of information crime is indisputable. It will be a formidable challenge to generate meaningfully normative consensus concerning much of this activity, to inhibit its commission, and to implement effective technological countermeasures and efficient penal responses to deter it. It is important to recognize that technocrime arises out of and is shaped by an ongoing contest between the powerful and the powerless over access to information, one of the foremost currencies of our environment today.

ENTERPRISE CRIME, CONTREPRENEURIAL CRIME, AND TECHNOCRIME, IN SUM

Are the activities discussed in this chapter forms of white collar crime? The answer might be: "No, and yes." Syndicated crime has not been conventionally characterized as a form of white collar crime, but the section of this chapter addressing *enterprise crime* demonstrated many points of intersection between traditional forms of "organized" crime and legitimate organizations or businesses. For some observers, the boundaries between organized crime (in the traditional sense) and white collar crime are eroding, and may eventually disappear.

In the second section of this chapter, intersections between traditional forms of professional crime, and especially classic confidence schemes or "cons," and business enterprises that have some legitimate aspects are explored. Swindles and scams may be absolute, wholly defrauding people, or relative, giving less in terms of services or products than expected. The term *contrepreneurial crime* nicely captures this spectrum of activities.

Finally, *technocrime* encompasses a wide range of illegal and harmful activities carried out by using advanced forms of technology, especially computers. In this section, an effort was made to discriminate between such forms of crime that do and do not fall within the realm of white collar crime. It should be obvious that the problem of crimes committed in cyberspace will increase in the future and will increasingly be a key element of different forms of white collar crime.

In sum, this chapter has attempted to expose readers to some hybrid and marginal but also highly significant manifestations of white collar crime.

KEY TERMS

big con, 181

computer crime, 191

contrepreneurial crime, 181

enterprise crime, 173

fence, 183

identity theft, 193

La Cosa Nostra, 173

Mafia, 173

organized crime, 173

penny stock fraud, 186

Ponzi scheme, 185

professional criminal, 180

pump and dump, 187

pyramid scheme, 185

syndicated crime, 174

technocrime, 191

telemarketing fraud, 189

DISCUSSION QUESTIONS

1. What is the notion of hybrid white collar crime? What are some of the different principal meanings of organized crime and syndicated crime? What are the main dimensions of enterprise crime, as a hybrid of syndicated crime and white collar crime?

2. How does syndicated crime become interrelated with governmental crime? What are the principal facts that lead to syndicated crime infiltration of legitimate businesses, and what are some consequences of such infiltration? What are some recent forms of syndicated crime involvement with legitimate businesses?

3. Identify the principal attributes of professional criminals and some of the main historical trends relating to such criminals. What justification, if any, can be advanced for differentiating between traditional professional criminals and contemporary contrepreneurs? What are some of the most enduring varieties of contrepreneurial crime?

4. Identify the principal defining elements of technocrime. Which specific facets of the modern technology/computer revolution promote white collar crimes, and which facets impose constraints on such crime? What are some of the emerging forms of technocrime, and what trends should we anticipate in the realm of technocrime?

5. Compare enterprise crime, contrepreneurial crime, and technocrime in terms of their basic attributes. Identify some of the key areas in which these different forms of crime intersect. Is there any reliable way of assessing which of these forms of crime does the most harm? Which do you regard as most likely to flourish in the years ahead, and why?

Explaining White Collar Crime

Theories and Accounts

When respectable members of society and major corporations are accused of white collar crimes, some people find it hard to understand. Why do smart people with decent incomes, or big businesses with good reputations, risk shame, ruin, and possibly prison or the destruction of their business? In 2005, for example, a former head of a multibillion-dollar corporation, at one point worth about a billion dollars himself, was convicted for complicity in a massive corporate accounting fraud and sentenced to 25 years in prison. A venerable accounting firm that had been in business for almost 90 years, employing 85,000 people, collapsed in the wake of a criminal conviction (Belson 2005; Byrne 2002b). How does this happen?

More generally, how do we best explain white collar crime? This straightforward question has inspired a wide range of responses, from a simple human motivation (greed) to complex structural explanations (e.g., "structural embeddedness" or "contradictions"). Only human beings attempt to explain the behavior of others instead of simply responding to it. Attempts to explain criminal behavior and crime—or behavior and activity that

deviate from accepted norms—extend far back in history. In modern times, a theory typically serves as a framework for criminologists' efforts to explain crime. A *theory* is a formal version of an explanation, although it is not necessarily a comprehensive explanation. It attempts to explain a class of events, whereas an explanation might simply attempt to make sense of a specific event (Goode 2005; Vold, Bernard, and Snipes 2002). In the conventional view, a good theory can be tested and fits the evidence provided by research (Williams and McShane 1998).

Previous chapters on the varieties of white collar crime include many references to explanations for such crime, but this chapter provides a much more systematic review of applicable theories and perspectives. Given the broad array of activities encompassed by the term *white collar crime*, it should be evident that no single theory fits all white collar crimes. Before proceeding with an examination of some of the specific perspectives on or theories of the causes of white collar crime, it is necessary to identify some of our underlying assumptions and the kinds of questions we should be asking.

UNDERLYING ASSUMPTIONS AND POINTS OF DEPARTURE

Every attempt at explanation invokes certain metaphysical, ontological, and epistemological assumptions about the ultimate nature of reality and being, and how we come to know and understand our world (Mandelbaum 1987). For example, is reality subjective (in the mind of the observer) or objective (independent of the observer)? Is "causation" simply a human construct, or is it something that can be definitively and objectively established? With regard to human beings, do they have a free will (voluntarism), or is this simply an illusion because all human behavior is instead a function of various internal and external forces (determinism)? Or is some mixture of free will and determinism closest to the truth? Are human beings naturally self-interested and greedy or naturally socially concerned and altruistic? Are we fundamentally rational and guided by reason or irrational and influenced principally by emotions? Or is it simply the case that human nature is endlessly malleable and has no fixed tendencies? Is society itself best thought of as an integrated system bound together by a high level of consensus, or is it more accurately portrayed as a contested terrain of conflicting interest groups, with the more powerful tending to dominate the less powerful? And are the norms and rules that govern human groups rooted in absolute, eternal moral laws, or are they simply products of a particular time and place and relative to the context in which they were created? These are but a few of the many enduring questions with which social philosophers have grappled through the ages. It is important to understand that almost anything we might say about white collar crime is rooted in our assumptions, whether explicit or implicit, concerning such questions.

The social and behavioral sciences have largely embraced the assumption that much about human activity and existence is explainable and that it is desirable to produce ever more rigorous, testable explanations. An alternative position is that human activity is more easily interpreted than explained and that it is endlessly variable or contradictory. Regardless, we have no single, comprehensive explanation of the causes of white collar crime; rather, we have at least provisionally identified some factors that appear to be correlated with or promote such crime.

WHAT DO WE WANT TO EXPLAIN?

When we are attempting to explain white collar crime, what exactly requires explanation? The conventional answer is that we must explain *criminality*, or what makes individuals or organizations commit white collar crimes. Such an answer focuses on individual or organizational motivations and on the forces that promote motivations and lead to the commission of white collar crimes.

A second answer is that we must explain the *crime*, or the event itself. One aspect of this approach addresses the issue of why the incidence of white collar crime varies among occupations and industries, within occupations and industries, or across time and space. Situational factors that contribute to the commission of white collar crime are especially important on this level of analysis. Criminal behavior has been treated as both an individual (or organizational) propensity and as an event; more sophisticated explanations treat it as a combination of both dimensions. Among the elements cited to explain criminal behavior are motivation (the will to deviate), freedom from social constraints (impunity relating to losses), skill, and opportunity (Sheley 1983). These factors may interact in different ways.

A third answer to the question of what must be explained, one that has received greater emphasis in recent decades, is that *criminalization*, the process whereby particular activities, entities, and individuals come to be defined as criminal, must be explained first (Gibbs 1987). This approach focuses on the origins of white collar crime laws or regulations and on the investigation, prosecution, and adjudication of white collar offenses (Vold et al. 2002). The capacity of white collar individuals

> **B O X 8.1** **The Demonic Explanation**
>
> The earliest explanation of criminality, which could be called demonic or spiritualistic, does not lend itself to empirical verification (Pfohl 1985; Vold et al. 2002). At the core of this explanation was the belief that other worldly influences caused criminal behavior. Such beliefs significantly influenced the response to crime, which for much of history was largely reactive. Exorcism, trials by ordeal, and penal measures involving corporal and capital punishment to exterminate evil spirits were important parts of this reaction. The motives for prosecuting "criminals" were not always pure. During the Renaissance (15th through 17th centuries), many thousands of Europeans were charged with witchcraft so
>
> that their accusers had reason to confiscate their property (Currie 1968).
>
> Criminologists today are unlikely to invoke the demonic explanation for criminality, but it is hardly extinct. Some people with fundamentalist religious beliefs continue to equate criminality with sin and otherworldly influences, but these beliefs are not limited to fundamentalists. Richard Quinney (1980), a prominent critical criminologist, has suggested that much that is wrong with our existence today—including, presumably, the rapacious conduct of white collar criminals—reflects a "sacred void" in the face of relentless secular and materialist forces.

and organizations to prevent or deflect criminalization of their harmful activities is one of the recurrent themes of this perspective. Because these matters are explored in some depth in Chapters 9, 10, and 11, they will be only briefly treated here, principally in terms of their intersection with causal explanations.

A truly substantial explanation for white collar crime must address each of these matters, and ideally it must explore the variety of interrelationships involved in white collar crime as criminality, as an event (a crime), and as criminalized activity. Another basic issue, originally raised by Sutherland (1940), is whether crime can be explained by a general theory that is applicable to both conventional and white collar crime or whether white collar crime must be explained by special theories applicable only to this type of crime.

Yet another issue in the explanation of white collar crime is the appropriate explanatory level. In *macro-level* explanations, the focus is on the conditions within society or the organization that promote white collar crime—on structural factors. In *micro-level* explanations, the focus is on the offenders and their individual propensities and choices. In *meso-level*, or intermediate, explanations, situational factors (e.g., specific circumstances) are examined. Some core questions at the

various levels include: What type of society or political economy produces the most white collar crime? What type of organization is most likely to promote white collar crime? Which situational factors are most closely associated with white collar crime? Which individual attributes are most fully correlated with involvement in white collar crime? In the sections that follow, we will examine some principal efforts to explain white collar criminality, crime, and criminalization.

EXPLAINING WHITE COLLAR CRIMINALITY

The most basic theories of criminality hold that criminals are different in some fundamental way from noncriminals. Such theories then attempt to identify the nature of the difference. On a sociological level, criminality, the propensity to commit crimes, is shown to vary among different segments of the population or among different organizations. We will explore biogenetic, psychological, and sociogenic explanations of criminality. Box 8.1 considers an early spiritual theory on criminality.

The Biogenetic Explanation

A *biogenetic explanation* of criminality became especially influential in the 19th century, although its roots can be traced to much earlier times (Vold et al. 2002). At its core was the notion that criminals are inherently different from other people, even down to their appearance. This explanation was promoted by Austrian anatomist Franz Joseph Gall's phrenology and Italian criminologist Cesare Lombroso's concept of the "born criminal" as an atavistic (less fully evolved) type. Criminals could be identified by their "primitive" appearance.

The significance of this notion of criminality is that it has persisted in the public imagination long after it was discredited by criminological research. Racist and ethnic elements were often added to the stereotypical conception of the criminal. Because white collar offenders typically do not "look like criminals," jurors and others may be less likely to impute criminality to them.

During much of the 20th century, biogenetic explanations of criminality, focusing on factors ranging from body type to brain chemistry, were discredited or overshadowed by other forms of explanation. A revival of interest in such explanations since the late 1970s reflects the influences of the emerging field of sociobiology and widely accepted findings of scientific research that such conditions as schizophrenia, clinical depression, and alcoholism have important biogenetic roots. Contributing to this renewed interest is a more conservative political and cultural ambience that is receptive to these kinds of explanations (Wilson 1975; Wilson and Herrnstein 1985). Most of the discussion of biogenetic factors applies these factors to certain classes of conventional offenders.

Biogenetic explanations have been challenged as having too simplistic a view of crime and of the relationship between biology and human behavior (Katz and Chambliss 1991). The pervasiveness of white collar crime would seem to offer a powerful refutation of the proposition that criminality can be generally explained by biogenetic explanations. No legitimate studies have examined the biological makeup of white collar offenders, although Jeffery

(1990) has suggested that future research might explore the possible role of the brain. To date, there is simply no evidence that biogenetic factors play a role in white collar criminality.

Psychological Explanations

Criminality has also been explained as a psychological phenomenon. In this approach, the focus is on personality, mental processes, the enduring effects of early childhood traumas, and the like. The single most famous psychological explanations of human conduct were advanced by Sigmund Freud.

From a *Freudian approach*, crime, including white collar crime, can be viewed as a reflection of the eternal conflict between the desires of the individual and the needs of civilization (Freud 1930). In one of his few specific discussions of crime, Freud (1923) suggested that individuals may commit crimes to bring upon themselves punishment for a preexisting sense of guilt. The fact that at least some white collar offenders have engaged in such self-destructive acts of illegality lends this notion some credibility. More specifically, white collar crime in a Freudian approach could be linked with defects in the superego (the conscience), the ego (the balancing voice of reason, or the idealized self), or the id (aggressive and libidinous innate drives). Many limitations of the Freudian model of the self have been identified, but the core notion of tensions and conflicts among different aspects of the self makes some sense intuitively and can be hypothetically associated in a limited way with white collar criminality.

Many but not all psychological theories follow the Freudian lead in emphasizing the importance of early childhood experience in shaping adult attitudes and behavior. Whether white collar criminality can be linked to childhood experiences has not been subjected to systematic study. To the extent that one's moral sensibility is shaped by childhood socialization, there may be some connection.

Personality Personality traits are among the most examined of all psychological explanations of white collar crime. Sutherland (1949) specifically repudiated the psychological level of explanation for white collar crime by pointing out that corporate patterns of lawbreaking are independent of specific individual personalities and that not all corporate divisions governed by a white collar criminal with a specific personality will engage in lawbreaking. Recent students of white collar crime are divided between those who regard personality as a negligible factor, especially for corporate crime, and those who believe it is significant in accounting for why some people commit white collar offenses while others in the same position do not (Coleman 2006; Croall 2001; Piquero et al. 2005). Contradictory possibilities exist: On the one hand, corporations may recruit conformists who are predisposed to go along with corporate crime; on the other hand, nonconformists might more readily commit white collar crimes against their employers.

For the most part, the relatively few studies exploring the relevance of personality for involvement in white collar crime have not produced any clear evidence of psychological abnormality, and most white collar offenders appear to fall within the range of normal personality types. A few studies have suggested that white collar offenders are somewhat more likely to display such personality attributes as a tendency toward risk taking and recklessness, ambitiousness and drive, and egocentricity and a hunger for power (Coleman 2006; Punch 2000; Snider 1993). Obviously such personality traits can be correlated with legitimate success as well, although we have much still to learn about risk taking as a desirable or undesirable trait (Wheeler 1992). Personality traits sometimes needed to get to the top, such as egocentricity, and reinforced in those who are at the top, such as paranoia and megalomania, can also contribute to excessive and illegal actions by some high-level corporate executives (Punch 2000). Extremely successful leaders of major corporations, such as Microsoft's Bill Gates, may have difficulty displaying contrition for wrongdoing due to a "messianic" faith in their mission—the same quality that contributed to their ambition, drive, and tenacity in building their business in the first place (Harmon 2002b). Gates specifically seemed to find it impossible to apologize for the anticompetitive practices of Microsoft, as established in legal proceedings.

A psychologist who has worked with white collar offenders finds them to be clever, easily frustrated, aloof, and creative in rationalizing their illegal conduct (Criddle 1987). One study comparing some 350 incarcerated white collar crime offenders with an equal number of white collar executives reports that the offenders have greater tendencies toward irresponsibility, lack of dependability, and disregard for rules (Collins and Schmidt 1993). White collar crime prisoners interviewed by a professor of business ethics and law attributed their involvement in white collar crime to greed, a feeling of invincibility, and poor judgment (Ellin 2002). It has also been speculated that white collar criminals may quite often have an especially pronounced "fear of falling" (or failing) or be less able to defer gratification and exercise self-control (Gottfredson and Hirschi 1990; Piquero 2004; Wheeler 1992). A recent study has produced some evidence that a "desire for control" may play a significant role in corporate criminal decision making (Piquero et al. 2005). More specifically, in a sampling of managers and MBA students, those who manifested a "desire for control" as part of their personality were also more likely to indicate an intention to commit violations in the context of corporate decision making. But most students of white collar crime apparently believe that those who emphasize personality type in explaining white collar crime still have the burden of proving their case.

The closely related concepts of character and identity may also have some relevance (Gunkel 1990). Personality is most typically associated with the behavioral characteristics of an individual; character and identity are associated with an individual's nature, especially his or her moral or ethical qualities. Attention to character suggests that white collar offenders can certainly be viewed as responsible moral agents who make choices rather than as hapless victims of external circumstances, but these choices must be understood in the context of various social conditions and influences (Martin

---

B O X 8.2 **Mental Illness, Drug Addiction, and Intellectual Aptitude: Factors in White Collar Crime?**

Conventional criminality has been associated with personal pathologies such as mental disorder and substance abuse, and with a lower than average IQ (Wilson and Herrnstein 1985). Are such factors linked to involvement in white collar crime?

Individuals with visible symptoms of mental illness are often precluded from occupying white collar positions of any importance and would thus have few opportunities to commit many types of white collar crime. Of course, on rare occasions some form of psychosis or affective disorder could play a role in the commission of a white collar crime. When an individual holding an important white collar position commits a crime that appears to be at odds with past professional behavior or seems "irrational," mental illness may be blamed. In the fascinating case of a major film studio head who embezzled tens of thousands of dollars,

many of his associates insisted that the crime could only be explained in terms of mental or emotional problems (McClintick 1982). The lawyer for a New York City union leader who embezzled $1.7 million attributed it to depression or a bipolar disorder (Greenhouse S. 1998b). To date there is only speculation, but no solid evidence, that drug addiction might play a role in some white collar crime cases (Cowles 1992).

The idea that conventional offenders may have lower IQs than nonoffenders has been challenged on many grounds, including alleged cultural biases of the IQ test and the fact that those caught committing crimes are not necessarily the smarter criminals. People who commit white collar crimes may need above-average intelligence both to qualify for their white collar positions and to carry out complex crimes.

1999). A study by Paternoster and Simpson (1996) found that moral considerations, presumably guided by good moral character, play a role in the decision making of prospective and actual corporate managers, with regard to engaging in illegal behavior on behalf of the corporation. Other things being equal, we would expect that individuals with good "character" in the sense of moral integrity are less likely to commit white collar crimes than are those who lack such character.

Character and personality may have played some role in the crimes of Adolf Hitler and associates in the Holocaust and of Richard Nixon and associates in the Watergate affair (Fest 1970; Woodward and Bernstein 1977). Biographical accounts of such notorious white collar offenders as Michael Milken (securities manipulations), Charles Keating (thrifts fraud), and Leona Helmsley (income tax evasion) identify several personality and character traits, such as obsessions with power and control, narcissism, a sense of superiority, and indifference to conventional rules of conduct, as contributing factors in their criminal conduct (Binstein and Bowden 1993; Pierson 1989; Stewart 1991).

An account of multimillionaire investment banker Martin Siegel's involvement in the Wall Street insider trading crimes of the 1970s refers to his singular insecurity (perhaps rooted in his father's bankruptcy in his youth), his limitless compulsiveness, and his obsession with maintaining an image of breathtaking success (Vise 1987). At the other end of the affluence scale, it seems reasonable to hypothesize that if two low-level employees react quite differently to opportunities to commit illegal acts against an employer, personality or character is one factor in the different responses even though other factors may well be more important. Some white collar crime does seem to be difficult to explain without reference to personality and character. Box 8.2 examines other possible factors.

Sociogenic Explanations

Some theoretical and empirical work that adopts a *sociogenic* framework also addresses the matter of criminality, especially in terms of alleged differences in criminal propensities among members of different social classes or groups. Gottfredson and Hirschi

---

B O X 8.3   White Collar Delinquency

In a rare study of white collar delinquency—specifically, illegal copying of audio albums, videos, and computer software—Hagan and Kay (1990) found that the presence of power, a positive orientation toward risk taking, and the absence of control (parental, in this case) are correlated with such delinquency. Males from the employer class (i.e., males with a parent who was a business owner) were found to be somewhat more likely than others (e.g., females from the employee class) to engage in illegal copying. Various methodological limitations and factors such as subjects' access to copying equipment and knowledge of how to operate it are confounding factors in such a study.

(1990) suggested that varying levels of self-control are fundamental factors in people's choices to commit crimes and that low social control (the inability to defer gratification) is more pronounced among lower-class individuals. People who commit white collar offenses also have low self-control, but in Gottfredson and Hirschi's interpretation, those in the white collar classes typically have more attractive options than lawbreaking, and thus the rate of such crime is relatively low.

Some commentators argue that the conventional view that criminality is more pronounced among lower-class individuals than among middle- and upper-class individuals is not dictated by theory or supported by empirical observation; others have suggested that middle-class criminality for the most part is relatively trivial in nature (Goode 2005; Tittle 1983; Tittle, Villemez, and Smith 1978). Still other criminologists, including Hagan (1989b) and Thio (1988), have developed "structural" or *power theories* of crime, which claim that criminality is more pronounced among the powerful and privileged than among the powerless and underprivileged. In this interpretation, the advantaged have stronger deviant motivations, enjoy greater deviant opportunities, and are subject to weaker social controls (see Box 8.3). The claim about stronger deviant motivations is based on the contention that the powerful are potently conditioned to aspire to material success; accordingly, they experience relative deprivation much more strongly than do the underprivileged or powerless. Revelations early in the 21st century of illegal or unethical practices by so many top corporate executives, board members, auditors, stock analysts, and investment bankers could lend some support to this position.

ORGANIZATIONAL CRIMINALITY AND THE CRIMES OF ORGANIZATIONS

Sociological theories focus, in particular, on explaining the "behavior" of *social entities*: groups, organizations, and societies. Much white collar crime—especially the most substantial and serious forms, including state-organized and corporate crime—is carried out on a group or organizational level. Organizations, arguably the dominant attribute of modern societies, have been characterized as rational systems with specific goals, as natural systems oriented toward self-survival, and as open systems of interdependent entities shaped by their external environment (Scott 1992). Organizational theories of crime are often provisional because it is difficult to collect enough relevant data to test them (Shover and Bryant 1993; Vaughan 1998). More systematic study is needed.

Organizational Responsibility

When we engage in the common practice of referring to organizations or networks of organizations as actors, we are not simply speaking of a sum of people and their individual actions but of patterned institutional practices (Gross 1980; Hall 1987). However, even though we may say that Ford produced unsafe cars or Hooker Chemical polluted the environment, this practice is somewhat problematic and controversial. In his pioneering study *White Collar Crime* (1949), Sutherland moved back and forth rather freely between discussing the crimes of people of the upper socioeconomic classes and the crimes of corporations. He wrote of white collar crime as a form of "organized" crime, and he wrote of the "criminality of corporations" independent of specific reference to individual executives. In *Corporate Crime*, the largest-scale and most prominent study of such crime since Sutherland, Clinard and Yeager (1980) specifically defined corporate crime as *organizational crime*. Throughout their study, they treated corporations as actors, although they recognized that the boundaries between illegal corporate acts and illegal acts carried out by executives for their own benefit can be blurred.

Donald Cressey (1989), a prominent contributor to the white collar crime literature, criticized his former mentor Sutherland, and Clinard and Yeager as well, for attributing human capabilities to corporations rather than distinguishing them from real people. Even though Sutherland had acknowledged that corporations could not suffer from human psychiatric disorders, he also (somewhat illogically) wrote of corporate criminality as though it occurred independently of the decisions and actions of human beings. Cressey insisted that we must recognize that corporations are not people, cannot learn, do not have motivations, and cannot form intent. For Cressey, causal principles used to explain the criminality of individuals cannot be used to explain the criminality of corporations; statistical correlations between structural variables (such as industry, financial status, and size) and corporate criminality cannot produce causal propositions.

Many students of white collar crime have insisted that a corporation can be regarded as directly responsible for a crime. In one statement of a widely adopted position, Gross (1980) argued that corporations "take on lives of their own." They develop a need to create orderly markets,

and they socialize their executives to respond with criminal actions to circumstances in which profits are threatened. Corporations resocialize their managers to adopt values and orientations compatible with the goals of the corporation; a corporate culture develops that is independent of individual corporate managers (Punch 2000; Slapper and Tombs 1999; Yeager and Reed 1998). In one view, then, corporate crime as organizational crime must be explained in terms of organizational factors (Gobert and Punch 2003; Kramer 1982), which profoundly influence individual decisions.

In a specific response to Cressey's critique, Braithwaite and Fisse (1990) defended the notion that corporations can take criminal action and can be properly held responsible for such action. They argued that a mixture of observable and abstracted characteristics defines both individuals and corporations; corporations collectively carry out spectacularly complex tasks that no single individual involved can carry out independently. Thus, collective decisions are not simply the sum of individual decisions. Corporate policies and procedures are the equivalent of corporate intentionality, and although corporations may not have feelings and emotions, they do possess autonomy and thus can properly be held responsible for their decisions. Braithwaite and Fisse (1990) concluded that as a practical matter, modern societies must hold corporations legally responsible for their actions. If corporations can formulate policy, they can also be affected by punishment. If we punish replaceable individuals only, we will not deter corporate crime.

On the other hand, it must be acknowledged that in a strictly literal sense a corporation cannot act. The decisions and actions of specific human beings set into motion all activities of governmental agencies and business entities. Organizational crimes are offenses committed by officers of organizations on behalf of the organization; individuals are integrated into roles within organizations, and organizations generate patterns of activity (Finney and LeSieur 1982; Gross 1980; Shover and Hochstetler 2002). In this view, individual identity is often subordinated to the demands of the organization. To the extent that the organization trains, indoctrinates, and persuades its members to engage in criminal activities, these crimes can be regarded as crimes of the organization rather than of individuals (Hall 1987). Middle managers of corporations, in one interpretation, are "coerced" to commit illegal actions by pressures to meet corporate performance expectations (Sharpe 1995). Such coercion does not exonerate individual managers but may mitigate their responsibility. The tension between focusing attention on organizations or individuals can never be fully resolved.

Are corporate decisions that result in illegal and harmful outcomes best described as rational calculations to accomplish corporate goals? Paternoster and Simpson (1996) found considerable support for rational choice calculations; in their interpretation, the decisions to engage in corporate crime are best understood in terms of the cost-benefit assessments of individual corporate managers, tempered by concern with being shamed and moral sentiments. Vaughan (1998) has suggested that corporate managers have most commonly been regarded as *amoral calculators* (p. 23), but in her interpretation, other factors may lead to the decision making that has harmful consequences. Rather, organizations over time come to adopt and promote decision making that is inherently risky and that will inevitably sometimes have unforeseen, catastrophic consequences (Vaughan 1999). Famously, Vaughan has challenged a standard account of the decision making that led to the Challenger explosion and has argued that managers were conforming to high levels of risky decision making that had become "normalized" within NASA and its contractors rather than deliberately violating rules and established guidelines (Vaughan 1996, 1998). In her view, such factors as coincidence, disorganization, incompetence, fumbling, misunderstanding, and ignorance in some combination can play roles in the harmful decisions of organizations.

The entire organization is seldom involved in corporate crime, and the majority of personnel do not directly participate (Hall 1987). But the organization and its resources make possible the crimes of even a small number of its officers or employees. Organizations create opportunities for illegal conduct by disproportionately serving affluent, accessible victims; by generating impersonal transactions; by creating and allocating resources; by providing strategic devices to facilitate and cover up illegalities; and by conditioning the development of new normative prescriptions capable of being violated (Shapiro 1980; Slapper and Tombs 1999; Vaughan 1998). Organizations may also be held directly accountable for forms of harm that are a consequence of their failure to put into place effective systems for managing risk (Gobert and Punch 2003). Organizations attempt, often successfully, to influence the legal environment within which they operate, to enhance the predictability and stability of their economic environment, and to shield themselves from civil and criminal liability (Gross 1980). Furthermore, the following rationalizations for violating regulations or breaking laws are typically generated on the corporate level: The laws or regulations are incomprehensible, excessively complex, too costly, unnecessary, and unjustified. They improperly interfere with free enterprise. Competitors are violating the laws with impunity, and the violations are economically necessary or even beneficial and do little real harm to individuals (Clinard and Yeager 1980; Reichman 1989). The increasing availability and attractiveness of such rationales promote corporate criminality.

The Various Dimensions of Organizational Criminality

Different levels of organizational analysis are relevant to understanding organizational crime. On a social psychological level, the organization is viewed as a context or environment that can influence individuals' attitudes and behavior in a criminal direction. On a structural level, the organization is viewed as having structural features and social processes (e.g., subunits and specialization) that facilitate the commission of crime. On an ecological level, the organization is viewed as part of an environment or interdependent system that has *criminogenic tendencies* (Scott 1992; Shover and Hochstetler 2002).

Some organizations are *crime coercive* (they literally compel others to commit crimes), whereas others are *crime facilitative* (they provide conditions that promote criminal conduct) (Needleman and Needleman 1979). Some industries or networks of organizations have been described as inherently criminogenic due to special conditions and industry norms (Clinard and Yeager 1980; Tillman and Indergaard 1999). For example, the liquor industry has a three-tiered system of distillers, wholesalers, and retailers. Distillers put formidable sales-quota pressures on wholesale distributors, who then engage in price fixing with each other and kickbacks to retailers, who in turn make illegal deals with distillers and pay bribes to local law enforcers, all in the interest of trying to survive and profit in an inadequately policed industry (Denzin 1977). In the auto industry, manufacturers impose pressures on their dealers to generate high sales volumes, and the resulting low profits induce dealers to enhance profits through fraudulent servicing of cars and fudging on warranties. Kickback deals with used-car dealers and manipulation of registered sale prices to cut taxes are also characteristic of the industry (Farberman 1975; Leonard and Weber 1970). In the case of the international pharmaceutical industry, bribery results from fears that products that cost millions of dollars to develop will not be approved for marketing (Braithwaite 1984). In the securities industry, new regulations and pressures to innovate generate new demands for information and transform existing networks and relationships so that incentives to engage in law-breaking are no longer effectively held in check by traditional constraints and controls (Reichman 1993). Corporate retrenchment and other forms of market restructuring in the health insurance business create opportunities for insurance fraud, also facilitated by social networks providing key intelligence about the marketplace (Tillman and Indergaard 1999).

Theories of corporate crime have either attempted to explain why some corporations commit crimes and others do not or have addressed the apparent overall increase in corporate illegalities at particular periods of time (Shover and Bryant 1993; Tombs 2005). Some relevant internal variables include the size of the corporation, the financial performance of the corporation and the degree of its emphasis on profit, the diffusion of responsibility through different divisions and departments, and a corporate subculture that promotes loyalty and deference to the interests of the corporation. On the matter of size, for example, research has found that the more complex, impersonal, and decentralized character of larger corporations is associated with greater involvement with illegal activity; other research has suggested that larger corporations have the resources and expertise to comply with the law more easily than do smaller corporations (Coleman 1992; Shover and Bryant 1993; Simpson 1993). The preponderance of evidence seems to support the notion that corporations that are doing poorly financially are more likely to engage in illegal activity (Coleman 1992; Shover and Bryant 1993).

According to a study of the nursing home industry, for-profit organizations are more likely to engage in violations of the law than are non-profit organizations (Jenkins and Braithwaite 1993). When corporations tend to reward short-term success more than they penalize long-term failure, when middle managers experience relentless pressure from above to maximize profits, and when such managers are shielded from responsibility for at least some of the harmful effects of their decisions, illegal activity is also promoted (Clinard 1983; Ermann and Lundman 1982; Jenkins and Braithwaite 1993). The corporate crime wave of the late 1990s and early 21st century, including the Enron case, was clearly influenced by an intensification of emphasis upon and massive financial rewards for producing short-term gains in stock price by whatever means (Fusaro and Miller 2002; Mitchell 2001). Top management tends to signal its expectations rather than give specific orders to break the law, and middle managers tend to adapt to the prevailing corporate morality that reflects changing corporate needs (Clinard and Yeager 1980; Jackall 1988; Shover and Bryant 1993). Altogether, middle managers believe that these internal factors take precedence over external moral values or expectations in guiding their actions on the job. In Enron, WorldCom, and other cases surfacing early in the 21st century, the apparent

---

B O X   8.4   **Diffusion Theory and Intermediate Fraud**

Wayne Baker and Robert Faulkner (2003) seek to explain intermediate fraud by *diffusion theory*. Intermediate fraud is fraud that develops in a business that was initially set up to be legitimate, not fraudulent, but ultimately engaged in fraudulent activity. Diffusion theory focuses on how a fraud spreads among investors via social networks. Specifically, Baker and Faulkner examine the factors that promoted a major fraud of investors by the Fountain Oil and Gas Company. A series of dry holes caused growing financial distress for this company and led to misrepresentation of company finances to raise funds from

investors, with subsequent embezzlement of the funds. A series of factors, including product attributes, buyer attributes and behavior, seller attributes and behavior, structure of the social network, and method of propagation, are explored in connection with this fraud. These factors—for example, the relatively high risk involved in oil well investment, the higher socio-economic status of the investors, and the extent to which investors are linked with each other in a social network—are found to have both facilitated the initial legitimate success of the business as well as the subsequent fraud.

---

direct involvement of CEOs and other high-level executives in wrongdoing was one of the especially distinctive features of these cases.

Externally, a variety of factors are related to corporate crime, including the economic climate, political and regulatory environment, level of industry concentration, style and strength of product distribution networks, product differentiation, and normative traditions within industries (Clinard and Yeager 1980; Keane 1993; Simpson 1993). Corporations are more likely to engage in corporate crime when legitimate opportunities to achieve their goals are blocked but illegitimate opportunities are available, when the local community is relatively tolerant of violations, when regulatory law is weak and ineffective, and when the political or economic climate promotes aggressive pursuit of profit (Braithwaite 1989a; Gunkel and Eitle 1989; Shover and Bryant 1993). Although it would seem logical that increased external pressure to make a profit would encourage a corporation to engage in illegal behavior, existing studies offer mixed support for this proposition (Simpson 1993). It seems likely, however, that any studies undertaken of the corporate crime wave of the early 21st-century period will reveal some correlation between levels of expectation for profitable financial statements and illegal or unethical accounting manipulations to meet those expectations.

Diffusion theory addresses some of the factors mentioned here (see Box 8.4).

An organization's location in an "ecosystem" of other similar organizations is another dimension of its external environment (Kunkel 1989; Tillman and Indergaard 1999). In one interpretation, rooted in a resource dependence model, more-dependent corporations are more likely to engage in misconduct in response to external pressures, especially when alternatives to the misconduct are limited and the organization's structure facilitates such misconduct (Zimmer 1989). In another interpretation, the *structural embeddedness* of financial organizations and corporations within networks that were largely beyond the reach of traditional forms of social control significantly contributed to the large-scale financial crimes of the 1980s (Reichman 1989; Zey 1993). In the recent era, excessive risk taking, competition, and the increasing size and complexity of corporations may contribute to both corporate breakdowns and related patterns of corporate illegality (Skeel 2005). Price fixing in the electrical industry was apparently enhanced by centralization of cartel authority in that industry (Faulkner et al. 2003). In some industries—e.g., the securities industry—low ethical standards or distorted values may also contribute to high levels of wrongdoing (Augar 2005; Morgenson 2002e; Tomasic and Pentony 1989). Altogether, more attention is now directed toward the network of alliances among organizations and the criminogenic pressures and opportunities that may arise within these networks. The corporate crimes of the early 21st-century period exemplify networks of alliances between corporations, auditing firms, investment banking houses, and other institutions; at least those at the top of these institutions derived benefits from cooperating explicitly or implicitly with each other in the production of false financial statements and inflated claims about stock values.

EXPLAINING WHITE COLLAR CRIME: THEORIES AND PERSPECTIVES

Many explanations of white collar crime focus more on the crime rather than on criminality. Most of these explanations are sociological, and they emphasize differences in circumstances or opportunities over differences among individuals. From this perspective, we may wish to explain differences in levels of involvement in white collar crime among different classes of individuals, professions, corporate organizations, and industries.

Sociological theories often emphasize structural factors. A *structural perspective* in criminology focuses either on social conditions that account for specific forms of criminal behavior or on how the distribution of power and resources influences how crime is defined and generated (Cullen 1983; Hagan 1989b). Pertinent structural questions include the following: Which forces produce laws that define white collar crime and a justice system that effectively implements and enforces those laws? Which forces produce a set of opportunities for illegal conduct? Which forces promote motivations and rationalizations that are conducive to illegal behavior or activity?

Some white collar crime is carried out by individuals acting alone, but much of it is a cooperative activity, involving two or more individuals. Certain forms of white collar crime lead to networks of people with the specialized knowledge required to carry out the crime (Waring 2002). Securities fraud

calls for one or more people who know how to file forms with the SEC, embezzlement requires accounting skills, and bid rigging necessitates access to restricted information. Co-offending, then, is characteristic of much white collar crime, just as it is characteristic of much conventional crime.

General Theories of Crime and White Collar Crime Theory

Can the same theories explain both white collar crime and conventional crime, or must different types of crimes be explained by different types of theories? Criminologists have been divided on this question. Sutherland was inspired to pursue the study of white collar crime partly because he recognized that the popular criminological theories of his time, which focused on poverty and social pathologies as basic causes of crime, did not explain the involvement of upper-class individuals and corporations in illegal conduct. Sutherland (1940) advanced his theory of differential association as a *general theory* that could account for both conventional and white collar crime. In the recent era, Michael Gottfredson and Travis Hirschi (1990) have also advanced a general theory of crime, centered on the consequences of parenting practices and levels of self-control. They also claim—as did Sutherland—that their theory can be applied as well to white collar crime as to conventional forms of crime. Some of the particulars of their theory, and the critique of the theory as it applies to white collar crime, are addressed in Box 8.5.

The general theories of crime have been criticized on various grounds, especially for attempting to explain different types of activities too simplistically and broadly. Although general theories may have some success in accounting for natural and physical phenomena, they are less usefully applied to the enormously variable realm of human activity (Weatherburn 1993). For example, no general theory provides a clear basis for explaining variations between conventional and white collar crime rates over time. An alternative perspective is that the explanation of white collar crime requires theories fundamentally different from those applied to conventional crime and that

---

B O X 8.5 Low Self-Control and White Collar Crime

In their book *The General Theory of Crime*, Michael Gottfredson and Travis Hirschi (1990) identify poor parenting and low self-control as the key factors in explaining crime—all crime. This general theory, or low self-control theory, of crime has been among the most popular and widely discussed of the recent era (Marcus 2004; Pratt and Cullen 2000). Gottfredson and Hirschi claim that individuals with low self-control—when given the opportunity to do so—will engage in criminal conduct, as well as other forms of deviant behavior, in the interest of achieving immediate gratification. They claim that this theory applies to white collar crime as well as to conventional crime. They also claim that white collar crime is relatively rare because people in white collar positions have a set of values and legitimate ways of obtaining gratification that deflect them from criminality.

Many objections can be raised to this theoretical approach to explaining white collar crime (Friedrichs and Schwartz, forthcoming; Spahr and Allison 2004). It relies upon false measures of white collar crime. It fails to recognize that some activities may be crime in one context but not another. It adopts notions of self-interest and self-control that are so broad they could be applied to all human activity, but do not explain much criminal activity. And it fails to take into account the capacity of corporate organizations to shape perceptions of self-interest, motives, and opportunities for wrongdoing (Geis 2000; Reed and Yeager 1996; Simpson and Piquero 2003; Yeager and Reed 1998). Hirschi and Gottfredson define white collar crime principally in terms of low-level embezzlements and frauds committed by relatively poor individuals; they fail to address many elite forms of white collar crime, including corporate crime. They fail to consider that corporate managers who engage in illegal activities may put their self-interest in jeopardy, and they do not explain why most white collar offenders typically do not commit conventional crimes (Benson and Moore 1992; Grasmick, Tittle, Bursick, and Arneker 1993; Reed and Yeager 1991). Indeed, much of the white collar crime discussed in this text is much better understood as a response to a high level of organizational control (over managers and employees) than as a function of low self-control. Such crime is often complex, involves planning, and is oriented toward long-term gains. There is little reason to believe that white collar crime is well-explained in terms of poor parenting and individual low self-control.

---

specific types of white collar crime require specific explanatory theories. Perhaps an intermediary position is that only up to a point and on a high level of generality, some common motivation (i.e., a desire for personal gain) may be shared by the inner-city youth who mugs a passerby and the Wall Street investment banker who engages in insider trading. But this does not take us far toward understanding the different patterns of involvement in illegal activities, the complex of circumstances that give rise to illegality, and the distinctive self-concepts and rationalizations of the range of white collar offenders.

Classical Criminology and Rational Choice

In the late 18th century, a variety of influential views of human nature, principles of justice, and economic activity were articulated. In his essay *On Crimes and Punishments (Dei Delitti e Elle Pene)*, published in 1764, the Italian nobleman and economist Cesare Beccaria called for a reformed criminal justice system based on rational, equitable principles toward which rational human beings could orient themselves. In *An Introduction to the Principles of Morals and Legislation* (1789), the English philosopher Jeremy Bentham, partially inspired by Beccaria, developed a utilitarian philosophy that incorporated the idea of humans who engage in a calculus to maximize pleasure and minimize pain.

The core notions of humans as capable of making rational choices and of a system of justice with equitable punishments that fit the crime have long been central to the operation of our criminal justice system (Norrie 1986). In 1759, the Scottish moral philosopher and economist Adam Smith wrote *The Theory of Moral Sentiments*, advancing the view of human beings as inherently self-interested actors who are not immune to the cultivation of moral character. This image has been embraced in some form by mainstream economists through the present era. Of course, many economists today reject the notion of humans as purely rational and recognize the influence of cultural, moral, and psychological factors (Rubinstein 1992; Sen 1977; Simon 1987). In the social sciences, one increasingly common view is that human behavior reflects a mixture of rational choice, emotions, and value commitments (Etzioni 1987). Still, the notion of humans as essentially rational and self-interested actors is the dominant view of white collar offenders in the law and in the public consciousness.

The classical assumptions about human nature have recently been embraced (with some qualifications) by neoclassical criminologists and proponents of *rational choice*, routine activities, and social control perspectives (Clarke and Felson 1993; Hirschi 1986; Trasler 2005). These criminologists essentially see criminal offenders as people who reason and plan strategically, adapt to particular circumstances, and weigh costs and benefits. Individuals who commit crimes are not averse to breaking laws if they see an opportunity they perceive to have a low likelihood of sanctions and the expectation of personal benefits. Proponents of this perspective do not necessarily deny that other factors—such as constitution (e.g., biogenetic inheritance), development (e.g., family influences), and social context (e.g., labor markets)—limit rationality and play a role in criminal behavior (Cornish and Clarke 1986; Wilson and Herrnstein 1985), but they also believe that rational choices account for a good proportion of criminal conduct. Herman Simon (1976) introduced the concept of *bounded rationality* or "limited rationality" to take into account the fact that choices of individuals and organizations are often based on incomplete or defective information and are only "rational" relative to the information available.

Rational choice assumptions would appear to be especially applicable to white collar offenders (Bartollas and Dinitz 1989; Piquero et al. 2005). If we assume that humans have the capability of making rational choices, then those who are better educated and better positioned in life would seem to have an advantage in considering and acting on various options. It is perhaps paradoxical, then, that those who have prominently promoted the neoclassical and rational choice perspective have focused most of their attention on conventional offenders, not white collar criminals.

Alternatively, the notion that human behavior is guided primarily by rational considerations may not apply in many circumstances when humans may be confused and uncertain how to act, may lack clear precedents, and may be driven by emotions rather than reason.

Alternative Dimensions of Crime and Choice

Raymond Paternoster and Sally Simpson (1993, 1996) have characterized corporate crime as criminal activity that is rooted in instrumental and strategic choices made by risk-averse managers who weigh various options' perceived costs and benefits to themselves. These choices involve a broad range of considerations, but the manager's view that laws or rules are unreasonable contributes to the choice not to comply. Whatever their preferences may be, managers are often subjected to various pressures to act collectively on behalf of the corporation (Simpson and Piquero 2003). This type of rational assessment of risks and benefits in the context of external occupational pressures can be applied to other types of white collar offenders as well.

Routine activities theory also incorporates an assumption of rational decision making in its approach to crime. This theory focuses on crime events as a consequence of the presence of motivated offenders, suitable victims or targets, and the absence of capable guardians or protectors of property. Marcus Felson is a leading proponent of this approach. In his influential text *Crime and Everyday Life* (2002), Felson argues that white collar crimes can be renamed "crimes of specialized access" (p. 95). In his interpretation, the legitimate features of work roles are the key to understanding a broad range of white collar crimes because the work role provides the specific opportunity for illegal actions.

BOX 8.6   The Moral and Sensual Attractions of White Collar Crime

A phenomenological or hermeneutic approach to crime stresses the choices confronting people who engage in crime, although this approach is at odds with the classical assumptions about rationality. Katz (1988), for example, disparaged the traditional socio-logical emphasis on background factors and treats crime and criminality in terms of emotions and "fore-ground" factors, including the "moral and sensual attractions" of committing crimes. He suggested that emotional processes parallel to those that entice people into committing robberies and murders may well apply to white collar offenders, although we have too few credible autobiographical accounts to verify this proposition (Katz 1988). At least some white collar offenders may be attracted by the emotional thrill of engaging in criminal conduct, especially when they assume risks disproportionate to any prospective pay-off. Reichman (1993) suggested that Drexel Burnham, which was at the center of the securities industry crimes of the 1980s, may have created a culture of action, chaos, and control parallel to that of the street criminals Katz studied. Punch (2000) also suggested that at least some corporate managers who engage in illegal activities may find the conspiratorial aspects of the lawbreaking exciting. On the other hand, Braithwaite (1992) argued that Katz is mistaken in suggesting that societal material and economic condi-tions are irrelevant to understanding another set of emotions—humiliation and rage—that can inspire criminal behavior.

Both conventional street crimes and white collar crimes are then regarded as outcomes of "routine activities." Box 8.6 offers an alternative view of crime as a magnet for thrill seekers.

Social Control and Bonds

Social control theories adopt assumptions about human nature that are fundamentally at odds with those of most etiological theories. *Social control theory* reverses the conventional question of why someone engages in criminal behavior and instead asks why someone *does not* engage in criminal behavior (Hirschi 1969). The answer is that people with strong bonds (attachment, commitment, involvement, and belief) to conventional institu-tions (such as the family, the school, and the church) are constrained from engaging in delin-quent or criminal conduct. The assumptions of control theory—that a natural inclination toward committing crimes is broadly diffused—would seem to be at odds with Hirschi and Gottfredson's (1989) general theory, which suggests that levels of self-control vary among individuals (Green 1990: 86). These control theory assumptions about human nature are generally compatible with those of rational choice theory, although they are very much at odds with sociological theories that regard human beings as social animals shaped by their environment (Hirschi 1986). In one test of control theory as applied to white collar crime, Lasley (1988) found that automobile corporation execu-tives with strong corporate attachments and com-mitments were less likely to report that they had committed white collar offenses against their employers than were peers with weaker bonds. If social control theory is in fact valid, we would expect that corporate executives with stronger bonds to the corporation are more likely to engage in corporate crimes on behalf of the corporation.

Social Process and Learning

Sutherland (1947) promoted a theory of *differential association*, which views criminal behavior as learned through contact with others with a law-violating orientation. This theory applies to both conventional and white collar crime. Sutherland formulated a list of nine interrelated propositions on the process and content of learning to be a criminal. In some respects, white collar crime may be better understood by reference to differential association than is true of conventional crime and delinquency, both because of the broader range of learning options generally available to the white collar offender and the complex nature of the offenses themselves. Modifications of differential association—such as Glaser's (1956) emphasis on differential identification (with a criminal role model) and Akers's (1985) emphasis on reinforcement (conditioning to engage in criminal behavior when it is experienced as rewarding)—can also be applied to the white collar offender.

An overriding limitation of this theoretical approach is that it does not adequately account for structural origins of the illegal patterns of behavior and appears to confuse a process of involvement in criminal behavior with a cause of such behavior (Geis and Goff 1987; Goode 2005). The theory does not address the problem that some white collar crime is individualistic (e.g., embezzlement) and that collective forms of white collar crime are committed by individuals who hold many attitudes that are favorable to obeying laws (Coleman 2002; Goode 2005). Both common sense and empirical evidence support the proposition that a learning process plays a significant role in much white collar crime. For example, a study of student white collar crime—cheating—found strong support for differential association, compared with other theories, to explain this conduct (Vowell and Chen 2004). But Sutherland's theory hardly provides us with a comprehensive explanation of white collar crime.

Interactionism and Labeling

Interactionist or labeling perspectives on crime are derived from a symbolic interactionist tradition emphasizing that meaning emanates from human interaction (Blumer 1969; Mead 1934, 1964). *Labeling theory*, which was especially influential in the 1960s and 1970s, has been principally concerned with the process of societal reaction to perceived crime (or the designation of particular individuals as criminals) rather than with the standard etiological question, "What made them do it?" (Schur 1971). Seminal concepts such as the dramatization of evil, *secondary deviance*, and master status do have some implications for understanding patterns of involvement in crime, including white collar crime (Becker 1963; Lemert 1951; Tannenbaum 1938).

The first point relevant to white collar crime is that powerful individuals and organizations are more likely than the powerless to be able to avoid being labeled as deviant or criminal, or to be able to negotiate more successfully the terms of any effort to so stigmatize them (Schur 1971; Waegel, Ermann, and Horowitz 1981). The ability to shield one's harmful activities from a stigmatizing label might contribute to self-justification and ongoing involvement in such activity (Benson 1990). On the other hand, Lemert's (1951) concept of secondary deviance refers to adaptations that occur after an individual has been labeled a deviant or a criminal; such individuals may adopt a deviant self-image, leading to further deviation and criminal activity. In this perspective, the imposition of the criminal label itself is a significant cause of criminal behavior.

The claim that the labeling process itself inspires more criminal behavior than it deters has been challenged on various grounds, and it is difficult to demonstrate empirically (Goode 2005; Moyer 2001; Vold et al. 2002). White collar offenders who have been processed by the criminal justice system typically have more legitimate options than do conventional offenders and are likely to be able to minimize the full effects of *stigma*. In a classic study of the effects of legal stigma, Schwartz and Skolnick (1964) found that physicians accused of malpractice were far less likely to suffer harmful consequences to their occupational status than were unskilled workers charged with assault. On the other hand, Benson (1984), in a subsequent study of convicted white collar offenders, found that professionals who occupy a position of trust, such as doctors and attorneys, may suffer significant stigmatizing consequences, whereas business executives may largely avoid such consequences. The ways in which offenders present themselves to society may also affect how they are labeled (see Box 8.7).

Neutralizations, Rationalizations, and Accounts

The interrelated concepts of neutralization, rationalization, and accounts play a central role in efforts to make sense of white collar criminality. White

---

B O X 8.7   The "Presentation of Self" and White Collar Crime

Goffman (1959, 1963) adopted a theatrical metaphor to explore the ways in which human beings engage in "the presentation of self in everyday life" in attempting to manage the impression others have of them. If we follow Goffman, the commission of white collar crime often depends on the offender's success in conveying an image of respectability and trustworthiness—in essence, in playing a role. If the offender carries off this role, opportunities to commit white collar crime are

expanded and the likelihood of detection and prosecution minimized. Goffman also investigated the means people use to shield themselves from stigma and to manage stigma that cannot be avoided. This *dramaturgic perspective* offers one approach to the specific strategies white collar offenders use to anticipate, deflect, or manage stigma, and these strategies may well be intertwined with their ongoing choices about engaging in white collar crime.

---

collar offenders tend not to be classic "outlaw" types—that is, people who are contemptuous of law and conventional standards of proper conduct. White collar criminals most typically conform to most laws and social conventions and are unlikely to identify with or endorse the activities of conventional offenders. How, then, do they become lawbreakers?

One important step is adopting a "vocabulary of motives": excuses, justifications, disclaimers, and denials (Mills 1940; Nichols 1990; Scott and Lyman 1968). Useful distinctions have been made between excuses, which tend to be defensive (e.g., an appeal to accidents), and justifications, which are positive interpretations of actions, such as an appeal to higher loyalties (Scott and Lyman 1968). Another useful dichotomy differentiates between *neutralizations*, which pertain to future or ongoing behavior, and *accounts*, which are invoked after the behavior has occurred (Nichols 1990). Despite these distinctions, these and related terms are often used interchangeably.

Donald Cressey, in his classic work on embezzlers, *Other People's Money* (1953), assigned central importance to *rationalizations* in explaining the conduct of white collar offenders. Cressey found that embezzlers were often individuals in positions of trust who, when confronted with a financial problem, embezzled money while rationalizing that they were only "borrowing" it.

Box (1983) showed that five "techniques of neutralization," which were developed by Sykes

and Matza (1957) to demonstrate how juvenile delinquents drift between commitments to conventional and delinquent norms and rationalize their illegal activities, are also invoked by corporate officials to rationalize and justify their illegal behavior. First, corporate officials may deny responsibility for any intentional wrongdoing by claiming that the relevant laws are vague or ambiguous, that the incident was an accident, or that other parties made the key decisions. Second, they may deny injury by rationalizing that their activities have actually been economically beneficial. Third, they may deny the existence of a victim by claiming that no one was really harmed by their activity. Fourth, they may condemn the condemners by claiming that laws are an unwarranted interference with free enterprise. And fifth, they may appeal to higher loyalties by affirming that the needs of their corporation and its stockholders—or their families—should take precedence over obedience to mere laws. In support of the relevance of such rationalizations, Benson (1985a) found that convicted antitrust offenders tended to claim they were merely following established practices in their business or that prevailing business conditions left them no choice but to violate the law. Willott, Griffin, and Torrance (2001) found that economic crime offenders resented being lumped together with "common" criminals; rather, their crimes were a consequence of an unlucky combination of forces such as the recession or a "screw-up" in the context of a crisis. They attributed their illegal actions to their need to be successful for the sake of their family, their employees and dependents, and their professional status. They attributed pursuit of criminal charges against them to the envy of government bureaucrats.

Thus, a wide range of white collar offenders invoke rationalizations. The type of rationale favored tends to vary by offense. Tax violators, for example, claim that "everybody does it," whereas defrauders claim that someone else was really to blame (Benson 1985a). In the E. F. Hutton check-kiting case, different rationalizations were invoked by executives on different levels of the firm (Nichols 1990). Those in different professions, such as law, engineering, and accounting, are likely to adopt different rationales as well (Grabosky 1990). Rationalizations are especially important in political white collar crime cases, such as Watergate and Iran-Contra, insofar as the perpetrators persuade themselves that national security or the long-term national interest requires them to break laws (Cavender, Jurik, and Cohen 1993; Wise 1973). By one interpretation, diffusion of responsibility, "plausible denial," and scapegoating were all elements of a dynamic process of constructing accounts as the Iran-Contra plot unfolded, and these accounts played a role in shaping the direction of the illegal action (Cavender et al. 1993). Because rationalizations, neutralizations, and accounts most typically surface after the crimes have been committed, it is not always clear to what extent they facilitated the lawbreaking in the first place or whether they developed later as attempts to excuse wrongdoing.

STRUCTURAL STRAIN AND THE STRUCTURE OF OPPORTUNITY

Émile Durkheim's (1893) original conception of *anomie* referred to a situation of normlessness, a breakdown of the guidelines for conventional behavior during rapid social change. The insider trading crimes of the 1980s have been linked with an anomic situation that fostered "the unbridled pursuit of pecuniary rewards" (Lilly, Cullen, and Ball 1989: 67).

Merton's (1957) revised notion of anomie—one of the most familiar explanations of crime—refers to an enduring situation in a society in which a generalized goal of material success is promoted, but the means to achieve such success legitimately are not equally distributed. Merton gives the label "innovative" to one class of adaptations that those who lack equal access to legitimate means (i.e., a good education and occupation) use to achieve material success; among those "innovations" is illegal behavior. Although this explanation for criminal behavior has most typically been associated with the economically disadvantaged, Merton came to recognize that much white collar crime is not visible or known and that the 19th-century robber barons and their successors used illegal or unethical innovations to realize their economic goals (Merton 1968). Merton had previously noted that the emphasis in science on originality may lead to "innovative" (and unethical or illegal) actions by scientists, including stealing ideas and generating false data, if they are under intense pressure to produce original scientific results.

If success is far more heavily emphasized in the higher strata of society and if its measurement is virtually open-ended, Merton's theory of anomie is even more applicable to white collar crime than it is to conventional crime. A study of employee theft in a nursing home, for example, found some support for strain theory (Van Wyk, Benson, and Harris 2000). Anomie theory has been applied quite specifically to understanding the "innovative" corporate use of illegal strategies to realize goals that cannot be achieved legitimately (Keane 1993; Passas 1990; Vaughan 1983). Furthermore, the commission of crimes by privileged segments of society and their broader immunity to prosecution can contribute significantly to an anomic climate in society, as less privileged people become cynical or confused about the prevailing rules (Passas 1990). White collar crime in this sense both reflects and promotes anomie.

Others have produced variants of Merton's theory. Cohen (1955) formulated status deprivation theory, and Cloward and Ohlin (1960) advanced differential opportunity theory. Both of these theories were applied to lower-class juveniles, but some connections with white collar crime can be made.

Status deprivation theory is especially concerned with explaining the nonutilitarian, malicious, and negativistic character of some lower-class delinquency as an alternative way of achieving status. White collar crime tends to be uniformly characterized as utilitarian, instrumental, and goal-oriented toward positive objectives, but some of it—for example, sabotage by disgruntled employees—may reflect responses to being deprived of a legitimate status.

Differential opportunity theory contends that the particular form of illegal conduct, whether it be theft, drug dealing, or gang conflict, is significantly a function of the structure of opportunity. Braithwaite (1992) noted that Cloward and Ohlin neglected the fact that criminals can actively create illegitimate opportunities, and this point is perhaps especially applicable to the powerful and privileged. Some white collar crime may be best understood as a response to a situation in which the attractions of particular illegitimate opportunities outweigh those of legitimate opportunities.

CONFLICT THEORY AND CRIMINOGENIC SOCIETIES

Conflict theory has been principally concerned with the process of criminalization. *Conflict theory* rejects the consensus theory notion of the social world as an organic or integrated system. In its so-called "nonpartisan" form, conflict theory is concerned with identifying how the values and interests of different groups conflict because the more powerful groups in society are disproportionately able to influence the character and content of the law (Vold et al. 2002). In this view, the behavior of the powerless is most likely to be defined as criminal. This theory would seem to offer little by way of explaining white collar crime and criminality, unless we recognize that the "white collar world" is heterogeneous and that the possession of power is a relative matter. Certainly the values and interests of the various white collar strata are at odds with those who make the laws. The neo-Marxist or radical version of conflict theory, which will be explored next, provides an explanation of the roots of criminal behavior that is at odds with mainstream theories.

The Structure of Contemporary Capitalist Society and White Collar Crime

The most basic form of structural explanation for white collar crime focuses on the nature of society itself. In particular, some students of white collar crime view capitalist society as a fundamental source of inspiration for such crime. One principal version of conflict theory is *Marxist*, or neo-Marxist, *theory*.

Karl Marx and his collaborator Friedrich Engels did not regard crime in any form to be a necessary or inevitable feature of human society (Greenberg 1981; Matthews 2003; Quinney 1977). Rather, crime is essentially a product of a class society, and of capitalism in particular; to the extent that humans manifest such patterns of behavior, capitalism promotes these tendencies in human beings. The capitalist system dehumanizes people, transforms many objects and dimensions of the human environment into commodities, and promotes "false needs" that generate a significant amount of property crime.

In the Marxist view, the worst crime is committed in the name of capitalism: the systematic exploitation of the working class. In his *The Condition of the Working Class in England* (1895, 1958), Engels contends that the ownership class is in fact guilty of murder because it is fully aware that workers in factories and mines will die violent, premature deaths due to unsafe conditions. The private ownership of capital results in many socially injurious acts that in today's terms can be labeled *crimes of capital* (Michalowski 1985: 314).

Beyond crimes that are intrinsic to capitalism, Marx, Engels, and their intellectual heirs have suggested that crime by rich and poor alike is a rational, inevitable response to an economic system that fosters greed, egoistic or individualistic tendencies, competitiveness, and debasement of humans (Bonger 1916; Gordon 1971; Lynch, Michalowski, and Groves 2000). Whenever the capitalist system undergoes an economic crisis, pressures to commit crimes increase (Reiman and Headlee 1981). The alienating and inauthentic dimensions of contemporary capitalism promote complex patterns of collaborative crime between elite organizations and governmental power holders (Simon 2006). Corporations specifically, operating in an environment of unequal distribution of market power and relentless pressure to increase profit or growth, violate laws when the potential benefits of doing so outweigh the potential costs (Barnett 1979, 1981b; Slapper and Tombs 1999). State regulation of corporate activity is significantly inhibited by the disproportionate influence of corporations in making and administering laws and by the state's need to foster capital accumulation. As capitalism becomes increasingly globalized, it becomes even less subject to state regulation in its relentless drive to expand markets and maximize profits (Pearce and Tombs 2002; Tombs and Whyte 2003).

Limitations of the Marxist Account   There are two obvious limitations of a structural, Marxist explanation for white collar crime. First, it does not explain either the existence of significant levels of white collar crime in socialistic countries or significant variations among different capitalist countries. Second, it is not helpful in explaining why some individuals and organizations within capitalist societies engage in white collar crime while others do not.

On the first point, Braithwaite (1988) has noted that much corrupt and criminal activity equivalent to corporate and occupational crime occurs in socialist countries. In the former Soviet Union, corrupt practices of state bureaucrats could be attributed to *performance pressures* to meet production targets; such pressures are the equivalent of competitive pressures in a capitalist system. But an overemphasis on competitive pressures overlooks

the fact that at least some white collar crime is fostered by cooperation, such as price fixing among corporations, rather than by competition. Moreover, any attempt to explain white collar crime in terms of the effects of a capitalist system must also acknowledge that capitalist societies today deviate considerably from the classical model of capitalism; for that matter, contemporary socialist societies deviate from the original model as well (Bohm 1982). Capitalist corporations do not necessarily have uniform interests, and at least some forms of corporate crime can work against corporate interests.

Explanations of white collar crime that focus on societal attributes as a whole need not be restricted to the organization of the political economy. U.S. society has been described as criminal or criminogenic on the basis of its modern, urbanized, bureaucratized character, which promotes impersonality and instrumentalism; its competitiveness; and its frontier cultural values, which promote toughness and resistance to authority (Schur 1969; Barron 1981). U.S. society is suffused with contradictions and conflicts pertaining to its religious, ethnic, racial, and gender-related heritage, and its political system celebrates democracy in an environment with a gross maldistribution of real power. White collar crime must be understood in terms of these structural attributes. (See Box 8.8.)

Radical and Critical Perspectives on White Collar Crime

Although contemporary radical thought is often characterized as directly based on Marxist theory, this is not uniformly the case. Reiman (1982), for example, argued that Marxism is materialist in explaining white collar crime as resulting from the organization of material production, whereas radicalism is idealist, at least when it explains white collar crime as a function of the intentions of elites. Sutherland was said to have in his outlook a radical strain that reflected his populist outlook. The radical criminology that developed in the 1970s was significantly influenced by Marxism, but it also

---

B O X 8.8   Economic Wilding, Capitalism, and White Collar Crime

The 1980s, the so-called Reagan–Bush era, has been characterized as a celebration of classical American capitalism. In the official rhetoric, such virtues as self-reliance, entrepreneurship, and individual initiative were promoted. But in an alternative critique, a form of "economic wilding"—Charles Derber (2004: 10) defined it as "the morally uninhibited pursuit of money by individuals or businesses at the expense of others"—became rampant. Certainly an epidemic of white collar crime occurred; the S & L fraud and insider trading cases are but two of the more publicized examples. According to Derber, this "individualism run amuck" has parallels with, and impacts on, other forms

of "wilding" lower down in the social order, including inner-city violence and pervasive cheating among young people. The recent "corporate scandals"— including the Enron case—suggest that economic wilding is intensifying within American society.

In a somewhat parallel vein, Rothstein (1992) suggested that the "real looters" of the recent era were not rioting inner-city youths but the high-level corporate executives who reaped enormous rewards for themselves while causing much economic devastation for workers, consumers, and taxpayers. Again, much evidence for the intensification of this form of "looting" is cited at a number of points in this book.

---

sought to explain the crimes of governmental and corporate elites in terms of willful abuses of power within a contemporary American context (Inciardi 1980a; Lynch, Michalowski, and Groves 2000). Much of the radical criminological work of this period examined the criminalization process as opposed to the "causes" of crime.

Since the early 1980s, new perspectives emerged within an evolving *radical* or *critical criminology* (Friedrichs 1998b; Lynch, Michalowski, and Groves 2000; Schwartz and Hatty 2003). These perspectives include left realism, peacemaking criminology, feminist criminology, and postmodernist criminology. Neither the causes of crime in the conventional sense nor white collar crime itself have been important preoccupations of these perspectives; they have been more concerned with how crime is conceived of or constituted, and appropriate responses to it.

An emerging *postmodernist criminology* challenges the strong tendency of conventional criminological perspectives to impose meaning on criminal conduct and events (Arrigo 2003; Schwartz and Friedrichs 1994) (see Box 8.9). *Constitutive criminology* is a new perspective that draws on postmodern thought among other theoretical traditions to emphasize the fundamental instability of meaning in a human world in which realities are constantly deconstructed and then reconstructed (Henry and Milovanovic

1991). Crime in this view must be regarded not as something that is caused but as an outcome of processes of interaction involving individuals and groups. As applied specifically to corporate crime, Henry and Milovanovic (1994) focus on how middle managers have tended to deflect primary responsibility for their involvement in illegal and unethical practices by engaging in denial and finger pointing. Such discursive practices divide human beings from each other and create opportunities to compartmentalize responsibility and accountability.

Feminist criminology is a critical criminological perspective that offers a particular viewpoint in explaining white collar crime. The white collar world has traditionally been predominantly a male world, and white collar criminals have been mainly white males. White collar crime has not been a primary concern of feminist criminology; rather, it has especially focused on exposing the overall patterns of patriarchy and male dominance in the realms pertaining to crime and the legal system. Direct forms of male violence against women, such as rape and spouse abuse, have been a major preoccupation of feminist criminology. Nevertheless, Daly (1989) observed that women are underrepresented among white collar offenders and that different motivations (e.g., family financial need) play a more important role in at least some white collar crime by females. Messerschmidt (1993) specifically

---

B O X 8.9   White Collar Crime in a Postmodern World

Postmodernist writers share the premise that the present era represents a fundamental break with the conditions of modernity, although the full scope of this break is a matter of some dispute. The challenge is to establish connections between such alleged postmodern conditions as the *hyperreal* and the contemporary character of white collar crime. In a discussion of the film *Wall Street*, which dealt with insider trading, Denzin (1990) observed that the film illustrates the *commodification*, the transformation into commodities of everything from information to human feelings, in "the postmodern moment" (p. 37).

Illusions, including the ultimate illusion of money, replace a more substantial dimension of "reality." Wall Street itself, the locus of some of the largest-scale white collar crime, is described in the language of postmodernist analysis as "a site where a political economy of signs ceaselessly circulates across an imaginary computerized space where nothing is any longer real" (Denzin 1990: 40). Such observations are indicative of one form of a postmodernist approach to understanding white collar crime, an approach that rejects any comprehensive or holistic explanation for such crime.

---

suggested that corporate crime reflects patriarchal patterns that exclude women from decision-making roles and promote a form of masculinity celebrating aggressive pursuit of material success. It is far from clear, however, that replacing men with women in corporate positions will result in less corporate crime (Snider 1993). The true extent to which gender plays a role in generating white collar crime may not be resolved until women are much more fully represented in the decision-making ranks in the corporate world. Box 8.10 considers women as victims of white collar crime.

EXPLAINING CRIMINALIZATION AND WHITE COLLAR CRIME

Explaining criminal behavior and crime has historically been the primary focus of criminology. In the 1960s and 1970s, this began to change with the development of theoretical perspectives that focused on criminalization. Investigations of criminalization pose questions on several levels of analysis. First, how does certain harmful activity come to be defined as criminal, whereas other equally or more harmful activity is not? The criminal law is not simply regarded as a given; rather, its particular form and content must be explained. Second, how do some individuals or organizations that engage in harmful conduct come to be labeled criminal, whereas others who engage in the same conduct are not labeled criminal? And third, what are the consequences of being so labeled?

In a legalistic sense, no crime exists until and unless there is formal recognition that a type of activity should be designated a crime. Therefore, we must explain why certain activity comes to be defined as white collar crime and why other activity that is just as harmful is not considered a crime. This aspect of criminalization is explored more fully in Chapter 9.

The criminalization process has been directly linked with patterns of engagement in white collar crime. For example, in one interpretation of the perspective of Adam Smith, white collar crime is a product of lawmaking that interferes with the natural operation of a free market economy (Jesilow 1982a). In this view, such laws will work to the advantage of wealthy corporations, which have the resources to confront and evade regulation more effectively. Thus, more white collar crime is to be expected when the market is fixed and has no free competition, when labor is regulated, and when regulatory law is pervasive and unpredictable. The law itself, in this sense, promotes white collar crime, and the public welfare is better served when exploitative activities of corporations and businesses

---

B O X 8.10   Women as a Special Class of Victims of White Collar Crime

Another dimension of the connection between gender and white collar crime is the provocative claim that in certain respects women are especially vulnerable to being victims of such crime, particularly in its corporate form (Gerber and Weeks 1992; Hinch and DeKeseredy 1992). The thesis is that women are overrepresented in lower-level corporate jobs in which vulnerability to injury is greater, that they are more likely to be sexually harassed and assaulted on the job, and that at home they disproportionately use harmful pharmaceutical and household products. In this account,

concerns for women's health and safety are not accorded a high priority in a capitalist, patriarchal society in which women are underrepresented in the corporate decision-making process. With the increasing globalization of corporate capitalism, women in developing countries are disproportionately vulnerable to being victimized and exploited (Wonders and Danner 2002). They suffer from economic displacement, unfair labor practices and unsafe working conditions, environmental harm, and some consequences of militarism.

---

are controlled by outraged consumers in a free market.

The seminal critic of capitalism, Karl Marx, did not favor criminalization as a response to exploitative and harmful corporate activities. For Marx, law by its very form was likely to favor privileged segments of society (Cain and Hunt 1979). Among other functions, it legitimates and shields economic exploitation and harm. In this sense, the law helps promote what we call white collar crime. Such crime can be obliterated only by abolishing the private ownership of property and transforming society so that people live in egalitarian, cooperative relationships with each other. In such a society, Marx argued, there is no need for criminal law.

The failure to criminalize some forms of harmful white collar activity, such as "tax avoidance," can help promote such activity, and in this negative way the law promotes white collar crime in the nonlegal sense of the term *crime* (McBarnet 1992). The removal of legal controls can create a whole range of new criminal opportunities. The deregulation of the U.S. savings and loan industry in the early 1980s certainly contributed to staggering losses through fraudulent activities within these institutions (Calavita and Pontell 1990; Pontell and Calavita 1993). Legal reforms in the later half of the 1990s, including passage of the Private Securities Litigation Reform Act of 1995 and repeal of the Glass/Steagall Act in 1999, contributed to the environment that

facilitated the wave of corporate scandals of the early 21st century (Henriques and Eichenwald 2002; Labaton 2002b).

INTEGRATED THEORIES OF WHITE COLLAR CRIME

A number of students of white collar crime have attempted to develop *integrated theories* of such crime that incorporate insights from different theoretical traditions and account for white collar crime on several different levels.

James William Coleman (1987) developed an integrated theory that centers on the coincidence of appropriate motivation and opportunity. A culture generates motives for lawbreaking when it emphasizes "possessive individualism," competition, and materialism; justifies rationalizations; and removes unified restraining influences. A built-in structure of opportunity renders white collar crime both less vulnerable to legal controls and sanctions (due to the disproportionate power of elites in the formulation and administration of the law) and open to a variety of attractive possibilities for disregarding or violating the laws that do exist. In the private sector, the attractiveness of illicit opportunities increases as profitability declines; the organizational rhetoric of condemning illegal activity comes into conflict with the conditions (diffusion of responsibility, deniability, and lack of authentic objections) that promote such activity. Various factors, including the structure of opportunity, the nature of financial reimbursement, and the occupational subculture, can render some occupations more conducive to illegality than others. Accordingly, white collar crime is most pervasive in societies that have a culture of competition, in organizations that are financially pressured, and in occupations with special opportunities and subcultural values that promote illegality.

John Braithwaite (1989a) based his integrative theory on two traditions: structural Marxist theory (first articulated by Dutch criminologist Willem A. Bonger), which links both white collar and conventional crime with the promotion of egoism in capitalist societies; and differential association theory (first developed by Sutherland), which holds that both white collar and conventional crime are learned relative to differential opportunity. Accordingly, nations with high levels of inequality of wealth and power will have high rates of both white collar and conventional crime because they produce a broad range of illegitimate opportunities that are more rewarding than legal opportunities. Organizational crime specifically is a response to relatively more attractive illegitimate opportunities and the subcultural value system that rationalizes taking advantage of them. For Braithwaite, the theoretical challenge is to construct a "tipping point" explanation that predicts when a stake in noncompliance outbalances a stake in conformity with the law. His critical tipping factor is *differential shaming*: Conduct tips in the direction that avoids the more potent shaming (disapproval), whether it comes from within the organization or from the state. Involvement in white collar criminal conduct can then be understood as a function of relative vulnerability to shaming; crime flourishes in organizations that shield members from shaming and pressure them to produce and is controlled in organizations that take proactive measures to expose law violators to shame. Braithwaite accordingly regarded differential shaming as the missing link

integrating two contradictory traditions (subcultural and control).

AN INTEGRATED, MULTILEVEL APPROACH TO UNDERSTANDING THE ENRON ET AL. CASES

The wave of corporate crime cases of the early 21st century, here called "Enron et al."—was collectively the largest-scale white collar crime wave in recent years, overshadowing the insider trading and S & L cases of the 1980s. Although it is not possible to say exactly what proportion of losses were due specifically to criminal activity, by any estimate the losses from unethical and illegal actions by high-level corporate executives were in the billions of dollars. Many different explanations have been offered for this corporate crime wave, ranging from economic determinism to intentional wrongdoing. Several different levels of explanation can be applied to these crimes (Friedrichs 2004). First, we consider the *structural* level.

Enron, WorldCom, Adelphia, Global Crossing, and other corporations are products of a capitalist political economy promoting free market competition, the pursuit of profit, and the expansion of markets, or growth. In the most recent era, an enormous emphasis on stock price maximization emerged. The late 1990s bull market created expectations of substantial stock price growth and put CEOs under immense pressure to produce numbers that would promote such price growth or at least not lead to a price decline. If quarterly reports were below expectations, the corporate stock price would get hammered, generating substantial losses and making it more difficult to raise further capital. During the same time, stock option plans, bonuses, and other extravagant forms of rewarding top executives greatly expanded. An escalating stock price was arguably the surest way to riches for these corporate managers, providing strong additional incentives for encouraging aggressive or blatantly fraudulent accounting in producing corporate financial statements. In the political realm, deregulatory legislation promoted by politicians who in many cases were receiving large political campaign funding donations from corporate interests contributed to a sense of immunity by corporate executives and auditors for financial manipulations they might undertake. A postmodern cultural environment fostered an increasing disconnect between traditional criteria for reality toward "hyperreal" orientations privileging simulations and abstract projections as "real." Finally, on a structural level, the crimes involved were facilitated by a network of escalating relationships and interdependencies between corporations, accounting firms, investment banking houses, stock brokerages and analysts, and law firms, with inherently corrupting conflicts of interest.

On an *organizational* level, an environment of intense competitiveness, intimidation toward compliance with the organizational agenda established by the company leadership, and the promotion of a strong ethos of corporate pride, loyalty, and superiority was also significant. Executive retention plans, pay incentive structures, rejection of old economy corporate models, and the use of complex financial instruments such as derivatives contributed to an environment fostering the relentless pursuit of higher returns, however fabricated, over integrity and other considerations.

On a *dramaturgic* level, Enron exemplified the projection of an image of ultrarespectability through Chairman Ken Lay's top-level political contacts, conspicuous local philanthropy, and the naming of Houston's stadium as Enron Field, for example. This image may have reinforced the sense within the company that its business practices were legitimate and immune from serious external oversight.

On an *individualistic* level, at least some of those at the center of the worst cases within these corporations appeared to be amoral risk takers, egocentric or sociopathic individuals with delusions of grandeur who were driven to "succeed" and were greedy for both material symbols of their financial success and for racking up the largest possible numbers to demonstrate to themselves (and others) their degree of success.

EXPLAINING WHITE COLLAR CRIME, IN SUM

White collar crime is clearly a complex, multifaceted phenomenon. No single theory or explanation can comprehensively explain all forms or instances of white collar crime. We should always be clear about what it is exactly that we are trying to explain: criminality, crime, or criminalization. The overarching view of this text is that the complexity and diversity of white collar crime precludes any single comprehensive theory or explanatory scheme. We have seen how difficult it is to overcome the methodological barriers to demonstrating conclusively the validity of competing theories of white collar crime; in some cases, the empirical evidence has been contradictory. We also touched on various definitional, conceptual, metaphysical, and typological problems that complicate the challenge of developing viable theoretical explanations.

Even though much theorizing is necessarily interpretive, some theories are more fundamental and powerful than others. Some forms of white collar crime are best understood on one level of explanation, and others on another. The individualistic and occupational forms of white collar crime, for example, lend themselves more readily to explanation within the framework of traditional, mainstream theories.

Organizational and corporate forms of white collar crime generate special difficulties. The real challenge is to identify how the macro levels and micro levels connect and interact to produce such white collar crime (Vaughan 1992, 1999). Numerous factors, ranging from external pressures to organizational position to regulatory patterns of response, may be involved in individual decisions to commit crimes on behalf of organizations. Given the large number of possible variables, we cannot easily expect to explain organizational crime with propositions that have the reliability of a scientific law.

If, on the one hand, it is true that organizations are *not* persons and that only actual humans can in the final analysis make decisions and take action, it is also quite evident that once corporate policies, norms, and goals are in place, they produce powerful forces that seem to dictate certain actions, including criminal actions, independent of the particular inclinations of individuals. In the section of this chapter addressing organizational crime, we have touched on some of the complex of factors that might explain organizational or corporate crime. Adopting extreme positions on either side of the issue—that is, either treating corporations as no different from individuals *or* focusing exclusively on individual decision makers—is likely to produce a distorted view. In some contexts, then, it makes more sense to speak of organizations, in other contexts of individuals, but in either case we should avoid confusing the matter by using ambiguous or inappropriate references.

Can we only invoke the core motivation of "greed" to largely explain white collar crime? The essential thesis of this chapter is that such a simplistic, one-dimensional explanation does not take us far in understanding either the endlessly complex mixture of factors that may be involved in such crime or the different ways of even thinking about what we are trying to explain. Motivation is only one element. We must continue to refine our understanding of the interrelationships among criminality, crime, and criminalization as they apply to white collar crime.

KEY TERMS

accounts, 214

amoral calculators, 206

anomie, 215

biogenetic explanation, 201

bounded rationality, 211

commodification, 219

conflict theory, 216

constitutive criminology, 218

crime coercive/facilitative, 206, 207

crimes of capital, 216

criminality, 199

criminalization, 199

criminogenic tendencies, 206

criminology, 218

differential association, 212

differential opportunity theory, 216

differential shaming, 221

diffusion theory, 208

dramaturgic perspective, 214

feminist criminology, 218

Freudian approach, 201

general theory, 209

hyperreal, 219

integrated theory, 220

labeling theory, 213

macro-/meso-/micro-level explanations, 200

Marxist theory, 216

neutralizations, 214

organizational crime, 205

performance pressures, 217

postmodernist criminology, 218

power theory, 204

radical/critical criminology, 218

rational choice, 211

rationalizations, 214

routine activities theory, 211

secondary deviance, 213

social control theory, 212

social entities, 204

sociogenic explanation, 203

status deprivation theory, 216

stigma, 213

structural embeddedness, 208

structural perspective theory, 209

DISCUSSION QUESTIONS

1. What are the principal objectives of a theory of white collar crime? Identify and discuss some of the main underlying assumptions for any such theory. What are the different answers to the question of what we want to explain with regard to white collar crime?

2. Evaluate the notion that white collar offenders are intrinsically different from nonoffenders. What are the principal elements of the demonic, biogenetic, psychological, and sociogenic perspectives on this question and the evidence for an answer to the question within these perspectives? Which individualistic attributes of white collar offenders do you regard as meriting further systematic study, and why?

3. Identify and discuss the principal arguments on both sides of the question of whether there is such a thing as corporate or organizational criminality. Which factors seem most important in explaining the crimes of corporations or organizations? What can be said in favor of and against the idea of a general theory of crime, especially as it applies to understanding white collar crime?

4. Choose three of the following theoretical perspectives on crime, or white collar crime: rational choice, social control, social learning, interactionism (labeling), neutralization, and structural strain. What are the principal underlying assumptions involved, and in what ways are these perspectives more useful to explaining white collar crime or conventional crime? Which theoretical perspective do you find most useful for understanding white collar crime, and why?

5. Evaluate critically the contribution of the conflict perspective, in its Marxist, radical, and contemporary critical forms, to the understanding of white collar crime. How can a focus on criminalization contribute to our understanding of white collar crime? What are the value and the limitations of an integrated theoretical approach?

Law and the Social Control of White Collar Crime

Do various forms of white collar crime develop and inspire laws in response to them, or do laws develop that designate certain forms of economic activity as criminal? The conventional view is that law—formal *social control*—develops in response to deviant or harmful activity. Some contemporary theoretical perspectives (e.g., conflict theory and labeling theory) have suggested that the opposite is true—that institutions of social control come to define certain activity as deviant or criminal, sometimes quite arbitrarily (Cohen 1985)—and there is considerable evidence to support this view. The relationship between law and objectively harmful activities of the white collar strata is complex. This chapter attempts to sort through some of the elements involved in this relationship.

SOCIAL CONTROL AND WHITE COLLAR CRIME

Even though social control in the form of proscriptions against conventional crimes such as murder, assault, and robbery has existed from at least the time of earliest recorded history, the range of activities defined as white collar crimes have inspired a more limited and typically belated formal response. Throughout much of history, the organization of economic and professional life was far simpler than has been true in modern times, and accordingly the opportunities to defraud, embezzle, or cause harm to others through economic activities have been far more limited. After all, a predominantly agricultural economy of self-sustaining family farms hardly promotes white collar crime. In small, homogeneous communities, people who engage in economic transactions have enduring relationships that include both informal controls and self-serving motivations not to defraud. Political structure also plays a role: Many of the worst white collar offenses in history have been committed in nondemocratic societies by political and economic elites who have not had a strong incentive to impose formal controls on their own predatory practices. Still, it is inaccurate and simplistic to imagine that the legal response to white collar crime is entirely a modern phenomenon. White collar crime can be seen both as a product of failed social control and as a product of highly successful social control. In the first view, it represents the failure of formal and informal institutions of social control to prevent or deter corporations and individuals from engaging in socially harmful conduct. Such external controls have often been either absent or only superficially

225

enforced. In the second view, corporate and other organizational forms of white collar crime may reflect the high level of control over individual human conduct that such entities achieve. These crimes often result from conformity to organizational norms.

White collar crime, especially in its corporate form, poses some unique challenges for proponents of more social control and less social control. The sections that follow consider the character of the most formal type of social control—law—in its response to white collar crime.

FORMAL LAW AND WHITE COLLAR CRIME

In the ongoing debate about the proper meaning of the term *white collar crime*, one camp advocates a narrow definition referring to certain violations of *criminal law* (Orland 1980; Tappan 1947). Sutherland (1940, 1949), however, insisted that the term should be applied more broadly to forms of white collar harm that are not specifically prohibited by criminal law but rather by some other form of law (e.g., civil law or administrative law). Sutherland's basic argument was that because corporations and other elements of the white collar world have too much influence over the criminalization process, the narrower conception of white collar crime allows these powerful segments of society to impose their own limits on our view of crime. Many subsequent students of the phenomenon have adopted some form of Sutherland's argument (Kauzlarich 1992; Schwendinger and Schwendinger 1970; Simon 2006). Even when laws attempting to control certain forms of corporate activities are adopted, elite interests often have the power to influence the meaning of the laws, as when tax evasion becomes tax avoidance (McBarnet 1992). In this view, law is a terrain of contested meaning. As a society becomes larger, more complex, and more heterogeneous, the historical tendency is to rely increasingly on law, the most formal type of social control (Friedrichs 2006). The application of

law has certainly expanded greatly in the response to white collar crime, although the appropriateness of this expansion is the subject of much ongoing debate. Historically, it has proven more difficult to formulate and apply criminal laws to harms committed in a business or professional context than to conventional forms of harm such as assault and burglary. Unlike most conventional crime, what we call white collar crime typically occurs in the context of legitimate and productive activities, and the proper lines of demarcation between acceptable and unacceptable practices (e.g., effective and fraudulent advertising) are not always clear (Croall 2001; McBarnet 2004).

In the Western, capitalist tradition, the premier philosopher of capitalism, Adam Smith (1776, 1937), argued that the free market, not the legal system, is the best and most efficient means for preventing or minimizing harmful conduct by businesses. One form of white collar criminal law that is logically consistent with Smith's position is *antitrust law*, which is directed against monopolistic practices that interfere with the operation of a truly competitive free market. Jesilow (1982a) pointed out that Smith had no illusions about the willingness of many businesspeople to do harm to consumers; Smith seemed to believe that most laws directed at them would simply be manipulated and evaded by more powerful businesspeople, which would lead to more harm rather than less. Some criminologists cite inherent limitations in the formal legalistic response to white collar crime and call for greater reliance on alternative means of social control (Braithwaite 2005; Simpson 2002). Critical criminologists—on the political left—have generally favored tough laws against corporate crime in particular, although this is somewhat of a dilemma as they generally oppose the expansion of state power through criminalization (Alvesalo and Tombs 2002). Conservatives and libertarians have generally opposed the expansion of white collar crime laws, or "the criminalization of almost everything," in one complaint (Healy 2004). The concern that laws regulating and restricting business practices are economically counterproductive was especially pronounced during the Reagan era in the

1980s and during the George W. Bush administration beginning in 2001.

As globalization increases and national boundaries become less and less important for many forms of business, the importance of social control on the international level increases (Barak 2001; Braithwaite and Drahos 2000; Michalowski and Kramer 1987). The larger the framework of social control, however, the more difficult it becomes to formulate laws that can be implemented and can garner broad support.

The extent to which social control should be directed toward individuals, groups, organizations, or some combination of these is another issue. Traditionally, social control has focused on the behavior of individuals, but the incidence of corporate white collar crime, in particular, has highlighted the need to control organizations.

THE HISTORICAL ORIGINS
OF WHITE COLLAR CRIME LAWS

Involvement of law in commercial matters dates from the earliest period of recorded history. According to Drapkin (1989), the first known legal documents were contracts of land sales and other transactions conducted around 2400 B.C. in ancient Mesopotamia. We also have evidence of concern with commercial misconduct in the form of a tablet (dated approximately 2050 B.C.) containing the code of a ruler, Ur–Nammu, that lays out guidelines for a uniform system of weights and measures and prohibits various forms of economic exploitation. Codes from this time stipulate punishments imposed on those who caused injury in the performance of their occupational duties. The Old Testament (e.g., Proverbs 11:25; Deuteronomy 25:13; Leviticus 25:14) includes proscriptions against deceitful and unfair market practices (Geis 1988; Levine 1980). The classical Greek lawmaker Solon (7th century B.C.) established laws against embezzling from the state, and the Roman statesman Cicero (1st century B.C.) discussed the obligations of "insiders" in grain

transactions (Drapkin 1989; Vermeule 1983). Such proscriptions and initiatives suggest, at a minimum, a clear recognition in ancient societies of economic crimes that differed from conventional forms of assault and robbery.

English common law, which evolved over hundreds of years and is an important foundation of American law, addressed occupational offenses less clearly than conventional forms of harm such as homicide and assault. In feudal England (1100–1400), the marketplace was heavily regulated, primarily to protect the interests of the Crown and the nobility (Michalowski 1985). Feudal merchants (*pies poudreux*, or "dusty feet") were at a serious disadvantage in a system that regarded profit as dishonorable or sinful (Sheldon and Zweibel 1980; Tigar and Levy 1977). Much control of English merchant activities was informal, but in the late Middle Ages specific laws were enacted to protect consumers; these laws prohibited regrating, engrossing, and forestalling, which were practices entailing either buying up market goods for sale at a profit or buying them up before they reached the market to drive up prices (Geis 1988). During this period, boards and guilds were empowered to establish fair prices (Sheldon and Zweibel 1980: 189). Following the "Black Death" in the 14th century, with its devastating impact on the pool of laborers, new laws prohibited giving or receiving excessive wages, refusing to work at the proper wage level, or refusing to work at all (Bellamy 1973; Chambliss 1964). Box 9.1 profiles an early example of white collar crime.

The previous paragraphs identified some early laws addressing harmful commercial practices, but they were sporadically enforced and seemed to be principally intended to protect the interests of the ownership class (Geis 1988; Michalowski 1985; Snider 1993). The law was not structured to respond effectively to the exploitative and harmful practices of businesses as corporate entities, and many harmful commercial and occupational practices were not addressed.

In the United States, two essentially contradictory forces relevant to white collar crime laws emerged in the 19th century in response to the country's accelerating transformation into an

---

B O X   9.1   The Carrier's Case and the Law of Employee Theft

The famous Carrier's case (1473) provided a foundation for the modern law of theft (Hall 1952). Instead of transporting bales of wool from one place to another, the carrier, the defendant in the case, broke open the bales and helped himself to the contents. English laws of the time did not specifically prohibit the use of goods already legally in one's possession for one's own purposes. The court ruled against the carrier and in doing so established a legal distinction between possession and ownership. This legal distinction was clearly responsive to the needs of an emerging class of merchants and traders, and it provided a precedent for subsequent laws prohibiting employee theft, embezzlement, and related acts.

These acts by employees became a matter of increasing concern to the ownership class, and a series of laws passed in England in the 17th and 18th centuries specifically criminalized such activities (Sharpe 1984). Initially these laws had a somewhat narrow focus, but they became a basis for general laws prohibiting occupational offenses. For example, the Servant Theft Statute (1520), which originally made theft of a master's property a felony, was eventually applied to employees generally. An embezzlement statute passed in England in 1742, which originally applied only to employees of the Bank of England, became a basis for a general embezzlement statute enacted at the end of the 18th century (Coleman 2002).

---

industrialized, urbanized, mass society. On the one hand, this expanding capitalist economy tended to give entrepreneurs and all manner of economic enterprises a free hand in creating new wealth and a booming economy (Friedman 1977; Hurst 1956). On the other hand, the workers, consumers, and investors in this increasingly large and complex society were especially vulnerable to being exploited, defrauded, or harmed by corporations, businesses, and professionals. Toward the end of the 19th century in particular, Congress enacted laws regulating and criminalizing a wide range of business practices. Periodic widespread anger over harmful working conditions, dangerous products, fraudulent sales, or environmental damage led to a series of white collar crime laws (Snider 1993). These legal reform campaigns were sometimes inspired by social critics, journalistic muckrakers, or highly publicized "catastrophes."

The U.S. Supreme Court has historically waxed and waned in its response to regulatory law, which addresses harmful business practices. For example, the Court originally upheld the body of state regulatory legislation passed in the latter half of the 19th century, but a more conservative Court shifted to a position favoring the rights of corporations, a pattern that in some form has continued through much of the 20th century into the early

years of the 21st century (Friedman 2002; Hall 1989). The tension between laws that emphasize economic development and those that favor regulating or criminalizing harmful practices is still very much with us.

CONTEMPORARY LEGISLATIVE LAWMAKING AND WHITE COLLAR CRIME

Lawmaking is a complex process that may reflect a variety of influences. Specific white collar crime laws emerge out of particular historical circumstances and may reflect various mixtures of consensual, rationalistic, and power-based dimensions; however, most contemporary theories of lawmaking also recognize the central role of power, especially in terms of the role of interest groups (Friedman 1977; Friedrichs 2006). In a useful study of white collar crime lawmaking, Savelsberg (1994) attempted to demonstrate that such legislation reflects the activities of lobbying by special interest groups more than the objective needs of society.

An *instrumentalist perspective* on lawmaking advances the view that in a capitalist society, law reflects the elite class's control over the state and is intended to serve the purposes of that class (Quinney 1974). This provocative challenge to a conventional view of law as rooted in democratic consensus is controversial and difficult to reconcile with many laws that appear to work against the immediate interests of major capitalist corporations. An alternative progressive perspective, which has been designated *structuralist*, recognizes that the state is "relatively autonomous" and is committed to the system's long-term survival rather than to advancing the specific, immediate interests of capitalist elites and entities (Collins 1984; Lynch, Michalowski, and Groves 2000). In this account, the state implements white collar crime law, including corporate crime law, to help sustain the system and legitimize the state in the eyes of its citizens. But there may well be tensions among state officials in terms of their concern with the system's long-term legitimacy or immediate well-being. Calavita and Pontell (1994) suggested that the state has generally been more tolerant of traditional corporate crimes in the manufacturing sector—mainly taking action in response to grassroots political demands—than of financial crimes such as the S & L frauds that enriched individuals at the expense of the economic system. Gerber, Jensen, and Fritsch (1997) argued that American politicians initially ignored the S & L frauds due to fear that it might harm their election prospects. They only addressed the issue after a key election to contribute to the preservation of long-term economic stability. Box 9.2 considers how white collar crime laws are forged when business interests conflict.

The Influence of Business on the Lawmaking Process

Because the evolution of white collar crime law is complex, laws governing economic crimes are likely to be products of various competing constituencies, and thus powerful economic interests do not always prevail (Neuman 1998; Savelsberg 1987). Nevertheless, business has generally had disproportionate influence over the lawmaking pro-

cess. The more limited legal response to white collar crime relative to conventional crime reflects in part the considerable input businesspeople have in implementing white collar crime laws; the class of people to whom conventional offenders typically belong has virtually no involvement in making conventional criminal law (Bakan 2004; Croall 2001). The politicians who make the laws often depend on business leaders and corporations for financial support for their campaigns, for personal gifts and favors, and for post-political career employment or contracts. Quite a number of legislators have become lobbyists (typically for business interests) after leaving office (Abramson 1998; Birnbaum 1992). And responsiveness to at least some business interests is often politically expedient when many of a politician's constituents are dependent on major corporations or are pro-business.

The business and corporate world does not fully control the lawmaking process, and the level of business's political influence has fluctuated in the course of modern U.S. history (Vogel 1989). In the 20th century, three major eras featuring laws regulating various forms of business conduct can be identified: the Progressive Era (1900s), when municipal reform groups were among the principal agitators for change; the New Deal Era (1930s), when the trade union movement played an especially important role; and the Great Society Era (1970s), during which various public interest groups lobbied for new legal initiatives. Vogel (1989) demonstrated that during periods with relatively strong economies (e.g., the 1960s) businesses are vulnerable to more regulation because during such periods higher expectations of business performance tend to develop and businesses cannot credibly claim that they are unable to afford to reform harmful practices. During an economic recession, in contrast, people tend to put a higher priority on jobs than on cracking down on the harmful conduct of business. However, developments early in the new century seemed to contradict this proposition. In 2002, in response to broadly diffused public anger over the series of revelations of corporate accounting misrepresentations and fraud, corporate elite greed, and other such wrongdoing, Congress and

---

BOX 9.2   The Dialectical Perspective on Lawmaking

William Chambliss advanced a *dialectical perspective* of lawmaking that views it as a process directed toward the resolution of various contradictions, conflicts, and dilemmas confronting society in a particular historical context (Chambliss and Courtless 1992; Chambliss and Seidman 1982). This theory provides useful explanations of laws regulating the meatpacking industry in the early 20th century and of more recent antipollution laws. In the dialectical view, conflicts between a public increasingly angry about unhealthful meat or dangerous forms of pollution and the short-term economic interests of meatpacking corporations or corporate polluters can be resolved by laws that ensure the general public welfare while protecting long-term economic interests of the larger corporations.

Corporate and business interests are hardly monolithic. Indeed, the large meatpackers supported the regulations because these laws helped restore public confidence in their product and drove many small competitors who were unable to meet the new expenses involved out of business (Kolko 1963; Poveda 1992). Manufacturing corporations that depended on

unclogged rivers for transporting goods favored the first laws against water pollution (Yeager 1991a). The securities industry has supported laws directed at practices such as insider trading that promote a loss of trust among investors and potential investors. In 2002, Henry Paulson Jr., CEO of the major investment banking firm, Goldman Sachs, called for some basic legal reforms in corporate laws as an important step in restoring public confidence in the securities markets, but most top businesspeople were resisting such reforms (Byrne 2002a; Glater 2005a). In general, businesses support laws regarded as promoting a more stable and predictable business environment. However, when regulatory laws' negative effects on profits outweigh benefits, businesses, especially in the manufacturing segment, tend to oppose these laws (see Box 9.3 on the Sarbanes-Oxley Act as an illustration of this thesis). Although the dialectical theory may be more directly applicable to some white collar crime laws than to others, it provides a general sense of the interrelated factors that guide the ongoing process of lawmaking in this realm.

---

the Bush administration initiated some regulatory reforms directed at corporations, accounting practices, and other players in the major financial markets (Bumiller 2002c). These reforms were being adopted during a period of some economic distress and anxiety, with elements of a recession. In this period, a precipitous decline of an estimated $7 trillion in stock values over a little more than two years was in some significant measure attributed to wrongdoing among financial elites. The percentage of Americans who were shareholders—in mutual funds and retirement funds, in particular—had grown exponentially in the recent era, and accordingly far more people could make a direct connection between sharp declines in their quarterly statements and the widely publicized allegations of white collar crime within major corporations and associated financial institutions. But by 2005, corporations and financial institutions were actively challenging the recent reforms and new regulatory rules (Glater 2005; Norris 2004). The cycle of reform and backlash against reform has been ongoing.

Legislators must necessarily be responsive to many constituencies, some of whom are harmed by business practices or are antagonistic toward business generally. In recent times in particular, relatively well-organized groups (e.g., environmental or consumer groups) have lobbied for laws that criminalize or otherwise penalize business practices they view as harmful or threatening. These groups operate as "moral entrepreneurs" that advocate white collar crime laws in the public interest. Although various social movements have promoted new laws throughout U.S. history, the tendency to seek social change through legal reform has intensified since the late 1950s (Friedrichs 2006; Handler 1978).

The relative success of the civil rights movement in challenging the legal status of segregation was one important source of inspiration for social movements representing disadvantaged and beleaguered constituencies. Most of these social movements' law reform initiatives did not focus on white collar crime in the narrower sense but were directed instead toward imposing more regulation of and greater control over a range of potentially harmful business practices. Even though these social movements, including consumer and environmentalist movements, have sought to influence legislative, judicial, and administrative lawmaking, they have perhaps been most successful in the courts (Handler 1978: 232). Powerful economic interests often have considerable advantages in the legislative and administrative arenas because politicians depend on their support. Reflecting pressure from such interests and conservative ideological commitments, the Republican-dominated Congress passed in 1995 a series of laws with several intentions: to shift more tort cases to federal jurisdiction; to discourage product-liability lawsuits by imposing responsibility for defendants' legal fees on plaintiffs who lose cases and by sanctioning lawsuits deemed frivolous; to impose limits on punitive damages in tort cases; and to make it more difficult for investors to establish fraud in cases against brokers (Labaton 1995a; Lewis N. A. 1995a, 1995b, 1995c). In 2005, the U. S. Senate passed a law, originally passed in the House, limiting the ability of people to file class action lawsuits against corporations (Labaton 2005a). Various business and financial interests that were major donors to the president and legislators' campaigns and had well-funded lobbying operations pushed for these reforms. Many commentators have suggested that the earlier legal reforms contributed to an environment that produced the corporate scandals of the early 21st century. Congress imposed new constraints on corporate and business practices during this period in response to widespread public anger and concern. However, lobbyists opposed to fundamental reforms continued to exercise formidable clout, and legislators aligned with business interests continued to block or stall at least some reform initiatives, such as those on off-shore tax havens (Johnston 2002d; Labaton and Oppel 2002; Morgenson 2002d). With the American Jobs Creation Act of 2004, Congress passed a law allowing corporations to avoid over $3 billion in taxes by "repatriating" their foreign profits without paying American taxes on these profits (*New York Times* 2005a). The claims that this law would create jobs, as its title suggests, has been vigorously challenged (Lefroy 2005). In 2005, the Bush administration was accused of having put national security in jeopardy by having bowed to

chemical industry opposition to a strong law to reduce the risk of terrorist attacks on chemical plants (*New York Times* 2005b). The regulatory laws that have been passed may be watered down or overridden by subsequent legislation; they may or may not be vigorously enforced by an administration unsympathetic to tough laws and penalties. No one should underestimate the potency of antiregulatory interests (see Box 9.3).

Finally, government agencies or entities may actively lobby for white collar crime laws, inspired either by self-interest, as occurs when an enforcement agency seeks to expand its reach and influence, or by a principled perception of a need for new laws (Lofquist 1993b). The Federal Trade Commission (FTC) expanded its regulatory mandate in 1950 by successfully mobilizing various resources to ensure passage of a key piece of antitrust legislation, the Celler-Kefauver Act (Luchansky and Gerber 1993). The SEC in 2002, in the face of widespread anger about various forms of securities misrepresentation by corporations and inadequate auditing by accounting firms, promoted some new initiatives to address these concerns (McNamee and Borrus 2002). But such initiatives by regulatory agencies ultimately contend with political pressures originating with business interests calling for modifying or eliminating these new rules (Norris 2004). Regulatory agencies do not operate within a political vacuum.

ALTERNATIVE SOURCES AND FORMS OF LAW AND LAWMAKING

The legislative branch is not the only source of laws, of course. Four alternative sources and forms of law and lawmaking are discussed in this section.

The Constitution and Constitutional Law

The U.S. Constitution and many state constitutions do not specifically address white collar crime. Still, the Constitution provides a basic framework for the response to white collar crime through the establishment of a federal court system, its allocation of

BOX 9.3   The Sarbanes-Oxley Act

In response to the firestorm of public anger over the corporate scandals of 2001–2002, beginning with the exposure of massive financial statement misrepresentations at Enron, Congress passed the Sarbanes-Oxley Act at the end of July 2002 (Brickey 2003; Moohr 2003; Recine 2002). Among other provisions, the Act calls for increased oversight duties for corporate fraud, the requirement that corporate CEOs and CFOs personally certify corporate financial statements, and adjustments of the Federal Sentencing Guidelines to implement longer prison sentences for high-level corporate executives convicted of corporate financial fraud. The Act also led to the establishment of a Public Company Accounting Oversight Board to oversee the auditing of corporations. This board was granted more power than the previous policing entity, which had obviously failed to prevent the release of fraudulent corporate financial statements. The overriding purpose of the Sarbanes-Oxley Act was to restore public confidence in such statements and to encourage investment in corporate stocks. This would be best accomplished if corporate and auditing misconduct was deterred by the stiffer penalties for such misconduct. It remained to be seen whether the initiatives implemented by the Act would have a real impact over the long term. Was this simply political symbolism, or was substantive reform really involved? Would corporate and accounting lobbyists succeed in watering down the provisions of the Act? Would regulatory and prosecutorial forces be adequately funded and supported to pursue offenders? Several years after adoption of the Sarbanes-Oxley Act, early assessments suggested that some industries seemed to benefit from the Act, while others were negatively impacted; some practices promoted by the Act were being adopted, but this law was not achieving all its intended effects (Rezace and Jain 2005; Schwartzkopf and Miller 2005). For one critic, the Sarbanes-Oxley Act is a form of "Congressional window-dressing" because it relies principally upon a historically failed policy of corporate self-governance (Weissmann 2005). But by 2005, many business leaders were complaining about the costs of complying with the Sarbanes-Oxley Act, and pressure was building for modifications in the implementation of this Act (Glater 2005). A general counsel for Nasdaq defended Sarbanes-Oxley as a necessary initiative to restore public confidence in the stock market (Greco 2005).The long-term effects of the Sarbanes-Oxley Act remain to be determined.

powers to the different branches of the government, and its imposition of limitations, especially in the Bill of Rights, on the exercise of governmental power in the investigation and prosecution of criminal cases. Because a somewhat disproportionate percentage of white collar crime cases are federal cases, the Bill of Rights' protections for those accused of crimes apply directly to these defendants. The Fourteenth Amendment extended due process protection to defendants in the far more common state cases.

The Commerce Clause of Article I, Section 8 of the Constitution authorized Congress to make laws regulating commerce between the states and provided one basis for federal intervention in the affairs of private businesses; at the same time it also became a basis for challenging states' attempts at regulating business activity. In its celebrated decision in *Marbury v. Madison* (1803), the U.S. Supreme Court established both the supremacy of the Constitution and the

Court's own right of judicial review in determining whether laws passed by other bodies were or were not constitutional. Accordingly, a broad body of *constitutional law* has developed, and some of this law has direct bearing on white collar crime cases.

One of the great paradoxes in constitutional history deserves mention here. Shortly after the end of the Civil War, the Fourteenth Amendment was ratified to ensure that newly emancipated slaves were not for all practical purposes re-enslaved by state laws that deprived them of due process. In the latter part of the 19th century, former slaves rarely had the financial resources needed to protect themselves by invoking this amendment, but businesses did. Lawyers for wealthy corporations vigorously fought off the federal government's efforts to intervene in some of their unscrupulous business activities by arguing that the corporations' Fourteenth Amendment guarantee of due process protection was being violated (Hall 1989).

In the 20th century, the U.S. Supreme Court has withheld from corporations certain protections, such as the privileges and immunities clause of the Fourteenth Amendment and due process protection of liberty (First 1990). Still, the statutory laws addressing various forms of white collar crime, including the Sherman Antitrust Act, have been especially vulnerable to challenges on the grounds that they are unconstitutionally vague. Indeed, many individuals and corporations in white collar crime cases have contested the charges on the grounds that constitutional provisions were violated or that an infringement on constitutional rights has occurred (Schroeder 2002). For example, defendants in environmental crime cases have challenged the state by invoking the commerce clause, the due process clause, the Fourth Amendment prohibition of unreasonable search and seizure, and the Fifth Amendment double jeopardy clause (when both civil and criminal actions are pursued) (Jalley, Moores, Henniger, and Maragani 2002). These constitutional challenges fail more often than they succeed, but they have not been uniformly unsuccessful.

Case Law

Case law that is a product of appellate court opinions has played an important role in the realm of white collar crime for several reasons. Statutory laws pertaining to white collar crime often include ambiguous elements, due to both the difficulty sometimes involved in differentiating between legitimate and illegitimate business practices and the compromises made in response to lobbying by special interests. Defendants in white collar crime cases are often better able to finance a full-scale appeal of criminal convictions than are conventional crime defendants. At the same time, public interest groups have often been more successful in the courts than in the legislative arena because the courts, especially the federal courts, are somewhat more insulated from politics and more open to principled arguments. Since the late 1950s, a period of judicial activism has effectively encouraged litigation by a growing number of activist groups, and by the 1970s, public interest law firms interested in pursuing test cases before the courts had emerged (Handler 1978).

The claim that the courts directly bring about important social change is not uniformly accepted (Rosenberg 1991). The counterargument is that change is likely to occur only when court decisions are complemented by social and political forces that are already moving society in that direction. Furthermore, both federal and state appellate court judges are often selected less for their legal brilliance than for their perceived ideological orientation; judges with a conservative orientation have traditionally been regarded as pro-business. During the late 19th century, after World War I, and during the Reagan–Bush era (1981–1992), especially large numbers of conservative, pro-business justices were appointed. The U.S. Supreme Court opinion in *Santa Clara v. Southern Pacific Railroad* (1886), which held that a corporation was entitled under the Fourteenth Amendment to the same protections as "natural persons," has been interpreted as a reflection of the subservience of the Court to big business in the late 19th century (Horwitz 1992). Of course, in many other cases the courts have upheld statutes regulating and criminalizing certain business activities (Friedman 2002).

Some areas of white collar crime law are more fully developed in the case law than in statutory law. For example, the insider trading laws are principally a product of a series of judicial opinions (Brodsky and Kramer 1997). The courts have in other cases interpreted statutory laws in a manner that extends the scope of the criminal liability of corporations and other white collar actors (Bucy 2002). A court opinion determined that the Racketeer-Influenced and Corrupt Organizations Act (RICO) could be applied to businesspeople and was not restricted to traditional mobsters (Geary 2002; Sacks, Coale, and Goldberg 2005). This Act is discussed more fully later in this chapter.

Executive Lawmaking

The executive branch is less directly involved in making law than the other two branches of the government, at least in the traditional sense. Still, this branch contributes to making much white collar crime law. Executive branch personnel have considerable input in the legislative process by providing many experts who testify before legislative committees and assist in the drafting of legislation. The executive branch can use its political clout to lobby for laws it favors, and the chief executive can veto legislation, although the use of this power is somewhat uncommon with respect to criminal law.

Most importantly, *executive lawmaking* occurs through this branch's control of agencies that investigate, enforce, and prosecute crime. Any laws the executive branch fails to enforce and prosecute in effect do not "exist." Thus, the Reagan administration's lack of interest in enforcing many provisions of antitrust law rendered it nonexistent during this period (Labaton 2000c). The George W. Bush administration was criticized from the outset for its perceived lack of interest in vigorous enforcement of environmental laws (Burns and Lynch 2004; Seelye 2002a, 2002b). This executive branch power is especially important with respect to white collar crime because indifference to, and even hostility toward, at least some white collar crime laws has been a recurrent pattern.

The executive branch appoints all federal judges and many state-level judges as well; especially important are Supreme Court justices and appellate court judges. Despite the legislative branch's confirmation powers, the executive branch has considerable discretion in determining which judges will interpret the law.

The executive branch also plays the same role in appointing the top people in many regulatory agencies, who in turn "make" much of the law that applies to white collar crime in the broadest sense. The executive branch has the power to administer penal sanctions, and chief executives on both the federal and the state levels have the power to pardon. Here again, these powers are especially significant for white collar offenders, who have traditionally benefited from correctional classification procedures that most often direct them to minimum-security facilities. White collar offenders have had great advantages in the parole process because they are more likely than conventional offenders to have a social background and demeanor that enables them to make a favorable impression on parole boards. Because of these factors, an executive branch agency, the parole board, often effectively compromises or diminishes the legal sanctions adopted by the legislative branch and imposed by the judicial branch. The pardoning power of the chief executive is also likely to favor the wealthy and influential.

The single most notorious use of the pardon in recent U.S. history was surely Gerald Ford's pardon of Richard Nixon as criminal charges relating to the Watergate matter were still under consideration. President Bill Clinton was also widely criticized and subjected to a criminal investigation when he pardoned several white collar criminals during his final hours in office, with the case of the vastly wealthy commodities trader Marc Rich, a fugitive from American justice for many years, receiving special attention (Johnston and Lacey 2001).

Administrative Law

The regulatory agencies that produce state and federal *administrative law* are among the less conspicuous participants in our legal system. This type of law is of special importance in any discussion of white collar crime insofar as many of the activities commonly classified under that heading are violations of administrative rather than statutory law. There is, however, some dissension over whether administrative law is really law in the conventional sense or more appropriately viewed as a body of rules produced by a special type of governmental entity (Luneburg 1990).

The delegation of broad, policy-making powers to administrative agencies is one of the basic characteristics of contemporary U.S. government (Bryner 1987). As the scope and complexity of matters regulated by the government has expanded, Congress has tended to pass acts that provide only a framework for responding to some problem; the appropriate regulatory agency is then authorized to create the detailed, relevant rules (*Guide to American Law* 1983). Administrative agency rule making is generally less visible than the lawmaking of official government branches and is accordingly somewhat vulnerable to abuse. In some cases, agencies act with a good deal of autonomy and may formulate rules either on the basis of perceived need or to advance internal agency careers and objectives. On the other hand, administrative agencies may also be very much under the influence of powerful executive or legislative branch officials or corporate interests with whom agency administrators have personal and professional ties.

Agencies produce rules of several different forms, including procedural rules that guide agency organization and operations, interpretative rules that embody the agency's interpretation of regulatory statutes, and legislative rules that are specific substantive statutes that the agency has been authorized to enact (*Guide to American Law* 1983). Agencies have enjoyed considerable discretion in this rule-making process, although overruling by the courts, new legislative action, or executive branch initiatives pose potential constraints.

The history of American administrative law dates from the first years of the Republic. In 1790, Congress delegated to the president certain legislative powers, such as prescribing rules and regulations to govern trade with Native Americans. In 1813, these powers were extended to other executive branch officials, such as the treasury secretary (Bryner 1987). For most of the 19th century and into the first two decades of the 20th century, the use of this power was quite limited. Although administrative law has been challenged periodically by some of its targets and legal authorities, the Supreme Court has upheld its basic constitutionality.

The peculiar character of administrative agencies in a system of checks and balances has been one source of concern. These agencies may be created by and act like the legislative branch, operate as part of the executive branch, and function (at times) like the judicial branch, as in this example:

> [T]he Securities and Exchange Commission is a regulatory agency that formulates laws like a legislature. . . . The commission enforces its rules the way the executive branch of government does—by prosecuting violators. . . . The commission acts as judge and jury when it conducts adjudicative hearings to determine violations or prescribe punishments. (*Guide to American Law* 1983: 78)

The New Deal era of the 1930s produced a great upsurge of regulatory activity and some expansion of administrative law. During this period, concern over improper use of discretionary powers by regulatory agencies led to legislative efforts to impose some constraints on these powers. The 1946 Administrative Procedure Act, the culmination of these efforts, stipulated that regulatory agencies are independent entities in the executive branch, granted aggrieved parties the right to seek judicial review, and distinguished between rule making and adjudication (Bryner 1987).

The overriding purpose of the Administrative Procedure Act was to ensure that regulatory agencies would act fairly, with appropriate attention to due process, but it also imposed some limits on judicial powers to rule on or overturn agency actions (*Guide to American Law* 1983). The specific parameters of administrative rules and decision-making processes have been an ongoing source of controversy. On the one hand there is general agreement that regulatory agencies confront a bewildering variety of situations that cannot be clearly anticipated by appropriate laws. On the other hand there is a historical concern that such agencies will accrue excessive and inappropriate powers they may abuse.

Administrative courts have become an attractive alternative to traditional courts for prosecution of some forms of white collar crime. The burden of proof is more modest, no jury is involved, and administrative court judges are especially equipped to settle cases more efficiently; furthermore, the clout of administrative law penalties, including fines of $1 million a day, has become more formidable.

A SELECTIVE REVIEW OF SUBSTANTIVE WHITE COLLAR CRIME LAWMAKING

In this section, we consider the specific development of white collar crime law in three significant areas: antitrust, occupational health and safety, and environmental damage. We also examine the controversial application of the RICO law to white collar crime cases.

Antitrust Law

In his celebrated *The Wealth of Nations* (1776), Adam Smith articulated the philosophical premises for a capitalist, free-market economy. Smith argued that the entire community benefits when individual entrepreneurs compete freely with each other because they are motivated to produce the highest-quality goods at the lowest possible price in the interest of enticing consumers to buy their products. In the United States at the end of the 19th century, more than 100 years after the publication of Smith's book, capitalism was booming on a scale probably unimagined by Smith, who lived in a predominantly agricultural society in which craftsmen, not industrial factories, produced most consumer dry goods. One of the ways in which the evolving industrial capitalism distorted Smith's vision was through the growth of immensely rich and powerful corporations that acquired monopolies or near-monopolies in oil, steel, railroads, and other markets.

In the years following the Civil War, the emergence of *trusts* was especially disturbing. Trusts, which were legal entities or holding companies for corporations engaged in the same type of business, fixed prices, controlled production, and organized geographical monopolies for an entire industry (Bohlman, Dundas, and Jentz 1989). The Standard Oil Company, presided over by John D. Rockefeller, was perhaps the most famous and wealthiest of these trusts. It drove small competitors out of business by undercutting their prices; once its competition was eliminated, it could raise prices and rates at will.

Considerable popular sentiment against the big trusts developed during this period among small businessmen, consumers, and farmers who paid exorbitant rates to railroads to transport their goods, all of whom suffered from this enormous concentration of economic power (Coleman 1985). During the years following the Civil War, the country suffered through stock market crashes and periods of economic depression blamed at least in part on the maneuvers of the trusts and other members of the economic elite. The national reach of monopolistic corporations and trusts was increasing in an era of rapidly expanded contacts among states. In this political and economic environment, the call for national antitrust laws increased greatly (Labaton 2000c).

Antitrust law, broadly defined as law that regulates economic competition, was not an invention of the 19th century. Evidence of efforts by kings to prohibit monopolistic practices in the markets can be found as far back as the 12th century in the English common law tradition. From the 15th century through the 18th century, a number of British cases firmly established several fundamental principles of antitrust law: that state-granted monopoly is bad, that cartels harm the public good, that free entry into the markets is good, and that reasonable restraints on marketing practices are desirable and permissible (Fox 1990).

In the new American Republic, individual states attempted to prohibit monopolistic practices, but the increasingly national character of the 19th-century economy limited the effectiveness of such laws. In a message to Congress in 1888, President Grover Cleveland warned that trusts, combinations, and monopolies were becoming "the people's master" (Van Cise 1990). Two years later, Congress passed the Sherman Act (named for the senator who introduced it; in Canada, a similar Combines Investigation Act had been passed in 1889). This Act, rooted in perceived common law principles that banned efforts to "prevent full and free competition," also prohibited combinations that tended to raise the cost to the consumer and actions causing a "restraint in trade" that could lead to monopolies (Van Cise 1990: 986–997). The Sherman Act gave private parties the right to sue for treble damages for violations of the act and gave the state in which such violations occurred the power to criminally prosecute and to seek injunctions (First 1990). Although the initial penalties were a maximum of one year in prison and fines of up to $5,000 per offense for individual offenders only, these penalties were increased in 1974 to a maximum three-year prison sentence for a felony conviction and fines of $100,000 for individuals and $1 million for corporations.

From the start, people have debated the nature of the underlying motivation behind the Sherman Act: whether it was a genuine desire to create an authentic free-market economy to benefit consumers or whether it was intended to provide a merely symbolic (and somewhat cynical) response to popular hostility toward the trusts but not to threaten the basic structure of a capitalist system that favored major corporations (Coleman 1985; Peritz 1996). Antitrust law has not been antagonistic to capitalism per se but rather to grossly abusive practices within the capitalistic system, and it has been tolerant of oligopolies, or domination of markets by a small number of major corporations, while opposing outright monopolies (Mensch and Freeman 1990). The rather imprecise language of the Sherman Act has allowed for quite different interpretations of its purpose, ranging from promoting greater economic efficiency to eliminating transfers of wealth from consumers to monopolists (Geis 2005c; Kauper 1990; Neuman 1998).

In the century following adoption of the Sherman Act, several new laws, including the Clayton Act (1914), the Robinson-Patman Act (1936), and the Celler-Kefauver Act (1950), were passed to address various perceived limitations of the original antitrust law. Early criminal prosecutions of corporations for violations of the Sherman Act were few and rarely successful (Geis 2005c; Whalley 1990); powerful, wealthy corporations neutralized or challenged various provisions of the Sherman Act and other antitrust laws. Throughout their history, the enforcement of these laws has been uneven and significantly dependent on both the political philosophy of the administration in power and prevailing economic circumstances (Ellis and Wyatt 1992; Jamieson 1994; Whalley 1990). Overall, antitrust was a much bigger issue with the American public in the early 20th century than at the end of the century. Antitrust prosecution was aggressive in the 1960s but much less so in the 1990s; it remained a contentious area of law in the 2000s (Epstein and Picker 2005; Labaton

2000c). In some periods, the primary mission of antitrust prosecutions has been to protect consumers; in other times it has been to protect individuals and business enterprises from arbitrary and unfair economic power used against them (Brinkley and Hobson 1998; Greve 2005; Waller 1997). In more recent times, civil antitrust suits have become much more common. Indeed, the highest profile antitrust case of the recent era—against Microsoft—was pursued in this way (Gordon 2002). Microsoft was accused of using unfair tactics against its competitors; critics of the prosecution of the Microsoft case questioned whether consumers were really harmed by the dominance of Microsoft (Piraino 2000).

Early in the 21st century, concerns with monopolistic practices persist. For example, the chairman of the Federal Trade Commission expressed his perception that an increase of mergers of hospitals and groups of doctors may be an important contributing factor in rising health care costs, and accordingly such mergers merited scrutiny by this agency (Abelson 2002b). The Department of Justice was pursuing fewer cases, but these cases tended to be bigger and more likely to have an international dimension (Cooper and Dedjinou 2005). The Department's approach encouraged voluntary corporate compliance with antitrust law; criminal prosecution has been reserved for clear, intentional violations of the law. Nevertheless, debate about the fairness and efficiency of antitrust law and its enforcement is bound to continue.

Occupational Safety and Health Laws

A great deal of evidence suggests that each year workers by the thousands die prematurely from occupationally related accidents and illnesses and that workers by the millions are seriously injured or become ill due to occupational conditions. At least a significant percentage of these deaths, injuries, and illnesses can be attributed to willful practices of employers, but they have rarely been held accountable.

Even though protective legislation concerning working conditions (e.g., the length of the working day for children) was first introduced in Great Britain in the early 19th century, little substantial legal protection for workers existed before 1970. Szasz (1984) largely attributed this absence of laws to industry's mobilization against such legislation, its ability to control access to much of the information necessary for the development of any such laws, and its considerable success in blaming workers for on-the-job injuries and illnesses. For much of the 20th century, corporate management was able to deflect passage of occupational safety and health laws by creating a network of organizations, such as the National Council for Compensation Insurance, that it claimed addressed the problems arising from such injuries and illnesses (Nader 2004; Szasz 1984).

This all began to change in the late 1960s. The relatively healthy economy of the times freed workers to focus on noneconomic issues; a rising work-related injury rate began to receive some attention; and new research was beginning to clearly document the relationship between work-related conditions (e.g., exposure to asbestos) and disease (Szasz 1984). Donnelly (1982) claimed that the agitation of rank-and-file workers over the neglect of worker health and safety by employers and labor leaders alike was the decisive factor leading to the Occupational Safety and Health Act of 1970. Ralph Nader (2004) and his associates worked actively for the passage of this law.

In one interpretation, the OSHA legislation was more of a symbolic gesture toward labor than a serious effort to protect workers (Calavita 1983). The affected industries initially attempted to derail implementation of the Act, then adopted defensive strategies to limit the reach of the OSHA agency, and finally launched an aggressive deregulatory campaign against OSHA and similar agencies (Szasz 1984). By the time Ronald Reagan was elected president in 1980, the political and economic climate had changed considerably, and a movement toward deregulation took place. Although the OSHA legislation was not repealed, its implementation was much more limited (Calavita 1983). OSHA has remained especially controversial, with a Congressman in 1995 introducing legislation to

disarm what he characterized as "the Gestapo" at the agency (Anderson 1995). Early in the new century, OSHA was most likely to seek a criminal prosecution if a death resulted from a business's engagement in willful violations of its rules or if a business made false representations about compliance with OSHA rules, although such prosecutions remain relatively rare (Kosanovic and Barnes 2005). This brief history demonstrates that laws related to corporate crime are responsive to rapidly shifting circumstances and political forces.

Environmental Protection Laws

The first law to criminalize the dumping of wastes into navigable waters, the Refuse Act of 1899, was passed to protect business interests by ensuring their unobstructed use of waterways. Before the 1960s, environmental protection laws were largely responsive to economic interests; they were not inspired by a desire to criminalize pollution practices harmful to citizens generally.

By the late 1960s, a set of circumstances favorable to such criminalization had developed (Burns and Lynch 2004; Yeager 1991a). A politically active middle class became increasingly concerned with environmental damage. A series of oil spills and other dramatic environmental disasters were featured in the media. New scientific tools had been developed to detect industrial pollution. Finally, organized lobbying could now be directed at the greater concentration of power at the federal level. In one interpretation, such initiatives, in response to an emerging environmentalist movement, reflected a shift from industrial to postindustrial values, which emphasize quality of life and environmental protection over accumulation of material wealth and natural resource exploitation (Hedman 1991).

The Environmental Protection Agency (EPA) was established by executive order in 1970, and throughout the 1970s, a series of environmental protection laws were passed, although criminal prosecutions of environmental offenders did not ensue until late in the decade during the Carter administration (Burns and Lynch 2004; Hedman

1991; Shover and Routhe 2005). In 1981, both the EPA and the Justice Department established special criminal enforcement units for environmental crime, and since the mid-1980s, Congress has elevated some environmental violations to felonies, with increased jail time and fines (Oliveira, Schenck, Cole, and Janes 2005). Today virtually all environmental statutes include criminal provisions, although they differ on the degree of liability; thus, violations of the Clean Air Act, which simply require that the violation was "knowing," are more easily criminally prosecuted than are violations of the Clean Water Act, for which demonstration of willful negligence is required (Cohen 1992). The strict liability aspect of environmental offenses and the Clinton Administration's promotion of an "attempted environmental crime" law were criticized (Carmichael 1996; Gray, Marzulla, and Shanahan 1998). In the mid-1990s, Congress approved standards based upon cost-benefit analysis for environmental regulation, and a new regulatory framework was established to give businesses more flexibility in preventing pollution, if they could improve on existing safeguards (Cushman 1995, 1996).

In the 1980s, criminal prosecutions of environmental offenders rose dramatically, despite the conservative Reagan administration's overall aversion to intervening in the conduct of private enterprise (Burns and Lynch 2004). Initially, the Reagan administration attempted to curtail the enforcement of environmental crime laws, but this effort backfired in 1983 with the widely publicized scandal of lax and corrupt EPA practices and the resignation or jailing of top agency officials. The subsequent, somewhat more vigorous response of the Reagan and George H. W. Bush administrations to environmental crime can be viewed both as a reaction to this scandal and recognition that Americans were becoming increasingly concerned about environmental destruction. A 1990 survey, for example, found that more than 70 percent of Americans favored jail terms for deliberate violations of pollution laws (Hedman 1991). Most of the enforcement effort, however, was directed at smaller, less powerful corporations; some 70 percent of those indicted were higher-level executives of such corporations (Adler and Lord 1991; Cohen 1992). Criminal cases were most likely to be pursued if significant environmental harm occurred, and culpable conduct could be identified (Oliveira et al. 2005). But many factors are taken into account in determining how to pursue cases, with considerable emphasis upon voluntary compliance with laws.

Many constraints have limited full implementation of the environmental laws enacted since the early 1980s, including inadequate budgets, court challenges, interagency jurisdictional conflicts, executive cost-benefit reviews, and "neutral" administrative procedures that are vulnerable to manipulation by corporate interests (Adler and Lord 1991; Burns and Lynch 2004; Yeager 1991b). Regulatory agencies have often been unwilling or unable, for better or worse, to implement environmental crime laws fully, and judges have been reluctant to impose on environmental offenders the criminal penalties permitted by the law (Adler and Lord 1991; Cohen 1992; Shover and Routhe 2005). In the recent era, judges were also finding some constitutional problems with private claims pursued in environmental cases and were cutting back on these private lawsuits (Glaberson 1999a). On a practical level, environmental offenders have the resources to challenge unfavorable judgments; ideological concerns focus on imposing on corporate entities criminal sanctions for actions that may not have been intended, especially on the basis of indirect liability; and environmental harm is not always easily identifiable and measurable (Gray et al. 1998). The George W. Bush administration, responding to formidable lobbying by corporate interests, was easing up on the imposition of tough antipollution standards (Nader 2004; Seelye 2002a). This administration generally promoted development over the preservation of nature (*New York Times* 2005). A federal appeals court in June 2005 upheld the Bush administration's policy of allowing power plants greater flexibility in controlling air pollutant emissions (Janofsky 2005c). Environmentalists were alarmed by such policies, although this court also struck down some polluter-friendly loopholes.

In 1980, Congress established the "Superfund" through the Comprehensive Environmental Response, Compensation, and Liability Act (Burns and Lynch 2004). This fund collected taxes from corporations to pay for cleaning up sites damaged by toxic pollutants. By the early 1990s, it seemed evident that much money had been spent with little to show for it (Barnett 1993). By 1995, the corporate tax to fund the Superfund had expired, and by 2002, cleanup funds were largely exhausted (Seelye 2002b). Businesses had long complained about the Superfund tax. But the unwillingness of the George W. Bush administration to seek a reauthorization of the Superfund tax had two clear implications: Fewer sites would be cleaned up, and ordinary taxpayers would have to bear the burden of whatever cleanups occurred (Browner 2002). The prospects for effectively addressing the toxic waste site problem were not especially good. Above all, tension persists between the objective of providing a safe, clean environment and the economic concerns about the costs in terms of jobs and prices of tough environmental law enforcement.

The RICO Law

In 1970, as part of the Organized Crime Control Act, Congress enacted a special section on Racketeer-Influenced and Corrupt Organizations (RICO) to provide prosecutors with a more effective weapon for combating organized crime (Poulin 1990; Sacks et al. 2005). The *RICO law* prohibits acquisition, operation, or income from an "enterprise" (any individual, associated group, or corporation) through a "pattern" (two or more offenses within a 10-year period) of "racketeering activity," common-law crimes, including those prohibited by any state, that are punishable by a year or more in prison (Albanese 1991; Rhodes 1984).

This powerful prosecutorial tool broadens federal criminal jurisdiction to include violations of state law; allows for important exceptions to the statute of limitations; permits the introduction of a broad range of evidence to demonstrate "criminal association," even if this evidence would normally be excluded from consideration; and provides for substantial forfeiture of property and freezing of assets, including attorney's fees (Sacks et al. 2005; Poulin 1990). More specifically, individuals convicted under the RICO law face up to 20 years in prison, fines of up to $25,000, forfeiture of any interest in the enterprise involved, treble civil damages, and dissolution of the enterprise.

RICO was used with considerable, if not uniform, success against syndicated crime figures in the 1970s and 1980s. Unfortunately, those convicted under this law were frequently elderly syndicated crime leaders whose imprisonment led to violent confrontations between would-be successors. Critics have argued that the tough provisions of RICO have inspired an even higher level of crime syndicate infiltration of relatively safe legitimate business and that in the long run the public may be even more fully victimized by more sophisticated, larger-scale scams (Albanese 1991).

Other concerns about RICO are especially relevant to white collar crime. First, since its implementation, either the criminal or the civil provisions of RICO have been used most frequently against individuals and groups who do not fit the conventional image of organized crime, including aggressive unions, anti-abortion protesters, and marijuana growers (Poulin 1990; Brickey 1990). The single most common targets of RICO prosecutions and lawsuits have been white collar offenders involved in some form of commercial or financial fraud or dispute, tax evasion, embezzlement, or bribery (Poulin 1990; Rhodes 1984). However, RICO suits against tobacco companies and HMOs have failed (Sacks et al. 2005). Second, the federal courts, including the U.S. Supreme Court, have essentially upheld such broad applications of RICO and ruled that it is up to Congress to change the law if it believes it is being misapplied (Geary 2002; Mansnerus 1989; Mannino 1990). Nevertheless, the late Chief Justice William Rehnquist complained bitterly about the burden of dealing with a flood of these cases, labeling RICO as "very possibly the single worst piece of legislation on the books" (Poulin 1990: 859, 864).

The business community in particular has expressed outrage at being frequent RICO targets.

BOX 9.4 White Collar Crime Law and the Legal Curriculum

The development of much of white collar crime law is relatively recent, and white collar crime has been an especially dynamic area of law since the 1970s. The latest legal developments pertaining to substantive white collar crimes and relevant procedural issues are reviewed annually in *American Criminal Law Review*. Attention to white collar crime law has not traditionally been a specific focus of law school curricula and attendant casebooks, although this is beginning to change with the appearance of such books as Harry First's *Business Crime: Cases and Materials* (1990); Jerold Israel, Ellen Podgor, Paul Borman, and Peter J. Henning's *White Collar Crime: Law and Practice*, 2nd edition (2003); Ellen S. Podgor and Jerold H. Israel's *White Collar Crime in a Nutshell*, 3rd edition (2004); J. Kelly Strader's *Understanding White Collar Crime*,

2nd edition (2002); Pamela Bucy's *White Collar Crime: Cases and Materials* (1998); and Kathleen F. Brickey's *Corporate and White Collar Crime—Cases and Materials* (2002). Of course, selected white collar crime issues have been examined in standard law courses (and accompanying casebooks) concerning such broader matters as corporate law, securities regulations, taxation, and the like. The full-fledged integration of white collar crime law into the legal education curriculum is still in its infancy, but it seems likely that the massive coverage of Enron and other corporate cases in early 2000s will contribute to the expansion of attention to white collar crime in law schools. Law professors interested in white collar crime issues have established a useful White Collar Crime Prof blog at http://lawprofessors.typepad.com/whitecollarcrime_blog/.

A New York businessman who underpaid state sales taxes on retail gasoline sales was convicted under RICO, was forced to forfeit close to $5 million and was liable for a federal fine up to twice that amount, and received a two-year sentence (Poulin 1990). Princeton/Newport Partners, an investment partnership, was indicted on creating false long-term capital gains, with a $13-million tax write-off on false losses, and was forced to liquidate in the face of severe RICO penalties and forfeitures (Labaton 1989c). The judge in this case imposed brief sentences of three to six months and scaled down a jury forfeiture award from $3.8 million to $1.5 million.

Critics of RICO, especially as applied to white collar crime offenders, contend that its broad language grants the state too much discretionary leeway; that it was never intended that businesspeople would be prosecuted as "racketeers"; that the forfeiture provisions are draconian, punitive, and out of proportion to the offenses; that the civil RICO suits are quasi-criminal sanctions that do not adequately differentiate between conduct requiring compensation and conduct requiring condemnation; that defense attorneys can easily be overwhelmed by the government's documentation and cannot effectively advise their clients; and that

businesspeople may be frightened into making deals to settle their case before trial and may have to liquidate or lose their businesses, with innocent consumers and customers bearing the costs (Brickey 1990; Geary 2002; Schneider 2005c).

In the early 1990s, business interests and other critics of RICO put pressure on Congress to amend the law to sharply limit its application to white collar crime (Labaton 1991). But these efforts failed; indeed, the highest proportion (48 percent) of RICO cases in recent years have been white collar cases (Schneider 2005c). The ongoing controversy over RICO usefully compels us to focus on the relationship between white collar crime and organized crime and the differences—if any—between "banksters" and mobsters. Box 9.4 offers an overview of white collar crime's treatment in law school curricula.

CIVIL AND CRIMINAL LAW AND WHITE COLLAR CRIME

Civil law has played a much larger role in responding to white collar "crime" than to conventional crime. In principle, *civil law* (tort) concerns itself with private, individual harms and objective responsibility, whereas criminal law focuses on public, social harms and morally culpable conduct (Hall 1943; Friedrichs 2006). Still, the line of demarcation between the private and the public is often quite blurred, especially when it concerns the harms caused by corporations, businesses, and professionals.

The distinction between civil and criminal law emerged quite clearly in 14th- and 15th-century England. It was well established by the middle of the 18th century when the English jurist William Blackstone produced his celebrated commentary on the common law (Mann 1992b). Columbia University law professor John Coffee Jr. (1992), who observed that criminal laws are legislative acts whereas the civil law is largely created by judges, identified several other differences between criminal and civil law: (1) the role of intent is greater in criminal law; (2) criminal law focuses on the creation of risk rather than on actual harm; (3) criminal law insists on greater evidentiary certainty and is less tolerant of procedural informality; (4) criminal law relies on public enforcement (although this is tempered by prosecutorial discretion); and (5) criminal law involves the deliberate imposition of punishment and the maximization of stigma and censure. Criminal sanctions are intended to express society's outrage over harmful behavior by both punishing morally blameworthy parties and deterring such conduct among others (Spurgeon and Fagan 1981); civil actions focus mainly on compensating an injured party for some measurable harm suffered.

Conversely, it is possible to emphasize the similarities between criminal and civil law, or between crimes and torts. Blum-West and Carter (1983) identified an enormous overlap between criminal and civil law in terms of rules of liability, moral judgments, and types of behavior involved. Furthermore, government prosecutors and administrative agencies initiate civil actions against white collar offenders. Strictly speaking, criminal prosecution is exclusively the prerogative of the government, but in some circumstances, such as those provided by RICO, private parties can "prosecute" civilly criminal wrongs and seek severe punitive sanctions (Mann 1992b). In the view that de-emphasizes the differences between civil and criminal law, both types of law require intent and have somewhat parallel rules for establishing culpability, although ordinary negligence is sufficient in tort cases, whereas most state laws require more for establishing criminal liability. Even if moral condemnation is generally greater for crimes than for torts, it is not uniformly so. Contrary to conventional rhetoric, tort sanctions are often punitive. The public/private interest distinction is artificial because both types of interest are typically involved in criminal and civil cases. Blum-West and Carter (1983) accordingly argued that we should not confuse the study of harmful behavior with the study of processes whereby some troublesome behaviors are classified as crime and others as tort.

Even though the lines of demarcation between civil and criminal law in their responses to white collar offenses have greatly eroded, ongoing debate centers on whether the civil law is encroaching more on criminal law concerns or whether the criminal law is encroaching on civil and regulatory areas (Coffee 1992). Those who view the matter of white collar crime primarily in moralistic terms are likely to favor a criminal law approach, which emphasizes the wrongfulness of white collar offenses and their equivalence with conventional crime. Others view the white collar crime issue more pragmatically, with an emphasis on effectively limiting the harmful consequences of such activity, and they are likely to be more favorably disposed toward the civil law approach. Former U.S. Attorney General Richard Thornburgh (2000) argued that civil lawsuits are a more efficient and flexible way of addressing product liability than criminal prosecution. Civil lawsuits are certain to remain a major element in the response to white collar wrongdoing.

LAW, CORPORATIONS, AND THE CONCEPT OF CRIMINAL LIABILITY

A central issue for a system of criminal law is the imputation of criminal liability or responsibility. Historically, the notion of criminal liability has

---

B O X 9.5 **Law Professor Stuart Green and the Moral Theory of White Collar Crime**

Although some law professors have now produced case books on white collar crime (see Box 9.4), relatively few have been interested in the broader issues pertaining to such crime. Stuart Green, L. B. Porterie Professor of Law at Louisiana State University, is an exception to this proposition. In a series of law review articles—and a forthcoming book—Green has explored the alleged overcriminalization of regulatory offenses, demonstrating their moral complexity (Green 1997); how moral concepts inform the law of perjury, fraud, and false statements (Green 2001); the various paradoxes that arise in connection with the application of criminal sanctions to the protection of intellectual property rights (e.g., in connection with allegations of plagiarism) (Green 2002); the tradi-

tional disconnect between notions of cheating and of crime, and the increasing incorporation of the moral notion of cheating in white collar crime law (Green 2003); the invocation of the term *white collar crime* within the law, as well as the complex moral and conceptual issues that arise in connection with white collar crime in relation to law (Green 2004); the legal status of threats made by Enron's Chief Financial Officer in connection with investment partnerships he set up (Green 2005a); and the moral content of such acts as obstruction of justice, contempt, and misprision of felony (Green 2005b). White collar crime issues bring into especially sharp relief some of the most complex challenges with which our system of law must contend.

---

been principally associated with "natural persons," although originally it seems to have referred to groups rather than individuals and implied an external relationship between the offense and the responsible party rather than a state of mind (Lilly and Ball 1982). The notion of an individual capable of forming criminal intent, or *mens rea*, developed as a key element in the legal conception of crime; moral responsibility was imputed to the individual. In the modern, Anglo-American tradition, the natural person is assumed to be capable of making voluntary choices for which he or she must be held responsible, unless some relevant "excusing condition" (e.g., youth or insanity) is present. A vast wealth of social science and behavioral research over the past century or so has identified the many ways in which human behavior is powerfully influenced—some would argue, absolutely determined—by factors ranging from genetic inheritance to early childhood experiences to situational peer pressures (some implications of this research are explored in Chapter 8). Individual white collar crime offenders are generally assumed to have willfully and voluntarily engaged in illegal behavior, although they may be better positioned than conventional offenders to invoke excusing conditions. It seems paradoxical that disadvantaged members

of society, who have limited opportunities and experience many harmful pressures, have more often suffered from the consequences of imputation of criminal liability than have privileged members of society, who have a much wider range of choices. In assessing the level of culpability of individual white collar offenders, some judges and jurors may hold them to a higher standard than conventional offenders, whereas others may empathize more readily with pressures that may have encouraged the criminal conduct. (See Box 9.5 for a review of one law professor's approach to white collar crime).

Corporate Criminal Liability

The question of whether corporations, as opposed to the individual personnel of corporations, should be held responsible for illegal acts has been a contentious issue in our legal history (Geis 2005b; Geis and DiMento 2002). Even the appropriate legal meaning of a corporation has been a matter of long-standing debate. Alternative views center on whether a corporation is an entity with an existence separate from shareholders and other participants or is simply an aggregation of natural individuals; whether it is an artificial creation of state law or a natural product of private initiative; and whether its activities have broad social and political ramifications that justify a substantial body of corporate law or primarily involve private relations between shareholders and managers, with these relations being the proper focus of the law (Millon 1990). In the most recent era, a movement toward imposing corporate criminal liability has generally intensified (DiMento, Geis, and Gelfand 2000–2001; Gobert and Punch 2003). (See Box 9.6 for a discussion of the status of corporate criminal responsibility in countries other than the United States.)

Corporate criminal liability is largely a 20th-century phenomenon. Under the common law tradition, a corporation could not face criminal charges; until the 15th century, in fact, the law recognized only "natural persons" (Coleman 1982). In the Anglo-American tradition, a recognition of *juristic persons* has only gradually emerged since the 11th century, with the breakdown of the hierarchical structure of feudal societies. Churches came to be recognized as entities independent of landowners who built them, towns began to assume distinctive rights and responsibilities, and the notion of "the Crown" was differentiated from the personhood of the monarch (Coleman 1982). The legal construct of a "trust" as a means of holding and passing on land separate from all the restrictions of traditional laws of inheritance and taxation also emerged during the medieval period. New corporations were formed to supervise the exploration and settlement of the colonies. In America, corporations grew rapidly with the establishment of the new republic because states were eager to attract them and shaped their laws in ways that facilitated their charters.

Although legal historians disagree somewhat on this matter, it appears that corporations have been held civilly liable, at least up to a point, for the harm they caused since early in their development; the notion of corporate criminal liability developed much more slowly (Belbot 1993; Bernard 1984). One seminal root of corporate civil and criminal liability was the ancient common-law doctrine that masters had legal responsibility for the wrongful acts of their servants.

Through at least the middle of the 18th century, English legal authorities held that private cor-

porations could not form criminal intent and could not be indicted or held directly responsible for crimes, although their members could be (Coffee 1983; Geis and DiMento 2003). The doctrine of *ultra vires* held that corporate powers are limited to what is authorized by the corporate charter, and thus the corporation could not be held responsible for executive actions not so authorized (Millon 1990). Accordingly, for much of history, a corporation could avoid liability by denying that harmful acts could be blamed on it because its corporate charter did not authorize them. Conversely, managers of corporations came to recognize that it was in their interest that the corporations—not themselves—assume liability for any harm done (Stone 1975). During the 19th century, it became increasingly apparent that the law must more clearly impute liability for the growing range of harms emanating from corporate growth. Box 9.6 compares the development of corporate criminality liability in several legal systems.

In Great Britain and the United States alike, railroads were held criminally responsible for harmful actions in the 19th century, but the notion of corporate criminal intent was not clearly recognized by the U.S. Supreme Court until *New York Central and Hudson River Railroad Co. v. U.S.* (1909), in which the railroad had violated the 1903 Elkins Act prohibiting the granting of rebates in interstate commerce (Coffee 1983; Geis 2005b). The Elkins Act, which amended previous prohibitions on railway rebates, was widely supported by the railroads because it could benefit them all by deterring selective rate cutting for big shippers (First 1990). One of the provisions of the Elkins Act was that rail executives would not be liable to jail sentences, as it was thought that such liability would inhibit them from testifying against each other. But the New York Central decision paved the way for applying legislative statutes directed at persons to corporations as well, so that by 1917, in *State v. Lehigh Valley Railroad Co.*, the Court accepted the long-resisted notion that a corporation could be held directly liable for a criminal charge of manslaughter (Coffee 1983; Parisi 1984).

B O X 9.6   A Comparative Perspective on Corporate Criminal Responsibility

The doctrine of holding corporations criminally responsible did not develop in civil law countries. In countries with a civil law system, the corporation was seen as an aggregate of individuals, precluding the notion of a juristic person; the tradition of judicial interpretation in common-law countries, which played a central role in the extension of criminal law liability to corporations, did not exist in civil law countries (Bernard 1984; Lederman 1985). In a parallel vein, Braithwaite and Fisse (1985) noted the paradoxical fact that even though Japan has a collectivist culture, Japanese law emphasizes individual responsibility for organizational crimes, whereas law in the United States, with an individualistic culture, allows for corporate responsibility for such crime. Altogether, the assignment of responsibility for corporate misconduct is complex. In a study in the United States, Russia, and Japan, some variations in such assignment were found between citizens of different countries, with Russians less likely to blame corporations than Americans or Japanese (Sanders and Hamilton 1997). Corporations were judged most responsible for wrongdoing when superior officers were judged most responsible.

The criminal liability of a corporation for the actions of its employees, or "agents," has come to be based on two major theories. The *imputation theory* holds that the corporation is liable for the intent and acts of its employees (generally excluding acts intended to benefit the employee only), on any level in the corporate hierarchy; the *identification theory* holds that liability is direct insofar as corporate actors are acting on behalf of the corporation (Parisi 1984; Walt and Laufer 1991). On somewhat parallel grounds, corporations have been held criminally liable for the conduct of their subsidiaries; for example, in 1990 the Exxon Corporation was successfully prosecuted for the conduct of a subsidiary, Exxon Shipping Company (Iracola 1995).

The imputation theory, the older and more widely adopted federal criminal law view, is known more specifically as the *respondeat superior rule* (Bucy 2002; Lederman 1985). Originally developed in tort law, this rule ascribes corporate criminal responsibility when a corporate agent (1) has committed a crime, (2) is acting within the scope of his or her authority, and (3) has the intent to benefit the corporation (Coffee 1983; Drew and Clark 2005). To obtain a conviction, a prosecutor need not necessarily identify the specific individuals responsible for the illegal act and need not demonstrate any actual benefit for the corporation from these acts, although as a practical matter it is more difficult to obtain a conviction in the absence of identifiable human culprits and material corporate benefits (Coffee 1983). One study of jurors' assessments of responsibility in business tort cases found that jurors preferred to deal with responsibility in terms of individual actors, but they also believed that corporations should be held to a higher level of responsibility than individuals (Hans and Lofquist 1992). This study found that a complex of factors, including the content of particular cases, influenced jurors' assessments of responsibility.

The *respondeat superior* doctrine, which is a rather controversial expansion of the notion of vicarious responsibility, is essentially a product of case law, not statutory law (Bucy 2002; Lederman 1985). In the case of *U.S. v. Hilton Hotels Corporation* (1972), the U.S. Court of Appeals established that a corporation can be held liable for employees' actions even when such actions are committed contrary to express corporate instructions. The rationale for this principle is to prevent corporations from immunizing themselves from liability by *official* (as opposed to actual) prohibitions on illegal actions (First 1990; Coffee 1983).

The identification theory was advanced by the Model Penal Code and has been adopted by some state legislatures and courts (Friedlander 1990; Walt and Laufer 1991). If the corporation is to be held liable, identification theory requires proof of higher authority, specifically when common-law crimes are involved (First 1990; Walt and Laufer 1991). Under this theory, the practical challenge for prosecutors is to establish that the corporate actors who initiated or carried out the illegal activity were at a high enough level in the corporate hierarchy to be said to be acting for the corporation (Benjamin and Bronstein 1987; Drew and Clark 2005). The corporation is exonerated if a high-level managerial employee took specific steps ("due diligence") to prevent the commission of the illegal activity (Walt and Laufer 1991). Different states have adopted different criteria for establishing which offenses and which managerial employees are included in the codes.

Some commentators have adopted a third theory of corporate criminal liability, arguing that criminal intent can be imposed on a corporation when a corporate "personality" or "ethos" advances procedures and practices that either promote or fail to prevent illegal activities (Fisse 1991; Foerschler 1990; Friedlander 1990). To date, this view has not been adopted by lawmaking bodies and courts.

Corporate Personhood and Corporate Decision Making

Just as modern law in the Anglo-American tradition has assigned criminal responsibility to the corporation, it has also accorded to corporations most if not all of the constitutional rights guaranteed to "natural persons" (Mitchell 2001; Nader and Mayer 1988). The concept of *corporation* encompasses both vast entities with state-like power and resources and modest entities that are effectively the alter ego of an individual or a small group of individuals (Flynn 1987). Some commentators call for stripping all corporations, which are goal-directed entities, of rights enjoyed by natural persons, perhaps by a constitutional amendment (Benjamin and Bronstein 1987; Nader and Mayer 1988). Corporations have rather hypocritically sought formal recognition as "persons" entitled to constitutional protections while seeking to avoid being criminally

sanctioned in the manner of "natural persons" (Barrile 1993b; Mitchell 2001). Corporate status as a "juristic person" has significantly benefited corporations even while it has imputed criminal responsibility to them.

The legal paradigms for the treatment of corporations have tended to be divided between a holistic view of the corporation as analogous to a person and the atomistic view of the corporation as an aggregate of individuals (Dan-Cohen 1992). Perhaps the most commonly embraced holistic view of the corporation equates it with the classic "economic man," a rational actor that seeks to maximize profit (First 1990; Metzger and Schwenk 1990). Still, it has been argued that such views are wrong insofar as they fail to capture the complex nature of corporations; an alternative view looks to organizational theory to produce a true picture of the dynamics of corporate decision making (Foerschler 1990). The economics Nobel Prize winner Herbert Simon, for example, has long claimed that the rational-actor model does not remotely describe processes of human decision making in complex situations; in particular, the "risky shift" phenomenon suggests that collective corporate decision making may result in less rational and riskier choices than individual corporate actors would make (Metzger and Schwenk 1990). An organizational process model of corporate decision making emphasizes task specialization, the diffusion of responsibility within an organization, and *bounded rationality*, the search for "good-enough" solutions as opposed to ideal solutions. The bureaucratic politics model of such decision making sees individual decisions as leading to coalitions that produce corporate decisions through a process of negotiation (Foerschler 1990; First 1990). These views of corporate decision making lend support to the position that corporations institutionalize certain practices that render them liable for their criminal acts in ways that cannot be equated either with individual acts or with the sum total of a large number of individual acts.

Foerschler (1990) proposed the following criteria for determining corporate intent: (1) Did a corporate practice or policy violate the law?

B O X　9.7　**The Corporate Criminal Liability Controversy**

An enduring controversy concerns the question of whether the imputation of corporate criminal liability is either sensible or just. Those who favor the doctrine of corporate criminal liability claim it is a necessary means of providing incentives for corporate compliance with the law and deterring corporate misconduct. Corporate processes affect decision making within corporations, this side contends. In addition, criminal procedure rules can be viewed as favoring a targeting of the corporate entity, corporations can be transformed more easily than individuals, and corporations have more assets to address wrongdoing than do individuals.

Those who oppose the doctrine of corporate criminal liability claim that corporations cannot have *mens rea*, that it is unfair to punish innocent parties (e.g., shareholders, employees), and that the doctrine protects guilty individuals. They also argue that civil liability is more efficient and effective, and that the criminal liability doctrine does not work (Bucy 2002;

DiMento et al. 2000–2001; Poling and White 2001). They claim it is difficult to demonstrate that corporate criminal liability is ultimately more effective than individual criminal liability.

On balance, it would seem to be a mistake to eliminate corporate criminal liability. Only if the corporation itself is liable will it have powerful enough incentives to establish appropriate preventive, disciplinary, and reward policies to minimize executive and employee involvement in criminal conduct. If the corporation is not criminally liable, executives are encouraged to violate or fail to comply with laws in ways that are beneficial to the corporation. At the same time, it would be helpful to have more empirical evidence on the question of whether the doctrine of corporate criminal liability deters corporate crime (Geis and DiMento 2003). To date, the empirical literature on this question is remarkably thin.

---

(2) Was it reasonably foreseeable that the corporate practice or policy would result in a corporate agent's violation of the law? (3) Did the corporation adopt a corporate agent's violation of the law? Whether or not we embrace this model for the assignment of corporate criminal liability, we can agree that the law should adapt itself to the realities of corporate decision making. Box 9.7 recaps continued debate over corporate criminal liability.

LAW AND THE SOCIAL CONTROL
OF WHITE COLLAR CRIME,
IN SUM

In this chapter, we have examined some basic propositions about white collar crime and law. Law is a product of a complex of forces, and no one-dimensional, simplistic explanation of the basis

of specific laws satisfactorily addresses its application to white collar crime. Lawmaking entities enjoy relative autonomy but tend to reflect the concerns of special interests. Laws directed at white collar crime may reflect normative or instrumental objectives, or some combination of the two. Further, tensions often exist between short-term needs (e.g., business prosperity) and long-term needs (e.g., the legitimation of the system).

In the realm of white collar crime laws, the objectives of the state and the business world may well clash, and conflicts often arise among segments of the business or professional communities. Even if powerful private interests are generally unable to dictate what laws should be made, they disproportionately influence lawmaking. Because many segments of the business or professional communities benefit from the existence, and sometimes from the enforcement, of white collar crime laws made on many different governmental levels, the symbolic purpose of the law may outweigh its practical, formal purpose.

KEY TERMS

administrative law, 234

antitrust law, 226

bounded rationality, 246

case law, 233

civil law (tort), 241

constitutional law, 232

corporate criminal liability, 244

criminal law (crime), 226

dialectical perspective, 230

executive lawmaking, 234

identification theory, 245

imputation theory, 245

instrumentalist perspective, 228

juristic persons, 244

respondeat superior doctrine, 245

RICO law, 240

social control, 225

structuralist perspective, 229

trusts, 236

ultra vires doctrine, 244

DISCUSSION QUESTIONS

1. What are some of the principal challenges involved in the social control of white collar crime? Which forms of social control are most likely to be effective in controlling white collar crime? What are some possible limitations of law as a means of controlling white collar crime?

2. Discuss some of the principal historical developments in the origins and evolution of white collar crime law. Which factors promoted and which factors hindered the development of white collar crime law in the United States? How does the dialectical perspective on lawmaking contribute to one's understanding of this development?

3. Identify the principal sources of lawmaking pertaining to white collar crime and the specific influences involved in this lawmaking process. What are the distinctive features of administrative lawmaking? Discuss the key

developments for one of the following areas of white collar crime law: antitrust law, occupational safety and health law, environmental protection law, or RICO law.

4. What are the essential differences and similarities between civil and criminal law in relation to white collar crime? What have the principal trends been in terms of a civil and criminal law response to such crime? Why, specifically, is it more appropriate to rely upon either civil or criminal law as a means of dealing with white collar crime?

5. What is the basic significance of the issue of criminal liability as it relates to white collar crime? Discuss the principal approaches to the matter of corporate criminal liability and the main arguments for and against corporate criminal liability. How do corporations benefit from and pay a price for having "personhood" attributed to them?

10

Policing and Regulating White Collar Crime

By any measure, the proportion of apparent white collar crimes that are officially investigated and prosecuted is lower than for conventional crime. In the simplest terms, what occurs in the street is more visible and more easily investigated than what occurs "in the suite" (i.e., in corporate and professional offices). In this chapter, we examine the process of policing white collar crime, beginning with the most public form of policing by the criminal justice system and moving to the least official and visible form, self-policing.

Two important ways in which white collar crime differs from conventional crime are the broad range of agencies involved in policing it and the much larger role of institutions and entities outside the criminal justice system. Much policing of white collar crime is handled by public regulatory agencies and various private policing agencies or entities. Self-policing plays a much larger role in the response to white collar crime than it does in the realm of conventional crime. Furthermore, although potential and actual white collar offenders have some influence over the process of policing these crimes, they do not entirely control it. At least in the public sector, policing and regulatory agencies have some degree of autonomy. For various reasons, they will sometimes take aggressive action against corporate, business, and professional offenders.

CRIMINAL JUSTICE SYSTEM POLICING: LAW ENFORCEMENT

Historically, white collar crime has not been a principal concern of law enforcement agencies. For many forms of white collar crime, the police have lacked jurisdiction, expertise, and resources. In some countries, such as Israel and Finland, the police have much broader jurisdictional powers to investigate a wide range of white collar crimes, or have been more strongly encouraged to investigate it, than is the case in the United States (Alvesalo 2002; Stotland 1981). White collar crime investigative units have been established in some U.S. urban police departments (Stotland 1982). Local police typically do not have the resources to address complex white collar crime cases (Schlegel 2000), though they are well positioned to play a key role in the pursuit of certain categories, including consumer fraud, fraudulent insurance claims, and local environmental safety violations. Howard E. Williams (1997), a lieutenant with the Austin, Texas police department who specializes in white collar crime, has produced a guide for local officers investigating such cases. Among other matters, this volume reviews techniques of auditing, suspect interviews, specific forms of evidence in white collar crime cases, methods to prove illicit transactions, and preparation of investigative reports in white collar crime cases. In the current era, local police and sheriff's departments must increasingly respond to complaints of Internet fraud (Burns et al. 2004). Traditionally, local law enforcement agencies have had neither the expertise nor the resources to address this form of white collar crime, but increasingly they recognize the need to develop competencies in this area.

Many factors limit substantial involvement of conventional police forces in white collar crime cases. The principal training of police personnel is oriented toward conventional crime; police officers are more likely to be attracted to the more dramatic forms of street crime than to white collar crime. Indeed, police officers who investigate white collar crime may be disparaged by other police officers who deal with "real" crime (Alvesalo 2002).

White collar crime cases are especially likely to require a greater investment of time than typical conventional crime cases with a lower probability of a successful resolution (Schlegel 2000). Because the investigation of such crime calls for forms of competence and expertise, such as accounting knowledge, that traditional policing agencies often lack, the chances of failure and of being perceived as incompetent are therefore considerably higher. It has been traditionally difficult for police to differentiate between legal and illegal business practices. To combat this problem, police must closely examine legal codes concerning business practices and transactions. As a police investigator notes, "In traditional crime investigations, the police are searching for the *criminal*, but in cases of white collar crime they are searching for the *crime*" (Alvesalo 2002: 158).

Public and political pressure are less likely to be intense for arrests for white collar crime than for predatory violence or drug dealing. Indeed, political pressure is more likely to be exerted in blocking or derailing white collar crime investigations than in conventional crime cases, and the police can operate effectively against white collar crime only to the extent that they are relatively free of political influence (Stotland 1981). Finally, media images of the consequences of serial murders and other such crimes are more likely to generate powerful and immediate public outrage and fear than are any images relating to most white collar crime.

State and Federal Enforcement Agencies

Because of the complex, often interjurisdictional character of much white collar crime, federal agencies have played a much larger role in the investigation of these crimes than have local police agencies. The role of the state police in the investigation of white collar crime has been relatively limited. State police agencies were established in a number of states in the early 20th century, in part to restore order in mining communities and other areas of labor unrest (Johnson 1981; Lynch, Michalowski, and Groves 2000). In at least some states, they apparently operated with a pro-business bias and may have been accessories to corporate crimes against labor.

During the course of the 20th century, many states established their own police forces. In the recent era, state police agencies have provided important support services to local police agencies and have investigated crimes occurring outside local jurisdictions, but typically these crimes have not been white collar crimes. About two thirds of the states have established white collar crime units or planned to do so (Schlegel 2000). With the help of the National White Collar Crime Center, state law enforcement agencies are able to have information stored in a database for easy access, resulting in state law enforcement information sharing (National White Collar Crime Center 2005).

If urban police forces are the principal public policing agency responding to street crime, then federal policing agencies make the most substantial response to white collar crime. Altogether, more than two dozen federal agencies have investigative jurisdiction over white collar crime, including governmental corruption cases (Pence 1986; Schlegel 2000); the lines of jurisdiction among these agencies are not sharply drawn. Furthermore, the prosecutorial arm of the federal government often engages in investigative inquiry on its own. The principal federal investigative agencies are the Federal Bureau of Investigation (FBI), the Inspectors General, the U.S. Postal Inspection Service, the U.S. Secret Service, the U.S. Customs Service, and the Internal Revenue Service Criminal Investigative Division.

The federal investigative agencies are charged with bringing the most serious cases—those in which criminal prosecution is warranted—to the attention of the U.S. Department of Justice or one of the 94 U.S. Attorneys with offices in all 50 states and U.S. territories. Only the Department of Justice or a U.S. Attorney can initiate a federal criminal prosecution.

Several sections of the Department of Justice Criminal Division investigate and supervise the prosecution of white collar crime, most notably the Fraud Section and the Public Integrity Section. The Fraud Section acts as a "rapid response team, investigating and prosecuting complex white collar crime cases throughout the country"; the Public Integrity Section oversees the federal effort to address governmental corruption of public officials (U.S. Department of Justice 2005). The Organized Crime and Racketeering Section might also become involved in white collar crime investigations. In addition to the Criminal Division, several other Justice Department divisions pursue white collar crime cases, including the Tax Division, the Land and Natural Resources Division, the Antitrust Division, the Civil Rights Division, and the Civil Division.

Other governmental institutions that play a role in the investigation of some form of white collar crime, especially internal governmental corruption, include the General Accounting Office (GAO), which audits executive branch spending; the Merit Systems Protection Board, which investigates and pursues whistle-blower complaints; and the Independent Prosecutor (or Counsel), who investigates and prosecutes criminal acts of high-level governmental officials (Mollenhoff 1988). The Freedom of Information Act, which was passed in 1966 and amended in 1974, has also played a role in uncovering illicit governmental activity in providing a means of access to many governmental records.

The FBI

The FBI grew from a small, somewhat corrupt Justice Department division into one of the world's largest, most efficient, and most highly regarded policing agencies during the almost 50-year reign (1924–1972) of J. Edgar Hoover. During this period, however, white collar crime (with the exception, perhaps, of bank fraud and embezzlement) was not the focus of much FBI attention.

Hoover and his associates, who had the typical biases of conservative, white, middle-class males of their time, were principally concerned with highly visible forms of professional crime, such as bank robbery and kidnapping, and the activities of alleged subversives (Kelly 2002; Theoharis 2004). Hoover was a master of good public relations, and he preferred to allocate FBI resources to crimes that were relatively easy to investigate and most likely to produce impressive enforcement statistics; thus, the investigation of complex white collar crimes, for which the outcome is uncertain, was not a top priority (Poveda 1990). In the final two years of the Hoover regime, white collar crime was not even mentioned in the FBI annual reports, although accounting and fraud cases were included under "other criminal investigations" (Poveda 1990). Even though a good deal of information about corrupt and improper dealings of various politicians and businesspeople came to Hoover's attention, he preferred maintaining confidential files on this information for his own purposes over referring it for prosecution. It is widely believed that no president in Hoover's later years was prepared either to force him to resign or fire him because he was privy to too much damaging information.

Hoover's death in 1972 coincided with declining confidence in traditional institutions such as government and big business and with the emergence of the Watergate affair. At least partly in response to these developments, Hoover's successors as FBI director claimed that they made white collar crime a higher priority (Kelly 2002; Poveda 1990). But FBI claims of allocating greater resources to white collar crime investigations have been questioned and largely attributed to reclassifying activities (Simon and Swart 1984).

The *Abscam* case, involving an FBI "sting" operation in which seven members of Congress were videotaped accepting bribes from "sheiks," was a widely publicized but controversial (on grounds of entrapment) initiative against corruption (Marx 1991). During the Reagan administration in the 1980s, protecting the government and major financial institutions from fraud took precedence over protecting consumers and taxpayers from the harmful activities of corporations and government agencies (Poveda 1990). By the late 1980s and early 1990s, 1,600 FBI agents were detailed to investigate various forms of white collar and governmental crime, with S & L and health care frauds receiving increasing attention. FBI attention to white collar crime increased somewhat during the Clinton era of the 1990s, including the FBI investigation of the Clintons' suspect Whitewater land deal (Schlegel 2000; Stewart 1996). Following the attack on America on September 11, 2001, a certain proportion of FBI resources assigned to white-collar crime cases were shifted to the war on terrorism. But the FBI has also played some role in investigating the series of corporate scandals, beginning with the Enron case late in 2001 (Farrell 2003). Younger agents, with some sophisticated training in forensic accounting, took the lead in this investigation. In 2003, the FBI established a Corporate Fraud Hotline to make it easier for members of the public to report allegations of corporate fraud directly to the FBI (FBI 2003). The FBI's expertise in investigating such crime continues to evolve.

The Inspectors General

One response to the growth of attention to crime and corruption by and against governmental agencies was the creation by a 1978 congressional act of *Inspectors General* to be attached to a variety of government departments and agencies (e.g., Housing and Urban Development, the Veteran's Administration, and, as of 1982, the Defense Department).

The Inspectors General have been granted authority to conduct audits and investigations of departments or agencies to which they are attached (IGNet 2003). Even though Inspectors General are granted some autonomy and certain powers and are expected to report to the Attorney General and to Congress any internal wrongdoing that comes to their attention, it is not clear that they can root out internal corruption effectively because they are part of the department they are investigating. Nevertheless, in the wake of 9/11 the Inspector General's Office attached to the EPA reported that the agency, at the behest of the White House, had deceived New York City citizens about health risks associated with the dust and debris following the attack (Krugman 2003). The Inspector General offices are also empowered to ensure that the programs administered by their departments are not abused, and in this responsibility they have been more successful, obtaining a significant percentage of convictions resulting in millions of dollars in fines (U.S. President's Council on Integrity and Efficiency 1988). More specifically, Inspectors General have investigated submission of false records by contractors, bribery, and nepotism (Torres 1985). Many cases of health-related fraud investigated by this office are resolved with civil penalties and exclusions of those engaged in fraud from the department's programs for a period of time.

The U.S. Postal Inspection Service

White collar crime is far more likely to involve the use of the U.S. mail than is true of conventional crimes. The U.S. Postal Inspection Service is generally identified as the oldest federal law enforcement agency. Postal "surveyors" were appointed in the colonial postal system, and the inspection service was developed early in the 19th century. In 1872, Congress enacted a mail fraud statute in response to an epidemic of mail swindles that were beyond the jurisdictional reach of local prosecutors.

Since then, the U.S. Postal Inspection Service, which is charged with maintaining the overall security and integrity of the mail system, has played an important role in investigating white collar crimes that involve some use of the mail (Kahn 1973; U.S. Postal Inspection Service 2003). It employs 2,000 postal inspectors and operates five forensic laboratories. This investigative entity has jurisdiction over embezzlements, identity frauds, lotteries, mail frauds, money laundering, and workers compensation frauds involving a postal element, and it now has jurisdiction over electronic frauds as well. Clearly, many of these schemes are at the margins of occupational and professional crime and are accordingly forms of contrepreneurial white collar crime. Mail fraud charges have sometimes been effective in major white collar crime cases involving securities and banking deposits because mail-related evidence may be especially solid. Although the U.S. Postal Service can neither prosecute frauds nor officially mediate disputes concerning frauds, its investigation alone can deter such schemes, and it can refer cases for criminal prosecution.

The U.S. Secret Service, U.S. Customs Service, and U.S. Marshals Service

The Secret Service investigates white collar crimes that involve counterfeiting or forgery of any form of federal currency or warranted financial instrument (Long 2005; Pence 1986). The U.S. Customs Service investigates money laundering, falsified import or export documents, illegal product dumping, and foreign corrupt payment (Pence 1986). The specific roles of these agencies in white collar crime cases have been little studied to date.

The U.S. Marshals Service is assigned to various federal justice agencies and has both law enforcement and court-related duties (Jonas 2005; U.S. Department of Justice 2003; Walker 1983). Some 94 marshals and 2,500 deputies work out of 400 offices in the United States and its territories. One of their duties has been to pursue and capture fugitives from federal justice, which traditionally has meant offenders such as bank robbers. In more recent years, however, U.S. marshals have increasingly engaged in the pursuit of white collar crime fugitives (Copetas 1986). A cadre of marshals has been trained in crucial aspects of high finance (e.g., stocks, commodities, international banking) because their success in capturing high-profile white collar crime fugitives often depends on their successful penetration of a sophisticated, high-finance environment. In some cases, major offenders who have fled abroad have been lured by a ruse involving the prospect of a lucrative deal to a meeting with an undercover marshal in a location where they can be captured and returned to U.S. jurisdiction. U.S. marshals played a key role in bringing fugitive financier Martin Frankel (who defrauded insurance companies out of hundreds of millions of dollars) back from Germany, where he had fled (Haber 2001). They also took custody of some of his American property and arranged for its sale to compensate victims.

The Internal Revenue Service's Criminal Investigative Division

Representing a substantial aspect of white collar crime, tax frauds or misrepresentations involving corporations, businesses, and individuals are investigated by the Internal Revenue Service (IRS). Tax audits and investigations may precipitate investigations of other types of corporate and occupational crime when they uncover evidence of substantial income that cannot be ascribed to legitimate sources. It is virtually a given that financially oriented white collar crimes of all types, including political corruption, generate income that is not reported on tax returns. Sometimes demonstrating that people have illegally evaded taxes is the easiest way to convict those under investigation for other crimes. In one celebrated case in the 1970s, Vice President Spiro Agnew pleaded no contest to one count of tax evasion in a plea bargain arising out of the investigation of his acceptance of bribes.

Even though the IRS's Criminal Investigation Division now has fewer than 3,000 agents, down from 4,000 in the 1980s, its agents are widely regarded as particularly smart and capable (Burnham 1989; U.S. Treasury 2003). The IRS's investigative powers are especially broad, reflecting the high priority Congress has assigned to the efficient collection of taxes, and IRS agents can seize evidence much more easily than can FBI or Drug Enforcement

Administration investigators. Businesspeople may be intimidated into cooperating with a criminal investigation when confronted with the prospect of a tax audit (Burnham 1989). The IRS also claims to have the best white collar crime lab in the country (Hershey 1990b). This *forensic crime lab* has the capability of reconstructing shredded documents, enhancing voices on tapes, and analyzing altered documents, fingerprints, ink, paper, and polygraphs. It has played a role in exposing illegal trading at the Chicago futures market and fraudulent activity at the Bank of Credit and Commerce International (BCCI), among other major white collar crimes.

The overwhelming majority of tax cases investigated by the IRS are generally disposed of as civil matters (Burnham 1989). By some accounts, the IRS pursues too many low-level and politically selected cases and not enough major corporate tax fraud cases. Still, the fear or anticipation of an IRS tax fraud investigation must be a concern of a wide range of white collar offenders. Early in the 21st century, the IRS announced its intention of devoting more attention to enforcing the tax laws, especially against wealthy taxpayers, and to cooperating more fully with state agencies in tax fraud cases (Johnston 2002f, 2003a, 2003b). By this time, the IRS's auditing staff was 20 percent reduced from 1995, despite a significant growth in the number of tax returns. The IRS acknowledged that up to this point it was auditing far more returns of the working poor than of wealthy taxpayers; it also acknowledged that wealthy taxpayers were often cheating, especially through investments and partnerships, and sometimes with the connivance of abusive tax scheme promoters and accounting firms.

THE REGULATORY SYSTEM RESPONSE

Sutherland and other early students of white collar crime recognized that the dominant legal response to crimes by businesses was regulatory rather than penal (Thomas 1982). More broadly, regulation has become such a central feature of our economy that some commentators now characterize the economic system as one of "regulatory capitalism" (Levi-Faur 2005). Regulatory enforcement occurs in only a very small percentage of the cases in which it could be applied, and it has far less of the moral disgrace and stigma associated with the criminal justice system. The lines of demarcation among the criminal, civil, and regulatory justice systems are not always sharp, but the regulatory justice system has a lower profile and is less likely to involve an adversarial confrontation between two parties than are the criminal and civil justice systems.

Regulation has been broadly defined as any attempt by the government to control the behavior of citizens, corporations, or subgovernments, but there is no real consensus on its meaning. Regulation typically involves the imposition of official standards and rules on some form of productive human activity, including an enforcement mechanism and some type of sanctions (Kerwin 1990). It may involve rate setting, licensing, and financial disclosure requirements. A distinction is often made between *economic regulation*, which addresses market relations (e.g., securities, antitrust matters, interstate commerce) and attempts to ensure stability in this realm, and *social* (or protective) *regulation*, which addresses harmful consequences to workers, consumers, and citizens of productive activities (Croall 2001; Snider 1987; Yeager 1987). Although significant interaction occurs between these two forms of regulation, the social form in particular has expanded greatly since the early 1970s. Because social or protective regulation is much less likely than economic regulation to serve business interests and involves an inherent conflict between the regulator and the regulated, it met with far more resistance from business interests (Barnett 1990; Szasz 1984). Social regulation typically arises following a crisis, tragedy, or panic over some industrial condition or practice (Snider 1987). In response to public pressure, the government reluctantly develops regulatory agencies and rules, which the affected industry initially resists and then lobbies to limit in scope. Regulatory laws and enforcement practices are often weak at the outset but may become more potent over time.

There is no single theory or model of regulation. One approach views regulation primarily as a rational means of protecting the public interest (Frank and Lombness 1988; Posner 1984; Snider 1987). A second economic approach to regulation emphasizes a cost-benefit analysis oriented toward efficiency, although this perspective does not necessarily address the important question of how costs and benefits are defined (Meidinger 1987). A third, essentially political, approach views regulation primarily in terms of competing interests and the extension of power. Neo-Marxist versions of a political approach to regulation see it as a mechanism for maintaining elites' power and privileges. In this view, regulated agencies are dominated by the industries they are supposed to regulate.

The Origins and Evolution of Regulation

Some form of marketplace regulation was characteristic of even ancient civilizations. Throughout the feudal period in Europe, the market was heavily regulated on behalf of the crown. The American experience with regulation has been one of ongoing tension between calls for more or less regulation of a wide range of activities.

Some enthusiasm for congressional intervention in the marketplace existed in the earliest days of the American republic, with the Commerce clause (Article 1, Section 8) of the Constitution providing a basic point of departure for such regulation. Early regulation largely favored commercial and manufacturing interests, and such agencies as the Army Corps of Engineers and the Patent and Trademark Office were mainly intended to promote and encourage economic growth (Hall 1989; Kerwin 1990). Much of the 19th century was dominated by a laissez faire economic philosophy and involved little regulation in the modern sense. The Interstate Commerce Commission (ICC), which was established in 1887 to regulate the railroad industry, was the first federal regulatory agency specifically charged with overseeing potentially harmful corporate activity. The ICC, the first U.S. regulatory agency, was abolished in 1996 as no longer meeting the needs of the times (*New*

York Times 1996). Many of its remaining functions were transferred to the new National Surface Transportation Board.

During the latter part of the 19th century, various states attempted to regulate other business activities, including insurance agencies and employment practices for women and children (Hall 1989). Between 1890 and 1910, most states instituted occupational licensing for various occupations in addition to doctors, lawyers, and teachers, who had already been subjected to licensing laws (Hall 1989). Whereas the U.S. Supreme Court had previously upheld state regulatory legislation, in the late 19th century it became more conservative, adopted a broad interpretation of the rights of corporations, and severely curtailed state regulation (Hall 1989). Increasingly, an evolving national economy led to a transfer of the primary regulatory responsibility for larger corporations from the states to the federal government, although states have continued to play a major role in regulating smaller businesses and individual occupations.

Regulatory cycles have occurred throughout U.S. history. The first major period of federal regulatory expansion in the 20th century occurred during the Progressive era (1900–1914), when populist sentiments against the abuses of big business became sufficiently intense to promote significant government intervention in harmful corporate and occupational activities on behalf of the public interest. In reality, however, much of the regulation developed during this period was supported by and benefited the newly regulated big businesses.

A second major period of regulatory initiatives occurred during the New Deal era of the 1930s, at least in part inspired by the belief that the 1929 stock market crash and the economic depression that followed resulted from unregulated abuses by financiers and major corporations. In an effort to reestablish confidence in failed banks and the stock market, the Federal Home Loan Bank Board (FHLBB), the Federal Deposit Insurance Corporation (FDIC), and the Securities and Exchange Commission (SEC) were established during this period. These agencies were granted considerable autonomy, although this has hardly made them immune to either political pressures or lobbying by corporate and business interests.

A third major stage of expanding federal regulation began in the relatively affluent Great Society era of the 1960s and early 1970s. The predominantly social regulation of this period was responsive to a growing awareness of and organized protest over harmful corporate activities by consumers, environmentalists, and workers (Szasz 1984). The Consumer Product Safety Commission (CPSC), the Environmental Protection Agency (EPA), the Occupational Safety and Health Administration (OSHA), and the Mining Enforcement and Safety Administration were all established between 1970 and 1973. These agencies operate under more direct control of the executive branch than is true of the New Deal agencies, and they tend to be more directly responsive to the political agenda of the incumbent administration.

A reasonably high level of consensus on the desirability of government regulation in many new areas eroded in the second half of the 1970s. During this period, a deterioration of the economy occurred, resulting in rising inflation and declines in industrial productivity and U.S. competitiveness abroad. This enabled critics to much more effectively advance the argument that federal regulation had become oppressive and economically harmful.

In 1980, Ronald Reagan ran for president on a platform that was highly critical of a bloated government, and his election was a major factor in the deregulatory era of the 1980s. During this decade, regulation was scaled back or severely constrained in many areas, including consumer protection and antitrust, especially when politically dominated agencies were able to act on a discretionary basis (Burns and Lynch 2004; Schechter 1990). The 1980s is now quite widely viewed as a period during which enormous damage to the environment, the workplace, and financial institutions occurred, at least in good part due to excessive deregulation.

The Clinton administration during the 1990s was somewhat more favorably disposed toward regulation than the previous Republican administrations but was a disappointment to some supporters who hoped for more aggressive regulatory oversight. The George W. Bush administration was quite open about its hostility to aggressive regulation as applied to the business realm, favoring the appointment of heads of regulatory agencies with a pro-business outlook (Alvarez 2001; Schroeder and Steinzor 2005). Circumstances following exposure of wrongdoing at Enron and other corporations, which could in part be attributed to a relative absence of regulatory oversight, forced the administration to support some stronger regulatory initiatives in 2002 (Walczak et al. 2002). It remained to be seen whether the "New Century" era would eventually produce major new regulation (see Box 10.1).

The Creation and Operation of Federal Regulatory Agencies

Federal regulatory agencies are created by congressional action, specifically by an "enabling" statute. Some agencies are structured as executive branch departments and others as relatively independent entities, although it is not clear that the latter structure is less susceptible to political influence than the former (Frank and Lombness 1988).

Regulatory agencies are typically directed by a commission, the members of which are appointed by the president and subject to congressional confirmation. Because they are political appointees, these top agency administrators generally serve only during the term of their presidential sponsor; the managerial personnel below them, however, are more often civil servants who work for the agency over an extended period of time (Snider 1987). The managerial personnel of these agencies may be required to have appropriate technical expertise, although the degree of emphasis on such expertise and the autonomy of the agency vary.

Regulatory agencies have three basic functions: rule making, administration, and adjudication (Frank and Lombness 1988). Congress first delegated the power to make regulatory rules (for trade with Indians) to the president in 1790 and to other executive branch officials in 1813 (Bryner 1987). In 1911 (in *U.S. v. Grimaud*), the U.S. Supreme Court upheld the constitutionality of regulatory agency rule making (challenged on the claim that legislative powers cannot be delegated), ruling that the agencies are simply

BOX 10.1   The Contemporary Debate on Regulation

The general tendency in an expanding and increasingly complex society is for regulation to grow (Levi-Faur 2005; Niskanen 2002; Snider 1987). Today an ongoing debate centers on the moral rightness, desirability, and expediency of regulation. Is there too much or too little regulation? Are specific regulatory statutes, agencies, policies, and actions defensible? Opponents of regulation claim that it infringes on Americans' freedom and economic rights; that at least some regulated activity (e.g., insider trading) is essentially victimless; that regulation is economically inefficient; and that alternative processes exist for dealing with harmful activities that are organizationally more effective and more efficient than regulation and incorporate greater accountability and due process (Bardach and Kagan 1982; Dorn and Manne 1987; Niskanen 2002).

More specifically, governmental regulation has been accused of stifling innovation, accelerating inflation, increasing unemployment, and decreasing international competitiveness. In February 1995, the Republican-dominated House of Representatives approved legislation requiring regulatory agencies to base their rules and actions primarily on economic calculations as opposed to health-based factors (Cushman 1995). This legislation, which was opposed by the Clinton administration, called for an elaborate system of risk assessments and the justification of financial costs to industries that result from regulatory activity. A conservative Joint Center for Regulatory Studies was established in 1998 to monitor cost-benefit aspects of regulation (Passell 1998). Early in the 21st century, the massive costs of inadequate regulation of corporations and securities were quite evident, and concerns about environmental harm were also expanding.

The accurate measurement of the costs and benefits of regulation is complex. Various parties have incentives to inflate costs or conceal benefits, and there is no single way of interpreting either costs or benefits (Bardach and Kagan 1982; Hahn and Hird 1991; Snider 1987). It is especially difficult to measure some long-term benefits of regulation, particularly in matters of health, safety, and environmental protection.

Furthermore, there is no complete consensus on regulatory purposes and goals. A leftist or progressive critique has argued that the principal objective of regulatory agencies in a capitalist society is to maintain broad popular legitimation of the system while promoting corporate accumulation of profits (Henry 1991; Snider 1987); this is accomplished by adopting regulation that only symbolizes governmental oversight, because regulatory agency effectiveness is severely limited by inadequate budgets and pro-industry regulatory board members who develop specific rules that favor industry interests.

Proponents of regulation contend it is necessary in a complex society in which anticompetitive forces with economically undesirable consequences can develop unless the state intervenes, because individuals and communities have neither the necessary information nor the means to protect themselves from a wide range of directly harmful or threatening corporate and business activities (Tolchin and Tolchin 1983). Furthermore, corporations have an uncommon measure of power in shaping perceptions of risks because the capability of assessing both risk-related information and realistic options for self-protection are not equally distributed in society. Defenders of regulation argue that factors ranging from bad management to declining markets, not the great expansion of federal regulation in the 1970s, were the principal causes of the economic distress of that period (Tolchin and Tolchin 1983).

In this view, businesses actually benefit from federal regulation because without it they would likely face a much greater number of conflicting state regulations and more civil suits from workers, consumers, and citizens. Even if such regulation cannot be shown to "pay" in terms of short-term market efficiency, other interests, such as protecting workers and the environment, should take precedence. Many polls reveal general public support for regulatory protection, especially in health, safety, and environmental matters (Hahn and Hird 1991; Tolchin and Tolchin 1983). Altogether, the pro-regulatory argument holds that regulation prevents and deters much activity that could be labeled white collar crime and that in its absence much harm occurs.

filling in the details of legislative laws (Frank and Lombness 1988). Since that time, rather extensive rule making by various regulatory agencies has been promoted by other Supreme Court decisions and has been generally accepted, although not without recurrent challenges and complaints (Bryner 1987).

Regulatory rule making has been supported on the grounds that it allows for more flexible responses to developing circumstances and often requires specialized scientific or technical knowledge that resides in regulatory agencies. It also frees Congress of the enormous burden of passing thousands of rules and diminishes the political consequences of unpopular or contested rules (Clinard and Yeager 1980). On the other hand, the legislative oversight process for regulatory rule making has become quite cumbersome, and the rule-making process can be distorted by many political or other inappropriate considerations (Bryner 1987; Clinard and Yeager 1980). Industry and business lobbying groups, for example, often succeed in delaying for many years the implementation of new rules they find threatening to their interests.

In recent years, federal regulatory agencies have been issuing as many as 7,000 rules and regulations annually, as compared with some 300 public laws enacted annually by Congress (Bryner 1987; Weidenbaum 2000). Many of these rules are relatively minor. In contrast to criminal laws, regulatory rules are likely to be more ambiguous, tend to focus on the risk (not the occurrence) of harm, and are geared toward strict liability, not criminal intent.

The investigatory process of regulatory agencies typically involves a mixture of reactive and proactive strategies. More visible offenses, especially those involving formal complaints, generally take priority over the more complex, costly proactive investigations in which agencies take the initiative (Frank 1984b; Frank and Lombness 1988). Violations come to the attention of regulatory agencies from many sources, including consumer complaints, government investigations, congressional committee investigations, business competitors, the media, and employees (Clinard and Yeager 1980).

When it is determined that hearings are appropriate, regulatory agencies can act quite informally in many circumstances without observing due process guidelines. A fairly large body of law, codified in a basic way by the Administrative Procedure Act (APA) in 1946, governs formal agency proceedings (Moore, Magaldi, and Gray 1987). Agency hearings most typically take the form of quasi-criminal proceedings

and are less formal than regular court hearings and trials (Metzger, Mallor, Barnes, and Phillips 1986). An administrative judge or hearing examiner, independent of agency personnel, presides at these hearings. Defendants can have attorneys, but they are not entitled to a jury trial. Administrative judges and hearing examiners are empowered to impose various orders or sanctions on defendants, including cease-and-desist orders, which are equivalent to injunctions; special orders, such as directives intended to correct past conduct or product recalls; consent orders, or negotiations regarding certain actions; summary orders, such as prevention of the sale of food; and license suspension or revocation (Clinard and Yeager 1980; Frank and Lombness 1988).

Administrative agencies can impose some direct sanctions or civil fines. Cases may also be referred for criminal action or may lead to civil suits. Appeals from hearing decisions must first go through an internal agency appeal process and only then are eligible for appellate court review, although appellate courts have typically been reluctant to overturn agency decisions (Metzger et al. 1986). When agency decisions are overturned, the basis for such reversals is likely to be a determination that the decision was fundamentally arbitrary, capricious, or discriminatory; was not based on substantial evidence; violated applicable constitutional safeguards; or exceeded the statutory authority of the agency.

The Regulatory Agency's Philosophy: Compliance versus Deterrence

Regulatory enforcement and decision-making styles vary greatly in terms of regulatory philosophy, regulatory officials' assessments of compliance and noncompliance, and the actions officials take when they identify violations (Braithwaite 2000; Frank and Lombness 1988; Kagan 1989). Many cases are dropped because it is impractical to pursue them further; cases that are pursued may be dealt with by administrative action or civil action or referral for criminal prosecution (Clinard and Yeager 1980). In the 1970s in particular, federal regulatory agencies seemed more willing to support the application of criminal sanctions (Thomas 1982). But for regulatory agencies generally, the invocation of law has typically been a "last resort" (Hawkins 2002). At the outset of the 21st century, many constraints on referrals for criminal prosecution remained in place.

Regulatory personnel on all levels may be considered antagonists by the regulated and may act quite autonomously. A study by Frank (1984a) found that threats and assaults against regulatory inspectors were not uncommon; in this respect, regulatory inspectors may have more in common with traditional enforcement agents than is generally thought to be the case. On all levels, a vigorous enforcement approach to regulatory violations typically encounters both practical and philosophical constraints.

Regulatory agencies, then, confront a basic choice between emphasizing *compliance* (persuasion and cooperation) or *deterrence* (prosecution and punishment) (Braithwaite 2002b; Grabosky 1997; Gunningham 1987). In one conceptual scheme, regulatory agencies extend along a continuum from particularistic nonenforcers who engage in cooperative fostering of self-regulation to rulebook enforcers who emphasize command and control (Braithwaite, Walker, and Grabosky 1987). In another scheme, four regulatory agency policing styles have been characterized as service, watchman, legalistic, and free agent (Frank 1984b). The first two styles favor persuasion; the service style displays greater proactive initiative and technical competence than the watchman style, which is industry dominated and reactive. The legalistic and free agent styles are prosecutorial, but the legalistic is more mechanistic and formal whereas the free agent style is more informal and autonomous.

Traditionally, most regulatory personnel have probably thought of themselves less as a police force and more as governmental agents who seek to gain voluntary compliance with regulatory standards (Frank and Lombness 1988; Hawkins 2002). Regulatory agencies typically adopt some mixture of cooperative and punitive approaches (Barnett 1990; Haines 1997; Parker 2002). Informality and bargaining—and a norm of accommodation—take precedence over the strict implementation of legal rules for most regulatory agencies (Gunningham and Kagan 2005; Haines 1997). Still, the degree to which cooperative versus punitive strategies should be adopted has been heatedly debated.

Many interacting factors shape regulatory enforcement styles. These factors include the technical, economic, and legal problems encountered in regulatory implementation; features of the "task environment"; and the political environment of the regulatory agency (Kagan 1989). Regulatory laws vary considerably, for example, in their stringency, specificity, and objectives they are promoting. The regulatory task environment takes into account such concrete factors as the visibility of violations, the size and sophistication of the regulated enterprises, the costs of compliance, and the seriousness of risks of harm. Regulatory agencies often develop different strategies for different corporations, based on their perception of whether the corporation is basically good or bad (Scholz 1984). According to Kagan and Scholz (1983), regulatory personnel tend to categorize corporate offenders as amoral calculators, who break laws to maximize profit; political citizens, who disagree on principle with regulatory rules or laws; and the organizationally incompetent, whose lawbreaking is a product of mismanagement and incompetence. Circumstances (such as an industrial catastrophe), corporate pressures, and cultural values also influence an agency's orientation toward implementation of regulations (Meidinger 1987; Reichman 1992). The response of the regulated business and pressures from third parties may also play a role (Grabosky 1997).

Criticisms of Regulatory Agencies

Politics is often a potent element in the regulatory agency appointment process, at least on the higher levels of agency staffing. Perhaps unsurprisingly, the ideological commitments of agency administrators apparently have important impacts on agency policies and practices. During the Reagan administration, for example, the Environmental Protection Agency was accused of pursuing a conservative political agenda rather than focusing on environmental protection (Barnett 1990, 1993). Similar allegations surfaced during the early years of the George W. Bush administration (Browner 2002).

Although regulatory agencies have been criticized as too responsive to a political agenda, they have also been characterized as being run by appointed bureaucrats with too much power, too little competence, and too little accountability (Bryner 1987). Citing low government salaries in comparison to private sector pay, critics charge that regulatory agencies can recruit only mediocre employees. Industry representatives claim this leads to inefficient, even absurd, overregulation, whereas critics of industry claim that regulatory personnel are too easily misled and tend to underregulate. In one illustration of the latter concern, modestly compensated government accountants, accustomed to auditing rather straightforward home mortgages, were grossly misled and manipulated by the savings and loan fraudsters of the 1980s, resulting in losses in the billions of dollars.

Grabosky (1995a) has argued that regulation can be counterproductive, producing self-fulfilling prophecies, overdeterrence, fear generation, perverse incentives, and opportunity costs. Counterproductive regulation can be explained by bad science, bad planning, implementation failure, lack of coordination, and bad politics. Accordingly, the implementation of any regulation should be carefully considered through rigorous analysis, and some measure of skepticism is appropriate in response to new regulatory initiatives, Grabosky contended.

It is commonly conceded that regulatory agencies are greatly understaffed and underfunded. Public pressure for agency action is small relative to that for conventional crime, and business interests have traditionally lobbied for various limitations on agency powers and budgets (Clinard and Yeager 1980; Conklin 1977). OSHA, for example, has several hundred inspectors with responsibilities relating to several million businesses. The SEC has an annual budget in the tens of millions of dollars to police financial transactions in the hundreds of billions of dollars. These agencies increasingly rely on computers to uncover illegal activities (Reichman 1987), but this use of computer technology raises concerns about excessive government intrusion and invasions of privacy. By the mid-1990s, efforts to harness the SEC had accelerated, and in 1999, it experienced budget cuts (Henriques 1995; Morgenson 1999). The wave of corporate securities-related frauds of the early 2000s surely reflected in some part such constraints on the SEC. Even with significant budgetary increases, the SEC was likely to find itself overwhelmed by its responsibilities (*New York Times* 2002f). The Corporate Finance Division alone, for example, is expected to review the filings of 15,000 companies annually.

Even though small businesses may be intimidated by government regulators, there is good reason to believe that larger corporations often have an advantage over regulatory agencies. In view of the enormous economic consequences of many regulatory actions, the potential and reality of corruption are ever present. Corruption may be direct or indirect, ranging from outright bribes to prospects of post-government jobs with lucrative salaries (Conklin 1977; Snider 1987). The meat industry provides the salaries for inspectors; and this arrangement—however cost-effective for the government—is obviously conducive to corruption (Coleman 2002: 141). Regulatory personnel may also be compromised by their subservience to powerful political officials, who may in turn put pressure on them on behalf of corporate and individual benefactors. This pattern was exemplified in the "Keating Five" case involving five U.S. senators who pressured thrift regulators on behalf of Charles Keating, the head of a major thrift who had donated heavily to their political campaigns. Enron CEO Kenneth Lay, as a major donor to the political campaigns of George W. Bush and many other politicians, exercised tremendous influence over the selection of energy regulatory administrators, energy policy deliberations, and energy-related legislation (Bradley 2002; Van Natta and Banerjee 2002; Wayne 2002a).

Other Factors in Regulatory Response

Beyond the specific problem of agency capture (see Box 10.2), other factors affect the regulatory response to corporations. In a study of the EPA,

BOX 10.2   Agency Capture

The concept of *agency capture* has been variously applied to situations in which little disruption of industry profits occurs, the level of regulation is minimal and acceptable to industry, and enforcement of regulatory law is lenient (Frank and Lombness 1988). More specifically, suspicions of agency capture occur when regulatory agency officials with a pro-industry bias are appointed (or when such officials can anticipate lucrative private industry careers following their government service), and when various forms of inducement or influence (political or psychological) are evident.

Some studies have found that a significant percentage of agency appointees come from the industry they are now charged with regulating or that when these appointees leave government service they often take jobs in these industries (Conklin 1977; Freitag 1983). Other observers (see, for example, Ayres and Braithwaite 1991) have argued that agency capture, signified by close and cooperative relationships with regulated industries, cannot simply be equated with corruption and does not necessarily lead to corruption.

Some typical criteria for identifying agency capture have been criticized. Industry interests are not necessarily unified or in conflict with public interests, although nonindustry interests may not be adequately represented within regulatory agencies (Clinard and Yeager 1980; Frank and Lombness 1988). Regulatory agency policies that may appear to signify "capture" may instead reflect a distaste for confrontation and a view of social welfare shared by the regulators and the regulated alike (Ayres and Braithwaite 1991; Laufer 2002).

Despite such reservations about the notion of agency capture, regulatory agencies have in various instances been co-opted by the industries or businesses they are supposed to be regulating. Since at least the 1970s, several policies and strategies have been adopted to minimize the chances of agency capture, including prohibiting entry into regulated industries for a significant period of time after regulatory agency service, limiting agency discretion with more specific statutes, and promoting a professional identity for agency personnel (Frank and Lombness 1988). Such measures may have diminished but have not eliminated the problem of agency capture.

Yeager (1987) found evidence of a strong structural bias in the regulatory process that favors larger, more powerful corporations. This bias exists because only the larger corporations are likely to have the resources to afford technical and legal experts who can challenge and negotiate with agency experts, and only the larger corporations can easily absorb (with their large volume of production) the formidable costs of compliance with regulatory requirements. Regulatory agency inspectors tend to regard larger corporations as more responsible and less prone to violations than small corporations (Haines 1997; Lynxwiler, Shover, and Clelland 1983). As a practical matter, cases brought against large corporations are more complex and time consuming and are likely to confront the formidable political clout of such corporations (Snider 1987). The important implication of Yeager's (1987) analysis is that the regulatory system reflects, reproduces, or reinforces social inequalities of wealth and power; the structural bias toward large corporations leads to underestimations of the level of violations committed by such corporations in official sanctioning data.

Altogether, regulatory agencies often find themselves contending with countervailing pro-regulatory and anti-regulatory forces, and as a matter of survival they may steer a middle course between these forces (Haines 1997; Hawkins and Thomas 1983). A complex of factors, ranging from political pressures to professional pride to personal greed, is involved in the regulatory process.

Prominent Regulatory Agencies and Their Functions

In this section, we briefly examine the origins and functions of five important federal regulatory agencies: the FDA, FTC, SEC, EPA and OSHA, and the CPSC.

Food and Drug Administration (FDA) The FDA, which is presently a part of the Department of Health and Human Services, has its seminal origins in the Food and Drug Act of 1906, which mandated public protection from hazardous (adulterated or mislabeled) foods, drugs, cosmetics, and medical devices (*Federal Regulatory Directory* 1990; Hawthorne 2005). The FDA, originally the Federal Bureau of Chemistry, was given considerably broader powers following a dramatic incident in 1937, when more than 100 people died after taking a dose of an alleged cure-all medication, elixir of sulfanilamide (Clinard and Yeager 1980). Another equally dramatic incident in the early 1960s—the discovery that pregnant women who had taken the drug Thalidomide gave birth to grossly deformed infants—led to further legislation that strengthened the FDA.

The FDA today regulates, inspects, monitors, tests, and develops guidelines for a wide range of foods, drugs, cosmetics, and medical devices. In many cases, the manufacturer actually conducts the tests, and the FDA has no direct control over this testing process (Coleman 1989). Its field inspectors are authorized to inspect any plant that produces products falling under the agency's jurisdiction. It can respond to perceived violations of its rules with a warning letter, recall order, injunction against further manufacture or distribution, citation threatening criminal action unless appropriate information is provided, direct seizure of prohibited goods, and/or recommendations for the imposition of civil monetary penalties or the initiation of criminal prosecution.

The FDA's effectiveness has been inhibited over the years both by its focus on small companies rather than on powerful, major corporations and by corruption in the form of FDA generic drug reviewers' acceptance of bribes from drug companies. The FDA has been criticized on the one hand for holding up approval of experimental drugs to treat AIDS and on the other hand for not requiring adequate testing of new medical devices. Accordingly, the FDA has been portrayed in conflicting ways: "Protector of the consumer? Pawn of industry? Pure scientists? Political plaything?"

(Hawthorne 2005). The FDA will continue to be at the center of a certain amount of political controversy.

Federal Trade Commission (FTC) The FTC was created as an independent agency in 1914 as the federal government's principal weapon against the trusts (*Federal Regulatory Directory* 1990; Salinger 2005). It has also been empowered to contend with unfair and deceptive business practices, including deceptive advertising, that defraud consumers. The FTC is empowered to issue trade regulation rules, which in their final form have the force of law, and it has broad powers to require businesses to produce various forms of information. Its overall charge—to prevent unfair competition and anticompetitive mergers—is so broad that it has stimulated considerable debate and litigation over the proper interpretation of its mandate (Coleman 2002). The commission issues advisory opinions to businesses that inquire about the potential liability of some of their planned practices.

The FTC can initiate proceedings against businesses that have engaged in practices prohibited by the agency's rules and can seek civil penalties or injunctions against businesses, although it is often able to simply negotiate a consent order calling for the cessation of the prohibited practice. The FTC has been attacked by consumer advocates for its relatively feeble and inefficient protection of consumers and by various business and professional groups for its perceived interference with their legitimate operations (Clinard and Yeager 1980). In recent years, the FTC has had to devote a disproportionate amount of time to addressing mergers but claims to be mainly focused on aiding consumers rather than breaking up corporations solely because they are large (Brinkley and Hobson 1998; Labaton 2000b). In an increasingly globalized world, it has played a role in the establishment of the International Competition Network to address antitrust issues across borders (Cooper and Dedjinou 2005). Addressing deceptive advertisements or offerings remains the most visible activity of the FTC.

The Securities and Exchange Commission (SEC)   The SEC was established in 1934 as one governmental response to the massive stock manipulations and frauds that contributed to the 1929 stock market crash (Cheng 2005c; Seligman 1982; Shapiro 1984). The agency got off to a strong beginning under its first three chairmen, Joseph P. Kennedy (father of President Kennedy), James M. Landis (a former Harvard Law dean), and William O. Douglas (subsequently a celebrated and controversial U.S. Supreme Court Associate Justice for 37 years). It is headquartered in Washington, DC, with branch offices in 15 U.S. cities.

The SEC, which is an independent regulatory agency composed of five commissioners, was given broad responsibilities to regulate and police the securities markets (Shapiro 1984). Some of its responsibilities include serving as a repository and examiner for registration statements filed by companies planning to sell stock to the general public; providing information on securities to investors; advising on some bankruptcy reorganizations; and investigating and initiating action when federal securities laws are violated and frauds are committed.

The specific methods used by SEC staff attorneys to investigate securities matters and the complex of factors involved in their decision-making process on responding to cases have been exhaustively explored in Susan Shapiro's pioneering *Wayward Capitalists: Targets of the Securities and Exchange Commission* (1984). One important finding was that the SEC rarely refers cases for criminal prosecution (only 6 out of 100 parties investigated ultimately find themselves in criminal court), preferring instead to resolve cases by various other means (Shapiro 1984, 1985). The SEC's enforcement powers are limited; it does not, for example, have legal access to evidence developed in grand jury inquiries into securities cases, and it must go to court and have a judge authorize any restraining orders or injunctions it seeks to impose (Eichenwald 1990c). Cases are referred to the SEC enforcement division by entities such as the American Stock Exchange and company executives who suspect securities violations, but the division also initiates some actions based on its own surveillance and review of press reports of stock sales and purchases (Cheng 2005c). Transnational securities-related violations are a growing and complex challenge for the SEC enforcement division.

The SEC has been criticized by some as unnecessary; others have regarded it as insufficiently vigilant and aggressive (Herman 1985; Seligman 2002). The SEC does not have full investigative powers; for example, it cannot use wiretaps (Kadlec 2001a). Although some sophisticated new forms of technology facilitate SEC investigations, this technology also makes new scams possible (Eaton 1997a). The SEC is also constrained because it is not empowered to bring criminal cases directly.

In the many decades of its existence, the SEC has clearly gone through periods of lethargy and relatively limited effectiveness (Morgenson 1999; Seligman 1982; Shapiro 1984) (see Box 10.3). Its funding and staffing have always been somewhat limited in view of its responsibilities for policing security markets involving literally hundreds of billions of dollars.

Environmental Protection Agency (EPA)   The EPA was established in 1970 as an independent executive branch agency headed by an administrator appointed by the president (Burns and Lynch 2004). The establishment of this agency was clearly a response to growing public concern with harm to the environment that rose sharply after a dramatic oil spill off the coast of Santa Barbara, California, early in 1969.

The EPA has mandated responsibilities to set standards and monitor practices relating to air quality, water quality, and the disposal of various forms of hazardous waste. It has been an especially large, visible, and controversial agency, attacked both by environmentalists who complain that it has not been sufficiently aggressive in protecting the environment and by business interests who complain that it imposes unreasonable costs and enforces unnecessary regulations. The EPA promotes voluntary compliance with environmental protection standards and encourages state and local initiatives in environmental matters. If polluters

---

B O X   10.3   The SEC in Recent Years

During the early years of the Reagan administration, the SEC was seen as retreating from its traditional role as protector of investors (Kerwin 1990; Seligman 1982). In the late 1980s, the SEC became somewhat more visible during a period of great growth of corporate takeovers, when a selective crackdown on insider trading cases was one major agency response (Kerwin 1990; Nash 1986). In the 1990s, the SEC remained quite conspicuous in policing various forms of financial crime, although it faced periodic cuts in its funding (Henriques 1994b; Morgenson 1999). In the late 1990s, SEC Chair Arthur Levitt was criticized by some as too tough, but the market thrived (Wayne 2001). Levitt pushed through the Fair Disclosure regulation prohibiting corporations from providing financial information to Wall Street analysts in advance of the public, and he opposed the "Contract for America" effort to make it more difficult for investors to sue. But he was unsuccessful in his efforts to impose more controls on accounting firms and to ban inherent conflicts of interest arising when such firms both conduct audits and provide consulting services. This failure may well have contributed to the circumstances giving rise to the corporate scandals of the 2000s.

The SEC was allegedly "in a coma" during the first year of the George W. Bush administration (*New York Times* 2002f). The appointment in 2001 of Harvey Pitt, a high-profile securities lawyer and a top lobbyist for the accounting industry, was controversial (Labaton 2001a). Although Pitt claimed to be committed to initiating various reforms, including the reduction of costs and discouraging of offshore investments, he was characterized as "the Reluctant Reformer" (McNamee and Borrus 2002). Pitt was forced to resign in November 2002 as a consequence of selecting as

chair of the new auditing oversight board William Webster, who headed the audit committee of a corporation being investigated for auditing fraud (Labaton 2002e, 2002f, 2002h). A government report described the SEC as "dysfunctional" during Pitt's tenure, and critics complained that the SEC staff was recommending watering down new rules for lawyers and accountants in response to lobbying pressure (Labaton 2002h; Labaton and Glater 2003). William Donaldson, a former securities company founder and CEO and Chair of the New York Stock Exchange, was SEC Chairman from 2003–2005 (Risen 2003). Donaldson surprised some observers by focusing on issues largely ignored by his predecessor: corporate governance, stock exchanges, executive compensation, and hedge funds. In his first year, the SEC filed almost 700 cases, a significant increase over previous years. But Donaldson's policies also alienated some Republican SEC commissioners and politicians. In June 2005, President George W. Bush appointed Representative Christopher Cox of California as the new Chairman of the SEC (Labaton 2005b). Cox, a former corporate lawyer, was known to be a "big business" advocate, a recipient of major contributions from the business and accounting industries, and someone who had opposed tougher accounting rules, taxes on dividends and capital gains, and was a sponsor of a bill to make investor lawsuits more difficult. Some commentators were concerned that he would not pursue aggressively the regulation of the securities markets. The SEC continues to contend with overwhelming responsibilities, inadequate resources, and inherent conflicts of interest (for example, when former enforcement chiefs resign to work as corporate lawyers defending Wall Street firms).

---

do not respond to orders to cease harmful activities, the agency can initiate informal negotiations, and if these efforts are unsuccessful, it can initiate civil proceedings. The EPA also has a criminal investigation unit that can initiate criminal prosecution for willful environmental criminals. Civil penalties may include revocation of licenses and permits and substantial fines. In the rather rare criminal cases, imprisonment can be imposed in addition to fines.

The EPA's reach expanded quite significantly during the 1970s. But in the early years of the Reagan administration, it was the subject of a scandal involving lax enforcement of environmental regulations and corrupt dealings with regulated industries (Burns and Lynch 2004). Rita Lavelle, a political appointee who headed the Superfund environmental cleanup program, was convicted on criminal charges of perjury and sentenced to six months in prison. The

---

B O X 10.4 **Protecting the Environment: Alternatives to Relying Upon the EPA**

Most people would agree that the long-term protection of the environment is one of the major challenges facing our society. In their landmark book *Environmental Crime: A Sourcebook*, Ronald Burns and Michael Lynch (2004) acknowledge the need for some basic reforms of the Environmental Protection Agency as one part of this endeavor, including a revised, clearer charter; enhanced environmental monitoring and data collection; increased funding; and a transformed organizational culture. But we have to avoid overreliance upon a regulatory agency in addressing the environmental challenges. They also call for increased environmental crime research, an increase in interdisciplinary study of environmental issues, greater societal consideration of sustainable development, and an increased focus on global environmentalism. The pursuit of "environmental justice" and the preservation of the environment require mobilization of human communities on all levels and cooperative endeavors between many different governmental and private sector entities.

---

evidence demonstrated that Lavelle and some of her EPA associates were more concerned with accommodating the administration's corporate supporters and maintaining positive ties with potential future employers in regulated industries than with fulfilling the EPA's mandate. In response to public concern and congressional pressure, the EPA became somewhat more vigilant in subsequent years. During the Clinton years, environmental criminal cases increased quite significantly, although some commentators regarded these cases as "overreach" (Carmichael 1996; Gray et al. 1998). During the same period, however, Congress was promoting more cost-benefit analysis in relation to environmental regulation and promoting a regulatory framework giving business more flexibility in preventing pollution (Cushman 1995, 1996). During the early years of the George W. Bush administration, the Superfund to clean up major toxic sites had largely dried up, and the administration was apparently responding to long-standing complaints from the energy industry and other businesses about the costs of environmental measures (Browner 2002; Seelye 2002a, 2002b). This administration was widely criticized for not supporting a stronger EPA and broader protections against environmental damage (Burns and Lynch 2004; Schroeder and Steinzor 2005). The long-term effectiveness of the EPA was increasingly in question (see Box 10.4).

Occupational Safety and Health Administration (OSHA) OSHA, established as a Labor Department agency in 1971, has been one of the most controversial federal regulatory agencies (*Federal Regulatory Directory* 1990; Holst 2005). OSHA was authorized to develop and enforce procedures and standards for workplace health and safety and to compensate for limitations of alternative remedies such as workers compensation, civil tort suits, and criminal prosecutions. The Occupational Safety and Health Act that established OSHA also gave states the option of developing their own enforcement plans, and as of 2003, 25 states had federally approved plans (OSHA 2003). At least some of these states (e.g., California) have agencies that pursue cases much more aggressively than does the federal agency (Brill 1992). Occupational health and safety standards in states that have not developed their own plans are enforced by the federal agency.

Some commentators have argued that OSHA was created primarily as a symbolic concession to labor forces rather than as a consequence of a serious governmental commitment to improve workplace conditions (Calavita 1983; Donnelly 1982). The agency has jurisdiction over most employers, although in 1976 most small businesses were exempted from OSHA's record-keeping requirements. In addition to developing protective standards and overseeing employer record keeping, OSHA is empowered to conduct workplace inspections (typically without advance notice) and issue citations for violations (Mendeloff and Gray 2005). It can recommend to the Occupational Safety and Health Review Commission the imposition of monetary civil penalties up to $10,000 per violation and jail terms up to six months per violation.

During the 1980s, OSHA was criticized for failing to take adequate steps against hazardous workplace conditions, and from a progressive point of view, it was virtually criminally negligent in failing to enforce regulations (Brill 1992; Calavita 1983; Frank 1993). In the 1980s, OSHA principally relied on inspections rather than on vigorous enforcement, and it concentrated more on worker safety than on health hazards (Viscusi 1986). Regulating direct, visible safety hazards that cause physical injury has in fact proven much easier than addressing unsafe conditions that may cause health problems over an extended period of time (Frank 1993). Different studies have established evidence that OSHA inspections can impact measurably on reducing worker injuries and increasing workplace safety (Gray and Scholz 1993; Mendeloff and Gray 2005). For the five years through 2004, OSHA claimed that enforcement actions had increased and injuries and illnesses had declined (OSHA 2004). But OSHA has continued to be a prime target of attack by businesspeople and conservative politicians for imposing unwarranted economic burdens. It has also been criticized by labor for failing to adopt stronger standards to protect workers (Wahl and Gunkel 1999). The business and politically conservative constituencies have been quite successful in limiting OSHA's potential effectiveness.

Consumer Product Safety Commission (CPSC)
This agency was established in 1972 at the height of the consumer movement, when an estimated 20 million Americans a year were being injured while using consumer products (*Federal Regulatory Directory* 1990; Holtfreter 2005c). The agency, which originally had five commissioners, was given the responsibility of protecting the public from dangerous products, assisting in the evaluation of

products, setting standards, and sponsoring investigations of the causes of and means for preventing product-related deaths, illnesses, and injuries. The agency is expected to monitor the enforcement of consumer product standards. It is empowered to impose civil fines but is much more likely to negotiate consent agreements with producers of dangerous or defective products. It can order bans on products or demand that they be redesigned. Although the agency was accorded considerable autonomy to minimize the chances of "capture," from the outset administrations antagonistic to its mission have attempted to impose constraints on it. During the Reagan administration, the CPSC experienced drastic budget cuts and massive staff reductions and went into a state of virtual paralysis. In the 1990s, there was some revival of support for the agency. The George W. Bush administration attempted to appoint a new head of the CPSC in 2001 who was criticized for her past disregard to the safety of children (Alvarez 2001). Concern reemerged at this time that the agency would be geared more toward the interests of manufacturers and not consumers.

PRIVATE POLICING

Private policing in the white collar crime arena has a long history. Many of the functions of modern police forces were once carried out by employees and servants of the powerful and privileged. Throughout much of the modern history of private police forces, they may have been used more often as an instrument whereby corporations committed crimes (e.g., against employees) than as a means of ferreting out and pursuing white collar crime cases, especially at the higher executive levels.

Since World War II, private policing has grown exponentially (Shearing and Stenning 1987; Williams J. W. 2005). Some important interconnections exist between public and private police, and some commentators argue that the lines of demarcation between them cannot always be easily drawn; other commentators emphasize the differences between public and private policing (Marx 1987; Williams J. W. 2005). Public and private police may join forces in criminal investigations, as when the FBI and IBM security collaborated on a computer-secrets theft case. Private police may be hired to investigate crimes that public police do not have time to investigate, or public police investigations may be subsidized by private entities. Some investigative units may be public/private hybrids, as is the case with the Law Enforcement Intelligence Unit, a private organization of public police. Finally, much intermixing of public and private policing personnel occurs; for example, many private policing agencies are headed by retired public police (Marx 1987). All such interrelationships are especially pronounced in the white collar crime realm.

The private security industry is a vast, multibillion-dollar enterprise, with at least twice as many employees as public policing agencies in the United States (Timm and Christian 1991). Of course, a great deal of this massive private security effort is devoted to the physical protection of business assets and has nothing to do with white collar crime. But a certain proportion of such private policing focuses on external or internal frauds or embezzlements by employees and outside parties. Only a small pro portion of private policing is directed at the illegal or improper activities of the corporate executives who typically hire and control private police. Indeed, security departments of major corporations may be confronted with the ethical and practical dilemma of responding to the discovery that their employer is suppressing research findings of injurious effects from their product or is engaging in some other form of illegal or harmful conduct (Nalla and Newman 1990). Internal security departments may not report to external enforcement agencies high-level corporate wrongdoing that comes to their attention.

When it comes to business, executives are socialized to think more in terms of "loss" than of crime (Stenning 1988); they are oriented toward preventing loss and using resources efficiently to maximize profit. Whenever possible, they prefer to avoid formally invoking the notion of crime

because criminalization typically generates many costs and complications. One security executive in a large corporation asserted that only 1 in 10 frauds within the company is likely to come to the attention of the security department (Cunningham, Straucher, and Van Meter 1991). Many middle-level executives and managers fear that reports of fraud and other employee illegalities in their department will reflect poorly on them, and they prefer to handle these matters directly.

In recent years especially, private security firms that specialize in the pursuit of white collar criminals have proliferated (Shuger 1992; Treaster 1997b; Williams J. W. 2005); the various financial scandals of the 1980s were a boon for such investigators, and the corporate scandals of the 2000s also increased demand for their services. Perhaps the most prominent of these investigative firms is Kroll Associates of New York, which received considerable publicity for locating Saddam Hussein's assets in bank accounts and corporate investments around the world (Byron 1991). Kroll Associates, which is typically hired by law firms or insurance companies attempting to investigate suspected white collar crime, has also undertaken hundreds of due diligence reports (seeking possible fraud and other improprieties) for investment banking houses anticipating the sale of a corporation's bonds or stocks. Kroll was involved in the investigation of Lincoln Savings & Loan, the Orange County derivatives investments, and kickbacks at Kmart, among other cases (Treaster 1997b). Kroll Ontrack, a division of Kroll, as well as many other firms, was specializing in Internet investigations on behalf of major corporations (Stewart 2004b). The work of forensic accountants (see Box 10.5) is crucial in many white collar crime cases.

In recent years, several dozen white collar crime investigative firms were billing hundreds of millions of dollars annually (Glater 2001c). Corporations found it increasingly in their interest to pay for thorough background investigations of their executives (Kuczynski 2002b). A celebrated executive of this period, "Chainsaw Al" Dunlop, was believed to have overseen major accounting fraud at Sunbeam, leading to huge losses for

---

B O X 10.5 Forensic Accountants as Fraud Detectives

Forensic accountants are specifically trained to investigate financial fraud. *Forensic accounting* in some form has been traced back to the early 19th century (Crumbley 2001). Originally such accountants testified in court cases involving fraud, but in recent years they have increasingly become "financial detectives" proactively investigating possible financial fraud. The field of forensic accounting has grown substantially in recent years. The first forensic accounting textbook was published in 1982, and forensic accounting courses (and concentrations) have been added to the curriculum of many colleges and universities (Crumbley 2001). The Association for Certified Fraud Examiners, founded in 1988, early in the 21st century had several thousand members and was growing rapidly (Glater 2001a; Wells 1993b). It publishes a bimonthly magazine, *The White Paper*.

Following the exposure of the Enron case and subsequent corporate scandals, the need for more aggressive forensic accounting as a standard feature of audits was increasingly obvious (Anastasi 2003; Buckhoff and Hansen 2002; O'Gara 2004). Such accounting calls for painstaking examination of financial records, with substantial use of computers and data banks. Many private business clients, hoping to be spared embarrassment and possible lawsuits, want investigators to produce evidence that will prompt financial restitution rather than a criminal indictment.

In a parallel vein, private insurance company fraud units have become an important factor in response to insurance-related fraud (Ghezzi 1983). Because such special investigation units (SIU) often use investigative procedures that would render evidence inadmissible in courts, such cases rarely go to court.

---

investors; he had earlier been fired from two companies following allegations of overseeing accounting fraud, but Sunbeam was not aware of this when he was hired as CEO.

Private police are often constrained from responding to apparent criminality in the same way as public police might, and they may be called in either because businesses do not want to involve the police or have yet to be successful in the case. According to a private investigator who specializes in white collar crime cases, the client's principal objective is often limited to locating and recovering stolen funds (Grant and Wolf 1988). Although recovery rather than revenge or "administering justice" is also a primary objective for some victims of conventional crime, it appears to be a more important factor in white collar cases. Furthermore, businesses are often reluctant to press charges against an insider, especially a top executive, who has defrauded the company due to concerns about bad publicity, possible declines in the company's stock value, and embarrassment about their own misplaced trust (Grant and Wolf 1988). Accordingly, private policing in a corporate or business setting is often directed toward concealing rather than broadly exposing white collar crime.

THE ROLE OF LAWYERS AND ACCOUNTANTS IN POLICING WHITE COLLAR CRIME

In commenting on the massive fraud committed over a period of years by Charles Keating's Lincoln Savings and Loan, Federal Judge Stanley Sporkin asked:

> Where ... were the outside accountants and attorneys when these transactions were effectuated? What is difficult to understand is that with all the professional talent involved (both accounting and legal), why at least one professional would not have blown the whistle to stop the overreaching that took place in this case. (Monse 1992: 4–5)

Following the exposure of massive financial misrepresentations at Enron and other corporations in the 2000s, the same question arose, although now the answer to many observers seemed to be: "They were all too often centrally involved in the wrongdoing" (Eichenwald 2002g; Glater 2002b; Jennings 2004). Accountants and lawyers are obviously not supposed to contribute to the perpetration of illegal acts, but do they have an obligation to blow the whistle on their clients when they become aware of illegal conduct? The question of the policing obligations of professionals such as lawyers and accountants is considered here.

Lawyers and Professional Ethics

Lawyers are typically thought of principally in terms of their obligation to defend clients against investigations and adjudications. But are there circumstances in which a lawyer is obliged to play a policing role? This is a complicated and contentious issue (Brown 1996; Shapiro 2002). Lawyers contend with complex and sometimes ambiguous ethical obligations with regard to client confidentiality and knowledge of illegal conduct. For lawyers who act as both counsel and corporate managers, these ethical issues are compounded.

As a general rule, a lawyer is prohibited from misrepresenting facts, knowingly offering false evidence, or furthering a fraud (Gerson 1992; Hughes 1993). American Bar Association (ABA) canons on a lawyer's ethical obligations when he or she discovers that a client has perpetrated a fraud have been quite confusing, however, and appear to prohibit an attorney's participation in client misconduct while simultaneously discouraging the attorney's investigation of client activities (Belbot 1991; Monse 1992). *ABA rules of professional conduct* adopted in the 1980s require lawyers to call on clients to rectify ongoing frauds they become aware of and to inform affected parties if clients fail to do so, unless a privileged lawyer–client communication is involved or disclosure would be detrimental to the client's interests (Steinberg 1991). It is difficult to conceive of a situation in which these two constraints would not apply. The courts have increasingly recognized that if lawyers who serve as in-house counsel feel compelled to resign from a company for ethical reasons, they may have some recourse against the company. If they remain silent in the face of company conduct that they know to be illegal, they may be liable for criminal charges at some point (Brown 1996). Altogether, lawyers operate today in a legal environment that requires close attention to such issues.

The ABA has traditionally rejected proposed new rules that would require lawyers to reveal to legal authorities a client's acts whenever either substantial financial harm was possible or the lawyer's services had been used to further some fraud (Belbot 1991). While lawyers are permitted to report clients' activities that could lead to imminent death or substantial bodily harm, they are not absolutely required to do so by ABA rules. Some commentators argue that lawyers should be required to report client conduct that endangers the public, and many states do in fact require such disclosure (Boxer 2001; Gillers 2001; Glaberson 2001a). In 2003, in part in response to the corporate scandals of this time, the ABA approved a new standard permitting lawyers to disclose confidences about the crimes of employees if it is deemed necessary to protect the company (Glater 2003). Lawyers are concerned about the erosion of their clients' trust, but legal ethicists are worried about the public interest and the erosion of public trust.

Rules that require lawyers to be "stool pigeons" against their clients have been attacked as unfair and harmful (Frankel 1992). One basic objection to requiring attorneys to police their clients, especially white collar crime defendants, is based on the complexity of laws, rules, and regulations, which may make it difficult for clients to clearly discriminate between legal and illegal actions (Belbot 1991). If clients know that under some circumstances their lawyer will report them and testify against them, they may withhold information a lawyer needs to mount an effective defense.

The ABA rules can also be viewed as intended to shield lawyers from liability rather than to protect the broader public from fraudulent activity. These rules hold that when a corporate board or high-level management insists on committing fraudulent and illegal activity, counsel should resign from representation; however, the specific obligations of counsel following such resignations are less clear. In the celebrated OPM Leasing case involving a massive fraud of business clients who were leasing computer services, the original lawyers did not in any way inform successor counsel that their client was engaged in an ongoing fraud; their actions are certainly controversial (Steinberg 1991). Altogether, the actions of lawyers in major recent white collar frauds have provided little basis for confidence that lawyers will protect the public from fraud by their clients.

In more recent years, government prosecutors have more aggressively pursued the position that lawyers who advised clients engaged in ongoing massive frauds are themselves responsible. The dramatic losses involved in the savings and loan catastrophe of the 1980s were an important source of inspiration for this policy and brought some of the ethical issues of legal representation into sharp focus (Monse 1992). In early 1992, the federal government sued a leading New York law firm (Kaye, Scholer, Fierman, Hays, and Handler) and its former managing partner for $275 million and sought to freeze their assets over its representation of Charles Keating, the convicted head of a savings and loan institution guilty of large-scale frauds (Hughes 1993; Labaton 1992a). The government's argument was that the lawyers involved both improperly advised the savings and loan company that some of its investments were permissible and were guilty of conflicts of interest. The lawyers repeatedly misled thrift examiners and engaged in obstructionist tactics for a savings and loan operation whose losses would ultimately cost the taxpayers $2 billion. The government's position is that a lawyer's obligations to a client are compromised if the client is supported in some way by taxpayer money and that a bank examination should not be equated with an adversarial proceeding (Gerson 1992; Hughes 1993; Labaton 1992b). Some parallel questions arose about the role of lawyers—and some prestigious law firms—in the more recent cases involving Enron and other corporations (Glater 2002b). A prestigious Houston law firm, Vinson & Elkins, served as Enron's legal counsel during the years when it was engaging in major financial misrepresentations (Schwartz 2002). Some critics contended that Vinson & Elkins was too closely tied to Enron and was complicit in some of the wrongdoing.

The courts have been divided concerning counsel's disclosure obligations, and in most jurisdictions today, lawyers do not have a specific obligation to blow the whistle on their clients (Steinberg 1991). Furthermore, after a sharply divided U.S. Supreme Court in 1994 ruled against the long-standing practice of permitting investors to file "aiding and abetting" accusations against lawyers representing securities defrauders, the lawyers for one group of defrauded investors simply accused the defendant's lawyers of direct complicity (Henriques 1994a). The outrage over the size and scope of losses in major cases in the recent era, from Lincoln Savings and Loan to Enron and WorldCom, has generated a call for a greater responsibility on the part of lawyers to police their clients under certain circumstances (*New York Times* 2002g). The corporate responsibility legislation passed by Congress in 2002 requires lawyers to report "evidence of a material violation of securities law or breach of fiduciary duty," in sequence to the company's general counsel, chief executive, and board of directors (Cramton, Cohen, and Koniak 2004; Glater 2002a). Lawyers increasingly may be vulnerable to charges and various penalties for their failure to report certain forms of wrongdoing by clients and for direct or implicit involvement in their clients' wrongful conduct.

Accountants and Auditing Responsibilities

Accountants also face conflicts in their obligations to clients and as discoverers of fraudulent activities. Accountants are sometimes brought in by management specifically when it suspects embezzlement or internal fraud, or when such matters as suspicious insurance claims arise. As a result, forensic accounting (see Box 10.5) has become an increasingly common specialty (Kleinfeld 1990; Manning 2005; Wells 1992).

Accountants are much more commonly brought in by corporations and businesses to conduct audits certifying the soundness and accuracy of financial statements and reports. Annual audits are required by the SEC for all companies traded on the stock market (Wells 1993a). Inevitably, accountants become aware of fraudulent misrepresentations in such statements and reports; all too often they have quietly dropped such accounts or deliberately overlooked these misrepresentations. When accountants produce reports certifying the soundness and accuracy of these business financial statements, they can wittingly or unwittingly become parties to an ongoing fraud because investors, regulators, and others may take actions premised on the accountants' or auditors' certification.

The legal liability to third parties of auditors that have been negligent or active participants in the production of misleading financial statements is rooted in common-law principles and the securities acts (Elliott and Willingham 1980). The traditional standard has been that auditors are responsible for detecting managerial misrepresentations that would produce misleading financial statements, *if* such errors are detected by *generally accepted accounting principles*, or GAAP (Elliott and Willingham 1980). Article 203 of the Accountants' Code of Professional Conduct says that auditors may depart from these standards to prevent financial statements from being misleading; this has been described as possibly "the most ignored rule in accounting" (Norris 2002a). In the case of the savings and loan crisis, Richard Breeden (1991), chairman of the SEC, argued that the accounting standards widely applied to the thrifts were inherently defective and produced a misleading picture of their assets and liabilities. Some parallel issues arose in connection with the wave of corporate scandals surfacing in the early 2000s and the certifying of corporate financial statements that in many cases turned out to be misleading at best (*New York Times* 2002c, 2002d).

In response to increasing criticism of their profession, the chief regulatory body for accountants asserted in 1988 that accountants have a responsibility to look actively for financial fraud inside companies they audit (Berg 1988). This body, the American Institute of Certified Public Accountants, has nevertheless emphasized that accountants cannot be expected to uncover all instances of fraud, and it voted overwhelmingly in 1992 to maintain the policy of prohibiting members from volunteering confidential client information to government agencies (McCarroll 1992). Thus, accountants were required to inform managerial authorities but not outside

entities of any fraud they have discovered (Elliott and Willingham 1980). However, the corporate scandals of the early 2000s clearly exposed the limitations of rules of this type, and in all too many cases, accountants as auditors appeared to be cooperating with management's desire to produce grossly misrepresented financial statements rather than uncovering and drawing attention to such misrepresentations.

As is true for lawyers, the obligation of client confidentiality has taken precedence over other considerations. Of course, the fact that auditors are investigating possible improper and illegal activities by those who pay for their services is a built-in conflict of interest (Wells 1993a). In the case of corporations with publicly held stock, the client should be the stockholders, but in fact, management is far more likely to be regarded as the client (Largay 2002). Major accounting firms such as Ernst & Young have been criticized for providing tax shelter advice to top corporate executives (Glater and Labaton 2003). In the recent era, conflicts of interest have often been greatly magnified when the accounting firm also derives a substantial income from providing consulting services to the businesses it is auditing. In one high-profile case, the Arthur Andersen firm received more income ($27 million) from the Enron Corporation in 2000 for consulting services than the income it received for auditing the company (Byrne 2002b). Furthermore, when an accounting firm as consultant provides advice to a corporation on how to organize and structure its finances, the accounting firm may very well be in a position of auditing much of its own work. This blatant conflict of interest was addressed by the Sarbanes-Oxley Act in 2002, which prohibits accounting firms from performing audits and some consulting services for the same client (Labaton 2002a). The accounting industry was unable to defeat this bill in the post-Enron environment, but it lobbied hard against some appointments to the Public Company Accounting Oversight Board set up to police the accounting industry (Quinn 2002). The profitability of accounting firms seemed to remain the highest priority. The members of the new board were also criticized for granting themselves high salaries—higher than the president's—as their first official act in 2003 (Labaton 2003a).

Accounting professionals generally adhere to the position that the corporate management prepares and must assume basic responsibility for financial statements and that accountants or auditors merely issue opinions based on information provided to them (Jennings, Reckers, and Kneer 1991). Increasingly, however, government agencies are investigating the criminal and civil liability of accountants in long-running frauds of corporations and businesses they have audited (Wells 1993a). In the early 1990s, accounting firms faced 4,000 liability suits and more than $15 billion in damages, primarily in S & L cases, and members of Congress called for legislation requiring accountants to blow the whistle on lawbreaking clients (McCarroll 1992; Wells 1993a). The legislative initiatives at that time largely failed, however, and some 10 years later, with confidence in the independence of accounting firms as auditors largely diminished in the face of the corporate scandals of the early 2000s, legislators focused more on prohibiting conflict of interest situations and imposing more oversight on the activities of the accounting industry (Benston 2003; Labaton 2002g). For some commentators, authentic auditing independence can only be achieved by establishing a Corporate Accountability Commission that assigns auditors and pays them from fees assessed to corporations (*Business Ethics* 2002b).

SELF-REGULATION: INTERNAL CONTROLS AND PROFESSIONAL ASSOCIATIONS

The notion of *self-regulation*, or private policing directed at one's own company or professional peers, is something that generally distinguishes white collar crime from conventional crime; that is, conventional criminals are not typically expected to police or regulate their own illegal conduct. In some respects, organized crime and crime syndicates may be said to engage in periodic self-policing when they act

against fellow criminals who violate their rules. In addition to whistleblowers (Chapter 1), informers in the whole range of conventional crime cases are "policing" their criminal associates, although often with wholly selfish motives. But only in the corporate and legitimate occupational realm do we find official, internal enforcers of codes or laws pertaining to the conduct of employers and employees.

Self-regulation is important because government does not have the resources or expertise to police or regulate fully all the activities of corporations, retail businesses, professionals, and legitimate white collar and blue collar entrepreneurs. On the one hand, many corporate crimes are instigated or inspired by the highest levels of authority in the corporation, and obviously these executives are unlikely to encourage investigation of such activity (Clinard 1983). On various levels, however, corporate executives may cultivate "concerted" or "strategic" ignorance of certain specific, culpable actions as a way of protecting themselves and the corporation from criminal charges (Katz 1980a; Lowell and Arnold 2003). White collar crime lawyers advise top executives to avoid involving themselves too directly in internal investigations when allegations of corporate wrongdoing arise as a way of minimizing the executives' exposure in any subsequent prosecution (Magnuson 1992). Thus, in many circumstances the chief executives of corporations either discourage self-policing or distance themselves from any self-policing inquiries.

On the other hand, Braithwaite and Fisse (1987) pointed out that, contrary to what we might expect, corporations often expend resources to police themselves because (1) they are not uniformly indifferent to an ethical obligation to do so, (2) they have a powerful self-interest in maintaining a good public reputation, and (3) they want whenever possible to preempt the imposition of the less palatable alternative of governmental regulation. Braithwaite and Fisse contended that self-policing can be much more thorough and effective, involving more substantial resources and broader access, than external policing and may be able to impose tough internal sanctions. But because the willingness of corporations to police themselves is far from a sure thing, they favored

---

B O X 10.6   **The Role of Corporate Boards in Self-Regulation**

Corporate boards of directors are supposed to play a key role in ensuring that corporate management is not engaging in actions harmful to the interest of shareholders and is not engaged in unwarranted forms of self-dealing. In theory, the board is selected by shareholders to monitor management, approve compensation for CEOs, and, if necessary, fire them; in practice, it often merely ratifies the policies of management (Lohr 2002a; Surowiecki 2004). In many cases, the independence of boards has been compromised by the fact that they are all too often selected by CEOs, who choose fellow club members, customers, suppliers, and consultants, among others. These directors have a mutually beneficial professional or personal relationship with the CEO and may feel beholden to the CEO for the privileges they enjoy as board members. Concern about the performance of boards as watchdogs is hardly new, but it intensified following disclosures in Enron and other cases of the early 2000s where corporate boards either failed to block various forms of financial fraud or were in some way complicit in these frauds (Abelson 2002a; Veasey 2003). A Congressional committee criticized directors

of ImClone for allowing Samuel Waksal, its former CEO, to remain at the company, even after they learned of his acts of forgery and other wrongdoing.

From 1999 on, the SEC imposed rules requiring boards of directors to assume increasing responsibility for the financial reporting process, although the long-standing structure of such boards clearly inhibited the adoption of this role in many cases (Dallas 2003; Rowlands 2002). Board members have become increasingly conscious of their liability when corporations engage in wrongdoing that the board is supposed to stop (Stellin 2002). Former board directors of WorldCom agreed in 2005 to pay millions of dollars toward settling investor lawsuits (Glater 2005h; Morgenson 2005c). Corporate CEOs and executives accordingly became more reluctant to serve on corporate boards (Holstein 2005). Some commentators believe that if we are to have truly independent boards, directors must be selected by a nominating committee of nonmanagement directors, boards should have their own financial advisors and lawyers, and CEOs should not serve on or dominate the boards (Lohr 2002a).

---

enforced self-regulation, a policy proposal addressed in Chapter 12. The wave of corporate scandals in the early 2000s clearly demonstrated, however, that many major American corporations are either unable or unwilling to police themselves (Walczak et al. 2002). Box 10.6 considers the board's role in self-regulation.

Self-Regulation in Financial Firms

In-house policing units have been established in many major financial firms. In the 1950s, a prominent stock brokerage was suspended by the SEC for 30 days for failing to adequately supervise brokers who defrauded clients. Since that time, stock brokerage and investment banking firms have hired compliance officers who are responsible for monitoring the firm's activities and ensuring that its personnel comply with pertinent laws and regulations (Cowan 1991; Weber and Fortun 2004).

Throughout much of this period, compliance officers occupied a fairly modest status within their firm, especially insofar as they were not involved in directly generating income for the firm, but the various scandals and investment banking house collapses of the late 1980s and early 1990s inspired a new appreciation of the potential benefits of a strongly backed compliance staff. This concern intensified considerably with the corporate scandals of the early 2000s. Membership in the Ethics Officer Association doubled between 2000 and 2005, from a little over 600 to 1200 (*Business Ethics* 2005). In May 2005, compliance lawyers on Wall Street (often former prosecutors) were identified as the "new legal stars," newly empowered and richly compensated in the wake of the corporate scandals (Steinhauer 2005). Historically, many investment banking firms and stock brokerages tend to refrain from exercising vigilance when individual employees appear to be making money, although in some cases improper or illegal conduct is involved (Eichenwald 1995b). Compliance officers in brokerages or banking houses who report apparent violations have been fired; revenue production has typically taken precedence over compliance (Morgenson 2002b). The failure of stock analysts associated with some major investment banks to produce truly objective and independent stock ratings was one factor in the massive corporate scandals of the early 2000s, but compliance officers at these firms were unable or unwilling to prevent investment bankers from interfering with stock analysts (Morgenson 2002b). With revenue significantly down following the exposure of such widespread wrongdoing in major corporations and the world of high finance, compliance officers could conceivably experience even more pressure to look the other way when confronted with evidence of unethical but revenue-producing practices. However, in the wake of the corporate scandals, compliance officers themselves were potentially liable in corporate fraud cases (Steinhauer 2005). Would the "newly empowered" compliance officers really impact policy, or would they prove to be just a new form of window dressing?

Self-Regulation and the Professions

Self-regulation has been a hallmark of professionalism (Abel 1988b; Moore 1970). Because of the historical tendency to assume that only professionals have the specialized knowledge needed to judge the professional behavior of their peers, the state has often deferred to peer judgments. Although criminal prosecution is always the prerogative of the state, crimes committed in their occupational capacities by such professionals as physicians and lawyers may be recognizable as such only by fellow professionals.

Even though professional associations such as the American Medical Association (AMA) and the American Bar Association (ABA) have no formal disciplinary powers beyond expulsion from association membership, such professional associations and their state affiliates formulate codes of conduct, form committees or boards to evaluate allegations of

professional misconduct, and are empowered to revoke licenses and the right to practice. Professional associations have traditionally been much more concerned with promoting the economic and other interests of the profession than with vigorously policing misconduct of professionals.

State and federal laws often prohibit aggressive legal actions against physicians for many forms of professional misconduct (Brinkley 1985). States typically delegate licensing and disciplining powers to a state board of examiners that is heavily influenced by medical societies through recommendations for membership and suggestions for standards of practice (Bene 1991). Although at least half the states have laws requiring state medical associations to report disciplinary actions to state boards, they apparently rarely do so (Brinkley 1985). State medical boards or agencies tend to be understaffed and underfinanced, and any actions taken against physicians are likely to be complicated, expensive, and time consuming. Board members, fearful of lawsuits, rarely invoke their powers against fellow physicians for alleged professional misconduct. In many states in a given year, no physician is stripped of a medical license; in other states, this sanction is imposed on no more than a handful of physicians (Brinkley 1985). Despite some recent increase in concern with medical crime and incompetence (not always so easily separated), the evidence suggests that a system of control that heavily relies on peer review has been exceptionally feeble.

In the case of the legal profession, until well into the 20th century professional discipline was principally a matter of informal peer control (Abel 1988b). Although the ABA promulgated around the turn of the century ethical rules that have been subjected to much revision and refinement over the years, the ABA seems to have been much less concerned with their actual enforcement. Furthermore, clients have either lacked the necessary knowledge to institute formal complaints against their attorneys or have been beneficiaries of their misconduct (Abel 1988b). Complaints made against lawyers most typically involve false advertising, fee abuse, neglect, misappropriation, and lack of communication (Schneyer 1991a).

As is the case for physicians, only a few lawyers each year are subjected to professional disciplinary action, although the number of such *disbarments* has increased somewhat in recent years. In New Jersey in 2000, 46 lawyers were disbarred (Holt 2001). The targets of disciplinary action are most often solo practitioners, some of whose flagrantly unethical or illegal actions have always been an embarrassment to the profession. The disproportionate disciplining of solo practitioners is significant given the fact that an increasingly large percentage of lawyers now practice within large law firms (Schneyer 1991b). There clearly are, then, many limitations on the existing self-policing practices of the legal profession.

Self-regulation or self-policing has the obvious advantages of economic efficiency and, in principle, appropriate expertise. Businesses and professions have found it advantageous to control themselves, but history suggests that such self-regulation or self-policing is unlikely to be extensive or effective unless formidable external pressures compel businesses and professions to take this responsibility more seriously.

POLICING AND REGULATING WHITE COLLAR CRIME, IN SUM

This chapter has surveyed some of the special challenges in policing white collar crime, as well as the wide range of entities involved in its policing. The limited role of local police agencies, relative to the significantly greater role of state and especially federal enforcement agencies, is shown to be the reverse of how conventional crime is policed. The specific roles of different federal enforcement entities, ranging from the FBI to the Internal Revenue Service's Criminal Division, were reviewed here.

The role of regulatory agencies in policing white collar crime was explored at some length in this chapter, insofar as they play a central role in policing some of the most significant and consequential forms of white collar crime. It was necessary here to devote some space to the ongoing controversies on the appropriate role and enforcement philosophy of these agencies. The specific responsibilities of the major relevant regulatory agencies were identified.

Private policing, and policing by professionals, also plays a larger role in relation to white collar crime than is true of conventional crime. The problem of conflicts of interest that arise in such policing is necessarily addressed.

Finally, self-regulation or self-policing is much more typical in the realm of white collar crime than as a means of addressing conventional forms of crime. Some reasons why this is so receive attention here.

In sum, the policing and regulating of white collar crime produce many challenges and complications that are less likely to arise in response to conventional crime. The evolution of the current cumbersome and decentralized manner of policing and regulating white collar crime into something more efficient and effective is likely to be one of the important challenges facing the justice system in the 21st century.

KEY TERMS

ABA rules of professional conduct, 269

Abscam, 252

agency capture, 261

compliance strategy, 259

deterrence strategy, 259

disbarment, 275

economic regulation, 254

forensic accounting, 268

forensic crime lab, 254

generally accepted accounting principles (GAAP), 271

Inspectors General, 252

private policing, 266

professional misconduct, 274

regulatory cycles, 255

self-regulation, 272

social regulation, 254

DISCUSSION QUESTIONS

1. Identify some of the principal disincentives for local police involvement with white collar crime. What state and federal enforcement agencies have played a role in the investigation of white collar crime? Which factors inhibit, and which factors contribute to, their effectiveness?

2. Distinguish between economic regulation and social regulation. What were the original objectives of regulation, and which historical factors have shaped the development of regulation? What are some of the principal arguments on both sides of the historical debate about regulation?

3. Describe the origins of federal regulatory agencies and their principal functions. Contrast the rationales behind agency philosophies of compliance or deterrence. Identify some of the principal criticisms of regulatory agencies. Discuss the significance of the concept of *agency capture*.

4. Identify three federal regulatory agencies with specific responsibilities relating to white collar crime; describe the jurisdictions of these agencies. Which agencies appear to be most effective, and which agencies appear to be least effective—or even counterproductive—and why? What factors specifically influence how agencies operate?

5. What are the principal differences and points of intersection between private policing and public policing? What are some of the principal issues arising in connection with the policing responsibilities of lawyers and accountants? What are the benefits and limitations of self-policing approaches?

Prosecuting, Defending, and Adjudicating White Collar Crime

Only a small percentage of white collar crimes are prosecuted and adjudicated by the criminal justice system. This relatively low level of formal processing reflects class biases inherent in our system, the greater resources available to people accused of white collar offenses, the complexity and costliness of prosecuting such cases, and the existence of alternative forms of response deemed more efficient or appropriate.

Still, at least some white collar crime cases do end up in the criminal courts. The state's needs to maintain or enhance its status as legitimate and deserving of compliance and to uphold the claim that in a democratic society the law applies equally to rich and poor lead to selective prosecution of white collar crime cases. Some segments of the corporate and white collar community benefit from prosecution of especially flagrant white collar crimes because it reinforces the notion that such crimes are principally the actions of a few "bad apples." Accordingly, attention is deflected from some of the structural sources and the pervasiveness of white collar crime. Indeed, the failure to respond more effectively to conventional crime has been labeled a *Pyrrhic defeat* that deflects public anger

from the far more substantial harms committed by corporate and governmental criminals (Reiman 2004). Still, criminal justice system personnel have some autonomy and may pursue white collar crime cases on behalf of their own values, interests, and goals.

PROSECUTION AT THE LOCAL, STATE, AND FEDERAL LEVELS

Local Prosecutors

The prosecutor, a key figure in the American criminal justice system, has formidable discretionary power over which criminal cases will be prosecuted and which charges will be pursued. Local prosecutors have traditionally directed most of their time and attention to the broad range of conventional crime cases, including assaults, thefts, burglaries, and robberies. This pattern is a consequence of several factors. Local police agencies deal principally with these types of cases and refer them to prosecutors for further action. Victims of such crimes are especially likely to report their cases to the criminal justice system. The voters, who elect and reelect district attorneys or chief prosecutors, are especially concerned with seeing conventional criminal offenders convicted and behind bars. And prosecutors have been socialized and trained, for the most part, to think of crime in conventional terms.

Sutherland and others have long argued that businesspeople and corporations are well positioned to use their influence to avoid prosecution for their crimes. But until quite recently, relatively little has been known about the local prosecution of white collar crime cases. Michael L. Benson and Francis T. Cullen's *Combating Corporate Crime* (1998) is the major study on local prosecutors and white collar crime and builds on some of the authors' earlier work, with William J. Maakestad and Gray Cavender.

The relatively low level of attention to white collar crime by local prosecutors results from several factors. Local prosecutors do not typically regard such crime as especially serious; in one survey, less than 4 percent of urban prosecutors considered corporate crime a "very serious" problem, and half did not regard it as at all serious (Benson and Cullen 1998). Cases involving direct violence and illicit drugs take priority with more local prosecutors. Corporate and finance crime cases in particular require large expenditures of time and special investigative skills, involve greater difficulties in establishing criminal intent, and pose problems in obtaining appropriate witness or victim cooperation (Benson, Cullen, and Maakestad 1993; Benson and Cullen 1998). These cases may require sifting through masses of dull and difficult-to-understand records, and the evidentiary issues are especially complex (Bucy 1994). A decision to prosecute a corporation requires a major commitment of finite resources. As a practical matter, a more substantial local prosecutorial response would require more sharing of information, automation, computer networks, and regional laboratories (Benson and Cullen 1998; Benson, Cullen, and Maakestad 1992, 1993). Accordingly, the local prosecution of corporate crime is significantly a

function of the level of resources and expertise available to a local prosecutor's office.

Prosecutors can rationalize their failure to take on corporate crime on the basis that such cases are the responsibility of various state or federal agencies, and to the extent that these agencies are pursuing a case, local prosecutors are far less likely to get involved (Benson and Cullen 1998). And local prosecutors may be reluctant to antagonize powerful business interests (Gurney 1985). The evidence suggests that whenever *economic crime units* (ECUs) have been established as a device for more effectively prosecuting white collar crime, the units place protecting the property interests of corporations and other organizations ahead of protecting individual citizens from corporate wrongdoing and harm (Gurney 1985). Furthermore, many local prosecutors eventually go into private practice and thus become dependent on local businesses and corporations as clients and sources of income. Despite such obstacles and rationales, some criminal prosecutions of corporations occur, although typically these are relatively small corporations.

Most local prosecutors handle only a few corporate crime cases a year, but this still adds up to several thousand cases annually in the United States (Benson and Cullen 1998). When prosecutors pursue white collar crime cases generally, they are most likely to be consumer frauds, insurance frauds, false claims, environmental offenses, securities frauds, and tax frauds and illegal payments cases, in roughly that order (Benson, Cullen, and Maakestad 1990a). However, individual local prosecutors might only have one case in each of these categories (and in some cases, none) in any given year. In his study of home health care fraud, Brian K. Payne (2003) identified 10 problems that prosecutors contend with in such cases: proof problems, witness problems, record chasing, complexity, insufficient statutes, minor losses, offender sympathy, time, victim biases, and funding. Such problems surely arise in connection with prosecuting other white collar crime cases (Payne 2005a). Nevertheless, in the most recent era prosecutors have increasingly pursued physicians who have engaged in conduct in their practice with physically harmful consequences for their patients (Liederbach, Cullen, Sund, and Geis 2001). Prosecuting such prestigious professionals was less politically tenable in the past. At the same time, prosecutors take many factors into account before pursuing cases against physicians (Ziegler and Lovrich 2003). Despite growing fear among physicians of being prosecuted in connection with prescribing pain relief medication, such prosecutions are rare and only likely to be undertaken in extreme circumstances.

Since the 1970s, local prosecutors have apparently become more concerned about white collar crime, probably as a reflection of greater public concern and because of changes in law and federal policy that extend both prosecutorial powers and local jurisdiction in such cases (Benson and Cullen 1998; Payne 2005). In the 1990s, for example, local prosecutors more actively pursued environmental crime cases and were more willing to proceed with only circumstantial evidence (Burns and Lynch 2004; Rebovich and Nixon 1994). Prosecutors tend to have some autonomy in choosing cases to pursue, although in politically sensitive cases interference from powerful politicians can occur (Levi 1996). Prosecution may be inspired by authentic moral outrage, a concern with equal justice, a desire to educate the public, and the hope of deterring such conduct by signaling a willingness to prosecute (Benson and Cullen 1998; Schudson, Onellion, and Hochstedler 1984). Prosecution is most likely in cases involving individual defendants and organizational victims, in which physical harm to human beings or substantial economic harm has occurred and involving multiple offenses or large numbers of victims (Benson and Cullen 1998; Gurney 1985; Schudson, Onellion, and Hochstedler 1984). It is easier to prosecute individuals than organizations, but organizational victims can augment the investigative resources of the prosecutor's task force.

Indignation and public anger are greater in cases involving physical harm and substantial economic harm, and it is also easier to prove cases involving multiple victims. In the case of organizations, prosecutors are confronted with the intimidating task of sorting through masses of accumulated records; the relevant records of individuals are likely to be less complex and more manageable.

Economically depressed communities are apparently less willing to prosecute corporate and business crimes if jobs may be lost as a consequence (Benson et al. 1992). However, some types of white collar offenders may be more vulnerable during periods of economic distress. For example, Arnold and Hagan (1992) found that solo practitioner lawyers who engage in professional misconduct are more likely to be prosecuted during a recession, perhaps in part because they are easy targets for frustration and anger during such a time. Conversely, economically stable and prosperous communities are more likely to have the resources to prosecute sophisticated business crime and are less likely to be tolerant of harmful corporate conduct.

Although obtaining a conviction is normally the primary criterion for measuring prosecutorial success, other worthwhile goals can be accomplished when corporations are prosecuted, even if they are not convicted (see Box 11.1). To the extent that the public is outraged by corporate crimes, prosecutors can reap favorable publicity (and better prospects of reelection) by prosecuting these cases.

State Attorney Generals

Even though state attorney generals have greater resources to pursue significant white collar crime cases than do local and county prosecutors, their resources have remained limited. Some 80 percent of state attorney generals in one survey indicated that they had the jurisdiction to investigate and prosecute white collar crime cases, but through the 1980s, the defendants were overwhelmingly individuals or individuals doing business as an organization (Ayers and Frank 1987). Fraudulent transactions were the most common white collar crimes handled, followed by theft or embezzlement in a white collar setting. Slightly less than half the white collar crime cases were disposed of by a criminal prosecution; the remainder of the cases were

---

B O X   11.1   The Pinto Case: Prosecuting the Ford Motor Company

In 1978 the part-time Elkhart County (Indiana) prosecutor, Michael Consentino, a conservative Republican, sought and got an indictment against the Ford Motor Company on the grounds that criminal negligence in the design of its Pinto (in which the gas tank was unprotected in the rear of the car) was the principal cause of the death of three teenage girls (Cullen et al. 1987). The prosecutor attributed Ford's acquittal in this case to the enormous legal resources available to the corporation and its attendant ability to keep much of the critical evidence out of the trial (Kramer 1985). Although this prosecutor, an elected official with a private practice on the side, had some justifiable concerns about the negative reactions of his conservative constituents and clients to this indictment, he claimed that his perception of Ford's responsibility for the tragedy motivated him to pursue the case.

---

dropped or handled by civil or administrative procedures. In the relatively few cases in which state prosecutors pursued corporations, they often did so in a cooperative venture with local and federal prosecutors in a process known as *cross designation* (Schudson et al. 1984). More typically, when corporate crime had to be handled on the state level, a civil or administrative approach was preferred.

State attorney generals identified several key factors in the decision to prosecute, including the amount of money involved, the number of victims, their belief in the guilt of the accused, and the likelihood of prosecutorial success, as opposed to political or public relations considerations (Ayers and Frank 1987). The overall hardening of state attorney generals toward white collar offenders may well reflect shifting public sentiments, and these state prosecutors are surely aware of the public relations aspects of prosecuting certain highly visible white collar crime cases. On one hand, state attorney generals have the resources to handle certain types of white collar crime cases that local prosecutors may lack; on the other hand, they typically contend that complex corporate crimes should be pursued at the federal level. One exception is profiled in Box 11.2.

Federal Prosecutors

Virtually by default, then, federal prosecutors have assumed the primary responsibility for pursuing major white collar crime cases. The 94 U.S. Attorneys, one for each federal judicial district, are appointed by the president (with the considerable input of U.S. senators) and are in charge of major federal prosecutions. With only a few conspicuous exceptions, U.S. Attorneys did not focus on white collar crime prosecutions until the 1970s, when the pace of federal prosecutions of white collar crime cases increased quite dramatically (Katz 1980a). During this period, for example, the U.S. Attorney's office for the Eastern District of New York began prosecuting a series of powerful local politicians for such crimes as double billing, tax evasion, embezzlement, kickbacks, and extortion (Katz 1980a). It also prosecuted corporations and corporate executives for charges involving adulterated food, bribery, negligent handling of hazardous products, and illegal campaign contributions, and it greatly increased the frequency of its prosecutions of defrauders of government agencies and programs, including the Small Business Administration and Medicaid.

In the shifting public attitudes promoted by the exposure of the Watergate affair in the early 1970s, ambitious federal prosecutors found it increasingly appealing to pursue white collar crime, and this policy shift became somewhat institutionalized in the 1980s (Coffee 1988b; Katz 1980a). (Ironically, the U.S. Justice Department and its highest officials or former officials became targets of allegations of complicity in political white collar crime during Watergate, and former Attorney General John Mitchell was convicted and imprisoned on such

---

B O X 11.2 New York Attorney General Eliot Spitzer and Wall Street

New York Attorney General Eliot Spitzer was especially active in investigating and pursuing cases of alleged wrongdoing in the world of high finance in the wake of the corporate scandals of the 2000s (Cassidy 2003; Fishman 2005a). Spitzer comes from privileged circumstances, had an Ivy League education, and worked for some years as a mergers and acquisition lawyer. In 2002, with a staff of fewer than 20 lawyers working on securities cases, Spitzer extracted a $100 million fine from Merrill Lynch in settling charges that the huge investment bank engaged in corrupt and dishonest practices by recommending stocks of client companies despite being aware that the stock was overvalued. Spitzer has also taken on the insurance industry, the mutual funds industry, major pharmaceutical corporations, and corporate polluters. Spitzer has not won all his cases—for example, a jury acquitted a former BankAmerica broker on charges of improper mutual funds trading (Gasparino 2005b)—but he has

succeeded in obtaining large settlements and concessions in many of the cases he has pursued.

Some critics complained that Spitzer was engaging in political opportunism; others argued that he was going too easy on Wall Street firms by not seeking criminal indictments. Spitzer claimed that he was more concerned with imposing real reform on how Wall Street firms did business than with high-profile criminal prosecutions of a select group of Wall Street executives. Spitzer was declared "Crusader of the Year" by *Time* magazine at the end of 2002 (Ignatius 2002–2003). To some legislators, Spitzer seemed to be engaging in legislating rather than prosecution. To some critics, Spitzer was inappropriately engaging in corporate management by forcing policy changes with threats of indictment (Orland 2004). Whether or not his approach was appropriate, he was described in some quarters as the most feared man on Wall Street.

---

charges.) At a Senate Judiciary Committee hearing in 1986, the Justice Department claimed dramatic increases in white collar crime prosecutions and the development of specialized expertise and prosecutorial units within the department (Committee on the Judiciary 1987). Other data generated by the FBI indicated a decline in white collar crime convictions between 1983 and 1986 (Caringella-MacDonald 1990).

Throughout the 1980s and into the 1990s, the conservative Republican Reagan and the first Bush administrations showed little commitment to prosecuting white collar crime. Still, relatively autonomous U.S. attorneys generated some momentum in this realm, vigorously pursuing S & L fraud, insider trading, and criminal corruption directed at high-level government officials and politicians. The application of RICO to white collar crime and emerging federal sentencing guidelines were among the new arsenal of potent prosecutorial weapons. The Clinton administration in the 1990s was somewhat more ideologically attuned to pursuing white collar crime cases, and a dramatic increase in the pursuit of antitrust cases in particular

occurred during the early years of this administration (Labaton 1995b). The antitrust case against Microsoft in the late 1990s was arguably the highest-profile case undertaken during the Clinton years (Auletta 2001; Heilemann 2001). But the Clinton administration developed other priorities, and federal prosecutors continued to be somewhat constrained by the complexities of pursuing corporate crime cases (France and Carney 2002; Leaf 2002). The George W. Bush administration could hardly have been more ideologically resistant to aggressively pursuing corporate crime, and its Justice Department retreated from the initiative to break up Microsoft (A. Cohen 2001b). In the wake of the corporate scandals of 2001–2002, and especially in light of its numerous ties to Enron, this administration was compelled to embrace some tough rhetoric and calls for prosecution of corporate executives (Norris 2002c). But it seemed to critics that this response was wholly driven by political pressures, was clearly not reflected in such areas as environmental crime, and would not be sustained if public concern about corporate crime declined or was deflected by other threats.

Prosecutors continued to be subjected to formid-able corporate lobbying efforts to discontinue the pursuit of cases against corporations (Khanna 2004). However, by the mid-2000s, relatively autonomous federal prosecutors had pursued and won dozens of major white collar crime cases (Berenson 2004d). Prosecutors lost a few cases but were more often than not successful in obtaining guilty pleas or verdicts.

The various federal agencies are one source of referrals for federal criminal prosecution. Even though a great deal of evidence of white collar crime activity comes to the attention of the Internal Revenue Service, the Environmental Protection Agency, and the Securities and Exchange Commis-sion, these agencies are not always eager to refer cases to the Justice Department. In one sense, any such referral is an admission of failure on their part; once the Justice Department takes on a case, the regulatory agency loses control of it. In addition, the SEC is conscious of the need to meet higher standards of proof in criminal cases and is often skeptical that criminal prosecution will result in the most satisfactory resolution of a case involving secu-rities (Shapiro 1985). Nevertheless, during a recent 10-year period, the SEC referred over 600 cases to the Department of Justice for possible prosecution (Leaf 2002). In recent years, federal prosecutors have also developed a more cooperative relationship with the EPA and OSHA in the pursuit of employers who flout safety laws, putting workers at risk (Bar-stow and Bergman 2005).

Federal prosecutors in the recent era have increasingly cooperated with other entities, such as state and local prosecutors in "parallel proceedings" against corporate offenders, or simultaneous pro-ceedings arising out of the same circumstances (Lowell and Arnold 2003). They are also authorized to bring civil proceedings against white collar offen-ders (Mann 1992b). Because monetary penalties are often imposed in white collar crime cases, a prose-cutor may have a much better chance of successfully resolving a civil case that imposes civil penalties equivalent to (if not exceeding) applicable criminal sanctions. The role of civil suits in white collar crime cases is more fully explored later in this chapter.

The Prosecution of Antitrust Cases

Violations of antitrust law are one form of white collar crime that exemplify the need for federal prosecution. The prosecution of antitrust cases, directed at various anticompetitive business prac-tices, has been highly selective and especially influ-enced by the political ideology of the incumbent administration (Clinard and Yeager 1980; Davis 2005). Corporate antitrust cases tend to be large and complicated, stretching across various juris-dictions and lasting an extended period of time. Antitrust cases initiated by the Federal Trade Commission are more likely to be settled by nego-tiation and agreement, whereas the Department of Justice's Antitrust Division tends to be more enforce-ment oriented (Jamieson 1994). After an initial investigation of a substantive complaint and the circulation of evidentiary memos, the determination to prosecute is based on the quality of the evidence, amount of interstate commerce, size of the parties involved, and likely impact of such prosecution on the department's reputation (Scott 1989). In most cases, a criminal prosecution is not pursued; when it is, a "no contest" plea and small fine are typical.

Once federal prosecutors begin to turn on the heat in price-fixing cases, conspirators tend to be eager to cooperate by testifying against associates to minimize their own exposure to sanctions. A 1974 revision of the Sherman Act that provided for felony provisions in antitrust cases led to fewer cases, less plea bargaining, and more acquittals. In recent years, the Justice Department has pursued fewer antitrust cases, but the cases pursued tend to be big cases and more often have an international dimen-sion (Cooper and Dedjinou 2005). The Justice Department attempts to encourage voluntary com-pliance by corporations and only seeks criminal indictments in cases where clear, intentional viola-tions are involved.

The Prosecution of Environmental Crime

Throughout most of our history, the parties responsible for myriad types of environmental destruction have not been subjected to criminal prosecution, although private parties have traditionally initiated civil suits against corporations and other entities whose polluting activities caused harm. The Rivers and Harbors Act (1899), considered the first congressional expression of intent to criminalize polluting activity, did not lead to any serious, measurable prosecutorial activity against environmental criminals for the first seven decades of the 20th century (Shover and Routhe 2005; Starr 1991). In the late 1960s and early 1970s, an environmentalist movement emerged, reflecting a shift from industrial values promoting exploitation of natural resources to postindustrial values favoring environmental protection (Hedman 1991). For most of the 1970s, a wave of new laws and the newly established Environmental Protection Agency were the principal legal system manifestations of this value shift. Still, little actual criminal prosecution of environmental offenders occurred.

During the relatively conservative Nixon and Ford administrations, the EPA resisted referring environmental cases to the Department of Justice for criminal prosecution; only 25 federal criminal cases were prosecuted on environmental charges during all of the 1970s (DiMento 1993). Only during the Carter administration (1977–1981) did criminal prosecutions increase. During the 1980s, the level of criminal investigative and prosecutorial resources directed toward environmental crime expanded considerably, despite the conservative Reagan administration; by 1985, up to 50 cases a year were being referred to the Department of Justice for criminal action (DiMento 1993). This expansion reflected autonomous momentum against such crime, fueled in part by considerable public outrage over revelations in 1983 of corrupt dealings between high-level EPA officials and corporate polluters.

In one interpretation, however, Department of Justice prosecutions of environmental criminals had leveled off during the first Bush administration (Adler and Lord 1991). The Clinton administration imposed a somewhat higher priority on pursuing environmental cases, and in 2000, that administration's final year, the EPA referred 236 cases to the Department of Justice for criminal prosecution,

resulting in the imposition of $122 million in fines (Jalley et al. 2002). A criminal case is most likely to be pursued when significant environmental harm is linked with culpable conduct, although many other factors may come into play. Despite some modest increases in prosecutions, fines, and prison sentences for individual corporate executives, there has been a systematic reluctance to imprison environmental offenders or to fine corporate environmental offenders more than a fraction (1 to 5 percent) of the statutory maximum for these offenses. The George W. Bush administration was criticized for pulling back on the enforcement and prosecution of environmental cases (Burns and Lynch 2004). Nevertheless, the EPA has some 200 criminal investigators who build cases for federal prosecutors, and some significant prison sentences were imposed in environmental cases in the recent era (Barstow and Bergman 2005). Ongoing public concern was sure to be one influence on future prosecutions.

Special Prosecutors (Independent Counsel)

Cases of governmental crime or political white collar crime are inherently problematic for prosecutors, who may be accused of either conducting vendettas against political enemies or failing to prosecute fully political allies or superiors. Special prosecutors, or *independent counsels*, have sometimes been appointed in politically sensitive cases to act free from direct supervision by the administration in power (Harriger 1992).

The Watergate affair illustrated the potential problems involved in prosecuting governmental and political white collar crime (Silverstein 1988). The Justice Department officials originally investigating the Watergate break-in had to report to President Nixon, who was himself deeply involved in covering it up. Under great public pressure in 1973, Nixon appointed a special prosecutor, Archibald Cox, but when Cox attempted to subpoena incriminating White House tapes later that year, Nixon fired him—or persuaded the solicitor general to fire him after the attorney general and his deputy resigned rather than do so. This "Saturday

Night Massacre" was a key factor in Nixon's resignation in 1974. The next two Watergate Special Prosecutors, Leon Jaworski and Henry Ruth, directed the case through the conviction and imprisonment of some key conspirators, although neither sought an indictment against Nixon himself.

The office of special prosecutor was formally created by the Ethics in Government Act of 1978; some further amendment of the office resulted from the Independent Counsel Reauthorization Act of 1987 (Laughlin 1989). The formal creation of the special prosecutor's office was clearly a response to the Watergate affair and its investigation (Nolan 1990). It was intended to address the obvious, inherent potential for a conflict of interest when the Justice Department, with its various ties to other divisions of the executive branch, is faced with prosecuting criminal allegations against powerful people in that branch (Baker 1992; Clayton 1992; Rogovin and Rogovin 1993).

Under the Independent Counsel Reauthorization Act, the U.S. Attorney General, after receiving allegations of illegalities by a government official covered by the Act, is required within a certain period of time to either determine that there is no substance to the allegations or notify the special division of the Court of Appeals for the District of Columbia, which is authorized to appoint and oversee a special (or independent) prosecutor. In *Morrison v. Olson* (108 S. Ct. 2597 1988), the U.S. Supreme Court ruled that this office was not a violation of the Constitution's separation of powers doctrine (Laughlin 1989); no increase in congressional power at the expense of executive power is involved.

Special prosecutors investigated the Iran-Contra arms case during the Reagan administration, the first Bush administration's handling of a billion-dollar bank fraud case involving illegal loans to Iraq, and various allegations against President Clinton (Sciolino 1992; Spencer 1993; Stewart 1996). But the aggressive pursuit of President Clinton by Independent Counsel Kenneth Starr, ultimately focusing especially on Clinton's involvement with intern Monica Lewinsky and leading to the effort to impeach the president, was widely criticized on

many grounds (Walsh 1998). This prosecutorial investigation was seen by many as heavily politicized, costly ($40 million or more), and generally harmful in its relentless pursuit of allegations relating to sexual misconduct. The independent counsel law itself was also widely criticized, and not only by targets of these prosecutors, as unnecessary, unfair, and ineffective (Carter 1988; O'Sullivan 1996; Smith 1992). Efforts in 1999 to introduce a reformed Independent Counsel law, imposing some limitations on jurisdiction, time frame, and budgets, were unsuccessful (Committee on Governmental Affairs 1999). But independent prosecutors continue to be appointed in some politically sensitive cases. For example, in 2005 an independent prosecutor investigated allegations of disclosure of classified information to reporters by high-level White House officials (Rich 2005b). Inherent conflicts of interest exist when high-level government officials are investigated by a Justice Department with close political ties to those officials.

THE ROLE OF THE GRAND JURY IN WHITE COLLAR CRIME CASES

The grand jury is more important in white collar crime cases than in conventional cases because a grand jury indictment is constitutionally required in the federal system, in which a higher proportion of white collar crime cases are prosecuted. In some cases, both federal and state grand juries hear testimony in the same case (Thomas 2003). Many state courts have eliminated grand juries.

In principle, one of the traditional rationales for grand jury indictments—to act as a buffer against vindictive, improper prosecution—is especially applicable in certain classes of white collar crime. A grand jury ideally acts as a check on politically motivated prosecution; it may also be more appropriate for a grand jury of anonymous citizens to return indictments in sensitive cases involving the powerful than for a politically vulnerable prosecutor to seek an indictment in such cases.

B O X 11.3 "Perp Walks" for White Collar Crime Defendants

Top executives of Adelphia and WorldCom were arrested in 2002, handcuffed, and marched into court in front of journalists and television cameras (Weiser 2002a). Conventional crime defendants have certainly been subjected to such "perp walks," but they have been less commonly applied to white collar crime defendants. On the one hand, the arrest procedures have been justified as standard practice when individuals are charged with serious offenses, which should be evenly applied without regard to the social status of the accused or the specific character of the offense. On the other hand, critics complain that perp walks, especially if they are deliberately staged for the benefit of the press, are prejudicial to the rights of the accused, bias potential jurors against them, and are gratuitous attempts to shame these defendants.

A second rationale for grand juries in white collar crime cases emphasizes the secrecy of the inquiry. Ideally, allegations about illegal activities by reputable organizations and individuals should be examined behind closed doors; if these allegations are wholly unsupported, the profoundly damaging publicity of a public inquiry is avoided. Finally, special grand juries are sometimes impaneled to investigate major ongoing criminal enterprises, including various forms of governmental or business crime, and the broad subpoena powers of a grand jury enable it to conduct such investigations especially thoroughly.

The grand jury, then, is an important element of white collar crime prosecution. The accused in such cases are especially concerned with avoiding indictment, and defense lawyers have attempted to challenge the traditional, strict constraints on their participation in grand jury hearings (First 1990). On the prosecutorial side, the subpoena powers of the grand jury may be essential for gathering evidence in complex cases in which a mass of documents and many witnesses are involved. In the government case against the accounting firm Arthur Andersen in 2002 for illegal document destruction, lawyers for Andersen claimed that the government was using a federal grand jury improperly to gather evidence and prepare for trial, after the firm had already been indicted (Eichenwald 2002d). The government lawyers claimed it was permissible for the grand jury to engage in an ongoing inquiry in the case, with the possibility of additional charges as a consequence. Still, prosecutors are often ambivalent about grand juries, finding them useful in certain situations and cumbersome in others. Box 11.3 addresses a phenomenon that occurs well outside the confines of a grand jury—the "perp walk."

DEFENDING WHITE COLLAR CRIMINALS

It is commonly assumed that one of the main differences between defendants in conventional crime cases and white collar crime defendants is that the latter can afford private lawyers and accordingly get a much better defense. This is typically true but not uniformly so (Weisburd et al. 1991). For example, antitrust defendants always have private counsel; embezzlement defendants often do not.

Defendants with private counsel usually have an advantage, but an indigent defendant who is represented by a highly experienced public defender could conceivably get a better defense than a white collar defendant with modest means who hires a lawyer with relatively little experience in such cases. On the upper end of the scale, of course, wealthy white collar crime defendants and corporate defendants can hire the best available legal counsel, which likely gives them a significant advantage but does not guarantee a favorable result. In his highly publicized securities fraud case, Michael Milken hired a team of some of the

---

B O X 11.4   David Boies and White Collar Crime Cases

David Boies and his firm, Boies, Schiller and Flexner, have been at the center of many major white collar crime cases (Donovan 2005; Liptak 2002a). The firm of 150 lawyers charges $700 an hour and takes in about $100 million in revenue annually. The firm has been retained to represent Adelphia, Tyco International, Qwest, and Andrew Fastow, former Chief Financial Officer of Enron. About 20 percent of this firm's cases are class action lawsuits, although it has both defended and attacked corporations in such cases, winning a $512 million settlement from the Sotheby and Christie's auction houses, for example. Boies was retained to represent the government in its attempt to break up Microsoft; he also represented Al Gore in his challenge to the Florida vote in the 2000 presidential election. White collar crime defense lawyers, then, do not necessarily take the defense side in all cases or limit themselves to criminal law. Rather ironically, in 2005, Boies—the self-styled "white knight" of white collar crime cases—found himself accused of conflicts of interest when it came out that a document management firm partially owned by offspring of his was recommended to his firm's clients without disclosing the financial interest of his family members (Glater and Sorkin 2005). Lawyers representing clients sued by Boies on behalf of a client corporation also claimed incompetence or improper withholding of documents by the document management firm.

---

best lawyers in the country. Despite legal bills of $1 million a month or more in the final years of his case, Milken ended up with a $600 million fine and a 10-year prison sentence, although this sentence was subsequently reduced substantially (Labaton 1990a; Stewart 1993). In more recent cases, some former corporate CEOs—including Martha Stewart, John Rigas, Bernie Ebbers, and Dennis Kozlowski—were convicted of serious charges despite having top-of-the-line defense attorneys. And lawyers who defend clients accused of white collar crimes complain that many existing procedural rules and practices—including prosecutorial freedom to "dump" thousands of documents on them without specifying which will be part of the case, greater difficulty in obtaining government witness lists, and limitations on use of witness prior statements—impose substantial burdens on defense attorneys (Morvillo, Bohrer, and Balter 2005). These critics argue that the procedural criminal law should more fully recognize the differences between conventional and white collar crime cases.

White collar crime defense work has become a fully recognized (if still somewhat uncommon) legal practice specialty (see Box 11.4). Defense lawyers tend to be somewhat divided between those who adopt a conciliatory, cooperative strategy with prosecutors and those who attempt to intimidate them by threatening all-out legal combat (Lewis 1992). Some practical guides to white collar crime defense provide advice on strategies for controlling case information and minimizing client criminal liability (Bailey and Rothblatt 1984; Lawless 1988; Magnuson 1992). Although the general rule is to avoid commenting to the media in high-profile cases, a proactive public relations campaign may be adopted as part of the defense strategy (Kasinof 1991; Magnuson 1992). Regardless, the overall objective is to minimize damage at every stage of the criminal justice procedure.

The major study of the white collar crime bar is Kenneth Mann's *Defending White-Collar Crime: A Portrait of Attorneys at Work* (1985), which studied defense lawyers who handled white collar crime cases in the Southern District of New York between 1974 and 1978. White collar crime defense was apparently the fastest-growing specialty in the legal profession during this period. Many lawyers who chose this specialty were graduates of elite law schools who had gained firsthand experience with white collar crime cases by serving as assistant U.S. attorneys. They were drawn to the specialty of defense counsel because it is quite lucrative (up to $300 an hour at that time), allows for solo practice or affiliation with a small firm (as opposed to a large organization), and often produces intrinsically fascinating cases with complex issues and high stakes. The specific kinds of cases handled by these lawyers include securities fraud, tax fraud, embezzlement, corruption, bribery, conspiracy to defraud, criminal regulatory violations, antitrust violations, and bankruptcy fraud.

According to Mann's study, much earlier involvement in the case is one of the primary differences between white collar crime defense work and conventional crime defense work. Because a major objective of these defenses is to control information, defense lawyers seek to ascertain what the prosecution knows and try to keep harmful evidence from being revealed. Clients and other potential witnesses are instructed to refrain from disclosing anything that does not have to be disclosed. White collar crime lawyers often employ investigators to learn as much as possible about the case, beyond even what the prosecutors may know, hoping to be in a position to dissuade the government from even seeking an indictment. Because white collar crime prosecutions require such a large commitment of government time and resources, the prosecution may be receptive to a well-informed argument that it will not be able to obtain a conviction or that the client has not really violated laws.

Alternatively, defense lawyers may seek to head off an indictment in exchange for the client's cooperation with prosecutors. A defense lawyer's previous experience as a prosecutor or a regulatory agency lawyer is often especially useful at this stage, both in terms of finely honed skills as a negotiator and personal connections with the prosecutors in the case. If the client is indicted anyway, defense lawyers are likely to explore the best possible deal in return for a guilty plea, emphasizing that the government will expend formidable resources if it is to mount a successful prosecution. Corporate lawyers in particular may use their clout to try to get hostile judges off particular cases and to block the participation of hostile witnesses and lawyers wherever possible (Nader and Smith 1996). If the case goes to trial, white collar defense lawyers attempt to exploit their superior financial resources to challenge the prosecution's case at every possible step. They may attempt to take advantage of the

greater ambiguity of the pertinent white collar crime laws and the great complexity of white collar cases generally. Defense lawyers—especially in cases involving complicated financial deals, as in the Enron case—can argue that what their client is accused of is not in fact a crime as defined by law (Eichenwald 2002c). And in the case of high-level corporate executives, defense lawyers will often argue that the defendant executive relied upon the advice of lawyers and accountants—that is, "professional reliance"—and so cannot be guilty of criminal intent (Seglin 2003). In civil lawsuits, however, a claim by top corporate executives that they did not know—or understand—what was going on within their corporation may work against them, as it can be argued that they are being well compensated to know (Eichenwald 2002c). For lower-level white collar executives, defense lawyers may claim that they were "just following orders" and cannot be held accountable for the illegal orders themselves (Glater 2005e).

Since white collar defendants often have relatively good reputations, defense lawyers may stress their "good character" and argue that a person with such a good character would be highly unlikely to engage in illegal or unethical conduct (Glater 2004b). As in all criminal trials, a key decision has to be made on whether or not the defendant should take the stand as a witness (see Box 11.5). Attacking the credibility of prosecution witnesses is still another tactic commonly adopted by defense lawyers when white collar crime cases go to trial (Hanley 2001a). Such witnesses frequently have some form of complicity in the crime being prosecuted and are attacked because they have been granted immunity from prosecution. The impeachment of prosecutorial witnesses is also a standard tactic in many conventional crime cases, but such cases are also more likely to have independent witnesses and forensic evidence. Scientific evidence in white collar crime cases—for example, relating to the consequences of limited exposure to asbestos—may be especially vulnerable to challenge (Glater 2002c). Defense lawyers in white collar crime cases must also avoid alienating jurors (mostly ordinary citizens) with overly technical cases or an elitist

---

B O X   11.5   **To Testify or Not to Testify**

All criminal case defendants have a Fifth Amendment right not to testify during their own trials. In conventional crime cases, a criminal defendant with a long record of criminal convictions is often well advised not to testify because the prosecution can attempt to impeach the credibility of the defendant witness by asking questions about that record. White collar crime defendants would appear to have some advantages as witnesses in their own defense, both because they are less likely to have previous criminal records and are more likely to be articulate and present themselves in a favorable way. However, they may also open themselves up to direct questioning on matters that cannot be easily explained away.

In the recent high-profile white collar crime cases, defendants made different choices on whether or not to take the stand. Investment banker Frank Quattrone was convicted on obstruction of justice charges despite testifying in his own defense at both his trials; jurors apparently did not find his testimony credible (Sorkin 2004c). Dennis Kozlowski, former

CEO of Tyco, was convicted of looting the company of hundreds of millions of dollars, despite testifying in his own defense (Sorkin 2005b). In the original trial on these charges, which ended with a hung jury, he had chosen not to testify. Former WorldCom CEO Bernard Ebbers was convicted on corporate fraud charges in 2005, with his testimony that he did not understand the company's finances and technology widely ridiculed (Belson 2005c; Glater and Belson 2005). After all, Ebbers had accepted hundreds of millions of dollars in compensation for leading this company.

Martha Stewart, in her trial on obstruction of justice charges, had made the choice not to testify but was convicted anyway (Hays and Eaton 2004). On the other hand, HealthSouth CEO Richard Scrushy was acquitted of corporate fraud charges after a trial where he did not take the stand (Romero and Whitmire 2005). Accordingly, there are possible rewards and risks involved in this decision, with no formula for sure success.

---

image (Belson and Glater 2005). Accordingly, some such lawyers adopt a deliberately "folksy" style in the interest of persuading the jury to accept their arguments on behalf of clients.

At the sentencing stage, white collar crime attorneys usually play a much larger role than conventional crime defense lawyers because defendants typically have many credible accomplishments to counterbalance their illegal acts. Again, defense lawyers may emphasize the ambiguous nature of the offense and the often more diffuse character of responsibility or blameworthiness in these cases. Michael Milken's lawyers orchestrated a letter-writing campaign by numerous prominent people attesting to Milken's good character and deeds, and they argued that at most he had committed technical violations on behalf of some clients in the context of overwhelmingly legitimate business dealings (Stewart 1991). Similarly, in the case of A. Alfred Taubman, the principal owner and former chairman of Sotheby's auction house, defense lawyers produced 90 letters in his support from

such prominent individuals as former President Gerald Ford and former Secretary of State Henry Kissinger, and emphasized his many charitable contributions and his poor health at age 78 (Vogel and Blumenthal 2002). The judge sentenced Taubman to a year and a day in prison and a $7.5 million fine for his central role in fixing auction house commissions in cooperation with his major competitor. In the case of Bernard Ebbers of WorldCom, his lawyers produced 169 letters of support on his behalf, and a plea for leniency was put forth on the basis that Ebbers had "lost everything" and was suffering from heart problems (Belson 2005e). Ebbers received a stiff prison sentence anyway. If defense lawyers are unsuccessful in sparing their client a prison sentence, however, they may have some influence over where their clients serve their sentence (Kuczynski 2001). This is typically not the case with conventional offenders.

Finally, white collar crime lawyers play an important role at the appeal stage because the complexity of many white collar crime cases may generate a wider range of options for appealing a conviction. If a client has financial means, a lawyer can devote a great deal of time to the appeal process.

White collar crime defense lawyers can find themselves caught in the middle of various ethical conundrums. One concern is the source of lawyers' fees. In at least some white collar crime cases, there is reason to suspect that the fees come from illegally obtained funds. White collar crime lawyers are now more vulnerable concerning the source of their fees. Section 1957 of the *Money Laundering Control Act* (1986) makes lawyers liable for criminal prosecution if they deposit client fees in excess of $10,000 that they know to come from criminally derived sources (Mann 1985; Lawless 1988). White collar criminal defense lawyers must now ensure that they obtain their fees without putting themselves in legal jeopardy.

In corporate crime cases, the question of whether the corporate counsel represents the corporation or individual executives may arise (Clinard and Yeager 1980). When counsel's primary responsibility is to the corporation, then individual executives may find that corporate counsel attempts to shift blame for the illegality to them personally as a way of shielding the corporation from criminal liability. It is not unethical for corporations to employ defense lawyers to represent accused corporate executives; however, the individual interests of the accused executives may be at odds (Clinard and Yeager 1980). A prominent Wall Street lawyer, Martin Lipton, has played so many roles with clients—including advisor on mergers and acquisitions, counselor to CEOs, corporate governance expert, and consultant on executive compensation—that conflict-of-interest questions have been raised (Thomas 2005c). But defense lawyers for corporations have also been accused of much broader forms of unethical behavior, including their strategy of seeking protective court orders and confidential settlements (Nader and Smith 1996). The confidential agreements may help to protect the reputation of the corporation, but they also deny the public important information about harmful practices of corporations and may lead to further injury.

ADJUDICATING WHITE COLLAR CRIME: PLEA BARGAINING AND TRIAL

The great majority of conventional criminal cases in most jurisdictions are resolved by plea bargaining. In some jurisdictions, well over 90 percent of the indictments for crimes are disposed of in this way. The process of negotiation in white collar crime cases is much more intense before charges are filed; indeed, formal charging of a white collar client is more likely to be regarded as a failure than is true in conventional crime cases (Mann 1985).

When the defense's arguments against charging fail, however, a strong incentive exists to plead guilty because of the low likelihood of winning cases for which such arguments have failed. Given the larger measure of resources that typically must be devoted to successfully prosecuting white collar crime cases, it makes sense that prosecutors will principally pursue formal charges only in cases in which formidable evidence for conviction exists. An analysis of sentencing data for 1,597 white collar crime cases in seven federal courts suggests that in complex cases the accused can often avoid punishment or incarceration if they are willing to plead guilty and cooperate with the efficient processing of their case (Albonetti 1994). White collar defendants are especially likely to be intimidated by the prospect of a prison sentence and may resist pleading guilty if such a sentence is involved. Michael Milken strongly resisted a negotiated plea because of his unwillingness to go to prison (Kornbluth 1992; Stewart 1993). By the time he finally entered into plea negotiations, he had lost much of his original negotiating leverage, and thus he received a stiff prison sentence, which was reduced because of his post-conviction cooperation in other cases. On the other hand, John McNamara, a Long Island car dealer who admitted defrauding General Motors of $436 million, was allowed to keep almost $2 million in assets and remain in business when he agreed early on to plead guilty and testify against former local officials, who were subsequently acquitted of bribery charges (Marks 1995). In the corporate crime cases of the 2000s, the standard tactic of offering some form of consideration to executives at the center of the wrongdoing, in return for guilty pleas and testimony against higher-level executives, was also applied (Eichenwald 2002b). Scott Sullivan, the Chief Financial Officer of WorldCom, pleaded guilty and testified against the CEO, Bernard Ebbers, and accordingly received a much lighter sentence—five years—than he would have had he been convicted at trial (Bayot and Farzad 2005).

White collar crime defendants might be expected to have greater confidence in their lawyers than would be true of conventional crime defendants, and the lawyers themselves are more likely to have economic incentives to take white collar (as opposed to conventional) crime cases to trial. From a strategic point of view, the white collar crime defense may believe that in court it can exploit ambiguities in the law, the complex or problematic nature of the evidence, and the defendant's respectable appearance and reputable standing in the community more effectively than would be true in a conventional crime case. The prosecutor may resist making plea bargaining arrangements in those few white collar crime cases in which formal charges are filed, both because of the greater visibility of the case and the prosecutor's confidence that the evidence will support the charges. Altogether, there appears to be somewhat less cooperative negotiation and somewhat more adversarial confrontation in white collar crime cases as compared to conventional crime cases.

The percentage of all white collar crime cases that advance to trial is small (Weisburd et al. 1991). Nevertheless, white collar crime defendants are more likely to plead not guilty and go to trial than is true of conventional crime defendants.

When the state widens the net and seeks more indictments against more individuals, defendants apparently become intimidated and are more likely to plead guilty (Adler and Lord 1991). In environmental crime cases, for example, the percentage of cases settled by plea bargaining more than doubled following a substantial increase in indictments in such cases.

THE ROLE OF THE TRIAL JURY

Controversy concerning trial juries centers on their representativeness, possible biases, and competence. On the issue of representativeness, neither conventional crime defendants nor high-status white collar crime defendants are likely to face juries literally made up of their peers. Are typical jurors more or less likely to be favorably disposed toward corporate and occupational crime defendants? Some evidence suggests that in criminal cases, jurors are more likely to hold corporations more blameworthy than individual executives for wrongdoing (Hans 1989). In other circumstances, especially in civil liability cases, jurors resist holding corporations responsible for harmful consequences that they believe individual plaintiffs should have anticipated; thus, with some recent exceptions, juries have refused to hold tobacco companies responsible for the harmful consequences of smoking. Jurors are not necessarily biased against corporations because they have *deep pockets* (MacCoun 1996). Although jurors may expect more of corporations than of individuals, they are also wary of plaintiffs attempting to capitalize on juror sympathy and to seek compensation to which they are not entitled (Hans 2000). Most jurors are neither anti-business nor pro-plaintiff (see Box 11.6).

A body of research strongly suggests that jurors are most likely to be sympathetic toward people like themselves. Some research has established that higher-status, better-educated, older males are more likely than others to be selected as jury forepersons (Wrightsman 1991). If it is also true that forepersons with such personal attributes tend to exercise some influence over other jurors, then middle-class white collar crime defendants might be expected to have a marginal advantage with juries because jurors generally (and more influential jurors in particular) may see defendants as more similar to themselves than would be the case with defendants in conventional crime cases. The types of crimes for which white collar crime defendants are charged—income tax evasion is a classic example—may not seem to jurors so remote from things they have done themselves or could imagine

---

B O X 11.6 Jurors and Punitive Damages

The role of jurors in determining the appropriate punishment for convicted corporate offenders has been a contentious topic of ongoing debate (Liptak 2002b; Sunstein et al. 2002). In the United States, almost uniquely, the jury sets the amount of punitive damages. The law itself has provided clear guidance to jurors on how to establish the correct amount when a determination is made to award punitive damages, and juries have taken quite different approaches to establishing the amount to be awarded. Although the awarding of such damages is quite rare—it occurs in about 4 percent of these cases—in some high-profile instances, jurors have awarded extreme or extravagant amounts as punishment (Glaberson 2001b). For example, in August 2005, a jury in Texas voted for a $229 million punitive damages fine against the pharmaceutical giant Merck, in a case involving its painkiller Vioxx and a patient on that drug who died (Berenson 2005c). In most cases where such damages are awarded, however, they are quite rational and not arbitrary or extreme (Graddy 2001). The notion of "Robin Hood" juries imposing huge punitive damage awards on corporate defendants and awarding them to ordinary plaintiffs seems to be largely a myth.

---

doing, especially compared to the alleged crimes of inner-city muggers.

Of course, it is also true that elite white collar offenders may inspire deep-seated resentment on the part of jurors. In a mock jury study involving 160 undergraduates, highly esteemed medical specialists were found to be especially vulnerable to jurors' negative bias in homicide cases, but in more moderate criminal cases involving Medicaid fraud, their status seemed to work in their favor (Rosoff 1989). The effects of jurors' bias are not simple, and prestige may work either for or against white collar crime defendants. And defendants may attempt to directly influence jurors' perceptions of them. In the 2005 trial of HealthSouth CEO Richard Scrushy, with predominantly black jurors, it was noted that he joined a black church shortly before the trial and that some black ministers accompanied him to the courtroom (Whitmire 2005). The jurors, however, claimed that it was the lack of credibility of prosecution witnesses that led them to acquit Scrushy of corporate fraud charges.

Another basic question about trial juries concerns their competence. Judge Jerome Frank once claimed that a jury applies law it does not understand to facts it cannot get straight (Vidmar 1989). To the extent that this sweeping claim holds any truth, it is more likely to apply to complex white collar cases than to conventional crime cases. Even though considerable research suggests that in most cases juries perform quite competently and focus on the legally relevant evidence as opposed to extra-legal factors (Hans 1989), this finding must be qualified somewhat for criminal and civil white collar cases.

Some studies of juries have found that they are able to follow judge's instructions, when explained; they are neither overwhelmed by nor dismissive of expert testimony; and their deliberations impact on their punitive award assessments (Diamond and Casper 1992). On the other hand, a number of studies of complex criminal and civil cases involving corporations or high-level frauds found that jurors could not accurately remember important scientific, medical, and economic information; reacted more to witnesses' personal attributes than to their testimony; and misunderstood the judge's instructions (Hans 1989; Hans and Vidmar 1986; Institute for Civil Justice 1992). A law professor argues that the jury in the case of the Andersen accounting firm in 2002 found against the firm because it did not understand the professional obligations of an Andersen lawyer (Gillers 2002). Jurors in cases against corporations must evaluate collective responsibility, which is a more complicated concept than individual responsibility (Hans 1989). For those reasons, many defendants choose a bench trial (before a judge only) over a jury trial, especially if they are offering a "technical" defense that a judge might be able to appreciate more objectively.

B O X 11.7   **Reversal of Arthur Andersen Conviction Due to Jury Charge by Judge**

On May 31, 2005, the U. S. Supreme Court overturned the conviction of the Arthur Andersen accounting firm in connection with obstruction of justice charges against the firm (Greenhouse 2005). In the face of a criminal investigation of Enron, for which Andersen served as auditor, Andersen employees shredded numerous documents. The Supreme Court, however, declared that the law upon which the government based its case, the Victim and Witness Protection Act, prohibits one party from "corruptly persuading" another to destroy documents, but the judge's charge to the jury in this case failed to clarify that, in order to convict, it had to be persuaded that Andersen employees knowingly violated the law. This finding of the Court did not rule on whether or not Andersen should have been indicted and whether or not it was actually innocent of the charges against it, only that the judge's charge to the jury was improper.

In criminal cases requiring a unanimous jury verdict, it is worth remembering that a single juror can derail a jury from reaching a verdict, resulting in a hung trial. In one notorious case, a six-month trial of two Tyco executives (Dennis Kozlowski and Mark Swartz), accused of defrauding the company of some $600 million, the judge declared a mistrial after a renegade juror declared that she had received a threatening letter (McEntegart 2004; Sorkin 2004a). This single juror, a retired teacher and lawyer, disagreed with all the other jurors who were apparently prepared to vote to convict the defendants. A retrial had to be held.

Overall, the evidence does not suggest that juries are either significantly more or less likely than judges to acquit white collar crime defendants or impose tougher penalties (Glaberson 2001b; Levi 1987). One commentator has suggested that juries in federal cases are more likely to convict than juries in state cases are because in the former cases, prosecutors get both the first and last word (Magnuson 1992). Far more remains to be learned about the role of juries in white collar crime cases.

JUDGES AND THE SENTENCING OF WHITE COLLAR CRIMINALS

The judge is the principal officer of the court. Aristotle equated the judge with "living justice." One of the great 20th-century associate justices of the U.S. Supreme Court, Benjamin Cardozo (1921), said that "in the long run, there is no guarantee of justice except the personality of the judge." In conventional crime cases, judges typically deal with defendants who are different from themselves and have committed offenses quite removed from their own patterns of behavior; this is not necessarily the case in white collar crime cases. Judges presiding over these cases often confront special challenges. The trial is likely to take longer, and testimony and evidence will more often be dry and tedious. Given the greater complexity of the law, the more ambiguous elements of intent and culpability, and the greater sophistication of defense lawyers involved in white collar crime cases, judges are more vulnerable to error. In particular, the judge's charge to the jury is often open to challenge (see Box 11.7).

SENTENCING

Two beliefs about the judicial sentencing of white collar offenders have been widely adopted over the years. One belief is that white collar offenders are treated more leniently at sentencing than are conventional offenders; the other is that sentencing is idiosyncratic and haphazard (Clinard and Yeager 1980). At least some evidence can be produced in support of either view.

Many methodological problems are involved in comparing conventional and white collar crime sentences, including inconsistency in defining such crimes, the variable socioeconomic status of white collar crime defendants, and different patterns of processing; for example, white collar crime cases are far more likely to be federal than state cases (Eitle 2000; Hagan and Nagel 1982). Nevertheless, traditionally the harshest sentences have been imposed on conventional offenders such as murderers, rapists, muggers, and burglars. Sentencing leniency may be offered in exchange for testimony and evidence necessary for other convictions. Because such cooperation is more important in complex white collar crime cases than in conventional crime cases, sentencing disparity favoring the white collar defendants results (Nagel and Hagan 1982). The tough "three strikes and you're out" laws have been directed at conventional offenders, not at white collar crime offenders (Geis 1996). It is worth noting that the harshest of all sentences, the death penalty, has never been imposed on a convicted white collar offender in the United States.

Traditionally, judges have been reluctant to impose tough sentences on businesspeople, apparently believing that they are generally well intentioned even if they have somehow broken the law (Conklin 1977; Leaf 2002). Judges may believe that the shame of criminal prosecution is punishment enough for many such offenders; they often allow businesspeople to remain in the community, where they can resume productive activity and can generate income to make restitution to victims. They may take into account the older age and poorer health of some white collar crime defendants and consider the perceived suffering of families, employees, or other dependents. Some judges may be persuaded by the defendant's articulate expression of contrition, good past record, and absence of directly threatening attributes, and they may perceive that the offense itself was illegal without being fundamentally immoral. Or they may feel the defendant is the scapegoat for an organizational misdeed (Croall 2001; Mokhiber 1988; Wheeler, Mann, and Sarat 1988). All such beliefs, however, contribute to a double standard of criminal justice relative to socioeconomic status.

Two major factors in any sentencing decision are the seriousness of the offense and the record of the accused. A basic paradox confronting judges in white collar crime cases is the contradiction between a serious offense (most typically involving substantial financial harm) and a defendant who is a respected member of the community, has never before been in trouble with the law, belongs to various worthwhile community organizations, and has a good family life (Wheeler, Mann, and Sarat 1988).

On some level, judges are also more likely to experience some sense of empathy—apparently more as a function of identification with common values rather than from similar background—with defendants in white collar crime cases than in cases involving conventional criminals (Croall 2001). On the other hand, because some judges are conscious of their empathy for such offenders, they may lean over backwards to avoid being biased in their favor. They sometimes will consider white collar defendants more culpable than conventional defendants because they expect more of people with a respectable and trusted status, like themselves. White collar crime offenders are more likely to be fined or put on probation than are conventional offenders (Weisburd, Waring, and Chayet 2001). Although community service sentences are not typical, they are more common in white collar crime cases (Croall 2001; Mokhiber 1988). Such sentences imposed on wealthy financiers convicted of securities-related crimes and tax frauds have included running a computer camp, setting up a homeless shelter, and teaching golf to handicapped youths (Lyne 1993). Indeed, a new specialized service identifies community organizations willing to provide such community service assignments to convicted white collar offenders. Dozens of experts in "sentencing mitigation," known as "post-conviction specialists," play a role in the effort to secure an alternative sentence for white collar offenders, although the success of such efforts has been disputed (Kuczynski 2001; Mitchell R. 2002). Sentencing Concepts Inc. requests home confinement and electronic monitoring for its clients. A consultant to Albert J. Pirro Jr., a well-connected Westchester, New York, lawyer convicted of tax fraud in 2000, recommended an alcohol rehabilitation facility for this client, who ended up serving 11 months (of a 29-month sentence) at a Florida prison camp, with the balance of time served in a halfway house.

Much evidence from government reports and scholarly studies supports the contention that white collar criminals are considerably less likely to go to prison than are conventional offenders and that the prison sentences they receive are of shorter duration (Croall 2001; Tillman and Pontell 1992). If one adopts a broad classification of white collar offenders to include low-level fraudsters, this generalization may be less true (Weisburd, Waring, and Chayet 2001). But the prison time served by white collar offenders averages one year, in comparison to almost four years on average for some conventional offenders (e.g., those convicted of robbery). S & L executives who stole more than $100,000 received prison sentences averaging 36 months, compared to more than 55 months for burglars and 65 months for first-time drug dealers (Smith G. B. 2002). James McDermott, a former CEO of an investment bank who pleaded guilty in an insider trading case, served five months of an eight-month sentence in a minimum-security facility. In countless instances over the years, inner-city residents convicted of nonviolent crimes have received long prison sentences, while wealthy corporate and finance executives involved in cases involving losses of millions of dollars have received no prison time at all (Leaf 2002). In May 2005, a man was freed from prison in North Carolina after serving 35 years, having originally been convicted of stealing a black-and-white TV set (Associated Press 2005); no white collar crime offenders, even those complicit in frauds involving vast sums of money, have ever served anything close to that length of time in prison. And no corporate executives ever went to prison for some of the most notorious corporate violence cases, including the Ford Pinto case and the Hooker Chemical Love Canal case. In the Film Recovery Systems case involving the death of a worker exposed to cyanide, the prison sentences imposed by the judge were set aside on appeal

(Barrile 1993a). Although the Aviation Maintenance Company was charged with murder and manslaughter in connection with grossly negligent practices that apparently caused a plane crash with great loss of life, no one went to prison (Bragg 1999b; Wald 1999a). It is often difficult to establish criminal intent in such cases. And if corporate and white collar offenders are convicted, they are more likely to obtain reversals of their conviction on appeal than is the case for conventional offenders.

Explaining Disparities in Sentences for White Collar Offenders

Not surprisingly, some types of white collar offenses elicit harsher sentences than others. Judges are especially tough on people who violate a public trust, although a violation of any occupational trust is typically considered a serious matter as well (Croall 2001; Hagan and Nagel 1982). In a study of white collar offenders processed in a federal court, individuals convicted of crimes such as mail fraud or fraud against a government agency received sentences equivalent in seriousness to conventional crime sentences, whereas most white collar offenders (e.g., those convicted of price fixing) received more lenient treatment (Hagan and Nagel 1982). In another study, CEOs and fraudsters were less likely to elicit a punitive response than were managers and other personnel (Eitle 2000). This study suggested that those in positions of authority and control were less vulnerable to tough sentences than other white collar offenders.

Considerable variation also exists among white collar offenses in the likelihood of receiving probation or fines. In one study, 90 percent of bank embezzlers but only 50 percent of antitrust offenders received probation; 100 percent of antitrust offenders but only 15 percent of bank embezzlers were fined (Weisburd et al. 1991). Most fines are modest and reflect the offender's perceived ability to pay. White collar offenders who have victimized the government are most likely to be fined. Only about 12 percent of the white collar crime offenders in the study were ordered to pay restitution (a proportion roughly equivalent to that for conventional crimes), mostly in cases such as bank embezzlement in which the level of harm was quite small (Weisburd et al. 1991).

Finally, the likelihood of a prison sentence depends significantly on the type of white collar crime involved. In a study of federal white collar crime defendants, Weisburd and colleagues (1991) found that 20 percent of antitrust violators went to prison (generally for short terms), whereas two thirds of the securities fraud offenders received prison sentences. It is clear from these data that it is difficult to generalize about the sentences imposed on individuals classified as white collar offenders.

The influence of a person's class on white collar crime has been much disputed. Part of the difficulty is a lack of consensus on the appropriate meaning of "class" (Benson 1989; Croall 2001; Eitle 2000). Studies conducted by Wheeler, Weisburd, and Bode (1982) and Weisburd and colleagues (1991) produced the surprising finding that higher-status white collar crime offenders received more severe sentences than lower-status white collar crime offenders. The explanation for such a counterintuitive finding may well be that the small number of high-status offenders who get to the formal sentencing stage in a criminal justice proceeding are vulnerable to tough sentences because their offenses are substantial and their visibility high.

Hagan and Parker (1985) concluded that higher-level corporate executives were less likely than subordinate managers to be indicted, tried, and ultimately sentenced for white collar crimes because the law makes it more difficult to establish criminal culpability for higher-level executives. Giving tough sentences for high-level offenders who are indicted, tried, and convicted, aided by attendant high levels of publicity, allows a judge to send a direct message to offenders' peers; the 10-year prison sentence imposed on Michael Milken is one example. But in recent years, in some high-profile cases, unusually stiff prison sentences have been imposed. In 2004, Jamie Olis, a former mid-level executive of Dynergy, received a 24-year prison sentence in connection with a scheme to disguise the corporation's financial problems,

costing investors (and pensioners) millions of dollars (Romero 2004). In 2005, John Rigas, the former head of the Adelphia cable company, and one of his sons (the former Chief Financial Officer) were sentenced to 15 and 20 years in prison respectively for their role in looting the company of hundreds of millions of dollars and concealing its debt (Farzad 2005b). In July of the same year, former WorldCom CEO Bernie Ebbers was sentenced to 25 years in prison after being convicted of having played a central role in his company's multibillion dollar fraud, which led to the largest bankruptcy in American history (Belson 2005f). And in September 2005, former Tyco CEO Dennis Kozlowski was sentenced to $8^1/_3$ to 25 years in a state prison for his role in looting his company of some $150 million (Sorkin 2005e). It remained to be seen, however, whether such sentences would survive appeals and how much time would actually be served.

Some judges are especially outraged when a privileged, powerful member of society engages in illegal actions. Hagan and Parker's (1985) study was conducted after the Watergate affair, and at least some judges may have been responding to a heightened public concern with the crimes of the privileged and powerful. Indeed, in another study of federal sentencing practices during this period, white collar offenders were more likely to receive prison sentences in the post-Watergate period than before, although the sentences were shorter on the average (Hagan and Palloni 1986). Judges in the recent corporate crime cases had to consider their sentencing options in the context of widely diffused public anger and disgust with the greedy and unprincipled actions of some high-level corporate executives (Glater 2002a). The stiff sentences mentioned earlier reflect this.

Stiff sentences for high-level offenders do not seem to be uniform practice. A study by Benson and Walker (1988) did not lend support to the finding that higher-status offenders get tougher sentences. Rather, the findings of Wheeler and colleagues (1982) may result from the fact that this study was conducted in urban federal districts with an especially high volume of white collar crime cases presided over by liberal judges. In an analysis of 1,597 white collar crime cases in federal courts, Albonetti (1994) concluded that offenders of higher social status were generally more likely to avoid punishment than were those of lower social status, although this outcome appears to be related more to the complexity of their cases, which provides them with bargaining leverage, than to a class bias operating in their favor. But lower-status offenders do not uniformly get the harshest punishments (Eitle 2000).

The principal study to date on the sentencing of white collar criminals is *Sitting in Judgment* (1988) by Stanton Wheeler, Kenneth Mann, and Austin Sarat, based on interviews with 51 federal judges. The kinds of white collar crimes these judges most typically adjudicated included bribery, income tax fraud, mail and wire fraud, price fixing, false claims and statements, and bank embezzlement. Even though judges often considered the sentencing of white collar offenders to be especially complicated, Wheeler, Mann, and Sarat (1988) identified an "informal common law" of sentencing for white collar crime offenses. The federal judges generally agreed that harm, blameworthiness, and consequence are the three basic factors involved in sentencing in these cases. More specifically, judges believed that they must assess the level and nature of the harm caused by the defendant's actions, the individual's culpability in the illegal activity, and the actual consequences for both the defendant and the community of any sanctions imposed. They also tended to agree on the importance of considering the totality of circumstances and factors in a case, as opposed to basing sentences on the formal charges alone. But even if there was fairly broad agreement on general principles, it does not follow that the judges agreed how exactly to resolve contradictions among equally valid principles or how much weight should be given to each case's numerous factors in arriving at an appropriate sentence.

Sentencing Organizational Offenders

Organizational offenders represent only a small proportion of criminal defendants. During one four-year period (1984–1987), only 1,569 organizational defendants out of a total 200,000 criminal defendants, or less than 1 percent, went to trial in the U.S. district courts (Parker 1989); organizational defendants typically represent an even smaller proportion of the caseload in state and local courts. Furthermore, most of these organizations are relatively small corporations, even though major corporations have been the focus of so much attention in corporate crime studies (Cohen 1989). Organizations are sentenced for fraud, antitrust, environmental, national defense, tax, and other offenses, related to monetary, food and drug, racketeering, and property crimes (U.S. Sentencing Commission 1990).

Because no centralized source of data on corporate crime exists, assessing criminal sentences for organizational crime is difficult. According to one study, almost 90 percent of the corporate offenders in the study sample were fined, about 15 percent were ordered to pay restitution, and almost 20 percent were ordered to make civil or other types of payments (Cohen 1989). Some 30 percent of the organizations were put on probation for a period averaging a little more than 40 months; only 1 percent were ordered to perform community service, and about 6 percent received some form of suspension of licensure (Cohen 1989).

The seriousness of a fine as a criminal sanction is meaningful only in relation to the harm caused and the resources of the organization fined. The average fine imposed on organizations totaled only 76 percent of the harm caused, in addition to any other sanctions such as restitution (Cohen 1989). Furthermore, corporations that caused the largest amount of harm paid fines that were a considerably lower percentage of the cost of the harm caused than did corporations that caused more modest monetary harm. Because most of these organizations ultimately incorporate these fines into their business expenses, any punitive or deterrent effect is seriously diluted.

In many cases, corporations evade payment of their fines (Mokhiber 1988). Even Exxon's enormous criminal fine of $100 million, paid in conjunction with a $1.1 billion civil settlement for the Valdez oil spill in Alaska, was dismissed by the corporate chairman as something that "will not curtail any of our plans"; indeed, Exxon stock rose dramatically after the announcement of this settlement (Adler and Lord 1991). A fine of more than $7 million in the Waste Management case in 2001—and acceptance of an injunction against further wrongdoing—did not deter the Andersen accounting firm from involvement in further wrongdoing at Enron; Andersen had also paid more than $200 million to settle shareholder claims in the Waste Management case (Eichenwald 2002g). A major investment banking firm, Citigroup, was fined over $100 million in connection with the collapse of Enron and subsequently agreed to pay $2 billion to settle Enron investors' claims (Cresswell 2005b). Many other corporations and investment banking houses paid large fines or settlements in the wake of the corporate scandals of the 2000s.

Sentencing Guidelines and White Collar Offenders

The adoption of federal and state *sentencing guidelines* was one of the most significant developments in criminal justice in the 1980s. The *Sentencing Reform Act of 1984,* one part of the Comprehensive Crime Control Act, marked the formal adoption of federal sentencing guidelines, which went into effect on November 1, 1987 (Hutchison and Yellen 1991). A U.S. Sentencing Commission was created to oversee the production, implementation, and revision of the guidelines. Congress's official objective in forming the commission and endorsing the guidelines was to create a more honest, uniform, and fair sentencing scheme. The U.S. Supreme Court upheld the constitutionality of the guidelines and the Sentencing Commission in *Mistretta v. United States* (488 U.S. 361 1989). In 2005 in *United States v. Booker,* the Court held that the U.S. Sentencing Guidelines violate the Sixth Amendment when they allow judicial finding of facts (rather than jury-established facts) to influence the sentencing decision (Allenbaugh 2005). Accordingly, the future of the sentencing guidelines was somewhat unsettled at this time.

The sentencing guidelines appear to have constrained judicial discretion in sentencing (despite allowing for some "departures" that must be justified) and increased the average amount of time spent in prison without clearly reducing disparity among sentences imposed on comparable offenders (Heaney 1991). The adoption of federal sentencing guidelines increased the fines and jail sentences for white collar crime offenders, but through the early 1990s, such offenders were still only receiving a fraction of the maximum sentences allowable (Adler and Lord 1991). Indeed, under the sentencing guidelines, pickpockets and muggers faced higher fines and longer jail sentences than did environmental criminals whose dumping of hundreds of gallons of hazardous waste caused some $40,000 in damage and resulted in the hospitalization of 12 people (Adler and Lord 1991; Piquero and Davis 2004). On the other hand, one commentator argues that low-culpability environmental violators are still at risk under the sentencing guidelines for receiving inappropriately tough sentences (O'Hear 2004). Two factors built into the sentencing guidelines—previous criminal record and the use of direct violence—inevitably favor white collar offenders because such factors are far more likely to be present in conventional crime. In November 2001, however, the U.S. Sentencing Commission drastically increased white collar crime sentences (Bowman 2001; Mitchell R. 2002). For example, under the old guidelines, frauds involving more than 50 people or losses in excess of $100 million called for a 5- to 6.5-year sentence; under the new guidelines the sentencing range was 19.5 to 24.5 years. Parole was eliminated, and good time reductions were limited to 15 percent of the sentence. In 2002, with the Sarbanes-Oxley Act, Congress doubled the maximum sentence for some forms of corporate-related fraud (Lichtblau 2003). The U.S. Sentencing Commission implemented these harsher terms in 2003, in the face of some controversy: Prosecutors complained that the harsher terms should be applied to other white collar crime offenses as well, while defense attorneys complained they were excessive.

Judges generally believe they should have greater flexibility in tailoring sentences to fit specific offenders and circumstances. This might be especially true in white collar crime cases, in which complex and contradictory factors are often involved. *Sentencing consultants* have profited by deciphering the sentencing guidelines that judges use and then assisting well-heeled defendants, such as Leona Helmsley, in formulating appeals to have their sentences reduced (Zagorin 1993). Some 100 sentencing consulting firms have formed a National Association of Sentencing Advocates.

The sentencing guidelines were formulated principally with individual violators of the federal criminal code in mind. Two dimensions of white collar crime that posed particular challenges for the Sentencing Commission are regulatory offenses and organizational offenders. The initial guidelines identified and addressed the most significant regulatory offenses (Hutchinson and Yellen 1991); other technical violations, some of which have serious consequences, were addressed in a separate system.

After several years of study and hearings, the U.S. Sentencing Commission promulgated sentencing guidelines for organizations in 1991 (Piquero and Davis 2004). A study of sentencing of organizations prior to the establishment of these guidelines found a wide disparity in sentences imposed on organizations and considerable disagreement between experts on how to best approach sentencing organizations (Murphy 2002). Even though the common-law tradition provided little guidance for sentencing corporations, the Sentencing Commission has insisted that the goals and purposes applied to "natural persons," including deterrence, punishment, and restitution, can be applied to organizations (Chaset and Weintraub 1992; U.S. Sentencing Commission 1988, 1989). The sentencing guidelines for organizations provide incentives for organizations to put into place truly effective compliance programs, with the major objective of promoting good corporate citizenship (Murphy 2002). The guidelines included organizational probation as one important, if controversial, sentencing option (Lofquist 1993a). The sentencing guidelines for corporations strongly encourage

them to cooperate with prosecutors in return for various forms of consideration (Laufer 2002). In some cases, this leads to the scapegoating of subordinate employees of the corporation.

In a typical year, only a handful of corporations are actually sentenced (Chaset and Weintraub 1992). In one recent year, for example, 304 organizations were sentenced (Murphy 2002). Due to the complexities involved in the sentencing of organizations, the original sentencing guidelines provided only a framework for fines of antitrust offenders (Parker 1989). The practical effect of the commission's organizational sentencing guidelines is to increase the size of fines and eliminate some of the sentences formerly available to judges in such cases. Despite a firestorm of protest from influential corporations, fine amounts increased significantly as a consequence of the adoption of the guidelines from a mean of $155,916 (median: $17,500) in 1988 to a mean of $1,595,836 (median: $100,000) in 2000, or a tenfold increase (Murphy 2002). According to a study carried out by Nicole Piquero and Jason Davis (2004), the legal factors specified by the guidelines are basic determinants of the sentences imposed on organizational offenders, but some extralegal factors (such as corporate solvency) also play a significant role. Ten years after implementation of the organizational guidelines, the chair of the U.S. Sentencing Guidelines Commission claimed success in deterring corporate crime (Murphy 2002). The corporate crime wave of the 2000s, however, suggests that any such success has hardly been uniform.

WHITE COLLAR CRIMINALS IN THE CORRECTIONAL SYSTEM

Individual white collar offenders are rarely sent to prison. Of the total federal prison population of more than 150,000 early in the 21st century, only a few more than 1,000 were classified as white collar offenders; by some calculations, white collar offenders actually declined as a proportion of the prison population early in the new century (Leaf 2002). This relative decline at least partly reflected the effects of mandatory drug-sentencing laws.

When white collar offenders are incarcerated, they are almost always sent to minimum-security prisons or prison camps, where the conditions are quite different from those in maximum-security prisons filled with conventional offenders. These prisons—two examples are Allenwood in Pennsylvania, and Lompoc in California—have sometimes been characterized as "country clubs" or *Club Fed*. Although they look more like a campus than a fortress, have a scenic setting, contain fairly extensive recreational facilities, and lack prison cells (Lounsberry 1991; Senior 2002), the inmates are not at liberty to leave the grounds, must accept banal work assignments, are quartered with other inmates in small cubicles or dormitories, and have limited choices concerning food and other amenities. In recent years, some "privileges"— furloughs, flexible family visits, and telephone time— have been restricted (Senior 2002). White collar crime offenders complain that some guards seem to take pleasure in humiliating them, and they must struggle against noise, boredom, and lack of privacy. Such incarceration is likely to be experienced as punitive, then, but it is substantially less punitive than the experience of the typical conventional career criminal in a maximum-security prison such as Attica or Leavenworth. In the post-Enron era, however, some convicted former executives were being sent to high-security prisons (Murphy 2004; Porter 2004; Sorkin 2005d). In such an environment, white collar offenders were especially vulnerable to extortion and assaults by hardened conventional crime inmates.

The assumption that white collar offenders who have lived in comfortable, even lavish circumstances and have enjoyed a respectable status suffer more from both the material deprivations and shame of imprisonment than do conventional offenders has not been well studied. Benson and Cullen (1988) cast some doubt on the validity of this "special sensitivity" thesis in their study of a small sample of 14 white collar offenders who had been incarcerated. Their interviews revealed that

these offenders had adjusted remarkably well to their prison experience and seemed to be quite free of emotional problems rooted in this experience. Benson and Cullen suggested that individuals with more education, greater family ties, and noncriminal identities may adapt better to prison than do individuals without these advantages. Furthermore, white collar offenders are more likely than conventional offenders to have had experience adapting to the expectations of a formal organization, and accordingly they may more easily conform to prison rules and regulations. One of the study participants who did time in a federal prison put it this way:

> Once you're past the first initial period, it's really not so bad. I mean sitting in prison, I got all the food, three square meals a day. I really have no problems, no worries.... Yeah, it's punishment, but its effect as punishment is gone after the first few days. I mean you're afraid of going to prison till you get to prison, and once you're in prison, you really don't want to go back to prison, but once you're there for a couple of months, you just kind of get into it. You live. You're there. You survive.... (Benson and Cullen 1988)

Such an account may be bravado and atypical; caution is warranted in drawing any conclusions from such a limited sample. But this study suggests that conventional wisdom about the impact of the prison system on white collar offenders may be wrong and that conventional lower-class offenders may suffer as much or even more. Indeed, by some accounts, some white collar offenders may actually have years added to their lives by being compelled in prison to eat a healthier, more balanced diet and exercise regularly. Arguably the highest-profile white collar crime inmate in recent years—Martha Stewart—claimed to have had an affirmative experience after five months in prison and used her imprisonment to soften her public image (Glater 2005b; Hays 2005b). She was also reported to have increased her net worth and lost weight in prison.

Still, no one should doubt that white collar offenders experience significant humiliation and

---

B O X 11.8   House Arrest as Punishment

Diana Brooks, the former CEO of Sotheby's who pleaded guilty and cooperated with prosecutors in a case involving the fixing of commissions on art sales, was sentenced to a $350,000 fine and six months of house arrest (Kuczynski 2002a; Shanahan 2002). Since the house in question is a 12-room, $5 million apartment on the Upper East Side of Manhattan, not everyone would agree that this was a significant punishment. Brooks was allowed to leave her apartment for grocery shopping and some scheduled appointments. Martha Stewart was also sentenced to five months of home confinement—subsequently extended—following her five months in prison (Hays

2005). And she was also spending this time on her luxurious estate, contending with restrictions similar to those imposed on Diana Brooks.

Home detention is increasingly used in recent years for white collar offenders, especially in response to the prison-crowding crisis. Those sentenced to home detention are typically required to wear an ankle bracelet. By any reasonable measure, they are far better off than those who are incarcerated. However, some evidence suggests that they do tend to experience a psychological burden in response to their humiliation, restricted circumstances, and more direct exposure to the unconstrained circumstances of ordinary members of society.

---

dramatically changed conditions in their daily lives when they are incarcerated. Michael Milken, who had spent the latter part of the 1980s as a billionaire and one of the most powerful financiers in America, had to share a small dormitory room with several other men at Pleasanton Federal Penitentiary. He was assigned such tasks as cleaning bathrooms, mopping floors, tidying up the trash area, and scouring rust off signs (Kornbluth 1992). Dennis Levine (1991a), one of the key figures in the 1980s insider trading cases, described a humiliating strip search, assignment to a small cubicle with a soiled mattress and a Mafioso cellmate, his initial job scrubbing toilets and urinals (for 11 cents an hour), and the poor prison food that greeted him at Lewisburg, a federal prison camp. Joseph Timilty, a prominent Boston politician sentenced to four months in a federal penitentiary in Pennsylvania, kept a diary detailing some of the daily humiliations and adjustments he experienced (Timilty and Thomas 1997). Box 11.8 discusses an alternative to incarceration—home detention.

Once white collar offenders leave prison, many return either to similar jobs or to lucrative new challenges (Clinard and Yeager 1980). The overall consequences of conviction and imprisonment for a white collar offense vary, of course. Some ex-convicts find themselves taking humble jobs at drastically lower incomes than they previously

earned (Stewart 2004a). In an era where it has become easier to conduct comprehensive background checks, especially over the Internet, it has become more difficult to conceal a prison term (Dahle 2004). Michael Benson (1984) found that professionals and public sector employees were more likely to suffer "a fall from grace," or a loss of occupational status, than were private businesspeople.

In general, however, the options available to white collar offenders who have served time are broader than those available to conventional crime "ex-cons." At least some of them may once again become involved in illegal or ethically questionable business activities. Dennis Levine was back in business as a financial advisor in New York and living in a Park Avenue condominium not long after his release from prison; *60 Minutes* aired a segment claiming that he was engaged in unethical dealings that cost two businesspeople, who had hired him to assist them in obtaining major loans, a substantial amount of money (Reibstein 1991). In other cases, however, the experience of incarceration may have a redemptive effect. After Michael Fury, a real estate lawyer, spent 18 months in a federal penitentiary for bank fraud, he became an ordained Protestant minister (Steinberg 1993a). Some former white collar crime convicts earn thousands of dollars giving talks about their experiences (Stewart

2004). But most white collar crime convicts surely have regrets about having gotten themselves into this type of trouble.

CIVIL SUITS

Much of the recent response to what is broadly classified as white collar crime has taken the form of civil (or private) lawsuits. Such suits, and the threat of such suits, continue to be a principal mechanism for attempting to control and punish white collar crime. It is unclear whether a traditional public/private distinction in law makes sense in a contemporary environment in which for-profit corporations make decisions that impose serious risks on the general public (Bender 1990).

Nevertheless, civil lawsuits seeking millions of dollars from white collar offenders, who often have substantial assets, have become more common (Friedman 2002; Institute for Civil Justice 1992). Such suits may occur in conjunction with criminal prosecution; alternatively, white collar offenders, especially corporations, may avoid criminal prosecution and sanctions by agreeing to make a civil settlement of claims against them.

Civil lawsuits initiated by private parties against corporations, businesspeople, or professionals alleged to be responsible for some harm have often faced a formidable challenge because defendants typically have the resources to mount a powerful defense and the laws governing liability are somewhat narrowly interpreted. Civil cases can take years to resolve. Early in the 20th century, industrial accidents were claiming an estimated 35,000 lives annually and causing 2 million injuries, but only a small fraction of these incidents resulted in lawsuits, and most victims were poorly compensated, if at all (Lieberman 1983). By the end of the century, only a small proportion of victims filed suit (Conlin 1991) because the obstacles to the successful pursuit of such legal actions remained considerable.

The civil lawsuits most directly relevant to white collar crime are tort cases, in which compensation, and sometimes punitive damages, are sought in response to some injury, damage, or loss (Freedman 2002; Sherman 1987). Even though most tort suits concern matters usually unrelated to white collar crime, many cases involve such crime in the broad sense. For example, malpractice suits against physicians increased overall in recent years, and average jury awards tripled from 1994 to 2000 to $3.5 million (Freedman 2002). Average awards in product-liability lawsuits also increased dramatically, although in some accounts too much attention has been paid to a relatively small number of such cases with high awards, and the facts of these cases have sometimes been distorted (Friedman 2002; Glaberson 1999b; Koenig and Rustad 2001). In addition, complex litigation involving multiple parties and causes of action, novel legal theories, and difficult technical evidence is on the rise (Institute for Civil Justice 1992). In part, this increase can be attributed to a movement in tort jurisprudence since the 1960s away from contract principles that imposed more responsibility on plaintiffs and toward principles such as *enterprise liability*, a form of strict liability that imposes more responsibility on manufacturers, professionals, and other potential defendants and displays a greater concern with compensating injured parties (Croley and Hanson 1991; Hall 1989; Huber 1988).

Targets of tort lawsuits, from manufacturers facing product liability claims to physicians facing malpractice suits, have frequently complained of a *civil liability crisis* or "litigation explosion" directed at them. They cite as harmful consequences of this crisis: plant closings, product discontinuances, abandoned medical practices, and price increases (Friedman 2002; Institute for Civil Justice 1992). Others have persuasively taken issue with people who blame the tort crisis on lawsuit-happy litigants, greedy lawyers, irresponsible juries, and "bleeding heart" judges. These critics have argued that the liability crisis is caused by corporate violence and irresponsibility and the relentless forces that place corporate profits ahead of all other considerations (Bender 1990). These critics note that only a small percentage of those who threaten to file lawsuits actually do so, that outcomes of such lawsuits are

---

B O X   11.9   SLAPPs: Strategic Lawsuits against Public Participation

Some real estate developers, alleged polluters, public servants, and other parties who have been opposed by citizens' groups have initiated their own civil lawsuits—called *strategic lawsuits against public participation (SLAPPs)*—to discourage these citizens groups from pursuing actions against them (Bishop 1991; Donson 2000; Pring and Canan 1996). Major multinational corporations have also adopted this strategy. In one high-profile case, McDonald's sued protestors who had distributed anti-McDonald's leaflets outside a restaurant (Vick and Campbell 2001). It is surely intimidating—and potentially costly—for small groups of private citizens to find themselves sued by an immensely wealthy and powerful corporation. Should such corporations be permitted to initiate these lawsuits against private citizens, or is the prospect of such a lawsuit likely to deter some groups that wish to expose harmful corporate practices?

---

typically unsuccessful, that atypical plaintiff victories are often distorted or exaggerated by media reporting, and that tort lawsuits are a necessary counterbalance to the extraordinary power of major corporations (Abel 1988a; Glaberson 1999c; Koenig and Rustad 2001). In this view, tort liability provides an important incentive for safer practices on the part of businesses and professionals, compensates the injured, and informs consumers about dangerous goods and services (Abel 1988a; Bender 1990; Swartz 1987). A study conducted by a Harvard Medical School professor and colleagues produced some solid evidence that medical malpractice suits have a deterrent effect in terms of reducing negligent injuries (Hiatt 1991).

In 1992, a bill that would have made it more difficult for consumers to sue manufacturers over defective products was defeated in the U.S. Senate (Meier 1992d). On the other hand, the securities industry and legal and accounting professions in 1995 pushed through a bill in Congress to make it more difficult for investors who had sustained losses to sue them (Lewis N. A. 1995b, 1995d). Various commentators have suggested that this and other legal reforms contributed to the environment fostering the wave of corporate and accounting scandals of the early 2000s, with billions of dollars of losses (Mayer 2002). Despite the legal constraints, Arthur Andersen and many other entities were targets of massive civil lawsuits as a consequence of the Enron collapse and other corporate meltdowns linked with fraudulent financial

reporting (Glater 2001d). Many such civil lawsuits are ultimately settled by some form of a "consent agreement," where the defending company agrees to pay settlements and costs, and other terms (Holtfreter 2005b). On the other hand, some corporations have adopted an aggressive legal approach to combating civil lawsuits (see Box 11.9).

Despite recent legislative and jurisprudential reforms that aided plaintiffs in tort cases, wealthy corporate defendants still have a considerable advantage in such lawsuits, and it is questionable whether plaintiffs will benefit from recent reforms indefinitely (Bender 1990; Friedman 2002). With respect to product liability, for which the economic stakes are especially large, the evidence suggests that since the mid-1980s, the courts have reverted to favoring defendants, and conservative scholars have called for a return to principles of contract and negligence (Croley and Hanson 1991; Labaton 1989d). Also since the mid-1980s, legislation in various states has imposed caps on awards (especially for punitive damages), time limits for filing cases, and in some cases, restrictions on contingency fees (Institute for Civil Justice 1992). In April 2003, the U.S. Supreme Court established new constitutional limits on punitive damages, ruling that juries could not consider a defendant's wealth when setting such awards (Greenhouse 2003b).

Recent research does not support claims by business and professional interests that the punitive awards imposed on them were unjust (Koenig and Rustad 2001; Sunstein et al. 2002). Punitive

---

B O X 11.10   William Lerach: Shareholder Hero or Economic Terrorist?

William Lerach is a San Diego lawyer who has initiated hundreds of lawsuits against corporations, mainly for fraud (Greider 2002; Kaplan and Murr 1996; Toobin 2002). Lerach and his law firm, Milberg Weiss, claimed that these corporations made false or blatantly misleading public statements about their financial status, causing huge losses to their stock investors when a more accurate picture of the corporation's finances emerge and the stock price plummets.

These lawsuits were initially directed in particular against high-tech corporations. Lerach argues that corporations have too often been run for the benefit of CEOs and other insiders, who are afflicted with character flaws and a basic lack of integrity. He has not only sought billions of dollars in class action lawsuits for his clients but claims to have also compelled corporations to adopt internal reforms to make corporate finances more transparent to shareholders. In the view of at least some observers, the wave of corporate scandals of the 2000s provided strong evidence in support of Lerach's claims. Unsurprisingly, Lerach and his firm initiated lawsuits against Enron, WorldCom, Global Crossing, and Qwest. In 2004, Lerach split from his principal partner, Melvyn Weiss, and in 2005, federal investigators were pursuing possible criminal charges against him and his firm for alleged illegal kickbacks to key plaintiff witnesses (O'Brien and Glater 2005). Whether this investigation was politically motivated or substantively warranted was a matter of controversy.

Corporate executives and venture capitalists have been outraged by Lerach's lawsuits for years, labeling him a "parasite," "pond scum," and a "cunning economic terrorist" (Kaplan and Murr 1996; Nocera 2005; Toobin 2002). His lawsuits were an important source of inspiration for these parties to lobby for passage of the *Private Securities Litigation Reform Act*, adopted by Congress in 1995 over President Clinton's veto, which made it substantially more difficult to initiate shareholder lawsuits. Supporters of this legislation called these lawsuits extortion, charging that they principally enriched greedy lawyers—nobody denies that Lerach and his firm have taken in huge fees—and stifled business initiative and growth. Some critics have challenged Lerach's claims that he is trying to impose reform on corporations to benefit shareholders, insofar as he greatly profits from existing practices. But it seems indisputable that a well-funded, aggressive SEC during the recent era might have meant far less work for lawyers like William Lerach.

---

damage awards are made in less than 5 percent of civil cases, less than 9 percent of product liability cases, and less than 3 percent of medical malpractice suits (Conlin 1991; Glaberson 2001b). Furthermore, the substantial majority of product liability and medical malpractice cases are won by the defendants, not the plaintiffs (Conlin 1991; Koenig and Rustad 2001; Perez-Pena 1994). Box 11.10 profiles a lawyer who has won many cases against major corporations.

Citizen Suits and Class Action Suits

"Citizen suits" and large-scale class action civil suits against major corporations have become far more common following a liberalization of federal rules in 1966 and congressional implementation of federal citizen suits (Friedman 2002; Lieberman 1983; Simon 1991).

Citizen suits allow private parties who have been injured or threatened to petition the court to enjoin the harmful activity and, under some statutes, to seek assessments of civil fines payable to the U.S. Treasury (Simon 1991). Environmentalist groups initiated several such suits after 1982 in response to their frustration with the Environmental Protection Agency's indifference concerning enforcement actions.

Class action lawsuits, in contrast, involve a group of directly injured parties seeking compensation and possible punitive damages from an organization. When a major corporation, or even the government, is charged with some form of harmful conduct, individual plaintiffs are typically at a formidable disadvantage due to the much more limited resources at their disposal. When a large group of victims of the same harmful conduct join in a class action against a major organization, their collective resources can be formidable. Class action lawsuits grew dramatically from 1966 on as a consequence of a change in federal law (Friedman 2002). First-class lawyers are often prepared to devote much time and effort on a contingency basis (i.e., taking a significant percentage of the monetary award if they win and nothing if they lose) to a case in which they may ultimately recover millions of dollars in fees.

Some early major class action lawsuits against corporations include the Agent Orange case against Dow Chemical and the U.S. government, the asbestos case against the Manville Corporation, and the Dalkon shield case against A. H. Robins (Brodeur 1985; Perry and Dawson 1985; Purdy 2005b; Schuck 1986). More recently, the tobacco companies and corporations such as Enron, which seemingly defrauded investors, have been the target of major class action lawsuits (Meier 1997b; Zellner and Forest 2001). Although some class action lawsuits have resulted in judgments in favor of the plaintiffs for hundreds of millions or even billions of dollars, the lawyers involved may have been the primary beneficiaries (Browning 2003a; Meier and Oppel 1999). Several corporations sued in class action suits, including Manville and A. H. Robins, filed for bankruptcy to limit their financial liability (Delaney 1989; Sobol 1991). Distribution of damage awards often takes years and may result in as little as several thousand dollars, or much less, for each plaintiff (Browning 2003a). The formidable costs and frustrations involved in these cases generated considerable pressure to reform the law, use alternatives to adjudication, and resolve claims more efficiently and equitably (Freedman 2002; Galen 1992; McGovern 1990). In 2005, the U.S. Senate passed a bill designed to sharply limit class action lawsuits against American corporations, although it also extended some further rights to plaintiffs in such suits (e.g., to insure that class members understand their rights and get valid compensation for their losses) (Labaton 2005a). This bill was strongly endorsed by President George W. Bush, although the merits of class action lawsuits continued to be debated

(*Congressional Digest* 2005). It seems likely that civil law responses to white collar crime will undergo various changes in the years ahead (see Box 11.11).

Collateral Civil Suits

The federal government, especially its regulatory agencies, often finds it more practical or efficient to pursue corporate wrongdoers and some classes of white collar criminals through *collateral civil suits*, either in conjunction with or in place of criminal prosecution. Major environmental damage cases, such as the Exxon *Valdez* oil spill, and insider trading cases, including the Ivan Boesky and Michael Milken cases, have involved civil law settlements of hundreds of millions of dollars. Both the federal government and various state governments initiated major civil lawsuits against the big tobacco companies and against Microsoft (Broder 1997a; Cohen A. 2001a; Lichtblau 2005). This tactic is deemed more feasible and more productive in such cases than criminal prosecution.

Civil lawsuits on many different levels were initiated against Enron, WorldCom, Adelphia, and others, along with investment banking houses and stock analysts, in the wake of the corporate scandals of the 2000s. New York Attorney General Eliot Spitzer initiated a major lawsuit against Merrill Lynch, for example, and state officials in other states initiated parallel investigations (McGeehan 2002e). Both criminal and civil cases were pursued. Ten Wall Street investment banking firms settled SEC, state, and market regulator charges against them by agreeing to pay $1.4 billion, but they still faced major private lawsuits (Labaton 2003b). Richard Scrushy, former CEO of HealthSouth, was acquitted of criminal charges of fraud in July 2005 but still faced various civil lawsuits (Whitmire 2005b). Corporate executives convicted of criminal charges in corporate fraud cases also still faced such lawsuits.

The government and its agents have traditionally been legally shielded from many kinds of civil lawsuits, largely on the premise that government

> **BOX 11.11** The Role of Mediators and Arbitrators in the Settlement of Complaints
>
> When people believe they have been cheated or mistreated in some form, the matter is often resolved informally. Sometimes a *mediator* is used to referee and possibly facilitate the resolution of such disputes. *Arbitrators* play an important role in the settlement of many complaints that might otherwise result in criminal changes or civil lawsuits (Morgenson 2001b; Winninghoff 1994). A broad range of financial institutions, including brokerage houses and banks, have required investors and consumers to sign agreements that they will take complaints to binding arbitration rather than to court (Meier 1997c).
>
> Investors have sometimes been skeptical about the neutrality of arbitrators, worrying that they will favor the financial institution. In fact, the relevant industry establishes the rules for such proceedings. Complainants are more limited in arbitration proceedings in terms of the types of evidence allowed and on appeal rights. Investors win only a little more than half the arbitration cases and receive judgments substantially smaller than they would receive in court (Jacobs and Siconolfi 1995). Arbitration is not always a quicker or even less costly way to resolve complaints. However, under federal law, the investor who pursues a federal fraud case is required to prove that the broker had criminal intent in the investing decision that led to a loss; in arbitration, the investor sometimes wins by demonstrating that the broker recommended unsuitable investments or that the broker was not adequately supervised.
>
> In the first half of 2001, almost 4,000 cases—a 25 percent increase over the previous year—were heard by the National Association of Securities Dealers, the nation's largest system for handling investor grievances. Whether such a trend reflects a fairer and more efficient resolution of investor complaints or a device to deflect full accountability for dishonest brokers will surely continue to be debated.

operations would be seriously hampered if such lawsuits were permitted. Still, in recent years the courts have permitted some civil suits against government officials.

PROSECUTING AND ADJUDICATING WHITE COLLAR CRIME, IN SUM

This chapter notes that, as is the case with policing, the prosecution of white collar crime is disproportionately a federal responsibility. Nevertheless, some recent increases in local prosecutors' attention to white collar crime cases were also discussed. On the federal level, issues involved in prosecuting some specific forms of white collar crime, including antitrust and environmental offenses, were addressed, as was the controversial role of special prosecutors.

The mid-section of this chapter reviewed the role of grand juries and trial juries, defense counsel, and judges in the process of trying white collar crime cases, as well as the status of plea bargaining in such cases. The various novel issues that arise in the sentencing of white collar offenders were also addressed, as was the adaptation of white collar offenders who are incarcerated.

The final part of this chapter attended to the proportionally larger role of civil lawsuits, including class action suits, in response to white collar and corporate wrongdoing. In sum, many different agencies and entities respond to white collar crime. This response is far less concentrated and centralized than is true for conventional crime; far less consensus exists on the most appropriate means of responding to white collar crime. Despite all of the recent initiatives against white collar crime, for the most part it is still less likely to be investigated, to be subjected to enforcement or prosecution, or to result in harsh sanctions than is conventional crime. The development of increasingly effective criminal justice and alternative responses to white collar crime will be one of the major challenges for our legal system in the years ahead.

KEY TERMS

arbitrators, 305

citizen suits, 303

civil liability crisis, 301

class action
lawsuits, 303

Club Fed, 299

collateral civil
suits, 304

cross designation, 280

deep pockets, 290

economic crime units
(ECUs), 278

enterprise liability, 301

independent
counsel, 283

mediator, 305

Mistretta v. *United States*
(1989), 297

Money Laundering
Control Act
(1986), 306

Private Securities
Litigation Reform Act
(1985), 303

Pyrrhic defeat, 277

sentencing
consultants, 298

sentencing
guidelines, 297

Sentencing Reform
Act of 1984, 297

strategic lawsuits
against public
participation
(SLAPPs), 302

DISCUSSION QUESTIONS

1. What principal factors have inhibited local
    prosecutors from pursuing white collar crime
    cases? When they do pursue such cases, which
    factors seem to persuade them to do so? What
    is the role of state attorney generals in the
    pursuit of white collar crime cases?

2. Identify some of the principal historical trends
    in the response of federal prosecutors to white
    collar crime, including reference to the major
    ideological and strategic factors influencing this
    response. What are the principal arguments
    that have been advanced in favor of and in
    opposition to special prosecutors or
    independent counsel? Similarly, what are some
    principal rationales for and against the use of
    grand juries in white collar crime cases?

3. In what ways does white collar crime defense
    work differ from conventional crime defense
    work? What major factors influence the

decision to plea bargain or go to trial with a
white collar crime case? What is your assessment of the objectivity and likely competence
of trial juries in white collar crime cases?

4. How does the judging process differ, if at all, in
    white collar crime cases, relative to conventional
    crime cases? What are some of the principal
    factors governing the sentencing of white collar
    crime offenders? What arguments can be
    advanced for and against the introduction of
    sentencing guidelines into the sentencing
    process for white collar offenders?

5. What seems to be the fate of white collar
    offenders who are sent to prison? What role have
    civil suits played in the response to white collar
    crime, and what are the major recent trends
    pertaining to such suits? Identify some of the
    principal arguments on behalf of or in opposition
    to class action suits and collateral civil suits.

12

Responding to the Challenge
of White Collar Crime

Early in the 21st century, we have every indication that white collar crime is pervasive and in many forms may well be on the rise. This text has attempted to "map" the white collar crime terrain. It has addressed some of the formidable problems in conceptualizing and studying white collar crime. It has identified the extraordinary range of activities that can either be characterized as forms of white collar crime or are associated with it. And it has described the massive economic, physical, social, and psychological harm caused by white collar crime. What, then, can be done about it?

RAISING CONSCIOUSNESS ABOUT WHITE COLLAR CRIME

The first step in any program for a more effective response to white collar crime calls for an elevated level of consciousness. A persistent thesis in the white collar crime literature is that the response to such crime is more limited and less severe than the response to conventional crime. This text has suggested many reasons for a more attenuated response, and it has cited some evidence for a growing recognition of the seriousness of white collar crime. The

challenge is to cultivate this recognition in a way rooted more in reality than in rhetoric.

Criminologists or criminal justicians can play a role in fostering broader attention to white collar crime in the media by engaging in *newsmaking criminology* (Barak 1994), which calls for criminologists to appear on television and radio shows, write for and make themselves available for interviews with the popular press, and accordingly reach out to a broader public audience. Grassroots organizations can continue to play a larger role in responding to corporate crime, as is evident in the environmental movement directed at corporate pollution and the antiglobalization movement (Cable and Benson 1993; Shover and Routhe 2005; Welton and Wolf 2001). The more the seriousness and the many harmful consequences of white collar crime are understood, the more effective any specific response to it is likely to be. The corporate scandals of the early 2000s certainly received a massive level of attention from the media and some attention from political entities. Millions of Americans were directly affected in the form of lost jobs and huge losses in investments and retirement funds. It remained to be seen whether this would translate into an enduring elevation of public interest in and concern with white collar crime.

POLICY OPTIONS
FOR RESPONDING
TO WHITE COLLAR CRIME

White collar crimes inspire an especially broad range of responses, from outrage to pragmatism to apathy. Apathy toward such crime is probably more widespread than it is for conventional crime, especially when people do not consider themselves to be affected by it. A cynical form of resignation to such crime is likely in people who regard humans as naturally corrupt, and some people believe the state should not intervene at all in many activities defined as white collar crime. Others view white collar crime as a reflection of regulatory overreach; such "crime" is largely an artifact of law (Healy 2004; Parker 1997; Reynolds 1985). White collar crime differs in a fundamental way from conventional crime because it is closely associated with productive, desirable activities. One concern is that excessively restrictive and punitive responses toward such crime, especially in its corporate form, will deter such productive activities more than it will deter prohibited activities. Some conservative critics and corporate leaders claim that governmental action and new laws adopted in response to corporate scandals cause more harm than they resolve (Glater 2005d; Shackelford 1993; Walczak et al. 2002). Thus, a basic tension exists between interventionist and noninterventionist strategies. Fisse and French (1985) suggested that a pragmatic, "incrementalist" approach with a mixture of laws, regulation, and negotiation could serve as a middle ground.

Responses to white collar crime may be directed toward structural, organizational, or individualistic levels; that is, they may address fundamental conditions in the social structure, organizational factors, or individual orientations that promote white collar crime. Likewise, responses to white collar crime may address social control (e.g., legal reform), opportunity structures (e.g., occupational conditions), or cognitive states (e.g., motivations). Responses to white collar crime may be essentially normative, utilitarian, or coercive. In other words,

they may attempt to persuade (normative), appeal to reason or offer practical inducements (utilitarian), or rely on threats of intervention and punishment (coercive). Similarly, responses to white collar crime may be essentially preventive (keeping the criminal activity from occurring in the first place), regulatory (operant while the criminal activity is in progress), or retaliatory (put into effect after the criminal activity has occurred). Rationales for responding formally to white collar crime include retribution (revenge), incapacitation, deterrence, and rehabilitation.

Responses to white collar crime range from very informal to highly formal. They may rely on public opinion and shaming, self-policing, private negotiations, citizens group boycotts, civil lawsuits, administrative regulation, or the criminal justice system.

The most effective and enduring solutions to white collar crime are structural, normative, and preventive. Structural, normative, and preventive strategies must operate on several different levels. First, they must attempt to diminish or eliminate motivations for committing white collar crimes. Second, they must attempt to transform the ethical and normative climate that helps promote such crime. Third, they must attempt to diminish the conditions that provide opportunities for such crime.

RESPONDING TO WHITE COLLAR
CRIME AS A MORAL ISSUE

Moral outrage is an understandable response to white collar crime. That large and powerful corporations would knowingly flout the law and defraud or endanger the lives of employees, customers, and citizens is outrageous. Anger and disgust are natural reactions to the greed of educated or affluent professionals, entrepreneurs, and retailers who engage in such activities.

Even if moral outrage at white collar crime is justifiable and perhaps necessary, it is less clear that social policies fueled primarily by such outrage are

---

B O X 12.1   Do Moral Appeals Work?

In the popular imagination, white collar crime reflects immoral and unethical choices. Are *moral appeals* a feasible means of promoting higher levels of compliance with the laws governing white collar crime, or are they too idealistic?

In a study of moral appeals through the mass media to promote taxpayer compliance, Mason and Mason (1992) identified several advantages over alternative approaches. They are relatively inexpensive; they may reach some of the many potential offenders who will not be dissuaded by enforcement efforts and sanctions; and

they are politically appealing because they are less alienating than conventional enforcement. But can such an approach have a measurable impact? In an oft-cited early study, Schwartz and Orleans (1967) found that moral appeals were more effective than threats; a subsequent replication by McGraw and Scholz (1991) found that moral appeals did not affect behavior, even if they influenced what people say about cheating. Mason and Mason (1992) found some evidence that media appeals to induce taxpayers to focus on the fairness of their conduct have some potential for success.

---

the most effective ways of responding to it (Fisse and French 1985: Simpson 2002). One tension in the ongoing debate about the appropriate response to white collar crime pits those who believe that moral idealism should provide the point of departure (see Box 12.1) against those who believe that practical realism should be the primary basis of social policy. Social policies based principally on moral outrage can have unintended harmful consequences for innocent parties. The conundrums and contradictions in formulating justifiable and effective social policy responses are especially pronounced with respect to white collar crime. We should be wary of policy proposals that are either excessively sanctimonious and self-righteous or excessively fainthearted and practical.

Business Ethics Courses in the Curriculum

One response to the perception of an ethics crisis in U.S. business was the much wider introduction of *business ethics* courses. Harvard University offered a course as early as 1915 that addressed ethical issues in business, but this appears to have been an anomaly (Alsop 2003). Business ethics courses first began to be introduced into the business curriculum in the 1950s, although such courses were not uniformly offered in the decades that followed (Weber 1990). Between the early 1970s and early 1980s, the number of business ethics courses in U.S. educa-

tional institutions increased fivefold, especially at the graduate level, and the call for strong ethics programs intensified during the 1980s (Hoffman 1989; Palmer 1986; Pitch 1983). The corporate crime scandals of the early 2000s inevitably inspired a surge in demand for business ethics courses (Healy 2002; Reeves 2002; Stewart 2004a). Significant numbers of students began to express concern about the absence of attention to ethics in the business school curriculum (Browning 2003b). In some business schools, seasoned executives and board members have been invited to participate in classes addressing ethics issues (Sorkin 2002a). Ideally, these business ethics courses promote values that put integrity and concern with the well-being of others ahead of personal or corporate enrichment and advantage.

Unfortunately, it is not clear that integrating business ethics into the curriculum will measurably elevate the ethical behavior of businesspeople. One view is that by the time students get to business or professional school, their ethical mindsets are fully developed; thus, ethical conduct is a matter of early training and character formation (Hutcheson 1990; Prentice 2002). A review of several studies suggested that any improvements in students' ethical awareness and reasoning after formal exposure to business ethics courses was apparently short-lived (Weber 1990). In the wake of the corporate scandals of the early 2000s, some MBA programs claimed that they were paying more attention to character and integrity in their admissions process (Browning 2002). Business schools today must offer ethics courses to be accredited, and the Harvard and Columbia University Business Schools are among those that have now made an ethics course mandatory for their students (Wu 2004). Nevertheless, ethics education remains marginalized from the essence of the business school curriculum (Shiller 2005). An image of humans as naturally calculating and selfish prevails, and most business courses promote a mindset where attention to the bottom line trumps all other considerations (Mangan 2002). Some business professors seem to believe that if businesspeople concern themselves with broader ethical issues, they will be defeated by their competition. Prentice (2002) argues that teaching business students business law—and the consequences of failing to comply with law—is more effective than attempting to teach ethics. Perrow (2002) suggests that, to be effective, ethics education for business students must attend to the contexts that promote or limit unethical behavior and the structural and political sources of ethical behavior in business. The contextual forces at work within a business or organization are likely to be more potent than exposure to one or more business ethics courses.

Business Ethics within the Business World

Business ethics has become a big business itself. Many publications and conferences address business ethics. Some people consider the notion of "business ethics" to be an oxymoron. An ongoing debate concerns business's principal ethical obligation: Is it maximizing the financial return to owners (shareholders) or the broader social responsibility to promote society's well-being (*Economist* 2005; Madsen and Shafritz 1990; Mangan 2002)? Businesses, especially larger corporations, have become conscious of a need to at least appear concerned with ethical conduct, although some internal ethical issues, such as employee layoffs, drug screening tests, and performance evaluations, do not involve white collar crime in the conventional sense.

Historically, corporations have lacked a formal mechanism for guiding and monitoring ethical decision making. Until recently, only a small minority of major corporations established ethics committees, ethical ombudsmen, and ethics judiciary boards (Hoffman 1989; Ross I. 1992). Through the 1990s, a growing number of major corporations and financial firms hired ethics or compliance officers, although the influence of these officers remained questionable (Kelley 1998). In fact, some compliance officers in brokerages or investment banking houses who reported apparent violations were fired (Morgenson 2002b). Revenue production takes precedence over compliance, and in an environment of decreasing revenue in the early 21st century, compliance departments could be under even more pressure to look the other way when rule violations come to their attention.

In addition to ethics or compliance officers, many larger businesses have established compliance programs that include a code of ethics and mechanisms for processing inquiries and complaints about questionable corporate activities. Only about a fourth of major corporations have specific ethics training programs for employees.

A code of ethics is the single most common element of corporate ethics programs (Metzger, Dalton, and Hill 1993). However, these codes mainly emphasize the corporation's legal responsibilities so that it can minimize its legal exposure in the event of unethical actions by employees. Of course, another important objective of these ethics codes and programs is to discourage unethical and illegal behavior against the corporation itself.

The success of any program incorporating a code of conduct significantly depends on the extent to which the targeted parties are consulted on and help formulate the codes rather than simply having the codes imposed upon them (Findlay and Stewart 1992). Even though corporate ethics programs are generally intended to reach individual consciences, recognizing that an organization's ethical ambience is a key element of corporate crime requires programs that address ethics collectively. The implementation of such programs always raises the question of whether they represent a serious commitment to ethical corporate conduct

---

B O X   12.2   Can a Corporation Be Ethically Transformed? The Case of Tyco

Tyco, a multibillion dollar conglomerate holding a wide range of companies involved in everything from electronics to fire security, was among the more ethically challenged companies of the recent era. Its former chief executive officer and chief financial officer were convicted in 2005 on charges of looting the company of some $150 million, and the company itself was alleged to have engaged in aggressive accounting practices and offshore tax evasion strategies. In 2002, Erich Pillmore was appointed to the new position of senior vice president of corporate governance (Kelly 2005). He attempted to institute a fundamental ethical transformation of the company.

Several hundred executives at the top of the company were replaced. An ombudsman for complaints within the company was established, as was a new head of environmental health and safety. A Sarbanes-Oxley process employing 3,000 people was introduced; audit staff more than doubled; the compensation package was overhauled; new caps were imposed on bonuses; new cash disbursement controls were put into place; a new ethics code was adopted; and new integrity training was instituted. Whether all these steps will turn out to be showcasing or will in fact achieve a basic ethical transformation of this company remains to be seen.

---

or are just "window dressing" intended to curry favorable public opinion or minimize legal exposure (Kelley 1998; Young 1981). Some critics have complained that too much attention is focused on elaborate rules of ethics and the appearance of ethical conduct rather than on real transgressions (Morgan and Reynolds 1997). Even if the commitment to ethical conduct is sincere, ethical considerations may not prevail over a corporation's financial interests. Some studies have even suggested that pressures to reach profit-related goals were greater, and federal agency citations more numerous, for companies with ethical codes than for those without them (Clinard 1990; Metzger et al. 1993). Unless there are specific incentives to reward ethical behavior, conduct codes are unlikely to have any positive effect:

> As long as you have a business culture that puts people in impossible situations—"your division has to grow 7 percent in the next year or else we're going to be No. 2 in the field and if we are, you're going to be job hunting"— you're going to have people shipping inferior goods, juggling the books, bribing when they have to, trampling workers beneath them and generally conducting themselves in the time honored tradition. Results, and only results, count. (Gary Edwards, in Wilkes 1989:24)

Some observers hope that over time more corporations will adopt the view that good ethics is good business, and investors have been cautioned about investing in the stock of unethical companies, as stock value can decline precipitously when problems are exposed (Lim 2005) (see Box 12.2). Even though corporations that foster a morally defensible internal environment appear to enjoy some long-term benefits due to enhanced employee morale and loyalty (Etzioni 1988b; Frederick 1999; Metzger et al. 1993), it would clearly be a mistake to rely on corporations to embrace voluntarily morally superior ethical standards.

SECURING COMPLIANCE AND SANCTIONING WHITE COLLAR CRIME

What are the best ways to secure compliance with laws and regulations directed at minimizing the harm done by corporations, entrepreneurs, and professionals? Ongoing debates in the realm of white collar crime center on the circumstances under which intervention does and does not make sense and the degree to which coercive and noncoercive means of inducing compliance should be used.

BOX 12.3   Shaming as a Response to White Collar Crime

A moralistic or normative response to white collar crime is ideally preventive, but it may come about as a reaction to such crime. John Braithwaite (1989c, 1993a, 2000) reintroduced the ancient notion of "shaming" into the dialogue concerning responses to crime generally. In his view, one of the reasons why punishment has largely failed to reduce the crime rate is that it has been "uncoupled" from its moral roots—shame. Thus, for individuals and corporations alike, shaming from without (e.g., by state agencies) and from within (e.g., by corporate colleagues) is a *normative form* of social control that has the potential to be far more effective than other forms of social control, especially coercion.

White collar individuals and corporations are concerned with their reputations, as a function of self-esteem or corporate pride and for economic reasons. An evolving societal consensus on the criminality of actions such as environmental damage has made those responsible for such crimes even more vulnerable to

shaming through adverse publicity and identification as a wrongdoer (Braithwaite 1993a).

In Braithwaite's (1989c, 2000) view, the shaming process should be reintegrative. *Reintegrative shaming* pulls the individual or organization back into the community rather than stigmatizing and pushing the offender away from the community and into further crime and deviance. Ideally, it is carried out by the peer community of the offending individual or organization. Reintegrative shaming emphasizes that certain deeds and actions may be wrong but that individuals and organizations can be redeemed. The effectiveness of such a strategy, however, tends to presuppose a rather high level of consensus on the perceived shamefulness of white collar crimes, and this assumption has been challenged (Uggen 1993). Individual white collar and corporate offenders are likely to rationalize their illegal activity and to characterize attempts to shame them as unjustifiable forms of persecution.

A variety of specific sanctions can be used to respond to white collar crime. The term *sanction* is most commonly equated with punishment, but strictly speaking, sanctions may be positive or negative. *Positive sanctions* include grants, bounties, fees, tax credits, loan guarantees, prizes or rewards, favorable administrative consideration, praise, inducements, incentives, indulgences, and compensatory power (Grabosky 1993, 1995b; Smith and Stalans 1991). Positive sanctions are not commonly used by the criminal law; when they are used, they are mainly intended to induce cooperation in a criminal prosecution or to encourage whistleblowers to come forward.

In 1986, Congress updated the False Claims Act of the Civil War era, thereby lifting the award ceiling and enabling whistleblowers to sue employers for damages (Diamant 2002; Ross I. 1992). This has proven quite effective in generating suits filed on behalf of whistleblowers, with defense contractors among the primary targets of these suits. Millions of dollars in rewards for coming forward raises some concern that whistleblowers may be overrewarded or may even lie to obtain a large award.

Positive sanctions can be directed toward potential lawbreakers as well (Friedland 1989; Grabosky 1995b). In a study of regulation of nursing homes, Makkai and Braithwaite (1993) found that the use of praise by nursing home inspectors for positive accomplishments helped improve levels of compliance with regulatory standards. A subsequent study suggested more complex patterns of compliance, however, with some of the regulated opting to disengage with the regulatory process (Braithwaite, Braithwaite, Gibson, and Makkai 1994). A review of research on tax compliance by Smith and Stalans (1991) found that positive incentives, such as respectful treatment and praise, were more likely to produce compliance than were monetary rewards and other material inducements. Such findings are consistent with a basic axiom of modern psychology: that rewarding good behavior is generally more effective than punishing bad behavior.

Positive sanctions have many advantages. They increase freedom of choice and are more likely to be perceived as legitimate and less likely to be alienating. They can facilitate learning of desired behavior, induce necessary cooperation and assistance from third parties, and foster collective pride in an organization (Freiburg 1987; Grabosky 1993; Ross I. 1992). Informal rewards such as praise and letters of recognition may be especially useful in securing compliance from businesses (Braithwaite 2002b). On the other hand, such incentives can be manipulative and paternalistic, as when they appear to offer bribes to engage in morally proper conduct. They can foster a climate of distrust within an organization and can be costly and vulnerable to fraud (Grabosky 1993). Rewards are less useful in the regulation of business than they are in markets generally (Braithwaite 2002b).

A wide range of *negative sanctions* is more commonly applied to white collar crime. In the case of individual offenders, negative sanctions range from imprisonment to fines to occupational disqualification; in the case of organizations, they include loss of charter, fines, and adverse publicity. Although negative sanctions are most readily associated with the criminal law, they may also be applied through civil and administrative law and by nongovernmental systems of social control. Negative civil sanctions include damages, divestiture orders, restitution, compensation, confiscation, injunctions, warnings, cease and desist orders, licensure revocation, suspension, cancellation, and fines (Freiburg 1987; Gobert and Punch 2003). Some sanctions may mix positive and negative elements. For example, a requirement of community service or restitution is a form of punishment for the perpetrator but directly benefits the community or victims of white collar crimes. For an argument for a sanction with mixed positive and negative elements, see Box 12.3.

LAW AND THE COERCIVE RESPONSE TO WHITE COLLAR CRIME

The use of the criminal law in response to white collar crime is generally more open to dispute than it is with respect to conventional crime. On one side of the argument are people who favor broader application of criminal law to harmful corporate and occupational activities by using a more prosecutorial and punitive approach; on the other side are people who favor decriminalizing some currently recognized forms of white collar crime and relying less on invoking criminal law in response to other offenses.

Since the 1970s, the criminal law has in fact been more broadly applied to corporate wrongdoing such as worker safety violations, toxic dumping, and environmental pollution. Coffee (1991) argued that this trend unnecessarily entangles in a criminal process individuals and corporations who have not consciously chosen to do harm. Goldstein (1992) suggested that the label "criminal" can lose some of its stigmatizing power if it is too readily applied to individuals or organizations not considered criminal by the general public.

In his influential *Where the Law Ends* (1975), Christopher Stone adopted the thesis that the effectiveness of the law in responding to corporate crime has inherent limitations. The law was originally developed to deal with individuals, not organizations. A built-in time lag in the application of the law is not well suited to addressing or preventing ongoing harm. The more threatening the law becomes to corporations, the more incentive such organizations have either to contest it and make its implementation especially costly or to withdraw from productive activity. Because corporations have many means of either shielding themselves from or minimizing the impact of efforts to control them by law, we should explore all available alternatives to the criminal law. Sally Simpson's (2002) *Corporate Crime, Law, and Social Control*, a review of studies of corporate crime deterrence, also concludes that the criminal law has basic limitations as an effective device for addressing corporate crime. And James Gobert and Maurice Punch (2003), in *Corporate Crime Reconsidered*, elaborate upon the complex legal challenges arising from corporate crime cases, including issues of jurisdiction for transnational corporations, special difficulties in demonstrating criminal intent, and questions of the competence of ordinary juries in these cases.

Civil Suits and Penalties

The use of civil procedures allows prosecutors to avoid meeting the criminal law's stringent standards for establishing proof and culpability; at the same time, the severity of judgments that can be imposed in civil proceedings is comparable to or exceeds criminal penalties. Furthermore, collecting a substantial civil judgment is far more economical than imposing prison sentences. At present, substantial overlap exists between civil and criminal proceedings and sanctions (Cohen 1992); one response to this situation is a call for more systematic coordination of civil and criminal sanctions, especially as applied to corporations (Yellen and Mayer 1992). One suggestion is that criminal sanctions could be lessened in cases in which civil penalties are especially punitive.

Private parties who have been injured by white collar offenders have always had the option of a civil lawsuit, but as a practical matter they have often lacked the necessary financial resources. Historically, it has been especially intimidating for injured private parties to take on large corporations, but in the second half of the 20th century, class action lawsuits (see Chapter 11) were permitted in certain cases and have become a significant device for responding to some forms of white collar crime. In these suits, a large class of plaintiffs—many thousands, in some cases—join in a lawsuit, and an attorney or law firm takes the case on a contingency basis, collecting a significant percentage of any successful judgment but nothing in lost cases. Whether the plaintiffs or the lawyers are the primary beneficiaries of these suits continues to be debated.

Historically, corporations have often found it less costly to contend with civil lawsuits than to limit profits by fully complying with the law or correcting the hazards they created (Frank and Lynch 1992). At the same time, an expansion of tort law has compelled corporations to correct at least some hazards involving the workplace or products (Rustad and Koenig 2002). Thus, it is difficult to state a general principle concerning the relative effectiveness of civil suits as a deterrent to corporate crime or to ascertain whether they result in more or less substantial punishment for offending corporations.

Compliance versus Punitive Approaches to Corporate Crime

Ongoing debate centers on whether a response to white collar crime, the corporate form in particular, that relies on invoking criminal law as punishment is more appropriate and effective than a cooperative regulatory response that attempts to avoid using criminal sanctions. Serious students of corporate crime generally agree that corporations are guided by self-interest and will mostly resist efforts to impose regulations on them and that some mixture of strategies is required to minimize the harm they do (Gobert and Punch 2003; Lofquist, Cohen, and Rabe 1997; Pearce and Snider 1995). The debate, however, centers principally on the extent to which cooperative and punitive measures should be emphasized.

The *compliance approach* favors cooperative strategies and is rooted in the assumption that a cooperative strategy is both a practical necessity and a more effective way of limiting the harm of corporate activities. At least some proponents of this approach disavow policy advocacy and consider their work a reflection of the realities of regulatory enforcement practices (Grabosky 1995a; Hawkins 1990). Whether or not specific policy endorsements are involved, the reality in this view is that punitive approaches are costly and risky and deflect regulatory personnel from their primary mission of inspecting corporate operations and inducing corporations to abandon or diminish harmful practices (Hawkins 1990; Simpson 2002). Compliance advocates consider punitive approaches to be based on false assumptions about how corporations operate (e.g., by purely rational calculations), and punitive sanctions are most likely to affect relatively low-level corporation managers.

Proponents of the compliance approach cite considerable evidence indicating that corporate harmful practices have declined over time, particularly in countries such as Great Britain that have emphasized a cooperative approach over a punitive strategy (Hawkins 1990, 2002). The pragmatic argument is that enforcement resources should be allocated in the most efficient manner and should have as their primary objective the reduction of harmful corporate activity (Gray and Scholz 1991; Simpson 2002). Proponents of a *punitive approach* are accused of ignoring empirical evidence and the realities of regulatory enforcement practices. Another reality in this view is that the harsh application of punitive sanctions to corporations inspires a corporate backlash against regulation generally, with broadly harmful consequences (Hawkins 1990, 1991). In sum, persuasion works better than coercion.

In contrast, some citizens' advocates such as Ralph Nader, some mainstream criminologists, and progressive criminologists in particular argue that the criminalization of harmful corporate activity is long overdue and that the imposition of tough, punitive sanctions is either an essential component or the only strategy that is likely to have an impact on corporate crime (Clinard 1990; Leaf 2002; Pearce and Snider 1995). In the progressive criminologists' view, the capitalist mode of production inevitably promotes violations of law, and as a result, regulatory violations are widespread for all types of corporations (Pearce and Tombs 2002). Furthermore, recent corporate takeovers and merger activity have put severe pressures on management to place short-term profits ahead of health and safety concerns (Mitchell 2001; Pearce and Tombs 1990; Skeel 2005). This approach holds that although a broad range of regulatory strategies, including preventive strategies, should be used, only the early, strict, and consistent enforcement of criminal law, with punitive sanctions for serious violations, can be effective against the immense power of corporations.

Above all, the compliance approach enables corporations to evade or reduce their responsibility for a range of enormously harmful endeavors (Pearce and Tombs 1990; Snider 1993). The position taken here is that the law—criminal law, in particular—must continue to be a central feature of the response to white collar crime. It is the only mechanism of social control that can adequately express appropriate moral outrage at the most serious white collar crimes: corporate and occupational crimes. The relatively recent extension of a criminal law response to environmental crimes is justifiable, even necessary, during a period when the harmful consequences of such offenses become ever more evident. On the other hand, a certain irony exists when progressive criminologists, who are generally antagonistic toward the capitalist state, call for stronger state action.

The objectives and effectiveness of the criminal law require dispassionate evaluation. Traditionally, the principal objectives of such law have been retribution, incapacitation, deterrence, and rehabilitation. We consider some issues involved in the realization of these objectives in the following sections. See Box 12.4 for a discussion of the concept of "just deserts."

DETERRENCE AND WHITE COLLAR CRIME

Even though deterrence is surely one of the central objectives of the criminal justice system, little consensus exists on how and whether legal sanctions have a deterrent effect. Indeed, various criminologists have come down on opposite sides of this issue, and the evidence to support deterrence is equivocal (Croall 2001; Simpson 2002; Wright 1994). *Deterrence* has been defined in different ways; for our purposes, we consider the deliberate decision to refrain from engaging in illegal activity out of fear of legal sanctions (Moore 1987; Simpson 2002).

The deterrent effect of sanctions has been long recognized to be a function of their certainty, severity, celerity, and uniformity; the first factor, certainty, is the most important (Simpson and Koper 1992). Increasingly sophisticated contemporary literature on deterrence distinguishes between *actual* (objective) and *perceptual* (subjective) deterrence— that is, between the real probabilities of being sanctioned and the more powerful, perceived likelihood of being punished (Wright 1994). The

B O X 12.4 "Just Deserts" and Corporate Crime

In the 1970s, some students of criminal justice policy concluded that if the system could not dependably either rehabilitate or deter offenders, it should instead ensure that offenders receive the penalty they deserve. This *just deserts* approach is associated with the ancient rationale of retribution for wrongdoing.

A recent version of just deserts emphasizes the element of public reprobation for wrongdoing over the earlier notion of restoring a balance of justice. Schlegel (1988, 1990) contended that the application of this model to corporations has been largely neglected but is both justifiable and effective. Sanctions for corporate crime must be sufficiently severe to convey the appropriate level of social condemnation. In this view, punishment plays a crucial role in deterring crime and powerfully endorses and revives important values. Schlegel held that principles of just deserts, if correctly applied, fulfill the basic requirements of justice.

The just deserts approach as applied to corporations has been challenged on several grounds. In *Not*

Just Deserts: A Republican Theory of Criminal Justice, Braithwaite and Pettit (1990) argued that the punitive response built into this model in practice metes out harsher sanctions to conventional offenders than to corporate offenders. Further, no government has the enormous resources needed to enforce the law and administer punishments to corporations according to the just deserts formula; rather, its regulators are necessarily constrained by pragmatism (Braithwaite and Pettit 1990). Braithwaite (1982b) argued that such a model inevitably results in injustices: Corporations are punished unjustly for the deeds of individuals or small groups of corporate officers and employees acting against the interests of the corporation, and employees and stockholders are punished for corporate acts undertaken without their endorsement and against their interest. A just deserts approach has the potential of expanding rather than reducing the scope of injustice.

---

research literature also suggests that *formal* sanctions are less of a deterrent than *informal* ones, although an important interactive effect occurs when formal sanctions trigger subsequent informal sanctions (Simpson 2002; Wright 1994). A traditional distinction has been made between *general deterrence*, in which potential offenders (i.e., the general public) are persuaded to refrain from illegal actions by the use of legal sanctions; and *specific deterrence*, in which punished offenders are dissuaded from the commission of further offenses by the imposition of legal sanctions.

Any theory of deterrence adopts, in some form, the classical criminological model of human beings as rational creatures capable of making a calculated, cost–benefit analysis of prospective criminal activity (Simpson 2002). Our criminal law essentially adopts this model, although a mass of social and behavioral science research has either cast serious doubt on its validity or identified many factors that compromise and limit rational choice. Clearly, a great deal of crime is not deterred by the threat of criminal sanctions.

Chambliss (1967) made a distinction between *instrumental crimes* (e.g., theft) and *expressive crimes* (e.g., substance abuse). Because instrumental crimes are directed toward material gain whereas expressive crimes are directed toward the satisfaction of some enticement, emotional need, or compulsion, Chambliss posited that it should be easier to deter instrumental crimes, although some students of deterrence disagree (see, for example, Andenaes 1974). The alternative view holds that the extent to which one offense is linked to either subcultural support or moral condemnation is more relevant to deterrence than whether the offense is instrumental or expressive.

White collar crime is typically viewed as a quintessentially instrumental (or rational) crime, and accordingly, proponents of Chambliss's view would expect white collar crime to be more amenable to deterrence than many forms of conventional crime (Simpson and Koper 1992). Furthermore, as Braithwaite and Geis (1982) observed, deterrence of white collar offenders should logically be more feasible than deterrence of conventional offenders because their illegal activity is less likely to be an integrated part of their lifestyle, they have more to lose materially, they are more likely to look to the future, and they are more likely to be concerned about their reputation. In adopting one version of this perspective, Bene (1991) argued that attorneys in particular should be susceptible to deterrence by appropriate fines because they often commit economic crimes; they are sophisticated, intelligent, and attuned to cost-benefit analysis; they are somewhat risk averse (to preserve the investment in their careers); and they are relatively well off and stand to lose much if caught committing a crime.

Such arguments make good logical sense, but it is difficult to demonstrate conclusively that the threat of criminal sanctions deters white collar crime. In their study of convicted white collar crime offenders, Weisburd and Waring (2001) found no evidence that the offenders' later behavior was affected by time spent in prison. Clearly, given the pervasiveness of white collar crime, a great deal of it has not been deterred. Furthermore, the perceived improbability of detection and punishment of white collar offenders surely compromises any deterrent effect. Can corporations be deterred from criminal conduct? Corporations, as collective, goal-oriented enterprises, are commonly assumed to be more rational than traditional individual offenders, and accordingly, they should be more responsive to deterrence. Braithwaite and Geis (1982) identified some of the differences between conventional crime and corporate crime that are relevant to the question of whether corporations can be deterred and rehabilitated. On the one hand, corporate crime is more difficult to detect, and corporate offenders are more difficult to convict; on the other hand, corporate offenders are more capable of being apprehended, deterred, incapacitated, and rehabilitated. Some evidence suggests that the imposition of more severe sanctions can inhibit corporations from reoffending (Simpson and Koper 1992). Logically, corporations should be more responsive than individuals to any scheme that diminishes the likelihood that crime will pay.

This rather optimistic view of the potential for deterring corporations has been questioned, pri-

marily on the basis that because corporate decision making is guided by a complex of factors relating to economic pressures, particular opportunities, and the need to survive, it does not simply take the form of rational calculations based on maximizing profit (Moore 1987; Stone 1975). Furthermore, as a practical matter the legal system can impose only limited controls on corporations, although it occasionally prosecutes corporate executives. In *Corporate Crime, Law, and Social Control*, a major study of the issue of corporate crime and deterrence, Sally S. Simpson (2002) concluded that on balance deterrence does not work for corporations or their managers. But the claim arising from this conclusion—that a criminal law response to corporate crime does not work—has been challenged on the grounds that criminal sanctions also serve purposes related to justice and fairness, independent of any deterrent effect (Johnson D. T. 2002).

According to one study, top management may be guided more by self-interest than by rational determinations of the corporation's interest. Executives may have professional loyalties that override corporate loyalty and will not necessarily make rational decisions in any case. They may not even have control over middle-management personnel who actually violate laws (Braithwaite and Makkai 1991). Decisions of top corporate managers may be driven more by emotions such as envy and pride than by dispassionate consideration of possible sanctions. Despite acknowledging that we have much to learn about how managers differentiate between personal and corporate vulnerability to sanctions and how reputation-related and economic sanctions have different effects, the study's authors concluded that deterrence works better on the corporate than on the individual level.

Altogether, we still lack an even remotely adequate base of knowledge and understanding of how the complex of factors involved in corporate behavior interact and of just which policies actually deter corporate illegality (Simpson and Koper 1992). For a proposal that criminologists can nevertheless play a more direct role in responding to certain forms of high-level white collar crime, see Box 12.5.

B O X 12.5   A "Chief Criminologist" for the SEC?

Professor William K. Black (2004), a former federal regulator and recently a professor at the University of Texas, has proposed that the SEC should appoint a Chief Criminologist. He attributes the gross failure of the SEC to anticipate and prevent such economic catastrophes as the S & L debacle and the Enron fraud at least in part to the fact that the SEC did not have the benefit of criminological knowledge and policy advice. Criminologists know how such "control frauds" originate, how they are sustained, which environmental characteristics produce waves of such frauds, and how some other disciplines—for example, economics—offer approaches to the challenges of control fraud that are false and damaging. In light of the staggering losses that control frauds produce, Black argues that it is a costly absurdity not to incorporate criminologists with white collar crime expertise in discussions about regulatory policy within government agencies such as the SEC.

REHABILITATION, PROBATION, AND ENFORCED SELF-REGULATION

Rehabilitation is the most recent rationale for penal responses to crime. The rehabilitation of white collar crime offenders involves some paradoxes. One important component of rehabilitative programs has been to provide convicted offenders with the education and job training they need to be able to support themselves by legitimate activities. For many white collar offenders, their educational credentials and job skills were often instrumental in putting them in a position to commit crimes in the first place. In some cases, white collar offenders are barred from returning to their original profession following release from prison, but the correctional system is rather unlikely to have the resources to provide these offenders with vocational preparation for an alternative career. To the extent that white collar offenders become rehabilitated in prison, such rehabilitation is much more likely to be a result of the old notion of expiation for their sins—that is, a personal realization of the wrongfulness of their conduct and a willful repudiation of such conduct in the future. In some cases, counseling and group therapy might play a role, but successful reintegration of a law-abiding citizen into mainstream society is more likely to result from factors external to the correctional process, such as whether the offender has a supportive family and good job prospects. Some commentators have suggested that rehabilitation may be more effective and more applicable to organizations than to individuals (Croall 2001; Gobert and Punch 2003; Slapper and Tombs 1999). Of course, any rehabilitation of organizations such as corporations must necessarily take place outside of correctional institutions.

Probation

Probation has typically been regarded as more appropriate for individual white collar offenders than for conventional offenders (Weisburd et al. 1991). The reasons are obvious. The white collar offender is unlikely to be viewed as a direct physical threat to the community, which is the least controversial rationale for incarcerating someone, and is much more likely to be viewed as capable of remaining in the community as a constructive, gainfully employed citizen. Probation officers for white collar offenders are said to typically "go through the motions" rather than to undertake serious supervision of such probationers (Benson 1985b). However, probation as a response to individual white collar crimes may be regarded as excessively lenient, and it may leave offenders in a position to continue engaging in harmful conduct.

The notion of probation for organizations dates from the early 1970s (Lofquist 1993a). It was first imposed in *U.S. v. Atlantic Richfield Co.* (1971), apparently as a result of a judge's confusion about

---

B O X 12.6   The "Devil's Advocate" and Corporate Probation

Ideally, enforced self-regulation operates preventively. A related notion proposed by Metzger and Schwenk (1990) calls for adoption of the ancient device of a "devil's advocate" (used by the Catholic church in canonization procedures) as an element of corporate probation. The objective is to cultivate an internal critique and exposure mechanism within corporate organizations. Such a strategy could conceivably be imposed on companies guilty of repeated, serious offenses and would probably be most appropriate for large, diversified corporations. Metzger and Schwenk (1990) seemed to believe that such a strategy would be both less intrusive and less costly than alternatives (e.g., corporate restructuring) that might be imposed after a corporate conviction.

---

the precedents concerning nonmonetary sanctions (Lofquist 1993b). Subsequent attempts to apply it to corporations were vigorously challenged in the courts, which conceded that corporations could refuse to be subjected to probation and could choose instead to pay a fine or meet other provisions of their sentences. In the early 1990s, the U.S. Sentencing Commission formally established organizational probation as an option, partly as a concession to sentencing commissioners who favored tougher penalties for organizations and were unhappy with the scaling down of the fine schedule in response to business and political lobbying (Lofquist 1993a, 1993b). The original purpose of organizational probation was to ensure that the corporation remained in legal compliance and followed through on orders to pay fines and restitution; now it can be applied more proactively to intervene in and attempt to transform organizational operations. Organizational probation is still relatively new, and its effectiveness as a means of rehabilitating corporate criminals has not been fully evaluated. In recent years, the substantial majority of corporations sentenced by federal courts were put on probation (U.S. Sentencing Commission 2005). Box 12.6 discusses one special proposed condition for corporations on probation.

Enforced Self-Regulation

For many years, Braithwaite (1982b, 1990, 2002a) has advocated enforced self-regulation by corporations. With the concepts of "restorative justice" and "responsive regulation," Braithwaite (2001) has argued that a restorative justice system that privileges cooperative initiatives may deter, incapacitate, and rehabilitate more effectively than a punitive system. A basic premise for Braithwaite's call for self-regulation is that as a practical matter the state cannot effectively inspect and regulate vast numbers of corporations; indeed, corporate inspectors are often better trained and better qualified than government inspectors. Furthermore, corporations typically have "multiple selves"; that is, at least some corporate executives are concerned with responsible, ethical behavior and the long-term reputation of the corporation, and we should attempt to reach these parties. Even though some corporations are not capable of effectively regulating themselves, some are prepared to support compliance programs fully (Braithwaite and Fisse 1987). All of the preceding principles are especially applicable to the growing number of transnational corporations.

Braithwaite (1982b) contends that although corporations cannot typically be expected to adopt self-regulation on an entirely voluntary basis, they will be responsive to *enforced self-regulation*. In this scheme, a corporate compliance director would be required to report to a relevant regulatory agency and would be criminally liable for failing to do so. Braithwaite's (1990, 2002a) *enforcement pyramid*, which combines persuasion and punishment, imposes increasingly punitive sanctions on corporations that fail to take advantage of opportunities for compliance. The sequence of the enforcement pyramid is (1) persuasion, (2) warning letter, (3) civil penalty, (4) criminal penalty, (5) license suspension, and (6) license revocation. Grabosky's (1997) three-dimensional pyramid incorporates more fully the activities of the regulated and of third parties. The concept of *tripartism* calls for regulation specifically fostering participation of nongovernmental groups, such as public interest groups (Ayres and Braithwaite 1991). Among the perceived advantages of this enforced self-regulation are that rules would be tailored to specific companies and could be adjusted more easily for changing conditions. Rules and regulations could be more innovative, comprehensive, and consistent, and companies would be more committed to rules they helped formulate and more willing to assume more of the costs associated with their enforcement. Offenders would be more easily caught, more effectively sanctioned by corporate discipline, and more easily prosecuted by the government when necessary. Altogether, in Braithwaite's view, corporations would have a formidable incentive to comply, as opposed to engaging in a costly, time-consuming, and embarrassing attempt to counter an enforced investigation and prosecution.

Critics such as Gunningham (1995a, 1995b) have suggested that in most documented cases of self-regulation, corporations have mainly been focused on placating the public and deflecting intervention by the state, rather than meaningful self-regulation. Gunningham contended that one must tailor the appropriate form of regulation to the specific circumstances; he favors a "co-regulation" model. Gobert and Punch (2003) have pointed out that self-regulation can only work if company executives and employees are truly committed to it and truly autonomous and efficient internal compliance measures can be put into place. Braithwaite has acknowledged the concerns of some critics and skeptics of his enforced self-regulation model but has argued that the enforcement component successfully counters their objections. Furthermore, Braithwaite (1993c) cited empirical evidence supporting the self-regulation model: that some transnational pharmaceutical corporations adhere to higher standards than are required in many of the countries in which they

operate. Box 12.6 suggests a variation on enforced self-regulation.

The courts could require a corporation (or an entire industry) to prepare a report identifying reasons for an offense, those responsible for it, and specific measures to be taken to address the problem (Braithwaite 1993c; French 1989). Although at least one version of this approach allows corporations a "first free bite" (by shifting attention away from their initial offense), and even though it imposes a greater burden on the justice system, this approach replaces reliance on industry standards, which may set the bar too low, with reliance on the adequacy of the corporation's response.

FINES, RESTITUTION, AND COMMUNITY SERVICE

White collar crimes are mainly thought of as a form of economic crime, and economic sanctions have been especially commonly imposed on convicted offenders. These economic sanctions can take different forms, including the forfeiture of assets (or illegal profits) and mandatory restitution to victims. Most typically, economic sanctions take the form of criminal or civil fines, especially in corporate crime cases, in part because corporations per se obviously cannot be incarcerated (Cohen 1991; Croall 2001; Gobert and Punch 2003). The use of fines has traditionally been strongly favored by conservatives, who argue that considerations of economic efficiency should be paramount (Romano 1991). If one adopts the premise that a business is essentially an economic institution, then it follows that it should be most responsive to appropriate economic sanctions.

Fines can be punitive, deter lawbreaking, and even rehabilitate if they enable the corporation, business, or individual offender to pay for the harm done and compensate victims. Although fines are likely to be cost efficient for the justice system, some basic policy choices must be made. When criminal acts are carried out through a corporation and fines are imposed, who should be the targets of the fines:

the corporation, the managers and employees who are directly responsible, or both? Questions of deterrence and of fairness are involved in these choices.

Many additional issues are involved in imposing fines, including the challenge of setting the appropriate amount and determining whether the fine should be based on losses to society or gains to offenders (First 1990; Gobert and Punch 2003). Conservative economists generally favor the first choice, even allowing corporations to profit from their illegal activity so long as they pay identifiable costs. They also argue that the threat of excessive fines against corporations may inhibit managers from undertaking activities that in the long run might prove to be socially beneficial (Macey 1991). On a more practical level, an excessive fine may not be collectable, may ruin the business, and may well inspire a political backlash (Croall 2001). Excessive fines may also seem to strip the punishment of corporations of any serious moral component by treating the issue as a purely economic one. On the other hand, too low a fine may be treated as a "cost of business" and is unlikely to have significant deterrent effect.

Sentencing Guidelines for Fines

The U.S. Sentencing Commission's attempts to establish guidelines for fines took into account various factors, including the amount of loss the offense caused (sometimes diffuse and difficult to calculate), the offense "multiple" (difficulty of detecting and prosecuting, to ensure that the fine is both a deterrent and a just punishment), and the enforcement costs involved (Cohen 1992; Murphy 2002). Taken together, these factors produce a total monetary sanction of restitution, forfeitures, and fines. The Sentencing Guidelines for Organizations generally called for significantly higher fines than those traditionally imposed, and they reflected a dramatic increase since the mid-1980s in the size of fines for organizations (Cohen 1991, 1992). During a recent 10-year period, over $2 billion in fines were imposed on organizations in accordance with these guidelines; the median size of fines imposed on organizations was a little over $100,000 (Murphy 2002; U.S. Sentencing Commission 2005). The growing recent trend of imposing punitive civil fines equivalent to or larger than criminal fines has generated some controversy over whether prosecutors are using civil sanctions inappropriately—that is, imposing criminal penalties without having to meet the rigorous evidentiary standards of the criminal court (Mann 1992b).

Are fines truly effective and equitable, or are they mainly treated as a cost of doing business? Metzger and Schwenk (1990) argued that fines are likely to have little effect on the managers who make crime-related decisions; corporations may indemnify agents for any individually imposed fines resulting from illegal activity taken on behalf of corporations (Stone 1989). The costs of fines imposed on a corporation can be largely passed on to customers or shareholders. And one of the many ironies involved in the imposition of fines is that those shareholders who know the corporation will be fined are least likely to experience a punitive loss because they will have sold their shares before stock values drop. Judge Diana E. Murphy (2002), Chair of the U.S. Sentencing Commission, has declared that the imposition into the early 21st century of fines of increasing size has been successful in deterring corporate crime and encouraging corporate compliance with the law. It is difficult, however, to produce definitive evidence in support of such a claim.

Various alternatives to traditional fines have been proposed, including equity fines, day fines, installment fines, pass-through fines, and superadded liability (Gilbert and Russell 2002; Metzger and Schwenk 1990). Of these alternatives, equity fines, or stock dilution, are regarded as an especially interesting alternative. *Equity fines* call for convicted corporations to issue equity securities (special shares) and place them with a state-run victim compensation board, which in turn can liquidate these securities when they can realize a maximum return (Coffee 1981a). Such fines avoid the limitations imposed by the corporation's current cash assets, potentially allow for a more powerful deterrent effect because they threaten future earnings, limit harm mainly to corporate owners (and shareholders), and spare consumers and other wholly innocent parties.

In the case of individual white collar crime offenders, fines unaccompanied by prison sentences have been justified on various grounds. In addition to saving the taxpayers the cost of imprisoning such offenders, many people view fines as both most appropriate for economic crimes not involving direct violence and more effective than alternatives in preventing recidivism (Bene 1991). Of course, fines may also be regarded as insufficiently punitive and fundamentally inequitable because conventional offenders are much more likely to serve time in prison. Furthermore, even when a substantial fine is imposed, it does not necessarily follow that it will actually be collected (Pizzo and Muolo 1993); some individuals ordered to pay fines or restitution of hundreds of thousands of dollars pay nothing by claiming bankruptcy.

Restitution

White collar offenders, particularly business organizations or corporations, are especially well positioned to make restitution to victims and to pay compensation for the losses they have caused. On the one hand, *restitution* can be especially appealing because it is constructive and economically efficient (i.e., the offender, not the taxpayer, pays for losses attributable to the illegal activity). On the other hand, restitution and compensation in the absence of more direct criminal sanctions can overemphasize the economic aspects of white collar crime.

Community Service

Finally, both individual and organizational offenders may be required to perform community service (Croall 2001; First 1990; Gobert and Punch 2003). Again, the most appealing dimension of this sanction is that a direct, positive benefit accrues to the community without significant costs. Physicians and lawyers can be compelled to donate their professional services to clinics serving underprivileged populations; businesses can be directed to undertake community cleanup and neighborhood enhancement projects; corporations can be required to establish programs that provide goods and services to needy organizations. Community service orders must be closely monitored, however, to ensure that the convicted offender does not transform the community service into a public relations coup. Further, community service, especially if it is the only sanction imposed, may allow the offender to rationalize that something other than a crime was involved.

OCCUPATIONAL DISQUALIFICATION

Loss of license or *occupational disqualification* can be a fairly drastic penalty for an individual. It is punitive and intended as a deterrent, and it also incapacitates offenders by depriving them of opportunities for committing their occupationally related crimes.

Some commentators consider occupational disqualification to be a particularly appropriate sanction for executives convicted of corporate crimes because it avoids some of the practical limitations of other sanctions (Croall 2001; McDermott 1982). In this view, disqualification is the direct equivalent of a substantial fine for convicted executives who either cannot afford to pay direct fines or who could be indemnified by their corporate employer. It is especially likely to have both specific and general deterrent effects, and it should prevent individual executives from continuing illegal activities within the corporation.

If occupational disqualification of corporate executives is to be effective, it must be administered from outside the corporation because corporations may be reluctant to disqualify their own executives (Coffee 1980). The corporation is likely to be more concerned with maintaining employee morale and fulfilling corporate objectives, and it may fear what disqualified executives can reveal about the corporation's misconduct. On the other hand, even if executives are disqualified by an outside entity, the corporation may simply replace them and resume its pattern of misconduct. Disqualified executives blocked from legitimate professional employment may be sufficiently desperate or embittered to resort to other forms of illegal activity.

B O X 12.7   Contractual Disqualification for Corporations

The U.S. government has repeatedly awarded lucrative contracts to corporations that have been found guilty of some form of criminal conduct, including defrauding the government. Barring corporations from receiving government contracts after they have been found guilty of repeated lawbreaking might have a significant deterrent effect (*Business Ethics* 2002b). The Project on Government Oversight has specifically recommended contract suspensions or debarments for companies with more than one criminal or civil judgment finding against them within a three-year period. President Clinton issued regulations to this effect during his final days in office in 2000 (*Business Ethics* 2002a). Although some government bureaucrats, especially in the Department of Defense, may complain that certain corporations are uniquely qualified to fulfill the terms of some contracts, it seems absurd to continue rewarding companies that repeatedly engage in fraud or misrepresentation.

Despite such reservations, occupational disqualification has a place in the arsenal of sanctions for white collar crime, whether it is permanent or imposed for a specified period of time. Even though several of those convicted in the celebrated insider trading cases of the 1980s were permanently banned from the securities industry (Stewart 1991), such a penalty did not necessarily preclude their involvement in other types of business opportunities. For physicians and lawyers, however, loss of license or disbarment can have especially devastating consequences; thus, such sanctions are relatively rare events in these professions, at least partly because of a reluctance to impose a penalty seen as having potentially draconian consequences. Box 12.7 considers a form of corporate disqualification.

INCARCERATION

Compared to conventional offenders, relatively few white collar criminals are sent to prison. A standard joke in the white collar crime literature is that many corporations have a "vice president in charge of going to prison," a "fall guy" for the corporation. The imprisonment of white collar crime offenders is quite controversial. Some arguments in favor of incarceration are that the high level of intent, calculation, and rationality and the extended period over which these crimes occur certainly merit the purely punitive dimension of prison. White collar offenders fear the prospect of prison perhaps more than any other sanction, and thus it has a powerful deterrent effect on both convicted and prospective offenders. The scope of harm caused by white collar offenders is often great enough to merit so serious a punishment as incarceration. Furthermore, it is simply unfair (and an inspiration for cynicism) to send conventional offenders to prison in large numbers without imposing the same sanction on white collar offenders who have caused equivalent or greater harm. Finally, the victims of white collar crimes, especially those who have suffered direct losses and injuries, may expect or demand imprisonment for convicted offenders.

Conversely, among the various arguments advanced against the use of imprisonment in white collar crime is that the rehabilitation dimension of imprisonment, which is one rationale for its existence, simply does not apply to white collar offenders. The humiliation and loss of status and position suffered by white collar offenders are on the average substantially greater than those sustained by conventional offenders, and imprisonment is a gratuitous, additional punishment. It is wasteful to put people in prison, especially highly competent business executives, professionals, and other skilled and well-educated people who could be making constructive contributions to society. White collar offenders are not "dangerous" in the direct, predatory sense, and accordingly they need not be incarcerated. A final argument is that it is more beneficial to victims of white collar crimes to require offenders to earn money legally outside prison and make restitution, which also saves taxpayers the costs of incarceration.

Thus, the "rational" arguments against imprisoning white collar offenders are many, but if it is indeed true that corporate executives and other white collar offenders fear imprisonment most, then incarceration is probably necessary in at least some cases (Clinard 1990; Leaf 2002; Smith 2002). Early in the 21st century, in the wake of corporate scandals that devastated the investments, pensions, and savings of millions of Americans, the public seemed to be more supportive of hard time for corporate criminals; prosecutors were seeking longer sentences; and Congress passed the Sarbanes-Oxley Act dramatically raising the prison sentences for certain kinds of white collar crime (Glater 2002a; Recine 2002). Long prison sentences were in fact imposed in some of these case: for example, 15 years in one case (for an 80-year–old man), 8 to 25 years in another, and 25 years in a third (Sorkin 2005e). While some commentators questioned both the fairness and the deterrent effectiveness of such draconian sentences, it is worth noting that a poll of high-level corporate executives uncovered strong support for these sentences (Norris 2005b). These executives believed themselves to be victims of crimes of corporate CEOs, insofar as the reputations of all such executives are sullied by these crimes of greed.

ORGANIZATIONAL REFORM AND CORPORATE DISSOLUTION

Some of the most harmful white collar crime is committed by or through an organization; large corporations are especially noteworthy in this respect. One ongoing debate centers on whether we should punish only the culpable individual executives within an organization or the organization itself. In the case of corporate crime, it is generally difficult to identify the guilty party and to ascertain whether illegal acts were committed to benefit the corporation as a

whole, some specific division within the corporation, or individual corporate executives (Braithwaite 2001; Gobert and Punch 2003; Lofquist et al. 1997).

Prosecutors may sometimes determine that both the organization and some of its executives are appropriate targets (Benson and Cullen 1998; Stone 1989). Many principled and practical reasons have been advanced for prosecuting organizations as well as individual executives. The organization must be deterred from future crimes and is better able to compensate victims of its crimes than are individual executives (DiMento et al. 2000–2001). Prosecutors can often secure more effective cooperation when they have the option of prosecuting both the organization and individual executives. One view holds that if much of the most significant white collar crime is organizational or corporate in form, then preventive efforts must be directed toward the organizational structure.

Numerous proposals have been advanced to reform or transform corporations to make them more accountable and less likely to engage in harmful and illegal actions: imposing a legal obligation to report activities that may cause death, injury, or loss; requiring effective compliance programs; redefining the rights of corporations to prevent them from using purely individual rights to protect themselves; limiting corporate ownership and control over the media; mandating that corporations' misdeeds be publicized and promoting more direct consumer pressure on corporations; freeing lawmakers from corporate PAC influence; strengthening whistle-blower laws to protect those within corporations who expose harmful and illegal practices; requiring that a percentage of fines be used to support independent corporate watchdogs; mandating public directors or worker representatives for corporate boards; and compelling corporations to undertake socially beneficial projects using their special skills.

Other proposals include requiring corporations to make restitution to their victims; discouraging investments in criminally recidivist corporations and prohibiting criminal companies from receiving government grants, licenses, or contracts; decreasing the size of corporations; and requiring federal chartering of corporations to allow for more potent federal

---

BOX 12.8   Citizen Works Proposals for Cracking Down on Corporate Crime

Citizen Works (www.citizenworks.org) is an activist organization founded by Ralph Nader. It has recently advanced the following specific proposals for cracking down on corporate crime:

1. Track the extent and cost of corporate crime
2. Increase corporate crime prosecution budgets
3. Ban corporate criminals from government contracts
4. Crack down on corporate tax avoidance
5. Restore the rights of defrauded investors
6. Democratize corporate governance
7. Rein in excessive executive pay

8. Regulate derivatives trading
9. Expand disclosure
10. End conflicts of interest on Wall Street
11. Fix the pension system
12. Foster a national discussion on corporate power

In addition to calls to crack down on corporate crime and rein in imperial CEOs, Ralph Nader (2005) calls for a broader attack on excessive corporate power by shoring up the civil justice system, regulating in the public interest, reintroducing serious trust busting (with the media as a primary target), getting corporations out of elections, and reclaiming the Constitution.

---

oversight and to close up loopholes in some state chartering standards (Clinard and Yeager 1980; Coleman 2002; Mokhiber 1988). Some specific reform proposals emanating out of the corporate scandals of the early 2000s included: independent accounting boards, a more muscular SEC, CEO/CFO certification, shareholder approval of stock options, auditor independence, more outsider directors, curbs on insider sales, expensing stock options, limiting company stock in 401(k)s, banning corporate moves offshore, regulating derivatives, disgorging ill-gotten gains, and incarcerating CEOs and CFOs who sign off on false financial statements (Walczak et al. 2002). These lists of proposed reforms are extensive but hardly exhaustive; they provide some sense of the broad range of possibilities for change. See Box 12.8 for some recently proposed reforms.

All corporate reform proposals are inevitably controversial on ideological grounds; that is, they are seen by some as unacceptable and economically destructive forms of intervention in the free-market system. For example, conservative critics of the federal chartering proposal fear a movement toward public ownership of corporations and an increase in the cost of doing business. Among progressives, however, reform proposals are largely regarded as delusions because they can always be co-opted or counteracted by powerful corporations and because

structural transformation of the capitalist system and nationalization of corporations are necessary if corporate crime is to be addressed in any substantial way (Barnett 1981a; Pearce and Tombs 2002). By any criteria, the reform proposals face formidable practical barriers. It remains difficult to demonstrate that such measures, when implemented, can be truly effective in preventing or limiting corporate crime. Even if it can be agreed that the overriding objective in addressing white collar crime on the organizational level is to diminish or eliminate organizational pressures and opportunities to commit illegalities, there are clearly many different opinions on how this should be accomplished.

Perhaps the most extreme sanction that can be imposed on a corporation is "capitalist punishment," or the forced dissolution of the corporation (Mokhiber 1988; Russell and Gilbert 1999; Schwartz and Ellison 1982). Such a sanction would seem to be justified for corporations involved in massively harmful activities over some extended period. As a practical matter, however, this penalty is widely regarded as too extreme and too harmful to too many innocent parties, such as workers, stockholders, and suppliers. *Corporate dissolution* is not the same as the execution of a "natural person" insofar as a corporation cannot suffer pain directly and its key personnel can hypothetically regroup after a dissolution and seek

---

BOX 12.9   A Stakeholder Model for Corporations: Costco and Whole Foods

Corporations too often engage in various forms of corporate crime when they privilege the pursuit of profit and economic benefits for corporate management and owners above all other considerations. Costco Wholesale is America's fifth-largest retailer, and Whole Foods is on the threshold of becoming a Fortune 500 company (Gertner 2004; Greenhouse 2005e). Both corporations have certainly been profitable, but their CEOs claim that they are more focused on benefit to stakeholders—including customers, employees, and community members—than to shareholders and the expectations of Wall Street analysts. Such analysts find it objectionable that Costco's average pay of $17 an hour is 42 percent higher than that of its nearest rival, Sam's Club, and that it offers its workers a generous health and dental plan and also contributes generously

to the retirement plan of its workers. It refrains from marking up branded items more than 14 percent (some stores mark up 50 percent or more) and pays its CEO $350,000 a year (modest relative to the size of the corporation). Whole Foods' stakeholder philosophy emphasizes customer and employee satisfaction, with employees receiving higher than average salaries ($29,000 a year) for the grocery industry and no corporate officer earning more than 14 times the salary of average employees. It also donates 5 percent of profits each year to charity, adopts environmentally friendly practices, and pays employees to engage in community service. Such corporations at least suggest that it is possible for a large, profitable corporation to adopt policies that benefit rather than harm citizens, customers, and employees.

---

to reestablish the corporation with a new name and a new charter in a new location. Some major corporations have in fact dissolved following revelations of their involvement in large-scale financial crime, either as a consequence of their internal corruption and frauds, fines and bad publicity from criminal prosecution, or both. The Equity Funding Corporation (insurance fraud), the American Continental Corporation (thrift and real estate fraud), and Drexel Burnham (insider trading) are but three examples of multimillion dollar corporations or financial entities that collapsed largely due to their involvement in white collar crime. Arthur Andersen, the accounting firm, dissolved as a company following conviction of criminal charges in 2002. See Box 12.9 for a discussion of two corporations that have embraced a new model for corporate policies.

RESPONDING TO RESIDUAL FORMS OF WHITE COLLAR CRIME

This text has addressed a range of hybrid and marginal forms of white collar crime, including: state-corporate crime, crimes of globalization, finance crime, techno-

crime, enterprise crime, contrepreneurial crime, and avocational crime. Each of these different forms of crime requires responses tailored to the specific character of that type of crime, ranging from the strengthening of consumer protection laws to the transformation of global economic policy. No single formula for responding to such diverse types of harmful activity is available.

CONTROLLING GOVERNMENTAL CRIME

Governmental crime has been treated here as a cognate form of white collar crime. Such crime, especially when it is committed at the highest levels of government, is extraordinarily difficult to control because those who are committing the crimes also often have disproportionate power to shield themselves from criminal investigation and prosecution. We must confront the basic paradox that even though we depend on governmental entities and agencies to control white collar crime, the state, its agencies, and politicians generally are the sources of some of the most serious and harmful

---

B O X   12.10   Responding to White Collar Crime Internationally

Much of our knowledge of white collar crime is somewhat parochial and lacks a comparative or international perspective; the literature on white collar crime is disproportionately American. As the business environment becomes ever more global, business crime will increasingly take advantage of the gaps and shortcomings of national laws and of limited international control structures (Braithwaite and Drahos 2000; Eatwell and Taylor 2000; Pearce and Tombs 2002). Accordingly, international organizations such as the United Nations and cooperative international responses to the major forms of white collar crime will become more important; the whole concept of regulation must be reconsidered today in light of expanding globalization (Danielsen 2005; Gilbert and Russell 2002; Picciotto 2002). At least some efforts to realize new international controls—for example, the creation of a "new world order"—may simply serve to extend the interests of powerful nations and transnational corporations (Chomsky 1993). Alternatively, the

potential for international law to play a generally positive role in responding to a range of emerging challenges has also been claimed (Falk 2004). But any efforts to develop authentically effective international responses to white collar crime will draw upon more systematic study of the different national styles of responding to such crime, the particular context within which these styles exist, and their relative successes. The context of globalization—an increasingly interdependent and interconnected world—will surely be central to these interpretations.

Altogether, it is clear that white collar crime must be addressed on many different levels. Surely it merits a higher priority than it has been historically accorded by society at large, the justice system, and the criminal justice curriculum. Ultimately, an effective response to white collar crime requires basic transformations in the structure of the capitalist political economy, the character of corporations and businesses, and the ethics of professions and individuals alike.

---

crime. When a state comes to be viewed as fundamentally criminal and corrupt, the ultimate response may be a popular uprising or a coup by disenchanted groups. In nondemocratic societies, this may be the only real option for challenging state crime.

Ideally, international tribunals would have both the jurisdiction and the means to mount an effective response to state crime. Tribunals addressing genocidal actions in Rwanda and Kosovo and the establishment of a permanent International Criminal Court at the outset of the 21st century were encouraging developments in response to at least some major forms of state crime, although the long-term effectiveness of such endeavors remains to be established (Minow 1998; Morris 2001; Ratner and Abrams 2001). Much of the response to state crime continues to rely on an international free press and various international organizations for monitoring state crime and corruption and generating pressure for action through exposure and shaming. Historically, high-level state criminals have had to answer directly for their crimes to an

international court only following their military defeat and capture, as did the surviving Nazi leadership brought to trial at Nuremberg after World War II. Some commentators suggest that abolishing the state itself would be the best way to reduce or eliminate state crime, but the enduring anarchist dream of living in a world without states is unlikely to be realized (Martin 1995). At the outset of the 21st century, responses to perceived state crimes were carried out by superpowers such as the United States and its allies (although the United States was itself viewed by many people as a criminal state), entities such as the United Nations and NATO, and international tribunals. Establishing a form of response widely endorsed as legitimate by people in many parts of the world, and avoiding the perpetration of gross abuses of power while enforcing international laws and accords, stood as a great challenge for the future (Gilbert and Russell 2002). Box 12.10 contemplates an international response to white collar crime.

The existing means of financing political campaigns are widely recognized to promote corrupt arrangements between public officials and corporations or other entities that donate money to their campaigns. Even though campaign-financing reforms have been undertaken periodically, they have hardly eliminated the problem of corrupt public officials. Although a ban on "soft money" went into effect in November 2002, some commentators anticipated that wealthy and powerful entities would be able to identify loopholes that would enable them to maintain their traditional disproportionate influence over the political process (Samples and Basham 2002). The soft money ban was overturned as unconstitutional by the U.S. Court of Appeals in May 2003, but was subsequently upheld by the U.S. Supreme Court later that year (Schifferes 2003; Urofsky 2005).

The "revolving-door" syndrome, in which people move between governmental regulatory positions in which they wield considerable influence over private-sector activities and lucrative positions in the industry or business they once regulated, is an obvious source of corruption. Despite laws and presidential directives intended to minimize this syndrome, it continues to be a problem. On all levels of governmental work, from the top down to police officers and municipal repair crews, a disparity exists between the relative power or illegal opportunities of government employees and their legal compensation.

STRUCTURAL TRANSFORMATION AS A RESPONSE TO WHITE COLLAR CRIME

In one fatalistic view, human nature is inherently corrupt, and thus no form of human intervention can obliterate the basic impulses that contribute to the commission of white collar crimes. In a more optimistic view, a substantial reduction of white collar crime requires a transformation of society's political, economic, and cultural structure. James William Coleman (2006) considered a fundamental repudiation of the "culture of competition" and a restructuring of social and economic relationships as a necessity to diminish markedly the scope of white collar crime.

Critics of the existing capitalist system regard as complicit in inequality: unemployment, overwork, poverty, diminished democracy, and environmental degradation, as well as corporate crime (Padgett 2005). David Simon (2006) contended that a *structural transformation* of our society into an "economic democracy" is the only appropriate response to elite deviance and all the interrelated problems of a modern capitalist society. A progressive political and economic transformation requires nationalization of certain industries, fundamental tax reform, income redistribution, and sound ecological policies. In this view, a society organized according to the general principles of democratic socialism is much more likely to foster a genuine sense of community and concern and to discourage selfish and predatory conduct. The opportunities for large-scale private enterprises to engage in various forms of exploitative and harmful activity would be greatly curtailed. Organizational and individual energy would be channeled into cooperative and productive endeavors.

Those who contend that a structural transformation is necessary if white collar crime, especially in its elite and corporate forms, is to be curtailed in a substantial and enduring way are surely correct on some level. All smaller scale reforms—new laws, different sanctions, and innovative educational programs—are likely to have only limited effect. Still, some limitations of structural transformation must be acknowledged. First, it may be viewed as utopian and somewhat out of touch with reality, insofar as relatively little support for such a transformation in the United States is apparent. Second, structural transformations undertaken out of progressive aspirations have all too often led to corrupt, totalitarian societies, especially in the 20th century; the Soviet Union is a prominent example. Third, any political and economic transformation that is to realize progressive goals must be accompanied by a cultural transformation that redirects human values and priorities. Those who call for a democratic socialist system often underestimate the importance of such cultural transformation.

RESPONDING TO THE CHALLENGE OF WHITE COLLAR CRIME, IN SUM

Moral indignation and a fair measure of outrage are often justified and can be productive in combating white collar crime up to a point, but such emotional responses must be tempered with pragmatism. Severe condemnation and harsh, selectively applied penal measures are necessary elements in the response to white collar crime, as are all strategies that maximize voluntary compliance. This chapter has identified a range of responses to white collar crime that fall between harsh penal measures and noninterventionist inducements for compliance.

Fostering a culture that promotes trust and offers incentives to refrain from cheating or engaging in illegal conduct is an overriding challenge in effectively addressing white collar crime. As a practical matter, more substantial training of enforcement personnel, greater funding, and a better reward structure are needed. Prosecutors and judges need more options and resources to take effective action against white collar offenders. Responding to white collar crime should be a higher priority. Still, we must not ignore the evidence suggesting that we cannot and should not rely excessively on responses rooted in a coercive criminal justice system.

How can we resolve the tensions between the pragmatist and progressive, the realist and idealist approaches to white collar crime? This is not an easy dilemma to resolve. The position adopted here could be described as progressive pluralism, which calls for moving against white collar crime on two tracks simultaneously. On the one hand, we must generate a much broader consciousness of the harm caused by white collar crime. Only with a much more widespread consciousness of this harm is it possible to undertake the structural and cultural transformation necessary as a precondition for substantially reducing the scope of white collar crime. At the same time, we must address the immediate challenge of white collar crime with an appropriate mixture of punishment and persuasion, a wide range of demonstrably effective sanctions, and any authentic means of promoting self-regulation.

A CONCLUDING NOTE: TRUSTED CRIMINALS AND WHITE COLLAR CRIME IN THE 21ST CENTURY

As we move through the 21st century, white collar crime in the broadest sense endures as a major threat to our physical and financial well-being. The proposition that white collar crime is a complex phenomenon has been a guiding premise of this book. We have rejected one-dimensional, simplistic, and dogmatic proclamations about white collar crime; instead, we have emphasized the multiple dimensions of such crime and have recognized that it generates public policy conundrums.

The crimes of large and powerful organizations such as corporations are especially pernicious. In a complex world of diminishing resources and increasing interdependency, the notion that corporations are devoid of social responsibility—and are justified in being exclusively oriented toward maximizing profit—is likely to become increasingly intolerable. But the response to white collar crime occurs in a dynamic political environment of countervailing forces pitting progressive reforms against conservative restraints. In the early years of the 21st century in the United States, for example, we saw some legislative initiatives directed at especially blatant corporate and accounting industry practices that facilitated certain forms of white collar crime on a massive scale. At the same time, efforts by a conservative administration and legislative leadership sought to scale back various forms of regulation and to protect corporate and finance industry interests. We also witnessed some campaign financing reforms but none that truly addressed the vastly disproportionate political influence of large corporations and wealthy individuals.

A wave of recent corporate scandals resulted in virtually unprecedented media attention to some forms of white collar crime, but in the face of other ongoing threats, including international terrorism, it was far from clear that attitudes and policy responses toward white collar crime would undergo a fundamental shift into high gear. In an evolving postmodern world of the 21st century, the ongoing revolutionary transformations in computerization and telecommunications will create broad new opportunities for white collar crime, and such crime will increasingly take on a global character. Many other factors, including a "graying" population and fundamental changes in the structure of corporations and occupations, will contribute to a significant expansion of white collar crime. The challenge of responding effectively to such crime is likely to intensify.

KEY TERMS

business ethics, 309

compliance approach, 314

corporate dissolution, 325

deterrence, 316

enforced self-regulation, 319

enforcement pyramid, 319

equity fines, 321

expressive crimes, 316

instrumental crimes, 316

just deserts, 315

moral appeals, 309

negative sanctions, 313

newsmaking criminology, 307

normative form, 312

occupational disqualification, 322

positive sanctions, 312

punitive approach, 315

rehabilitation, 318

reintegrative shaming, 312

restitution, 322

structural transformation, 328

tripartism, 320

DISCUSSION QUESTIONS

1. Identify some specific strategies that might elevate consciousness about white collar crime. What are some of the major policy options for responding to white collar crime generally? Which overall strategy, if any, is most likely to succeed, and why?

2. What are the major elements of a moralistic response to white collar crime, and what are some limitations of an emphasis on business ethics? How would you evaluate Braithwaite's call for relying upon reintegrative shaming? What are some benefits and limitations of both positive sanctions and negative sanctions in response to white collar crime?

3. Discuss the arguments made for and against greater reliance upon formal law as a means of dealing with white collar crime. What are some recent trends in the use of civil law in response to

white collar crime? Identify and evaluate principal arguments on both sides of the cooperative versus punitive approach debate.

4. How can the different objectives of the penal system—retribution, incapacitation, deterrence, and rehabilitation—be fulfilled in connection with white collar crime? Can they be reconciled? Discuss the specific role of the following as responses to these questions: just deserts, general deterrence, probation, self-regulation, fines, restitution, community service, occupational disqualification, incarceration, and corporate dissolution. Which strategies do you regard as most effective and justifiable, and why?

5. What are some of the most important specific strategies for responding to the following forms of residual (hybrid and marginal) white collar crime: state-corporate

crime, finance crime, technocrime, enterprise crime, contrepreneurial crime, and avocational crime? What, if anything, can be done about state crime and political white collar crime? Overall, what kinds of structural transformations might diminish the problem of white collar crime, and why are you optimistic or pessimistic about our chances of addressing this problem successfully in the future?

Appendix
White Collar Crime in Films

This list is an inventory of white collar crime films produced since 1930, as compiled by Lawrence T. Nichols of West Virginia University. An earlier version of this list was published in "White-Collar Cinema: Changing Representations of Upper-World Deviance in Popular Films," pp. 61–84, Volume 11, *Perspectives on Social Problems* (Amsterdam: JAI Press, 1999). This list, which has been updated from 1999 by Professor Nichols, is reproduced here with his permission. The article "White-Collar Cinema" presented several major findings: (1) Earlier white collar crime films (before the 1960s) focus more on individuals, whereas later films focus more on systemic problems. (2) With regard to genre, the main form of white collar crime films has been drama (as opposed to action, which is more prominent in organized crime and terrorism movies). (3) With regard to theme, the primary emphasis has been on corruption rather than greed or violence. (4) The number of white collar crime films has increased greatly since the 1930s, as the United States has become more and more a white collar society. (5) Even so, the number of white collar crime films is still far less than that of other crime films, especially movies about street crime. (6) The article suggests that more-violent types of crime are more amenable to the motion picture format because these involve rapid movement, as in car chases and shootouts. (7) If, therefore, film producers wish to develop the white collar crime film, they may be expected to blend in elements of action films.

Period	Title	Violations
1931–1939	Mr. Smith Goes to Washington	Political corruption
	Night Court	Crooked judge
1940–1949	All My Sons	Military contract fraud
	Chicago Deadline	Reporter vs. political corruption
	Citizen Kane	Corporate/political corruption
	Double Indemnity	Insurance fraud, murder
	I Wake Up Screaming	Crooked cop
	Meet John Doe	Media fraud
	Parole, Inc.	State government corruption
	The Great McGinty	Political machine corruption
	The Inspector General	Political corruption in Russia

1950–1959	On the Waterfront	Union corruption
	Rogue Cop	Police corruption
	Seven Days in May	Military coup
	The Last Hurrah	Political machine corruption
1960–1969	Ada	Political corruption
	Cool Hand Luke	Corrupt prison system
	Elmer Gentry	Religious fraud
	Judgment at Nuremberg	Government violence
1970–1979	All the President's Men	Watergate scandal
	And Justice for All	Corrupt judge
	Assassination of Trotsky	State-sanctioned murder
	China Syndrome	Corporate greed, fraud
	Executive Action	Government conspiracy to kill JFK
	Magnum Force	Police vigilantism
	Murder by Decree	State-sponsored murder
	Murder of Fred Hampton	Police vigilantism, corruption
	One Man Jury	Police vigilantism
	Save the Tiger	Insurance fraud
	Serpico	Police whistleblower
	Three Days of the Condor	CIA corruption
	Walking Tall	Local political corruption
1980–1989	Above the Law	Police corruption
	Absence of Malice	Unethical journalism
	Act of Vengeance	Union corruption
	American Justice	Government corruption
	And Nothing But the Truth	Political corruption
	Best Little Whorehouse in Texas	Local government corruption

	Best Seller	Corporate violence
	Brubaker	Corrupt state prison system
	Code of Silence	Police vigilantism
	Eight Men Out	Fraud in professional athletics
	Gorky Park	Government corruption in Soviet Union
	House on Carroll Street	Government illegality
	Huey Long	Political corruption (Louisiana)
	Legal Eagles	Fraud in professional art
	Marie	Whistleblower in state government
	No Way Out	Government violence
	Protocol	Government corruption
	Salvador	Government violence
	Salvation	Religious fraud
	Romero	Government violence
	Tank	Government corruption
	The Killing Fields	Government violence (Cambodia)
	The Shakedown	Police corruption
	Tin Men	Fraudulent sales practices
	To Kill a Priest	Government violence (Poland)
	Trading Places	Insider trading
	Wall Street	Insider trading
	Whistleblower	Government violence (Britain)
	Witness	Police corruption
1990–1999	A Civil Action	Environmental crime
	Article 99	VA hospital abuses
	Backdraft	Corrupt firefighter
	Broken Trust	Judicial corruption
	City Hall	Political corruption

1990–1999 *(continued)*

Class Action	Unsafe products
Clear and Present Danger	Political corruption (drug war)
Conspiracy Theory	Political conspiracy
Copland	Police corruption
Disclosure	Sexual harassment on job
Enemy of the State	Political corruption
Excessive Force	Police corruption
Extreme Justice	Police vigilantism
Extreme Measures	Hospital fraud
Glengarry Glen Ross	Real estate fraud
Godfather, III	Vatican bank corruption
Havana	Government corruption (Cuba)
Hoffa	Union corruption
Internal Affairs	Police corruption
Krippendorf's Tribe	Research fraud
JFK	Political conspiracy
L.A. Confidential	Police/political corruption
Leap of Faith	Religious fraud
Mission Impossible	Double agent
My Fellow Americans	Political corruption

Nixon	Political corruption
Other People's Money	Corporate raiders
Presumed Innocent	Government corruption
Quiz Show	Corporate fraud
Rising Sun	Corporate violence (Japan)
Sneakers	Computer hackers
The Firm	Legal profession fraud
The Fugitive	Medical fraud
The Insider	Unsafe products/ whistleblower
The Pelican Brief	Government violence
Wag the Dog	Government/media misinformation

2000– 2005

Antitrust	Monopolistic practices
Boiler Room	Stock fraud
Dark Blue	Police corruption in Los Angeles
Erin Brockovich	Environmental crime
Lucky Numbers	Lottery fraud
Minority Report	Police corruption (futuristic)
Shattered Glass	False reporting
Silver City	Police corruption

References

Abadinsky, H. (1981; 1985; 2000) *Organized crime.* Boston: Allyn & Bacon.

Abadinsky, H. (2005) "Organized crime," pp. 1068–1074 in R. A. Wright and J. M. Miller (Eds.), *Encyclopedia of criminology.* Volume II. New York: Routledge.

Abel, R. L. (1988a) "The crisis is injuries, not liability," pp. 31–41 in W. Olson (Ed.), *New directions in liability law.* New York: The Academy of Political Science.

Abel, R. L. (1988b) "United States: The contradictions of professionalism," pp. 186–243 in R. L. Abel and P. S. C. Lewis (Eds.), *Lawyers in society: The common law world.* Berkeley: University of California Press.

Abelson, R. (2001) "In hindsight, plenty of unasked questions arose about the company board." *New York Times* (November 30): C6.

Abelson, R. (2002a) "Enron's board quickly ratified far-reaching management moves." *New York Times* (February 22): C6.

Abelson, R. (2002b) "U.S. to step up antitrust effort on health care." *New York Times* (August 18): A1.

Abelson, R., and Freudenheim, M. H. (2005) "Scrushy for the defense?" *New York Times* (April 7): C1.

Abelson, R., and Glater, J. D. (2003) "New York will sue 2 big drug makers on doctor discount." *New York Times* (February 13): A1.

Abramson, J. (1998) "The business of persuasion thrives in nation's capital." *New York Times* (September 29): A1.

Abramson, J. (2002) "I am woman, hear me roar in the Enron scandal." *New York Times* (January 27): Wk3.

Ackerman, K. D. (2005) *Boss Tweed: The rise and fall of the corrupt pol who conceived the soul of modern New York.* New York: Carroll & Graf.

Adams, J. R., and Frantz, D. (1992) *A full-service bank: How BCCI stole billions around the world.* New York: Pocket Books.

Adams, W., and Brock, J. W. (1989) *Dangerous pursuits—Mergers and acquisitions in the age of Wall Street.* New York: Pantheon Books.

Adler, F., Mueller, G. O. W., and Laufer, W. S. (1998) *Criminology* (3rd ed.). Boston: McGraw-Hill.

Adler, M. D. (2005) "Against 'individual risk': A sympathetic critique of risk assessment." *University of Pennsylvania Law Review* 153: 1121–1250.

Adler, R. W., and Lord, C. (1991) "Environmental crimes: Raising the stakes." *The George Washington Law Review* 59: 781–861.

Agee, P. (1988) "Remarks: The role of the CIA, anti-communism and the U.S." Institute for Media Analysis, Harvard University, November 11–13.

Agence France-Presse. (2004) "Indonesia: Suharto tops list of embezzling leaders." *New York Times* (March 26): A5.

Akers, R. L. (1985) *Deviant behavior: A social learning approach* (3rd ed.). Belmont, CA: Wadsworth.

Alario, M., and Freudenberg, W. (2003) "The paradoxes of modernity: Scientific advances, environmental problems, and risks to the social fabric." *Sociological Forum* 18: 193–214.

Alatas, S. H. (1990) *Corruption: Its nature, causes and functions.* Aldershot, UK: Avebury.

Albanese, J. S. (1982) "What Lockheed and La Cosa Nostra have in common: The effect of ideology on criminal justice policy." *Crime & Delinquency* 28: 211–232.

Albanese, J. S. (1991) "Organized crime: The mafia myth," pp. 201–218 in J. F. Sheley (Ed.), *Criminology: A contemporary handbook.* Belmont, CA: Wadsworth.

Albanese, J. S. (1998) *Organized crime in America.* (3rd ed.). Cincinnati, OH: Anderson.

Albanese, J. S., Das, D., and Verma, A. (Eds.). (2003) *Organized crime: World perspectives.* Upper Saddle River, NJ: Prentice Hall.

Albonetti, C. A. (1994) "The symbolic punishment of white-collar offenders," pp. 269–282 in G. S. Bridges and M. A. Myers (Eds.), *Inequality, crime, and social control.* Boulder, CO: Westview Press.

Allen, H. E., Friday, P. C., Roebuck, J. B., and Sagarin, E. (1981) *Crime and punishment.* New York: Free Press.

Allenbaugh, M. (2005) "The Supreme Court's new blockbuster U.S. Sentencing Guidelines decision: A clear Sixth Amendment ruling, with an invitation to Congress to create a better remedy." *FindLaw's Legal Commentary* (January 4): 1–4.

Allison, G. (2004) *Nuclear terrorism: The ultimate preventable tragedy.* New York: Henry Holt.

Almeida, P., and Stearns, L. B. (1998) "Political opportunities and local grassroots environmental movements: The case of Minamata." *Social Problems* 45: 37–60.

Alsop, R. (2003) "Right and wrong." *Wall Street Journal* (September 17): 1.

Alter, J. (1995) "Blowing smoke at CBS." *Newsweek* (December 4): 45.

Altheide, D. L. (2002) *Creating fear: News and the construction of crisis.* Hawthorne, NY: Aldine de Gruyter.

Altheide, D. L., Adler, P. A., Adler, P., and Altheide, D. A. (1978) "The social meaning of employee theft," pp. 90–124 in J. Johnson and J. Douglas (Eds.), *Crime at the top: Deviance in business and the professions.* Philadelphia: Lippincott.

Altman, D. (2002) "When insiders' sales are a long-term plan." *New York Times* (May 19): B11.

Altman, L. (1994) "Researcher falsified data in breast cancer study." *New York Times* (March 14): A1.

Alvarez, L. (2001) "Democrats reject Bush's choice to head product safety panel." *New York Times* (August 3): A1.

Alvesalo, A. (1999) "A sitting duck or a Trojan horse? Critical criminology and white collar crime control." *The Critical Criminologist* 9 (Spring) 5–7.

Alvesalo, A. (2002) "Downsized by law, ideology and pragmatics—Policing white collar crime," pp. 149–164 in G. W. Potter (Ed.), *Controversies in white-collar crime.* Cincinnati, OH: Anderson.

Alvesalo, A., and Tombs, S. (2002) "Working for criminalization of economic offending: Contradictions for critical criminology?" *Critical Criminology* 11: 21–40.

Anastasi, J. (2003) *The new forensics—Investigating corporate fraud and the theft of intellectual property.* New York: John Wiley.

Andenaes, J. (1974) *Punishment and deterrence.* Ann Arbor: University of Michigan Press.

Andersen. (2000) *Study of restatement matters: An analysis of the industries and accounting issues underlying public company restatements.* Chicago: Author.

Anderson, A. G. (1979) *The business of organized crime: A cosa nostra family.* Stanford, CA: Hoover Institution Press.

Anderson, D. L. (Ed.) (1998) *Facing My Lai—Moving beyond the massacre.* Kansas City: University of Kansas Press.

Anderson, J. (2005a) "A new inquiry into big board specialists." *New York Times* (February 7): C1.

Anderson, J. (2005b) "Merrill to pay Florida couple $1 million." *New York Times* (March 1): C3.

Anderson, M. (1992) *Imposters in the temple.* New York: Simon & Schuster.

Anderson, S. (1995) "OSHA under siege." *The Progressive* (December) 26–28.

Andrew, C., and Gordievsky, O. (1990) *KGB—The inside story.* New York: HarperCollins.

Andrews, E. L. (1997) "None prove so stubborn as a giant spurned." *New York Times* (January 11): A37.

Andrews, E. L. (2003) "Senate panel backs bill to give tax windfall to U.S. companies." *New York Times* (October 2): A1.

Andrews, E. L. (2004) "House approves $140 billion in tax breaks." *New York Times* (June 18): C1.

Andrews, S. (1996) "Michael Milken just wants to be loved." *New York Times* (June 10): 20–30.

Anechiarico, F. (1990) "Remembering corruption." *Corruption and Reform* 5: 109–124.

Angier, N. (1997) "In a culture of hysterectomies, many question their necessity." *New York Times* (February 17): A1.

Anonymous. (1971) "Criminal deviancy in a small business: Superior TV, " pp. 198–207 in H. T. Buckner (Ed.), *Deviance, reality and change*. New York: Random House.

Applebome, P. (1992) "Art and commerce: A college's turbulent tale." *New York Times* (August 23): A36.

Applebome, P. (1993a) "G.M. is held liable over fuel tanks in pick-up trucks." *New York Times* (February 5): A1.

Applebome, P. (1993b) "Alabama governor found guilty of ethics charges and is ousted." *New York Times* (April 23): A1.

Arenson, K. W. (1995) "Ex-United Way leader gets 7 years for embezzlement." *New York Times* (June 23): A14.

Arnold, B. L., and Hagan, J. (1992) "Careers of misconduct: The structure of prosecuted professional deviance among lawyers." *American Sociological Review* 57: 771–780.

Arnold, B. L., and Kay, F. M. (1995) "Social capital, violations of trust—and the vulnerability of isolates: The social organization of law practice and professional self-regulation." *International Journal of the Sociology of Law* 23: 321–346.

Aronowitz, S., and Gautney, H. (Eds.) (2003) *Implicating empire—Globalization and resistance in the 21st century world order*. New York: Basic.

Arrigo, B. A. (2003) "Postmodern justice and critical criminology: Positional, relational, and provisional science," pp. 43–56 in M. D. Schwartz and S. Hatty (Eds.), *Controversies in critical criminology*. Cincinnati, OH: Anderson.

Ashman, C. R. (1973) *The finest judges money can buy*. Los Angeles: Nash Publishing.

Associated Press. (1988) "U.S. says big meatpacker cheated workers." *New York Times* (April 2): A10.

Associated Press. (1991) "Oil firms face trial on price fixing." *Scranton Times* (June 3): A1.

Associated Press. (1995) "Murder charges dropped in cyanide death." *Scranton Times* (June 26): 11.

Associated Press. (1996) "Daiwa Bank admits guilt in cover-up." *New York Times* (February 29): D1.

Associated Press. (1999) "U.S. plans to retry Keating on Savings and Loan fraud." *New York Times* (January 12).

Associated Press. (2001a) "Deaths at work fall by nearly half in 20 years." *New York Times* (April 27): A14.

Associated Press. (2001b) "Johns Hopkins is investigating study in India by professor." *New York Times* (July 31): A15.

Associated Press. (2002a) "Big contractor settles lawsuit in fraud case." *New York Times* (February 9): A14.

Associated Press. (2002b) "Whistle-blowers being punished, a survey shows." *New York Times* (September 3): A14.

Associated Press. (2004) "For some whistleblowers, big risks pay off." *New York Times* (November 29): A11.

Associated Press. (2005) "Freedom for a 35-year inmate whose crime was stealing a TV." *New York Times* (May 29): A20.

Associated Press (2006) "Priest admits to stealing $140,000 from Trenton parish." *New York Times Online* (February 24).

Atlas, R. D. (2002) "Big board issues its ideas on corporate governance." *New York Times* (June 7): C4.

Atlas, R. D. (2003) "Bank of America official said to have resigned." *New York Times* (September 12): C5.

Atlas, R. D. (2004) "Fund executive accepts life ban in trading case." *New York Times* (May 21): A1.

Aubert, V. (1952) "White collar crime and social structure." *American Journal of Sociology* 58: 263–271.

Augar, P. (2005) *The greed merchants*. London: Penguin.

Auletta, K. (2001) *World War 3.0—Microsoft and its enemies*. New York: Random House.

Aulette, J. R., and Michalowski, R. (1993) "Fire in Hamlet: A case study of a state-corporate crime," pp. 171–206 in K. D. Tunnell (Ed.), *Political crime in contemporary America: A critical approach*. New York: Garland.

Ayers, K., and Frank, J. (1987) "Deciding to prosecute white collar crime: A national survey of state attorneys general." *Justice Quarterly* 4 (September) 425–440.

Ayres, I., and Braithwaite, J. (1991) "Tripartism: Regulatory capture and empowerment." *Law & Social Inquiry* 16: 435–496.

Azmy, B. (2005) "Squaring the predatory lending circle." *Florida Law Review* 57: 297–410.

Bacon, P., and Roston, E. (2003) "Stop calling us." *Time* (April 28): 56–58.

Bagli, C. V. (1997) "Sign a lease, pay the rent: No apartment." *New York Times* (August 25): B1.

Bagli, C. V., and Rashbaum, W. K. (2002) "28 city tax assessors indicted in decades-long bribe scheme." *New York Times* (February 26): A1.

Bailey, F. L., and Rothblatt, H. B. (1984). *Defending business and white collar crimes: Federal and state* (2nd ed.). Rochester, NY: Lawyers Cooperative Publishing Co.

Bakan, J. (2004) *The corporation—The pathological pursuit of profit and power.* New York: Free Press.

Baker, N. C. (1992) *Conflicting loyalties: Law and politics in the attorney general's office, 1789–1990.* Lawrence: University of Kansas Press.

Baker, W. E., and Faulkner, R. R. (2003) "Diffusion of fraud: Intermediate economic crime and investor dynamics." *Criminology* 41: 1173–1206.

Balen, M. (2003) *The secret history of the South Sea bubble: The world's first great financial scandal.* New York: HarperCollins.

Ball, D. (1970) "The problematics of respectability," pp. 326–371 in J. D. Douglas (Ed.), *Deviance and respectability: The social construction of moral meanings.* New York: Basic Books.

Banstetter, T. (2002) "Enron incites reports by whistle-blowers." *Scranton Times* (February 24): C6.

Barak, G. (1990) "Crime, criminology, and human rights: Towards an understanding of state criminality." *The Journal of Human Justice* 2: 11–28.

Barak, G. (1991) *Crimes by the capitalist state—An introduction to state criminality.* Albany NY: SUNY Press.

Barak, G. (1994) *Media, process and the social construction of crime.* New York: Garland.

Barak, G. (2001) "Crime and crime control in an age of globalization: A theoretical discussion." *Critical Criminology* 10: 57–72.

Barak, G., and Bohm, R. M. (1989) "The crimes of the homeless or the crime of homelessness? On the dialectics of criminalization, decriminalization, and victimization." *Contemporary Crises: Law, Crime and Social Policy* 13: 275–288.

Barboza, D. (1999a) "The great pork gap." *New York Times* (January 7): C1.

Barboza, D. (1999b) "$1.1 billion to settle suit on vitamins." *New York Times* (November 4): C1.

Barboza, D. (2001a) "Hyatt Hotel family will pay $460 million in S & L case." *New York Times* (December 11): C1.

Barboza, D. (2001b) "U.S. accuses Tyson Foods of seeking illegal workers." *New York Times* (December 20): A1.

Barboza, D. (2004) "Questions seen in seed prices set in the 90s." *New York Times* (January 6): A1.

Barboza, D., Eaton, L., and Henriques, D. B. (1999) "Penny-stock fraud is billion-dollar game." *New York Times* (November 19): A1.

Bardach, E., and Kagan, R. A. (1982) *Going by the book: The problem of regulatory unreasonableness.* Philadelphia: Temple University Press.

Barker, A. (1994) "The upturned stone: Political scandals and their investigation process in twenty democracies." *Crime, Law & Social Change* 21: 337–373.

Barker, T. (1996) *Police ethics: Crisis in law enforcement.* Springfield, IL: Charles C. Thomas.

Barker, T., and Carter, D. L. (Eds.) (1986) *Police deviance.* Cincinnati, OH: Pilgrimage.

Barlow, H. D. (1993) "From fiddle factors to networks of collusion: Charting the waters of small business crime." *Crime, Law & Social Change* 20: 319–337.

Barlow, H. D., and Kauzlarich, D. (2002) *Introduction to criminology* (8th ed.). Upper Saddle River, NJ: Prentice Hall.

Barnett, C. (2003) "The measurement of white-collar crime using Uniform Crime Reports (UCR) data." NIBRS Publications Series. Washington, D.C.: U.S. Department of Justice.

Barnett, H. C. (1979) "Wealth, crime, and capital accumulation." *Contemporary Crises* 3: 171–186.

Barnett, H. C. (1981a) "Review of Corporate Crime." *The Insurgent Sociologist* 11: 107–111.

Barnett, H. C. (1981b) "Corporate capitalism, corporate crime." *Crime & Delinquency* 27: 4–23.

Barnett, H. C. (1982) "The production of corporate crime in corporate capitalism," pp. 157–171 in

P. Wickman and T. Dailey (Eds.), *White-collar and economic crime*. Lexington, MA: Lexington.

Barnett, H. C. (1990) "Political environments and implementation failures: The case of Superfund enforcement." *Law & Policy* 12: 225–246.

Barnett, H. C. (1993) "Crimes against the environment: Superfund enforcement at last." *The Annals* 525: 119–133.

Barnhill, J. (2005) "Religious fraud, " pp. 679–685, in L. E. Salinger (Ed.), *Encyclopedia of white-collar and corporate crime*. Thousand Oaks, CA: Sage.

Barrile, L. (1993a) "Determining criminal responsibility of corporations." A paper presented at the Annual Meeting of the American Society of Criminology (San Francisco), November.

Barrile, L. (1993b) "A soul to damn and a body to kick: Imprisoning corporate criminals." *Humanity & Society* 17: 176–196.

Barron, J. (1989) "Unnecessary surgery." *New York Times Magazine* (April 16): 25–46.

Barron, M. (1981) "The criminogenic society: Social values and deviance," pp. 136–152 in A. S. Blumberg (Ed.), *Current perspectives on criminal behavior* (2nd ed.). New York: Knopf.

Barry, D. (1996) "Report urges outing leaders of San Gennaro feast." *New York Times* (January 18): B1.

Barstow, D. (2003) "U.S. rarely seeks charges for deaths in workplace." *New York Times* (December 22): A1.

Barstow, D. (2005) "Foundry pleads guilty to environmental crimes." *New York Times* (March 23): A12.

Barstow, D., and Bergman, L. (2003a) "At a Texas foundry, an indifference to life." *New York Times* (January 7): A1.

Barstow, D., and Bergman, L. (2003b) "A family's fortune, a legacy of blood and tears." *New York Times* (January 9): A1.

Barstow, D., and Bergman, L. (2005) "With little fanfare, a new effort to prosecute employers that flout safety laws." *New York Times* (May 2): A17.

Barstow, D., and Henriques, D. B. (2002) "Lines of profit and charity blur for companies with 9/11 tie-ins." *New York Times* (February 2): A1.

Bartlett, D. L., and Steele, J. B. (1998a) "Corporate welfare." *Time* (November 9): 34–54.

Bartlett, D. L., and Steele, J. B. (1998b) "Fantasy islands." *Time* (November 16): 79–93.

Bartlett, S. (1990) "Getting a mental grip on the dimensions of the savings disaster." *New York Times* (June 10).

Bartollas, C., and S. Dinitz (1989) *Introduction to criminology*. New York: Harper & Row.

Bartosiewicz, P. (2004) "How donated dollars turned into pennies." *New York Times* (July 15): Wk 5.

Bayer, A. E. (2001) "Academic faculty deviance," pp. 1–3 in P. A. Adler, P. Adler, and J. Corzine (Eds.), *Encyclopedia of criminology and deviant behavior*, Vol. 1. Philadelphia: Brunner-Routledge.

Bayot, J. (2002) "Retailers' suit says 2 issuers of credit cards acted illegally." *New York Times* (December 14): C1.

Bayot, J. (2003a) "Exxon is ordered to pay $11.9 billion to Alabama." *New York Times* (November 15): C3.

Bayot, J. (2003b) "Settlement is seen as changing the ways consumers use debit cards." *New York Times* (May 2): C1.

Bayot, J., and R. Farzad (2005) "WorldCom executive sentenced." *New York Times* (August 12): C1.

Beam, A. (2004) "Greed on trial." *The Atlantic Monthly* (June) 96–108.

Bearak, B. (2001) "Too true, buildings kill: Will India pay heed now?" *New York Times* (January 31): A3.

Beaty, J., and Gwynne, S. C. (1991) "The dirtiest bank of all." *Time* (July 29): 42–47.

Bebchuk, L. (2002) "Settling for less." *New York Times* (December 17): A21.

Bebchuk, L., and Fried, J. M. (2004) *Pay without performance*. Cambridge, MA: Harvard University Press.

Beccaria, C. (1764; 1819) *On crimes and punishments*. Philadelphia: Philip H. Nicklin.

Becker, E. (2004) "A World Bank mission to bring help to the poor." *New York Times* (April 22): Wk 1.

Becker, E. (2005) "Similar resume, different decade." *New York Times* (March 22): C1.

Becker, E. and Strom, S. (2005) "Groups pledge to account for tsunami aid." *New York Times* (February 25): A4.

Becker, H. L. (1963) *Outsiders: Studies in the sociology of deviance*. New York: Free Press.

Becker, P. J., Jipson, A. J., and Bruce, A. (2000) "The Pinto legacy: The community as an indirect victim of corporate deviance." *The Justice Professional* 12: 305–326.

Beckwith, D. (1987) "The high price of friendship." *Time* (December 28): 23.

Behar, R. (1990) "Catch us if you can." *Time* (March 26): 60.

Behar, R. (1991) "The thriving cult of greed and power." *Time* (May 6): 50–57.

Behar, R. (1992) "A lawyer's precipitous fall from grace." *Time* (March 16): 52.

Beirne, P., and Messerschmidt, J. (2005) *Criminology*. Los Angeles: Roxbury Publishing Co.

Belbot, B. A. (1991) "Whistleblowing and lawyers." *Journal of Contemporary Criminal Justice* 7: 154–166.

Belbot, B. A. (1993) "Corporate criminal liability," pp. 211–238 in M. B. Blankenship (Ed.), *Understanding corporate criminality*. New York: Garland.

Bell, D. (1962) "Crime as an American way of life: A queer ladder of social mobility," pp. 127–150 in *The end of ideology*. New York: Free Press.

Bell, R. (1992) *Impure science—Fraud, science, and political influence in scientific research*. New York: Wiley.

Bellafante, G. (1997) "Hide and go sue." *Time* (January 13): 81.

Bellamy, J. (1973) *Crime and public order in England in the later middle ages*. London: Routledge & Kegan Paul.

Bellini, J. (1986) *High tech holocaust*. London: David & Charles.

Belluck, P. (2001) "Prosecutors say greed drove pharmacist to dilute drugs." *New York Times* (August 18): A1.

Belluck, P. (2002a) "2 Harvard students accused of embezzling from theater club." *New York Times* (February 7): A20.

Belluck, P. (2002b) "A sentence for corruption ends an era in Providence." *New York Times* (September 7): A13.

Belsky, G. (1996) "Steer clear of these car repair rip-offs." *Readers Digest* (December) 134–137.

Belson, K. (2004a) "Grand Jury subpoenas documents from Nortel." *New York Times* (May 15): C1.

Belson, K. (2004b) "Lucent fined $25 million by S.E.C. in fraud case." *New York Times* (May 18): C1.

Belson, K. (2005a) "WorldCom's audacious failure and its toll on an industry." *New York Times* (January 18): C1.

Belson, K. (2005b) "Ebbers may testify. But should he?" *New York Times* (February 27): Bus 5.

Belson, K. (2005c) "Ebbers mounts an I-never-knew defense." *New York Times* (March 11): C1.

Belson, K. (2005d) "Ex-Chief of WorldCom is found guilty in $11 billion fraud." *New York Times* (March 16): A1.

Belson, K. (2005e) "Ebbers pleads for leniency in sentencing." *New York Times* (June 11): C13.

Belson, K. (2005f) "WorldCom head is given 25 years for huge fraud." *New York Times* (July 14): A1.

Belson, K., and Glater, J. (2005) "A folksy lawyer with a high-powered client." *New York Times* (February 17): C1.

Belson, K., and Schiesel, S. (2005) "Did the buck stop anywhere?" *New York Times* (March 4): C1.

Bender, L. (1990) "Feminist (re)torts: Thoughts on the liability crisis, mass torts, power, and responsibilities." *Duke Law Journal* (September) 848–912.

Bene, S. G. (1991) "Why not fine attorneys? An economic approach to lawyer disciplinary sanctions." *Stanford Law Review* 43: 864–941.

Benjamin, M., and Bronstein, D. A. (1987) "Moral and criminal responsibility and corporate persons," pp. 277–282 in W. J. Samuels and A. J. Miller (Eds.), *Corporations and society: Power and responsibility*. New York: Greenwood Press.

Bennett, G. (1987) *Crimewarps—The future of crime in America*. Garden City, NY: Anchor Press.

Bennett, J. T., and Dilorenzo, T. J. (1994) *Unhealthy charities: Hazardous to your health*. New York: Basic Books.

Benson, M. L. (1984) "The fall from grace: Loss of occupational status as a consequence of conviction for a white collar crime." *Criminology* 22: 573–595.

Benson, M. L. (1985a) "Denying the guilty mind: Accounting for involvement in white-collar crime." *Criminology* 23: 583–608.

Benson, M. L. (1985b) "White collar offenders under community supervision." *Justice Quarterly* 2: 429–438.

Benson, M. L. (1989) "The influence of class position on the formal and informal sanctioning of white collar offenders." *The Sociological Quarterly* 30: 465–479.

Benson, M. L. (1990) "Emotions and adjudication: Status degradation among white-collar criminals." *Justice Quarterly* 7: 515–528.

Benson, M. L., and Cullen, F. T. (1988) "The special sensitivity of white-collar offenders to prisons: A critique and research agenda." *Journal of Criminal Justice* 16(3) 207–216.

Benson, M. L., and Cullen, F. T. (1998) *Combating corporate crime: Local prosecutors at work.* Boston: Northeastern University Press.

Benson, M. L., Cullen, F. T., and Maakestad, W. J. (1990a) "Local prosecutors and corporate crime." *Crime & Delinquency* 36: 356–372.

Benson, M. L., Cullen, F. T., and Maakestad, W. J. (1990b) "The social movement against corporate crime: Assessing the role of local prosecutors." A paper presented at the Annual Meeting of the Academy of Criminal Justice Sciences (Denver), March.

Benson, M. L., Cullen, F. T., and Maakestad, W. J. (1992) "Community context and the prosecution of corporate crime," pp. 269–288 in K. Schlegel and D. Weisburd (Eds.), *White collar crime reconsidered.* Boston: Northeastern University Press.

Benson, M. L., Cullen, F. T., and Maakestad, W. J. (1993) "Local prosecutors and corporate crime." *NIJ Research in Brief* (January) 1–7.

Benson, M.L., and Kerley, K. R. (2001) "Life course theory and white collar crime," pp. 121–136 in H. N. Pontell and D. Shichor (Eds.), *Contemporary issues in crime and criminal justice.* Upper Saddle River, NJ: Prentice-Hall.

Benson, M. L., and Moore, E. (1992) "Are white-collar and common offenders the same? An empirical and theoretical critique of a recently proposed general theory of crime." *Journal of Research in Crime & Delinquency* 29: 251–272.

Benson, M. L., and Walker, E. (1988) "Sentencing the white-collar offender." *American Sociological Review* 53: 294–302.

Bentham, J. (1789; 1948) *An introduction to the principles of morals and legislation.* New York: Macmillan.

Benston, G. J. (2003) "The regulation of accountants and public accounting before and after Enron." *Emory Law Journal* 52: 1325–1353.

Bequai, A. (1978) *White collar crime: A 20th century crisis.* Lexington, MA: Heath.

Bequai, A. (1987) *Technocrimes.* Lexington, MA: Lexington.

Berenson, A. (2002) "The biggest casualty of Enron's collapse: Confidence." *New York Times* (February 10).

Berenson, A. (2003a) *The number—How the drive for quarterly earnings corrupted Wall Street and corporate America.* New York: Random House.

Berenson, A. (2003b) "Banks encourage overdrafts, reaping profits." *New York Times* (January 22): A1.

Berenson, A. (2003c) "Prosecutors investigating Freddie Mac." *New York Times* (June 12): C1.

Berenson, A. (2004a) "From haircuts to company jet, bosses' perks unveiled in court." *New York Times* (February 22): A1.

Berenson, A. (2004b) "There's a reason your mother told you not to lie." *New York Times* (March 7): Wk 14.

Berenson, A. (2004c) "Guilty verdicts give executives a new focus: Risk of prison." *New York Times* (March 8): C1.

Berenson, A. (2004d) "Despite 2 mistrials, success in pursuing white-collar crimes." *New York Times* (April 4): A1.

Berenson, A. (2004e) "Former executives of computer firm indicted in fraud." *New York Times* (September 23): A1.

Berenson, A. (2005a) "At Pfizer, the isolation increases for a whistle-blower." *New York Times* (June 6): C1.

Berenson, A. (2005b) "First Vioxx suit: Entryway into a legal labyrinth?" *New York Times* (July 11): C1.

Berenson, A. (2005c) "Jury calls Merck liable in death of man on Vioxx." *New York Times* (August 20): A1.

Berenson, A., and Vogel, C. (2002) "Ex-Tyco chief is indicted in tax case." *New York Times* (June 7): C1.

Berg, E. N. (1988) "Auditors must search for fraud under new rule." *New York Times* (February 10): 1A.

Berg, E. N. (1991) "$415 million settlement and pensions." *New York Times* (December 3): D1.

Berger, R. J., Free, M. D., Jr. and Searles, P. (2001) *Crime, justice, and society: Criminology and the sociological imagination.* Boston: McGraw-Hill.

Berke, R. L. (2002a) "Greed, pain, excesses: Oh, what a lovely issue." *New York Times* (January 27): Wk 1/1.

Berle, A. A., and Means, G. C. (1932) *The modern corporation and private property.* New York: Commerce Clearing House.

Berman, L. (2001) *No peace, no honor: Nixon, Kissinger, and betrayal in Vietnam.* New York: Free Press.

Bernard, T. J. (1984) "The historical development of corporate criminal liability." *Criminology* 22 (February) 3–18.

Bilimoria, D. (2001) "Corporate control, crime, and compensation: An examination of large corporations," pp. 297–312 in N. Shover and J. P. Wright (Eds.), *Crimes of privilege: Readings in white-collar crime*. New York: Oxford University Press.

Billstein, R., Fings, K., Kugler, A., and Levis, N. (2001) *Working for the enemy: Ford, General Motors, and forced labor in Germany during the Second World War*. New York: Berghahn.

Binstein, M., and Bowden, C. (1993) *Trust me: Charles Keating and the missing billions*. New York: Random House.

Birenbaum, A. (1977) "Medicine, social change, and deviant behavior," pp. 139–154 in E. Sagarin (Ed.), *Deviance and social change*. Beverly Hills, CA: Sage.

Birnbaum, J. H. (1992) *The lobbyists*. New York: Times Books.

Bishop, K. (1991) "Developers and others use new tool to quell protests by private citizens." *New York Times* (April 26): B9.

Black, E. (2001) *I.B.M. and the holocaust*. New York: Crown.

Black, W. K. (2004) "Why doesn't the SEC have a 'Chief Criminologist'?" *The Criminologist* 29 (November/December): 1, 3–4.

Black, W. K. (2005a) *The best way to rob a bank is to own one*. Austin, Texas: University of Texas Press.

Black, W. K. (2005b) "Control fraud as an explanation for white-collar crime waves: The case of the savings and loan debacle." *Crime, Law & Social Change* 43: 1–29.

Blair, C. (2001) *The environment—A revolution in attitudes*. Farmington Hills, MI: Gale Group.

Bloch, H. A., and Geis, G. (1962; 1970) *Man, crime and society*. New York: Random House.

Block, A. A., and Scarpitti, F. (1985) *Poisoning for profit: The mafia and toxic waste in America*. New York: Morrow.

Block, A. A., and Weaver, C. A. (2004) *All is clouded by desire: Global banking, money laundering and international organized crime*. Westport, CT: Praeger.

Bloomberg News (2005) "Exxon to pay $1.3 billion under ruling by justices." *New York Times* (June 24): A20.

Blum, D. (1988) "Rich kid, poor kid." *New York* (February 22): 48–55.

Blum, W. (2000) *Rogue state—A guide to the world's only superpower*. Monroe, ME: Common Courage Press.

Blumberg, P. (1989) *The predatory society: Deception in the American marketplace*. New York: Oxford University Press.

Blumenstyk, G. (2003) "Greening the world or 'greenwashing' a Republican?" *Chronicle of Higher Education* (January 10): A22–27.

Blumer, H. (1969) *Symbolic interaction: Perspective and method*. Englewood Cliffs, NJ: Prentice Hall.

Blum-West, S., and Carter, T. J. (1983) "Bringing white-collar crime back in: An examination of crimes and torts." *Social Problems* 30: 545–554.

Bohlen, C. (1997) "Albanian parties trade charges in the pyramid scandal." *New York Times* (January 29): A3.

Bohlman, H. M., Dundas, M. J., and Jentz, G. A. (1989) *The legal environment of business*. St. Paul: West Publishing.

Bohm, R. M. (1982) "Capitalism, socialism and crime," pp. 49–60 in H. E. Pepinsky (Ed.), *Rethinking criminology*. Beverly Hills, CA: Sage.

Bonger, W. A. (1916) *Criminality and economic conditions*. Boston: Little, Brown.

Bonner, R. (2005) "Deaths and a doctor's past transfix Australians." *New York Times* (June 19): A1.

Bonner, R., and O'Brien, T. L. (1999) "Activity at bank raises suspicions of Russia mob tie." *New York Times* (August 19): A1.

Boone, L. E. (1992) *Quotable business*. New York: Random House.

Boone, M. (1989) *Capital crime—Black infant mortality in America*. Newbury Park, CA: Sage.

Booth, C. (1993) "Nice work if you can get it." *Time* (March 8): 57.

Borkin, J. (1978) *The crime and punishment of I.G. Farben*. New York: Free Press.

Borosage, R. L. (2002) "Enron conservatives." *The Nation* (February 4): 4–5.

Bowie, N. E. (2005) "Digital rights and wrongs: Intellectual property in the information age." *Business and Society Review* 110: 77–96.

Bowman, F. O. (2001) "The 2001 Federal Economic Crime Sentencing Reforms: An analysis and legislative history." *Indiana Law Review* 35: 5–82.

Bowman, S. R. (1996) *The modern corporation and American political thought: Law, power and ideology*.

University Park, PA: Pennsylvania State University Press.

Box, S. (1983) *Power, crime and mystification*. London: Tavistock.

Boxer, S. (2001) "Lawyers are asking how secret is a secret?" *New York Times* (August 11): B7.

Boye, M. W. (1991) *Self-reported employee theft and counterproductivity as a function of employee turnover antecedents*. Ph.D. Dissertation, DePaul University.

Bradley, W. (2002) "Enron's end." *The American Prospect* (January 1–14) 30–31.

Bradlow, D. D. (1996) "The World Bank, the IMF, and human rights." *Transnational Law & Contemporary Problems* 6: 47–90.

Bradsher, K. (1999) "G.M. admits brake flaws after inquiry." *New York Times* (July 22): A10.

Bradsher, K. (2002) *High and mighty—SUVs: The world's most dangerous vehicles and how they got that way*. New York: Public Affairs.

Brady, J. (1983) "Arson, urban economy, and organized crime: The case of Boston." *Social Problems* 31: 1–27.

Brady, K. (1984) *Ida Tarbell: Portrait of a muckraker*. New York: Seaview.

Bragg, R. (1999a) "A Baptist leader is guilty of swindling and of theft." *New York Times* (February 28): A14.

Bragg, R. (1999b) "Politics hinted in Valujet crash charges." *New York Times* (July 15): A12.

Bragg, R. (2000) "Tobacco lawsuit in Florida yields record damage." *New York Times* (July 16): A1.

Bragg, R. (2002) "Workers feel pain and layoffs and added sting of betrayals." *New York Times* (January 20): A1.

Brainard, J. (2000) "As U.S. releases new roles on scientific fraud, scholars debate how much and why it occurs." *Chronicle of Higher Education* (December 8): A26.

Braithwaite, J. (1982b) "Enforced self-regulation: A new strategy for corporate crime control." *Michigan Law Review* 80: 1466–1507.

Braithwaite, J. (1984) *Corporate crime in the pharmaceutical industry*. London: Routledge & Paul Kegan.

Braithwaite, J. (1985a) "White collar crime," pp. 1–25 in R. H. Turner and J. F. Short, Jr. (Eds.), *Annual review of sociology*. Palo Alto, CA: Annual Reviews.

Braithwaite, J. (1985b) *To punish or persuade: The enforcement of coal mine safety*. Albany, NY: SUNY Press.

Braithwaite, J. (1988) "White-collar crime, competition, and capitalism: Comment on Coleman." *American Journal of Sociology* 94: 627–632.

Braithwaite, J. (1989a) "Criminological theory and organizational crime." *Justice Quarterly* 6: 333–358.

Braithwaite, J. (1989b) "The state of criminology: Theoretical decay or renaissance," pp. 155–166 in W. S. Laufer and F. Adler (Eds.), *Advances in criminological theory*, Vol. 2. New Brunswick, NJ: Transaction.

Braithwaite, J. (1989c) *Crime, shame and reintegration*. New York: Cambridge University Press.

Braithwaite, J. (1990) "Convergences in models of regulatory strategy." *Current Issues in Criminal Justice* 2: 59–66.

Braithwaite, J. (1992) "Poverty, power and white-collar crime: Sutherland and the paradoxes of criminological theory," pp. 78–107 in K. Schlegel and D. Weisburd (Eds.), *White-collar crime reconsidered*. Boston: Northeastern University Press.

Braithwaite, J. (1993a) "Shame and modernity." *The British Journal of Criminology* 33: 1–18.

Braithwaite, J. (1993b) "Pride in criminological dissensus." *Law & Social Inquiry* 18: 501–512.

Braithwaite, J. (1993c) "Transnational regulation of the pharmaceutical industry." *The Annals* 525: 12–30.

Braithwaite, J. (2000) *Regulation, crime, freedom*. Aldershot, UK: Ashgate.

Braithwaite, J. (2001) "Conceptualizing organizational crime in a world of plural cultures," pp. 17–32 in H. N. Pontell and D. Shichor (Eds.), *Contemporary issues in crime and criminal justice*. Upper Saddle River, NJ: Prentice Hall.

Braithwaite, J. (2002a) *Restorative justice and responsive regulation*. New York: Oxford University Press.

Braithwaite, J. (2002b) "Rewards and regulation." *Journal of Law & Society* 29: 12–26.

Braithwaite, J. (2005) *Markets in Vice, Markets in Virtue*. Leichhardt, Australia: The Federation Press.

Braithwaite, J., and Drahos, P. (2000) *Global business regulation*. Cambridge, UK: Cambridge University Press.

Braithwaite, J., and Fisse, B. (1985). "Varieties of responsibility and organizational crime." *Law & Policy* 7: 315–343.

Braithwaite, J., and Fisse, B. (1987). "Self-regulation and the control of corporate crime," pp. 221–246 in C. Shearing and P. C. Stenning (Eds.), *Private policing*. Newbury Park, CA: Sage.

Braithwaite, J., and Fisse, B. (1990) "On the plausibility of corporate crime theory," pp. 15–38 in W. S. Laufer and F. Adler (Eds.), *Advances in criminological theory*, Vol. 2. New Brunswick, NJ: Transaction.

Braithwaite, J., and Geis, G. (1982) "On theory and action for corporate crime control." *Crime & Delinquency* 28: 292–314.

Braithwaite, J., and Makkai, T. (1991) "Testing an expected utility model of corporate deterrence." *Law & Society Review* 25: 7–39.

Braithwaite, J., and Pettit, P. (1990) *Not just deserts—A republican theory of criminal justice*. Oxford, UK: Clarendon Press.

Braithwaite, J., Walker, J., and Grabosky, P. (1987) "An enforcement taxonomy of regulatory agencies." *Law & Policy* 9 (July): 315–343.

Braithwaite, V., Braithwaite, J., Gibson, D., and Makkai, T. (1994) "Regulatory styles, motivational postures and nursing home compliance." *Law & Policy* 16: 363–394.

Brecher, J. (1974) *Strike!* Greenwich, CT: Fawcett Books.

Breeden, R. C. (1991) "Thumbs on the scale: The role that accounting practices played in the savings and loan crisis." *Fordham Law Review* 59: 571–591.

Brenner, E. (1993) "Protecting elderly residents from predatory contractors." *New York Times* (May 23): Bus 1.

Brewer, L., and Hansen, M. (2004) *Confessions of an Enron executive: A whistleblower's story*. Bloomington, IN: AuthorHouse.

Brewton, P. (1992) *The mafia, the CIA, and George Bush*. New York: Shapolsky Publishers.

Brick, M. (2001) "U.S. Trust is fined $10 million in bank secrecy law case." *New York Times* (July 14): C1.

Brickey, K. F. (1990) "RICO forfeitures as 'excessive fines' or 'cruel and unusual punishments.'" *Villanova Law Review* 35: 905–928.

Brickey, K. F. (2002) *Corporate and white collar crime: Cases and materials*. New York: Aspen Law & Business.

Brickey, K. F. (2003) "From Enron to WorldCom and beyond: Life and crime after Sarbanes-Oxley." *Washington University Law Quarterly* 81: 357–402.

Brill, H. (1992) "Government breaks the law: The sabotaging of the Occupational Safety and Health Act." *Social Justice* 19: 63–81.

Brinkley, J. (1985) "Medical discipline laws: Confusion reigns." *New York Times* (September 3): A1.

Brinkley, J. (1988) "Other Reagan officials accused of improprieties." *New York Times* (March 28): A8.

Brinkley, J. (1999) "U.S. judge declares Microsoft is a market-stifling monopoly: Gates dissents, favoring talks." *New York Times* (November 6): A1.

Brinkley, J. (2000a) "U.S. judge says Microsoft violated antitrust laws with predatory behavior." *New York Times* (April 4): A1.

Brinkley, J. (2000b) "Microsoft break-up is ordered for antitrust law violations." *New York Times* (June 8): A1.

Brinkley, J. (2002) "Auditors say U.S. agencies lose track of billions." *New York Times* (October 14): A17.

Brinkley, J., and Hobson, L. M. (1998) "Aiding consumers is now the thrust of antitrust push." *New York Times* (March 22): A1.

Brinkley, J., and Lohr, S. (2001) *U.S. v. Microsoft*. New York: McGraw-Hill.

Brobeck, S., and Averyt, A. (1983) *The product safety book*. New York: Dutton.

Broder, J. M. (1997a) "2 top cigarette makers seek settlement." *New York Times* (April 17): A11.

Brodeur, P. (1985) *Outrageous misconduct: The asbestos industry on trial*. New York: Pantheon Books.

Brodsky, D. M., and Kramer, D. J. (1997) "Congress must define insider trading." *New York Times* (June 1): C7.

Brooke, J. (1996) "Officials say Montana 'Freemen' collected $1.8 million in scheme." *New York Times* (March 29): A1.

Brooks, J. (1987) *The takeover game*. New York: Dutton.

Brown, C. (Ed.) (2003) *Lost liberties: Ashcroft and the assault on personal freedom*. New York: The New Press.

Brown, D. (1971) *Bury my heart at Wounded Knee*. New York: Holt, Rinehart & Winston.

Brown, E. (2004) "Can for-profit schools pass an ethics test?" *New York Times* (December 12): Bus 5.

Brown, G. D. (2002) "The global threats to workers' health and safety on the job." *Social Justice* 29: 12–25.

Brown, H. L. (1996) "The dilemma of corporate counsel faced with client misconduct: Disclosure of client confidences or constructive discharge." *Buffalo Law Review* 44: 777–886.

Brown, S. E. (1982) "Hidden assaults and the tobacco industry." A paper presented at the Annual Meeting of the American Society of Criminology (Toronto), November.

Browner, C. (2002) "Polluters should have to pay." *New York Times* (March 1): A23.

Browning, F., and Gerassi, J. (1980) *The American way of crime*. New York: Putnam.

Browning, L. (2002) "M.B.A. programs now screen for integrity, too." *New York Times* (September 15): B4.

Browning, L. (2003a) "Class-action suits mean delays and, maybe, cash." *New York Times* (January 12): Bus 9.

Browning, L. (2003b) "Ethics lacking in business school curriculum, students say in survey." *New York Times* (May 20): C3.

Browning, L. (2005a) "Market place." *New York Times* (March 16): C2.

Browning, L. (2005b) "Court case gives rare look at tax shelter clients." *New York Times* (June 11): C1.

Brownlee, S., and Roberts, S. V. (1994) "Should cigarettes be outlawed?" *U.S. News and World Report* (April 18): 32–38.

Brownstein, R. (1981) "The toxic tragedy," pp. 1–59 in R. Nader, R. Brownstein, and J. Richard (Eds.), *Who's poisoning America—Corporate polluters and their victims in the chemical age*. San Francisco: Sierra Club Books.

Bryant, A., and Meier, B. (1996) "Taking a hard line amid the wreckage." *New York Times* (October 6).

Bryner, G. C. (1987) *Bureaucratic discretion: Law and policy in federal regulatory agencies*. New York: Pergamon Press.

Buckhoff, T., and Hansen, J. (2002) "Interviewing as a 'forensic-type' procedure." *Journal of Forensic Accounting* 3: 1–16.

Bucy, P. H. (1994) "The poor fit of traditional evidentiary doctrine and sophisticated crime: An empirical analysis of health care prosecution." *Fordham Law Review* 63: 383–477.

Bucy, P. H. (1998) *White collar crime: Cases and materials*. St. Paul, MN: West.

Bucy, P. H. (2002) "Corporate criminal responsibility," pp. 259–266 in J. Dressler (Ed.), *Encyclopedia of crime and justice*, Vol. 1 (2nd ed.). New York: Gale Group.

Bumiller, E. (2002b) "Bush faces scrutiny over disclosing '90 stock sale late." *New York Times* (July 4): A11.

Bumiller, E. (2002c) "Bush signs bill aimed at fraud in corporations." *New York Times* (July 31): A1.

Buranen, L., and Roy, A. M. (Eds.) (1999) *Perspectives on plagiarism and intellectual property in a postmodern world*. Albany, NY: SUNY Press.

Burd, S. (1999) "Loopholes in student-aid law may expose programs to fraud." *Chronicle of Higher Education* (January 15): A32.

Burnham, D. (1989) *A law onto itself—The IRS and the abuse of power*. New York: Random House.

Burns, J. F. (1998) "Bhutto clan leaves trail of corruption." *New York Times* (January 9): A1.

Burns, R. G. (1999) "Socially constructing an image in the automobile industry." *Crime, Law & Social Change* 31: 327–346.

Burns, R. (2002) "Toward a sourcebook of white collar crime statistics: A collection of environmental crime data." Presented at the Annual Meeting of the Academy of Criminal Justice Sciences (Anaheim, CA), March.

Burns, R. G. (2005) "Toward a sourcebook of white collar crime statistics." Presented at the Annual Meeting of the Academy of Criminal Justice Sciences (Chicago), March.

Burns, R. G., and Lynch, M. J. (2004) *Environmental Crime: A Sourcebook*. New York: LFB Scholarly Publishing.

Burns, R. G., and Orrick, L. (2002) "Assessing newspaper coverage of corporate violence: The dance hall fire in Goteborg, Sweden." *Critical Criminology* 11: 137–150.

Burns, R. G., Whitworth, K., and Thompson, C. (2004) "Assessing law enforcement preparedness to address Internet fraud." *Journal of Criminal Justice* 32: 477–493.

Burrough, B., and Helyar, J. (1989) *Barbarians at the gate: The fall of RJR Nabisco*. New York: Harper & Row.

Burroughs, J. (1997) *The legality of threat or use of nuclear weapons*. Munster: LIT.

Busch, A. (2000) "Unpacking the globalization debate: Approaches, evidence and data," pp. 21–48 in D. Hay and D. Marsh (Eds.), *Demystifying globalization*. New York: St. Martin's Press.

Business Ethics. (2002a) "When brilliant ideas become law: Punishing the corporate felon." *Business Ethics* (January/February): 6.

Business Ethics. (2002b) "Reforming corporate governance after Enron." *Business Ethics* (July/August): 6.

Business Ethics. (2005) "Ethics officers double in four years." *Business Ethics* (Spring): 9.

Butler, R. (2001) *The greatest threat—Iraq, weapons of mass destruction, and the crisis of global security.* New York: Public Affairs.

Butterfield, F. (2002a) "F.B.I. covered up for Boston mobsters, lawsuit asserts." *New York Times* (May 31): A17.

Butterfield, F. (2002b) "U.S. crime rate rose 2% in 2001 after 10 years of decreases." *New York Times* (October 29): A20.

Byrne, J. A. (2002a) "Restoring trust in corporate America." *Business Week* (June 24) 31–35.

Byrne, J. A. (2002b) "Fall from grace." *Business Week* (August 12): 51–56.

Byron, C. (1990) "Drexel's fall." *New York* (March 19): 31–40.

Byron, C. (1991) "High spy: Jules Kroll's modern gumshoes are on a roll." *New York* (May 13): 70–84.

Cable, S., and Benson, M. (1993) "Acting locally: Environmental injustice and the emergence of grass-roots environmental organizations." *Social Problems* 40: 464–477.

Cain, M., and Hunt, A. (1979) *Marx and Engels on law.* London: Academic Press.

Calavita, K. (1983) "The demise of the occupational safety and health administration: A case study in symbolic interaction." *Social Problems* 30: 437–448.

Calavita, K., and Pontell, H. N. (1990) "'Heads I win, tails you lose': Deregulation, crime, and crisis in the savings and loan industry." *Crime & Delinquency* 36: 309–341.

Calavita, K., and Pontell, H. N. (1993) "Savings and loan fraud as organized crime: Towards a conceptual typology of corporate illegality." *Criminology* 31: 519–548.

Calavita, K., and Pontell, H. N. (1994) "The state and white-collar crime: Saving the savings and loans." *Law & Society Review* 28: 297–324.

Calavita, K., Pontell, H. N., and Tillman, R. H. (1997) *Big money crime: Fraud and politics in the savings and loan crisis.* Berkeley: University of California Press.

Canedy, D. (2001) "Children are prey in a Medicaid dental scheme." *New York Times* (August 17): A1.

Caplowitz, D. (1967) *The poor pay more.* New York: Free Press.

Carbonell–Catilo, A. (1986) "The Philippines: The politics of plunder." *Corruption and Reform* 1: 235–243.

Cardozo, B. N. (1921) *Nature of the judicial process.* New Haven, CT: Yale University Press.

Caringella-MacDonald, S. (1990) "State crises and the crackdown on crime under Reagan." *Contemporary Crises* 4: 91–118.

Carlson, M. (1989a) "$1 billion worth of influence." *Time* (November 6): 27–28.

Carlson, M. (1989b) "A legal bank robbery." *Time* (November 27): 29.

Carlson, M. (1990a) "Money talks." *Time* (April 9): 18–20.

Carlson, M. (1990b) "Seven sorry senators." *Time* (January 8): 48–50.

Carmichael, K. D. (1996) "Strict criminal liability for environmental violations: A need for judicial restraint." *Indiana Law Journal* 71: 729–752.

Carpenter, T. (1989) *Missing beauty.* New York: Zebra Books.

Carson, G. (1973) "The income tax and how it grew." *American Heritage* 25: 4.

Carson, R. (1962) *The silent spring.* Boston: Houghton Mifflin.

Carter, S. L. (1988) "Comment: The independent counsel mess." *Harvard Law Review* 102: 105–142.

Carter, T. S. (1999) "Ascent of the corporate model in environmental-organized crime." *Crime, Law & Social Change* 31: 1–30.

Carvajal, D. (1995) "Gerulaitis death attributed to short pipe." *New York Times* (May 24): B5.

Carvajal, D. (1999) "Milken-supported libel suit against a writer is dismissed." *New York Times* (September 24): C6.

Cassidy, J. (2002) "The greed cycle." *The New Yorker* (September 23): 64–77.

Cassidy, J. (2003) "The investigation." *The New Yorker* (April 7): 55–73.

Caufield, C. (1996) *Masters of illusion: The World Bank and the poverty of nations.* New York: Henry Holt & Co.

Cavender, G., Jurik, N. C., and Cohen, A. K. (1993) "The baffling case of the smoking gun: The social ecology of political accounts in the Iran-Contra affair." *Social Problems* 40: 152–166.

Cavender, G., and Mulcahy, A. (1998) "Trial by fire: Media constructions of corporate deviance." *Justice Quarterly* 15: 697–717.

Cebulak, W. (1991) "White-collar crime in socialism: Myth or reality?" *Journal of Comparative and Applied Criminal Justice* 15: 109–120.

Chalk, F., and Jonassohn, K. (1990) *The history and sociology of genocide—Analyses and case studies.* New Haven, CT: Yale University Press.

Chambliss, W. J. (1964) "A sociological account of the law of vagrancy." *Social Problems* 12: 46–67.

Chambliss, W. J. (1967) "Types of deviance and the effectiveness of legal sanctions." *Wisconsin Law Review* (Summer) 703–714.

Chambliss, W. J. (1973) "The saints and the rough-necks." *Society* 11: 24–31.

Chambliss, W. J. (1988a) *On the take—From petty crooks to presidents* (2nd ed.). Bloomington: Indiana University Press.

Chambliss, W. J. (1988b) *Exploring criminology.* New York: Macmillan.

Chambliss, W. J. (1989) "State–organized crime." *Criminology* 27: 183–208.

Chambliss, W. J. (2004) "On the symbiosis between criminal law and criminal behaviors." *Criminology* 42: 241–252.

Chambliss, W. J., and Courtless, T. F. (1992) *Criminal law, criminology, and criminal justice.* Pacific Grove, CA: Brooks/Cole.

Chambliss, W. J., and Seidman, R. (1982) *Law, order, and power* (2nd ed.). Reading, MA: Addison-Wesley.

Chase-Dunn, C., Kawano, Y., and Brewer, B. D. (2000) "Trade globalization since 1795: Waves of integration in the World-System." *American Sociological Review* 65: 77–95.

Chaset, A. J., and Weintraub, B. B. (1992) "New guidelines for sentencing corporations." *Trial* (April) 41–44.

Chavez, L. (1982) "Toxic waste entrepreneur." *New York Times* (May 27): D1.

Chen, D. W. (1998) "Inspections cutting back on mail fraud based in Nigeria." *New York Times* (November 11): B1.

Chen, D. W. (2000) "Pirro sentenced to 29 months in U.S. prison." *New York Times* (November 2): B1.

Cheng, Hongming. (2005a) "Advertising fraud," pp. 9–14 in L. M. Salinger (Ed.), *Encyclopedia of white-collar and corporate crime.* Thousand Oaks, CA: Sage.

Cheng, Hongming (2005b) "Insider trading," pp. 427–432 in L. M. Salinger (Ed.), *Encyclopedia of white-collar and corporate crime.* Thousand Oaks, CA: Sage.

Cheng, Hongming (2005c) "Securities and Exchange Commission," pp. 723–725 in L. M. Salinger (Ed.), *Encyclopedia of white-collar and corporate crime.* Thousand Oaks, CA: Sage.

Chivers, C. J., and Arvedlund, E. B. (2005) "Russia tycoon given 9 years on tax charge." *New York Times* (June 1): A1.

Chomsky, N. (1993) "World order and its rules: Variations on some theories." *Journal of Law & Society* 20: 145–165.

Chomsky, N. (2001) *9-11.* New York: Seven Stories Press.

Chronicle of Higher Education. (2002) "Corruption plagues academe around the world." *Chronicle of Higher Education* (August 2): A32–A36.

Chua-Eoan, H. E. (1995a) "Going for broke." *Time* (March 13): 40–47.

Chua-Eoan, H. E. (1995b) "The predator's fall." *Time* (June 19): 36–37.

Church, G. J. (1994) "It's a jungle out there." *Time* (March 28): 27–29.

Church, G. J. (1997) "Elderscam: Reach out and bilk someone." *Time* (August 25): 54–57.

CJ International. (1986) "International white collar crime." *CJ International* 2: 1, 9.

Clark, J. P., and Hollinger, R. (1977) "On the feasibility of empirical studies of white collar crime," pp. 139–158 in R. F. Meier (Ed.), *Theory in criminology—Contemporary views.* Beverly Hills, CA: Sage.

Clark, J. P., and Hollinger, R. C. (1983) *Theft by employees in work organizations.* Washington, DC: National Institute of Justice.

Clarke, L. (1988) "Explaining choices among technological risks." *Social Problems* 35: 22–35.

Clarke, M. (1990) *Business crime—Its nature and control.* New York: St. Martin's Press.

Clarke, R. V., and Felson, M. (1993) "Introduction: Criminology, routine activity and rational choice," pp. 1–14 in R. V. Clarke and M. Felson (Eds.), *Routine activity and rational choice*. New Brunswick, NJ: Transaction.

Clayton, C. W. (1992) *The politics of justice: The attorney general and the making of legal policy*. Armonk, NY: M.E. Sharpe.

Clegg, R. (2000) "Photographs and fraud over race." *Chronicle of Higher Education* (November 24): B27.

Clinard, M. B. (1983) *Corporate ethics and crime: The role of the middle manager*. Beverly Hills, CA: Sage.

Clinard, M. B. (1990) *Corporate corruption: The abuse of power*. New York: Praeger.

Clinard, M. B., and Quinney, R. (1967; 1973) *Criminal behavior systems: A typology*. New York: Holt, Rinehart & Winston.

Clinard, M. B., and Yeager, P. C. (1978) "Corporate crime—Issues in research." *Criminology* 16: 255–272.

Clinard, M. B., and Yeager, P. C. (1980) *Corporate crime*. New York: Free Press.

Clines, F. X. (1993) "An unfettered Milken has lessons to teach." *New York Times* (October 16): A1.

Clines, F. X. (2002) "Ohio Congressman guilty in bribery and kickbacks." *New York Times* (April 12): A17.

Cloward, R. A., and Ohlin, L. E. (1960) *Delinquency and opportunity: A theory of delinquent gangs*. Glencoe, IL: Free Press.

Clymer, A. (1997) "Years of ethics flaws by Gingrich are cited; Speaker to pay $300,000." *New York Times* (January 18): A1.

Clymer, A. (2002) "A bid to change. An uncertain future." *New York Times* (February 14): A31.

Coffee, J. C., Jr. (1980) "Corporate crime and punishment: A non-Chicago view of the economics of criminal sanctions." *American Criminal Law Review* 17: 419–476.

Coffee, J. C., Jr. (1981a) "'No soul to damn; no body to kick': An unscandalized inquiry into the problem of corporate punishment." *Michigan Law Review* 79: 386–459.

Coffee, J. C., Jr. (1981b) "From tort to crime: Some reflections on the criminalization of fiduciary breaches and the problematic line between law and ethics." *American Criminal Law Review* 19: 117–172.

Coffee, J. C., Jr. (1983) "Corporate criminal responsibility," pp. 253–264 in S. Kadish (Ed.), *Encyclopedia of crime and justice*. New York: Free Press.

Coffee, J. C., Jr. (1988a) "Hush!: The criminal status of confidential information after McNally and Carpenter and the enduring problem of over-criminalization." *American Criminal Law Review* 26: 121–154.

Coffee, J. C., Jr. (1988b) *Statement on prosecuting white collar crime*. Proceedings of Symposium 87: White Collar/Institutional Crime—Its measurement and analysis. Sacramento, CA: Department of Justice, Bureau of Criminal Statistics and Special Services.

Coffee, J. C., Jr. (1991) "Does 'unlawful' mean 'criminal'?: Reflections on the disappearing tort/crime distinction in American law." *Boston University Law Review* 71: 193–245.

Coffee, J. C., Jr. (1992) "Paradigms lost: The blurring of the criminal and civil law models—and what can be done about it." *Yale Law Review* 101: 1875–1892.

Cohen, A. (2001a) "No split—But Microsoft's a monopolist." *Time* (July 9): 36–38.

Cohen, A. (2001b) "Microsoft uncut." *Time* (September 17): 42–44.

Cohen, A. K. (1955) *Delinquent boys: The culture of the gang*. New York: Free Press.

Cohen, M. A. (1989) "Corporate crime and punishment: A study of social harm and sentencing practices in the federal courts, 1984–1987." *American Criminal Law Review* 26: 605–662.

Cohen, M. A. (1991) "Corporate crime and punishment: An update on sentencing practices in the federal courts, 1988–1990." *Boston University Law Review* 71: 249–279.

Cohen, M. A. (1992) "Environmental crime and punishment: Legal/economic theory and empirical evidence on enforcement of federal environmental statutes." *The Journal of Criminal Law and Criminology* 82: 1054–1108.

Cohen, R. W., and Witcover, J. (1974) *A heartbeat away: The investigation and resignation of Vice President Spiro Agnew*. New York: Bantam Books.

Cohen, S. (1985) *Visions of social control—Crime, punishment, and classification*. Oxford: Polity Press.

Cohen, S. (1993) "Human rights and the crimes of the state: The culture of denial." *Australian & New Zealand Journal of Criminology* 26: 97–115.

Cohen, S. (2001) *States of denial—Knowing about atrocities and suffering*. Cambridge, UK: Polity Press.

Colapinto, J. (2001) "Ralph Nader is not sorry." *Rolling Stone* (September 13): 64–72.

Coleman, J. S. (1974) *Power and the structure of society.* New York: Norton.

Coleman, J. S. (1982) "Power and the structure of society," pp. 36–52 in M. D. Ermann and R. J. Lundman (Eds.), *Corporate and governmental deviance: Problems of organizational behavior in contemporary society* (2nd ed.). New York: Oxford University Press.

Coleman, J. W. (1985) "Law and power: The Sherman Antitrust Act and its enforcement in the petroleum industry." *Social Problems* 32: 264–274.

Coleman, J. W. (1987) "Toward an integrated theory of white-collar crime." *American Journal of Sociology* 93: 406–439.

Coleman, J. W. (1992) "The theory of white-collar crime: From Sutherland to the 1990s," pp. 53–77 in K. Schlegel and D. Weisburd (Eds.), *White-collar crime reconsidered.* Boston: Northeastern University Press.

Coleman, J. W. (2002, 2006) *The criminal elite* (5th ed., 6th ed.). New York: St. Martin's Press.

Colino, S. (1990) "Felony 101." *Student Lawyer* (October) 32–37.

Collins, H. (1984) *Marxism and law.* New York: Oxford University Press.

Collins, J. M., and Schmidt, F. L. (1993) "Personality, integrity and white collar crime: A construct validity study." *Personnel Psychology* 46: 295–311.

Collison, M. N. (1990) "Survey at Rutgers suggests that cheating may be on the rise at larger universities." *Chronicle of Higher Education* (October 24): A30.

Colmey, J., and Liebhold, D. (1999) "It's all in the family." *Time* (May 31): 68–69.

Colquhoun, P. (1795; 1969) *A treatise on the police of the metropolis.* Montclair, NJ: Patterson Smith.

Committee on Governmental Affairs. (1999) "Independent counsel reform proposed." Washington, DC: U.S. Senate.

Committee on the Judiciary, U.S. Senate. (1987) *Oversight of the problem of white collar crime: Hearings.* Washington, DC: U.S. Government Printing Office.

Comstock, A. (1880; 1969) *Frauds exposed.* Montclair, NJ: Patterson Smith.

Congressional Digest. (2005) "Class action lawsuits." *Congressional Digest* 84 (April) 97–125.

Conklin, J. E. (1977) *"Illegal but not criminal": Business crime in America.* Englewood Cliffs, NJ: Prentice Hall.

Conlin, R. B. (1991) "'Litigation explosion': Tempest in a teapot." *Trial* (November) 114–118.

Conly, C. (1990) *Organizing for computer-crime investigation and prosecution.* Washington, DC: National Institute of Justice Reports.

Connolly, J. (1996) "Who was using whom?" *New York* (February 12): 37–40.

Consumer's Research. (1990) "Telephone scams for the 1990s." *Consumer's Research* (May) 29–31.

Cookson, P. W., and Persell, C. H. (1985) *Preparing for power—America's elite boarding schools.* New York: Basic Books.

Cooper, K., and Dedjinou, A. C. (2005) "Antitrust violations." *Criminal Law Review* 42: 179–122.

Cooper, M. H. (1987) "Corporate takeovers," *Editorial Research Reports.* Washington, DC: Congressional Quarterly.

Copes, H., Kerley, K. R., Mason, K. A., and Van Wyk, J. (2001) "Reporting behavior of fraud victim's and Black's theory of law: An empirical assessment." *Justice Quarterly* 18: 343–363.

Copetas, C. (1986) "White-collar manhunt." *New York Times Magazine* (June 8): 45–46, 75–80.

Cornish, D., and Clarke, R. V. (1986) *The reasoning criminal: Rational choice perspectives on offending.* New York: Springer-Verlag.

Cottam, M., and Marenin, O. (1989) "Predicting the past: Reagan administration assistance to police forces in Central America." *Justice Quarterly* 6: 589–618.

Cottle, M. (2002) "Private practice." *The New Republic* (October 14): 12–16.

Court, J. (2003) *Corporateering—How corporate power steals your personal freedom . . . And what you can do about it.* New York: Jeremy Tarcher/Putnam.

Cowan, A. L. (1991) "Compliance officer's day in the sun." *New York Times* (October 20): F10.

Cowan, A. L. (2001) "Rich cashed in a world of chits to win pardon." *New York Times* (April 11): A1.

Cowan, A. L. (2004) "Onetime fugitive gets 17 years for looting insurers." *New York Times* (December 11): C3.

Cowan, A. L. (2005a) "Taking protest to a corporate chief's street, 3 activists face charges in Greenwich." *New York Times* (March 13): A40.

Cowan, A. L. (2005b) "Greenwich developer accused of defrauding banks." *New York Times* (July 28): B1.

Cowles, E. L. (1992) "Is the boardroom immune? An assessment of drug use on employment-related financial crime." A paper presented at the Annual Meeting of the American Society of Criminology (New Orleans), November.

Cowley, G. (1990) "Secondhand smoke: Some grim news." *Newsweek* (June 11): 59.

Cowley, G. (1997) "Bitter pill." *Newsweek* (October 6): 57.

Cramton, R. C., Cohen, G. M., and Koniak, S. P. (2004) "Legal and ethical duties of lawyers after Sarbanes-Oxley." *Villanova Law Review* 49: 725.

Cressey, D. R. (1953) *Other people's money*. Glencoe, IL: Free Press.

Cressey, D. R. (1969) *Theft of the nation*. New York: Harper & Row.

Cressey, D. R. (1980) "Management fraud, controls, and criminological theory," pp. 117–147 in R. K. Elliott and J. T. Willingham (Eds.), *Management fraud: Detection and deterrence*. New York: Petrocelli.

Cressey, D. R. (1989) "The poverty of theory in corporate crime research," pp. 31–55 in W. S. Laufer and F. Adler (Eds.), *Advances in criminological theory*, Vol. 1. New Brunswick, NJ: Transaction.

Cresswell, J. (2005a) "Paradise and money lost." *New York Times* (August 14): 3/1.

Cresswell, J. (2005b) "Citigroup agrees to pay $2 billion in Enron scandal." *New York Times* (June 11): A1.

Cresswell, J., and Dash, E. (2005) "Bank of America to buy MBNA, a prime issuer of credit cards." *New York Times* (July 1): A1.

Criddle, W. (1987) "They can't see there's a victim." *New York Times* (February 22): E3.

Crisp, W. R. (1997) "60 subscriptions, and no grand prize." *New York Times* (February 1): A19.

Croall, H. (2001) *Understanding white collar crime*. Buckingham, UK: Open University Press.

Croissant, J. L. (2001) "Can this campus be bought?" *Academe* (September–October) 43–48.

Croley, S. P., and Hanson, J. D. (1991) "What liability crisis: An alternative explanation for recent events in products liability." *Yale Journal of Regulation* 8: 1–112.

Crossette, B. (2002) "War crimes tribunal becomes reality without U.S. role." *New York Times* (April 12): A3.

Croteau, D., and Hoynes, W. (2001) *The business of media—Corporate media and the public interest*. Thousand Oaks, CA: Pine Forge Press.

Crumbley, D. L. (2001) "Forensic accounting: Older than you think." *Journal of Forensic Accounting* 2: 181–202.

Cullen, F. T. (1983) *Rethinking crime and deviance theory*. Totowa, NJ: Rowman & Allenheld.

Cullen, F. T., and Benson, M. L. (1993) "White collar crime: Holding a mirror to the core." *Journal of Criminal Justice Education* 4: 325–348.

Cullen, F. T., Clark, G., Link, B., Mathers, R., Niedospial, J., and Sheahan, M. (1985) "Dissecting white-collar crime: Offense type and punitiveness." *International Journal of Comparative and Applied Criminal Justice* 9: 16–27.

Cullen, F. T., Maakestad, W. J., and Cavender, G. (1987) *Corporate crime under attack: The Ford Pinto case and beyond*. Cincinnati, OH: Anderson.

Cunningham, W. C., Straucher, J. J., and Van Meter, C. W. (1991) *Private security trends—1970 to 2000*. Boston: Butterworth-Heineman.

Curra, J. (1994) *Understanding social deviance—From the near side to the outer limits*. New York: HarperCollins.

Current Biography Yearbook. (1986) "Ralph Nader," pp. 402–405 in *Current biography yearbook*. New York: H. W. Wilson.

Currie, E. P. (1968) "Crimes without criminals: Witchcraft and its control in Renaissance Europe." *Law & Society Review* 3: 7–32.

Currie, E., and Skolnick, J. (1988) *America's problems* (2nd ed.). Glenview, IL: Scott, Foresman.

Cushman, J. H. (1990) "United and Boeing held at fault in deaths on jet." *New York Times* (April 11): A14.

Cushman, J. H. (1993) "Paul, Weiss law firm to pay U.S. $45 million." *New York Times* (September 29): D1.

Cushman, J. H. (1995) "House approves a new standard for regulations." *New York Times* (March 1): A1.

Cushman, J. H. (1996) "Adversaries back pollution rules now on the books." *New York Times* (February 12): A1.

Dahle, C. (2004) "What is that felony on your resume?" *New York Times* (October 1): B11.

Dallas, L. L. (2003) "The multiple roles of corporate boards of directors." *San Diego Law Review* 40: 781–820.

Danielsen, D. (2005) "How corporations govern: Taking corporate power seriously in transnational regulation and governance." *Harvard International Law Journal* 46: 411.

Daly, K. (1989) "Gender and varieties of white-collar crime." *Criminology* 27: 769–793.

Dan-Cohen, M. (1992) "Responsibility and the boundaries of the self." *Harvard Law Review* 105: 959–1011.

Darrow, M. (2003) *Between light and shadow: The World Bank, the International Monetary Fund, and International Human Rights Law.* Portland, OR: Hart Publishing.

Dash, E. (2005a) "Ex-F.B.I. agent and trader are convicted." *New York Times* (January 25): C1.

Dash, E. (2005b) "Regulators start inquiry into data loss." *New York Times* (June 22): C1.

Davilo, M., Marquant, J. W., and Mullings, J. Z. (2005) "Beyond Mother Nature: Contractor fraud in the wake of natural disasters." *Deviant Behavior* 26: 271–293.

Davidson, A. (1990) *In the wake of the Exxon Valdez.* San Francisco: Sierra Club Books.

Davidson, B. (1961) *The African slave trade.* Boston: Little, Brown.

Davis, J. (2005) "Antitrust," pp. 42–44 in L. M. Salinger (Ed.), *Encyclopedia of white-collar and corporate crime.* Thousand Oaks, CA: Sage.

Davis, M. S. (1989) *The perceived seriousness and incidence of ethical misconduct in academic science.* Ph.D. Dissertation, Ohio State University.

Davis, R. G., Keil, B., and Keil, B. (1998) "What's wrong with this picture?" *New York Times* (March 9): 38–43, 73.

Delamarter, R. T. (1976) *Big blue—IBM's use and abuse of power.* New York: Dodd, Mead.

Delaney, K. J. (1989) "Power, intercorporate networks, and 'strategic bankruptcy.'" *Law & Society Review* 23: 643–666.

Delaney, K. J. (1992) *Strategic bankruptcy.* Berkeley: University of California Press.

Delaney, K. J. (1994) "The organizational construction of the 'bottom line.'" *Social Problems* 41: 497–518.

Deloughry, T. J. (1991) "Up to 300 institutions may be cut by U.S. from loan programs." *Chronicle of Higher Education* (May 22): A1.

Dentzer, S. (1984) "How Americans beat the tax man." *Newsweek* (April 16): 56–60.

Denzin, N. K. (1977) "Notes on the criminogenic hypothesis: A case study of the American liquor industry." *American Sociological Review* 42: 905–920.

Denzin, N. K. (1990) "Reading 'Wall Street': Postmodern contradictions in the American social structure," pp. 31–44 in B. B. Turner (Ed.), *Theories of modernity and postmodernity.* London: Sage.

DePalma, A. (1991) "A college acts in desperation and dies playing the lender." *New York Times* (April 17): A1.

DePalma, A. (1992a) "House inquiry is expanded into research overcharges." *New York Times* (January 20): B8.

DePalma, A. (1992b) "In trial, M.I.T. to defend trading student aid data." *New York Times* (June 24): A17.

DePalma, A. (1992c) "M.I.T. ruled guilty in antitrust case." *New York Times* (September 3): A1.

Derber, C. (2003) *People before profit.* New York: Picador.

Derber, C. (2004) *The wilding of America—Money, mayhem, and the new American dream.* Third ed. edition. New York: Worth Publishers.

Derber, C., Schwartz, W. A., and Magrass, Y. (1990) *Power in the highest degrees—Professionals and the rise of a new Mandarin order.* New York: Oxford.

Desnoyers, R. C. (2005) "Tax evasion," pp. 789–793 in L. M. Salinger (Ed.), *Encyclopedia of white-collar crime.* Thousand Oaks, CA: Sage.

Desruisseaux, P. (1999) "Cheating is reaching epidemic proportions worldwide, researchers say." *Chronicle of Higher Education* (April 30): A45.

Deutsch, C. H. (2002) "Xerox revises revenue data, tripling error first reported." *New York Times* (June 29): C1.

Dexter, L. A. (1970) *Elite and specialized interviewing.* Evanston, IL: Northwestern University Press.

Diamant, M. (2002) "False claims." *American Criminal Law Review* 39: 491–506.

Diamond, S. (1986) "NASA wasted billions, federal audits disclose." *New York Times* (April 23): A1.

Diamond, S. S., and Casper, J. D. (1992) "Blindfolding the jury to verdict consequences: Damages, experts, and the civil jury." *Law & Society Review* 26: 513–563.

DiMento, J. F. (1993) "Criminal enforcement of environmental law." *The Annals* 525: 134–146.

DiMento, J. F., Geis, G., and Gelfand, J. M. (2000–2001) "Corporate criminal liability: A bibliography." *Western State University Law Review* 28: 1–64.

Dinitz, S. (1982) "Multidisciplinary approaches to white collar crime," pp. 129–152 in H. Edelhertz and T. D. Overcast (Eds.), *White-collar crime: An agenda for research*. Lexington, MA: Lexington.

Dino, M. (2004) "Cooking the books in the restaurant business." *Crime and Justice International* (November/December) 29–30.

Dirks, R. L., and Gross, L. (1974) *The great Wall Street scandal*. New York: McGraw-Hill.

Ditton, J. (1977) *Part–time crime: An ethnography of fiddling and pilferage*. London: Macmillan.

Ditzen, L. S., Dobrin, P., and Eng, L. (1995) "U.S. state investigating collapsed charity." *The Philadelphia Inquirer* (May 17): 1.

Dodd, C. J., and Hager, C. (2001) "Can Bush and Putin control Russia's arsenal?" *New York Times* (November 13): A17.

Dodge, M. (2001a) "Fertile frontiers of medical fraud: A case study of egg and embryo theft," pp. 155–174 in H. N. Pontell and D. Shichor (Eds.), *Contemporary issues in crime and criminal justice*. Upper Saddle River, NJ: Prentice Hall.

Dodge, M. (2001b) "Slams, crams, jams, and other phone scams." *Journal of Contemporary Criminal Justice* 17: 358–368.

Domanick, J. (1989) *Faking it in America: Barry Minkow and the great ZZZ Best scandal*. Chicago: Contemporary Books.

Dong, E. (1991) "Confronting scientific fraud." *Chronicle of Higher Education* (October 9): A50.

Donnelly, P. G. (1982) "The origins of the occupational safety and health act of 1970." *Social Problems* 30: 13–25.

Donovan, K. (2005) *v. Goliath—The trials of David Boies*. New York: Pantheon.

Donson, F. J. L. (2000) *Legal intimidation: A SLAPP in the face of democracy*. London: Free Association Books.

Dooling, R. (2005) "The risk not taken." *New York Times* (April 3): Wk 13.

Dorman, M. (1975) *Vesco—The infernal money-making machine*. New York: Berkeley.

Dorn, J. A., and Manne, H. G. (Eds.) (1987) *Economic liberties and the judiciary*. Fairfax, VA: George Mason University Press.

Douglas, J. D. (1992) "Betraying scientific truth." *Society* (November/December) 76–82.

Douglas, L. P. (2001) *The memory of judgment—Making law and history in the trials of the Holocaust*. New Haven, CT: Yale University Press.

Douglas, M. (1990) "Risk as a forensic resource." *Daedalus* 119: 1–16.

Dowie, M. (1977) "Pinto madness." *Mother Jones* (September/October) 18–32.

Downie, L. (1976) *The new muckrakers*. Washington, DC: New Republic Book Co.

Doyle, J. (2000) *Taken for a ride: Detroit's big three and the politics of pollution*. New York: Four Walls/Eight Windows.

Draper, E. (1984) "Risk by choice? Knowledge and power in the hazardous workplace." *Contemporary Sociology* 13: 688–691.

Draper, E. (2003) *The company doctor: Risk, responsibility, and corporate professionalism*. New York: Russell Sage Foundation.

Draper, T. (1991) *A very thin line: The Iran-Contra affairs*. New York: Farrar, Straus & Giroux.

Drapkin, I. (1989) *Crime and punishment in the ancient world*. Lexington, MA: Lexington.

Drew, K., and Clark, K. A. (2005) "Corporate criminal liability." *American Criminal Law Review* 42: 277–303.

Driscoll, D. J. (1989) "The development of human rights in international law," pp. 41–56 in W. Laquer and B. Rubin (Eds.), *The human rights reader* (Rev. ed.). New York: New American Library.

Dudziak, M. L. (Ed.) (2003) *September 11 in history—A watershed moment?* Durham, NC: Duke University Press.

Duffy, M. (2002) "What did they know… And when did they know it?" *Time* (January 28): 16–22.

Duffy, M., and Dickerson (2002) "Enron spoils the party." *Time* (February 4): 19–25.

Dugger, C. (2004) "World Bank challenged: Are the poor really helped? *New York Times* (July 28): A12.

Duke, S. (1983) "Economic crime: Tax offenses," pp. 683–688 in S. Kadish (Ed.), *Encyclopedia of crime and justice*. New York: Macmillan and Free Press.

Dunne, T. (1999) "The spectre of globalization." *Indiana Journal of Global Legal Studies* 7: 17–34.

Durkheim, E. (1893; 1933) *Division of labor in society*. New York: Macmillan.

Durkheim, E. (1912; 1965) *The elementary forms of the religious life*. New York: Free Press.

Easterbrook, G. (2001) "The big one." *The New Republic* (November 5): 24–26.

Eaton, L. (1994) "U.S. says man bilked investors of $130 million." *New York Times* (May 18): D1.

Eaton, L. (1997a) "Crackdown on fraud intensifies." *New York Times* (January 2): C23.

Eaton, L. (1997b) "Marketplace." *New York Times* (February 27).

Eaton, L. (1997c) "Judge planning severe sentence for Hoffenberg in fraud case." *New York Times* (March 6): D1.

Eaton, L. (1997d) "States lead a crackdown on telemarketing brokers." *New York Times* (May 30).

Eaton, L. (1999a) "Assault with a fiscal weapon." *New York Times* (May 25): C1.

Eaton, L. (1999b) "Businessman convicted of fraud charge in huge leasing company failure." *New York Times* (June 11): B5.

Eatwell, J., and Taylor, L. (2000) *Global finance at risk: The case for international regulation.* New York: The New Press.

Eckholm, E. (2005a) "Excess fuel billing by Halliburton in Iraq is put at $108 million in audit." *New York Times* (March 15): A12.

Eckholm, E. (2005b) "Now you see it: An audit of KBR." *New York Times* (March 20): Wk 4.

Economist, The. (2005) "The good company." *The Economist* (January 22): 11.

Edwards, A., and Gill, P. (2002) "Crime as enterprise? The case of transnational organized crime." *Crime, Law & Social Change* 37: 203–223.

Eichenwald, K. (1990a) "Milken set to pay a $600 million fine in Wall Street fraud." *New York Times* (April 21): A1.

Eichenwald, K. (1990b) "Milken defends 'junk bonds' as he enters his guilty plea." *New York Times* (April 25): A1.

Eichenwald, K. (1990c) "S.E.C. complains about its limits." *New York Times* (April 30): 2D.

Eichenwald, K. (1991) "Judge who gave Milken 10 years backs a parole after he serves 3." *New York Times.*

Eichenwald, K. (1992) "Two sued by S.E.C. in bidding scandal at Salomon Bros." *New York Times* (December 3): A1.

Eichenwald, K. (1993a) "Prudential agrees to a settlement in securities fraud." *New York Times* (October 22): A1.

Eichenwald, K. (1993b) "New cloud over Prudential Bache." *New York Times* (December 17): D1.

Eichenwald, K. (1994a) "An inquiry broadens at Prudential." *New York Times* (May 16): D1.

Eichenwald, K. (1994b) "He told. He suffered. Now he's a hero." *New York Times* (May 29): 3/1.

Eichenwald, K. (1995a) *Serpent on the rock.* New York: Harper Business.

Eichenwald, K. (1995b) "Learning the hard way how to monitor trades." *New York Times* (March 9): C1.

Eichenwald, K. (1998a) "Former Archer Daniels executives are found guilty of price fixing." *New York Times* (September 18): A1.

Eichenwald, K. (1998b) "U.S. suit charges fraud by 2 hospital chains." *New York Times* (October 6): A1.

Eichenwald, K. (2000a) *The informant.* New York: Broadway Books.

Eichenwald, K. (2000b) "Hospital company agrees to pay $745 million in U.S. fraud case." *New York Times* (May 19): A1.

Eichenwald, K. (2001a) "Global conspiracy on construction bids defrauded U.S." *New York Times* (April 13): C1.

Eichenwald, K. (2001b) "Terror money hard to block, officials find." *New York Times* (December 10): A1.

Eichenwald, K. (2002a) "Enron paid huge bonuses in '01: Experts see a motive for cheating." *New York Times* (March 1): C1.

Eichenwald, K. (2002b) "Another quality of the corporate titan: Ignorance at the top." *New York Times* (March 3): Wk 3.

Eichenwald, K. (2002c) "White-collar defense stance: The criminal-less crime." *New York Times* (March 3): Wk 3.

Eichenwald, K. (2002d) "Grand jury being misused as investigator, Andersen says." *New York Times* (March 26): C1.

Eichenwald, K. (2002e) "Waste Management executives are named in S.E.C. accusation." *New York Times* (March 27): C1.

Eichenwald, K. (2002f) "Andersen witnesses defend intent of shredding." *New York Times* (June 1): C1.

Eichenwald, K. (2002g) "Andersen trial yields evidence in Enron's fall." *New York Times* (June 17): A1.

Eichenwald, K. (2002h) "Could capitalists actually bring down capitalism?" *New York Times* (June 30): 4/1.

Eichenwald, K. (2002i) "A powerful, flawed witness against Enron." *New York Times* (October 21): C1.

Eichenwald, K. (2004) "Archer Daniels said to settle sweetener price-fixing case." *New York Times* (June 18): C1.

Eichenwald, K. (2005a) *Conspiracy of fools: A true story.* New York: Broadway Books.

Eichenwald, K. (2005b) "Reform effort at businesses feels pressure." *New York Times* (January 14): A1.

Eichenwald, K. (2005c) "When the top seat is the hot seat." *New York Times* (March 10): C1.

Eichenwald, K. (2005d) "Big paycheck is Exhibit A." *New York Times* (June 19): A1.

Eichenwald, K., and Kolata, G. (1999a) "Drug trials hide conflicts for doctors." *New York Times* (May 16): A1.

Eichenwald, K., and Kolata, G. (1999b) "A doctor's drug studies turn into fraud." *New York Times* (May 17): A1.

Eichenwald, K., and Richtel, M. (2002) "Enron trader pleads guilty to conspiracy." *New York Times* (October 18): C1.

Einstadter, W. (1992) "Asymmetries of control: Surveillance, intrusion, and corporate theft of privacy." *Justice Quarterly* 9: 285–298.

Einwohner, R. L., and Spencer, J. W. (2005) "That's how we do things here: Local culture and the construction of sweatshops and anti-sweatshop activism in two campus communities." *Sociological Inquiry* 75: 249–272.

Eisenberg, D. (2000) "Anatomy of a recall." *Time* (September 11): 29–31.

Eisenberg, D. (2002a) "Dennis the Menace." *Time* (June 17): 47–48.

Eisenberg, D. (2002b) "Jail to the chiefs?" *Time* (August 12): 24–26.

Eitle, D. J. (2000) "Regulatory justice: A re-examination of the influence of class position on the punishment of white-collar crime." *Justice Quarterly* 17: 809–839.

Elias, R. (1986) *The politics of victimization—Victims, victimology and human rights.* New York: Oxford University Press.

Ellin, A. (2002) "Scared straight in business school." *New York Times* (January 13): Ed 7.

Elliott, R. K., and Willingham, J. J. (1980) *Management fraud: Detection and deterrence.* New York: Petrocelli Books.

Ellis, P. J., and Wyatt, J. R. (1992) "Antitrust violations." *American Criminal Law Review* 29: 175–193.

Emery, F. (1994) *Watergate.* New York: Times Books.

Engelberg, S. (1994) "In immigration labyrinth, corruption comes easily." *New York Times* (September 12): A1.

Engels, F. (1895; 1958) *The condition of the working class in England.* Translated by W. O. Henderson & W. H. Chaldner. Stanford, CA: Stanford University Press.

Epstein, R. A., and Picker, R. C. (2005) "Introduction: Antitrust." *University of Chicago Law Review* 72: 1–2.

Ericson, R. V., and Doyle, A. (2004) "Criminalization in private: The case of insurance fraud," pp. 99–124 in Law Commission of Canada, *What is a Crime? Defining criminal conduct in contemporary society.* Vancouver: University of British Columbia Press.

Erikson, K. (1976) *Everything in its path: Destruction of community in the Buffalo Creek flood.* New York: Touchstone.

Erlanger, S. (1998) "Suharto fostered rapid economic growth, and staggering graft." *New York Times* (May 22): A9.

Erlanger, S. (2001) "Lax nuclear security in Russia is cited as way for bin Laden to get arms." *New York Times* (November 12): B1.

Ermann, D., and Lundman, R. (1982) *Corporate deviance.* New York: Holt, Rinehart & Winston.

Ermann, D., and Lundman, R. (2002) *Corporate and governmental deviance: Problems of organizational behavior in contemporary society* (6th ed.). New York: Oxford University Press.

Esbenshade, J. (2004) *Monitoring sweatshops: Workers, consumers and the global apparel industry.* Philadelphia: University of Temple Press.

Etzioni, A. (1987) "How rational are we?" *Sociological Forum* 2: 1–20.

Etzioni, A. (1988a) *Capital corruption—The new attack on American democracy.* New Brunswick, NJ: Transaction.

Etzioni, A. (1988b) *The moral dimension: Toward a new economics.* New York: Free Press.

Evans, R. D., and Porche, D. A. (2005) "The nature and frequency of Medicare/Medicaid fraud and neutralization techniques among Speech, Occupational, and Physical Therapists." *Deviant Behavior* 26: 253–270.

Evans, S. S., and Lundman, R. J. (1983) "Newspaper coverage of corporate price-fixing." *Criminology* 21: 529–541.

Eviatar, D. (2005) "A big win for human rights." *The Nation* (May 9): 20–22.

Fabrikant, G. (2001) "Blockbuster settles suit on late fees." *New York Times* (June 6): C1.

Fabrikant, G. (2005) "Time Warner and S.E.C. settle for $300 million." *New York Times* (March 22): C1.

Fain, P. (2005) "Thanks, Enron: Auditors gain clout on campuses." *Chronicle of Higher Education* (June 10): A1.

Falconer, B. (2003) "Murder by the state." *The Atlantic Monthly* (November): 56–57.

Falk, R. (1993) "The making of global citizenship," pp. 39–52 in J. Brecher, J. B. Childs, and J. Cutler (Eds.), *Beyond the New World Order*. Boston: South End Press.

Falk, R. A. (2004) *The declining world order—America's imperial geopolitics*. New York: Routledge.

Falk, R. A., Kolko, G., and Lifton, R. J. (Eds.) (1971) *Crimes of war*. New York: Vintage.

Faludi, S. C. (1990) "Safeway LBO yields vast profits but exacts a heavy human toll." *Wall Street Journal* (May 16): 1.

Farberman, H. A. (1975) "A criminogenic market structure: The automobile industry." *The Sociological Quarterly* 16: 438–457.

Farrell, G. (2003) "FBI's new breed runs hot on Enron's trail." *USA Today* (January 28): B1.

Farrell, G. (2004) "Pfizer settles fraud case for $430 M." *USA Today* (May 14): B1.

Farzad, R. (2005a) "Wal-Mart sues ex-executive, saying he stole $500,000." *New York Times* (February 28): C3.

Farzad, R. (2005b) "Jail terms for 2 at top of Adelphia." *New York Times* (June 21): C1.

Fathi, N. (2002) "Bush's 'Evil' label rejected by angry Iranian leaders." *New York Times* (February 1): A10.

Faulkner, R. R., Cheney, E. R., Fisher, G. A., and Baker, W. (2003) "Crime by committee: Conspirators and company men in the illegal electrical industry cartel, 1954-1959."*Criminology* 41: 511–554.

Fawthrop, T., and Jarvis, H. (2004) *Getting away with genocide? Elusive justice and the Khmer Rouge tribunal*. London: Pluto Press.

Fay, S. (1999) The collapse of Barings. New York: W. W. Norton & Co.

FBI. (2002a) Crime in the United States—2001. Uniform Crime Reports. Washington, DC: Federal Bureau of Investigation.

FBI. (2002b) White collar crime study. U.S. Department of Justice http://www.fbi.gov.presrel.02.

FBI. (2005) Press release. http://www.fbi.gov/prcsrcl/kprcssrclo3/mueller.022505.htm.

Feder, B. J. (1982) "Manville submits bankruptcy filing to halt lawsuits." *New York Times* (August 27): 1.

Feder, B. J. (1990) "G.E. agrees to pay $16.1 million fine for Pentagon fraud." *New York Times* (July 27): A1.

Feder, B. J. (2005) "S.E.C. brings fraud suit against ex-Quest officials." *New York Times* (March 16): C1.

Feder, B. J., and Brick, M. (2002) "Enron says that shredding was stopped only recently." *New York Times* (January 30): A1.

Feder, B. J., and Eichenwald, K. (2004) "Ex-WorldCom chief is indicted by U.S. in securities fraud." *New York Times* (March 3): A1.

Federal regulatory directory (6th ed.). (1990) Washington, DC: Congressional Directory.

Feller, W. V. (2005) "Risk analysis," pp. 690–692 in L. M. Salinger (Ed.), *Encyclopedia of white-collar and corporate crime*. Thousand Oaks, CA: Sage.

Felson, M. (2002) *Crime and everyday life* (3rd ed.). Thousand Oaks, CA: Sage.

Felstiner, W. L. F., and Siegelman, P. (1989) "Neoclassical difficulties: Tort and deterrence for latent injuries." *Law & Policy* 11: 309–329.

Fendrich, R. P. (1992) "Bush's antitrust lawyers attack philanthropy." *Wall Street Journal* (July 27): A13.

Fest, J. (1970) *The faces of the Third Reich*. New York: Ace.

Fields-Meyer, T. (2005) "Fleecing the flock." *People* (February 28): 113–116.

Finckenauer, J., and Albanese, J. (2005) "Organized crime in North America," pp. 439–456 in R. Reichel (Ed.), *Handbook on Transnational Crime & Justice*. Thousand Oaks, CA: Sage.

Findlay, M., and Stewart, A. (1992) "Implementing corruption prevention strategies through codes of conduct." *Corruption and Reform* 7: 67–85.

Finkelstein, K. N. (2000) "Curtain falls on opera patron charged with fraud." *New York Times* (July 22): B1.

Finnegan, W. (2000) "After Seattle." *The New Yorker* (April 17): 40–51.

Finney, H. C., and Lesieur, H. R. (1982) "A contingency theory of organizational crime," pp. 255–299 in S. B. Bacharach (Ed.), *Research in the sociology of organizations*, Vol. 1. Greenwich, CT: JAI Press.

First, H. (1990) *Business crime—Cases and materials.* Westbury, NY: Foundation Press.

Fischel, D. (1995) *Payback—The conspiracy to destroy Michael Milken.* New York: Harper Business.

Fischer, R. A. (1996) *Them damned pictures—Explorations in American political cartoon art.* Archon Books.

Fisher, L. (1992a) "Accusation of fraud at Sears." *New York Times* (June 12): D1.

Fisher, L. (1992b) "Sears auto centers to halt commissions." *New York Times* (June 23): D1.

Fishman, S. (2005a) "Inside Eliot's Army." *New York* (January 10): 17–23.

Fishman, S. (2005b) "Mommy's little con man." *New York* (June 27): 17–21, 78.

Fisse, B. (1991) "Corporate criminal responsibility." *Criminal Law Journal* 15: 166–174.

Fisse, B., and French, P. A. (1985) *Corrigible corporations and unruly law.* San Antonio, TX: Trinity University Press.

Flynn, J. J. (1987) "The jurisprudence of corporate personhood: The misuses of a legal concept," pp. 131–160 in W. J. Samuels and A. S. Miller (Eds.), *Corporations and society—Power and responsibility.* New York: Greenwood Press.

Flynn, L. (2004) "Internet giants file 7 suits aimed at stopping spam." *New York Times* (October 29): C6.

Flynn, K. (2000) "An un-Brooklyn crime." *New York Times* (May 17): B1.

Foerschler, A. (1990) "Corporate criminal intent: Toward a better understanding of corporate misconduct." *California Law Review* 78: 1287–1311.

Fogg, P. (2005) "Grant-Theft auto." *Chronicle of Higher Education* (February 4): A7.

Forero, J. (2003) "Texaco goes on trial in Ecuador pollution case." *New York Times* (October 23): C1.

Fountain, J. W., and Wong, E. (2001) "Notre Dame coach resigns after 5 days and a few lies." *New York Times* (December 15): A1.

Fox, E. (1990) "The Sherman Antitrust Act and the world." *Antitrust Law Journal* 59: 109–118.

Fox, S. (1984) *The mirror makers.* New York: Vintage.

Fox, S. (1989) *Blood and power—Organized crime in twentieth century America.* New York: Morrow.

France, M. K., and Carney, D. (2002) "Why corporate crooks are tough to nail." *Business Week* (July 1): 35–38.

Francis, D. (1988) *Contrepreneurs.* Toronto: Macmillan of Canada.

Frank, E. (2000) "Global democratization: Spotlight on the United States." *New Politics* 8: 14.

Frank, N. (1984a) "Assaults against inspectors: The dangers of enforcing corporate crime." *Law & Policy* 6: 361–378.

Frank, N. (1984b) "Policing corporate crime: A typology of enforcement styles." *Justice Quarterly* 1: 235–252.

Frank, N. (1993) "Maiming and killing: Occupational health crimes." *Annals* 525: 107–118.

Frank, N., and Lombness, M. (1988) *Controlling corporate illegality.* Cincinnati, OH: Anderson.

Frank, N., and Lynch, M. J. (1992) *Corporate crime, corporate violence: A primer.* New York: Harrow & Heston.

Frankel, M. E. (1992) "Lawyers can't be stool pigeons." *New York Times* (March 14): 15a.

Frantz, D. (1987) *Levine & Co.—Wall Street's insider trading scandal.* New York: Avon Books.

Frantz, D. (1994) "Reports describe widespread abuse in farm program." *New York Times* (October 3): A1.

Frantz, D. (1998a) "Hospice boom is giving rise to new fraud." *New York Times* (May 10): A1.

Frantz, D. (1998b) "Sweepstakes pit gullibility and fine print." *New York Times* (July 28): A1.

Frantz, D. (1999) "Gaps in sea laws shield pollution by cruise lines." *New York Times* (January 3): A1.

Frederick, R. E. (Ed.) (1999) *A companion to business ethics.* Malden, MA: Blackwell Publishers.

Freedman, M. (2002) "The tort mess." *Forbes* (May 13): 91–98.

Freedman, S. G. (1982) "The town Manville built has mixed feelings." *New York Times* (September 1): B1.

Freiburg, A. (1987) "Reconceptualizing sanctions." *Criminology* 25: 223–256.

Freidson, E. (1970) *Professional dominance.* New York: Atherton Press.

Freidson, E. (1986) *Professional powers*. Chicago: University of Chicago Press.

Freitag, P. J. (1983) "The myth of corporate capture: Regulatory commissions in the United States." *Social Problems* 30 (April) 480–491.

French, P. A. (1989) "Enforced corporate responsive adjustments." *Legal Studies Forum* 13: 115–134.

Freud, S. (1923) *The ego and the id*. London: Hogarth Press.

Freud, S. (1930) *Civilization and its discontents*. London: Hogarth Press.

Freudenheim, M., and Lichtblau, E. (2003) "Former HealthSouth chief indicted by U.S." *New York Times* (November 5): C1.

Fried, J. J. (1991) "Unisys settles U.S. fraud case for $190 million." *Philadelphia Inquirer* (September 7): 7D.

Fried, J. P. (1996a) "Charge of fraud ends high life of a social duo." *New York Times* (May 5): 37.

Fried, J. P. (1996b) "Official stole charity funds, U.S. charges." *New York Times* (December 18): B1.

Fried, J. P. (1997a) "Financial advisor sentenced to 15 months and restitution." *New York Times* (March 16): B3.

Fried, J. P. (1997b) "Man who bilked friends and relatives of millions is sentenced to four years." *New York Times* (October 7): B3.

Fried, J. P. (2001) "Telemarketing schemes burn twice, taking money and then selling lists of 'suckers.'" *New York Times* (July 8): 24.

Friedland, M. L. (1989) *Sanctions and rewards in the legal system—A multidisciplinary approach*. Toronto: University of Toronto Press.

Friedlander, S. L. (1990) "Using prior corporate convictions to impeach." *California Law Review* 78: 1313–1339.

Friedman, L. M. (1977) *Law and society—An introduction*. Englewood Cliffs, NJ: Prentice Hall.

Friedman, L. M. (2002) *American law in the 20th century*. New Haven, CT: Yale University Press.

Friedrichs, D. O. (1983) "Victimology: A consideration of the radical critique." *Crime & Delinquency* 29: 283–294.

Friedrichs, D. O. (1985) "The nuclear arms issue and the field of criminal justice." *The Justice Professional* 1: 5–9.

Friedrichs, D. O. (1992) "White collar crime and the definitional quagmire: A provisional solution." *Journal of Human Justice* 3: 5–21.

Friedrichs, D. O. (1996) "Governmental crime, Hitler, and white collar crime: A problematic relationship." *Caribbean Journal of Criminology and Social Psychology* 1: 44–63.

Friedrichs, D. O. (Ed.) (1998a) *State crime*, Vols. I and II. Aldershot, UK: Ashgate.

Friedrichs, D. O. (1998b) "New directions in critical criminology and white collar crime," pp. 77–94 in J. I. Ross (Ed.), *Cutting the edge—Current perspectives in radical/critical criminology and criminal justice*. Westport, CT: Praeger.

Friedrichs, D. O. (1999) "White collar crime and the class-race-gender construct," pp. 141–158 in M. D. Schwartz and D. Milovanovic (Eds.), *Race, gender, and class in criminology—The intersections*. New York: Garland.

Friedrichs, D. O. (2000a) "Crime in high places: A criminological perspective on the Clinton case," pp. 281–300 in J. T. Ulmer (Ed.), *Sociology of crime, law, and deviance*. Amsterdam: JAI.

Friedrichs, D. O. (2000b) "The crime of the century? The case for the Holocaust." *Crime, Law & Social Change* 34: 21–41.

Friedrichs, D. O. (2001a; 2006) *Law in our lives: An introduction*. Los Angeles, CA: Roxbury Publishing Co.

Friedrichs, D. O. (2001b) "Corporate crime," pp. 89–94 in David Luckenbill and Dennis Peck (Eds.), *Encyclopedia of criminology and deviant behavior*, Vol. II. Philadelphia, PA: Brunner/Routledge/Taylor & Francis.

Friedrichs, D. O. (2002a) "State-corporate crime in a globalized world: Myth or major challenge?" pp. 53–72, in G. W. Potter (Ed.), *Controversies in white collar crime*. Cincinnati, OH: Anderson.

Friedrichs, D. O. (2002b) "Occupational crime, occupational deviance, and workplace crime: Sorting out the difference." *Criminal Justice* 2: 243–256.

Friedrichs, D. O. (2004) "Enron et al.: Paradigmatic white collar crime cases for the new century." *Critical Criminology* 12: 113–132.

Friedrichs, D. O., and Friedrichs, J. (2002) "The World Bank and crimes of globalization: A case study." *Social Justice* 29: 13–36.

Friedrichs, D. O., and Schwartz, M. D. (forthcoming) "Low self-control or high organizational control? The paradoxes of white-collar crime," in E. Goode (Ed.), *Evaluating the General Theory of Crime.* New York: Cambridge University Press.

Fritsch, J. (1992) "Prosecutors depict vast fraud scheme by L. I. car dealer." *New York Times* (April 16): B1.

Fritsch, J. (2001) "Guardianship abuses noted, including a $1,275 ice cream." *New York Times* (December 4): D3.

Fuerbringer, J. (1997) "Mr. Boesky goes to Main Street." *New York Times* (April 16): C11.

Fuerbringer, J. (2002) "How trail of big currency losses remained uncovered for 5 years." *New York Times* (March 5): C1.

Fuerbringer, J., and Rashbaum, W. (2003) "Currency fraud ran deep, officials say." *New York Times* (November 20): C1.

Fusaro, P. C., and Miller, R. M. (2002) *What went wrong at Enron.* New York: John Wiley & Sons.

Fyfe, J. (1988) "Police use of deadly force." *Justice Quarterly* 5: 165–205.

Galbraith, J. K. (1986) "A classic case of euphoric insanity." *New York Times* (November 23): E3.

Galen, M. (1992) "Guilty!" *Business Week* (April 13): 60–65.

Gambetta, D. (Ed.) (1988) *Trust: Making and breaking cooperative relations.* New York: Basil Blackwell.

Gans, H. J. (1979) *Deciding what's news—A study of CBS Evening News, NBC Nightly News, Newsweek and Time.* New York: Pantheon Books.

Ganzini, L., McFarland, B., and Bloom, J. (1990) "Victims of fraud: Comparing victims of white collar and violent crime." *Bulletin of the American Academy of Psychiatry and Law* 18: 55–63.

Garber, S., and Bowen, A. G. (1999) "Newspaper coverage of automotive product liability verdicts." *Law & Society Review* 33: 93–122.

Gardiner, J. A. (1986) "Controlling official corruption and fraud: Bureaucratic incentives and disincentives." *Corruption and Reform* 1: 33–50.

Garfield, R. (2002) "Economic sanctions, humanitarianism, and conflict after the Cold War." *Social Justice* 29: 94–107.

Garfinkel, H. (1956) "Conditions of successful degradation ceremonies." *American Journal of Sociology* 61: 420–424.

Garment, S. (1992) *Scandal—The culture of mistrust in American politics.* New York: Doubleday.

Gasparino, C. (2004) "Tough beat." *Newsweek* (October 11): 40–41.

Gasparino, C. (2005a) *Blood on the streets: The sensational inside story of how Wall Street analysts duped a generation of investors.* New York: Free Press.

Gasparino, C. (2005b) "Cracks in the crackdown." *Newsweek* (June 20): 46.

Gasparino, C. (2005c) "Good news: You're fired." *Newsweek* (July 25): 48.

Gaylord, B. (2002) "Investors hold bank liable for losses at currency firm." *New York Times* (March 16): C1.

Geary, W. R. (2002) "The legislative recreation of RICO: Reinforcing the 'myth' of organized crime." *Crime, Law & Social Change* 38: 311–356.

Gegak, T. T. (1997) "Stick 'em up? Not anymore. Now it's crime by keyboard." *Newsweek* (July 21): 14.

Geis, G. (1967) "White collar crime: The heavy electrical equipment antitrust cases of 1961," pp. 139–151 in M. Clinard and R. Quinney (Eds.), *Criminal behavior systems: A typology.* New York: Holt, Rinehart & Winston.

Geis, G. (1974) "Avocational crime," pp. 272–298 in D. Glaser (Ed.), *Handbook of criminology.* New York: Rand McNally.

Geis, G. (1984) "White collar crime and corporate crime," pp. 132–166 in R. Meier (Ed.), *Major forms of crime.* Beverly Hills, CA: Sage.

Geis, G. (1988) "From Deuteronomy to deniability: A historical perlustration on white-collar crime." *Justice Quarterly* 5: 7–32.

Geis, G. (1993) "The evolution of the study of corporate crime," pp. 3–28 in M. Blankenship (Ed.), *Understanding corporate criminality.* New York: Garland.

Geis, G. (1996) "A base on balls for white-collar criminals," pp. 244–264 in D. Shichor and D. Sechrest (Eds.), *Three strikes and you're out—Vengeance as public policy.* Thousand Oaks, CA: Sage.

Geis, G. (2000) "On the absence of self-control as the basis for a general theory of crime: A critique." *Theoretical Criminology* 4: 35–53.

Geis, G. (2005a) "Caveat emptor," pp. 146–147 in L. M. Salinger (Ed.), *Encyclopedia of white-collar and corporate crime.* Thousand Oaks, CA: Sage.

Geis, G. (2005b) "Corporate criminal liability," pp. 211–213 in L.M. Salinger (Ed.), *Encyclopedia of white-collar and corporate crime.* Thousand Oaks, CA: Sage.

Geis, G. (2005c) "Sherman Antitrust Act," pp. 741–743 in L. M. Salinger (Ed.), *Encyclopedia of white-collar and corporate crime.* Thousand Oaks, CA: Sage.

Geis, G., and DiMento, J. F. C. (2002) "Empirical evidence and the legal doctrine of corporate criminal liability." *American Journal of Criminal Law* 29: 341–375.

Geis, G., and Goff, C. (1982) "Edwin H. Sutherland: A biographical and analytical commentary," pp. 3–21 in P. Wickman and T. Dailey (Eds.), *White collar and economic crime.* Lexington, MA: Heath.

Geis, G., and Goff, C. (1987) "Edwin H. Sutherland's white-collar crime in America: An essay in historical criminology," pp. 1–31 in L. Knafla (Ed.), *Criminal justice history,* Vol. 7. Westport, CT: Meckler.

Geis, G., and Meier, R. F. (Eds.) (1977) *White-collar crime.* New York: Free Press.

Geis, G., Mobley, A., and Shichor, D. (1999) "Private prisons, criminological research and conflict of interest: A case study." *Crime & Delinquency* 45: 371–388.

Geis, G., Pontell, H. N., and Jesilow, P. (1988) "Medicaid fraud," pp. 17–39 in J. E. Scott and T. Hirschi (Eds.), *Controversial issues in crime and justice.* Beverly Hills, CA: Sage.

George, S. (2000) "Carte blanche, bete noire." *Dissent* (Winter) 13–15.

Geraghty, M. (1996) "Students, wooed by credit-card purveyors, often over-commit themselves, colleges find." *Chronicle of Higher Education* (November 8): A37.

Gerber, J., and Fritsch, E. J. (1993) "On the relationship between white-collar crime and political sociology." *Teaching Sociology* 21: 130–139.

Gerber, J., Jensen, E. L., and Fritsch, E. J. (1997) "Politics and white collar crime: Explaining government intervention in the Savings and Loan scandal." *Critical Criminology* 7: 59–73.

Gerber, J., and Short, J. F., Jr. (1986) "Publicity and the control of corporate behavior: The case of infant formula." *Deviant Behavior* 7: 195–216.

Gerber, J., and Weeks, S. L. (1992) "Women as victims of corporate crime: A call for research on a neglected topic." *Deviant Behavior* 13: 325–347.

Gerson, S. M. (1992) "When lawyers must disclose." *New York Times* (April 9): A25.

Gerth, J. (1988) "$69 million award in Ashland case." *New York Times* (June 14): D1.

Gerth, J., and Labaton, S. (1997) "Payment to an ex-Clinton aide is linked to big Chinese project." *New York Times* (March 6): A1.

Gertner, J. (2004) "The virtue in $6 heirloom tomatoes." *New York Times Magazine* (June 6): 44, 46, 48.

Ghezzi, S. G. (1983) "A private network of social control: Insurance investigation unit." *Social Problems* 30: 521–531.

Gibbons, D. C. (1979) *The criminological enterprise—Theories and perspectives.* Englewood Cliffs, NJ: Prentice Hall.

Gibbons, D. C. (1983) "Mundane crime." *Crime & Delinquency* 29: 213–228.

Gibbons, D. C. (2002) "Typologies of criminal behavior," pp. 1585–1591 in J. Dressler (Ed.), *Encyclopedia of crime and justice,* Vol. 4. New York: Gale Group.

Gibbs, J. P. (1987) "The state of criminological theory." *Criminology* 25: 821–840.

Gibney, F. (1978) "What's an operator?" pp. 9–22 in J. M. Johnson and J. D. Douglas (Eds.), *Crime at the top: Deviance in business and the professions.* Philadelphia: Lippincott.

Gilbert, M., and Russell, S. (2002) "Globalization of criminal justice in the corporate context." *Crime, Law & Social Change* 38: 211–238.

Gillers, S. (2001) "A duty to warn." *New York Times* (July 26): A25.

Gillers, S. (2002) "The flaw in the Andersen verdict." *New York Times* (June 18): A23.

Gilpin, K. N. (1998) "Antitrust suit filed against Visa and Mastercard." *New York Times* (October 8): C3.

Gilson, R. J. (1987) "The outside view of inside trading." *New York Times* (February 8): A23.

Gitlin, T. (1980) *The whole world is watching.* Berkeley: University of California Press.

Gitlin, T. (1983) *Inside prime time.* New York: Pantheon Books.

Giuliani, R. (1990) Interview: "From Milken to the Mafia." *Barron's* (November 26): 12–13, 24, 26.

Glaberson, W. (1987) "Wall Street informer admits his guilt in insider trading." *New York Times* (February 18): A1.

Glaberson, W. (1989a) "Millions, and friends' trust, vanish in Brooklyn betrayal." *New York Times* (November 21): B1.

Glaberson, W. (1989b) "Helmsley gets 4-year term for tax fraud." *New York Times* (December 13): B1.

Glaberson, W. (1990) "Court says job hazards may be a crime." *New York Times* (October 17): B1.

Glaberson, W. (1999a) "Novel antipollution tool is being upset by courts." *New York Times* (June 5): A1.

Glaberson, W. (1999b) "When the verdict is just a fantasy." *New York Times* (June 6): E1.

Glaberson, W. (1999c) "Looking for attention with a billion-dollar message." *New York Times* (July 18): Wk 3.

Glaberson, W. (2001a) "Lawyers consider easing restrictions on client secrecy." *New York Times* (July 31): A1.

Glaberson, W. (2001b) "A study's verdict: Jury awards are not out of control." *New York Times* (August 6): A9.

Glaberson, W. (2002) "Former justice pleads guilty to bribery charge." *New York Times* (August 6): B4.

Glanz, J., and Wong, E. (2003) "'97 report warned of foam damaging tiles." *New York Times* (February 4): 1.

Glasberg, D. S., and Skidmore, D. (1997a) *Corporate welfare policy and the welfare state: Bank deregulation and the savings and loan bailout.* Hawthorne, NY: Aldine de Gruyter.

Glasberg, D. S., and Skidmore, D. (1997b) "The dialectics of state economic intervention: Bank deregulation and the savings and loan bailout." *The Sociological Quarterly* 38: 67–93.

Glaser, D. (1956) "Criminality theories and behavioral images." *American Journal of Sociology* 61: 433–444.

Glaser, K., and Possony, S. T. (1979) *Victims of politics— The state of human rights.* New York: Columbia University Press.

Glassner, B. (2000) *Fear—Why Americans are afraid of the wrong things.* Boulder, CO: Perseus.

Glater, J. D. (2001a) "And now, a case for the forensic accountant." *New York Times* (May 27): C4.

Glater, J. D. (2001b) "Lawyers may reveal secrets of clients, bar group rules." *New York Times* (August 1).

Glater, J. D. (2001c) "A firm's revival comes in a crisis." *New York Times* (November 7): C1.

Glater, J. D. (2001d) "Accounting firm is bracing for an onslaught." *New York Times* (December 1): C2.

Glater, J. D. (2002a) "Mad as hell: Hard time for white-collar crime." *New York Times* (July 28): Wk 5.

Glater, J. D. (2002b) "Round up the usual suspects. Lawyers, too?" *New York Times* (August 4): Wk 4.

Glater, J. D. (2002c) "Defending a united Detroit on asbestos." *New York Times* (November 3): 3/1.

Glater, J. D. (2003) "Bar Association in a shift on disclosure." *New York Times* (August 13): C4.

Glater, J. D. (2004a) "Stewart's celebrity created a magnet for scrutiny." *New York Times* (March 7): A1.

Glater, J. D. (2004b) "Character to be major focus in Tyco trial." *New York Times* (May 6): C1.

Glater, J. D. (2005a) "A big new worry for corporate directors." *New York Times* (January 6): C1.

Glater, J. D. (2005b) "Crime and punishment, the celebrity version." *New York Times* (March 6): Wk 4.

Glater, J. D. (2005c) "Sorry, I'm keeping the bonus anyway." *New York Times* (March 13): 3/1.

Glater, J. D. (2005d) "Here it comes: The Sarbanes-Oxley backlash." *New York Times* (April 17): Bus 5.

Glater, J. D. (2005e) "For some, 'Just following orders' is a good defense." *New York Times* (June 24): C6.

Glater, J. D. (2005f) "Case isn't closed as Spitzer's office plans to retry Broker on 4 counts." *New York Times* (July 8): C3.

Glater, J. D. (2005g) "8 former partners of KPMG are indicted." *New York Times* (August 30): C1.

Glater, J. D. (2005h) "Oracle's chief in agreement to settle insider trading lawsuit." *New York Times* (September 12): C1.

Glater, J. D., and Belson, K. (2005) "Ebbers, on witness stand, may have lost his case." *New York Times* (March 16): C1.

Glater, J. D., and Labaton, S. (2003) "Auditor role in working for executives is questioned." *New York Times* (February 8): C1.

Glater, J. D., and Sorkin, A. R. (2005) "A lion of the courtroom hears his critics roar." *New York Times* (September 22): C1.

Glazer, M. P., and Glazer, P. M. (1989) *The whistle-blowers.* New York: Basic Books.

Gobert, J., and Punch, M. (2003) *Rethinking corporate crime.* New York: Cambridge University Press.

Goetz, B. (1997) "Organization as class bias in local law enforcement: Arson-for-Profit as a 'non-issue.'" *Law & Society Review* 31: 557–588.

Goff, C. (2001) "The Westray mine disaster: Media coverage of a corporate crime in Canada," pp. 195–217 in H. N. Pontell and D. Shichor (Eds.), *Contemporary issues in crime and criminal justice*. Upper Saddle River, NJ: Prentice Hall.

Goff, C., and Nason-Clarke, N. (1989) "The seriousness of crime in Fredericton, New Brunswick: Perceptions toward white-collar crime." *Canadian Journal of Criminology* 31: 19–34.

Goffman, E. (1959) *The presentation of self in everyday life*. New York: Doubleday.

Goffman, E. (1963) *Stigma: Notes on the management of spoiled identity*. Englewood Cliffs, NJ: Prentice Hall.

Gold, A. R. (1990) "State is called New York's no. 1 polluter." *New York Times* (March 3): A25.

Goldberg, C. (2000) "U.S. seeks millions in suit against advisers in Russia." *New York Times* (September 27): A12.

Goldin, D. (1995) "A brisk market develops in college term papers." *New York Times* (November 22): B5.

Goldstein, A. S. (1992) "White-collar crime and civil sanctions." *Yale Law Journal* 101: 1795–1874.

Gonzalez, J. (1991) "Senatorial privilege?" *New York Daily News* (September 24): C3.

Goode, E. (2005) *Deviant behavior* (7th ed.). Upper Saddle River, NJ: Prentice Hall.

Gordon, D. M. (1971) "Class and the economics of crime." *The Review of Radical Political Economics* 3: 51–72.

Gordon, J. S. (1991) "Understanding the S & L mess." *American Heritage* (February/March): 49–68.

Gordon, J. S. (1996) "American taxation." *American Heritage* (May/June): 63–84.

Gordon, R. L. (2002) *Antitrust abuse in the new economy—The Microsoft case*. Cheltenham, UK: Edgar Elgar.

Gorman, C. (1990) "This is a rescue?" *Time* (March 11): 58–59.

Gottfredson, M. R., and Hirschi, T. (1990) *A general theory of crime*. Stanford, CA: Stanford University Press.

Gottlieb, M., and Eichenwald, K. (1997) "Biggest hospital operator attracts federal inquiries." *New York Times* (March 28): A1.

Graber, D. (1980) *Crime news and the public*. New York: Praeger.

Grabosky, P. N. (1989) *Wayward governance*. Canberra: Australian Institute of Criminology.

Grabosky, P. N. (1990) "Professional advisers and white collar illegality: Toward explaining and excusing professional failure." *University of New South Wales Law Journal* 13: 73–90.

Grabosky, P. N. (1993) *Rewards and incentives as regulatory instruments*. Canberra, Australia: Australian National University.

Grabosky, P. N. (1995a) "Counterproductive regulation." *International Journal of the Sociology of Law* 23: 347–369.

Grabosky, P. N. (1995b) "Regulation by reward: On the use of incentives as regulatory instruments." *Law & Policy* 17: 257–282.

Grabosky, P. N. (1997) "Discussion paper: Inside the pyramid: Towards a conceptual framework for the analysis of regulatory systems." *International Journal of the Sociology of Law* 25: 195–201.

Grabosky, P. N. (2001) "Virtual criminality: Old wine in new bottles." *Social & Legal Studies* 10: 243–249.

Grabosky, P. N., Braithwaite, J., and Wilson, P. R. (1987) "The myth of community tolerance toward white collar crime." *Australian and New Zealand Journal of Criminology* 20: 33–44.

Grabosky, P. N. and Smith, R. G. (1998) *Crime in the digital age: Controlling telecommunications and cyberspace illegalities*. New Brunswick, NJ: Transaction.

Grabosky, P. N., Smith, R. G., and Dempsey, G. (2001) *Electronic theft: Unlawful acquisition in cyberspace*. Cambridge: Cambridge University Press.

Grabosky, P., and Wilson, P. R. (1989) *Journalism and justice: How crime is reported*. Sydney, Australia: Pluto Press.

Graddy, E. (2001) "Juries and unpredictability in products liability damage awards." *Law & Policy* 23: 29–45.

Grady, D. (2002) "U.S. lets drug tied to deaths back on market." *New York Times* (June 8): A1.

Grant, D. S., Jones, A. W., and Bergesen, A. J. (2002) "Organizational size and pollution: The case of the U.S. chemical industry." *American Sociological Review* 67: 389–407.

Grant, A., and Wolf, M. J. (1988) *Platinum crime*. New York: Pocket Books.

Grasmick, H. G., Tittle, C. R., Bursik, R. J., and Arneker, B. J. (1993) "Testing the core empirical implications of Gottfredson and Hirschi's general theory of crime." *Journal of Research in Crime & Delinquency* 30: 5–24.

Gray, C. B., Marzulla, R. J., and Shanahan, J. C. (1998) " 'Attempted' environmental crime: A flawed concept." *Journal of Law & Politics* 14: 363–381.

Gray, W. B., and Scholz, J. T. (1991) "Analyzing the equity and efficiency of OSHA enforcement." *Law & Policy* 13: 185–210.

Gray, W. B., and Scholz, J. T. (1993) "Does regulatory enforcement work? A panel analysis of OSHA enforcement." *Law & Society Review* 27: 177–214.

Greco, S. (2005) "Learning to love sox." *Corporate Counsel* (July): 16–17.

Green, G. S. (1990; 1997) *Occupational crime*. Chicago: Nelson Hall.

Green, J. (1997) *Risk and misfortune: A social construction of accidents*. London: UCL Press.

Green, M. J. (1975) *The other government—The unseen power of Washington lawyers*. New York: Grossman.

Green, M. J. (1984) *Who runs Congress?* New York: Dell.

Green, P. J. (2005) "Disaster by design: Corruption, construction and catastrophe." *British Journal of Criminology* 45: 528–546.

Green, P. J., and Ward, T. (2004) *State Crime*. London: Pluto Press.

Green, S. P. (1997) "Why it's a crime to tear the tag off a mattress: Overcriminalization and the moral content of regulatory offenses." *Emory Law Journal* 46: 1533–1615.

Green, S. P. (2001) "Lying, misleading, and falsely denying: How moral concepts inform the law of perjury, fraud, and false statements." *Hastings Law Journal* 53: 157–212.

Green, S. P. (2002) "Plagiarism, norms, and the limits of theft law: Some observations on the use of criminal sanctions on enforcing intellectual property rights." *Hastings Law Journal* 54: 167–242.

Green, S. P. (2004) "The concept of white collar crime in law and legal theory." *Buffalo Law Review* 8: 101–134.

Green, S. P. (2005a) "Theft by coercion: Extortion, blackmail, and hard bargaining." *Washburn Law Journal* 44: 553–582.

Green, S. P. (2005b) "Uncovering the cover-up crimes." *American Criminal Law Review* 42: 9–44.

Greenberg, D. (1981) *Crime and capitalism*. Palo Alto, CA: Mayfield.

Greenhouse, L. (2002) "Court to clarify definition of fraud in charitable fund-raising." *New York Times* (November 5): A18.

Greenhouse, L. (2003a) "Supreme Court to review Nike case in major look at free speech rights of corporations." *New York Times* (January 11): A12.

Greenhouse, L. (2003b) "Justices limit punitive damages in victory for tort revision." *New York Times* (April 8): A16.

Greenhouse, L. (2005) "Justices reject auditor verdict in Enron scandal." *New York Times* (June 1): A1.

Greenhouse, S. (1998a) "Cornell professor fights a slander suit." *New York Times* (April 1): A14.

Greenhouse, S. (1998b) "Depression caused union chief to take funds, his lawyer says." *New York Times* (December 15): B11.

Greenhouse, S. (1999) "Scandals affirm New York as union corruption capital." *New York Times* (February 15): B1.

Greenhouse, S. (2002) "Suits say Wal-Mart forces workers to toil off the clock." *New York Times* (June 25): A1.

Greenhouse, S. (2005a) "At a small shop in Colorado, Wal-Mart beats a union once more." *New York Times* (February 26): A8.

Greenhouse, S. (2005b) "Wal-Mart to pay U.S. $11 million in lawsuit on immigrant workers." *New York Times* (March): A1.

Greenhouse, S. (2005c) "Beyond the bargains, grievances." *New York Times* (June 6): B1.

Greenhouse, S. (2005d) "Fired officer is suing Wal-Mart." *New York Times* (July 1): C1.

Greenhouse, S. (2005e) "How Costco became the Anti-WalMart." *New York Times* (July 17): Bus 1.

Greenwald, C. (1980) *Banks are dangerous to your wealth*. Englewood Cliffs, NJ: Prentice Hall.

Greenwald, J. (1990) "Predator's fall." *Time* (February 26): 46.

Gregor, N. (1998) *Daimler-Benz in the Third Reich*. New Haven, CT: Yale University Press.

Greider, W. (1997) *One world, ready or not: The manic logic of global capitalism*. New York: A Touchstone Book.

Greider, W. (2000) "Time to rein in global finance." *The Nation* (April 24) 13–20.

Greider, W. (2002) "William Lerach's legal crusade against Enron and infectious greed." *The Nation* (August 5/12): 11–15.

Greve, M. S. (2005) "Cartel federalism: Antitrust enforcement by state attorney generals." *University of Chicago Law Review* 72: 99–122.

Griffin, J. (2002) *Mob nemesis: How the FBI crippled organized crime.* Amherst, NY: Prometheus Press.

Grisanti, M. L. (1989) "The Caesarean epidemic." *New York* (February 20): 55–61.

Grisham, J. (1991) *The firm.* New York: Dell.

Grogan, J. (2005) "An open letter." *New York Times* (May 11): A10–11.

Gross, D. (2005) "The crime: Slow job growth. A suspect: Enron." *New York Times* (September 11): 3/3.

Gross, E. (1980) "Organization structure and organizational crime," pp. 52–76 in G. Geis and E. Stotland (Eds.), *White-collar crime: Theory and research.* Beverly Hills, CA: Sage.

Gross, J. (2003) "Exposing cheat sheets, with student aid." *New York Times* (November 26): A1.

Guernsey, L (2002) "Where tips meet truth (sometimes)." *New York Times* (February 21): G1.

Guide to American Law, The. (1983) St. Paul, MN: West.

Gunkel, S. E. (1990) "Rethinking the guilty mind: Identity salience and white collar crime." A paper presented at the Annual Meeting of the American Society of Criminology (Baltimore, MD), November.

Gunkel, S. E. (2005) "Insider Trader Sanctions Act," pp. 432–433 in L. M. Salinger (Ed.), *Encyclopedia of white-collar and corporate crime.* Thousand Oaks, CA: Sage.

Gunkel, S. E., and Eitle, D. J. (1989) "Local state structure and corporate crime." A paper presented at the Annual Meeting of the American Society of Criminology (Reno, NV), November.

Gunningham, N. (1987) "Negotiated non-compliance: A case study of regulatory failure." *Law & Policy* 9 (January): 69–93.

Gunningham, N. (1995a) "Environment, self-regulation, and the chemical industry: Assessing responsible care." *Law & Policy* 17: 57–109.

Gunningham, N. (1995b) "Designing sustainable regulation: Towards an optimal regulatory mix." *Law & Society Association Meeting,* Toronto (June 1–4).

Gunningham, N., and Kagan, R. A. (2005) "Regulation and business behavior." *Law & Policy* 27: 213–218.

Gunsalus, C. K. (1997) "Rethinking unscientific attitudes about scientific misconduct." *Chronicle of Higher Education* (March 28): B4–5.

Gurney, J. N. (1985) "Factors influencing the decision to prosecute economic crime." *Criminology* 23: 609–628.

Gutman, R., and Rieff, D. (Eds.) (1999) *Crimes of war—What the public should know.* New York: W. W. Norton.

Haber, J. (2001) "Fugitive financier brought home to face the fire." *The Marshal's Monitor* (July/August).

Hafner, K., and Flynn, L. (2003) "Email swindle uses false report about a swindle." *New York Times* (June 20): A1.

Hagan, F. (1992) "From HUD to Iran-Contra: Crime during the Reagan Administration." A paper presented at the Annual Meeting of the American Society of Criminology (New Orleans), November.

Hagan, F. (1997) *Political crime—Ideology and criminality.* Boston: Allyn & Bacon.

Hagan, F. (2002) *Introduction to criminology* (5th ed.). Belmont, CA: Wadsworth/Thomson Learning.

Hagan, F., and Benekos, P. S. (1991) "The great savings and loan scandal: An analysis of the biggest financial fraud in American history." *Journal of Security Administration* 14: 41–64.

Hagan, J. (1983) *Victims before the law: The organizational dominance of criminal law.* Toronto: Butterworth.

Hagan, J. (1989a) "Why is there so little criminal justice theory? Neglected macro- and micro-level links between organization and power." *Journal of Research in Crime and Delinquency* 26: 116–135.

Hagan, J. (1989b) *Structural criminology.* New Brunswick, NJ: Rutgers University Press.

Hagan, J., and Kay, F. (1990) "Gender and delinquency in white-collar families: A power-control perspective." *Crime & Delinquency* 36: 391–407.

Hagan, J., and Nagel, I. H. (1982) "White-collar crime, white-collar time: The sentencing of white-collar offenders in the Southern District of New York." *American Criminal Law Review* 20: 259–289.

Hagan, J., and Palloni, A. (1986) "'Club Fed' and the sentencing of white-collar offenders before and after Watergate." *Criminology* 24: 603–622.

Hagan, J., and Parker, P. (1985) "White-collar crime and punishment." *American Sociological Review* 50: 302–316.

Hahn, R. W., and Hird, J. A. (1991) "The costs and benefits of regulation: Review and synthesis." *Yale Journal of Regulation* 8: 233–278.

Haines, F. (1997) *Corporate regulation: Beyond 'punish and persuade.'* Oxford, UK: Clarendon Press.

Hakim, D. (2001) "S.E.C. censures three big firms on charges of 'pumping.'" *New York Times* (August 11): C1.

Halberstam, D. (2001) *War in a time of peace—Bush, Clinton and the generals.* New York: Scribner's.

Halbfinger, D. M. (2005) "Taking on a giant (Whistle-blowers welcome)." *New York Times* (June 1): E1.

Halbrooks, C. (1990) "It can happen here." *Newsweek* (November 26): 10.

Hall, J. (1943) "Interrelations of criminal law and torts." *Columbia Law Review* 43: 753–779, 967–1001.

Hall, J. (1952) *Theft, law and society* (2nd ed.). Indianapolis: Bobbs-Merrill.

Hall, K. L. (1989) *The magic mirror—Law in American history.* New York: Oxford University Press.

Hall, R. H. (1987) *Organizations—Structures, processes and outcomes.* Englewood Cliffs, NJ: Prentice Hall.

Haller, M. H. (1990) "Illegal enterprise: A theoretical and historical interpretation." *Criminology* 28: 207–231.

Halliday, D. J. (2004) "U.S. policy and Iraq: A case of genocide," pp. 264–269 in A. Jones (Ed.), *Genocide, war crimes, and the west: History and complicity.* London: Zed Books.

Hamilton, V. L., and Sanders, J. (1996) "Corporate crime through citizens' eyes: Stratification and responsibility in the United States, Russia, and Japan." *Law & Society Review* 30: 513–547.

Hamilton, W. H. (1931) "The ancient maxim of caveat emptor." *Yale Law Journal* 40: 1133–1187.

Hammer, J. (1990) "Fear in the backroom." *Newsweek* (September 24): 64.

Handler, J. F. (1978) *Social movements and the legal system: A theory of law reform and social change.* New York: Academic Press.

Hanley, R. (1997) "Prudential fights to keep documents from some customers." *New York Times* (August 5): B1.

Hanley, R. (2001a) "Defense attacks credibility of witness in ex-financier's fraud trial." *New York Times* (March 17): A13.

Hanley, R. (2001b) "Former financier is guilty of money laundering and fraud." *New York Times* (April 17): B1.

Hans, V. (1989) "The jury's response to business and corporate wrongdoing." *Law and Contemporary Problems* 52: 177–201.

Hans, V. (2000) *Business on trial: The civil jury and corporate responsibility.* New Haven, CT: Yale University Press.

Hans, V., and Vidmar, N. (1986) *Judging the jury.* New York: Plenum.

Hans, V. P., and Lofquist, W. S. (1992) "Jurors judgments of business liability in tort cases: Implications for the litigation explosion." *Law & Society Review* 26: 85–116.

Hansell, S. (2003) "Spammers can run but they can't hide." *New York Times* (November 9): 3/1.

Hansell, S. (2004) "Technology: Online swindlers called 'phishers' lure the unwary." *New York Times* (March 24): A1.

Hardin, R. (2002) *Trust and trustworthiness.* New York: Russell Sage Foundation.

Harding, R. (1983) "Nuclear energy and the destiny of mankind—Some criminological perspectives." *Australian and New Zealand Journal of Criminology* 16: 81–92.

Harmer, R. M. (1975) *American medical avarice.* New York: Abelard Schuman.

Harmon, A. (2002a) "Piracy, or innovation? It's Hollywood vs. High Tech." *New York Times* (March 14): C1.

Harmon, A. (2002b) "Why Gates has trouble saying he's sorry." *New York Times* (April 29): C1.

Harmon, A. (2002c) "Judge backs terms of U.S. settlement in Microsoft case." *New York Times* (November 2): A1.

Harmon, A. (2003) "261 lawsuits filed on music sharing." *New York Times* (September 9): A1.

Harriger, K. (1992) *Independent justice: The federal special prosecutor in American politics.* Lawrence: University of Kansas Press.

Harris, A. R. (1991) "Race, class, and crime," pp. 95–120 in J. Sheley (Ed.), *Criminology: A contemporary handbook.* Belmont, CA: Wadsworth.

Harris, G. (2004) "As doctor writes prescription, drug company writes a check." *New York Times* (June 27): A1.

Harris, G. (2005a) "Drug industry's longtime critic says 'I told you so.'" *New York Times* (February 15): F5.

Harris, G. (2005b) "F.D.A. announces strong warnings for painkillers." *New York Times* (April 8): A1.

Harris, J. (1974) "The Marxist conception of violence." *Philosophy & Public Affairs* 3: 192–220.

Hasseldine, J., and Li, Z. (1999) "More tax evasion research required in the new Millennium." *Crime, Law & Social Change* 31: 91–104.

Hauber, A. R., Toonvliet, L. C., and Willemse, A. M. (1988) "The perceived seriousness of white collar crime and conventional crime." *Corruption and Reform* 3: 41–64.

Hawkins, K. (1984) *Environment and enforcement: Regulation and the social definition of pollution.* New York: Oxford University Press.

Hawkins, K. (1990) "Compliance strategy, prosecution policy and Aunt Sally." *British Journal of Criminology* 30: 444–466.

Hawkins, K. (1991) "Enforcing regulations: More of the same from Pearce and Tombs." *British Journal of Criminology* 31: 427–430.

Hawkins, K. (2002) *Law as a last resort: Prosecution decision-making in a regulatory agency.* Oxford, UK: Oxford University Press.

Hawkins, K., and Thomas, J. M. (1983) "Perspectives on regulation: Law, discretion, and bureaucratic behavior." *Law & Policy* 5 (January): 35–74.

Hawthorne, F. (2005) *Inside the FDA.* New York: John Wiley & Sons.

Hay, C. and Marsh, D. (Eds.) (2000) *Demystifying globalization.* New York: St. Martin's Press.

Hayes, P. (1987) *Industry and ideology—I. G. Farben in the Nazi era.* Cambridge, UK: Cambridge University Press.

Hayes, P. (1998) "State policy and corporate involvement in the Holocaust," pp. 197–218 in M. Berenbaum and A. J. Peck (Eds.), *The Holocaust and history.* Bloomington, IN: Indiana University Press.

Hayes, T. C. (1990) "Former savings executive sentenced to 30 years in jail." *New York Times* (April 6): D1.

Hayner, P. B. (2002) *Unspeakable truths.* New York: Routledge.

Hays, C. (2004) "5 months in jail, and Stewart vows, 'I'll be back.'" *New York Times* (July 17): A1.

Hays, C. (2005a) "No remorse. No regrets. No worries for Martha." *New York Times* (February 27): Bus 9.

Hays, C. (2005b) "Home sweet home confinement." *New York Times* (March 5): C1.

Hays, C., and Eaton, L. (2004) "Stewart found guilty of lying in sale of stock." *New York Times* (March 6): A1.

Healey, P. (2003a) "Appliance store owner jailed in fraud case." *New York Times* (November 11): B5.

Healey, P. (2003b) "Investigators say fraud ring staged thousands of crashes." *New York Times* (August 13): A1.

Healy, B. (2002) "Business ethics engulf lecture halls." *Scranton Times* (July 14): C6.

Healy, P. (2000) "College admission officers target fraudulent essays." *Scranton Sunday Times* (December 3): C7.

Healy, G. (Ed.) (2004) *Go directly to jail: The criminalization of almost everything.* Washington, D.C.: Cato Institute.

Heaney, G. W. (1991) "The reality of sentencing guidelines: No end to disparity." *American Criminal Law Review* 28: 161–232.

Hedges, C. (1999) "Leaders in Bosnia are said to steal up to $1 billion." *New York Times* (August 17): A1.

Hedges, C. (2000) "Immigrants seeking help with I.N.S. fall prey to con artists." *New York Times* (July 17): B1.

Hedman, S. (1991) "Expressive functions of criminal sanctions in environmental law." *The George Washington Law Review* 59: 889–899.

Heffernan, W. C., and Kleinig, J. (Eds.) (2004) *Private and public corruption.* Lanham, MD: Rowman & Littleheld.

Heidenheimer, A. J. (1977) "Definitions, conceptions and criteria of corruption," pp. 19–26 in J. Douglas and J. M. Johnson (Eds.), *Official deviance.* Philadelphia: Lippincott.

Heidenreich, J. G. (2001) *How to prevent genocide.* Westport, CT: Praeger.

Heilbrun, J. R. (2005) "Oil and water: Elite politicians and corruption in France." *Comparative Politics* (April): 277–296.

Heilemann, J. (2001) *Pride before the fall—The trials of Bill Gates.* New York: HarperBooks.

Helmkamp, J., Ball, J., and Townsend, K. (Eds.) (1996) *Definitional dilemma: Can and should there be a universal definition of white collar crime?* Morgantown, WV: National White Collar Crime Center.

Henderson, J. H., and Simon, D. R. (1994) *Crimes of the criminal justice system.* Cincinnati, OH: Anderson.

Henriques, D. B. (1990a) "The latest penny-stock shuffle." *New York Times* (April 1): Bus 1.

Henriques, D. B. (1990b) "A paradoxical anti-takeover bill." *New York Times* (April 8): 15.

Henriques, D. B. (1992) "Falsifying corporate data becomes fraud of the 90's." *New York Times* (September 21): A1.

Henriques, D. B. (1993) "Evidence mounts of rigged bidding in milk industry." *New York Times* (May 23): A1.

Henriques, D. B. (1994a) "Towers investors try aggressive new legal tack." *New York Times* (June 10): D1.

Henriques, D. B. (1994b) "Republicans may curb S.E.C. and fraud suits by investors." *New York Times* (December 12): A1.

Henriques, D. B. (1995) "Efforts to harness S.E.C. worry agency critics too." *New York Times* (October 23): A1.

Henriques, D. B. (1999) "A brutal turn in stock frauds." *New York Times* (November 2): B1.

Henriques, D. B. (2002) "A home lender in a settlement for $60 million." *New York Times* (March 22): A1.

Henriques, D. B., and Eichenwald, K. (2002) "A fog over Enron, and the legal landscape." *New York Times* (January 27): 3/1.

Henriques, D. B., and Fabrikant, G. (2002) "Deciding on executive pay: Lack of independence seen." *New York Times* (December 18): A1.

Henry, F. J. (1991) "Corporate violence: Government regulation and the possibilities of reform." *Free Inquiry in Creative Sociology* 19 (November): 145–153.

Henry, S. (1978) *The hidden economy.* London: Mark Robertson.

Henry, S., and Lanier, M. M. (Eds.) (2001) *What is crime? Controversies over the nature of crime and what to do about it.* Lanham, MD: Rowman and Littleheld.

Henry, S., and Milovanovic, D. (1991) "Constitutive criminology: The maturation of critical criminology." *Criminology* 29: 293–316.

Henry, S., and Milovanovic, D. (1994) "The constitution of constitutive criminology: A postmodern approach

to criminological theory," pp. 110–133 in D. Nelken (Ed.), *The futures of criminology.* London: Sage.

Herbert, B. (2005) "Truth and deceit." *New York Times* (June 2): A25.

Herling, J. (1962) *The great price conspiracy: The story of the antitrust violations in the electrical industry.* Washington, DC: Robert B. Luce.

Herman, E. S. (1982) *The real terror network—Terrorism in fact and propaganda.* Boston: South End Press.

Herman, E. S. (1985) Review essay: "The transformation of Wall Street." *ABF Research Journal* (Summer): 691–697.

Hernandez, R. (1995) "Yale says it sees an imposter in the Ivy." *New York Times* (April 12): B1.

Hershey, R. D., Jr. (1984) "Panel says U.S. can trim costs by $424 billion." *New York Times* (January 13): A1.

Hershey, R. D., Jr. (1990a) "Thrift office will open its cases." *New York Times* (July 6): D1.

Hershey, R. D., Jr. (1990b) "Tax sleuths turn to technology." *New York Times* (March 23): D1.

Hershey, R. D., Jr. (1994) "I.R.S. finds fraud grows as more file by computer." *New York Times* (February 21): A1.

Hershey, R. D., Jr. (1999) "The check is in the mail and so is a headache." *New York Times* (September 12): C12.

Heyman, J. (Ed.) (1999) *States and illegal practices.* Oxford, UK: Berg.

Hiatt, H. (1991) "Patients, doctors, and lawyers: Resolving the malpractice crisis." *Bulletin—The American Academy of Arts & Sciences* 44: 41–50.

Hickey, N. (1981) "Is television doing its investigative reporting job?" pp. 166–170 in B. Cole (Ed.), *Television today: A close-up view.* New York: Oxford University Press.

Hilberg, R. (1980) "The anatomy of the Holocaust," pp. 85–102 in H. Friedlander and S. Milton (Eds.), *The Holocaust: Ideology, bureaucracy and genocide.* New York: Kraus International Publications.

Hill, A. F. (2002) "Insider women with outsider values." *New York Times* (June 6): A31.

Hills, S. L. (1980) *Demystifying social deviance.* New York: McGraw-Hill.

Hills, S. L. (1982) "Crime and deviance on a college campus: The privilege of class." *Humanity & Society* 6: 257–266.

Hilts, P. J. (1993a) "Manufacturer admits selling untested devices for heart." *New York Times* (October 16): A1.

Hilts, P. J. (1993b) "Misconduct in science is not rare, a survey finds." *New York Times* (November 12): A22.

Hilts, P. J. (1996) *Smoke screen—The truth behind the tobacco industry cover-up.* Reading, MA: Addison-Wesley.

Hinch, R., and DeKeseredy, W. (1992) "Corporate violence and women's health at home and in the workplace," in B. Bolaria and H. Dickinson (Eds.), *The sociology of health care in Canada* (2nd ed.). Toronto: Harcourt Brace Jovanovich.

Hinduja, S. (2004) "Perceptions of local and state law enforcement concerning the role of computer crime investigative teams." *Policing: An International Journal of Police Strategies and Management* 27: 341–357.

Hirschi, T. (1986) "On the compatibility of rational choice and social control theories of crime," pp. 105–118 in D. B. Cornish and R. V. Clarke (Eds.), *The reasoning criminal—Rational choice perspectives on offending.* New York: Springer-Verlag.

Hirschi, T., and Gottfredson, M. (1989) "The significance of white-collar crime for a general theory of crime." *Criminology* 27: 359–371.

Hitchens, C. (2001) *The trial of Henry Kissinger.* New York: Verso.

Hitt, J. (2004) "America Kabuki: The ritual of scandal." *New York Times* (July 18): B7.

Hodson, R., and Sullivan, T. A. (2002) *The social organization of work.* Belmont, CA: Wadsworth.

Hoge, W. (1999) "Trial opens for Pinochet with listing of 35 crimes." *New York Times* (September 28): A8.

Hoge, W. (2000) "Pinochet is ruled unfit to be tried and may be freed." *New York Times* (January 12): A1.

Hoge, W. (2005a) "Panel says Annan didn't intervene in Iraq contract." *New York Times* (March 30): A1.

Hoge, W. (2005b) "U.N. Chief admits Oil-for-Food missteps." *New York Times* (September 8): A10.

Hoffman, W. M. (1989) "The cost of a corporate conscience." *Business and Society Review* 69: 46–47.

Holcomb, B. (1986) "Inside the boiler room." *New York* (August 4): 38–41.

Holland, R. C. (1995) "Public perceptions of white collar crime seriousness: A survey of an Australian sample." *International Journal of Comparative and Applied Criminal Justice* 19: 91–105.

Hollinger, R. C. (2001) "Computer crime," pp. 76–81 in D. Luckenbill and D. Peck (Eds.), *Encyclopedia of criminology and deviant behavior,* Vol. 2. Philadelphia: Brunner-Routledge.

Hollinger, R. C., and Lanza-Kaduce, L. (1988) "The process of criminalization: The case of computer crime laws." *Criminology* 26: 101–126.

Hollinger, R. C., Slora, K. B., and Terris, W. (1992) "Deviance in the fast-food restaurant: Correlates of employee theft, altruism, and counterproductivity." *Deviant Behavior* 13: 155–184.

Holst, A. (2005) "Occupational Safety and Health Act," pp. 577–579 in L. M. Salinger (Ed.), *Encyclopedia of white-collar and corporate crime.* Thousand Oaks, CA: Sage.

Holstein, W. J. (2005) "The big chill in the boardroom." *New York Times* (May 22): Bus 11.

Holt, L. B. (2001) "NJ Supreme Court discipline fewer attorneys in 2000. More disbarments, fewer suspensions." http://www.judiciary.statenj.us.

Holtfreter, K. (2005a) "Is occupational fraud 'typical' white-collar crime? A comparison of individual and organizational characteristics." *Journal of Criminal Justice* 33: 353–365.

Holtfreter, K. (2005b) "Consent agreements, decrees, and orders," pp. 195 in L. M. Salinger (Ed.), *Encyclopedia of white-collar and corporate crime.* Thousand Oaks, CA: Sage.

Holtfreter, K. (2005c) "Consumer Product Safety Act," pp. 199–200 in L. M. Salinger (Ed.), *Encyclopedia of white-collar and corporate crime.* Thousand Oaks, CA: Sage.

Holtfreter, K. (2005d) "Employee crime," pp. 281–288 in L. M. Salinger (Ed.), *Encyclopedia of white-collar and corporate crime.* Thousand Oaks, CA: Sage.

Honan, W. H. (1995) "Teacher tied to stolen manuscript pages faced prior ethical questions, colleagues say." *New York Times* (May 30): A11.

Hoover, E. (2003) "Pushing the envelope." *Chronicle of Higher Education* (October 17): A39.

Hope, K. R. (1987) "Administrative corruption and administrative reform in developing states." *Corruption and Reform* 2: 127–147.

Horn, S. (2005) "Counting corporate crooks." *New York Times* (July 16): A15.

Horning, D. (1970) "Blue-collar theft: Conceptions of property, attitudes toward pilfering, and work norms in a modern industrial plant," pp. 46–64 in E. O. Smigel and H. L. Ross (Eds.), *Crimes against bureaucracy*. New York: Van Nostrand Reinhold.

Horning, D. (1983) "Employee theft," pp. 698–704 in S. Kadish (Ed.), *Encyclopedia of crime and justice*. New York: Macmillan and Free Press.

Horwitz, M. J. (1992) *The transformation of American law, 1870–1960: The crisis of legal orthodoxy*. New York: Oxford University Press.

Hovencamp, H. (2004) "Sensible antitrust roles for pharmaceutical competition." *University of San Francisco Law Review* 39: 11–32.

Huber, P. (1988) "Tort reform by contract," pp. 174–185 in W. Olson (Ed.), *New directions in liability law*. New York: The Academy of Political Science.

Huber, P. (1990) "Pathological science in court." *Daedalus* 119: 97–118.

Hughes, E. C. (1964) "Good people and dirty work," pp. 23–36 in H. S. Becker (Ed.), *The other side: Perspectives on deviance*. New York: Free Press.

Hughes, J. A. (1993) "Law firm Kaye, Scholer, Lincoln S & L and the OTS." *Notre Dame Journal of Law, Ethics & Public Policy* 7: 177–222.

Hume, E. (1990) "Why the press blew the S & L scandal." *New York Times* (May 24): A25.

Humphries, D. (1981) "Serious crime, news coverage and ideology: Crime coverage in a metropolitan paper." *Crime & Delinquency* 27: 191–205.

Hurst, J. W. (1956) *Law and the conditions of freedom in the nineteenth century United States*. Madison: University of Wisconsin Press.

Hutcheson, M. (1990) "Teaching the right thing." *NYU Alumni Magazine* (Fall): 12–15.

Hutchison, T. W., and Yellen, D. (1991) *Federal sentencing law and practice—1991 supplement*. St. Paul, MN: West.

Hutter, B. M., and Lloyd-Bostock, S. (1990) "The power of accidents: The social and psychological impact of accidents and the enforcement of safety regulations." *British Journal of Criminology* 30: 409–422.

Ianni, F. A., and Reuss-Ianni, E. (1972) *A family business*. New York: New American Library.

Icahn, C. (1986) "Confessions of a raider." *Newsweek* (October 20): 51–55.

Ignatieff, M. (2005) "America the mercurial." *Legal Times* (March/April): 68–69.

Ignatius, A. (2002–2003) "Wall Street's top cop." *Time* (December 30/January 6): NPA.

IGNet (2003) *Inspectors General*. Available online: www.ignet.gov/igs/faq.html.

Inciardi, J. A. (1975) *Careers in crime*. Chicago: Rand McNally.

Inciardi, J. A. (1980a) *Radical criminology: The coming crises*. Beverly Hills, CA: Sage.

Inciardi, J. A. (1980b) "Youths, drugs and street crime," pp. 175–204 in F. Scarpitti and S. Datesman (Eds.), *Drugs and youth culture*. Beverly Hills, CA: Sage.

Institute for Civil Justice. (1992) *Annual report*. Santa Monica, CA: Rand.

Iracola, R. (1995) "Criminal liability of a parent company for the conduct of its subsidiary: The spillover of the Exxon Valdez." *Criminal Law Bulletin* 31: 3–18.

Irwin, G. (2003) "Stop thief!" *Scranton Times* (January 4): D1.

Isaacson, W. (1983) "The winds of reform." *Time* (March 7): 12–30.

Iseman, F. (1986) "Let corporate takeovers keep rolling." *New York Times* (December 1): A21.

Ishay, M. R. (2004) *The history of human rights*. Berkeley: University of California Press.

Israel, J. H., Podgor, E., Borman, P. D., and Henning, P. J. (2003) *White collar crime: Law and practice*. St. Paul, MN: West.

Ives, N. (2005) "Web marketers fearful of fraud in pay-per-click." *New York Times* (March 3): C1.

Jachcel, E. (1981) *Towards a criminological analysis of the origins of capital*. Ph.D. Dissertation, University of Sheffield.

Jack, R., and Jack, D. C. (1992) *Moral vision and professional decisions: The changing moral values of women and men lawyers*. New York: Cambridge University Press.

Jackall, R. (1988) *Moral mazes: The world of corporate managers*. New York: Oxford University Press.

Jackson, B. (1988) *Honest graft*. New York: Knopf.

Jackson, D. D. (1974) *Judges*. New York: Atheneum.

Jackson, J. H. (2000) *The jurisprudence of GATT and WTO*. Cambridge, UK: Cambridge University Press.

Jackson, P. G. (1990) "Sources of data," pp. 21–56 in L. Kempf (Ed.), *Measurement issues in criminology*. New York: Springer-Verlag.

Jacobs, M., and Siconolfi, M. (1995) "Investors fare poorly fighting Wall Street—And may do worse." *Wall Street Journal* (February 8): 1.

Jacobs, S. L. (2004) "Indicting Henry Kissinger: The response of Raphael Lemkin," pp. 214–229 in A. Jones (Ed.) *Genocide, War Crimes, and the West: History and Complicity*. London: Zed Books.

Jacobson, H., and Greca Green, R. (2002) "Computer crimes." *American Criminal Law Review* 39: 273–326.

Jacoby, T. (1988) "Going after dissidents." *Newsweek* (February 8): 29.

Jalley, E. M., Moores, P. B., Henninger, B. L., and Maragani, G. P. (2002) "Environmental crimes." *American Criminal Law Review* 39: 403–489.

Jamieson, K. M. (1994) *The organization of corporate crime*. Thousand Oaks, CA: Sage.

Janofsky, M. (2005a) "Court rules U.S. can't pursue $280 billion as tobacco penalty." *New York Times* (February 5): A1.

Janofsky, M. (2005b) "U.S. finishes tobacco racketeering case." *New York Times* (June 8): A14.

Janofsky, M. (2005c) "U.S. Court backs Bush's revisions in Clean Air Act." *New York Times* (June 25): A1.

Janofsky, M., and Johnston, D. (2005) "Limit for award in tobacco case sets off protests." *New York Times* (April 6): A1.

Jaroff, L. (1997) "Intellectual chain gang." *Time* (February 10): 64.

Jaschik, S. (1990) "As probe of tuition ends its first year, colleges are confused, cautious." *Chronicle of Higher Education* (August 15): A1.

Jehl, D. (2003) "Insiders new firm consults in Iraq." *New York Times* (September 30): A1.

Jeffery, C. R. (1990) *Criminology—An interdisciplinary approach*. Englewood Cliffs, NJ: Prentice Hall.

Jeffreys-Jones, R. (1989) *The CIA and American democracy*. New Haven, CT: Yale University Press.

Jenkins, A., and Braithwaite, J. (1993) "Profits, pressure, and corporate law-breaking." *Crime, Law & Social Change* 20: 221–232.

Jenkins, P. (1988) "Whose terrorists? Libya and state criminality." *Contemporary Crises* 12: 5–24.

Jennings, M. M. (2004) "The disconnect between and among legal ethics, business ethics, law, and virtue: Learning not to make ethics so complex." *University of Saint Thomas Law Journal* 1: 995–1040.

Jennings, M., Reckers, P. M. J., and Kneer, D. (1991) "The auditor's dilemma: The incongruous judicial notions of the auditing profession and actual auditor practice." *American Business Law Journal* 29: 89–122.

Jesilow, P. (1982a) "Adam Smith and white-collar crime." *Criminology* 20: 319–328.

Jesilow, P. (1982b) *Deterring automobile repair fraud: A field experiment*. Unpublished Ph.D. Dissertation, University of California, Irvine.

Jesilow, P., Pontell, H. N., and Geis, G. (1985) "Medical criminals: Physicians and white collar crime." *Justice Quarterly* 2: 149–166.

Jesilow, P., Pontell, H. N., and Geis, G. (1987) "Physician immunity from prosecution and punishment for medical program fraud," pp. 7–22 in W. B. Groves and G. R. Newman (Eds.), *Punishment and privilege*. New York: Harrow & Heston.

Jesilow, P., Pontell, H. N., and Geis, G. (1992) *Prescription for profit—How doctors defraud Medicaid*. Berkeley: University of California Press.

Johnson, B. T. (2000) "The World Bank does not provide effective development programs," pp. 116–122, in L. K. Egendorf (Ed.), *The Third World—Opposing viewpoints*. San Diego, CA: Greenhaven Press.

Johnson, D. R. (1981) *American law enforcement: A history*. St. Louis: Forum Press.

Johnson, D. T. (2002) *Review of: Corporate crime, law and social control*, by Sally S. Simpson, *Law & Politics Book Review* 12: 454–463.

Johnson, J., and Holub, M. (2003) "Corporate flight: 'Moving' offshore to avoid U.S. taxes." *Journal of Financial Crime* 10: 246–252.

Johnson, L. K. (1985) *A season of inquiry: The Senate intelligence investigation*. Lexington: University Press of Kentucky.

Johnson, M. (1986) *Takeover—The new Wall Street warriors*. New York: Belvedere Books/Arbor House.

Johnston, D. (1989) "Hastings ousted as Senate vote convicts judge." *New York Times* (October 21): A1.

Johnston, D. (1990) "100 possible cases of savings fraud given U.S. priority." *New York Times* (July 7): A1.

Johnston, D. (1995) "University agrees to pay in settlement on Medicare." *New York Times* (December 13): A18.

Johnston, D. (1996) "Former Interior Secretary avoids trial with a guilty plea." *New York Times* (January 3): A11.

Johnston, D. (1998a) "The old tax dodge." *New York Times* (April 15): C1.

Johnston, D. (1998b) "Reno seeks independent counsel for investigation of labor chief." *New York Times* (May 12): A1.

Johnston, D. (1999a) "$116 million punitive award against AETNA." *New York Times* (January 21): C1.

Johnston, D. (1999b) "Overtime policy earns date with law for Justice Department." *New York Times* (August 25): A1.

Johnston, D. (2002a) "Enron avoided income tax in 4 of 5 years." *New York Times* (January 17): A1.

Johnston, D. (2002b) "Affluent avoid scrutiny on taxes even as I.R.S. warns of cheating." *New York Times* (April 7): A1.

Johnston, D. (2002c) "A tax that's often ignored suddenly attracts attention." *New York Times* (June 5): C1.

Johnston, D. (2002d) "G.O.P. is moving to slow action on tax loophole." *New York Times* (June 18): C1.

Johnston, D. (2002e) "United Way official knew about abuses, memo says." *New York Times* (September 3): A12.

Johnston, D. (2002f) "Hunting tax cheats, I.R.S. vows to focus more effort on the rich." *New York Times* (September 13): A1.

Johnston, D. (2002g) "Departing chief says the I.R.S. is losing its war on tax cheats." *New York Times* (November 5): A1.

Johnston, D. (2003a) "Tax moves by Enron said to mystify the I.R.S." *New York Times* (February 13): C1.

Johnston, D. (2003b) *Perfectly legal: The covert campaign to rig our tax system to benefit the super rich—and cheat everyone else.* New York: Portfolio.

Johnston, D. (2005a) "Man of many names now called No. 1 tax cheat." *New York Times* (March 2): C1.

Johnston, D. (2005b) "Tax cheat sentenced to 6 years for defying I.R.S." *New York Times* (April 14): C3.

Johnston, D., and Lacey, M. (2001) "Aides say Clinton ignored pardon advice." *New York Times* (March 2): A19.

Jonas, W. (2005) "Marshal's Service, U.S.," pp. 955–957 in R. A. Wright and J. M. Miller (Eds.), *Encyclopedia of criminology.* New York: Routledge.

Jonassohn, K., with Bjornson, K. S. (1998) *Genocide and gross human violations in comparative perspective.* New Brunswick, NJ: Transaction.

Jones, A. (Ed.) (2004) *Genocide, war crimes, and the West: History and complicity.* London: Zed Books.

Jones, C. (2002) "Pharmacist admits diluting drugs." *USA Today* (February 27): 3a.

Jones, D. (1997) "48% of workers admit to unethical or illegal acts." *USA Today* (April 4): 1.

Jones, K. (1993) "Wal-Mart's pricing on drugstore items is held to be illegal." *New York Times* (October 13): A1.

Josephson, M. (1934) *The robber barons—The great American capitalists.* New York: Harcourt, Brace & World.

Joynson, R. B. (1994) "Fallible judgments." *Society* (March/April): 45–52.

Judson, G. (1992) "Real estate empire was built on illusion." *New York Times* (March 9): A1.

Judson, K. (1994) *Computer crime—Phreaks, spies and salami slicers.* Hillside, NJ: Enslow Publishing.

Judt, T. (2005) "The new world order." *New York Review of Books* (July 14): 14–18.

Kadlec, D. (2000) "Crimes and misdemeanors." *Time* (October 2): 52–54.

Kadlec, D. (2001a) "Wall Street's new honor code." *Time* (June 25): 73.

Kadlec, D. (2001b) "Power failure." *Time* (December 10): 68–69.

Kadlec, D. (2002a) "Who's accountable?" *Time* (January 21): 25–35.

Kadlec, D. (2002b) "BUY! I need the bonus." *Time* (May 20): 57–58.

Kadlec, D. (2005) "Down, but not out." *Time* (June 20): 52–55.

Kagan, R. A. (1989) "Editor's introduction: Understanding regulatory enforcement." *Law & Policy* 11: 89–119.

Kagan, R. A., and Scholz, J. T. (1983) "The criminology of the corporation and regulatory enforcement strategies," in K. Hawkins and J. Thomas (Eds.), *Enforcing regulation.* Boston: Kluwer-Nijhoff Publishers.

Kahn, E. J., Jr. (1973) *Fraud—The United States Postal Inspection Service and some of the fools and knaves it has known.* New York: Harper & Row.

Kahn, J. (1999a) "Phantom insurance empire yields puzzles (and $335 million gone)." *New York Times* (June 25): A1.

Kahn, J. (1999b) "Troubles at Kroll-O'Gara are attributed to in-fighting." *New York Times* (September 27): C10.

Kahn, J. (2000) "Globalization: Unspeakable, yes, but is it really evil?" *New York Times* (May 7): A4.

Kahn, J., and Finkelstein, K. G. (1999) "How bigger didn't turn out to be better in insurance scheme." *New York Times* (July 7): C3.

Kahn, P. W. (1987) "From Nuremberg to the Hague: The United States position in *Nicaragua* v. *United States* and the development of international law." *Yale Journal of International Law* 12: 1–62.

Kalette, D. (1990) "Dangerous lessons." *USA Today* (November 29): 1A.

Kane, J., and Wall, A. D. (2006) *The 2005 national public survey on white collar crime.* Fairmount, WV: National White Collar Crime Center.

Kang, D. C. (2002) *Crony capitalism: Corruption and development in South Korea and the Philippines.* Cambridge, UK: Cambridge University Press.

Kaplan, D. A. (2001) *The accidental president.* New York: William Morrow.

Kaplan, D. A., and Murr, A. (1996) "The lawyer CEOs love to hate." *Newsweek* (February 26): 63.

Kapstein, E. B. (1998/1999) "A global third way: Social justice and the world economy." *World Policy Journal* 15: 23–35.

Karmen, A. (2004) *Crime victims—An introduction to victimology* (5th ed.). Belmont, CA: Thomson Learning/Wadsworth.

Kasinof, J. (1991) "The chutzpah defense." *New York* (November 11): 38–44.

Katz, J. (1980a) "Concerted ignorance: The social psychology of cover-up," pp. 149–170 in R. K. Elliott and J. J. Willingham (Eds.), *Management fraud: Detection and deterrence.* New York: Petercelli.

Katz, J. (1980b) "The social movement against white-collar crime," pp. 161–184 in E. Bittner and S. Messinger (Eds.), *Criminology review yearbook,* Vol. 2. Beverly Hills, CA: Sage.

Katz, J. (1988) *Seductions of crime: Moral and sensual attractions of doing evil.* New York: Basic Books.

Katz, J. (1997) "Ethnography's warrants." *Sociological Methods and Research* 25: 391–423.

Katz, J., and Chambliss, W. J. (1991) "Biology and crime," pp. 244–271 in J. Sheley (Ed.), *Criminology: A contemporary handbook.* Belmont, CA: Wadsworth.

Kauper, T. E. (1990) "The justice department and the antitrust laws: Law enforcer or regulator?" *The Antitrust Bulletin* 35: 83–122.

Kauzlarich, D. (1992) "Epistemological barriers to the study of harms: A sociology of criminology." A paper presented at the Annual Meeting of the American Society of Criminology (New Orleans), November.

Kauzlarich, D. and Friedrichs, D. (2003) "Crimes of the state," pp. 109–120 in M. D. Schwartz and S. Hatty (Eds.), *Controversies in critical criminology.* Cincinnati, OH: Anderson.

Kauzlarich, D., and Kramer, R. C. (1993) "State-corporate crime in the U.S. nuclear weapons production complex." *Journal of Human Justice* 5: 4–25.

Kauzlarich, D., and Kramer, R. C. (1998) *Crimes of the American nuclear state: At home and abroad.* Boston: Northeastern University Press.

Kauzlarich, D., Kramer, R. C., and Smith, B. (1992) "Towards the study of governmental crime: Nuclear weapons, foreign intervention, and international law." *Humanity & Society* 16: 543–563.

Kauzlarich, D., Matthews, R. A., and Miller, W. J. (2001) "Toward a victimology of state crime." *Critical Criminology* 10: 173–194.

Kean, P. (1994) "Temps perdus." *Lingua Franca* (April): 49–53.

Keane, C. (1993) "The impact of financial performance on frequency of corporate crime: A latent variable test of strain theory." *Canadian Journal of Criminology* (July): 293–308.

Keller, B. (2002) "The monster in the dock." *New York Times* (February 9): A10.

Kelley, T. (1998) "Charting a course to ethical profits." *New York Times* (February 8).

Kelly, J. (2002) "The most dangerous institution." *American Heritage* (August/September): 30–38.

Kelly, M. (2005) "Ethical makeover." *Business Ethics* (Spring): 14–19.

Kempe, F. (1990) *Divorcing the dictator—America's bungled affair with Noriega.* New York: Putnam.

Kennedy, R. (1997) "Deadline fear puts many immigrants in fraudulent hands." *New York Times* (March 23): 39.

Kennedy, R. (2003) "Living here, but registered there." *New York Times* (January 3): B1.

Kerbo, H. R., and Inoue, M. (1990) "Japanese social structure and white collar crime: Recruit cosmos and beyond." *Deviant Behavior* 11: 139–154.

Kerr, P. (1991a) "Hard times prove fecund for swindlers." *New York Times* (June 7): B1.

Kerr, P. (1991b) "Vast amount of fraud discovered in worker's compensation system." *New York Times* (December 29): A1.

Kerr, P. (1992a) "Blatant fraud pushing up the cost of car insurance." *New York Times* (February 6): A1.

Kerr, P. (1992b) "Centers for head injury accused of earning millions for neglect." *New York Times* (March 16): A1.

Kerr, P. (1992c) "Insurers faulted on policy switch." *New York Times* (April 22): A1.

Kerr, P. (1993) "'Ghost riders' are target of an insurance sting." *New York Times* (August 18): A1.

Kerry, J. (1990) "Where is the S & L money?" *New York Times* (June 1): A29.

Kerwin, C. (1990) "Introduction." *Federal regulatory directory* (6th ed.). Washington, DC: Congressional Quarterly.

Kevles, D. J. (1998) *The Baltimore case: A trial of politics, science, and character.* New York: W. W. Norton.

Khanna, V. S. (2004) "Corporate crime legislation: A political economy analysis." *Washington University Law Quarterly* 82: 95–141.

Kilborn, P. T. (1986) "Big Trader to pay U.S. $100 million for insider abuses." *New York Times* (November 15): A1.

Kilgallon, C. (2003) "Charges of grand larceny, all in tiny bottles." *New York Times* (April 24): B3.

King, H., and Chambliss, W. J. (1984) *Harry King—A professional thief's journey.* New York: Wiley.

Kirchhoff, S. (2004) "More U.S. home buyers fall prey to predatory lenders." *USA Today* (December 6): 1A.

Kirkpatrick, D. D. (2002a) "As historian's fame grows, so do questions on methods." *New York Times* (January 11): A1.

Kirkpatrick, D. D. (2002b) "Writer leaves 'Newshour' in furor over book." *New York Times* (February 28): A23.

Kirkpatrick, D. D. (2005) "Senate leader explains his sale of a stock that then plummeted." *New York Times* (September 22): A29.

Klein, N. (2005) "The rise of disaster capitalism." *The Nation* (May 2): 9–11.

Kleiner, C., and Lord, M. (1999) "The cheating game." *U.S. News & World Report* (November 22): 55–66.

Kleinfeld, N. R. (1990) "Looking into accounting's heart of darkness." *New York Times* (April 15): 12E.

Kleinfeld, N. R. (1998) "Missing: One banker and $66 million." *New York Times* (May 3): 43.

Klockars, C. (1980) "The Dirty Harry problem." *Annals* 452: 33–47.

Kluger, R. (1996) *Ashes to Ashes: America's hundred-year cigarette war, the public health, and the unabashed triumph of Philip Morris.* New York: Knopf.

Knapp Commission. (1973) *Report on police corruption.* New York: George Braziller.

Knight-Ridder Newspapers. (1990a) "Insurance fraud probed." *Scranton Tribune* (June 11): 1.

Knight-Ridder Newspapers. (1990b) "Doctors costing patients billions." *Scranton Times* (June 21): 1.

Knight-Ridder Newspapers. (1995) "Health-care fraud fast-growing crime." *Scranton Times* (March 22): 1.

Knightly, P., Evans, H., Potter, E., and Wallace, M. (1979) *Suffer the children: The story of Thalidomide.* New York: Viking Press.

Koenig, T. and Rustad, M. (2001) *In defense of tort law.* New York: New York University Press.

Kohn, G. (1989) *Encyclopedia of American scandal.* New York: Facts on File.

Kolata, G. (1996a) "Sharp regional incongruity found in medical costs and treatments." *New York Times* (January 30): C3.

Kolata, G. (1996b) "Inquiry lacking due process." *New York Times* (June 25): C3.

Kolata, G. (2001) "Johns Hopkins admits fault in fatal experiment." *New York Times* (July 17): A16.

Kolata, G. (2002) "Assigning blame if fraud is found." *New York Times* (September 29): Wk 3.

Kolko, G. (1963) *The triumph of conservatism.* New York: Free Press.

Kornbluth, J. (1992) *Highly confident: The crime and punishment of Michael Milken.* New York: Morrow.

Kosanovic, M. R., and Barnes, C. E. (2005) "Employment-related crimes." *American Criminal Law Review* 42: 305–346.

Kramer, L. (1989) *Reports from the Holocaust: The story of an AIDS activist.* New York: St. Martin's Press.

Kramer, R. C. (1982) "Corporate crime: An organizational perspective," pp. 75–94 in P. Wickman and T. Dailey (Eds.), *White-collar and economic crime*. Toronto: Lexington Books.

Kramer, R. C. (1984) "Corporate criminality: The development of an idea," pp. 13–38 in E. Hochstedler (Ed.), *Corporations as criminals*. Beverly Hills, CA: Sage.

Kramer, R. C. (1985) "Pinto prosecutor interviews." *ACJS White Paper*. Omaha, NE: Academy of Criminal Justice Sciences.

Kramer, R. C. (1989) "Criminologists and the social movement against corporate crime." *Social Justice* 16: 146–164.

Kramer, R. C. (1992) "The space shuttle Challenger explosion: A case study of state-corporate crime," pp. 214–243 in K. Schlegel and D. Weisburd (Eds.), *White collar crime reconsidered*. Boston: Northeastern University Press.

Kramer, R. C., and Michalowski, R. J. (1990) "State–corporate crime." A paper presented at the Annual Meeting of the American Society of Criminology (Baltimore), November 7–12.

Kramer, R. C., and Michalowski, R. J. (1995) "The iron fist and the velvet tongue: Crime control policies in the Clinton administration." *Social Justice* 22: 87–100.

Kramer, R. C., Michalowski, R. J., and Kauzlarich, D. (2002) "The origins and development of the concept and theory of state-corporate crime." *Crime & Delinquency* 48: 263–282.

Kratcoski, P. C. (2001) "An international view of the extent, causes, and effects of government and police corruption: Summary of the proceedings from the IPFS Conference in Poland, 2001." *International Journal of Comparative and Applied Criminal Justice* 25: 215–223.

Krauss, C. (1994) "12 police officers charged in drug corruption sweep: Bratton sees more arrests." *New York Times* (April 16): A1.

Kristof, N. D. (1995) "South Korean ex-Chief arrested and apologizes in bribery case." *New York Times* (November 17): A1.

Kristof, N. D. (2005) "Day 113 of the President's silence." *New York Times* (May 3): A25.

Kristof, N. D. and Wu Dunn, S. (2000) "Two cheers for sweatshops." *New York Times Magazine* (September 24): 70–71.

Krimerman, L. I., and Perry, L. (Eds.) (1966) *Patterns of anarchy*. New York: Anchor Press.

Krugman, P. (2001a) "The big lie." *New York Times* (May 27): A9.

Krugman, P. (2001b) "Taking care of business." *New York Times* (October 28): A13.

Krugman, P. (2001c) "A defining issue." *New York Times* (December 4): A21.

Krugman, P. (2003) "Dust and deception." *New York Times* (August 26): A19.

Krugman, P. (2005) "The ugly American bank." *New York Times* (March 18): A21.

Kruttschnitt, C. (1985) "Are businesses treated differently? A comparison of the individual victim and the corporate victim in the criminal courtroom." *Sociological Inquiry* 55: 225–238.

Kuczynski, A. (2001) "For the elite, easing the way to prison." *New York Times* (December 9): 9/1.

Kuczynski, A. (2002a) "When home is a castle, and the big house, too." *New York Times* (August 17): 9/1.

Kuczynski, A. (2002b) "Companies dig deeper into executives' pasts." *New York Times* (August 19): A1.

Kuczynski, A., and Sorkin, A. R. (2002) "For well-heeled, stock tips are served with the canapés." *New York Times* (July 1): A1.

Kunen, J. S. (1994) *Reckless disregard—Corporate greed, government indifference, and the Kentucky school bus crash*. New York: Simon & Schuster.

Kunkel, K. R. (1989) *A structural approach to illegal corporate activity: The auto-producers, mail-order houses, meatpackers, and movie-makers from 1890–1950*. Ph.D. Dissertation, University of Missouri–Columbia.

Kwitny, J. (1979) *Vicious circles—The Mafia in the marketplace*. New York: Norton.

Labaton, S. (1988) "Drexel concedes guilt on trading; to pay $650 million." *New York Times* (December 22): A1.

Labaton, S. (1989a) "Does an assault on nature make Exxon a criminal?" *New York Times* (April 23).

Labaton, S. (1989b) "Five years after settlement, Agent Orange war lives on." *New York Times* (May 8): 1d.

Labaton, S. (1989c) "Uncertain future for RICO cases." *New York Times* (November 13): D2.

Labaton, S. (1989d) "Product liability's quiet revolution." *New York Times* (November 27): D2.

Labaton, S. (1990a) "Defiance didn't help defendants, it seems." *New York Times* (April 25): D8.

Labaton, S. (1990b) "Fraud uncovered in property sales in savings rescue." *New York Times* (June 21): A1.

Labaton, S. (1991) "Congress moves on price-fixing." *New York Times* (May 16): D2.

Labaton, S. (1992a) "U.S. moves to freeze assets at law firm for S & L role." *New York Times* (March 3): A1.

Labaton, S. (1992b) "Telling on clients." *New York Times* (March 5): D13.

Labaton, S. (1994a) "Plea is accepted in B.C.C.I. scandal." *New York Times* (July 9): A1.

Labaton, S. (1994b) "A Clinton friend admits mail fraud and tax evasion." *New York Times* (December 7): A1.

Labaton, S. (1995a) "GOP preparing bill to overhaul negligence law." *New York Times* (February 19): A1.

Labaton, S. (1995b) "At Justice, the taming of a whirlwind." *New York Times* (October 22): C1.

Labaton, S. (1998) "Friend of Clinton indicted a 2nd time; tax scheme cited." *New York Times* (May 1): A1.

Labaton, S. (1999a) "West Coast S & L wins $909 million from government." *New York Times* (April 10): A1.

Labaton, S. (1999b) "Justices throw out $1.5 billion asbestos settlement, citing possible conflict of interest." *New York Times* (June 24): A25.

Labaton, S. (2000a) "Top asbestos makers agree to settle 2 large lawsuits." *New York Times* (January 23): A22.

Labaton, S. (2000b) "Business awaits its regulator-in-chief." *New York Times* (October 8).

Labaton, S. (2000c) "Scholarly regulator guides antitrust law into New Age." *New York Times* (December 11): A18.

Labaton, S. (2001a) "White House picks chairman of S.E.C." *New York Times* (May 8): A1.

Labaton, S. (2001b) "The world gets tough on price fixers." *New York Times* (June 3): 3/1.

Labaton, S. (2001c) "Judge orders talks to settle Microsoft case." *New York Times* (September 29): C1.

Labaton, S. (2002a) "S.E.C. leader sees outside monitors for auditing firms." *New York Times* (January 18): A1.

Labaton, S. (2002b) "Who, exactly, got us into this?" *New York Times* (February 3): 3/1.

Labaton, S. (2002c) "Downturn and shift in population feed boom in white-collar crime." *New York Times* (June 2): A1.

Labaton, S. (2002d) "Bush doctrine: Lock 'em up." *New York Times* (June 16): Bus 1.

Labaton, S. (2002e) "S.E.C. chief seeks promotion: Chances look dim." *New York Times* (July 24): A1.

Labaton, S. (2002f) "Chief of S.E.C. is set to pursue former clients." *New York Times* (July 18): A1.

Labaton, S. (2002g) "Will reforms with few teeth be able to bite?" *New York Times* (September 22): Bus 4.

Labaton, S. (2002h) "Governmental report details a chaotic S.E.C. under Pitt." *New York Times* (December 20): A1.

Labaton, S. (2003a) "Six months later, new audit board holds first talk." *New York Times* (January 20): A1.

Labaton, S. (2003b) "10 Wall St. firms settle with U.S. in analyst inquiry." *New York Times* (April 29): A1.

Labaton, S. (2004a) "Fund misconduct is common, panel is told." *New York Times* (January 28): C1.

Labaton, S. (2004b) "De Beers agrees to guilty plea to re-enter the U.S. market." *New York Times* (July 10): C1.

Labaton, S. (2005a) "Senate approves measure to curb big class actions." *New York Times* (February 11): A1.

Labaton, S. (2005b) "Bush S.E.C. pick seen as friend of corporations." *New York Times* (June 3): A1.

Labaton, S., and Barboza, D. (1999) "U.S. outlines how makers of vitamins fixed global prices." *New York Times* (May 21): A1.

Labaton, S., and Bergman, L. (2000) "Documents indicate Ford knew of engine defects but was silent." *New York Times* (September 12): A1.

Labaton, S., and Feder, B. J. (2003) "U.S. proposal banning MCI from seeking federal work." *New York Times* (August 1): C1.

Labaton, S., and Leonhardt, D. (2002) "Whispers inside. Thunder outside." *New York Times* (June 30): C1.

Labaton, S., and Lohr, S. (2002) "U.S. and Microsoft in deal, but states hold back." *New York Times* (November 3): A1.

Labaton, S., and Oppel, R. A., Jr. (2002) "Enthusiasm ebbs for tougher laws in wake of Enron." *New York Times* (June 10): A1.

Labeff, E., Clark, R. E., Haines, V., and Dickhoff, G. M. (1990) "Situational ethics and college student cheating." *Sociological Inquiry* 60: 190–198.

Lacayo, R., and Ripley, A. (2002/2003) "Persons of the Year." *Time* (December 30/January 6): 30–34.

Lacey, M. (1999) "Tobacco industry accused of fraud in lawsuit by U.S." *New York Times* (September 23): A1.

LaFollette, M. C. (1992) *Stealing into print: Fraud, plagiarism, and misconduct in scientific publishing.* Berkeley: University of California Press.

LaFraniere, S. (2005) "Africa tackles graft, with billions in aid in play." *New York Times* (July 6): A1.

Laird, E. (2001) "Internet plagiarism: We all pay the price." *Chronicle of Higher Education* (July 13): B5.

Lamb, D. (1987) *The Africans.* New York: Vintage.

Lambert, B. (2004) "Locksmith accused of bilking L.I. hospital system for years." *New York Times* (June 19): B5.

Lambert, B. (2005a) "Audit describes 8 years of theft at L.I. schools." *New York Times* (March 3): A1.

Lambert, B. (2005b) "School's chief and roommate inflated bills in scam, officials say." *New York Times* (June 9): B6.

Lambert, B. (2005c) "L.I. school official helped son cheat on test, investigators say." *New York Times* (June 28): B1.

Landa, R. (1991) "The poor pay more." *New York Daily News* (April 15): C5.

Langenbacher, E. (2004) "The allies in World War II: The Anglo-American bombardment of German cities," pp. 116–133 in A. Jones (Ed.), *Genocide, war crimes and the West: History and complicity.* London: Zed Books.

Langewiesche, W. (1998) "The lessons of ValuJet 592." *The Atlantic Monthly* (March): 81–83.

Lanza-Kaduce, L. (1980) "Deviance among professionals: The case of unnecessary surgery." *Deviant Behavior* 1: 333–359.

Largay, J. A. (2002) "Lessons from Enron." *Accounting Horizons* 16: 153–156.

Lashinsky, A. (2001) "Bankrupt analysis." *New York Times* (November 30): A27.

Lasley, J. R. (1988) "Toward a control theory of whitecollar offending." *Journal of Quantitative Criminology* 4: 347–362.

Laub, J. H. (1983) *Criminology in the making: An oral history.* Boston: Northeastern University Press.

Laufer, W. S. (2002) "Corporate prosecution, cooperation, and the trading of favors." *Iowa Law Review* 87: 643–667.

Laughlin, P. F. (1989) "Ethics in Government Act." *American Criminal Law Review* 26: 789–805.

Lawless, J. (1988) "The white-collar defendant." *Trial* 24: 42–47.

Leaf, C. (2002) "Enough is enough." *Fortune* (March 18): 61–76.

Leape, L. L. (1989) "Unnecessary operations." *Health Services Research* 24: 351–408.

Leatherman, C. (1995) "A president under fire." *Chronicle of Higher Education* (November 3): 23–24.

Leatherman, C. (1999) "At Texas A & M, conflicting charges of misconduct tear a program apart." *Chronicle of Higher Education* (November 5): A18.

LeBillon, P. (2005) "Corruption, reconstruction and oil governance in Iraq." *Third World Quarterly* 26: 685–703.

Leckey, A. (Ed.) (2004) *The best business stories of the year.* New York: Vintage Books.

Ledbetter, J. (2003) "The boys in the bubble." *New York Times* (January 2): A17.

Lederman, E. (1985) "Criminal law, perpetrator and corporation: Rethinking a complex triangle." *Journal of Criminal Law and Criminology* 76: 285–341.

Lee, M. T., and Ermann, M. D. (1999) "Pinto 'madness' as a flawed landmark narrative: An organizational and network analysis." *Social Problems* 46: 30–47.

Leeds, J. (2005) "A money scandal that's rocking hip-hop." *New York Times* (August 7): 3/1.

Lefroy, G. (2005) *The great America job scam: Corporate tax-dodging and the myth of job creation.* San Francisco: Berrett-Koehler.

Lemert, E. (1951) *Social pathology.* New York: McGraw-Hill.

Leonard, W., and Weber, M. G. (1970) "Automakers and dealers: A study of criminogenic market forces." *Law & Society Review* 4: 407–424.

Leonhardt, D. (2000) "Credit card issuer will repay millions to some customers." *New York Times* (June 29): A1.

Leonhardt, D. (2002a) "For executives, nest egg is wrapped in a security blanket." *New York Times* (March 5): C1.

Leonhardt, D. (2002b) "Did pay incentives cut both ways?" *New York Times* (April 7).

Leonhardt, D. (2002c) "Watch it. If you cheat, they'll throw money." *New York Times* (June 9).

Lesce, T. (2000) *21st century fraud—How to protect yourself in the new millennium*. Port Townsend, WA: Companies Unlimited.

Leslie, C. (1989) "An ivy league cartel." *Newsweek* (August 27): 65.

Levi, M. (1987) *Regulating fraud—White-collar crime and the criminal process*. London: Tavistock.

Levi, M. (1991) "Public, business, and victim perceptions of white-collar crime and criminal justice." A paper presented at the International Law & Society Conference (Amsterdam), June.

Levi, M. (1992) "White-collar crime victimization," pp. 169–194 in K. Schlegel and D. Weisburd (Eds.), *White collar crime reconsidered*. Boston: Northeastern University Press.

Levi, M. (1996) "Equal before the law? Politics, power, and justice in serious fraud prosecutions." *Crime, Law & Social Change* 24: 319–340.

Levi, M. (2001) "Transnational white-collar crime: Some explorations of victimization impact," pp. 341–358 in H. N. Pontell and David Shichor (Eds.), *Contemporary Issues in Crime and Criminal Justice*. Upper Saddle River, NJ: Prentice Hall.

Levi-Faur, D. (2005) "The global diffusion of regulatory capitalism." *Annals* 598: 12–32.

Levin, N. (1973) *The Holocaust—The destruction of European Jewry, 1933–1945*. New York: Schocken Books.

Levine, D. B. (1991a) "The insider." *New York* (September 16): 38–49.

Levine, D. B. (1991b) *Inside out—An insider's account of Wall Street*. New York: Putnam.

Levine, R. (1988) "Hertz concedes it overcharged for car repairs." *New York Times* (January 26): A1.

Levy, B. (1968) "Cops in the ghetto: A problem in the police system," pp. 347–358 in L. H. Masotti and D. R. Bowen (Eds.), *Riots and rebellion: Civil violence in the urban community*. Beverly Hills, CA: Sage.

Levy, C. J. (1993) "Store founder pleads guilty in fraud case." *New York Times* (July 23): B1.

Levy, C. J. (2003a) "U.S. indicts doctor in fraud at state homes for mentally ill." *New York Times* (January 7): A1.

Levy, C. J. (2003b) "Doctor admits he did needless surgery on the mentally ill." *New York Times* (May 20): B1.

Levy, C.J. and Luo, M. (2005) "New York Medicaid fraud may reach into billions." *New York Times* (July 18): A1.

Levy, S., and Stone, B. (2005) "Grand theft identity." *Newsweek* (July 4): 39–47.

Lewis, B. C. (2004) "Prevention of computer crime amidst international anarchy." *American Criminal Law Review* 41: 1353–1372.

Lewis, C., and the Center for Public Integrity. (1998) *The buying of the Congress: How special interests have stolen your right to life, liberty, and the pursuit of happiness*. New York: Avon.

Lewis, C., and the Center for Public Integrity. (2000) *The buying of the president 2000*. New York: Avon.

Lewis, C., and the Center for Public Integrity. (2004) *The buying of the president 2004*. New York: HarperCollins.

Lewis, M. (2001a) "Jonathan Lebed's extracurricular activities." *New York Times Magazine* (February 25): 26.

Lewis, M. (2001b) "Faking it." *New York Times Magazine* (July 15): 32.

Lewis, N. A. (1992) "A lawyer beloved of the famous and troubled." *New York Times* (October 16): B18.

Lewis, N. A. (1995a) "House approves a major change in legal system." *New York Times* (March 8): A1.

Lewis, N. A. (1995b) "House passes bill that would limit suits of investors." *New York Times* (March 9): A1.

Lewis, N. A. (1995c) "House debates bill to limit damages on civil suits." *New York Times* (March 10): A1.

Lewis, N. A. (1995d) "Senate votes bill to curb lawsuits by stockholders." *New York Times* (June 29): A1.

Lewis, N. A. (2001) "Exiting job, Clinton accepts immunity deal." *New York Times* (January 20): A1.

Lewis, P. H. (1994) "Student accused of running network for pirated software." *New York Times* (April 9): A1.

Lichtblau, E. (2003) "Panel clears harsher terms in corporate crime cases." *New York Times* (January 9): C1.

Lichtblau, E. (2005) "U.S. seeks higher damages in tobacco industry suit." *New York Times* (July 19): A16.

Lichter, S. R., Lichter, L. S., and Rothman, S. (1991) *Watching America*. New York: Prentice Hall.

Lichterman, A., and Cabasso, J. (2002) "The end of disarmament and the arms races to come." *Social Justice* 29: 74–93.

Lieberman, D. (2002) "Millions of pirates are plundering satellite TV." *USA Today* (December 2): A1.

Lieberman, J. K. (1972) *How the government breaks the law.* New York: Penguin Books.

Lieberman, J. K. (1983) *The litigious society.* New York: Basic Books.

Liederbach, J. (2001) "Opportunity and crime in the medical professions," pp. 144–156 in N. Shover and J. P. Wrights (Eds.), *Crimes of privilege—Readings in white collar crime.* New York: Oxford.

Liederbach, J., Cullen, F. T., Sund, J. L., and Geis, G. (2001) "The criminalization of physician violence: Social control in transformation?" *Justice Quarterly* 18: 141–170.

Lilly, J. R., and Ball, R. A. (1982) "A critical analysis of the changing concept of criminal responsibility." *Criminology* 20: 169–184.

Lilly, J. R., Cullen, F. T., and Ball, R. A. (1989) *Criminological theory: Context and consequences.* Newbury Park, CA: Sage.

Lim, P. J. (2005) "Gauging that other company asset: Its reputation." *New York Times* (April 10): B6.

Lindgren, S-A (2002) "Economic crime in Sweden: An essentially contested issue." *Criminal Justice* 2: 363–383.

Lindsey, R. B. (1979) "Swindlers in Arizona said to make millions." *New York Times* (May 21): A1.

Ling, E. (1991) *Fraud and social change: Whistle-blowing and white-collar crime in a major corporation.* Ph.D. Dissertation, Ohio State University.

Liptak, A. (2002a) "Company in trouble? Just let him loose." *New York Times* (June 9): C1.

Liptak, A. (2002b) "Debate grows on jury's role in injury cases." *New York Times* (August 26): A1.

Lipton, E., and Nixon, R. (2005) "Many contracts for storm work raise questions." *New York Times* (September 26): A1.

Liu, M., Nordland, R., and Thomas, E. (2003) "The Saddam file." *Newsweek* (April 28): 21–31.

Lizza, R. (2002) "Keep away." *The New Republic* (January 28): 17–18.

Lofquist, W. S. (1993a) "Organizational probation and the U.S. Sentencing Commission." *Annals of the American Academy of Political & Social Science* 525: 157–169.

Lofquist, W. S. (1993b) "Legislating organizational probation: State capacity, business power, and corporate crime control." *Law & Society Review* 27: 741–784.

Logan, G. J. (1988) "Profile: Better business bureau." *Consumer's Research* (September): 29–31.

Logue, J. (1988) "Conclusion," pp. 254–265 in A. Markovits and M. Silverstein (Eds.), *The politics of scandal: Power and process in liberal democracies.* New York: Holmes & Meier.

Lohr, S. (1991) "At the end of a twisted trail, piggy bank for a favored few." *New York Times* (August 12): A1.

Lohr, S. (1998) "Gates, on Capital Hill, presents case for an unfettered Microsoft." *New York Times* (March 4): A1.

Lohr, S. (2002a) "New economy." *New York Times* (May 6): C24.

Lohr, S. (2002b) "For Microsoft, ruling will sting but not really hurt." *New York Times* (November 2): C1.

Lohr, S. (2003) "Whistle-blower changes sides to aid Hewlett, once a target." *New York Times* (January 13): C1.

Lohr, S. (2004) "Ex-Executives at Symbol are indicted." *New York Times* (June 4): C1.

Long, M. P. (2005) "Secret Service, U.S.," pp. 1473–1475 in R. A. Wright and J. M. Miller (Eds.), *Encyclopedia of Criminology.* New York: Routledge.

Long, S. B. (1981) "Social control in the civil law: The case of income tax enforcement," pp. 181–214 in H. Laurence Ross (Ed.), *Law and deviance.* Beverly Hills, CA: Sage.

Long, S. B., and Swingen, J. A (1991) "Taxpayer compliance: Setting new agendas for research." *Law & Society Review* 25: 637–689.

Longmire, D. R. (1982) "The new criminologist's access to research support: Open arenas or closed doors?" pp. 19–34 in H. E. Pepinsky (Ed.), *Rethinking criminology.* Beverly Hills, CA: Sage.

Lounsberry, E. (1991) "Federal prison at Allenwood becomes known as Club Fed." *The Sunday Scranton Times,* (September 15): 16.

Lowell, A. D., and Arnold, K. C. (2003) "Corporate crime after 2000: A new law enforcement challenge or déjà vu." *American Criminal Law Review* 40: 219–240.

Lowenstein, D. H. (2004) "When is a campaign contribution a bribe?" pp. 127–172 in W. C. Heffernan and J. Kleinig (Eds.), *Private and Public Corruption.* Lanham, MD: Rowman & Littleheld.

Lowenstein, R. (2002) "Heads I win, tails I win." *New York Times Magazine* (June 9) 102–104.

Lowenstein, R. (2004) "The company they kept." *New York Times Magazine* (February 1): 29–32, 62.

Luban, D. (1987) "The legacies of Nuremberg." *Social Research* 54: 779–830.

Luchansky, B., and Gerber, J. (1993) "Constructing state autonomy: The Federal Trade Commission and the Celler-Kefauver Act." *Sociological Perspectives* 36: 217–240.

Lueck, T. J. (1993) "20 New York schools to lose U.S. grants." *New York Times* (October 21): B3.

Lueck, T. J. (2004) "Nader calls for impeachment of Bush over the war in Iraq." *New York Times* (May 25): A21.

Lundberg, F. (1968) *The rich and the super-rich: A study in the power of money today.* New York: Lyle Stuart.

Luneburg, W. V. (1990) "State and federal administrative law." *Administrative Law Review* 42: 113–120.

Luo, M. (2005) "Hospital agrees to repay state $76.5 million." *New York Times* (May 18): B1.

Lupsha, P. A. (1986) "Organized crime in the United States," pp. 32–57 in R. J. Kelly (Ed.), *Organized crime—A global perspective.* Totowa, NJ: Rowman & Littlefield.

Lybarger, J., Klenowski, P., and Kane, J. (2001) "Identifying trends in white collar crime: A 20-year analysis of UCR data." A paper presented at the Annual Meeting of the Academy of Criminal Justice Sciences (Washington, DC), April.

Lynch, G., and Missal, M. J. (1987) "Recent civil and criminal prosecutions of insider trading violations," pp. 20–64 in H. L. Pitt (Ed.), *Insider trading—Counseling and compliance.* Clifton, NJ: Prentice Hall Law & Business.

Lynch, M. J., McGurrin, D., and Fenwick, M. (2004) "Disappearing act: The representation of corporate crime research in criminological literature." *Journal of Criminal Justice* 32: 389–398.

Lynch, M. J., Michalowski, R., and Groves, W. B. (2000) *The new primer in radical criminology: Critical perspectives on crime, power, and identity* (3rd ed.). Monsey, NY: Criminal Justice Press.

Lynch, M. J., Nalla, M. K., and Miller, K. W. (1989) "Cross-cultural perceptions of deviance: The case of Bhopal." *Journal of Research on Crime and Delinquency* 26: 7–35.

Lynch, M. J., Stretesky, P., and Burns, R. (2004) "Slippery business: Race, class and legal determinants of penalties against petroleum refineries." *Journal of Black Studies* 34: 421–440.

Lynch, M., Stretesky, P., and Hammond, P. (2000) "Media coverage of chemical crimes in Hillsborough County, Florida, 1987–1997." *British Journal of Criminology* 40: 112–116.

Lynch, M. J., Stretesky, P. B., and McGurrin, D. (2002) "Toxic crimes and environmental justice: Examining the hidden dangers of hazardous wastes," pp. 109–136 in G. W. Potter (Ed.), *Controversies in white-collar crime.* Cincinnati, OH: Anderson.

Lyne, B. (1993) "Giving the bad guys a shot at redemption." *New York Times* (March 28): F29.

Lynxwiler, J., Shover, N., and Clelland, D. J. (1983) "The organization and impact of inspector discretion in a regulatory bureaucracy." *Social Problems* 30: 435–436.

Lyons, R. D. (1982) "Time-sharing resorts under inquiry." *New York Times* (May 30): 37.

Maas, P. (1973) *Serpico.* New York: Bantam Books.

MacCoun, R. (1996) "Differential treatment of corporate defendants by juries: An examination of the 'deep pockets' hypothesis." *Law & Society Review* 30: 121–161.

Macey, J. (1991) "Agency theory and the criminal liability of organizations." *Boston University Law Review* 71: 315–340.

Machan, T. R., and Johnson, M. B. (Eds.) (1983) *Rights and regulation: Ethical, political and economic issues.* Cambridge, MA: Ballinger.

Mackay, R. E. (1996) "Victimology and rights theory." *International Review of Victimology* 4: 195–219.

MacNamara, D. E. J. (1991) "The victimization of whistle-blowers in the public and private sectors," pp. 121–133 in R. J. Kelly and D. E. J. MacNamara (Eds.), *Perspectives on deviance: Domination, degradation and denigration.* Cincinnati, OH: Anderson.

Madsen, A. (1984) *60 Minutes.* New York: Dodd, Mead.

Madsen, P., and Shafritz, J. M. (Eds.) (1990) *Essentials of business ethics.* New York: Penguin Books.

Magnuson, E. (1988a) "It's lovely at the top." *Time* (April 11) 25–26.

Magnuson, E. (1988b) "The Pentagon up for sale." *Time* (June 27) 16–18.

Magnuson, R. J. (1992) *The white-collar crime explosion: How to protect yourself and your company from prosecution.* New York: McGraw-Hill.

Makin, J. (1986) "Business ethics." *Public Opinion* (November/December): 4–6, 57.

Makinson, L. (1990) *Open secrets—The dollar power of PACS in Congress.* Washington, DC: Congressional Quarterly.

Makkai, T., and Braithwaite, J. (1993) "Praise, pride and corporate compliance." *International Journal of the Sociology of Law* 21: 73–91.

Mallaby, S. (2004) *The world's banker.* New York: Penguin Press.

Manchester, W. (1968) *The arms of Krupp.* Boston: Little, Brown.

Mandel, E. (1983) "Joint-stock company," pp. 241–244 in T. Bottomore (Ed.), *A dictionary of Marxist thought.* Cambridge, MA: Harvard University Press.

Mandelbaum, M. (1987) *Purpose and necessity in social theory.* Baltimore, MD: The Johns Hopkins University Press.

Manes, S., and Andrews, P. (1994) *Gates.* New York: Touchstone Books.

Mangan, K. S. (2002) "The ethics of business schools." *The Chronicle of Higher Education* (September 20) A14–16.

Manheim, J. (2000) *The death of a thousand cuts: Corporate campaigns and the attack on the corporation.* New York: Lawrence Erlbaum.

Mann, D., and Sutton, M. (1998) "Netcrime—More changes in the organization of thieving." *British Journal of Criminology* 38: 201–229.

Mann, K. (1985) *Defending white collar crime.* New Haven, CT: Yale University Press.

Mann, K. (1992a) "White collar crime and the poverty of the criminal law." *Law & Social Inquiry* 17: 561–572.

Mann, K. (1992b) "Punitive civil sanctions: The middle ground between criminal and civil law." *Yale Law Review* 101: 1795–1874.

Mann, M. (2005) *The dark side of democracy: Explaining ethnic cleansing.* Cambridge, UK: Cambridge University Press.

Mannino, E. F. (1990) "Less corn and more hell: The application of RICO to financial institutions." *Villanova Law Review* 35: 883–904.

Manning, G. A. (2005) *Financial investigation and forensic accounting* (2nd ed.). Boca Raton, FL: CRC Press.

Mansnerus, L. (1989) "As racketeering law expands, so does pressure to rein it in." *New York Times* (March 12): E4.

Manson, D. A. (1986) "Tracking offenders: White-collar crime." *Special reports.* Washington, DC: Bureau of Justice Statistics.

Marcus, B. (2004) "Self-control in the general theory of crime: Theoretical implications of a measurement problem." *Theoretical Criminology* 8: 35–55.

Maren, M. (1996) "Does not compute." *New York Magazine* (December 9): 49.

Margolick, D. (1992) "Till debt do us part." *New York Times Magazine* (December 16): 46.

Marklein, M. B. (2003) "Is there any truth to today's resume?" *USA Today* (February 4): D1.

Markoff, J. (1994) "Microsoft's barely limited future." *New York Times* (July 18): C1.

Markoff, J. (2002) "Verisign's marketing is subject of F.T.C. investigation." *New York Times* (August 7): C2.

Markoff, J. (2005) "Microsoft to pay I.B.M. $775 million in settlement." *New York Times* (July 2): C1.

Markovits, A., and Silverstein, M. (Eds.) (1988) *The politics of scandal: Power and process in liberal democracies.* New York: Holmes & Meier.

Markovskaya, A., Pridemore, W. A., and Nakajima, C. (2003) "Law without teeth: An overview of the problems associated with corruption in Ukraine." *Crime, Law & Social Change* 39: 193–213.

Marks, P. (1995) "Dealer's plea in G.M. fraud may be bargain of his life." *New York Times* (January 20): A10.

Markusen, E. (1992) "Genocide and modern war," pp. 117–148 in M. Dobkowski and I. Wallimann (Eds.), *Genocide in our time.* Ann Arbor, MI: Pierian Press.

Mars, G. (1982) *Cheats at work—An anthology of workplace crime.* London: Unwin.

Mars, G. (Ed.) (2001a) *Occupational crime.* Aldershot, UK: Ashgate.

Mars, G. (Ed.) (2001b) *Workplace sabotage.* Aldershot, UK: Ashgate.

Martin, B. (1995) "Eliminating state crime by abolishing the state," pp. 389–417 in J. I. Ross (Ed.), *Controlling state crime.* New York: Garland.

Martin, M. W. (1999) "Explaining wrong-doing in professions." *Journal of Social Philosophy* 30: 236–250.

Martz, L. (1987) "New doubts about Meese and the Contra inquiry." *Newsweek* (April 20) 29–30.

Martz, L. (1990a) "Bonfire of the S & Ls." *Newsweek* (May 21): 20–25.

Martz, L. (1990b) "S & Ls: Blaming the media." *Newsweek* (June 25): 42.

Marx, G. (1987) "The interweaving of public and private police in undercover work," pp. 172–193 in C. D. Shearing and P. C. Stenning (Eds.), *Private policing*. Newbury Park, CA: Sage.

Marx, G. (1988) *Undercover—Police surveillance in America*. Berkeley: University of California Press.

Marx, G. (1991) "When the guards guard themselves: Undercover tactics turned inward." *Policing and Society* 1: 1–22.

Marx, K. (1867) *Capital*, Vol. 1. Hamburg: Otto Meissner.

Masland, T., and Bartholet, J. (2000) "The lost billions." *Newsweek* (March 13): 38, 40.

Mason, K. A., and Benson, M. L. (1996) "The effects of social support on fraud victims' reporting behavior: A research note." *Justice Quarterly* 13: 511–524.

Mason, L., and Mason, R. (1992) "A moral appeal for taxpayer compliance: The case of a mass media campaign." *Law & Policy* 14: 381–399.

Massing, M. (2002) "Losing the peace?" *The Nation* (May 13): 11–18.

Matthews, R. A. (2003) "Marxist criminology," pp. 1–13 in M. D. Schwartz and S. Hatty (Eds.), *Controversies in Critical Criminology*. Cincinnati, OH: Anderson.

Matthews, R. A. (2006) "Ordinary business: State corporate crime—Nazi Germany," in R. Michalowski and R. Kramer (Eds.), *State-corporate crime: Wrongdoing at the intersection of business and government*. New Brunswick, NJ: Rutgers University Press.

Matthews, R. A., and Kauzlarich, D. (2000) "The crash of ValuJet flight 592: A case study in state-corporate crime." *Sociological Focus* 3: 281–298.

Mayer, J. (2002) "The accountant's war." *The New Yorker* (April 22–29): 64–71.

Mayer, J. (2004) "Contract sport: What did the Vice President do for Halliburton?" *The New Yorker* (February 16 & 23): 80–91.

Mazlish, B. (1999) "A tour of globalization." *Indiana Journal of Global Legal Education* 7: 5–16.

McBarnet, D. (1992) "Legitimate rackets: Tax evasion, tax avoidance, and the boundaries of legality." *The Journal of Human Justice* 3: 56–74.

McBarnet, D. (2004) *Crime, compliance, and control*. Aldershot, UK: Ashgate.

McCabe, D. L. (1992) "The influence of situational ethics on cheating among college students." *Sociological Inquiry* 62: 365–374.

McCabe, D. L., Trevino, L. K., and Butterfield, K. D. (1999) "Academic integrity in honor code and non-honor code environments." *Journal of Higher Education*, 70.

McCaghy, C. H., and Cernkovich, S. A. (1987) *Crime in American society* (2nd ed.). New York: Macmillan.

McCarroll, T. (1992) "Who's counting?" *Time* (April 13): 48–50.

McClintick, D. (1982) *Indecent exposure*. New York: Dell.

McCormick, J. (1999) "The sorry side of Sears." *Newsweek* (February 22): 35–39.

McDermott, M. F. (1982) "Occupational disqualification of corporate executives: An innovative condition of probation." *Journal of Criminal Law and Criminology* 73: 604–641.

McEntegart, P. (2004) "One angry man." *Time* (April 12): 47–48.

McEwen, T. (1990a) "The growing threat of computer crime." *Detective* (Summer): 6–11.

McEwen, T. (1990b) *Dedicated computer crime units*. Washington, DC: National Institute of Justice.

McFadden, R. D. (1987) "Judge sent poisoned candy: Man he sentenced arrested." *New York Times* (February 21): A1.

McFadden, R. D. (2004) "Rowland admits felony in office." *New York Times* (December 24): A1.

McFarland, A. S. (1984) *Common cause: Lobbying in the public interest*. Chatham, NJ: Chatham House.

McGeehan, P. (2002a) "Merrill Lynch under attack as giving out tainted advice." *New York Times* (April 9): C1.

McGeehan, P. (2002b) "S.E.C. begins investigation into analysts." *New York Times* (April 24): C1.

McGeehan, P. (2002c) "Merrill chief is apologetic over analysts; one dismissed." *New York Times* (April 27): C1.

McGeehan, P. (2002d) "The crux of reform: Autonomous stock rating." *New York Times* (October 7): C1.

McGeehan, P. (2002e) "States talk tough, Wall Street sweats." *New York Times* (October 20).

McGeehan, P. (2003) "For this chief, a loss would be a gain." *New York Times* (December 3): C1.

McGeehan, P. (2004) "Mountains of interest add to pain of credit cards." *New York Times* (November 11): A1.

McGinn, D. (2002) "Are you a tax chump or a tax cheat?" *Newsweek* (April 15): 38–39.

McGinn, D. (2000) "Waiting for the gavel to fall." *Newsweek* (March 6): 48.

McGovern, F. E. (Ed.) (1990) "Claims resolution facilities and the mass settlement of mass torts." *Law and Contemporary Problems* 53 (Autumn) 1–205.

McGraw, K. M., and Scholz, J. T. (1991) "Appeals to civic virtue versus attention to self-interest: Effects on tax compliance." *Law & Society Review* 25: 471–478.

McGuire, S. (2001) "Software pirates, beware." *Newsweek* (October 29): 68.

McLean, B. (2001) "Why Enron went bust." *Fortune* (December 24): 59–68.

McMillen, T. (1992) *Out of bounds*. New York: Simon & Schuster.

McMullan, J. L. (1982) "Criminal organization in sixteenth and seventeenth century London." *Social Problems* 29: 311–323.

McNamee, M., and Borrus, A. (2002) "The reluctant reformer." *Business Week* (March 25): 72–81.

McNish, J., and Stewart, S. (2005) *Wrong way: The fall of Conrad Black*. Woodstock, NY: Overlook Press.

McShane, M. D., and Williams, F. P. III (1992) "Radical victimology: A critique of the concept of victim in traditional victimology." *Crime & Delinquency* 38: 258–271.

Mead, G. H. (1934; 1964) *Mind, self and society: From the standpoint of a social behaviorist*. Chicago: University of Chicago Press.

Meidinger, E. (1987) "Regulatory culture: A theoretical outline." *Law & Policy* 9: 349–386.

Meier, B. (1992a) "Sharing of credit card numbers by merchants brings new fears of fraud." *New York Times* (March 28): 50.

Meier, B. (1992b) "Bronco accidents pose new questions for Ford on safety." *New York Times* (June 15): A1.

Meier, B. (1992c) "Crazy Eddie's insane odyssey." *New York Times* (July 19).

Meier, B. (1992d) "Bill to curb consumer lawsuits falls short." *New York Times* (September 13): E3.

Meier, B. (1992e) "Data show G.M. knew for years of risk in pickup trucks' design." *New York Times* (November 17): A1.

Meier, B. (1993) "Courtroom drama pits G.M. against a former engineer." *New York Times* (January 19): D1.

Meier, B. (1995) "The lion king of the lien." *New York Times* (June 29): D1.

Meier, B. (1997a) "Jury says ABC owes damages of $5.5 million." *New York Times* (January 23): A1.

Meier, B. (1997b) "Class action consciousness." *New York Times* (February 18): C1.

Meier, B. (1997c) "In fine print, customers lose ability to sue." *New York Times* (March 10): A1.

Meier, B. (1998a) "Files of R. J. Reynolds Tobacco show efforts on youth." *New York Times* (January 15): A12.

Meier, B. (1998b) "Data on tobacco show a strategy aimed at blacks." *New York Times* (February 6): A1.

Meier, B. (1999) "Metropolitan Live in accord for settlement of fraud suits." *New York Times* (August 19): A1.

Meier, B. (2004) "2 guilty in fraud at cable giant." *New York Times* (July 9): A1.

Meier, B. (2005) "Heart device sold despite flaw, data shows." *New York Times* (June 2): C1.

Meier, B., and Oppel, R. A., Jr. (1999) "State's big suits against industry brings battle on contingency fees." *New York Times* (October 15): A1.

Meier, R. F. (2001) "Geis, Sutherland, and white-collar crime," pp. 1–16 in H. N. Pontell and D. Shichor (Eds.), *Contemporary issues in crime and criminal justice*. Upper Saddle River, NJ: Prentice Hall.

Meier, R. F., and Short, J. F., Jr. (1982) "The consequences of white-collar crime," pp. 23–50 in H. Edelhertz and T. D. Overcast (Eds.), *White-collar crime: An agenda for research*. Lexington, MA: Lexington Books.

Meier, R. F., and Short, J. F., Jr. (1985) "Crime as hazard: Perceptions of risk and seriousness." *Criminology* 23: 389–399.

Meller, P. (2001) "Vitamin producers fined $752 million." *New York Times* (November 22): W1.

Meller, P. (2002) "Europe fines Nintendo $147 million for price fixing." *New York Times* (October 31): D1.

Mendeloff, J., and Gray, W. B. (2005) "Inside the black box: How do OSHA inspections lead to reduction in workplace injuries?" *Law & Policy* 27: 219–237.

Mendelsohn, R. S. (1979) *Confessions of a medical heretic.* New York: Warner Books.

Mendelson, M. A. (1974) *Tender loving greed.* New York: Random House.

Mensch, E., and Freeman, A. (1990) "Efficiency and image: Advertising as an antitrust issue." *Duke Law Journal* 20: 321–373.

Mercer, J. (1995) "Too good to be true." *Chronicle of Higher Education* (May 26): A33.

Meredith, R. (1997) "VW agrees to pay G.M. $100 million in espionage case." *New York Times* (January 10): A1.

Merton, R. K. (1957) "Social theory and anomie." *American Sociological Review* 3: 672–682.

Messerschmidt, J. (1993) *Masculinities and crime: Reconceptualization of theory.* Lanham, MD: Rowman & Littlefield.

Metzger, M., Dalton, D. R., and Hill, J. W. (1993) "The organization of ethics and the ethics of organizations: The case for expanded organizational ethics audits." *Business Ethics Quarterly* 3: 27–43.

Metzger, M. B., Mallor, J. P., Barnes, T. B., and Phillips, M. J. (1986) *Business law and the regulatory environment: Concepts and cases* (6th ed.). Homewood, IL: Irwin.

Metzger, M. B., and Schwenk, C. R. (1990) "Decision-making models, devil's advocacy, and the control of corporate crime." *American Business Law Journal* 28: 323–377.

Meyer, M. (1998) "Suharto family values." *Newsweek* (January 26): 48.

Michaels, J. W., and Miethe, T. D. (1989) "Applying theories of deviance to academic cheating." *Social Science Quarterly* 70: 870–885.

Michalowski, R. J. (1985) *Order, law and crime.* New York: Random House.

Michalowski, R. J., and Kramer, R. C. (1987) "The space between the laws: The problem of corporate crime in a transnational context." *Social Problems* 34: 34–53.

Michalowski, R. J. and Kramer, R. C. (Eds.) (2006) *State-corporate crime: Wrong-doing at the intersection of business and government.* New Brunswick, NJ: Rutgers University Press.

Michalowski, R., and Pfuhl, E. H. (1991) "Technology, property and law: The case of computer crime." *Crime, Law & Social Change* 15: 255–275.

Miethe, T. D. (1984) "Types of consensus in public evaluations of crime: An illustration of strategies for measuring consensus." *Journal of Criminal Law and Criminology* 75: 459–473.

Miethe, T. D. (1999) *Whistleblowing at work—Tough choices in exposing fraud, waste, and abuse on the job.* Boulder, CO: Westview Press.

Miethe, T. D., and Rothschild, J. (1994) "Whistle-blowing and the control of organizational misconduct." *Sociological Inquiry* 64: 322–347.

Milgram, S. (1963) "Behavioral study of obedience." *Journal of Abnormal and Social Psychology* 67: 371–378.

Miller, A. G. (1986) *The obedience experiments: A case study of controversy in social science.* Westport, CT: Praeger.

Miller, J., Engelberg, S., and Broad, W. (2001) *Germs—Biological weapons and America's secret war.* New York: Simon & Schuster.

Miller, K. S., and Gaines, L. K. (1997) "Scamming: An ethnographic study of workplace crime in the retail food industry." *The Justice Professional* 10: 3–17.

Miller, N. (1992) *Stealing from America: A history of corruption from Jamestown to Reagan.* New York: Paragon House.

Millon, D. (1990) "Theories of the corporation." *Duke Law Journal* 20: 201–262.

Mills, C. W. (1940) "Situated actions and vocabularies of motives." *American Sociological Review* 5: 904–913.

Mills, C. W. (1956) *The power elite.* New York: Oxford University Press.

Mindell, E. (1987) *Unsafe at any meal.* New York: Warner Books.

Minkow, B. (1997) *Buyer beware—A home encyclopedia.* Los Angeles: Penguin.

Minkow, B. (2005) *Cleaning up: One man's redemptive journal through the seductive world of corporate crime.* Nashville, TN: NelsonCurrent.

Minow, M. (1998) *Between vengeance and forgiveness—Facing history after genocide and mass violence.* Boston: Beacon Press.

Mintz, B. (1985) *The power structure of American business.* Chicago: University of Chicago Press.

Mintz, M., and Cohen, J. S. (1971) *America, Inc.* New York: Dell.

Mintz, M., and Cohen, J. S. (1976) *Power, Inc.* New York: Viking Press.

Misztal, B. A. (1996) *Trust in modern societies: The search for the bases of social order.* Cambridge, MA: Polity Press.

Mitchell, L. E. (2001) *Corporate irresponsibility.* New Haven, CT: Yale University Press.

Mitchell, L. E. (2002) "American corporations: The new sovereigns." *Chronicle of Higher Education* (January 18): B13–14.

Mitchell, R. (2002) "White-collar criminal? Pack lightly for prison." *New York Times* (August 11): Bus 4.

Moffatt, M. (1989) *Coming of age in New Jersey—College and American culture.* New Brunswick, NJ: Rutgers University Press.

Mogul, F. (1997) "5 indicted in $2.6 million embezzling case at a Sioux college." *New York Times* (February 26): D23.

Mohawk, J. C. (2000) *Utopian legacies: A history of conquest and oppression in the Western world.* Santa Fe, NM: Clear Light Publishers.

Mohr, C. (1983) "Spare parts for arms can cost an arm and a leg." *New York Times* (November 20): E7.

Mokhiber, R. (1988) *Corporate crime and violence—Big business power and the abuse of the public trust.* San Francisco: Sierra Club Books.

Mokhiber, R., and Weissman, R. (1999) *Corporate predators.* Monroe, ME: Common Courage Press.

Mollenhoff, C. R. (1988) "Essential institutions to combat fraud and corruption in government operations." *Corruption and Reform* 3: 125–134.

Monaghan, P. (1991) "Sociologists' close-up look at bigtime basketball depicts a world in which players' academic goals are subverted." *Chronicle of Higher Education* (February 6): A31.

Monaghan, P. (2001) "Professors settle suit with University of Denver over retracted article." *Chronicle of Higher Education* (September 7): A25.

Monastersky, R. (2002) "Atomic lies." *Chronicle of Higher Education* (August 16): A16–21.

Monastersky, R. (2005) "Scientific misbehavior is rampant, study of 3,000 researchers finds." *Chronicle of Higher Education* (June 17): A11.

Monse, M. D. (1992) "Ethical issues in representing thrifts." *Buffalo Law Review* 40: 1–64.

Moohr, G. S. (2003) "An Enron lesson: The modest role of criminal law in preventing corporate crime." *Florida Law Review* 55: 937–975.

Mooney, C. J. (1992) "Critics question higher education's commitment and effectiveness in dealing with plagiarism." *Chronicle of Higher Education* (February 12): A13, A18.

Moore, C. A. (1987) "Taming the giant corporation? Some cautionary remarks on the deterrability of corporate crime." *Crime & Delinquency* 33: 379–402.

Moore, G. A., Magaldi, A. M., and Gray, J. A. (1987) *The legal environment of business: A contextual approach.* Cincinnati, OH: Southwestern Publishing.

Moore, M. (2005) http://www.michaelmoore.com.

Moore, W. E. (1970) *The professions: Roles and rules.* New York: Russell Sage.

Morgan, P. W., and Reynolds, G. H. (1997) *The appearance of impropriety: How the ethics wars have undermined American government, business, and society.* New York: The Free Press.

Morgenson, G. (1999) "House cuts could force S.E.C. lay-offs." *New York Times* (August 3): C1.

Morgenson, G. (2001a) "Wall Street firms endorse ethics standards for analysts." *New York Times* (June 13): C1.

Morgenson, G. (2001b) "Why investors may find arbitrators on their side." *New York Times* (August 19).

Morgenson, G. (2001c) "Hands out, even in a time of crisis." *New York Times* (November 4).

Morgenson, G. (2002a) "More clouds over Citigroup on its dealings with Ebbers." *New York Times* (January 3): 3/1.

Morgenson, G. (2002b) "The enforcers of Wall Street? Then again, maybe not." *New York Times* (June 20): C1.

Morgenson, G. (2002c) "Investors want cops on the street." *New York Times* (May 26): C1.

Morgenson, G. (2002d) "A Wall Street push to water down securities law." *New York Times* (June 18): A1.

Morgenson, G. (2002e) "Trust shattered: Wall Street can't afford coincidences." *New York Times* (July 28).

Morgenson, G. (2003) "A year's debacles, from comic to epic." *New York Times* (December 28): 3/1.

Morgenson, G. (2004a) "The C.E.O.s mad, mad world." *New York Times* (March 7): 3/1.

Morgenson, G. (2004b) "Before Enron, there was Cendant." *New York Times* (May 9): 3/1.

Morgenson, G. (2004c) "A coming nightmare of homeownership?" *New York Times* (October 3): 3/1.

Morgenson, G. (2005a) "If directors snooze, now they may lose." *New York Times* (January 9): 3/1.

Morgenson, G. (2005b) "Chief quits post at giant insurer amid questions." *New York Times* (March 15): A1.

Morgenson, G. (2005c) "Morgan accord over World-Com costs $2 billion." *New York Times* (March 17): A1.

Morgenson, G. (2005d) "Who's preying on your grandparents?" *New York Times* (May 15): 3/1.

Morgenson, G. (2005e) "What are mergers good for?" *New York Times Magazine* (June 5): 56–62.

Morgenson, G. (2005f) "What's good for business if for no one else." *New York Times* (June 5): Bus 9.

Morgenson, G. (2005g) "An 'oops' at the bank of 'wow.'" *New York Times* (August 1): 3/1.

Morgenson, G. (2005h) "S.E.C. looks at company's retaliation on analysts." *New York Times* (September 23): C1.

Morgenson, G., and McGeehan, P. (2002) "Wall Street firms are ready to pay $1 billion in fines." *New York Times* (December 20): A1.

Morgenson, G., and Walsh, M. W. (2004) "How consultants can retire on your pension." *New York Times* (December 12): C1.

Morgenthau, T. (1989) "The S & L scandal's biggest blowout." *Newsweek* (November 6): 35–36.

Moriarty, J. (2005) "Do CEOs get paid too much?" *Business Ethics Quarterly* 15: 257–281.

Morris, M. (2001) "The United States and the International Criminal Court." *Law and Contemporary Problems* 64: 1–202.

Morvillo, R. G., Bohrer, B. A., and Balter, B. L. (2005) "Motion denied: Systematic impediments to white collar criminal defendant's trial preparations." *American Criminal Law Review* 42: 157–177.

Moss, M. (2004) "Erase debt now. Close your home later." *New York Times* (October 10): C1.

Moss, M. and Jacobs, A. (2004) "Blue skies and green yards, all lost to red ink." *New York Times* (April 11): A1.

Moyer, I. (2001) *Criminological theory—Traditional and nontraditional voices and themes.* Thousand Oaks, CA: Sage.

Mrkvicka, E. F. (1989) *The bank book.* New York: Harper & Row.

Mrozek, T. (1999) "Charles Keating pleads guilty to federal fraud charges; four criminal convictions resolve 10-year old case." *Press Release* (Central District of California April 6).

Mueller, G. O. W., and Adler, F. (1985) *Outlaws of the ocean.* New York: Hearst Maritime Books.

Mullins, C. W., Kauzlarich, D. and Rothe, D. (2004) "The International Criminal Court and the control of state crime: Prospects and problems." *Critical Criminology* 12: 285–308.

Mundy, A. (2001) *Dispensing with the truth: The victims, the drug companies, and the dramatic story behind the battle over fen-phen.* New York: St. Martin's Press.

Mundy, L. (1992) "The fixers—How they may have tampered with your pay." *Lingua Franca* (November/December): 1: 28–33.

Mundy, L. (1993) "The dirty dozen—Academia's skankiest funders." *Lingua Franca* (March/April): 1: 24–31.

Murphy, D. E. (2002) "The federal sentencing guidelines for organizations: A decade of promoting compliance and ethics." *Iowa Law Review* 87: 697–719.

Murphy, K. (2004) "A sunless year in a tiny cell." *New York Times* (June 20): Bus 5.

Murr, A. (1997) "Living high on the hog." *Newsweek* (October 27): 48.

Mydans, S. (2000) "Suharto is formally charged with corruption." *New York Times* (August 4).

Myers, G. (1907) *History of the great American fortunes.* New York: The Modern Library.

Nader, R. (1965) *Unsafe at any speed: The designed-in dangers of the American automobile.* New York: Grossman.

Nader, R. (2004) *The good fight.* New York: Regan Books.

Nader, R. (2005) "How to curb corporate power." *The Nation* (October 10): 20–24.

Nader, R., and Mayer, C. J. (1988) "Corporations are not persons." *New York Times* (April 4): 31.

Nader, R., and Smith, W. J. (1996) *No contest: Corporate lawyers and the perversion of justice in America.* New York: Random House.

Nagel, I., and Hagan, J. (1982) "The sentencing of white-collar criminals in federal courts: A sociolegal exploration of disparity." *Michigan Law Review* 80: 1427–1465.

Nalla, M., and Newman, G. (1990) *A primer in private security.* New York: Harrow & Heston.

Nasar, S. (1994) "Fallen bond trader sees himself as an outsider and a scapegoat." *New York Times* (June 5): A1.

Nash, D. T. (1987) *Medical mayhem.* New York: Walker.

Nash, N. C. (1986) "Suddenly, a sleepy SEC is wide awake." *New York Times* (November 23): 5E.

Nash, N. C. (1989a) "Savings regulators see fraud by head of failed institution." *New York Times* (November 1): A1.

Nash, N. C. (1989b) "Savings executive won't testify and blames regulators for woes." *New York Times* (November 22): A1.

Nash, N. C. (1989c) "Collapse of Lincoln Savings leaves scars for rich, poor and the faithful." *New York Times* (November 30): A22.

Nash, N. C. (1990a) "Losses at savings and loan in 1989 were the biggest ever." *New York Times* (March 27): A1.

Nash, N. C., and Shenon, P. (1989) "Figure in savings debacle: Victim or villain?" *New York Times* (November 9): A1.

National Advisory Commission on Civil Disorders. (1968) *Report.* New York: Bantam Books.

National Commission on Terrorist Attacks Upon the United States. (2004) *Final Report.* New York: Norton.

National White Collar Crime Center. (2005) "State-supported projects." http://www.nw3c.org.programs.html.

Navarro, M. (1996) "36 accused of bilking investors of $265 million in Florida." *New York Times* (August 24): A9.

Neckel, S. (1989) "Power and legitimacy in political scandal: Comments on a theoretical framework for the study of political scandals." *Corruption and Reform* 4: 147–158.

Needleman, M. L., and Needleman, C. (1979) "Organizational crime: Two models of criminogenesis." *The Sociological Quarterly* 20: 517–528.

Neier, A. (1998) *War crimes.* New York: Random House.

Nelken, D. (2002) "White collar crime," in M. Maguire, R. Morgan, and R. Reiner (Eds.), *The Oxford handbook of criminology.* New York: Oxford University Press.

Nelkin, D., and Brown, M. (1984) *Workers at risk—Voices from the workplace.* Chicago: University of Chicago Press.

Nelli, H. S. (1986) "Overview," pp. 1–9 in R. J. Kelly (Ed.), *Organized crime—A global perspective.* Totowa, NJ: Rowman & Littlefield.

Neuman, W. L. (1998) "Negotiated meanings and state transformation: The trust issue in the Progressive era." *Social Problems* 45: 315–335.

Newfield, J., and Barrett, W. (1988) *City for sale—Ed Koch and the betrayal of New York.* New York: Harper & Row.

Newman, A. (2002) "G.E.D. course was a fraud, a judge rules." *New York Times* (October 26): B1.

Newman, A. (2003) "Prosecutors see pattern of corruption in state court." *New York Times* (April 25): B1.

Newman, D. J. (1953) "Public attitudes toward a form of white-collar crime." *Social Problems* 4: 228–232.

Newman, D. J. (1958) "White-collar crime: An overview and analysis." *Law and Contemporary Problems* 23: 228–232.

Newport, J. P., Jr. (1989) "LBOs—Greed, good business—or both?" *New York Times* (January 2): G6.

New York Times. (1993) "The M.I.T. case: Time to back off." *New York Times* (September 27). A16.

New York Times. (1996) "The I.C.C. dies." *New York Times* (January 3): A14.

New York Times. (1997) "Bhopal's second tragedy." *New York Times* (January 15): A18.

New York Times. (1998) "No way to silence whistle-blowers." *New York Times* (January 20): A20.

New York Times. (2001) "False claims from fake crashes lead to charges against 172." *New York Times* (July 20): B5.

New York Times. (2002a) "Poor marks on the environment." *New York Times* (January 28): A14.

New York Times. (2002b) "Enronitis." *New York Times* (February 9): A18.

New York Times. (2002c) "Accountability for accountants." *New York Times* (June 4): A18.

New York Times. (2002d) "Accountants on trial." *New York Times* (June 19): A22.

New York Times. (2002e) "Those very public arrests of executives." *New York Times* (July 18).

New York Times. (2002f) "Policing Wall Street." *New York Times* (August 5): A14.

New York Times. (2002g) "Holding lawyers accountable." *New York Times* (August 15): A22.

New York Times. (2002h) "Underwriting fraud." *New York Times* (August 25): Wk 8.

New York Times. (2004a) "Corporate tax holidays." *New York Times* (April 13): A24.

New York Times. (2004b) "Those illegal farm subsidies." *New York Times* (April 28): A20.

New York Times. (2005a) "Corporate welfare runs amok." *New York Times* (January 30): Wk 16.

New York Times. (2005b) "Nature at bay." *New York Times* (May 9): A18.

New York Times. (2005c) "Corporate profit vs. public safety." *New York Times* (June 20): A14.

New York Times. (2005d) "Chile: Pinochet acquittal upheld." *New York Times* (September 16): A9.

New York State Organized Crime Task Force. (1988) *Corruption and racketeering in the New York City construction industry.* Ithaca, NY: ILR Press.

Nichols, L. T. (1990) "Reconceptualizing social accounts: An agenda for theory building and empirical research." *Current Perspectives in Social Theory* 10: 113–144.

Nichols, L. T. (1991) "'Whistleblower' or 'renegade': Definitional contests in an official inquiry." *Symbolic Interaction* 14: 395–414.

Nichols, L. T. (1999) "White-collar cinema: Changing representations of upper-world deviance in popular films," pp. 61–84 in *Perspectives on social problems*, Vol. 11. Amsterdam: JAI Press.

Nicholson, C. K. (1990) "Computer viruses: Information age vulnerability and the technopath." *American Criminal Law Review* 27: 525–543.

Niebuhr, G. (1998) "Baptist leader is charged with theft." *New York Times* (February 26): A12.

Nieves, E. (2001) "Court overturns jury award in '89 Exxon Valdez spill." *New York Times* (November 8): A14.

Niskanen, W. A. (2002) "A retrospective." *Regulation* (Summer): 4–5.

Nocera, J. (2005) "The lawyer companies love to hate." *New York Times* (July 2): C1.

Nolan, B. (1990) "Removing conflicts from the administration of justice: Conflicts of interest and independent counsels under the Ethics in Government Act." *Georgetown Law Journal* 79: 1–80.

Noonan, J. T., Jr. (1984) *Bribes.* Berkeley: University of California Press.

Nordheimer, J. (1996) "One day's death toll on the job." *New York Times* (December 22).

Norrie, A. (1986) "Practical reasoning and criminal responsibility: A jurisprudential approach," pp. 217–230 in D. B. Cornish and R. V. Clarke (Eds.), *The reasoning criminal.* New York: Springer-Verlag.

Norris, F. (1996) "An insider gets rich in trades, and walks." *New York Times* (September 8).

Norris, F. (1997) "The many lives made miserable by a low-down high roller." *New York Times* (March 9): Wk 3.

Norris, F. (2000a) "Accounting firm is said to violate rules routinely." *New York Times* (January 6): A1.

Norris, F. (2000b) "Accounting firm to pay a big fine." *New York Times* (June 20): A1.

Norris, F. (2000c) "Micro Strategy chairman accused of fraud by S.E.C." *New York Times* (December 15): W5.

Norris, F. (2001a) "A felon seeks vindication: Will Milken be pardoned?" *New York Times* (January 19): C1.

Norris, F. (2001b) "U.S. accuses former Cendant chiefs of fraud." *New York Times* (March 1): C1.

Norris, F. (2001c) "S.E.C. accuses former Sunbeam official of fraud." *New York Times* (May 6): A1.

Norris, F. (2001d) "An executive's missing years: Papering over past problems." *New York Times* (July 16): A1.

Norris, F. (2002a) "An old case is returning to haunt auditors." *New York Times* (March 1): C2.

Norris, F. (2002b) "Who wants to buy stock? Not the insiders." *New York Times* (May 31): C1.

Norris, F. (2002c) "Hard talk, softer plans." *New York Times* (July 10): A1.

Norris, F. (2003a) "6 from Xerox to pay S.E.C. $22 million." *New York Times* (June 6): C1.

Norris, F. (2003b) "His bonus was based on inflated profits. Will he give it back?" *New York Times* (October 10): C1.

Norris, F. (2004) "3 years after Enron, resistance to new rules grows." *New York Times* (December 17): C1.

Norris, F. (2005a) "Chief executive was paid millions, and he never noticed fraud?" *New York Times* (January 7): C1.

Norris, F. (2005b) "Why his peers say Kozlowski got off easy." *New York Times* (September 23): C1.

Nossiter, A. (1995) "A mistake, a rare prosecution, and a doctor is headed for jail." *New York Times* (March 16): A1.

Nussbaum, M. A. (2002) "Blowing the whistle: Not for the fainthearted." *New York Times* (February 10): C10.

O'Brien, T. (1998a) "Pastor Chuck's bully pulpit." *New York Times* (August 22): D7.

O'Brien, T. (1998b) "Fraud is rare, but check the tab anyway." *New York Times* (November 11): D1.

O'Brien, T. (1999a) "Stock hustlers thrive on the web." *New York Times* (August 23): A1.

O'Brien, T. (1999b) "Russian says officials funneled cash to bank in laundering case." *New York Times* (August 28): A1.

O'Brien, T. (2004) "Gone in sixty seconds." *New York Times* (October 24): 3/1.

O'Brien, T. (2005) "Mayday? Payday! Hit the silk!" *New York Times* (January 9): 3/1.

O'Brien, T., and Glater, J. D. (2005) "Robin Hoods or legal hoods? The government takes aim at a class-action powerhouse." *New York Times* (July 17): 3/1.

O'Brien, T., and Lee, J. (2004) "A seismic shift under the house of Fannie Mae." *New York Times* (October 3): 3/1.

O'Brien, T., and Treaster, J. B. (2005) "The insurance scandal shakes main street." *New York Times* (April 17): C1.

O'Connor, A. (2005) "Westchester druggist held in $4 million fraud." *New York Times* (August 4): B3.

O'Gara, J. D. (2004) *Corporate fraud—Case studies in detection and prevention.* New York: John Wiley.

O'Hear, M. M. (2004) "Sentencing the green-collar offender: Punishment, culpability, and environmental crime." *Journal of Criminal Law & Criminology* 95: 133–269.

Oliver, A. (1997) "On the nexus of organizations and professions: Networking through trust." *Sociological Inquiry* 67: 227–245.

Oliveira, A., Schenck, C., Cole, C., and Janes, N. L. (2005) "Environmental crimes." *American Criminal Law Review* 42: 347–426.

O'Malley, P. (Ed.) (1998) *Crime and the risk society.* Aldershot: Ashgate.

Oppel, R. A., Jr. (2002a) "Lawyer at Enron warned officials of dubious deals." *New York Times* (February 7): C1.

Oppel, R. A., Jr. (2002b) "Wall St. analyst faulted in Enron." *New York Times* (February 28): A1.

Oppel, R. A., Jr. (2002c) "S.E.C. taking closer look at Wall Street." *New York Times* (June 1): C1.

Oppel, R. A., Jr. (2002d) "Lawmakers turn to other efforts to deal with scandals." *New York Times* (July 26): C6.

Oppel, R. A., Jr., and Eichenwald, K. (2001) "Enron paid $55 million for bonuses." *New York Times* (December 6): C1.

Oppel, R. A., Jr., and Gerth, J. (2002) "Enron forced up California prices, documents show." *New York Times* (May 7): A1.

Oppel, R. A., Jr., and Sorkin, A. R. (2001a) "Enron admits to overstating profits by about $600 million." *New York Times* (November 1): C1.

Oppel, R. A., Jr., and Sorkin, A. R. (2001b) "Enron Corporation files largest U.S. claim for bankruptcy." *New York Times* (December 3): A1.

Orey, M. (1999) *Assuming the risks: The mavericks, the lawyers, and the whistle-blowers who beat big tobacco.* New York: Little, Brown.

Orland, L. (1980) "Reflections on corporate crime: Law in search of theory and scholarship." *American Criminal Law Review* 17: 501–520.

Orland, L. (2004) "Corporate misconduct vs. criminal behavior." *New York Times* (December 21): Op ed.

Ortega, B. (1997) "Some physicians do unnecessary surgery." *New York Times* (February 23): C1.

OSHA. (2003) OSHA website. www.osha.gov.

Ostling, R. N. (1992) "The tuition game." *Time* (November 9): 60.

O'Sullivan, J. (1996) "The Independent Counsel Statute: Bad law, bad policy." *American Criminal Law Review* 33: 463–509.

Outlaw, M. C., and Ruback, R. B. (1999) "Predictors and outcomes of victim restitution orders." *Justice Quarterly* 16: 847–869.

Padgett, T. (1989) "Big trouble in the pits." *Newsweek* (August 14): 36.

Padgett, T. (2005) "After Dot-Com, after WorldCom, after Enron, *After Capitalism.*" *Business Ethics Quarterly* 15: 329–340.

Palast, G. (2003) *The best democracy money can buy.* New York: Plume.

Palermo, P. F. (1978) *Lincoln Steffens.* Boston: Twayne.

Palmer, R. E. (1986) "Let's be bullish on ethics." *New York Times* (June 21): A31.

Papke, D. R. (1987) *Framing the criminal: Crime, cultural work and the loss of critical perspective.* Hamden, CT: Archon.

Parenti, C. (1999) *Lockdown America.* London: Verso.

Parisi, N. (1984) "Theories of corporate criminal liability," pp. 41–68 in E. Hochstedler (Ed.), *Corporations as criminals.* Beverly Hills, CA: Sage.

Parker, C. (2002) *The open corporation: Self-regulation and democracy.* Cambridge, UK: Cambridge University Press.

Parker, D. B. (1980) "Computer-related white-collar crime," pp. 199–200 in G. Geis and E. Stotland (Eds.), *White-collar crime: Theory and research.* Beverly Hills, CA: Sage.

Parker, J. S. (1982) "Social control and the legal profession," pp. 197–230 in P. Wickman and T. Dailey (Eds.), *White-collar and economic crime.* Lexington, MA: Lexington Books.

Parker, J. S. (1989) "Criminal sentencing policy for organizations: The unifying approach for optimal penalties." *American Criminal Law Review* 26: 513–604.

Parker, J. S. (1997) "The blunt instrument," pp. 71–97 in W. S. Lofquist, M. A. Cohen, and G. A. Rabe (Eds.), *Debating corporate crime.* Cincinnati, OH: Anderson.

Parloff, R. (2005) "Diagnosing for dollars." *Fortune* (June 13): 97–110.

Passas, N. (1990) "Anomie and corporate deviance." *Contemporary Crises* 4: 157–178.

Passas, N., and Goodwin, N. (Eds.) (2004) *It's legal but it ain't right: Harmful social consequences of legal industries.* Ann Arbor, MI: University of Michigan Press.

Passell, P. (1998) "Economic scene." *New York Times* (July 30): D2.

Paternoster, R., and Simpson, S. (1993) "A rational choice theory of corporate crime," pp. 37–58 in R. V. Clarke and M. Felson (Eds.), *Routine activity and rational choice.* New Brunswick, NJ: Transaction.

Paternoster, R., and Simpson, S. (1996) "Sanction threats and appeals to morality: Testing a rational choice model of corporate crime." *Law & Society Review* 30: 549–583.

Patterson, M. J., and Russell, R. H. (1986) *Behind the lives: Case studies in investigative reporting.* New York: Columbia University Press.

Pauly, D. (1987) "Travel scams: A costly trip." *Newsweek* (April 27): 48–49.

Payne, B. K. (2003) *Crime in the home health care field.* Springfield, IL: Charles C. Thomas.

Payne, B. K. (2005a) "Prosecution," pp. 640–643 in L. M. Salinger (Ed.), *Encyclopedia of white-collar and corporate crime.* Thousand Oaks, CA: Sage.

Payne, B. K. (2005b) "Telemarketing fraud," pp. 799–802 in L. M. Salinger (Ed.), *Encyclopedia of white-collar and corporate crime.* Thousand Oaks, CA: Sage.

Payne, B. K. (2005c) "Medicaid and Medicare," pp. 521–524 in L. M. Salinger (Ed.), *Encyclopedia of white-collar and corporate crime.* Thousand Oaks, CA: Sage.

Payne, B. K., and Gainey, R. Q. (2004) "Ancillary consequences of employee theft." *Journal of Criminal Justice* 32: 63–73.

Pear, R. (1991) "Study says fees are often higher when doctor has stake in clinic." *New York Times* (August 9): A1.

Pear, R. (1992a) "U.S. seeks millions back in charges." *New York Times* (January 13): A1.

Pear, R. (1992b) "Top infant–formula makers charged by U.S. over pricing." *New York Times* (December 12): A1.

Pear, R. (1999a) "U.S. is asking for patient's help in fight against Medicare fraud." *New York Times* (February 21): A1.

Pear, R. (1999b) "Whistleblowers likely to get stronger federal protection." *New York Times* (March 15): A1.

Pear, R. (1999c) "States called lax on tests for lead in poor children." *New York Times* (August 22): A1.

Pear, R. (2000) "Fraud in Medicare increasingly tied to claims payers." *New York Times* (September 20): A1.

Pear, R. (2002) "Investigators find repeated deception in ads for drugs." *New York Times* (December 4): A12.

Pear, R. (2004) "Investigators say drug makers repeatedly overcharged." *New York Times* (June 30): A19.

Pear, R. (2005a) "Huge bill fraud cited at clinics." *New York Times* (March 12): A1.

Pear, R. (2005b) "Buying of news by Bush's aides is ruled illegal." *New York Times* (October 1): A1.

Pear, R., and Eckholm, E. (1991) "When healers are entrepreneurs: A debate over costs and ethics." *New York Times* (June 2): A1.

Pearce, F. (1976) *Crimes of the powerful.* London: Pluto Press.

Pearce, F., and Snider, L. (Eds.) (1995) *Corporate crime: Contemporary debates.* Toronto, CN: University of Toronto Press.

Pearce, F., and Tombs, S. (1989) "Bhopal: Union Carbide and the hubris of the capitalist technology." *Social Justice* 16: 116–144.

Pearce, F., and Tombs, S. (2002) "States, corporations, and the 'new' world order," pp. 185–222 in G. Potter (Ed.), *Controversies in white-collar crime.* Cincinnati, OH: Anderson.

Pellow, D. N. (2001) "Environmental justice and the political process: Movements, corporations, and the state." *Sociological Quarterly* 42: 47–67.

Pence, L. L. (1986) "The federal enforcers: An overview of the prosecutors and investigators," pp. 1–50 in L. L. Pence, G. A. Feffer, and E. C. Hoffman III (Eds.), *White collar crime manual.* Washington, DC: Federal Publications.

Pennsylvania Crime Commission. (1991) *Organized crime—Report.* Harrisburg, PA: Commonwealth of Pennsylvania.

Perez-Pena, R. (1994) "U.S. juries grow tougher on plaintiffs in lawsuits." *New York Times* (June 17): A1.

Perez-Pena, R. (1995) "Audit finds fund misuse by York College president." *New York Times* (January 27): B3.

Peritz, R. J. (1996) *Competition policy in America, 1888–1992: History, rhetoric, law.* New York: Oxford University Press.

Perrow, C. (1984) *Normal accidents—Living with high-risk technologies.* New York: Basic Books.

Perrow, C. (2002) "Letter." *Chronicle of Higher Education* (October 18): B16–17.

Perrucci, R., Anderson, R. M., Schendel, D. E., and Trachtman, L. E. (1980) "Whistle-blowing: The professionals' resistance to organizational authority." *Social Problems* 28: 149–164.

Perry, S., and Dawson, J. (1985) *Nightmare: Women and the Dalkon shield.* New York: Macmillan.

Peters, J. W., and Hakim, D. (2005) "Ford's lending practices challenged in a lawsuit." *New York Times* (March 1): C2.

Petersen, M. (2001a) "Court papers depict scheme in drug billing." *New York Times* (February 20): C1.

Petersen, M. (2001b) "Nine West in settlement on shoe prices." *New York Times* (March 7): D1.

Petersen, M. (2001c) "2 drug makers to pay $875 million to settle fraud case." *New York Times* (October 4): C1.

Petersen, M. (2002a) "Vermont to require drug makers to disclose payments to doctors." *New York Times* (June 13): C1.

Petersen, M. (2002b) "U.S. prosecutors in Newark join investigation of Schering." *New York Times* (June 20): C1.

Petersen, M. (2003a) "Drug makers expand their Medicaid role." *New York Times* (April 23): C1.

Petersen, M. (2003b) "AstraZeneca pleads guilty in cancer medicine scheme." *New York Times* (June 21): C1.

Petersen, M., and Walsh, M. W. (2002) "States accuse Bristol-Meyers of fraud on Taxol." *New York Times* (June 5): C1.

Peterson, M. J. (1989) "An historical perspective on the incidence of piracy," pp. 41–60 in E. Ellen (Ed.), *Piracy at sea.* Paris: International Maritime Bureau.

Petzinger, T. (1987) *Oil & honor: The Texaco-Pennzoil wars.* New York: Berkley Books.

Peyser, M. (2002) "The insiders." *Newsweek* (July 1): 38–43.

Pfohl, S. (1985; 1994) *Images of deviance and social control.* New York: McGraw-Hill.

Pfost, D. R. (1991) "Reagan's Nicaraguan policy: A case study of political deviance and crime." *Crime & Social Justice* 27: 66–87.

Picciotto, S. (2002) "Introduction: Reconceptualizing regulation in the era of globalization." *Journal of Law and Society* 29: 1–11.

Pierson, R. (1989) *The queen of mean: The unauthorized biography of Leona Helmsley.* New York: Bantam Books.

Pillar, P. R. (2001) *Terrorism and U.S. foreign policy.* Washington, DC: Brookings Institution Press.

Pilzer, P. Z., and Deitz, R. (1989) *Other people's money*. New York: Simon & Schuster.

Piquero, N. L. (2004) "Motivations of white collar crime: Examining the fear of falling." A paper presented at the Annual Meeting of the American Society of Criminology (Nashville), November 17–20.

Piquero, N. L., and Davis, J. L. (2004) "Extralegal factors and the sentencing of organizational offenders: An examination of the Federal Sentencing Guidelines." *Journal of Criminal Justice* 32: 643–654.

Piquero, N. L., Exum, M. L., and Simpson, S. S. (2005) "Integrating the desire-for-control and rational choice in a corporate crime context." *Justice Quarterly* 22: 251–280.

Piraino, T. A., Jr. (2000) "Identifying monopolists' illegal conduct under the Sherman Act." *New York University Law Review* 75: 810–892.

Pitch, T. (1983) "Business ethics new appeal." *New York Times* (December 11): 3.

Pitt, H. L. (1987) *Insider trading—Counseling and compliance*. Clifton, NJ: Prentice Hall Law & Business.

Pizzo, S. (1990) "The real culprits in the thrift scam." *New York Times* (April 2): A17.

Pizzo, S., Fricker, M., and Muolo, P. (1991) *Insider job: The looting of America's savings and loans*. New York: Harper Perennial.

Pizzo, S. P., and Muolo, P. (1993) "Take the money and run." *New York Times Magazine* (May 9): 26, 56–62.

Platt, A., and Cooper, L. (1974) *Policing America*. Englewood Cliffs, NJ: Prentice Hall.

Podgor, E. S., and Israel, J. H. (2004) *White collar crime in a nutshell* (3rd ed.). Minneapolis, MN: West.

Poling, J. C., and White, K. M. (2001) "Corporate criminal liability." *American Criminal Law Review* 38: 525–554.

Pollack, A. (1999) "Restoring the junk bond king." *New York Times* (March 14): C3.

Pollack, A. (2002) "Drug factory of Johnson & Johnson under inquiry." *New York Times* (July 19): C1.

Pollack, A. (2003) "Sealed indictment is said to charge bank with fraud." *New York Times* (August 28): C1.

Pollack, K. M. (2002) *The threatening storm—The case for invading Iraq*. New York: Random House.

Pontell, H. N., and Calavita, K. (1993) "White-collar crime in the savings and loan scandal." *Annals* 525: 31–45.

Pontell, H. N., Jesilow, P. D., and Geis, G. (1982) "Policing physicians: Practitioner fraud and abuse in a government medical program." *Social Problems* 30: 117–125.

Pontell, H. N., Jesilow, P. D., Geis, G., and O'Brien, M. J. (1985) "A demographic portrait of physicians sanctioned by the federal government for fraud and abuse against Medicare and Medicaid." *Medical Care* 23: 1028–1031.

Pontell, H. N., Rosoff, S. M., and Lam, J. (2001) "The role of fraud in the Japanese financial crisis: A comparative study," pp. 321–340 in H. N. Pontell and D. Shichor (Eds.), *Contemporary Issues in Crime and Criminal Justice*. Upper Saddle River, NJ: Prentice Hall.

Pooley, E. (1993) "Scamming Wall Street." *New York Times* (June 7): 28–36.

Posner, R. (1984) "Theories of economic regulation," pp. 240–250 in A. I. Ogus and C. G. Veljanovski (Eds.), *Readings in the economics of law and regulation*. Oxford, UK: Clarendon Press.

Porter, B. (2004) "A long way down." *New York Times* (June 6): 50–58, 106–109.

Potter, G. W., and Kappeler, V. E. (1998) *Constructing crime*. Prospect Heights, IL: Waveland Press.

Poulin, A. B. (1990) "RICO: Something for everyone." *Villanova Law Review* 35: 853–864.

Poveda, T. G. (1990) *Lawlessness and reform: The FBI in transition*. Pacific Grove, CA: Brooks/Cole.

Poveda, T. G. (1992) "White-collar crime and the Justice Department: The institutionalization of a concept." *Crime, Law & Social Change* 17: 235–252.

Powell, B. (1986) "Can corporate America cope?" *Newsweek* (November 17): 64–65.

Power, S. (2002) *"A problem from Hell"—America and the age of genocide*. New York: Basic Books.

Power, S. (2004) "Dying in Darfur." *The New Yorker* (August 30): 57–73.

Prados, J. (1986) *Presidents' secret wars: CIA and Pentagon covert operations from World War II through Iranscam*. New York: Morrow.

Prashad, V. (2002) *Fat cats and running dogs: The Enron stage of capitalism*." Monroe, ME: Common Courage Press.

Pratt, T. C., and Cullen, F. T. (2000) "The empirical status of Gottfredson and Hirschi's general theory of crime: A meta-analysis." *Criminology* 38: 931–964.

Prentice, R. (2002) "An ethics lesson for business scandals." *New York Times* (August 20): Op ed.

Press, C. (1981) *The political cartoon*. London: Associated Press.

Press, E. (1996) "Look at the cost of white-collar crime, too." *New York Times* (April 26).

Preston, I. L. (1994) *The tangled web they weave—Truth, falsity, and advertisers*. Madison: University of Wisconsin Press.

Preston, J. and Miller, J. (2005) "Texan is indicted in Iraq oil sales by Hussein aides." *New York Times* (April 15): A1.

Priest, G. L. (1990) "The new legal structure of risk control." *Daedalus* 119: 207–228.

Pring, G. W., and Canan, P. (1996) *SLAPPS: Getting sued for speaking out*. Philadelphia: Temple University Press.

Pristin, T. (2000) "Chinese immigrants lose savings and hopes in a citizenship swindle." *New York Times* (February 24): B3.

Pristin, T. (2001) "Tales of lost homes surface in Queens." *New York Times* (February 8): B3.

Pulley, J. (2003) "Tainted gifts." *Chronicle of Higher Education* (January 3): A32–34.

Punch, M. (1996) *Dirty business—Exploring corporate misconduct*. London: Sage.

Punch, M. (2000) "Suite violence: Why managers murder and corporations kill." *Crime, Law & Social Change* 33: 243–280.

Purdom, T. S. (1998) "Ex-governor is sentenced to 2½ years." *New York Times* (February 3): A10.

Purdom, T. S. (2005) "'Deep Throat' unmasked himself: Ex-No. 2 at F.B.I." *New York Times* (June 1): A1.

Purdy, E. (2005a) "Computer hacking," pp. 190–193 in L. M. Salinger (Ed.), *Encyclopedia of white-collar and corporate crime*. Thousand Oaks, CA: Sage.

Purdy, E. (2005b) "Class-action lawsuits," pp. 168–171 in L. M. Salinger (Ed.), *Encyclopedia of white-collar and corporate crime*. Thousand Oaks, CA: Sage.

Purdy, E. (2005c) "Sweepstakes fraud," pp. 778–779 in L. M. Salinger (Ed.), *Encyclopedia of white-collar and corporate crime*. Thousand Oaks, CA: Sage.

Purdy, S. (2005) "Contractor fraud," pp. 200–204 in L. M. Salinger (Ed.), *Encyclopedia of white-collar and corporate crime*. Thousand Oaks, CA: Sage.

Quah, J. S. T. (2003) *Curbing corruption in Asia—A comparative study of six countries*. London: Eastern Universities Press.

Qinglian, H. (2004) "On systemic corruption in China and its influence," pp. 239–275 in W. C. Heffernan and J. Kleinig (Eds.), *Private and public corruption*. Lanham, MD: Rowman & Littlefield.

Quinn, J. B. (1999) "You're a big winner! (Not)." *Newsweek* (September 27): 49.

Quinn, J. B. (2002) "Is reform a bad joke?" *Newsweek* (October 14): 43.

Quinn, J. B. (2003) "Mutual funds greed machine." *Newsweek* (November 24): 45.

Quinney, R. (1963) "Occupational structure and criminal behavior: Prescription violations by retail pharmacists." *Social Problems* 11: 179–185.

Quinney, R. (1964) "The study of white collar crime: Toward a reorientation in theory and research." *Journal of Criminal Law, Criminology and Police Science* 55: 208–214.

Quinney, R. (1974) *Critique of legal order*. Boston: Little, Brown.

Quinney, R. (1977) *Class, state and crime*. New York: David McKay.

Quinney, R. (1979) *Criminology* (2nd ed.). Boston: Little, Brown.

Quinney, R. (1980) *Providence: The reconstruction of social and moral order*. New York: Longman.

Quint, M. (1995) "Aiming at insurance giants." *New York Times* (July 19): C1.

Raab, S. (1997) "Official says mob is shifting crimes to new industries." *New York Times* (February 10): A1.

Rabe, G. A., and Ermann, D. (1995) "Corporate concealment of tobacco hazards: Motives and historical context." *Deviant Behavior* 16: 223–244.

Rajagopal, B. (2003) *International law from below: Development, social movements, and third world resistance*. Cambridge, UK: Cambridge University Press.

Ramirez, A. (1992) "5 are indicted in computer credit theft." *New York Times* (July 9): A14.

Randall, D. M. (1987) "The portrayal of corporate crime in network television newscasts." *Journalism Quarterly* 64: 150–153.

Randall, D. M., Lee-Sammons, L., and Hagner, P. R. (1988) "Common versus elite crime coverage in network news." *Social Science Quarterly* 69: 910–929.

Ranelagh, J. (1986) *The agency—The rise and decline of the CIA.* New York: Simon & Schuster.

Rashbaum, W. K. (2004) "Officials say Mob stole $200 million using phone bills." *New York Times* (February 11): A1.

Rashbaum, W. K. (2005) "Judge is charged in money-laundering case." *New York Times* (August 31): B1.

Rashbaum, W. K., and Berenson, A. (2002) "Sale of home of Tyco figure gets 2nd look, prosecutors say." *New York Times* (June 8): C1.

Rashid, A. (2000) *Taliban.* New Haven, CT: Yale University Press.

Ratner, S. R., and Abrams, J. S. (2001) *Accountability for human rights atrocities in international law.* New York: Oxford University Press.

Rawlinson, P. (2002) "Capitalists, criminals, and oligarchs—Sutherland and the new 'Robber Barons.'" *Crime, Law & Social Change* 37: 293–307.

Reasons, C. E., and Chappell, D. (1987) "Continental capitalism and crooked lawyering." *Crime & Social Justice* 26: 38–59.

Rebovich, D., and Layne, J. (2000) *The national public survey on white collar crime.* Morgantown, WV: National White Collar Crime Center.

Rebovich, D., and Nixon, R. T. (1994) *Environmental crime prosecution: Results of a national survey.* Washington, DC: National Institute of Justice.

Recine, J. S. (2002) "Examination of the white collar crime penalty enhancements in the Sarbanes-Oxley Act." *American Criminal Law Review* 39: 1536–1570.

Reed, G. E., and Yeager, P. C. (1991) "Organizational offending and neoclassical criminology: A challenge to Gottfredson and Hirschi's general theory of crime." A paper presented at the Annual Meeting of the American Society of Criminology (San Francisco), November.

Reed, G. E., and Yeager, P. C. (1996) "Organizational offending and neo-classical criminology: Challenging the reach of a general theory of crime." *Criminology* 34: 357–382.

Reeves, F. (2002) "The ethical chase." *Pittsburgh Gazette* (October 5): A9.

Regenstein, L. (1986) *How to survive in America the poisoned.* Washington, DC: Acropolis Books.

Reibstein, L. (1991) "Hail felons well met." *Newsweek* (October 7): 44–45.

Reich, R. B. (1983) *The next American frontier.* New York: Times Books.

Reich, R. B. (1989) "America pays the price." *New York Times* (January 29): 32–40.

Reich, R. B. (2005) "Don't blame Wal-Mart." *New York Times* (February 28): A19.

Reichman, N. (1986) Review of James W. Coleman, *The Criminal Elite. Contemporary Sociology* 15: 379–380.

Reichman, N. (1987) "Computer matching: Toward computerized systems of regulation." *Law & Policy* 9: 387–413.

Reichman, N. (1989) "Breaking confidences: Organizational influences on insider trading." *The Sociological Quarterly* 30: 185–204.

Reichman, N. (1992) "Moving backstage: Uncovering the role of compliance practices in shaping regulatory policy," pp. 244–268 in K. Schlegel and D. Weisburd (Eds.), *White-collar crime reconsidered.* Boston: Northeastern University Press.

Reichman, N. (1993) "Insider trading," pp. 55–96 in M. Tonry and A. J. Reiss, Jr. (Eds.), *Beyond the law—Crime in complex organizations.* Chicago: University of Chicago Press.

Reiman, J. H. (1982) "Marxist explanations and radical misinterpretations: A reply to Greenberg and Humphries." *Crime & Delinquency* 28: 610–617.

Reiman, J. H. (1990; 1995; 2001; 2004) *The rich get richer and the poor get prison.* Boston: Allyn & Bacon.

Reiman, J. H., and Headlee, S. (1981) "Marxism and criminal justice policy." *Crime & Delinquency* 27: 24–47.

Reinertsen, R., and Bronson, R. J. (1990) "Informant is a dirty word," pp. 99–104 in J. Gilbert (Ed.), *Criminal investigation.* Columbus, OH: Merrill.

Reiss, A. J., Jr., and Biderman, A. (1980) *Data sources on white-collar law-breaking.* Washington, DC: U.S. Government Printing Office.

Rettig, S., and Passamanick, B. (1959) "Changes in moral values over three decades." *Social Problems* 6: 320–328.

Reuter, P. (1993) "The cartage industry in New York," pp. 149–202 in M. Tonry and A. J. Reiss (Eds.), *Beyond the law—Crime in complex organizations.* Chicago: University of Chicago Press.

Reuters. (2002) "Study: Internet use in U.S. homes routine." CNN (December 29) www.cnn.com. 2002/TECH/Internet.

Reynolds, M. (1985) *Crime by choice: An economic analysis.* Dallas, TX: The Fisher Institute.

Rezace, Z. and Jain, P. K. (2005) "Industry-wide effects of the Sarbanes-Oxley Act." *Journal of Forensic Accounting* 6: 147–162.

Rhodes, R. P. (1984) *Organized crime—Crime control vs. civil liberties.* New York: Random House.

Rich, B. (1994) *Mortgaging the earth: The World Bank, environmental impoverishment, and the crisis of development.* Boston: Beacon Press.

Rich, F. (2002) "The United States of Enron." *New York Times* (January 19): A19.

Rich, F. (2004) "He's firing as fast as he can." *New York Times* (March 14): Arts 1.

Richards, S. C., and Avery, M. J. (2000) "Controlling state crime in the United States of America: What can we do about the thug state?" pp. 31–58 in J. I. Ross (Ed.), *Varieties of state crime and its control.* Monsey, NY: Criminal Justice Press.

Richardson, L. (1996a) "Former charity head ordered to prison." *New York Times* (July 31): B3.

Richardson, L. (1996b) "Ex-car dealer sentenced." *New York Times* (August 10): 20.

Richardson, L. (1996c) "Suspect is arrested in cheating scheme for graduate tests." *New York Times* (October 29): A1.

Richtel, M. (2002) "Credit card theft is thriving online as global market." *New York Times* (May 11): A1.

Rider, B. A. K. (2000) "The control of insider trading— Smoke and mirrors!" *Dickinson Journal of International Law* 19: 1–45.

Rigakos, G. S. 1999. "Risk society and actuarial criminology: Prospects for a critical discourse." *Canadian Journal of Criminology* 41: 137–150.

Rimer, S. (2004) "When plagiarism's shadow falls on admired scholars." *New York Times* (November 24)

Ringer, R. (1994) "Banks report card on mutual funds." *New York Times* (October 29): C1.

Ripley, A. (2005) "10 questions for Jeffrey Wigand." *Time* (February 14): 8.

Rivlin, G. (2005) "Purloined lives." *New York Times* (March 17): C1.

Robb, C. (1990) *White-collar crime in modern England: Financial fraud and business morality, 1845–1929.* Ph.D. Dissertation, Northwestern University.

Roberg, R., Crank, J., and Kuykendall, J. (2000) *Police and society* (2nd ed.). Los Angeles: Roxbury Publishing Co.

Roberg, R. R., and Kuykendall, J. (1993) *Police and society.* Belmont, CA: Wadsworth.

Robinson, M. B. (2002a) *Justice blind? Ideals and realities of American criminal justice.* Upper Saddle River, NJ: Prentice Hall.

Robinson, M. B. (2002b) "An analysis of 2002 ACJS papers: What members presented about and what they ignored." *ACJS Today* (November/ December): 1–3, 6.

Robyn, L. (2002) "A critical model for the study of resource colonialism and native resistance," pp. 85–108 in G. Potter (Ed.), *Controversies in white-collar crime.* Cincinnati, OH: Anderson.

Rogovin, M., and Rogovin, W. M. (1993) "The office of attorney general: 'Not properly political.'" *The Journal of Law & Politics* 9: 317–328.

Rohde, D. (2000) "Ex-union president is sentenced to 3 to 9 years for stealing over $2 million." *New York Times* (June 6): B4.

Rohter, L., and Forero, J. (2005) "Unending graft is threatening Latin America." *New York Times* (July 30): A1.

Romano, J. (1992) "A state crackdown on insurance fraud." *New York Times* (December 27).

Romano, R. (1991) "Comment: Organization theory and the criminal liability of organizations." *Boston University Law Review* 71: 377–382.

Romero, S. (2004) "Ex-Executive of Dynergy is sentenced to 24 years." *New York Times* (March 26): C2.

Romero, S., and Atlas, R. D. (2002) "WorldCom files for bankruptcy: Largest U.S. case." *New York Times* (July 22): A1.

Romero, S., and Richtel, M. (2001) "Second chance." *New York Times* (March 5): E1.

Romero, S., and Whitmire, K. (2005) "Former chief of HealthSouth acquitted in $2.7 billion fraud." *New York Times* (June 29): A1.

Rose, R. J. (2004) *Slaves to fashion: Poverty and abuse in new sweatshops.* Ann Arbor: University of Michigan Press.

Rosefsky, R. S. (1973) *Frauds, swindles and rackets.* Chicago: Follett.

Rosenbaum, D. E. (1996) "Rostenkowski pleads guilty to mail fraud." *New York Times* (April 10): A20.

Rosenberg, G. H. (1991) *The hollow hope: Can courts bring about social change?* Chicago: University of Chicago Press.

Rosenmerkel, S. (2001) "Wrongfulness and harmfulness as components of seriousness of white-collar offenses." *Journal of Contemporary Criminal Justice* 17: 308–327.

Rosenthal, E. (1990) "Health insurers say rising fraud is costing them tens of billions." *New York Times* (July 5): A1.

Rosner, L. S. 1986. *The Soviet way of crime.* Westport, CT: Bergin & Garvey.

Rosoff, S. M. (1989) "Physicians as criminal defendants: Specialty, sanctions, and status liability." *Law and Human Behavior* 15: 231–235.

Rosoff, S. M., Pontell, H. N., and Tillman, R. (2002) *Profit without honor—White-collar crime and the looting of America* (2nd ed.). Upper Saddle River, NJ: Prentice Hall.

Ross, D. (2005) "Computer Fraud and Abuse Act," pp. 189–190 in L. M. Salinger (Ed.), *Encyclopedia of white-collar and corporate crime.* Thousand Oaks, CA: Sage.

Ross, E. A. (1907; 1973) *Sin and society: An analysis of latter day iniquity.* New York: Harper & Row.

Ross, H. L. (1961) "Traffic law violation: A folk crime." *Social Problems* 8: 231–241.

Ross, I. (1992) *Shady business: Confronting corporate corruption.* New York: The Twentieth Century Fund.

Ross, J. I. (1992) "Towards a conceptual clarity of police criminality." Unpublished manuscript, University of Lethbridge.

Ross, J. I. (Ed.) (2000) *Varieties of state crime and its control.* Monsey, NY: Criminal Justice Press.

Ross, J. I. (2003) *The dynamics of political crime.* Thousand Oaks, CA: Sage.

Rothman, R. (1978) *Inequality and stratification in the United States.* Englewood Cliffs, NJ: Prentice Hall.

Rothstein, R. (1992) "Who are the real looters?" *Dissent* (Fall): 429–430.

Rowan, R. (1986) "The 50 biggest Mafia bosses." *Fortune* (November 10): 24–38.

Rowlands, G. S. (2002) "Earnings management, the SEC, and corporate governance: Director liability arising from the Audit Committee report." *Columbia Law Review* 102: 168–207.

Royster, C. (2000) *The fabulous history of the dismal swamp company: A story of George Washington's time.* New York: Alfred Knopf.

Rozen, M. (2002) "Wayward son." *The American Lawyer* (December): 74–79.

Rozhon, T. (2005) "Wider net cast in sales inquiry." *New York Times* (May 11): C1.

Rozhon, T., and Treaster, J. (2002) "Insurance plans of top executives may violate law." *New York Times* (August 29): A1.

Rubin, B. (1987) *Modern dictator—Third world coup makers, strongmen, and populist tyrants.* New York: McGraw-Hill.

Rubinstein, D. (1992) "Structural explanation in sociology: The egalitarian imperative." *The American Sociologist* 23: 5–19.

Ruggiero, V. (2002) "Introduction: Fuzzy criminal actors." *Crime, Law & Social Change* 37: 177–190.

Russell, S. (2005) "Since September 11, all roads lead to Rome." *Critical Criminology* 13: 27–53.

Russell, S., and Gilbert, M. J. (1999) "Truman's revenge: Social control and corporate crime." *Crime, Law & Social Change* 32: 59–82.

Rustad, M., and Koenig, T. (2002) "Taming the tort monster: The American civil justice system as a battleground of social theory." *Brooklyn Law Review* 68: 1–122.

Rutenberg, J. (2000) "Local TV uncovered national scandal." *New York Times* (September 11): C17.

Sachs, S. (2001) "Welcome to America, and stock fraud." *New York Times* (May 15): A1.

Sack, K. (1993) "26 states and Fleet settle suit." *New York Times* (February 9): D1.

Sacks, M., Coale, T., and Goldberg, L. (2005) "Racketeer Influenced and Corrupt Organizations." *American Criminal Law Review* 42: 825–875.

Sale, H. A. (2004) "Banks: The forgotten partners in fraud." *University of Cincinnati Law Review* 73: 139–177.

Sale, K. (1977) "The world behind Watergate," pp. 240–252 in G. Geis and R. F. Meier (Eds.), *White-collar crime: Offenses in business, politics, and the professions.* New York: Free Press.

Sale, K. (1990) *The conquest of paradise*. New York: Knopf.

Salinger, L. (2005) "Federal Trade Commission," pp. 312–313 in L. M. Salinger (Ed.), *Encyclopedia of white-collar and corporate crime*. Thousand Oaks, CA: Sage.

Salpurkas, A. (1996) "Exxon is accused of 'astonishing ruse' in oil-spill trial." *New York Times* (June 14): C5.

Salzman, A. (2005) "Yale professor to step down in inquiry over billing." *New York Times* (January 11): B5.

Samples, J., and Basham, P. (2002) "Meet the new loopholes." *New York Times* (November 5): A27.

Sampson, A. (1973) *The sovereign state of ITT*. Greenwich, CT: Fawcett.

Samuelson, R. T. (1987) "Corporate socialism." *Newsweek* (December 28): 42.

Sanders, J., and Hamilton, V. L. (1997) "Distributing responsibility for wrongdoing inside corporate hierarchies: Public judgments in three societies." *Law and Social Inquiry* 22: 815–855.

Sanders, W. B. (1974) *The sociologist as detective: An introduction to research methods*. New York: Praeger.

Sarangi, S. (2002) "Crimes of Bhopal and the global campaign for justice." *Social Justice* 29: 47–52.

Sarasohn, J. (1993) *Science on trial: The whistleblower, the accuser and the Nobel laureate*. New York: St. Martin's Press.

Saul, S. (2005a) "Drug makers race to cash in on nation's fight against fat." *New York Times* (April 3): A1.

Saul, S. (2005b) "Bristol-Myers seen settling case by U.S." *New York Times* (June 6): C1.

Savelsberg, J. S. (1987) "The making of criminal law norms in welfare states: Economic crime in West Germany." *Law & Society Review* 21: 529–562.

Savelsberg, J. S. (1994) *Constructing white-collar crime: Rationalities, communication, power*. Philadelphia: University of Pennsylvania Press.

Schaeffer, R. K. (2003) *Understanding globalization: The social consequences of political, economic, and environmental change*. Lanham, MD: Rowman & Littlefield.

Schechter, R. E. (1990) "A retrospective on the Reagan FTC: Musings on the role of an administrative agency." *Administrative Law Review* (Fall): 489–517.

Schell, J. (1982) *The fate of the earth*. New York: Avon Books.

Schell, J. (2001) "The new nuclear danger." *The Nation* (June 25): 11–16.

Schell, J. (2003a) "American tragedy." *The Nation* (April 7): 4–5.

Schell, J. (2003b) *The unconquerable world: Power, nonviolence and the will of the people*. New York: Metropolitan Books.

Schelling, T. C. (1973) "Economic analysis and organized crime," pp. 75–104 in J. F. Conklin (Ed.), *The crime establishment*. Englewood Cliffs, NJ: Prentice Hall.

Schemo, D. J. (1993) "Software maker accused of using virus to compel client to pay bill." *New York Times* (November 23): A1.

Schemo, D. J. (2001) "University of Virginia hit by scandal over cheating." *New York Times* (May 10): A1.

Scheppele, K. L. (1988) *Legal secrets: Equality and efficiency in common law*. Chicago: University of Chicago Press.

Scherzer, M. (1987) "Insurance," pp. 185–200 in H. L. Dalton, S. Burns, and Yale AIDS Law Project (Eds.), *AIDS and the law*. New Haven, CT: Yale University Press.

Scheuerman, W. E. (1999) "Economic globalization and the rule of law." *Constellations* 6: 3–25.

Schiesel, S. (1998a) "Company gets record antitrust fine for price fixing in electrodes." *New York Times* (April 8).

Schiesel, S. (1998b) "Phone-carrier fraud brings big U.S. fine." *New York Times* (April 22): D1.

Schiesel, S. (2005) "Growth of wireless Internet opens new path for thieves." *New York Times* (March 19): A1.

Schifferes, S. (2003) "Court blocks campaign finance reform." *BBC News*. news.bbc.cu.uk.

Schjolberg, S., and Parker, D. B. (1983) "Computer crime," pp. 218–223 in S. Kadish (Ed.), *The encyclopedia of crime and justice*. New York: Macmillan and Free Press.

Schlegel, K. (1988) "Desert, retribution, and corporate criminality." *Justice Quarterly* 5: 615–634.

Schlegel, K. (1990) *Just deserts for corporate criminals*. Boston: Northeastern University Press.

Schlegel, K. (2000) "Transnational crime." *Journal of Contemporary Criminal Justice* 16: 365–385.

Schlesinger, A. (2004) "The making of a mess." *New York Review of Books* (September 23): 40–43.

Schlesinger, A., Jr., and Bruns, R. (1975) *Congress investigates*. New York: Chelsea House.

Schmitt, E. (1998) "Abuses are cited in trade of money for U.S. residence." *New York Times* (April 13): A1.

Schneider, A. (1999) "Why professors don't do more to stop students who cheat." *Chronicle of Higher Education* (January 22): A8.

Schneider, K. (1994) "Exxon is ordered to pay $5 billion for Alaska spill." *New York Times* (September 17): A1.

Schneider, S. (2005a) "Advance fee fraud," pp. 8–9 in L. M. Salinger (Ed.), *Encyclopedia of white-collar and corporate crime*. Thousand Oaks, CA: Sage.

Schneider, S. (2005b) "Organized crime," pp. 590–595 in L. M. Salinger (Ed.), *Encyclopedia of white-collar and corporate crime*. Thousand Oaks, CA: Sage.

Schneider, S. (2005c) "Racketeer Influenced and Corrupt Organizations," pp. 660–664 in L. M. Salinger (Ed.), *Encyclopedia of white-collar and corporate crime*. Thousand Oaks, CA: Sage.

Schneider, V. W., and Wiersema, B. (1990) "Limits and use of the Uniform Crime Reports," pp. 21–48 in D. L. Mackenzie, P. J. Baunach, and R. R. Roberg (Eds.), *Measuring crime: Large-scale, long-range efforts*. Albany, NY: SUNY Press.

Schneyer, T. (1991a) "Professional discipline in 2050: A look back." *Fordham Law Review* 60: 125–131.

Schneyer, T. (1991b) "Professional discipline in law firms." *Cornell Law Review* 77: 1–46.

Schoenberger, K. (2001) "When the numbers just don't add up." *New York Times* (August 19).

Schoenfeld, G. (2001) "Could September 11 have been averted?" *Commentary* (December): 121–129.

Scholz, J. T. (1984) "Voluntary compliance and regulatory enforcement." *Law & Policy* (October): 385–404.

Schroeder, C. H., and Steinzor, R. (Eds.) (2005) *A new progressive agenda for public health and the environment*. Durham, NC: Carolina Academic Press.

Schroeder, T. E. (2002) "Seventeenth survey of white collar crime." *American Criminal Law Review* 39: 201–1145.

Schuck, P. H. (1986) *Agent orange on trial: Mass toxic disasters in the court*. Cambridge, MA: Harvard University Press.

Schudson, C. B., Onellion, A. P., and Hochstedler, E. (1984) "Nailing an omelet to the wall: Prosecuting nursing home homicide," pp. 131–145 in E. Hochstedler (Ed.), *Corporations as criminals*. Beverly Hills, CA: Sage.

Schultz, J. (2003) *Reviving the fourth estates: Democracy, accountability, and the media*. New York: Cambridge University Press.

Schur, E. M. (1969) *Our criminal society*. Englewood Cliffs, NJ: Prentice Hall.

Schur, E. M. (1971) *Labeling deviant behavior—Its sociological implications*. New York: Harper & Row.

Schwartz, J. (2001) "Trying to keep young internet users from a life of piracy." *New York Times* (December 25): C1.

Schwartz, J. (2002) "Troubling questions ahead for Enron's law firm." *New York Times* (March 12): C1.

Schwartz, J., and Dobrzynski, J. H. (2001) "3 men are charged with fraud in 1000 art auctions on Ebay." *New York Times* (March 9): A1.

Schwartz, M. (1987) *The structure of power in America: The corporate elite as a ruling class*. New York: Holmes & Meier.

Schwartz, M. D., and Ellison, C. (1982) "Criminal sanctions for corporate misbehavior." *Humanity & Society* 6: 267–293.

Schwartz, M. D., and Friedrichs, D. O. (1994) "Postmodern thought and criminological discontent: New metaphors for understanding violence." *Criminology* 32: 201–226.

Schwartz, M. D., and Hatty, S. (Eds.) (2003) *Current controversies in critical criminology*. Cincinnati, OH: Anderson.

Schwartz, R. D., and Orleans, S. (1967) "On legal sanctions." *University of Chicago Law Review* 34: 274–290.

Schwartz, R. D., and Skolnick, J. H. (1964) "Two studies of legal stigma," pp. 103–118 in H. S. Becker (Ed.), *The other side*. New York: Free Press.

Schwarzkopf, D. L., and Miller, H. M. (2005) "Early evidence of how Sarbanes-Oxley implementation affects individuals and their workplace relationships." *Business and Society Review* 110: 21–45.

Schwendinger, H., and Schwendinger, J. (1970) "Defenders of order or guardians of human rights?" *Issues in Criminology* 5: 123–137.

Sciolino, E. (1992) "Attorney general names prosecutor in Iraq loans case." *New York Times* (October 17): A1.

Scott, D. W. (1989) "Policing corporate collusion." *Criminology* 27: 559–587.

Scott, M. B., and Lyman, S. (1968) "Accounts." *American Sociological Review* 22: 664–670.

Scott, W. R. (1992) *Organizations: Rational, natural and open systems*. Englewood Cliffs, NJ: Prentice Hall.

Seagull, L. M. (1995) "Whistle-blowing and corruption control: The GE case." *Crime, Law & Social Change* 22: 381–390.

Secretariat, The. (2005) "Economic and financial crimes; Challenges to sustainable development." *Eleventh United Nations Congress on Crime Prevention and Criminal Justice* (April 18-25), Bangkok.

Seelye, K. (2002a) "Regulators urge easing U.S. rules on air pollution." *New York Times* (January 8): A1.

Seelye, K. (2002b) "Bush slashing aid for E.P.A. cleanup of 33 toxic sites." *New York Times* (July 1): A1.

Seelye, K. (2005) "Felt is praised as a hero and condemned as a traitor." *New York Times* (June 2): A16.

Seglin, J. L. (2003) "When executives say they don't have a clue." *New York Times* (November 16): 3/6.

Seligman, A. (1997) *The problem of trust*. Princeton, NJ: Princeton University Press.

Seligman, J. (1982) *The transformation of Wall Street: A history of the Securities and Exchange Commission and modern corporate finance*. Boston: Houghton Mifflin.

Seligman, J. (2002) "Restoring the S.E.C." *New York Times* (November 10): Wk 13.

Seligson, M. A. (2002) "The impact of corruption on regime legitimacy: A comparative study of four Latin American countries." *Journal of Politics* 64: 408–433.

Selke, W., and Pepinsky, H. E. (1984) "The politics of police reporting in Indianapolis, 1948–1978." *Law and Human Behavior* 6: 327–342.

Sen, A. (1977) "Rational fools: A critique of the behavioral foundations of economic theory." *Philosophy and Public Affairs* 6: 316–345.

Senior, J. (2002) "You've got jail." *New York* (July 22): 29–33, 80–81.

Serrin, J., and Serrin, W. (2002) *Muckraking! The journalism that changed America*. New York: New Press.

Sessions, W. S. (1991) "Computer crime—An escalating crime trend." *FBI Law Enforcement Bulletin* (February): 12–15.

Sexton, J. (1994) "New York police often lie under oath, report says." *New York Times* (April 22): A1.

Shamir, R. (2004) "Between self-regulation and the Alien Tort Claims Act: On the contested concept of corporate social responsibility." *Law & Society Review* 38: 635–664.

Shanahan, G. (2002) "You say house arrest, I say paradise." *New York Times* (May 2): Home 1.

Shao, M. (1996) "SJC disciplines attorney for excessive fees." *Boston Globe* (August 13): 1.

Shackelford, D. B. (1993) "Commentary: The savings and loan crisis." *Law & Policy* 15: 195–198.

Shapiro, B. (2003) *Shaking the foundations: Investigative journalism through 200 years of outrage, invective, exposure, and vindication*. New York: Nation Books.

Shapiro, I., and Brilmayer, L. (Eds.) (1999) *Global justice*. New York: New York University Press.

Shapiro, S. P. (1980) *Thinking about white collar crime: Matters of conceptualization and research*. Washington, DC: U.S. Department of Justice.

Shapiro, S. P. (1984) *Wayward capitalists: Targets of the Securities and Exchange Commission*. New Haven, CT: Yale University Press.

Shapiro, S. P. (1985) "The road not taken: The elusive path to criminal prosecution for white-collar offenders." *Law & Society Review* 19: 179–217.

Shapiro, S. P. (1990) "Collaring the crime, not the criminal: Reconsidering the concept of white-collar crime." *American Sociological Review* 55: 346–365.

Shapiro, S. P. (2002) *Tangled loyalties: Conflict of interest in legal practice*. Ann Arbor, MI: University of Michigan Press.

Sharpe, A. N. (1995) "Corporate performance crime as structurally coerced action." *The Australian and New Zealand Journal of Criminology* 28: 73–92.

Sharpe, J. A. (1984) *Crime in early modern England: 1550–1750*. London: Longman.

Shatz, M. S. (1971) *The essential works of anarchism*. New York: Bantam Books.

Shaw, M. (2003) *War and genocide—Organized killing in modern society*. Cambridge, UK: Polity Press.

Sheak, R. (1990) "Corporate and state attacks on the material conditions of the working class." *Humanity & Society* 14: 105–127.

Shearing, C. D., and Stenning, P. C. (1987) *Private policing*. Newbury Park, CA: Sage.

Sheff, D. (1994) *Game over—How Nintendo conquered the world*. New York: Vintage.

Sheldon, J. A., and Zweibel, G. T. (1980) "Historical developments of consumer fraud law," pp. 185–202 in E. Bittner and S. Messinger (Eds.), *Criminology review yearbook*. Beverly Hills, CA: Sage.

Sheley, J. F. (1983) "Critical elements of criminal behavior explanation." *The Sociological Quarterly* 24: 161–186.

Shenk, J. F., and Klaus, P. A. (1984) "The economic cost of crime to victims." Special Report. Washington, DC: U.S. Department of Justice, Bureau of Justice Statistics.

Shenon, P. (2001) "Internet piracy is suspected as U.S. agents raid campuses." *New York Times* (December 12): C1.

Shenon, P., and Hulse, C. (2005) "DeLay is indicted in Texas case and forfeits G.O.P. house post." *New York Times* (September 29): A1.

Shepard, C. E. (1989) *Forgiven—The rise and fall of Jim Bakker and the PTL ministry*. New York: Atlantic Monthly.

Sherman, H. L., Jr. (1987) "Torts," pp. 418–431 in R. L. Janosik (Ed.), *Encyclopedia of the American judicial system*. New York: Scribner.

Sherman, L. W., and Langworthy, R. (1979) "Measuring homicide by police officers." *Journal of Criminal Law and Criminology* 4: 546–560.

Shichor, D. (1989) "Corporate deviance and corporate victimization: A review and some elaboration." *International Review of Victimology* 1: 67–88.

Shichor, D., Sechrest, D. V., and Doocy, J. (2001) "Victims of investment fraud," pp. 81–96 in H. N. Pontell and D. Shichor (Eds.), *Contemporary issues in crime and criminal justice*. Upper Saddle River, NJ: Prentice Hall.

Shiller, R. J. (2005) "How Wall Street learns to look the other way." *New York Times* (February 8): Op ed.

Shilts, R. (1987) *And the band played on—Politics, people, and the AIDS epidemic*. New York: St. Martin's Press.

Short, J. F., Jr. (2001) "Technology, risk analysis, and the challenge of social control," pp. 213–230 in H. N. Pontell and D. Shichor (Eds.), *Contemporary issues in criminology and criminal justice*. Upper Saddle River, NJ: Prentice Hall.

Short, P. (2005) *Pol Pot: Anatomy of a nightmare*. New York: Henry Holt.

Shover, N., and Bryant, K. M. (1993) "Theoretical explanations of corporate crime," pp. 141–176 in M. B. Blankenship (Ed.), *Understanding corporate criminality*. New York: Garland.

Shover, N., Clelland, D. A., and Lynxwiler, J. (1986) *Enforcement of negotiation: Constructing a regulatory bureaucracy*. Albany, NY: SUNY Press.

Shover, N., and Coffey, G. S. (2005) "Telemarketing predators: Finally, we've got their number." *NIJ Journal* 252: 14–18.

Shover, N., Coffey, G. S., and Hobbs, D. (2003) "Crime on the line." *British Journal of Criminology* 43: 489–505.

Shover, N., Fox, G. L., and Mills, M. (1991) *Victimization by white collar crime and institutional delegitimation*. Unpublished manuscript, University of Tennessee.

Shover, N., Fox, G. L., and Mills, M. (1994) "Longterm consequences of victimization by white-collar crime." *Justice Quarterly* 11: 75–98.

Shover, N., and Hochstetler, A. (2002) "Cultural explanation and organizational crime." *Crime, Law & Social Change* 37: 1–18.

Shover, N., and Routhe, A. S. (2005) "Environmental crime," pp. 321–371 in M. Tonry (Ed.), *Crime and Justice: A review of research*. Chicago: University of Chicago Press.

Shuger, S. (1992) "Public eye." *New York Times Magazine* (September 3): 57, 74–87.

Shukla, R. K., and Bartgis, E. E. (Forthcoming) "NASA," in E. Jensen and J. Gerber (Eds.), *Encyclopedia of white-collar crime*. New York: Greenwood Press.

Sieh, E. W. (1993) "Employee theft: An examination of Gerald Mars and an explanation based on equity theory," pp. 95–111 in F. Adler and W. S. Laufer (Eds.), *New directions in criminological theory*, Vol. 4. New Brunswick, NJ: Transaction.

Sifakis, C. (2001) "Weil, Joseph 'Yellow Kid,'" pp. 932–933 in *The encyclopedia of crime*. New York: Facts on File.

Silk, L. (1990) "The true cost of the bailout." *New York Times* (June 1): D2.

Silverman, M., Ree, P. R., and Lydecker, M. (1982) *Prescriptions for death: The drugging of the third world.* Berkeley: University of California Press.

Silverstein, M. (1988) "Watergate and the American political system," pp. 15–37 in A. Markovits and M. Silverstein (Eds.), *The politics of scandal: Power and process in liberal democracies.* New York: Holmes & Meier.

Simon, D. R. (2002) *Tony Soprano's America: The criminal side of the American dream.* Boulder, CO: Westview Press.

Simon, D. R. (2006) *Elite deviance* (8th ed.). Boston: Allyn & Bacon.

Simon, D. R., and Swart, S. L. (1984) "The Justice department focuses on white-collar crime: Promises and pitfalls." *Crime & Delinquency* 30: 91–106.

Simon, H. (1976) *Administrative behavior* (3rd ed.). New York: Free Press.

Simon, H. (1987) "Rationality in psychology and economics," in R. Hogarth and M. Reder (Eds.), *Rational choice.* Chicago: University of Chicago Press.

Simon, J. F. (1991) "Citizen suits for environmental enforcement." *Trial* (September): 30–33.

Simons, M. (2001) "Milosevic is given to U.N. for trial in war-crime case." *New York Times* (June 29): A1.

Simons, M. (2002) "Without fanfare or cases, International Court sets up." *New York Times* (July 1): A3.

Simons, M. (2005) "Sudan poses first big trial for World Criminal Court." *New York Times* (April 28): A12.

Simpson, S. S. (1993) "Strategy, structure and corporate crime: The historical context of anticompetitive behavior," pp. 71–94 in F. Adler and W. S. Laufer (Eds.), *New directions in criminological theory,* Vol. 4. New Brunswick, NJ: Transaction.

Simpson, S. S. (2002) *Corporate crime, law, and social control.* New York: Cambridge University Press.

Simpson, S. S. (2003) "The criminological enterprise and corporate crime." *The Criminologist* 4: (July/August): 1, 3–5.

Simpson, S. S., Harris, A. R., and Mattson, B. A. (1993) "Measuring corporate crime," pp. 115–140 in M. B. Blankenship (Ed.), *Understanding corporate criminality.* New York: Garland.

Simpson, S. S., and Koper, C. S. (1992) "Deterring corporate crime." *Criminology* 30: 347–376.

Simpson, S. S., and Koper, C. S. (1997) "The changing of the guard: Top management team characteristics, organizational strain, and antitrust offending, 1960–1988." *Journal of Quantitative Criminology* 13: 373–404.

Simpson, S. S., and Piquero, N. L. (2001) "The Archer Daniels Midland antitrust case of 1996: A case study," pp. 175–194 in H. Pontell and D. Shichor (Eds.), *Contemporary issues in crime and criminal justice.* Upper Saddle River, NJ: Prentice Hall.

Simpson, S. S., and Piquero, N. L. (2003) "Low self-control, organizational theory, and corporate crime." *Law & Society Review* 36: 509–548.

Sims, C. (1990a) "Phone fraud: It's still a big problem on campus." *New York Times* (January 3): B6.

Sims, C. (1990b) "U.S. accuses 2 Nynex companies of overcharging and fines them." *New York Times* (February 8): A1.

Sims, C. (1993) "Keating convicted of U.S. charges." *New York Times* (January 7): D1.

Sinclair, U. (1906; 1960) *The jungle.* New York: New American Library.

Singer, P. W. (2003) *Corporate warriors: The rise of the privatized military industry.* Ithaca: Cornell University Press.

Singer, P. W. (2004) "Nation builders and low bidders in Iraq." *New York Times* (June 15): Op ed.

Skeel, D. (2005) *Icarus in the boardroom: The fundamental flaws in corporate America and where they came from.* New York: Oxford University Press.

Sklar, J. N. (1964; 1986) *Legalism: Law, morals, and political trials.* Cambridge, MA: Harvard University Press.

Skogly, S. I. (2002) *The human rights obligations of the World Bank and the International Monetary Fund.* London: Cavendish Publishing Co.

Skolnick, J. H. (1969) *The politics of protest.* New York: Ballantine Books.

Slapper, G., and Tombs, S. (1999) *Corporate crime.* London: Addison Wesley Longman.

Sloan, A. (2001) "Lights out for Enron." *Newsweek* (December 10): 50–51.

Sloane, L. (1991a) "Rising fraud worrying car insurers." *New York Times* (November 16): 48.

Sloane, L. (1991b) "Beware postcards bearing gifts and 900 numbers." *New York Times* (December 14): A12.

Smigel, E. O. (1970) "Public attitudes toward stealing as related to the size of the victim organization," pp. 15–28 in E. Smigel and H. L. Ross (Eds.), *Crimes against bureaucracy*. New York: Van Nostrand Reinhold.

Smith, A. (1759; 1976) *The theory of moral sentiments*. Oxford, UK: Clarendon Press.

Smith, A. (1776; 1937) *An inquiry into the nature and causes of the wealth of nations* (E. Canaan, Ed.) New York: Modern Library.

Smith, C. (1990) "Rose sentenced to 5 months for filing false tax returns." *New York Times* (July 20): A1.

Smith, D. C., Jr. (1978) "Organized crime and entrepreneurship." *International Journal of Criminology and Penology* 6: 161–177.

Smith, D. K. (2004) "Online investing and the online consumer: State and decentered regulatory responses." *Law & Policy* 26: 371–374.

Smith, G. B. (2002) "Historically, bad execs do little jail time." *The Scranton Times* (July 23): 12.

Smith, G. K. (1992) "The independent counsel in the Iran/Contra affair: Why Gordon Liddy went to jail and Oliver North went to Disneyworld." *American Criminal Law Review* 29: 1261–1299.

Smith, J., and Moran, T. P. (2000) "WTO 101: Myths about the World Trade Organization." *Dissent* (Spring): 66–70.

Smith, K. W., and Kinsey, K. A. (1987) "Understanding taxpayers' behavior: A conceptual framework with implications for research." *Law & Society Review* 21: 639–663.

Smith, K. W., and Stalans, L. J. (1991) "Encouraging tax compliance with positive incentives: A conceptual framework and research directions." *Law & Policy* 13: 35–53.

Smith, R. G., Grabosky, P., and Urbas, G. (2004) *Cyber criminals on trial*. Cambridge, UK: Cambridge University Press.

Smith, R. W. (2004) "American self-interest and the response to genocide." *The Chronicle of Higher Education* (July 30): B6–9.

Smothers, R. (1996) "Nigerian sentenced in first of global business fraud schemes." *New York Times* (March 24): A34.

Smothers, R. (1999a) "65 accused of aiding health fraud." *New York Times* (February 3): 35.

Smothers, R. (1999b) "In plea deal, a banker outlines money laundering in Caymans." *New York Times* (August 3): A1.

Smothers, R. (2000) "Ex-regulator sentenced in tele-market fraud." *New York Times* (July 18): C2.

Smothers, R. (2001) "Former penny-stock financier on trial in bankruptcy fraud." *New York Times* (March 10): B7.

Smothers, R. (2005) "Former Hudson County leader gets 41 months in corruption case." *New York Times* (March 25): B5.

Snider, L. (1987) "Towards a political economy of reform, regulation, and corporate crime." *Law & Policy* 9: 37–68.

Snider, L. (1993) *Bad business—Corporate crime in Canada*. Scarborough, Ontario: Nelson Canada.

Snider, L. (2000) "The sociology of corporate crime: An obituary." *Theoretical Criminology* 4: 169–206.

Snider, L. (2001) "Crimes against capital: Discovering theft of time." *Social Justice* 28: 105–120.

Snider, L. (2003) "Researching corporate crime," pp. 49–68 in S. Tombs and D. Whyte (Eds.), *Unmasking the crimes of the powerful*. New York: Peter Lang.

Snizek, W. E. (1974) "Deviant behavior among blue-collar workers-employees: Work-norm violation in the factory," pp. 67–74 in C. D. Bryant (Ed.), *Deviant behavior—Occupational and organizational bases*. Chicago: Rand McNally.

Soble, R. J., and Dallos, R. E. (1974) *The impossible dream: The Equity funding story*. New York: Putnam.

Sobol, R. B. (1991) *Bending the law: The story of the Dalkon shield bankruptcy*. Chicago: University of Chicago Press.

Solomon, A. M. (1989) "The risks were too good to pass up." *New York Times Book Review* (October 29): 27–28.

Sorkin, A. R. (2002a) "Back to school, but this one is for top corporate officials." *New York Times* (September 3): A1.

Sorkin, A. R. (2002b) "When a trusted secretary takes more than a letter." *New York Times* (November 27): A1.

Sorkin, A. R. (2002c) "Life without a jet, and other laments." *New York Times* (December 15).

Sorkin, A. R. (2004a) "Judge ends trial when Tyco juror reports threat." *New York Times* (April 3): A1.

Sorkin, A. R. (2004b) "Ex-Secretary guilty of embezzling $7 million." *New York Times* (April 21): C4.

Sorkin, A. R. (2004c) "Wall Street banker is found guilty of obstruction." *New York Times* (May 4): A1.

Sorkin, A. R. (2005a) "Former chief of Tyco maintains innocence on eve of trial no. 2." *New York Times* (January 16): A1.

Sorkin, A. R. (2005b) "Ex-chief and aide guilty of looting millions at Tyco." *New York Times* (June 18): A1.

Sorkin, A. R. (2005c) "Judges cite concerns over trial of banker." *New York Times* (July 13): C1.

Sorkin, A. R. (2005d) "How long to jail white-collar criminals." *New York Times* (September 16): C1.

Sorkin, A. R. (2005e) "Ex-Tyco officers to get 8 to 25 years." *New York Times* (September 20): A1.

Sorkin, A. R., and Atlas, R. D. (2001) "Circling the wagons around Enron." *New York Times* (November 22): C1.

Spaeth, A. (1997) "The golden shaft." *Time* (May 19): 54–58.

Spahr, L. L., and Alison, L. J. (2004) "US Savings and Loan fraud: Implications for general and criminal culture theories of crime." *Crime, Law & Social Change* 41: 95–106.

Sparks, A. (1990) *The mind of South Africa*. New York: Knopf.

Sparrow, M. K. (1996) *License to steal—Why fraud plagues America's health care system*. Boulder, CO: Westview Press.

Sparrow, M. K. (1998) "Fraud control in the health care industry: Assessing the state of the art." *National Institute of Justice: Research in Brief*: 1–11.

Speer, D. L. (2000) "Redefining borders: The challenges of cybercrime." *Crime, Law & Social Change* 34: 259–273.

Spencer, J. W., and Triche, E. (1994) "Media constructions of risk and safety: Differential framings of hazard events." *Sociological Inquiry* 64: 199–213.

Spencer, S. (1993) "Lawrence Walsh's last battle." *New York Times Magazine* (July 4): 11.

Sperber, M. (2000) *Beer and circus—How big-time college sports is crippling undergraduate education*. New York: Henry Holt.

Spragins, E. E. (1997) "Scam scuttling." *Newsweek* (October 6): 79–81.

Springen, K. (1991) "A slippery pyramid?" *Newsweek* (July 22): 39.

Spurgeon, W. A., and Fagan, T. P. (1981) "Criminal liability for life—Endangering corporate conduct." *The Journal of Criminal Law and Criminology* 72: 400–433.

Staats, G. R. (1977) "Changing conceptualizations of professional criminals: Implications for criminology theory." *Criminology* 15: 49–65.

Stallbaumer, L. M. (1999) "Big business and the persecution of the Jews: The Flick concern and the Aryanization of Jewish property before the war." *Holocaust and Genocide Studies* 13: 1–27.

Stamler, B. (2003) "The gray area for nonprofits: Where legal is questionable." *New York Times* (November 17): D17.

Stanley, A. (1999) "How 2 priests got mixed up in a huge insurance scandal." *New York Times* (June 26): A1.

Starek, R. B. (1996) "Myths and half-truths about deceptive advertising." National Infomercial Marketing Association (October 15), Las Vegas.

Starobin, P. (1997) "Why those hidden cameras hurt journalists." *New York Times* (January 28): Op ed.

Starr, J. M. (1998) "Why study Vietnam?" pp. 213–222 in D. L. Anderson (Ed.), *Facing My Lai*. Kansas City: University of Kansas Press.

Starr, J. W. (1991) "Turbulent times at Justice and EPA: The origins of environmental criminal prosecutions and the work that remains." *The George Washington Law Review* 59: 900–915.

Steele, J. (2004) *Risks and legal theory*. Oxford, UK: Hart Publishing.

Steffens, L. (1904) *The shame of the cities*. New York: McClure, Phillips.

Steffensmeier, D. (1986) *The fence*. Totowa, NJ: Rowman & Littlefield.

Steffensmeier, D. (1989) "On the causes of 'white-collar' crime: An assessment of Hirschi and Gottfredson's claims." *Criminology* 27: 345–358.

Steier, R. (1993) "The price isn't always right." *New York Post* (February 26): 3.

Stein, B. (2005) "We were soldiers once, and broke." *New York Times* (July 17): 3/4.

Steinberg, A. (1972) *The bosses*. New York: Macmillan.

Steinberg, J. (1993a) "Risen from a 'Living Cemetery.'" *New York Times* (March 29): B1.

Steinberg, J. (1993b) "Connecticut store owner sentenced for tax fraud." *New York Times* (October 21): B1.

Steinberg, M. I. (1991) "Attorney liability for client fraud." *Columbia Business Law Review* 1: 11–26.

Steinhauer, J. (2005) "New legal stars guard Wall St. from scandals." *New York Times* (May 19): A1.

Stellin, S. (2002) "Directors ponder new tougher roles." *New York Times* (June 30): Bus 16.

Stenning, P. (1988) "Corporate policing: Some recent trends," pp. 37–45 in *Business and crime: A consultation*. Windsor, UK: Centre for Criminological & Sociolegal Studies, University of Sheffield.

Stern, G. M. (1976) *The Buffalo Creek disaster*. New York: Vintage.

Stern, J. (1999) *The ultimate terrorists*. Cambridge, MA: Harvard University Press.

Stern, P. M. (1972) *The rape of the taxpayer*. New York: Vintage.

Stern, P. M. (1980) *Lawyers on trial*. New York: Time Books.

Sterngold, J. (1990) *Burning down the house—How greed, deceit, and bitter revenge destroyed E. F. Hutton*. New York: Summit Books.

Sterngold, J. (1995) "Orange County bankruptcy: The poor feel the most pain." *New York Times* (December 5): A1.

Stevenson, R. W. (1991a) "Keating's trial begins with emotion flaring." *New York Times* (August 3): A35.

Stevenson, R. W. (1991b) "U.S. accuses G.E. of fraud in Israeli deal." *New York Times* (August 15): A1.

Stevenson, R. W. (1992a) "Keating is sentenced to 10 years for defrauding S & L customers." *New York Times* (April 11): A1.

Stewart, C. S. (2004a) "After serving time, executives now serve up advice." *New York Times* (June 1): C1.

Stewart, C. S. (2004b) "Fighting crime one computer at a time." *New York Times* (June 10): C5.

Stewart, J. B. (1987) *The prosecutors*. New York: Touchstone Books.

Stewart, J. B. (1991) *Den of thieves*. New York: Simon & Schuster.

Stewart, J. B. (1993) "Michael Milken's biggest deal." *The New Yorker* (March 8): 58–71.

Stewart, J. B. (1996) *Blood sport—The president and his adversaries*. New York: Simon & Schuster.

Stewart, J. B. (2001) "The Milken file." *The New Yorker* (January 22): 47–61.

Stewart, J. B. (2003) "Spend! Spend! Spend!" *The New Yorker* (February 17 & 24): 132–147.

Stiglitz, J. E. (2002) *Globalization and its discontents*. New York: W. W. Norton & Co.

Stohl, M., and Lopez, G. A. (Eds.) (1984) *The state as terrorist: The dynamics of governmental violence and repression*. Westport, CT: Greenwood Press.

Stolberg, S. G., and Harris, G. (2003) "Measure to ease imports of drugs is gaining in House." *New York Times* (July 22): A1.

Stone, A. (2002) "In poll, Islamic world says Arabs not involved in 9/11." *USA Today* (February 27): 1.

Stone, B. (2001) "Busting the web bandits." *Newsweek* (July 16): 55.

Stone, C. (1975) *Where the law ends*. New York: Harper.

Stone, C. (1989) "Choice of target and other law enforcement variables," pp. 203–223 in M. L. Friedland (Ed.), *Sanctions and rewards in the legal system: A multidisciplinary approach*. Toronto: University of Toronto.

Stone, M. (1986) "Insiders." *New York* (July 28): 26–34.

Stotland, E. (1981) "Can white-collar crime investigators be protected from improper pressures? The case of Israel." *Journal of Criminal Justice* 9: 265–288.

Stotland, E. (1982) "The role of law enforcement in the fight against white-collar crime," pp. 69–98 in H. Edelhertz and T. D. Overcast (Eds.), *White collar crime—An agenda for research*. Lexington, MA: Lexington.

Stout, D. (1995) "Defense lawyer pleads guilty to aiding cartel." *New York Times* (July 4): 8.

Stader, J. K. (2002) *Understanding white collar crime* (2nd ed.). Newark, NJ: Lexis/Nexis.

Strom, S. (2002) "Questions arise on accounting at United Way." *New York Times* (November 19): A1.

Strom, S. (2003) "Guilty plea due today in big United Way theft." *New York Times* (February 6): A24.

Stylianou, S. (2003) "Measuring crime seriousness perceptions: What have we learned and what else do we want to know." *Journal of Criminal Justice* 31: 37–56.

Sullivan, J. (2000) "School vendors charged with price fixing." *New York Times* (June 2): B3.

Sullivan, J., and Berenson, A. (2000) "Dozens named in stock fraud linked to mob." *New York Times* (June 15): C2.

Sullivan, T., and Hodson, R. (2002) *The social organization of work*. Belmont, CA: Wadsworth/Thomson Learning.

Sunstein, C. R., Hastie, R., Payne, J. W., Schade, D. A., and Viscusi, W. K. (2002) *Punitive damages—How juries decide*. Chicago: University of Chicago Press.

Surette, R. (1998) *Media, crime, and criminal justice* (2nd ed.). Belmont, CA: Wadsworth.

Surowiecki, J. (2004) "Board stiffs." *The New Yorker* (March 8): 30.

Sutherland, E. H. (1924) *Criminology*. Philadelphia: Lippincott.

Sutherland, E. H. (1937) *The professional thief*. Chicago: University of Chicago Press.

Sutherland, E. H. (1940) "White-collar criminality." *American Sociological Review* 5: 1–12.

Sutherland, E. H. (1945) "Is 'white-collar crime' crime?" *American Sociological Review* 10: 132–139.

Sutherland, E. H. (1947) *Criminology* (4th ed.). Philadelphia: Lippincott.

Sutherland, E. H. (1949) *White collar crime*. New York: Holt, Rinehart & Winston.

Sutton, A., and Wild, R.,(1985) "Small business: White-collar villains or victims?" *International Journal of the Sociology of Law* 13: 247–259.

Swanson, W., and Schultz, G. (1982) *Prime rip*. Englewood Cliffs, NJ: Prentice Hall.

Swarns, R. L. (1996) "After T.W.A. crash, a 'charity' springs up." *New York Times* (August 10): 26.

Swarns, R. L. (1997) "Former chief is charged with bilking foster agency." *New York Times* (May 13): B31.

Swartz, E. M. (1987) "Product liability and the captive consumers." *Case and Comment* (November/ December): 3–6.

Sykes, C. J. (1988) *Profscam: Professors and the demise of higher education*. Washington, DC: Regnery.

Sykes, G. M., and Matza, D. (1957) "Techniques of neutralization: A theory of delinquency." *American Sociological Review* 22: 664–670.

Szasz, A. (1984) "Industrial resistance to occupational safety and health legislation, 1971–1981." *Social Problems* 32: 103–116.

Szasz, A. (1986a) "The process and significance of political scandals: A comparison of Watergate and the 'Sewergate' episode at the Environmental Protection Agency." *Social Problems* 33: 202–217.

Szasz, A. (1986b) "Corporations, organized crime, and the disposal of hazardous waste: An examination of the making of a criminogenic regulatory structure." *Criminology* 24: 1–28.

Szockyj, E. (1990) "From Wall Street to Main Street: Defining insider trading as a social problem." A paper presented at the Annual Meeting of the American Society of Criminology (Baltimore, MD), November.

Szockyj, E., and Geis, G. (2002) "Insider trading: Patterns and analysis." *Journal of Criminal Justice* 30: 273–286.

Tager, M. (1988) "Corruption and party machines in New York City." *Corruption and Reform* 3: 25–39.

Tannenbaum, F. (1938) *Crime and the community*. New York: Columbia University Press.

Tappan, P. (1947) "Who is the criminal?" *American Sociological Review* 12: 96–102.

Tarbell, I. (1904; 1925) *History of the Standard Oil Co.* New York: Macmillan.

Taylor, S. (1983) "Ethics and the law: A case history." *New York Times Magazine* (January 9): 31–33, 46–49.

Taylor, S. (1985) "Criminal lawyers and lawyers who turn criminal." *New York Times* (March 19): A17.

Taylor, T. (1970) *Nuremberg and Vietnam: An American tragedy*. New York: Bantam Books.

Tedeschi, B. (2001) "Seller of online currency may have been victim of fraud." *New York Times* (August 27): C1.

Tedeschi, B. (2002) "E-Commerce report." *New York Times* (June 10): C7.

Tedeschi, B. (2003) "E-Commerce report." *New York Times* (January 27): C4.

Teuber, A. (1990) "Justifying risk." *Daedalus* 119: 235–254.

Theoharis, A. (2004) *The FBI and American democracy: A brief critical history*. Lawrence, KS: University Press of Kansas.

Thio, A. (1988; 2003) *Deviant behavior* (3rd ed.). New York: Harper & Row.

Thomas, J. M. (1982) "The regulatory role in the containment of corporate illegality," pp. 99–127 in

H. E. Edelhertz and T. D. Overcast (Eds.), *White-collar crime: An agenda for research.* Lexington, MA: Lexington.

Thomas, L. (2003) "2 grand juries are formed in bank case." *New York Times* (March 15): C1.

Thomas, L. (2004) "Psst. Why insider trading keeps going." *New York Times* (May 16): C1.

Thomas, L. (2005a) "Catch him if you can." *New York Times* (January 16): 3/1.

Thomas, L. (2005b) "Jury tallies Morgan's total of $1.45 billion." *New York Times* (May 19): C1.

Thomas, L. (2005c) "Counselor for all reasons." *New York Times* (July 28): C1.

Thomas, R. (1994) "Forget about the experts." *Newsweek* (October 31): 42.

Thompson, B. (2002) "Toward an understanding of academic deviance," pp. 73–84 in G. W. Potter (Ed.), *Controversies in white-collar crime.* Cincinnati, OH: Anderson.

Thompson, D. (2001) "California raps 'predatory lending.'" *Scranton Times* (November 4): C4.

Thornburgh, R. (1990) "Money laundering." *Vital Speeches of the Day* 56: 578–580.

Thornburgh, R. (2000) "Sue, but don't prosecute." *New York Times* (September 20): Op ed.

Thornton, E., Coy, P. and Timmons, H. (2002) "The breakdown of banking." *Businessweek* (October 7): 40–42.

Thottam, J. (2003) "Are they all crooked?" *Time* (November 17): 54–57.

Thurman, Q., and Vose, B. (2001) "Tax fraud," pp. 490–493 in D. Luckenbill and D. Peck (Eds.), *Encyclopedia of criminology and deviant behavior,* Vol II. Philadelphia: Brunner-Routledge.

Tibbetts, S. C. (1997) "Gender differences in students' rational decisions to cheat." *Deviant Behavior* 18: 393–414.

Tidwell, G. L. (1993) *Anatomy of a fraud.* New York: Wiley.

Tierney, K. J. (1999) "Toward a critical sociology of risk." *Sociological Forum* 14: 217–242.

Tigar, M., and Levy, M. R. (1977) *Law and the rise of capitalism.* New York: Monthly Review Press.

Tillman, R. (1998) *Broken promises—Fraud by small business health insurers.* Boston: Northeastern University Press.

Tillman, R. (2002) *Global pirates: Fraud in the offshore insurance industry.* Boston: Northeastern University Press.

Tillman, R., and Indergaard, M. (1999) "Field of schemes: Health insurance fraud in the small business sector." *Social Problems* 46: 572–590.

Tillman, R., and Pontell, H. N. (1992) "Is justice 'collar-blind'? Punishing Medicaid provider fraud." *Criminology* 30: 547–574.

Tilly, C. (1985) "War making and state making as organized crime," pp. 169–191 in P. B. Evans, D. Rueschmeyer, and T. Skocpol (Eds.), *Bringing the state back in.* Cambridge, UK: Cambridge University Press.

Timm, H. W., and Christian, K. E. (1991) *Introduction to private security.* Pacific Grove, CA: Brooks/Cole.

Tittle, C. R. (1983) "Social class and criminal behavior: A critique of the theoretical foundations." *Social Forces* 62: 334–373.

Tittle, C. R., Villemez, W. J., and Smith, D. A. (1978) "The myth of social class and criminality: An empirical assessment of the empirical evidence." *American Sociological Review* 43: 643–656.

Titus, R. M., Heinzelmann, F., and Boyle, J. M. (1995) "Victimization of persons by fraud." *Crime & Delinquency* 41: 54–72.

Toffler, B. L. (2003) *Final accounting: Ambition, greed, and the fall of Arthur Andersen.* New York: Broadway Books.

Tolchin, M. (1984) "One enlists in the campaign against waste." *New York Times* (February 28): A14.

Tolchin, S. J., and Tolchin, M. (1983) *Dismantling America—The rush to deregulate.* Boston: Houghton Mifflin.

Tolchin, S. J., and Tolchin, M. (2001) *Glass house: Congressional ethics and the politics of venom.* Cambridge, MA: Westview Press.

Tomasic, R., and Pentony, B. (1989) "Insider trading and business ethics." *Legal Studies Forum* 13: 151–170.

Tombs, S. (2005) "Corporate crime," pp. 240–244 in R. A. Wright and J. M. Miller (Eds.), *Encyclopedia of criminology.* New York: Routledge.

Tombs, S., and Hillyard, P. (2004) "Towards a political economy of harm: States, corporations, and the production of inequality," pp. 30–54, in P. Hillyard, C. Pantazis, D. Gordon and S. Tombs (Eds.),

Beyond criminology: Taking harm seriously. London: Pluto Press.

Tombs, S., and Whyte, D. (Eds.) (2003) *Unmasking the crimes of the powerful and scrutinizing states and corporations.* New York: Peter Lang.

Toobin, J. (2002) "The man chasing Enron." *The New Yorker* (September 9): 86–94.

Toobin, J. (2004) "A bad thing." *The New Yorker* (March 22): 60–72.

Torres, D. A. (1985) *Handbook of federal police and investigative agencies.* Westport, CT: Greenwood Press.

Tracy, P. E., and Fox, J. A. (1989) "A field experiment on insurance fraud in auto body repair." *Criminology* 27: 589–603.

Trasler, G. (2005) "Rational choice theory," pp. 1403–1407 in R. A. Wright and J. M. Miller (Eds.), *Encyclopedia of criminology.* New York: Routledge.

Traub, J. (1988) "Into the mouths of babes." *New York Times Magazine* (July 24): 18–20, 51.

Treaster, J. B. (1997a) "Patching the cracks in the rock." *New York Times* (February 23).

Treaster, J. B. (1997b) "Gumshoes with white collars?" *New York Times* (August 29): C1.

Treaster, J. B. (1999a) "Worry over insurance fraud extends to grave." *New York Times* (July 7): C1.

Treaster, J. B. (1999b) "Cendant settles fraud lawsuit for $2.8 billion." *New York Times* (December 8): A1.

Treaster, J. B. (2003) "As Hancock's profit declined, chief's pay rose to $21 million." *New York Times* (May 17): C1.

Treaster, J. B. (2005a) "Fraud in insurance is vast, Spitzer tells a state panel." *New York Times* (January 18): C2.

Treaster, J. B. (2005b) "Insurance broker settles Spitzer suit for $850 million." *New York Times* (February 1): A1.

Tresniowski, A., Kapos, S., and Comander, L. (2004) "Taken for a ride." *People* (June 21): 135–137.

Trillin, C. (2000) "Marisa and Jeff." *The New Yorker* (July 10): 26–33.

Truell, P. (1995a) "Cravath lawyer and brother charged with insider trades." *New York Times* (June 26): D1.

Truell, P. (1995b) "A Japanese bank is indicted in U.S. and also barred." *New York Times* (November 3): A1.

Truell, P. (1998) "Milken settles S.E.C. complaint for $47 million." *New York Times* (February 27): A1.

Truell, P., and Gurwin, L. (1992) *False profits: The inside story of BCCI, the world's most corrupt financial empire.* New York: Houghton Mifflin.

Turk, A. (1982) *Political criminality.* Beverly Hills, CA: Sage.

Turley, J. (2000) "'From pillar to post': The prosecution of American presidents." *American Criminal Law Review* 37: 1049–1106.

Turner, H. A. (1969) "Big business and the rise of Hitler." *American Historical Review* 75: 56–90.

Turow, S. (2004) "Cry no tears for Martha Stewart." *New York Times* (May 27): Op ed.

Tyler, G. (1981) "The crime corporation," pp. 273–290 in A. S. Blumberg (Ed.), *Current perspectives on criminal behavior.* New York: Knopf.

Uchitelle, L. (2002) "The rich are different. They know when to leave." *New York Times* (January 20): Wk 1.

Uggen, C. (1993) "Reintegrating Braithwaite: Shame and consensus in criminological theory." *Law & Social Inquiry* 18: 481–499.

Ulen, T. S. (1997) "The economic case for corporate criminal sanctioning," pp. 119–141 in W. S. Lofquist, M. A. Cohen, and G. A. Rabe (Eds.), *Debating corporate crime.* Cincinnati, OH: Anderson.

Unger, C. (2004) *House of Bush, House of Saud: The secret relationship between the world's two most powerful dynasties.* New York: Scribner.

Urofsky, M. I. (2005) *Money and Free Speech: Campaign Finance Reform and the Courts.* Lawrence, KS: University Press of Kansas.

U.S. Department of Justice. (1989) *White collar crime: A report to the public.* Washington, DC: U.S. Government Printing Office.

U.S. Department of Justice. (2003) "United States Marshals Service." http://www.usdoj.gov/marshals/.

U.S. Department of Justice. (2005) "Fraud Section: Problem Integrity Section." http://www.usdoj.gov/criminal/fraud.htm.

U.S. News & World Report. (2000) "Top 10 scams on the information highway." *U.S. News & World Report* (November 13): 16.

U.S. Postal Inspection Service. (2003) "Who we are." http://www.susps.com/postalinspectors/missmore.htm.

U.S. President's Council on Integrity and Efficiency, Committee on Investigations and Law Enforcement. (1988) *Report.* Washington, DC: U.S. Government Printing Office.

U.S. Senate. (1987) *Hearings before the committee on the judiciary: Oversight of the problem of white collar crime.*

Washington, DC: U.S. Government Printing Office.

U.S. Sentencing Commission. (1990) *Annual report.* Washington, DC: U.S. Sentencing Commission.

U.S. Sentencing Commission. (2005) *Organizational sentencing.* Washington, DC: U.S. Sentencing Commission.

Useem, M. (1983) *The inner circle: Large corporations and the rise of business political activity in the U.S. and U.K.* New York: Oxford University Press.

Valaskakis, K. (1999) "Globalization as theatre." *International Social Science Journal* 160: 153–164.

Vallabhaneni, S. (2000) Inertia of change in the World Bank: The Pak Mun Dam project as a case study. Honors Thesis. Providence, Rhode Island: Brown University.

Van Cise, J. G. (1990) "Antitrust past–present–future." *The Antitrust Bulletin* 35: 985–1008.

Van Duyne, P. C. (1993) "Organized crime and business crime enterprises in the Netherlands." *Crime, Law and Social Change* 19: 103–142.

Van Natta, D., and Banerjee, N. (2002) "Top G.O.P. donors in energy industry met Cheney panel." *New York Times* (March 1): A1.

Van Natta, D., and Wayne, L. (2002) "Several administration officials held Enron shares." *New York Times* (January 18): C6.

Van Wyk, J. A., Benson, M. L., and Harris, D. K. (2000) "A test of strain and self-control theories: Occupational crime in nursing homes." *Journal of Crime and Justice* 23: 27.

Vandenburgh, H. (1998) *Feeding frenzy: Organizational deviance in the Texas for-profit psychiatric hospital industry.* Baltimore, MD: University Press of America.

Vandenburgh, H. (1999) "Business-first behavior by Texas for-profit psychiatric hospitals," pp. 195–216 in *Perspectives on Social Problems*, 11. Greenwich, CT: JAI Press.

Vashita, A., Johnston, D. R., and Choudhury, M. S. (2005) "Securities fraud." *American Criminal Law Review* 42: 877–941.

Vaughan, D. (1980) "Crime between organizations: Implications for victimology," pp. 77–97 in G. Geis and E. Stotland (Eds.), *White collar crime: Theory and research.* Beverly Hills, CA: Sage.

Vaughan, D. (1983) *Controlling unlawful corporate behavior.* Chicago: University of Chicago Press.

Vaughan, D. (1992) "The macro–micro connection in white collar crime theory," pp. 124–148 in K. Schlegel and D. Weisburd (Eds.), *White collar crime reconsidered.* Boston: Northeastern University Press.

Vaughan, D. (1996) *The Challenger launch decision: Risky technology, culture, and deviance at NASA.* Chicago: University of Chicago Press.

Vaughan, D. (1998) "Rational choice, situated action, and the social control of organizations." *Law & Society Review* 32: 23–61.

Vaughan, D. (1999) "The dark side of organizations: Mistake, misconduct, and disaster," pp. 271–305 in *Annual Reviews of Sociology.* Palo Alto, CA: Annual Reviews.

Veasey, E. N. (2003) "Corporate governance and ethics in post-Enron WorldCom environment." *Wake Forest Law Review* 38: 839–854.

Ventura, H. E., Miller, J. M., and DeFlem, M. (2005) "Governmentality and the war on terror: FBI Project Carnivore and the diffusion of disciplinary power." *Critical Criminology* 13: 55–70.

Vermeule, C. (1983) "Crime and punishment in antiquity." *Harvard Magazine* (November/December): 64–70.

Vick, D. W., and Campbell, K. (2001) "Public protests, private lawsuits, and the market: The investor response to the McLibel case." *Journal of Law & Society* 28: 204–241.

Vidmar, N. J. (1989) "Foreword—Empirical research and the issue of jury competence." *Law and Contemporary Problems* 52: 1–8.

Villa, J. K. (1988) *Banking crimes.* New York: Clark Boardman.

Viscusi, W. K. (1983) *Risk by choice: Regulating health and safety in the workplace.* Cambridge, MA: Harvard University Press.

Viscusi, W. K. (1986) "The structure and enforcement of job safety regulation." *Law and Contemporary Problems* 49: 127–150.

Vise, D. A. (1987) "One of the market's best and brightest is caught." *The Washington Post* (March 2): 6–7.

Vitello, P. (2005) "Ex-schools chief on L. I. pleads guilty to stealing $2 million." *New York Times* (September 27): B1.

Vogel, C., and Blumenthal, R. (2001) "Art auction houses agree to pay $512 million in price-fixing case." *New York Times* (September 23): A1.

Vogel, C., and Blumenthal, R. (2002) "Ex-Chairman of Sotheby's gets jail time." *New York Times* (April 23): B1.

Vogel, D. (1989) *Fluctuating fortunes*. New York: Basic Books.

Vohra, N. K. (1994) "Downsizing sweeps the industry," pp. C75–C77 in *Industry surveys*. New York: Standard & Poor.

Vold, G. B., Bernard, T. J., and Snipes, J. (2002) *Theoretical criminology* (5th ed.). New York: Oxford University Press.

von Zielbauer, P. (2003) "Bridgeport mayor took what he could, ex-advisor says." *New York Times* (January 11): B5.

Vowell, P. R., and Chen, J. (2004) "Predicting academic misconduct: A comparative test of four sociological explanations." *Sociological Inquiry* 74: 226–249.

Wachsman, H. F. (1989) "Doctors who maim and kill." *New York Times* (August 25): A29.

Waegel, W. B., Ermann, M. D., and Horowitz, A. M. (1981) "Organizational responses to the imputation of deviance." *Sociological Quarterly* 22: 43–55.

Wahl, A-M., and Gunkel, S. E. (1999) "Due process, resource mobilization, and the Occupational Safety and Health Administration, 1971–1996: The politics of social regulation in historical perspective." *Social Problems* 46: 591–616.

Wakin, D. J. (2005) "Art patron left trail of angry investors." *New York Times* (June 2): E1.

Walczak, L., Dunham, R. S., and Dwyer, P. (2002) "Let the reforms begin." *Business Week* (July 22): 26–31.

Wald, M. L. (1988) "Using liability law to put tobacco on trial." *New York Times* (February 14): F11.

Wald, M. L. (1992) "Credit fraud a growing menace, survey finds." *New York Times* (July 8): C13.

Wald, M. L. (1995) "Fake replacement parts often used on airlines." *New York Times* (May 25): A18.

Wald, M. L. (1999a) "Murder charges filed by Florida in ValuJet crash." *New York Times* (July 14): A1.

Wald, M. L. (1999b) "Cruise line pleads guilty to dumping of chemicals." *New York Times* (July 22): A10.

Wald, M. L. (1999c) "State Farm is told to pay policyholder $456 million in auto-parts case." *New York Times* (October 5).

Waldman, M. (1990) *Who robbed America? A citizen's guide to the savings & loan scandal*. New York: Random House.

Waldman, S. (1989) "The HUD Rip-off." *Newsweek* (August 7): 16–22.

Walker, A. (1981) "Sociology and professional crime," pp. 153–178 in A. S. Blumberg (Ed.), *Current perspectives on criminal behavior*. New York: Knopf.

Walker, S. (1980) *Popular justice—A history of American criminal justice*. New York: Oxford University Press.

Walker, S. (1983) *The police in America*. New York: McGraw-Hill.

Walklate, S. (1989) *Victimology: The victim and the criminal justice process*. London: Unwin Hyman.

Wall, D. S. (2003) *Cyberspace crime*. Brookfield, VT: Ashgate.

Wallace, R. P., Lusthaus, A. M., and Kim, J. H. (2005) "Computer crimes." *American Criminal Law Review* 42: 223–276.

Wallechinsky, D. (2005) "The world's 10 worst dictators." *Parade* (February 13): 3–6.

Waller, S. W. (1997) "Market talk: Competition policy in America." *Law & Social Inquiry* 22: 435–457.

Walsh, A. (2005) "Biological theories of criminal behavior," pp. 106–109 in R. A. Wright and J. M. Miller (Eds.), *Encyclopedia of criminology*. New York: Routledge.

Walsh, J. (2005) "Japan," pp. 455–459 in L. M. Salinger (Ed.), *Encyclopedia of white-collar and corporate crime*. Thousand Oaks, CA: Sage.

Walsh, L. E. (1998) "Kenneth Starr and the Independent Counsel Act." *New York Review of Books* (March 5): 4, 6.

Walsh, M. (2004) "A hard-to-swallow lesson on pensions." *New York Times* (October 14): C1.

Walsh, M. (2005) "How Wall Street wrecked United's pension." *New York Times* (July 31): 3/1.

Walsh, M. F., and Schram, D. D. (1980) "The victim of white-collar crime: Accuser or accused?" pp. 32–51 in G. Geis and E. Stotland (Eds.), *White collar crime: Theory and research*. Beverly Hills, CA: Sage.

Walt, S., and Laufer, W. S. (1991) "Why personhood doesn't matter: Corporate criminal liability and sanctions." *American Journal of Criminal Law* 18: 263–287.

Walzer, M. (1977) *Just and unjust wars: A moral argument*. New York: Basic Books.

Walzer, M. (2004) *Arguing about war*. New Haven, CT: Yale University Press.

Waring, E. (2002) "Co-offending as a network form of social organization," pp. 31–47 in E. Waring and D. Weisburd (Eds.), *Crime and Social Organization*. New Brunswick, NJ: Transaction.

Warr, M. (1989) "What is the perceived seriousness of crimes?" *Criminology* 27: 795–821.

Washburn, J. (2005) *University, Inc.—The corporate corruption of higher education*. New York: Basic Books.

Wasik, M. (1991) *Crime and the computer*. Oxford, UK: Clarendon Press.

Wayne, L. (1996) "Former Lazard partner gets 33-month prison term." *New York Times* (December 20): D1.

Wayne, L. (2001) "Investors' advocate at the S.E.C." *New York Times* (January 30): C1.

Wayne, L. (2002a) "Enron, preaching deregulation, worked the statehouse circuit." *New York Times* (February 9): C1.

Wayne, L. (2002b) "America's for-profit secret army." *New York Times* (October 13).

Wayne, L. (2005) "An office and a gentleman." *New York Times* (June 19): C1.

Wayne, L., and Pollack, A. (1998) "The master of Orange County." *New York Times* (July 22): D1.

Weatherburn, D. (1993) "On the quest for a general theory." *Australian and New Zealand Journal of Criminology* 26: 35–46.

Webb, T. (1990) "Light sentences in S & L cases blasted." *Scranton Times* (July 19): 5.

Webber, A. M. (1995) "Gibraltar may tumble." *New York Times* (August 20): 11.

Webber, F. (1999) "The Pinochet case: The struggle for the realization of human rights." *Journal of Law & Society* 26: 523–537.

Weber, J. (1990) "Measuring the impact of teaching ethics to future managers: A review, assessment and recommendation." *Journal of Business Ethics* 9: 1183–1190.

Weber, J., and Fortun, D. (2005) "Ethics and compliance officer profile: Survey, comparison, and recommendations." *Business and Society Review* 102: 97–115.

Weidenbaum, M. (2000) "Federal regulatory policy, 1980–2000." *Society* (November/December): 86–89.

Weil, J. R., and Brannon, W. T. (1957) *"Yellow Kid" Weil—Con man*. New York: Pyramid.

Weiner, E. (1990) "Eastern Airlines indicted in scheme over maintenance." *New York Times* (July 26): A1.

Weiner, T. (1999) "Lobbying for research money, colleges bypass review process." *New York Times* (August 24): A1.

Weiner, T. (2003a) "Ex-leader stole $100 million from Liberia, records show." *New York Times* (September 18): A3.

Weiner, T. (2003b) "Free trade accord at age 10: The growing pains are clear." *New York Times* (December 27): A1.

Weinstein, M. M. (2005) *Globalization: What's new*. New York: Columbia University Press.

Weir, D., and Noyes, D. (1983) *Raising hell—How the Center for Investigative Reporting gets the story*. Reading, MA: Addison-Wesley.

Weisburd, D., Waring, E., with Chayet, E. (2001) *Whitecollar crime and criminal careers*. Cambridge, UK: Cambridge University Press.

Weisburd, D., Wheeler, S., Waring, E. J., and Bode, N. (1991) *Crimes of the middle class*. New Haven, CT: Yale University Press.

Weiser, B. (1997a) "Legal advocate, or illegal conspirator?" *New York Times* (January 8): B1.

Weiser, B. (1997b) "Federal inquiry widens in test scheme." *New York Times* (August 13): B2.

Weiser, B. (1997c) "Bear, Stearns is called an extortion target." *New York Times* (November 7): D2.

Weiser, B. (1997d) "Brokers and mob linked in swindle." *New York Times* (November 26): A1.

Weiser, B. (1997e) "Prison term for lawyer who overcharged U.S." *New York Times* (December 11): B3.

Weiser, B. (1998a) "2 charged with insider trading of Lotus stock in '98 scheme." *New York Times* (January 14): D1.

Weiser, B. (1998b) "Error by U.S. imperils witnesses in case over Wall Street mob ties." *New York Times* (February 3): A1.

Weiser, B. (1999) "Bankers Trust admits it misused money claimed by customers." *New York Times* (March 12): A1.

Weiser, B. (2002a) "Same walk, nicer shoes." *New York Times* (November 26): B1.

Weiser, B. (2002b) "Identity ring said to victimize 30,000." *New York Times* (November 26): A1.

Weiser, B. (2003) "Fund for officers' families was fraud, suspect admits." *New York Times* (June 17): B3.

Weiser, B., and McGeehan, P. (1999) "Executive's affair with stripper leads to insider trading charges." *New York Times* (December 22): A1.

Weisman, S. L. (1999) *Need and greed—The story of the largest Ponzi scheme in American history.* Syracuse, NY: Syracuse University Press.

Weiss, G. (2003) *Born to steal—When the Mafia hit Wall Street.* New York: Warner.

Weissmann, M. M. (2005) "Corporate transparency or Congressional window-dressing? The case against Sarbanes-Oxley as a means to avoid another corporate debacle: The failed attempt to revise meaningful regulatory oversight." *Stanford Journal of Law, Business & Finance* 10: 98–137.

Welch, M. R., Xu, Y., Bjarnason, T., Petec, T., O'Donnell, P., and Magro, P. (2005) "'But everybody does it . . .': The effects of perceptions, moral pressures, and informal sanctions on tax cheating." *Sociological Spectrum* 25: 21–52.

Wellford, C. F., and Ingraham, B. L. (1994) "White-collar crime: Prevalence, trends, and costs," pp. 7–90 in A. R. Roberts (Ed.), *Critical issues in crime and justice.* Thousand Oaks, CA: Sage.

Wells, J. T. (1992) *Fraud examination: Investigative and audit procedures.* New York: Quorum Books.

Wells, J. T. (1993a) "Accountancy and white-collar crime." *Annals* 525: 83–94.

Wells, J. T. (1993b) "From the chairman." *The White Paper* 7: 1.

Wells, J. T. (2004) *Corporate fraud handbook: Prevention and detection.* New York: John Wiley & Sons.

Welton, N., and Wolf, L. (2001) *Global uprising—Confronting the tyrannies of the 21st century.* New York: New Society Publishers.

Whalley, J. L. (1990) "Crime and punishment—Criminal antitrust enforcement in the 1990s." *Antitrust Law Journal* 59: 151–160.

Wheeler, S. (1992) "The problem of white-collar motivation," pp. 108–123 in K. Schlegel and D. Weisburd (Eds.), *White-collar crime reconsidered.* Boston: Northeastern University Press.

Wheeler, S., Mann, K., and Sarat, A. (1988) *Sitting in judgment: The sentencing of white-collar criminals.* New Haven, CT: Yale University Press.

Wheeler, S., Weisburd, D., and Bode, N. (1982) "Sentencing the white-collar offender: Rhetoric and reality." *American Sociological Review* 47: 641–659.

Whitaker, B. (2005) "After the storm, rebuilding the nest egg." *New York Times* (April 12): Ret 2.

Whitaker, L. (2000) *Understanding and preventing violence.* Boca Raton, LA: CRC Press.

White, D. M., and Averson, R. (1979) *The celluloid weapon.* Boston: Beacon Press.

White, E. M. (1993) "Too many campuses want to sweep student plagiarism under the rug." *The Chronicle of Higher Education* (February 24): A44.

White, L. C. (1988) *Merchants of death—The American tobacco industry.* New York: William Morrow.

Whiteside, T. (1972) *The investigation of Ralph Nader: General Motors vs. one determined man.* New York: Pocket Books.

Whitmire, K. (2005a) "Jurors doubted Scrushy's colleagues." *New York Times* (July 2): C5.

Whitmire, K. (2005b) "S.E.C. wants day in court with Scrushy." *New York Times* (July 8): C3.

Wilgoren, J. (2005) "Trial shows ex-governor in two lights." *New York Times* (September 29): A14.

Wilkes, P. (1989) "The tough job of teaching ethics." *New York Times* (January 22): E1, 24.

Williams, E. (1966) *Capitalism and slavery.* New York: Capricorn.

Williams, F. P., and McShane, M. D. (1988; 1998) *Criminological theory.* Englewood Cliffs, NJ: Prentice Hall.

Williams, H. E. (1997) *Investigating white-collar crime—Embezzlement and financial fraud.* Springfield, IL: Charles C. Thomas.

Williams, J. W. (2005) "Reflections on the private versus public policing of economic crime." *British Journal of Criminology* 45: 316–339.

Williams, K. (1989) "Researching the powerful: Problems and possibilities of social research." *Contemporary Crises* 13: 253–274.

Williams, M. (2005) "Computer offenses," pp. 212–219 in R. A. Wright and J. M. Miller (Eds.), *Encyclopedia of criminology.* New York: Routledge.

Williams, R. (1987) *Political corruption in Africa.* Aldershot, UK: Gower.

Willliamson, D. (2000) "Robbery," pp. 43–50 in L. Trumbull, E. H. Hendrix, and B. D. Dent (Eds.), *Atlas of crime.* Phoenix, AZ: Oryx Press.

Willott S., Griffin, C., and Torrance, M. (2001) "Snakes and ladders: Upper-middle class male offenders talk about economic crime." *Criminology* 39: 441–466.

Willson, S. B. (2004) "Bob Kerrey's atrocity, the crime of Vietnam and the historic pattern of US imperialism," pp. 164–180 in A. Jones (Ed.), *Genocide, war crimes and the West: History and complicity*. London: Zed Books.

Wilson, E. D. (1975) *Sociobiology*. Cambridge, MA: Harvard University Press.

Wilson, J. Q. (1961) "The economy of patronage." *Journal of Political Economy* 69: 369–380.

Wilson, J. Q., and Herrnstein, R. J. (1985) *Crime and human nature*. New York: Simon & Schuster.

Wilson, M. (2001) "Folk crime," pp. 235–238 in D. Luckenbill and D. Peck (Eds.), *Encyclopedia of criminology and deviant behavior*. Philadelphia: Brunner-Routledge.

Winerip, M. (1994) "Billions for school are lost in fraud, waste and abuse." *New York Times* (February 2).

Wines, M. (1997) "Supreme leader, pigeon in chief." *New York Times* (March 23).

Winninghoff, T. (1994) "In arbitration, pitfalls for consumers." *New York Times* (October 22): B7.

Winter, G. (2000) "Taking at the office reaches new heights." *New York Times* (July 12): BP1.

Wise, D. (1973) *The politics of lying*. New York: Vintage.

Wise, D. (1976) *The American police state—The government against the people*. New York: Random House.

Wolff, E. N. (2000) "Recent trends in the size distribution of household wealth," pp. 107–117 in J. N. Skolnick and E. H. Currie (Eds.), *Crisis in American institutions* (11th ed.). Boston: Allyn & Bacon.

Wolff, R. P. (1976) *In defense of anarchism*. New York: Harper Torchbooks.

Wolfgang, M., Figlio, R., Tracy, P., and Singer, S. (1985) *The national survey of crime severity*. Washington, DC: U.S. Government Printing Office.

Wolfson, M. (2001) *The fight against big tobacco—The movement, the state, and the public's health*. Hawthorne, NY: Aldine de Gruyter.

Wonders, N., and Danner, M. (2002) "Globalization, state-corporate crime, and women: The strategic role of women's NGOs in the New World Order," pp. 165–184 in G. W. Potter (Ed.), *Controversies in white-collar crime*. Cincinnati, OH: Anderson.

Wong, E. (2001) "An advisor to the stars is sentenced to prison." *New York Times* (February 8): B8.

Wong, E., and Eaton, L. (2001) "An advisor to the stars, but a fraud to all comers." *New York Times* (January 27): B1.

Woodiwiss, M. (2001) *Organized crime and American power: A history*. Toronto: University of Toronto Press.

Woodward, B., and Bernstein, C. (1977) *The final days*. New York: Avon Books.

World Bank. (2000) "The World Bank provides effective development programs," pp. 107–115 in L. K. Egendorf (Ed.), *The third world—Opposing viewpoints*. San Diego, CA: Greenhaven Press.

Wright, J. (1979) *On a clear day you can see General Motors*. New York: Avon Books.

Wright, J. P., and Cullen, F. (2000) "Juvenile involvement in occupational delinquency." *Criminology* 38: 863–896.

Wright, J. P., Cullen, F. T., and Blankenship, M. B. (1995) "The social construction of corporate violence: Media coverage of the Imperial Food Products fire." *Crime & Delinquency* 41: 20–36.

Wright, R. A. (1994) *In defense of prisons*. Westport, CT: Greenwood Press.

Wright, R. A., and Friedrichs, D. O. (1991) "White collar crime in the criminal justice curriculum." *Journal of Criminal Justice Education* 2: 95–119.

Wrightsman, L. (1991) *Psychology and the social system* (2nd ed.). Pacific Grove, CA: Brooks/Cole.

Wrong, M. (2001) *In the footsteps of Mr. Kurtz: Living on the brink of disaster in Mobutu's Congo*. New York: Harper Collins.

Wu, A. (2004) "Emotional striptease and other paths to ethics." *New York Times* (March 7): Bus 4.

Wyman, D. S. (1984) *The abandonment of the Jews—America and the Holocaust, 1941–1945*. New York: Pantheon Books.

Yardley, J. (2002) "Letters show Bush and Lay shared much." *New York Times* (February 16): C1.

Yardley, W., and Stowe, S. (2005) "A contrite Rowland gets a year for accepting $107,000 in gifts." *New York Times* (March 18): A1.

Yeager, P. C. (1987) "Structural bias in regulatory law enforcement: The case of the U.S. Environmental Protection Agency." *Social Problems* 34: 330–344.

Yeager, P. C. (1991a) *The limits of law: The public regulation of private pollution*. Cambridge, UK: Cambridge University Press.

Yeager, P. C. (1991b) "Law, crime and inequality: The regulatory state." A paper presented at the Annual Meeting of the American Society of Criminology (San Francisco), November.

Yeager, P. C., and Kram, K. E. (1990) "Fielding hot topics in cool settings: The study of corporate ethics." *Qualitative Sociology* 13: 127–148.

Yeager, P. C., and Reed, G. E. (1998) "Of corporate persons and straw men: A reply to Herbert, Green, and Larragoite." *Criminology* 36: 885–897.

Yellen, D., and Mayer, C. J. (1992) "Coordinating sanctions for corporate misconduct: Civil or criminal punishment?" *American Criminal Law Review* 29: 961–1024.

York, M. (2004) "Father and son faked removal of asbestos, workers say." *New York Times* (February 3): B1.

Young, M. (1991) *The Vietnam wars: 1945–1990*. New York: HarperPerennial.

Young, T. R. (1981) "Corporate crime: A critique of the Clinard Report." *Contemporary Crises* 5: 323–335.

Zagorin, A. (1993) "Get out of jail, not quite free." *Time* (May 24): 50.

Zagorin, A. (1997) "Charlie's an angel." *Time* (February 3): 36–38.

Zagorin, A., and Burger, T. J. (2004) "Beyond the call of duty." *Time* (November 1): 64.

Zaitzow, B. H., and Robinson, M. B. (2001) "Criminologists as criminals," pp. 229–235 in A. Thio and T. C. Calhoun (Eds.), *Readings in deviant behavior*. Boston: Allyn & Bacon.

Zeitlin, L. (1971) "A little larceny can do a lot for employee morale." *Psychology Today* 5: 22.

Zeller, T. (2005a) "Black market in credit cards thrives on Web." *New York Times* (June 21): A1.

Zeller, T. (2005b) "After the storm, the swindlers." *New York Times* (September 8): A1.

Zellner, W., and Forest, S. A. (2001) "The fall of Enron." *Business Week* (December 17): 30–35.

Zernike, K. (2003) "Students shall not download. Yeah. Sure." *New York Times* (September 20): A6.

Zey, M. (1993) *Banking on fraud: Drexel, junk bonds, and buyouts*. New York: Aldine de Gruyter.

Zhang, L. (2001) "White-collar crime: Bribery and corruption in China," pp. 23–35 in J. Liu, L. Zhang, and S. F. Messner (Eds.), *Crime and social control in a changing China*. Westport, CT: Greenwood Press.

Ziegler, S. J., and Lovrich, N. P. (2003) "Pain relief, prescription drugs and prosecution: A four-state survey of chief prosecutors." *Journal of Law, Medicine & Ethics* 31: 75–100.

Zielbauer, P. (2001) "Yale hospital faces inquiry on fraud." *New York Times* (March 31): B1.

Zielbauer, P. (2002) "After years of high life, swindler pleads guilty." *New York Times* (May 16): B1.

Zietz, D. (1981) *Women who embezzle or defraud: A study of convicted felons*. New York: Praeger.

Zimmer, C. R. (1989) *Resource dependence, differential association, and corporate misconduct*. Ph.D. Dissertation. The University of North Carolina at Chapel Hill.

Zitrin, R., and Langford, C. (1999) *The moral compass of the American lawyer*. New York: Ballantine Books.

Zuckerman, H. (1977) "Deviant behavior and social control in science," pp. 87–138 in E. Sagarin (Ed.), *Deviance and social change*. Beverly Hills, CA: Sage.

Zuckhoff, M. (2005) *Ponzi's scheme*. New York: Random House.

Name Index

Subject Index